The Immanent Utopia

The Immanent Utopia

*From Marxism on the State
to the State of Marxism*

Axel van den Berg

Princeton University Press

Princeton, New Jersey

Copyright © 1988
by Princeton University Press
Published by Princeton University Press,
41 William Street,
Princeton, New Jersey 08540
In the United Kingdom:
Princeton University Press, Guildford, Surrey

Library of Congress Cataloging-in-Publication Data
Van den Berg, Axel.
The immanent utopia: From Marxism on the state to the state of
Marxism / Axel van den Berg.
p. cm.
Rev. ed. of the author's doctoral thesis.
Bibliography: p.
Includes index.
ISBN 0-691-09438-1 (alk. paper) ISBN 0-691-02844-3 (pbk.)
1. Marx, Karl, 1818–1883. 2. Communist state. I. Title.
HX38.5.V266 1988
306'.2—dc19   88-9411

This book has been composed in Baskerville

Clothbound editions of Princeton University Press books
are printed on acid-free paper,
and binding materials
are chosen for strength and durability.
Paperbacks, although satisfactory
for personal collections,
are not usually suitable for library rebinding

Printed in the United States of America
by Princeton University Press,
Princeton, New Jersey

Voor Myn Moeder en Voor Myn Vader

Contents

vii

Acknowledgments

It is reassuring to discover in the prefaces to other books, among them some of the greats, that even the best-laid plans have a way of turning into products entirely different from what was originally intended. My projects seem to be unusually vulnerable to this kind of subversion. I began work on my M.A. thesis thinking I would assess the empirical evidence for theories announcing a resurgence of radicalism among workers in Western Europe, and ended up with a comparison of radical elitist and pluralist theories of capitalist democracy—arguing that they did not differ on empirical matters at all. Something similar happened in the course of my work on my Ph.D. dissertation, of which this book is the final product. I began with plans of testing the recent Marxist theories of the state by examining the genesis of various welfare-state programs in Canada. But when I began to work on an introductory chapter which was to survey the literature and derive some testable hypotheses from it, it turned out to be very hard indeed to come up with any, and increasingly so as the theories became of more recent date and hence, presumably, more sophisticated. As a result, I decided to write a theoretical critique of these theories instead, trying to determine why it was so hard to derive any distinctive empirical implications from them. Having now embarked upon a theoretical critique of Marxist theories I had to write a brief introductory chapter on Marx, Engels, and the Marxist "classics," of course. But as I started to work on that I stumbled on some amazing—to me, at least—parallels between the fragmentary remarks on the state by Marx and Engels and the more recent theories. Thus, in the end I found myself writing a far broader theoretical critique of Marxism in general. I suppose the similarity in the way I was distracted from my initial projects for both theses suggests something about the sincerity of my often stated commitment to empirical research.

At any rate, the route having been a long and tortuous one, I have incurred a large variety and number of debts. First, I am grateful to the Canadian Social Sciences and Humanities Research Council and the Québec Fonds pour la formation de chercheurs et de l'aide à la recherche for several years of fellowships that permitted me to pursue my doctoral studies interrupted by distractions of my own choosing only. Second, I thank McGill University for the Social Science Research Grant to support my efforts to turn the dissertation into a publishable manuscript.

If any of the arguments and analyses that follow turn out to hold any water this is no doubt to a large extent attributable to the innumerable fellow students, friends, colleagues, and students of my own who were willing to listen to my half-baked ramblings and help me turn them into something more or less coherent. A complete listing would be impossible, but at the very least it would include: Nancy Di Tomaso, Les Kennedy, Harvey Krahn, Gordon Laxer, Helen Levine Batten, Michael Lipkin, Graham Lowe, Cerise Morris, Gleema Nambiar, David Pariser, Dorothy Pawluch, Suzanne Peters, David Shewchuk, Joe Smucker, Jacqueline St.Clair-Stokes, Michael Sullivan, Julian Tanner, Carol Taylor, Ted Withers, and Steve Woolgar. For specific comments and criticisms of the dissertation and manuscript, without which the book would have been much worse, I am indebted to Jeffrey Alexander, Dick Batten, Stephen Bornstein, Richard Hamilton, Tony Masi, Rick Ogmundson, Jim Rule, Don Von Eschen, and Jim Wright, some of whom also belong on the preceding list, as they themselves know only too well. I am particularly grateful to Jeffrey Alexander and Richard Hamilton, without whose strong support and encouragement at crucial junctures this book might never have gone to press. But the greatest debt of gratitude by far I owe to Mike Smith, who saw the project through from start to finish, and whose characteristic blend of relentless criticism and unfailing support makes him the superb teacher, colleague, and friend that he is. For helping me with the often extraordinarily demanding word-processing, typing, indexing, and library work, I thank Margie Fedak, Kathleen Foley, Sherri Tepper, Steven Slimovitch and Jerzy Depa. I also owe a great deal to Barbara Westergaard for the truly magnificent job of copyediting she did on the unwieldy manuscript. Finally, a debt of a different kind, but probably the greatest of all, I owe to my wife Sylvie without whose support and love through years of obsessive work, illnesses, uprooting moves, and frustrations of all kinds, I would *never* have made it to this point.

The Immanent Utopia

Introduction

> What differentiates the bourgeois state from all previous
> organizations of social power is the fact that its dominational
> character is not obvious.
>
> (Gerstenberger 1978, 155–56)

Marxism is inherently incapable of taking the so-called super-structure seriously. It must either relegate such things as politics, culture and consciousness to mere "epiphenomena" of the economic "base" or else lose its own (theoretical) coherence by importing the "bourgeois" concepts needed to deal with them in a more satisfactory manner. For a long time, this has been the smug conventional wisdom among non-Marxists.

Undoubtedly, the orthodox version of "historical material-ism," as codified by Engels[1] and promulgated and strictly enforced by Kautsky, Plekhanov, and, at least in theory, Lenin, was not exactly conducive to viewing the superstructure as worthy of separate investigation (Levi 1981, 434; Miliband 1977, 7–12). Although nowadays widely discredited as a "vulgarization" of Marx's "real" ideas (e.g., Avineri 1968; Giddens 1971; Rader 1979; but cf. Alexander 1982b; Cohen 1978), it certainly held sway well into the twentieth century as the only permissible orthodoxy.

In addition, "dialectical materialism" was believed to provide all the answers a Marxist would ever need (see Kolakowski 1978a, ch. 15; Lichtheim 1965, 244–58)[2]. Such theoretical clo-

---

1   I try to ignore the heated debate over whether or not Engels's rendition corresponds faithfully to Marx's "true" ideas as much as possible (see, e.g. Avineri 1968, 65–69; Carver 1980; 1984a, b; Collins 1985, 56–62; Gouldner 1980, ch. 9; Horowitz and Hayes 1980; Kline 1984, 25–38; Kolakowski 1978a, 399–408; Levine 1975, 1983, 1985; Stanley and Zimmerman 1984).

2   Neither Marx nor Engels ever used the term "dialectical materialism." It was apparently introduced by J. Dietzgen in the 1870s and then popular-ized by Plekhanov and his once faithful pupil Lenin (see McLellan 1980, 152n). Kline (1984, 22, n. 42) dated its use to an 1891 article by Plekhanov, but has since discovered that the above tracing of the term is correct (corre-spondence with the author, October 26 and 29, 1985).

3

sure, although perhaps an important source of moral strength for Marxist activists in uncertain times (Gouldner 1980, 296–99; 1985, 137), fostered a habit of not asking questions to which the authorized texts did not provide a clear answer, a habit that was energetically reinforced by the Bolshevik guardians of orthodoxy after 1917 and seems to die hard even today (Bobbio 1978a, 7–16; Bridges 1974, 162; E. O. Wright 1975, 20; 1978, 138–39). Thus, neither the doctrine nor the intellectual climate fostered by orthodoxy was very favorable to systematic Marxist explorations of superstructural phenomena.[3]

This has been particularly awkward with respect to politics and the state. For, while sharing the anarchist vision of the eventual "withering away" of the state, Marxism has always contemptuously distanced itself from the political naiveties of its anarchist and "utopian" socialist competitors, insisting that the state must first be conquered by a politically organized proletariat, and its repressive machinery employed as ruthlessly as necessary, before it can be allowed to die of its own obsolescence (see, e.g., Lenin 1932, 52–54; Marx 1961, 236ff.; 1963b, 16–75; 1974, 269ff.; Marx and Engels 1959, 443–46, 459–70, 481–85; Marx, Engels, and Lenin 1967, 152ff.; Shaw 1974, 432–36).[4] Yet, in spite of this emphasis on the strategic importance of politics and the state, and endless debates about questions of political tactics and strategy, until very recently Marxists have largely failed to produce any systematic theoretical treatments of politics and the state (Anderson 1976, 114; Jessop 1977, 354; Miliband 1965, 278; 1977, 1–6; Therborn 1978, 47).

But now all this has changed. The loosening of Moscow's iron grip in the 1950s and the resurgence of radical politics in the 1960s have produced an extraordinary revival of what is now known as "Western Marxism" (Anderson 1976; Burawoy 1978; Flacks and Turkel 1978; Jacoby 1979; Long 1980; Stedman Jones, et al. 1977). Perhaps *the* central theme in this revival has

3   Following Giddens (1971, 185, n. 2; 1973, 198, n. 6; 1977, 369–70, n. 6) I use the adjective "Marxian" to refer to Marx's own writings and ideas only and "Marxism" and "Marxist" to refer to the doctrines of his self-proclaimed followers.
4   For a particularly provocative treatment of the difference between Marxism and "Bakuninism" with respect to politics, see Gouldner (1985, ch. 7).

been a concern to finally bring the superstructure within the
purview of Marxist theory *without* resorting to economistic reduction. Moreover, since about the mid-1960s the efforts to seriously "theorize" the superstructure—to use the current jargon—have been dominated by a series of debates, on an
unprecedented international scale and commanding the attention of an extraordinarily large audience, on the nature of politics and the state in capitalist society. Thus the 1970s have
rightly been hailed as "the decade of the theory of the state"
(Panitch 1979, 1). After close to two decades of intense debate,
there is now a very sizable Marxist literature on the state, complete with surveys, stock-takings, and (somewhat) critical assessments.[5] The consensus seems to be that there has been "notable
progress" (Milner 1977, 101) toward a viable, nonreductionist
Marxist theory of the state. Indeed, given the size of the literature and the amount of time passed, it would be somewhat embarrassing if there had not been.

However, as is so often the case in the paradigm-ridden social
sciences, such positive assessments come almost exclusively
from fellow Marxists or sympathisers, while "bourgeois" social
scientists have generally ignored the whole daunting literature
(for a notable exception, see Parkin 1979). It is time, then, for
a thorough, critical appraisal of the Marxist theory of the state
from a *non*-Marxist perspective. My principal aim is to assess
whether in the past two decades Marxist thinking about politics
and the state has advanced to the point that it now holds at least
the promise of a credible alternative to its "bourgeois" counter-
part(s). In other words, has there really been progress toward a
theory of the state that is both viable, in the sense of logically
consistent and empirically tenable, *and* still recognizably Marxist?

This immediately raises the thorny question of what we mean
by "recognizably Marxist." For the price paid for the renunciation of the erstwhile dogmas has been the proliferation of such

5   To mention only a few of the reviews: Alford (1975), Alford and Friedland
(1985), Carnoy (1984), Esping-Andersen, Friedland, and Wright (1976),
Gold, Clarence, and Wright (1975a, b), Holloway and Picciotto (1977,
1978), Jessop (1977, 1982), Koch (1980), Mollenkopf (1975), Skocpol
(1980), Weiner (1980), A. Wolfe (1974, 1977).

a diversity of conflicting "schools," theories, and interpretations that it has become exceedingly difficult to discern even the vaguest "family resemblance" (Bottomore 1979, 18).

Perhaps the distinctness of a doctrine like Marxism is bound to be subject to continuous erosion in a liberal society: "bourgeois" social science adopts those propositions from Marxism that are considered tenable in the light of empirical evidence, while Marxists modify and reinterpret received dogmas that come to be perceived as clearly untenable—until it becomes hard to tell the two apart—(cf. Bottomore 1975, 66–67). The basic propositions of "historical materialism" have been particularly vulnerable to this process of progressive decomposition. Toward the end of his life Engels became alarmed at the rigid versions of his doctrines being disseminated by some of his followers, which caused him to stress the "relative independence" of the superstructure from the economic base, although he still insisted that in the "reciprocal interaction" between them "economic necessity . . . *in the last instance* always asserts itself" (Howe 1976, 149, 157).[6] Since the "last instance" has yet to be further specified, this could easily be interpreted to mean that economy and polity "interact" in a way not unlike the conventional "bourgeois" conceptions. The meaning of most other previously distinctively Marxist notions has been similarly diluted. The very distinction between base and superstructure, or even between forces and relations of production, has been questioned in view of its tendency to lead to "vulgar determinism" (see, e.g., Avineri 1968, Corrigan, Ramsey, and Sayer 1978; Giddens 1971, 1977, 195–99; Meiksins Wood 1981; Ollman 1971; Rader 1979). Some Marxists have come to accept that class divisions may not be the only or even the "fundamental" division in capitalist society (see, e.g., Jessop 1977, 353–54, 1982, ch. 5; Przeworski 1977; Szymanski 1978), just as "bourgeois" social science has come to acknowledge routinely the importance of class conflict (e.g., Giddens 1973; R. F. Hamilton 1972; Lipset 1960; Parkin 1971, 1979). Meanwhile, the very definition of class used by some Marxists seems to have become virtually indistinguishable from "bourgeois" definitions (see,

6   Unless indicated otherwise, all emphases in quotations are in the original.

e.g., Abercrombie and Urry 1983; Carter 1985; Cottrell 1984; Walker 1978; E. O. Wright 1980, 1985). Not even the transitory nature of capitalism itself can be taken for granted anymore by Marxists, while, on the other side, its great defenders (Schumpeter, Von Hayek, Friedman) became anxiously aware of its very precariousness. Under these circumstances, then, it is becoming less and less clear "what makes Marxists and their inquiries distinctive" (Vaillancourt 1986, 2; cf. Bottomore 1975, 66–74; Heilbroner 1980, 19–22; Warshay 1981, 32–33).

This presents a fundamental problem for the kind of comparative assessment I wish to undertake. What minimum criteria does a theory have to satisfy to qualify as "recognizably Marxist"? Conversely, at what point does it become indistinguishable from its "bourgeois" counterparts? Rather than trying to settle this question a priori, which, given its obvious contentiousness, would be both futile and damaging to the rest of my arguments, I propose to make this the second major aim of this book: to try and uncover inductively, by way of a more or less comprehensive survey of conflicting Marxist theories of the state, what, if anything, they still have in common. What *does* make these theories "Marxist"?

This still leaves me with a "sampling" problem, however, namely which theories to choose as representative of Marxism and what to present as the "bourgeois" alternative. Fortunately, the existing literature is a considerable help here. First, there is little disagreement as to who have been the major contributors to the debates about the Marxist theory of the state. At a minimum, they include such authors as Miliband, Poulantzas, and Offe and, for those who take U.S. developments seriously, Domhoff, O'Connor, and some "poststructuralist" theorists. These are the authors who have brought such now (in)famous terms as "the capitalist state," "relative autonomy," "factor of cohesion," "state apparatus," "accumulation and legitimation function," and the like into circulation. Second, for all the differences between them, their theories do seem to have at least one thing in common: "virtually all Marxist treatments of the state begin with the fundamental observation that the state in capitalist society broadly serves the interests of the capitalist class" (Gold, Lo, and Wright 1975a, 31). This is clearly a minimum criterion for a "recognizably Marxist" theory of the state, without which it would not be considered distinctively Marxist. As I try to show in Chapter 1, it was Marx's basic assumption about the governments of his day, before the introduction of universal suffrage. Later on, as discussed in Chapter 2, Lenin extended the argument to "bourgeois" democracy, and, as can be seen from the subsequent chapters, the recent literature consists of a succession of attempts to explain why and how even now this "fundamental observation" stands, in spite of apparent evidence, such as the rise of the so-called welfare state, to the contrary.

This also provides me with a logical candidate for the "bourgeois" alternative to compare the Marxist theories to. American Marxists and radicals still use the complacent "pluralism" of the 1950s as a convenient straw man (see, e.g., Alford and Friedland 1985 and chapter 6 below). But this amounts to a pretty futile exercise not only because that kind of pluralism never did become the dominant non-Marxist theory outside the United States, but even more because not much could be learned from the comparison. It is obvious that we will find clear differences between Marxist theories of the state and this particular representative of "bourgeois" theory, as would be the case a fortiori with any theories drawn from even further on the right of the political spectrum. What might be called "liberal reformism" provides a much more instructive case precisely because it is much closer to Marxism and the results of the comparison can therefore not be predicted in advance. Where appropriate I give a more detailed description of what I take this position to be. Suffice it to say here that it agrees with many Marxists on the disproportionate political influence enjoyed by business interests, even when all citizens formally possess equal political power, but it rejects the Marxist tenet that the state necessarily serves the interests of the capitalist class and it takes the implementation of policies opposed by business, particularly welfare legislation, to be evidence refuting that tenet. This choice of "bourgeois" alternative is further justified in Chapter 2, where I document that Marxist thinking about the modern democratic state has been consciously formulated in opposition to just this kind of reformism.

Another point on which all reviewers of the debates seem to agree is on their cumulative, progressive character. There is a ³ general consensus that the earliest, so-called instrumentalist theory has been relegated to obsolescence by the far more sophisticated "structuralist" theories of the state which are, in turn, now due to be replaced by still more advanced "poststructuralist" approaches. This claim of steady theoretical progress over the past two decades is also critically assessed in what follows. It is my third major concern.

My three main concerns account for the main differences between my treatment of Marxist theories of the state and that of other recent surveys. First of all, my interest in assessing the claim of steady theoretical progress necessitates an approach that differs from those who take that progress for granted. While others offer a country-by-country survey (Carnoy 1984), or one organized according to objects or levels of analysis (Alford and Friedland 1985), I deliberately present the theories chronologically, in order to show how each theory grew out of a reaction against previous theories, allowing me to assess the *theoretical trajectory* followed over the years. Also, since I cannot *a priori* accept the inferiority of earlier theories to the current favorites, I discuss the former in some detail. Thus, whereas recent treatments mention the old, now allegedly obsolete "instrumentalist" theory only in passing references to its crudity or as a short-hand criticism of more recent theories still bearing its traces, I devote a whole chapter (3) to a detailed discussion of it. Similarly, whereas Carnoy (1984, ch. 4) emphasizes Poulantzas's later "dialectical" at the expense of his earlier "structuralist" theory, and Jessop (1982, 181–91) treats them as a single, evolving body of work (though he is by no means unaware of the contradictions between them), and Alford and Friedland (1985, 277–78, 334–35, 366–67) do not even seem to be aware of any difference between the two, I devote my longest chapter to a painstaking dissection of the earlier structuralism, on the grounds that *this* was by far the more internationally influential of the two and that, with respect to the central Marxist tenet that concerns me (that the state serves the interests of the capitalist class) the two approaches are completely contradictory.

There are other differences that stem from my critical focus on that central tenet. Carnoy (1984) offers a largely and it seems deliberately uncritical survey of political writings from a "class perspective" in various countries, without providing any rationale for his choice of authors. As a result, he discusses several theories that have no direct or distinct bearing on my central focus and actually chooses as representatives of the "class struggle" approach American writers concerned with the alleged current crisis of capitalism rather than the nature of the capitalist state (1984, 235–45). But on the whole Carnoy provides a useful alternative source for the reader to check the accuracy of my summaries of the theories we *both* cover.

The same can be said for Jessop's book (1982). Although ostensibly written from a rather orthodox Marxist starting point, his treatment is in some respects closer than any other to mine. Jessop is not primarily interested in those authors who are "engaged in theoretical combat with various liberal and pluralist positions" (15), he explicitly dismisses "instrumentalism" and virtually all theories of U.S. or British origin for their "extraordinary weakness" (xvi), and he reluctantly devotes a brief digression to Offe while discussing more orthodox German theorists, because Offe has only "an ambivalent and mediated relationship to orthodox Marxism" (106). Instead, Jessop discusses the "state monopoly capitalist" ("stamocap") theories officially authorized by the Communist parties in the 1950s and 1960s (ch. 2), the ultrafundamentalist "state derivation" debates (*Staatsableitungdebatte*) in Germany (ch. 3), and (primarily the late) Poulantzas as an example of the "neo-Gramscian" approach (ch. 4), while searching for elements of an adequate Marxist *methodology* for analyzing the capitalist state. None of these approaches, however, has had the impact on the international literature that the theories I discuss have had. Jessop seems to have chosen his theories for their apparent orthodoxy and what he considers to be their theoretical sophistication (xi–xvi). Yet his criticisms of them, and the very chronology he presents, run remarkably parallel to mine. The stamocap theories, it turns out, suffer from the same weaknesses as do instrumentalist theories; the "derivationists" who seek to "derive" "correctly" the "necessity," "form," and "functions" of the capitalist state from the economic categories found in *Das Kapital*—

which, as Jessop himself admits, "involves an incestuous process
of mutual criticism for having chosen the wrong starting point"
(137)—are criticized for being overly functionalistic, much in
the way I criticize (the early) Poulantzas and Offe; and the
"neo-Gramscian" approaches seem to be as theoretically indeterminate as the "class struggle" approaches I discuss in Chapter 6, many of which Jessop deliberately snubs as theoretically
poor U.S. cousins of their European counterparts. In fact, even
the cautious, non-class-reductionist, open-ended "method of
articulation" (ch. 5) that Jessop advocates has much in common
with my arguments. I leave it to the reader to draw the appropriate conclusions concerning the current state of Marxism
from these remarkable parallels.

Finally, a few comments on the differences between this book
and the recent volume by Alford and Friedland (1985) seem in
order. Since they, too, are comparing "bourgeois" to "class perspective" theories of the state, at first sight it might seem that
their effort should be very similar to mine. Instead, the two are
very different indeed. Alford and Friedland identify three
broad "world views," the "pluralist," "managerial," and "class"
perspectives, which they conceive as relatively self-contained
paradigmlike entities, each with its own epistemological and po-
litico-ideological presuppositions, proper domain of inquiry,
methodology, appropriate level of analysis, and "functional" as
well as "political" variants. Most of their book is taken up with
examples of theories belonging to each of the "world views,"
organized according to the authors' elaborate classification of
"levels of analysis," "home domains," "aspects of the state," and
"functional" versus "political" variants.

In fact, Alford and Friedland appear to be much more interested in demonstrating the utility of their classification schemes
than in surveying and analyzing theories of the state per se.
The theories they discuss seem to serve an illustrative purpose
only. As a result, they offer more of a *tour d'horizon* of a variety
of theories dealing with a wide range of areas from social movements to poverty, class formations, elites, bureaucracy, imperialism, democracy, economic crises, industrial conflict, and so
on, than any sustained analysis of recent theories of the state.
Alford and Friedland actually pay remarkably little attention to

the latter as conventionally understood. The central issue in recent debates, namely, how and why the formally democratic state nevertheless serves the interests of the capitalist class, is passed over in three pages (Alford and Friedland 1985, 333–36) without any in-depth analysis; major contributions are discussed only briefly (301–3, 317–21) or not at all, or only in quite different contexts (273–75, 387, 434–36). Thus the theories Alford and Friedland survey, and the aims of their survey, are clearly very different from mine.

Finally, at a more basic level, Alford and Friedland are not at all interested in weighing alternative theories in the way I propose to do. They consider this a futile exercise because the alternatives hail from entirely different, incommensurable "world views" which do not even agree on basic criteria of validity and verification. Instead, they want to combine the strengths of each perspective in a "higher synthesis." Not surprisingly, this higher synthesis turns out to consist of such lame commonplaces as that each perspective has its proper strengths and "domain," that the "class" perspective should not ignore political power and culture as independent factors, and so on (ibid., 388, 434, 441–42), while it also simply adopts large chunks of the "class" perspective without explicit justification. This is not surprising because the whole procedure is fundamentaly illconceived. Alford and Friedland subscribe to the current vogue of "postpositivist" theorizing which stresses the profound sociohistorical and philosophical roots of the differences between the various theoretical traditions in the social sciences, the inevitable "theoryladenness" of all concepts and all methodologies, and the like. But to expect to construct a "higher synthesis" acceptable to anyone but oneself out of this oversociologized view of social theories is to commit a monumental non sequitur. For if there *really* are no agreed-upon criteria of validity, utility, and the like, between the adherents of different "paradigms," what criteria can one use to construct a "higher" synthesis with? The best one could possibly do is to offer yet another self-contained, and, therefore, in the eyes of others entirely arbitrary, "world view," or else, and this is far more likely, simply a disguised version of one of the already existing ones. Thus, Alford and Friedland's own "synthesis" boils down to little more than a conventional Weberian-like call for a "multidimensional" approach, albeit expressed in the convoluted language of currently fashionable "theorization."

This kind of "postpostivism" necessarily leads to a dead end. The alternative is to assume that there *are* some basic principles on which adherents of different theories agree, and that it *is* possible to compare them critically on that basis. Only this kind of comparative analysis will help us better understand the real differences between them and whether they *are* capable of resolution on the basis of shared criteria or not, instead of *a priori* decreeing *none* of their differences resolvable in this way. I believe that there are at least two criteria of validity that most Marxists and non-Marxists would agree on: (1) logical consistency, and (2) (*pace* "postpositivism") some consistency with empirical reality that can be in principle falsified. Without these two commitments, however half-heartedly adhered to in the real world, there would indeed be little sense in comparing theories, or even discussing them for that matter. Having decided to discuss Marxist theories of the state and some "bourgeois" alternatives, I take it for granted from here on that at least these two basic principles are accepted by both sides.

Finally, as already suggested, I expect to be able to throw some light on the current state of Marxism more generally from this survey of theories of the state. These theories lend themselves particularly well to this purpose because of their novelty and their prominence in Marxist thinking in the past two decades. But I do believe that similar analyses could be applied to current debates among Marxists on class theory or Marxist economics, two areas in which Marxism has traditionally claimed greater strength, and that the conclusions would be remarkably similar to those I reach in the concluding chapter (see, e.g., Van Parijs 1980 and Robinson 1966 on Marxist economics; Gagliani 1981 and Parkin 1979 on class theory).

1 Marx and Engels on the State and Politics

> The social revolution of the nineteenth century cannot draw
> its poetry from the past, but only from the future.
>
> (Marx 1963a, 18)

The recent interest in the state has, not surprisingly, stimulated renewed efforts to collect, classify, and reanalyze everything Marx and Engels have ever written on the subject. No less predictably, such efforts invariably lead to the conclusion that their fragmentary remarks and journalistic pieces do contain a coherent and genuine Marxist theory of the state after all. There is now an extensive literature offering a variety of "authentic" theories of the state attributed to the founders of Marxism on the basis of various "correct" readings of their works. The different "genuine" theories proposed diverge as widely as do the various versions of Marxism, and the two are clearly related. One can interpret Marx's "mature" works in the light of his early works or vice versa, emphasize the simple generalizations or the more complex journalism, look for a complete theory or only elements thereof, assume total unanimity or certain differences between Marx and Engels, seek to justify a Leninist or a more reformist political strategy, and so on and so on; each perspective seems to yield a different "genuine" theory of the state (see, e.g., Avineri 1968; Chang 1931; Colletti 1975; Draper 1974, 1977, 1978; Hunt 1974, 1984; Jessop 1977; Lichtheim 1965; Löwith 1982; Maguire 1978; Mewes 1976; Miliband 1965; S. W. Moore 1957; Perez-Diaz 1978; B. D. Wolfe 1965).[1]

Here I will not try to add one more "correct" interpretation of Marx and Engels's views on the state and politics. The sheer diversity of such interpretations strongly suggests that Marx and Engels simply did not *have* a coherent theory of the state and that, consequently, the search for one is futile (cf. Jessop

[1] For a fairly comprehensive and dispassionate survey of Marx and Engels's views on the state, see McLellan (1980, 206–22).

14

1982, ch. 1). Rather than imposing an artificial coherence, I briefly present their best-known statements on the subject, as incoherent and inconsistent as they may appear. This will at least set a minimal standard that subsequent Marxist theorists must improve upon. In addition, those statements reveal certain basic assumptions underlying the thinking of Marx and Engels, which are more or less concealed in their more complete and polished theorizing on other subjects (notably Marx's economics) and which may help to explain why their political writings did not offer any clear-cut answers to the questions of strategy that came to dominate the political debates among their followers.

Marx and Engels on the State

One of the great debates of marxology concerns the exact relation between the "early" and the "mature" writings of Marx, with *The German Ideology*, Marx and Engels's first fully collaborative effort written in 1845–1846, conventionally thought to be the first of the "mature" works (see, e.g., Althusser 1969, 31–39; Draper 1977, 189; Jessop 1982, 9; Maguire 1978, 14). Depending on where one stands on the issue, one may consider the early writings either as of little interest except as "anticipations, forerunners, or harbingers to one extent or another" of the "developed Marxism" first expounded in *The German Ideology* (Draper 1977, 189; Miliband 1965, 279–83; Perez-Diaz 1978, 3–5), or as already containing so much of the essence of Marxism as to be indispensable for a correct understanding of the late writings (Avineri 1968; Colletti 1975; Fromm 1961, 69–79; Giddens 1971, 4–7; Löwith 1982, 68–99; Ollman 1971; Rader 1979). In what follows I present the early and then the mature writings more or less chronologically without committing myself to any particular view of the "essence" of Marxism just yet.

The "Early" Marx

Marx's earliest published writings are his articles for the short-lived liberal democratic *Rheinische Zeitung* (Marx 1977, 17–25) which are primarily of interest for anticipating some of the main themes in the manuscript known as the "Critique of Hegel's Philosophy of Right" (Marx 1975, 57–198).[2] In the best known of them he fiercely defends the freedom of the press and exposes the use of the state as protector of the interests of the rich, basing his argument on the very Hegelian argument that the "true nature," "concept," or "idea" of the state is to represent the "universal" interest, the community as a whole. In these articles, it is generally agreed, Marx does not yet show himself to be anything more than a for-the-time somewhat radical democrat (see Draper 1977, 36–76; Hunt 1974, 31–44; Kolakowski 1978a, 120–22; Perez-Diaz 1978, 15–28; Teeple 1984, ch. 1).

There is less agreement about the "Critique." In it, Marx accepts two of Hegel's assumptions: (1) that the sphere of "civil society," characterized by a Hobbesian "war of all against all" has separated itself from the state, and (2) that the true "essence" of the state is "universality," in other words, to formulate the true general interest as opposed to the manifold particular interests rampant in "civil society." What he rejects is Hegel's claim that the actually existing state, with its supposedly independent sovereign, its "universal class" of bureaucrats and its estates representing "civil society" in the legislative assembly, *does in fact* succeed in overcoming the unrestrained egoism and particularism of "civil society."[3] As Marx himself puts it, "Hegel should not be blamed for describing the essence of the modern state as it is, but for identifying what is with the *essence of the state*" (1975, 127).

Following Feuerbach, Marx argues that Hegel persistently inverts the "predicate" or "idea" and its subject.[4] The "idea" of the state does not impose itself on its personnel, the personnel determines the actual character of the state. The state is not an independent force following its own "essence" but a derivative of and abstraction from civil society, the embodiment of the

2   The title in the edition I refer to is "Critique of Hegel's Doctrine of the State." I continue to refer to it under the more conventional title.

3   Marx, however, may well have simplified Hegel's rather ambiguous position vis-à-vis the actual Prussian state: see Perez-Diaz (1978, 102–3, n. 54).

4   Teeple (1984, 47–48) questions the conventional wisdom that Marx's critique of Hegel was greatly influenced by Feuerbach.

split between particularism and universality, between private and public man. Since the state is wholly separated from civil society its claim to universality is necessarily false: universality can only be accomplished by the universal becoming the business of everyone, not just of a separate caste of bureaucrats and representatives. Universality can only be achieved by "true democracy." Only by "*unrestricted* active and passive *suffrage*" can civil society establish "its *political* existence as its authentic existence" and thus overcome the dichotomy between private and public by dissolving *both* civil society *and* the state (Marx 1975, 191; also Avineri 1968, 13–40; Draper 1977, ch. 3, 168–81; Giddens 1971, 4–7; Hunt 1974, 59–68; Kolakowski 1978a, 122–25; Levitt 1978, 16; Löwith 1982, 83–90; McLellan 1980, 119, 206–7, 213–15; Mewes 1976; Miliband 1965, 279–81; Perez-Diaz 1978, 28–32; Rader 1979, 62–70 165–69).

Some argue that Marx is "still committed to liberal radical political ideas" here (Jessop 1977, 354; 1982, 6; see also Lichtheim 1965, 37–38; Perez-Diaz 1978, 32). But Marx clearly goes *beyond* liberal democracy, no matter how "radical" (Avineri 1968, 38; Berki 1983, 36–37; Colletti 1975, 40–46; Maguire 1978, 10; Miliband 1965, 281; Springborg 1984; Teeple 1984, ch. 2). He seems already to demand some sort of direct, unmediated self-government of the entire community, uncorrupted by the selfish interests of private property, dissolving all distinctions and conflicts between private and public interests, "the first true unity of the particular and universal" (Marx 1975, 88). This does not mean, though, that the "Critique" already contains the whole of "mature" Marxism *in nuce*, as some have come close to saying (Avineri 1968, ch. 1), or even just the "mature" theory of the state (Colletti 1975, 45–46; Rader 1979, 165–69).

In the article "On the Jewish Question," written immediately after the "Critique," Marx already quite explicitly treats liberal-democratic political reform as insufficient by itself to achieve the truly universal "species-life" prescribed by man's "species being" (1975, 211–41). "Political emancipation," such as the elimination of religious and property qualifications for participation in the political community, proclamations of the "rights of man," and the like, is certainly a step forward, Marx argues, but it does not eliminate the effects of religion, property, and the "war of all against all" which ravage "civil society." It *does*, however, "perfect" the state by exposing as clearly as possible its illusory pretenses of embodying true universality, thereby rendering the contradiction between the imaginary community and the reality of rampant selfishness and struggle in "civil society" as sharp as possible. Thus he argues:

> The perfected political state is by nature the *species-life* of man in *opposition* to his material life. All the presuppositions of this egoistic life continue to exist *outside* the sphere of the state in *civil* society, but as qualities of civil society. Where the political state has attained its full degree of development man leads a double life, a life in heaven and a life on earth, not only in his mind, in his consciousness but in *reality*. He lives in the *political community*, where he regards himself as a *communal being*, and in *civil society*, where he is active as a *private individual*, regards other men as means, debases himself to a means and becomes a plaything of alien powers. (Marx 1975, 220)

As this "double life" becomes increasingly intolerable, Marx goes on to argue, it will become clear that beyond "political emancipation" lies "human emancipation," in which the "species-life" will be realized by the fusion of state and "civil society" into a single true community, reconciling private and public, particular and universal (see Draper 1977, 109–25; Hunt 1974, 68–74; Kolakowski 1978a, 125–27; Miliband 1965, 281; Teeple 1984, 100–8).[5] But Marx does not give any clear indication yet as to who was to bring about this "human" emancipation, or how.

In his subsequent writings Marx slowly worked out his answers to these questions. In "A Contribution to the Critique of Hegel's Philosophy of Right. Introduction"—the introduction to the unfinished "Critique," written during the winter of 1843–1844 and published together with "On the Jewish Question" in

---

5   As Bobbio (1978a, 30) points out, the unfortunate Marxist tradition of dismissing questions of civil and political rights as "bourgeois" superficialities can be traced to this fateful distinction between "political" and "human" emancipation, "which has become a convenient license for all aspiring dictators (with or without the proletariat)."

the one (double) issue of the *Deutsch-Französische Jahrbücher* edited by Marx and Arnold Ruge appearing in February 1844 (Marx 1975, 243–57)—Marx for the first time identifies the proletariat as the true "universal class," charged with the historical mission of the revolutionary transformation of society to effect the emancipation of mankind (cf. Hunt 1974, 74–84; Kolakowski 1978a, 127–31; Teeple 1984, 108–14). In the famous "Economic and Philosophical Manuscripts" and some notes on James Mill's *Elements of Political Economy*, both written in the spring and summer of 1844 but not published until 1932 and 1926 respectively (Marx 1975, 259–400; Fromm 1961, 71), "theoretical communism," that is, the argument that only the suppression of private property and of the division of labor can eliminate human alienation, is first developed (Kolakowski 1978a, 132–41; Teeple 1984, ch. 4).

These theoretical developments are reflected in the 1844 article entitled "Critical Notes on the Article 'The King of Prussia and Social Reform. By a Prussian' " (Marx 1975, 401–20) in which Marx interprets a weavers' revolt in Silesia as a "social revolution" against the "dehumanized life" separating the individual from "the *true* community of man, *human* nature" (479). Since the modern state cannot establish true community without abolishing itself, he argues, this social revolution will first of all have to consist of the *political* act of overthrowing "the existing ruling power." "But as soon as its *organizing functions* begin and its *goal*, its *soul* emerges, socialism throws its *political* mask aside" (420; see Teeple 1984, 114–17). In the last of his "early" writings and the first to which Engels contributed—*The Holy Family*, published in February 1845—Marx settles his last accounts with the Young Hegelians, without adding anything to his previous arguments as far as the state and politics are concerned—although the work does contain the first hints of the "materialist" interpretation of history (see Marx 1961, 223–28; 1977, 131–55; Draper 1977, 125–28; Kolakowski 1978a, ch. 7).

To conclude, then, the principal theme of these "early" writings seems to be a sustained polemic against any kind of dichotomy, any distinctions between private and public, civil society and state, particular and universal, individual and community, and so on. These distinctions are condemned in the name of some integral unity of them all, which is apparently inherent in man's "species being." This certainly still sounds rather vague and utopian (cf. Avineri 1968, 13–40; Kolakowski 1978a, 127; Mewes 1976; Rader 1979, 165–69). It is most of all in the elimination of this utopian tone that the "mature" writings differ from the early ones.

The "Mature" Theory of the State

As already mentioned, *The German Ideology*, although not published until 1932, is the first work in which the "materialist conception of history" is systematically set out and contains the first hints of a class theory of the state.[6] It is also the first work that is entirely written by Marx and Engels together. Thus, naturally, there are the inevitable scholastic debates over who was the true originator of which ideas, particularly with respect to the state which, however, can be safely ignored here without affecting the general argument (see, e.g., Avineri 1968, 203; Draper 1977, 181–86; Hunt 1974, 125–30; Maguire 1978, 11–13).

According to the argument in *The German Ideology*, the division of labor, as it has evolved involuntarily and unplanned, produces a "contradiction between the interests of the individual and that of the community," because of which "the latter takes an independent form as the State, divorced from the real interests of individual and community" (Marx 1977, 169). This state presents "an illusory communal life," which is, however, based on real social relations "and especially . . . on the classes, already determined by the division of labour, which in every such mass of men separate out, and of which one dominates all the others" (ibid.). Furthermore, "through the emancipation of private property from the community, the State has become a separate entity, beside and outside civil society; but it is nothing more than the form of organization which the bourgeois necessarily adopt both for internal and external purposes, for the mutual guarantee of their property and interests . . . the State is the form in which the individuals of a ruling class assert their

6   Marx himself never used the phrase "historical materialism." It was coined, according to Kline (1984, 24, n. 42) by Engels, as was the term "materialist conception of history."

common interests . . ." (Marx and Engels 1947, 59–60). Although these passages still show traces of Marx's early writings the movement toward the "classical" theory of the state as an instrument of class oppression is clear here.[7]

The exact meaning of this "classical" theory depends on how one views the relation between the economic base and the state generally, an extremely controversial issue in current marxology. Unfortunately, the question must be confronted here to some extent. On the one hand there are those who claim that Marxists, including Marx and Engels, treat the state as an "epiphenomenon" of the mode of production, as wholly or largely derivative of the economic base and the corresponding class structure (Keane 1978, 50–55; Kline 1984; Levi 1981, 434; Lichtheim 1965, 373–74; Spencer 1979, 173–74). This view is usually supported by citing one or more of the following *loci classici*. In *The German Ideology*, Marx and Engels claim that

> the material life of individuals, which by no means depends merely on their "will," their mode of production and form of intercourse,[8] which mutually determine each other—this is the real basis of the State and remains so at all the stages at which division of labour and private property are still necessary, quite independently of the

7   Hal Draper (1977, 190), anxious to rid Marx of what he calls "Hegelese," interprets these passages as precursors of Engels's later theory according to which the state emerged as a socially necessary institution which became, however, in the context of an emerging class society necessarily a *class* institution. But not only is this extremely implausible from the point of view of timing (Engels formulated his theory at least thirty years later, whereas only months before writing the present passages Marx was still writing pure "Hegelese"), it can also be proved plain wrong: right after the first passage quoted, Marx and Engels make it quite clear that the necessity of an "illusory 'general' interest in the form of the state" is attributable entirely to the fact that "individuals seek only their particular interest, which for them does not coincide with their communal interest" (Marx 1977, 170), and *not* to any necessity to take care of commonly agreed upon needs (see also Kolakowski 1978a, 159, 172, 178).

8   "Form of intercourse" here obviously refers to what are elsewhere called "relations of production," "social relations," or "relations of property," as they perform the exact same function as "fetters" upon the developing "forces of production" which must ultimately be replaced by new "forms of intercourse" (see Marx 1977, 178–79, 180–81; cf. Rader 1979, 199). The terminology itself, then, is not sufficient reason for giving a nonreductionist interpretation to this particular passage.

will of individuals. These actual relations are in no way created by the State power; on the contrary they are the power creating it. The individuals who rule in these conditions, besides having to constitute their power in the form of the State, have to give their will, which is determined by these definite conditions, a universal expression as the will of the State, as law—an expression whose content is always determined by the relations of this class, as the civil and criminal law demonstrates in the clearest possible way. (Marx 1977, 184)

The Poverty of Philosophy, written a year later (1846–1847), contains the famous passage:

Social relations are closely bound up with production forces. In acquiring new productive forces men change their mode of production; and in changing their mode of production, in changing the way of earning their living, they change all their social relations. The handmill gives you society with the feudal lord; the steammill, society with the industrial capitalist.

The same men who establish their social relations in conformity with their material productivity, produce also principles, ideas and categories, in conformity with their social relations. (Marx 1963b, 109)

By far the most often quoted is the passage from the "1859 Preface" to *A Contribution to the Critique of Political Economy*:

The general conclusion at which I arrived and which, once reached, became the guiding principle of my studies can be summarized as follows. In the social production of their existence, men inevitably enter into definite relations, which are independent of their will, namely relations of production appropriate to a given stage in the development of their material forces of production. The totality of these relations of production constitutes the economic structure of society, the real foundation, on which arises a legal and political superstructure and to which correspond definite forms of social consciousness. The mode of production of material life conditions[9] the general process of social, political and intellec-

9   I have deliberately used the least "reductionist" translation I know of here in order not to have to enter the debate over whether more conventional translations overstate the reductionism of the German original. Those

tual life. It is not the consciousness of men that determines their existence, but their social existence that determines their consciousness. (Marx 1975, 425)

In the third volume of *Capital*, finally, Marx states that

the specific economic form, in which unpaid surplus-labour is pumped out of direct producers, determines the relationship of rulers and ruled, as it grows directly out of production itself and, in turn, reacts upon it as a determining element. Upon this, however, is founded the entire formation of the economic community which grows up out of the production relations themselves, thereby simultaneously its specific political form. It is always the direct relationship of the owners of the conditions of production to the direct producers—a relation always naturally corresponding to a definite stage in the development of the methods of labour and thereby its social productivity—which reveals the innermost secret, the hidden basis of the entire social structure, and with it the political form of the relation of sovereignty and dependence, in short, the corresponding specific form of the state. This does not prevent the same economic basis—the same from the standpoint of its main conditions—due to innumerable different empirical circumstances, natural environment, racial relations, external historical influences, etc., from showing infinite variations and graduations in appearance, which can be ascertained only by analysis of the empirically given circumstances. (Marx 1967b, 791–92)

Now, it does not seem too frivolous to me to interpret these passages to mean that the level of development of the material means of production causes specific relations of production to come into existence, and that the latter, in turn, cause a specific superstructure to arise—allowing for a fairly narrow range of variation attributable to secondary, essentially exogenous factors such as climate (cf. Kolakowski 1978a, 338). But then again, this is not saying very much since *none* of the crucial terms is at all clearly defined. The meaning and conceptual boundaries of the three central variables—the forces of production, the relations of production, and the superstructure—are

---

translations render the German "*bedingt*" as "determines" rather than "conditions" (see, Balbus 1982, 22; Gouldner 1980, 224–25; Rader 1979, 15).

far from clear or obvious, and this is especially, and not a little paradoxically, true for the first two, the ones specific to Marxism. And even if these could be adequately sorted out, the exact nature of the "correspondence," "appropriateness," or "conformity" between them still remains to be specified (cf. Giddens 1979, 150–54). But however unclear the exact meaning of these passages, it *does* seem reasonable to assume that they were intended to have *some* definite meaning, an obvious point that the scores of exegetes and reinterpreters often seem to overlook.

It may be more realistic to redefine the "relations of production" or the even vaguer notion of "social existence" so as to include large chunks of the superstructure (Giddens 1971, 21–24, 40–45; Rader 1979, ch. 1), but that hardly helps to explain how those same relations can simultaneously be the "real basis" or "real foundation" *upon which* the superstructure "arises," or again the "forces creating it," unless they were partly to arise upon, or create themselves! To attribute some sort of "organic model" to Marx, in which all factors interact "dialectically," yet with a "causal hierarchy" in which an ill-defined "base" is in an unspecified sense "more important" than the other (cf. Avineri 1968, 41, 65–95; Giddens 1977, 195–99; Ollman 1971; Rader 1979, ch. 2), is tantamount, it seems to me, to saying that he had no model at all, other than a vague idea that all things are related. Similarly, S. W. Moore (1957, 26–29, 46–47) argues— quoting the late Engels's "corrections" of "vulgar" determinism mentioned in the *Introduction* above—that the economic base only prevails on the state "in the last instance," leaving much room for variation, and he adds: *"The crucial problem for the Marxian theory of the state is to investigate the limits of independent action by state power"* (47). Again, sensible though it is, this amounts to admitting that Marxism simply does not *have* a theory of the relation between economy and state other than that the effects of the economy should not be overlooked in explaining state action, a piece of advice that, arguably, may have been needed in the middle of the nineteenth century, but that has become little more than a platitude since then. If historical materialism means no more than this, why did Marx and Engels not say so themselves? Moreover, such an interpretation seems to deny the whole theory of conflicting forces and relations of production as the "motive force of history" which to Marx and Engels is the whole point to begin with (Marx 1975, 425–26; 1977, 178–81).

In general, all this raises the rather obvious question of why Marx and Engels would have repeated the same argument over and over again, over a time span of several decades and in almost identical terms, if all they meant to convey was the truism that things are interdependent, and why they should have persisted in formulating it in terms that can so easily be interpreted to mean something quite different. Of course, they also wrote journalistic pieces that seem squarely to contradict the reductionist interpretation of the relation between economy and state (Avineri 1968, 41; Rader 1979, 14–18). But does this necessitate a reinterpretation of the above passages to force them into conformity with those less systematic writings? For one thing, even in the most famous of them, *The Eighteenth Brumaire of Louis Bonaparte* and *The Class Struggles in France* (Marx 1963a; Marx and Engels 1959, 281–317), Marx clearly and explicitly *tries* to treat the state and politics as derivative of the class structure but simply fails (Spencer 1979). Second, such reinterpretations only raise the further and intriguing question why so many writers find the very thought of any inconsistencies anywhere in the work of Marx and Engels so utterly intolerable. Would it not be a lot simpler and more sensible to accept at least the possibility that their statements on the relation between state and economy are not entirely consistent, as one would with any other social theorist?

I will assume, then, that at least in part of their works and part of the time Marx and Engels considered the state and politics as wholly or largely a product of the economic base and more particularly of the class structure. How else can one interpret a particularly strong statement such as this one from *The Poverty of Philosophy*? "Truly, one must be destitute of all historical knowledge not to know that it is the sovereigns who in all ages have been subject to economic conditions, but they have never dictated laws to them. Legislation, whether political or civil, never does more than proclaim, express in words, the will of economic relations" (Marx 1963b, 83).

But how exactly "the will of economic relations" expresses itself in legislation is still open to interpretation. One can picture the class structure as a distribution of power that is slowly shifting in favor of the working class as a result of the development of the forces of production. Economic "dominance" would then be a matter of degree, and so would the class character of state policy: slowly shifting to reflect the changing balance of power in the economy (e.g., Stephens 1979, 4–5). This view is not entirely unfounded: Marx certainly supported any reform that would improve the lot of the workers and once even referred to the Ten Hours Bill as a great victory of "the political economy of the working class" over that of "the middle class" (Marx 1974, 79; see also 1977, 228–29). But there can be little doubt that on the whole he took a far more categorical view: the state is entirely controlled by either one class or another, but it is never "shared."

At any rate, the simplest interpretation of the Marxian theory of the state is the one propagated by Lenin and his followers (Chang 1931; Lenin 1932; S. W. Moore 1957) and consequently long considered to be the only possible one. Its *locus classicus* is the famous formula of the *Communist Manifesto*: "Political power, properly so called, is merely the organizing power of one class for oppressing another" (Marx 1977, 238), and the even more famous corollary according to which "the executive of the modern State is but a committee for managing the common affairs of the whole bourgeoisie" (ibid., 223). The emphasis here is on "merely" and "but." This version specifically argues that the function of the state, *any* state, is *"nothing but the oppression of one class by another"* (Chang 1931, 52, emphasis added). By rather selectively quoting from Engels's *Origin of the Family* and greatly simplifying the argument (although, as we shall see, also rendering it more logically consistent), Lenin (1932, 7–20 and *passim*) asserts that the state emerged historically only as a result of the emergence of irreconcilable class antagonism which could only be kept from destroying society altogether by a separate institution capable of forcefully suppressing one class at the behest of another (for Engels's rather more complex argument see Engels 1972, 159–64). Moreover, all class societies, since they are all riven by "irreconcilable" class antagonism, need a state "for the forcible holding down of the exploited class in the conditions of oppression . . . determined by the existing mode of production" (Engels 1939, 306). Conversely, all states are necessarily the instrument of the economically dominant class. Even the modern "bourgeois" democracies, Engels argues, are instruments of capitalist rule so long as the working class is not yet mature enough to emancipate itself (1972, 160–62). In a phrase that has recently become the subject of much debate Engels declares: "The modern state, whatever its form, is an essentially capitalist machine; it is the state of the capitalists, the ideal collective body of all capitalists" (1939, 304).

This version of the Marxian theory of the state amounts, then, to the claim that "the State, no matter what its form, is in origin and nature, in purpose and function, a class organ, an organization for the oppression of one class by another" (Chang 1931, 58). The obvious implication of this is that when, and *only* when, classes and their antagonisms have been abolished once and for all, the state, thus defined, will also cease to be necessary. In the famous words of Engels:

> When ultimately it becomes really representative of society as a whole, it makes itself superfluous. As soon as there is no longer any class of society to be held in subjection; as soon as, along with class domination and the struggle for individual existence based on the former anarchy of production, the collisions and excesses arising from these have also been abolished, there is nothing more to be repressed which would make a special repressive force, a state necessary. The first act in which the state really comes forward as the representative of society as a whole—the taking possession of the means of production in the name of society—is at the same time its last independent act as a state. The interference of the state power in social relations becomes superfluous in one sphere after another, and then ceases of itself. The government of persons is replaced by the administration of things and the direction of the processes of production. The state is not "abolished," *it withers away.* (Engels 1939, 306–7)

Thus, this "Leninist" interpretation is relatively straightforward. The state is *defined* as an exclusively repressive institution.[10] It originated with the emergence of classes as the instrument with which the economically dominant class could forcibly suppress all others. It necessarily persists and fulfills this function only so long as classes continue to exist. It will eventually be captured by the working class and used to abolish all classes, and hence all class antagonisms, and it will "wither away" by itself once this goal has been accomplished (cf. Chang 1931, ch. 3; Kolakowski 1978a, 58–61). Of course, as Engels suggests, institutions for the "administration of things and the direction of the processes of production" remain. Only the repressive functions of the state will disappear as the need to repress anyone disappears. As the *Communist Manifesto* has it, "the public power will lose its political character" (Marx 1977, 238; cf. Giddens 1973, 126; Kolakowski 1978a, 254–56; McLellan 1980, 211; Weiner 1980, 4). Clearly Marx and Engels believed that once classes were abolished social conflict would be reduced to such an extent as to render any special agency for its resolution, let alone one employing force, superfluous. This is one of the most persistent themes in the writings of both Marx and Engels, throughout their careers, including, as we have seen, the "early" writings of Marx, albeit without the class theory (see, e.g., Engels 1972, 162; Marx 1963b, 174; 1979, 336, 354; Marx and Engels 1959, 465).[11]

10   Draper describes the "objective relationship between the state and the class structure" as established by Marx and Engels thus: "The state is the institution, or complex of institutions, which bases itself on the availability of forcible coercion by special agencies of society in order to maintain the dominance of a ruling class, preserve existing property relations from basic change, and keep all other classes in subjection" (1977, 251). He adds that "in subjection" does not necessarily mean "cowering under a whip" but rather "in willing compliance, in passive acquiescence, or in ingrained dependence" (ibid.). But if *this* is the way the state resolves "irreconcilable" class antagonisms one is forced to wonder how "irreconcilable" they were to begin with (cf. Plamenatz 1963, 351–56). As we shall see, the central problem of the recent Marxist literature on the state is how to maintain that the state keeps the working class "in subjection" while conceding that it makes surprisingly little use of the "whip" in doing so.

11   Although Heller (1981) does somewhat overstate the case that Marx anticipated the abolition of *all* institutions mediating between the "associated producers," Giddens surely *under*states it when he asserts that Marx did not believe in the possibility of abolishing "all forms of division of interest between men" any more than "that conflicts between men can be abrogated" (1976, 102; cf. Altman 1981, 394–95). As the *persistent* theme of the aboli-

But clear and consistent as this theory of the state may appear, it is, the inevitable Leninist claims to the contrary notwithstanding, not the only one to be found in the writings of Marx and Engels. As it turns out, for explaining concrete, complex reality the theory is altogether too simplistic. Consequently, in those writings in which they attempt to deal with that reality, as well as in some of their more general statements, Marx and Engels often present a model that differs significantly from the simple theory. But what seems to have been gained in terms of realism is definitely lost in terms of logical consistency.[12]

First, Engels's explanation of the origin of the state is more complex than Leninists have claimed. Perhaps to accommodate Marx's notion of an "Asiatic" mode of production in which the state is actually the cause, not the result, of the class structure (Gouldner 1980, ch. 11), and no doubt also in view of the anthropological evidence he had been gathering,[13] Engels postulates two quite different theories of the relationship between the origins of classes and of the state. In addition to the theory that the state emerges *as a result* of the emerging division of labor and consequent class structure and class conflict, he suggests that even in tribal societies in which no clear class divisions yet exist, some individuals are entrusted with authority to perform functions in the common interest (e.g., conflict adjudication, protection of the rights of individuals, etc.). Out of this authority separate organs may develop that in time come to dominate society and create a class division between rulers and ruled which then develops further into greater and greater inequality of power and wealth. Thus, in the course of its development the state itself creates a ruling class of which it *becomes*

---

tion of politics clearly shows, Marx and Engels *did* come very close to believing just that (see also Fetscher 1961; McLellan 1969; Ollman 1977).

12   My treatment of the writings on the state of *both* Marx and Engels on an equal footing is not meant as an endorsement of any particular position in the continuous debate over the issue of whether Engels did or did not adequately represent the "authentic" Marx. Instead, I am only interested in establishing whether and to what extent there are elements of a common, more or less consistent theory of the state in the writings of each, *however* many inconsistencies and contradictions they may contain as well.

13   Although, as Jessop notes (1982, 17) a precursor of this more complex theory already appears in *The German Ideology*.

the instrument, although it also continues to perform functions originally assigned to it in the common interest (see Engels 1939, 165, 197–202; cf. Hunt 1984, 6–12).

There clearly are two conflicting theories of the interrelated emergence of classes and the state here: according to one the emergence of a rudimentary division of labor leads to growing economic inequality which, in turn, leads to more intense social (class) conflict which, finally, is suppressed by specialized institutions created by the wealthy to subject and control the poor and thus protect and maintain the privileges of the wealthy; according to the second, the causal sequence is the reverse: people originally entrusted with authority to fulfill commonly agreed upon functions use that authority also in their own particular interests *at the expense* of the common interest, until they come to form a separate stratum of wealthy rulers who use the power of the state to maintain and protect their power and privileges while continuing to perform certain indispensable social functions as well (cf. Gouldner 1980, 328–33). Engels appears to present these two accounts as two clearly distinct historical roads by which the same ultimate result was obtained. Draper (1977, ch. 11) tries to weld the two into one coherent theory according to which class and state formation occurs in a mutually reinforcing process each supporting as well as feeding upon the other. Hunt claims Engels reconciled what he aptly calls the "class state" with the "parasite state" view in a letter of 1890, in which Engels seems to conceive "the parasitic tendencies as a striving to be found in all states but fulfilled only in certain exceptional types" (Hunt 1984, 24). But for the exaggerated desire to present Engels's arguments as a perfectly coherent entity, there is in principle little wrong with these interpretations. To view the historical emergence of political and economic inequality as simultaneous, mutually reinforcing processes is probably quite reasonable.

But there is a problem. Adding the second causal sequence as another possibility, or fusing it with the first, completely undermines the intent and implications of the original theory. The theory becomes more acceptable only because there is nothing particularly Marxist about it anymore. In the original theory, the *exclusive raison d'être* of the state was the economically privileged class's need to forcibly subject the less privileged classes. The assertion that once this sole *raison d'être* was abolished the state, too, would disappear seemed at least a vaguely plausible implication.[14] But if the state can arise for reasons *other than* the "irreconcilable" antagonism of classes, there is absolutely no reason to believe the disappearance of classes will also lead to a "withering away" of the state. Thus, the "question whether it was the wealthy who made themselves rulers, or the rulers who made themselves wealthy" (Hunt 1984, 25) is a crucial one.

It might be argued that it is only a matter of definition: the state may be narrowly defined as only a repressive class agency or more broadly as including both purely administrative and purely repressive functions. Only the repressive functions are the product of class divisions and they will disappear along with them, while the administrative part of the broadly defined state remains. The original theory thus simply defines the state more narrowly than the second one, but other than that they are perfectly compatible, it would seem (cf. Elster 1985, 400–402).

But this clearly will not do either, for the whole point of the second theory was precisely that an initially purely "administrative" agency will become an independent power base for its incumbents by means of which they can form a new ruling class, because of "the parasitic tendencies . . . found in all states." If this could happen at the dawn of civilization when purely administrative functions were presumably very simple and thus the extra resources at the administrators' disposal very modest, it is even *more* certain to happen in a highly complex modern society in which administrative tasks require highly specialized agencies wielding and controlling enormous economic resources and power (see Plamenatz 1963, 356–67). Tragically, orthodox Marxists have ignored Engels's more complex theory of the origins of classes and the state and have thus never seriously contemplated its unsettling implications (cf. Gouldner

---

14   But no more than that. So far, no Marxist has adequately shown why the personnel of the state, even *if* originally hired solely by and for the privileged class, could not subsequently become autonomous of this class and pursue its own interests, if necessary *at the expense of* its former masters (cf. Levi 1981, 443; Parkin 1979, 126–29).

1980, 339–52, and ch. 12). It is an outright scandal that even those who *do* acknowledge the more complex theory *still* do not seem to be able to draw the obvious implication *even today* (Draper 1977, 260–62; Meiksins Wood 1981, 83).

Another troublesome implication is that even in existing class societies state incumbents need not necessarily be the exclusive instrument of the economically dominant class and may, in fact, be tempted to play one class off against the other to pursue their own interests (Levi 1981; Plamenatz 1963, 367–73). That this was more than just a theoretical possibility was brought out rather forcefully by the events of 1848–1850 in France and Germany. In trying to make sense of these events, Marx and Engels were forced to employ far more complex arguments than the simple class theory of the state allows, although the extent to which they were aware of this is a subject of much controversy (see, e.g., Elster 1985, 408–28; Maguire 1978; Spencer 1979). At any rate, in Marx's famous analyses of the events leading up to the rise of the second Empire in France, the state and politics appear as far from simple "expressions" of ruling-class needs in the class struggle.

On the contrary, although strenuously pretending to employ a systematic class-theoretical approach, Marx *in fact* explains the political events as resulting from a complex sequence of conflicts and alliances between a variety of groups and individuals motivated by all sorts of aspirations, desires and ideals, none of which easily fits the simple formulas of the class model (Marx 1963a; Marx and Engels 1959, 281–317; cf. Spencer 1979). Amid all this, the state does not appear as the willing instrument of the bourgeoisie at all, but as an autonomous force which tends to dominate society completely. As its bureaucratic and military organization is further developed with each major upheaval, Marx argues, the state becomes more and more an "appalling parasitic body, which enmeshes the body of French society like a net and chokes all its pores" (1963b, 121), until, under the second Bonaparte, it appears "to have made itself completely independent" (122; cf. Marx 1974, 206–8; Spencer 1979, 176–83).

However, the degree of independence Marx grants the state—and exactly from whom and what—is not very clear and subject to various interpretations. Marx clearly does not wish to present the Bonapartist state as neutral between classes. On the contrary, the whole tenor of his arguments is that the bourgeoisie was forced to accept a strong dictatorial, and hence somewhat uncontrollable, state to protect itself against a proletariat that for the first time appears as a credible threat to its privileges, although the evidence he presents does not clearly support his case (see Marx and Engels 1959, 313; Hunt 1984, 47–56; Perez-Diaz 1978, 53–83; Miliband 1965, 283–85; Spencer 1979). But it remains unclear in what sense and to what degree the state is independent from the bourgeoisie.

Many years later, Engels appears to generalize from this case in a famous passage in which he argues that since "the state arose from the need to hold class antagonism in check . . . it is, as a rule, the state of the most powerful, economically dominant class. . . . By way of exception, however, periods occur in which the ruling classes balance each other so nearly that the state power, as ostensible mediator, acquires, for the moment, a certain degree of independence from both" (Engels 1972, 160). He gives the second Empire as a typical case (ibid.). Clearly, however, Engels considers this to be a rare and transitory phenomenon. A few pages further he makes this clear once again, in another famous line: "The cohesive force of civilized society is the state, which in all typical periods is exclusively the state of the ruling class, and in all cases remains essentially a machine for keeping down the oppressed exploited class" (164). But how and to what degree the state becomes independent in such transitory cases of a class balance of power, and how the state becomes the instrument of the ruling class once again when "typical periods" return, Engels does not say.

There is yet another possible interpretation of the theoretical implications of "1848." Over two decades after the event Marx claimed that the second Empire "was the only form of government possible at a time when the bourgeoisie had already lost, and the working class had not yet acquired, the faculty of ruling the nation" (Marx 1974, 208). This suggests it might have been more than a mere transitory exception. Hal Draper has attempted to formulate a single coherent theory drawing on absolutely every line ever written by Marx and Engels that could possibly be of any relevance whatsoever. According to the resulting theory one particular class has undivided control over the state in "normal" times of relative stability, but in major periods of transition between one mode of production and another, when the class struggle is still undecided and in flux, the state acquires a degree of autonomy from all classes, allowing it to pursue its own, self-aggrandizing interests, though only to the extent that this does not seriously conflict with the interests of the economically dominant class (Draper 1977, chs. 15–23, esp. pp. 585–87). Moreover, for a variety of reasons, the state shows a greater tendency toward such autonomization in capitalist than in other modes of production (ch. 14).

But Draper's zeal to iron out all conceivable inconsistencies (cf. Gouldner 1985, 116–30) leads him to grossly overinterpret a few meager hints by Marx and Engels. Again one must wonder why Marx and Engels did not clearly state it themselves if this was indeed their "real" theory. Besides, the theory, whether rightly attributed to Marx and Engels or not, is of no more than antiquarian interest since it is obviously wrong: autonomization of the state has been frequent (one need only think of the reigns of, e.g., Attila, Peter the Great, Louis xiv, and so on) and even appears to be a secular trend, transitions to another mode of production have been rare indeed (cf. Gouldner 1980, 299–308). Finally, Draper's formulation does not really clarify anything since, like Marx and Engels themselves, he leaves the exact degree of "independence" from the "dominant" class, as well as the way it is obtained and lost again, completely obscure. If the state is really autonomous, why can it not undertake anything against that class's interests? If the class has the power to prevent that, in what sense is the state *ever* "autonomous"?

Thus, Marx's analyses of Bonapartism can be interpreted in at least three ways: it is a form of authoritarianism to which the exploiting class has recourse whenever its privileges are seriously threatened; it is characteristic of the power equilibrium between classes in times of major transitions; it is an occasional and transitory anomaly resulting from a temporary power equilibrium. The first is, it seems to me, the explanation Marx would have *liked* to give but could not, precisely because it does not square with the way the regime arose and achieved its autonomy.[15] The second rests on flimsy textual evidence and raises as many questions as it answers. Only the third interpretation appears plausible. It is, after all, the only one explicitly endorsed by Engels and is in line with the well-documented fact that Marx and Engels's attempts to come to grips with such phenomena as Bonapartism consist mainly of *ad hoc* theorizing (see Levi 1981, 462; Lichtheim 1965, 384, 396; Spencer 1979).[16] Since other interpretations do not offer any clear alternative theory of the relation between state and "ruling class," one has to conclude that while Marx and Engels were unable to validate their original, simple theory they did not develop any alternative either, in other words, they simply did not leave any coherent theory of the state.[17]

Thus, Marx and Engels's theorizing about the origins of the state and its relation to the class structure is either more or less logically consistent but clearly too simplistic, or else realistic but then it either flatly contradicts the original theory or else it lacks clarity and coherence. It remains to deal briefly with perhaps the most controversial aspect of the Marxian theory of the state: the state's role in the transition from capitalism to socialism.

Although Marx and Engels shared the eventual aims of anarchism, they always insisted that the root of the evil was the existence of classes and not the state itself and that, hence, the state could only be abolished by first using *it* to abolish classes (see, e.g., Marx, Engels, and Lenin 1967, 244–46). This argument clearly implies the "pure" class theory of the state: the state defined as "nothing but" an agency for the use of force by

15   Elster (1985, 411–22) calls this the "abdication theory of the state" and clearly shows (esp. 415–16) how hard it is to render it plausible and how easily it becomes indeterminate with respect to the interests of the bourgeoisie.

16   This interpretation also seems to accord with Hunt's somewhat inconclusive discussion (1984, 47–63). It should be noted that, given Marx and Engels's unshakable faith in the imminence of the transition to socialism (see below), Draper's interpretation and mine are not that far apart in practice, although Marx and Engels clearly did not consciously combine the two elements—temporary class stalemate and transition between modes of production—into a coherent overall theory of the state as Draper seems to suggest.

17   The *accuracy* of Marx's descriptions of the events of 1848 is, of course, another matter. It has recently been contested rather convincingly by Traugott (1985; see also Gouldner 1985, 100–13).

one class against another. Thus, in a critical note on Bakunin's *Statism and Anarchy* written in 1874, Marx argues that so long as other classes, and particularly the capitalist class, still exist, the proletariat, once having obtained government power, will still have to "employ *forcible* means, hence governmental means" (1974, 333). So the argument is essentially that the proletariat will have to gain control of the means of organized violence, which is the state, in order to use them to forcibly disown and subject the capitalist class, and only when it has succeeded in doing this will the need for using organized force against anyone, and hence the state *thus defined*, disappear.

Two analytically distinct issues are often confused in the heated debates on the transitional state. One deals with popular control of the state: did Marx and Engels envisage a majoritarian democracy or an elite dictatorship? The second concerns the treatment of the (capitalist) minority: how much violence and ruthlessness are necessary and advisable to force the former exploiters into subjection? Many critics of Marxism would argue that the two questions are inextricably linked and that sharp distinctions between them are hence useless. But one of the distinguishing aspects of Marxism until recently may well be the implicit belief, rightly or wrongly, that the two questions are entirely distinct and unrelated.

As for the first question, I do not think it can be shown that Marx or Engels *ever* advocated an "educational" dictatorship by a "vanguard" à la Babeuf, whether explicitly or implicitly, as some have claimed (e.g., Lichtheim 1965, 56–62, 372–77). In fact, they always carefully dissociated themselves from this authoritarian strategy, even during periods of extreme revolutionary enthusiasm (Hunt 1974, 84–92, 110–23). But they did advocate the notorious "*class dictatorship* of the proletariat as the necessary transit point to the *abolition of class differences generally*" (Marx and Engels 1959, 317) on several occasions, precisely during periods of social upheaval. Nevertheless, as careful consideration of *every* occurrence of the theme by Draper (1962) and Hunt (1974, ch. 9; see also Elster 1985, 443–49; Sowell 1985, 145–49; Wolfe 1965, 167–78) convincingly shows, there is no unequivocal evidence that they advocated a "dictatorship" in the modern sense of the word.

Of course, one can argue that this would vitiate the whole intent of proletarian "self-emancipation" as Draper (1974, 1977, ch. 13) does, but this is the least convincing argument for believing in Marx and Engels's basically democratic intentions. After all, it certainly did not stop the Bolsheviks from holding on to power by dictatorial means, in the name of the workers' and peasants' "true" interests, once they had lost majority support. A more convincing argument is the fact that Marx and Engels *never* make clear what they mean when they refer to the "dictatorship of the proletariat," as if to them the term was wholly unproblematic (Miliband 1965, 289). As Hunt (1974, ch. 9, 204–336) has shown, it seems most likely that by "dictatorship" they simply meant *unmitigated majority rule*, that is, democratic government without *any* institutional or legal restraints.[18] What is most striking, in fact, about the passages in which they consider the transitional "rule" or "dictatorship" of the proletariat is the complete absence of any hint that they ever considered direct proletarian rule as in any way problematic (cf. Elster 1985, 448). In the *Communist Manifesto* they simply equate raising "the proletariat to the position of ruling class" with winning "the battle of democracy" (Marx 1977, 237). Marx's notes on Bakunin, written more than a quarter of a century later, are remarkable in that they suggest he simply did not comprehend the latter's objections to his statist strategy, which he dismisses as "democratic twaddle, political drivel" (1974, 336) while flatly reiterating that the entire proletariat will indeed govern directly until all "political" government (i.e., coercion) will be obsolete (335–37).

There is, in fact, one, and *only* one, mention of the "dictatorship of the proletariat" with reference to a specific institutional arrangement, and it further reinforces the impression that it meant little more than (unmitigated, ruthless) proletarian majority rule. In his introduction of 1891 to the reissue of *The Civil War in France*—Marx's passionate obituary to the 1871 Paris

18   Of course, as Marx knew very well, the proletariat was not a majority anywhere during his lifetime. But he clearly expected it to become an overwhelming majority relatively rapidly (cf. Hunt 1974, 88) and believed, perhaps rather naively, it would be possible to form an alliance with the poor peasantry in the meantime (Marx 1974, 333–34).

Commune—Engels writes: "Of late the social-democratic Phil-istine has once more been filled with wholesome terror at the words: dictatorship of the proletariat. Well and good, gentle-men; do you want to know what this dictatorship looks like? Look at the Paris Commune. That was the dictatorship of the proletariat" (Marx and Engels 1959, 362).

After approvingly describing the ultra-democratic features of the Paris Commune (Marx 1974, 208–12), Marx proclaims that it was "essentially a working-class government . . . the political form at last discovered under which to work out the economical emancipation of labor" (212). Marx's sincerity here is the sub-ject of another one of those perpetual disputes of marxology. No doubt he privately had serious misgivings from the start about the true class nature of the Commune and its chances of survival (Hunt 1984, 100–108, 120–24). No doubt his pamphlet was in part a deliberate attempt at historical falsification, ob-scuring the role of its leaders who were mostly followers of Proudhon, Blanqui, and Bakunin, in order to claim the heroic episode for Marxism (see Marx 1977, 592–94; Lichtheim 1965, 112–21; B. D. Wolfe 1965, 105–47). But none of this necessarily discredits Marx's passionate praise for the type of direct de-mocracy that the Commune tried to implement (Avineri 1968, 239–49; Draper 1977, 314–18; Hunt 1974, 307; 1984, ch. 5; Perez-Diaz 1978, 55). Nor can it be claimed that the ultra-democratic vision of *The Civil War in France* was an unchar-acteristic temporary aberration (see, e.g., Lichtheim 1965, 112–21), if my argument that Marx simply did not *offer* a character-istic theory of proletarian rule anywhere else is correct. It is at best "uncharacteristic" in the sense that it is more specific than anything he wrote before or after on the subject.[19]

But if "dictatorship" of the proletariat meant some form of democratic majority rule, it certainly did not mean *liberal* de-mocracy, which brings us to the second question concerning the

19   As so often, the controversy over Marx's real intentions has political roots. The ultrademocratic passages in Marx's pamphlet served as a justification for the Leninist strategy of "smashing" the bourgeois state and replacing it with Soviet-type direct democracy (Lenin 1932; cf. Chang 1931, ch. 6) only to be ignored when they became a potential source of embarrassment for the Bolsheviks once they had come to power (see ch. 2).

transitional state. Hunt (1974, 315–16) claims that Marx and Engels referred to the repressive mission of the dictatorship of the proletariat only once in a relatively obscure polemic against anarchism, published in Italian in 1874 (see Marx 1974, 327–32; Marx and Engels 1959, 481–85), which was subsequently used to great effect by Lenin (1932, 51). But although especially Engels's contribution is indeed of a rare and brutal frankness, it is not as atypical as Hunt suggests. From their earliest "mature" works on it is quite clear that Marx and Engels expected the transitional state to suppress all resistance ruthlessly while abolishing private property in the means of production, and thereby all classes, by whatever means necessary. In fact, if the term "dictatorship" meant anything to them, it was this unprecedented, unrestrained majority despotism to end all despotisms, as Hunt himself clearly shows (1974, ch. 9; see also Alexander 1982b, 458–60).

For one thing, in all those passages in which they explain at all what they mean when they say that political power "properly so called" will disappear *after* it has been used by the proletariat to abolish all classes, Marx and Engels make it quite clear that they mean precisely *force* and *coercion*, as I have already argued above. In addition to those already cited, there is the following ominous passage in *The German Ideology*:

> Further, it follows that every class which is struggling for mastery, even when its domination, as is the case with the proletariat, postulates the abolition of the old form of society in its entirety and of domination itself, must first conquer for itself political power in order to represent its interest in turn as the general interest, which immediately it is forced to do. Just because individuals seek only their particular interest, which for them does not coincide with their communal interest, the latter will be imposed on them as an interest "alien" to them, and "independent" of them, as in its turn a particular, peculiar "general" interest; or they themselves must remain within this discord, as in democracy. (Marx 1977, 169–70)

One could scarcely find a better passage illustrating the meaning of "positive freedom" and its illiberal implications (Berlin 1969, ch. 3).

The *Communist Manifesto* announces that

> the proletariat will use its political supremacy to wrest, by degrees,
> all capital from the bourgeoisie, to centralize all instruments of
> production in the hands of the State, i.e. of the proletariat organ-
> ized as the ruling class; and to increase the total of production
> forces as rapidly as possible.
>
> Of course, in the beginning this cannot be effected except by
> means of despotic inroads on the rights of property, and on the
> conditions of bourgeois production. (Marx 1977, 237)

These "despotic inroads" are to include, besides centralization of control of all production and communication in the hands of the state, "confiscation of the property of all emigrants and rebels," establishment of "industrial armies," and massive de-urbanization (ibid.). Only after the proletariat "sweeps away by force the old conditions of production" will "public power . . . lose its political character" (238).

Similarly, in the "Address to the Communist League" of March 1850—famous for its battle cry "The Revolution in Permanence" and notorious for its extremely violent language and militant refusal to accept the fact that the revolutionary tide had by that time definitely turned—Marx and Engels call upon the workers of Germany "not [to] allow themselves to be misguided by the democratic talk of freedom for the communities, of self-government, etc." Instead, "it is the task of the really revolutionary party to carry through the strictest centralization," because "revolutionary activity . . . can proceed with full force only from the centre" (Marx 1977, 284).

Finally, if only for its brutal frankness, it may be useful to quote the Engels passage Hunt claims to be the only one of its kind: "A revolution is certainly the most authoritarian thing there is; it is the act whereby one part of the population imposes its will upon the other part by means of rifles, bayonets, and cannon—authoritarian means, if such there be at all; and if the victorious party does not want to have fought in vain, it must maintain this rule by means of the terror which its arms inspire in the reactionaries" (Marx and Engels 1959, 485).

Thus, the transitional "dictatorship of the proletariat" would clearly involve a highly centralized state apparatus tightly controlling all spheres of production and communication and capable and willing to suppress ruthlessly all minority opposition to the majority will of the proletariat as ruling class. Marx and Engels did not for a moment seriously consider the possibility that such a state could easily become an uncontrollable monster, no matter how democratic in form. And since they never thought this might become a problem, they also never doubted that the proletarian state would be impelled to abolish all classes only to then inevitably "wither away" by itself. It is this paradoxical combination of hard-nosed "realism" and utopian naiveté that has so perplexed their liberal critics.[20]

There is, however, a fairly simple explanation for the fact that Marx and Engels did not see any contradiction in arguing for an unprecedented concentration of state power, capable of unlimited use of force where necessary, and yet expect such a state to pose no obstacles to direct democratic control and its own eventual abolition. This explanation is that for all their equivocations and inconsistencies Marx and Engels really *did* adhere to the simple class theory I outlined above, according to which the *only possible raison d'être* of organized coercion is the existence of classes on the basis of private ownership of the means of production and that therefore any organized coercion to abolish this private property necessarily abolishes its own *sole raison d'être* and thus itself. All of which really amounts to saying that because they essentially believed in this simplistic class theory of all evil, Marx and Engels simply did not see the need to develop a coherent theory of the transition to socialism and of postcapitalist politics (cf. Bottomore 1979, 71–73; Gouldner 1980, 346–52).

After this fairly comprehensive survey, I trust I have made my point: the writings of Marx and Engels do not contain a

---

20   One article that interprets the notion of the "dictatorship of the proletariat" in much the same way as I have then goes on to argue that such liberal critics are guilty of "separating mechanically what Marx and Engels tried to unite dialectically" (Ehrenburg 1980, 24). Apparently these critics fail to understand that the "dictatorship of the proletariat" and the "withering away of the state" form a "dialectical unity of opposites in Marx's theory of the proletarian state" (21, emphasis omitted). I am not quite sure what this means, however, other than that quasi-Hegelian jargon is remarkably well-suited for "dialectically" eliminating any troublesome problems one does not care to think through by more conventional means.

coherent theory of politics and the state. The closest thing appears to be what I have described as the simple class theory, but it was even then so obviously at odds with reality that Marx and Engels were frequently forced to deviate from it and add various modifications. These modifications, however, either totally destroy the original theory or do not add up to any coherent alternative. Their rather vague statements about the transitional "dictatorship of the proletariat" suggest that they never really abandoned the simple model. Marx's early writings on the state, finally, appear to be in an entirely different category. They seem to amount to a still rather utopian protest against any separation of public and private, particular and universal, in the name of some abstract philosophical notion of complete "universality."

However, there does appear to be one theme that permeates both the early and the "mature" writings on the state: the eventual abolition of politics and the state altogether. Of course there are important differences. The early writings are very abstract and utopian. It is not clear in them what exactly "human emancipation" means—other than a state of total unity, harmony and bliss—nor who is going to bring it about. The mature writings appear to be much more hard-nosed and realistic. "Human emancipation" is turned into the self-emancipation of the oppressed proletariat after long and fierce struggles in which it will take over the state, or construct its own, with which it will forcibly abolish all classes. Once this has been accomplished all conflicts stemming from class divisions will naturally have disappeared and hence so will the organized coercion necessary to repress such conflicts (cf. Maguire 1978, 226–38).

Yet, despite this important difference between the early and the "mature" writings (see also Berki 1983), there is a remarkable continuity which has, of course, not been lost on those who stress the more "humanist" early writings (Avineri 1968, 43–52; Colletti 1975, 40–46; Giddens 1971, 6–7, 19–20; Hunt 1974, 125–30; Kolakowski 1978a, 130; Löwith 1982; Rader 1979).[21]

---

21 Although the argument by Shaw (1974, 431), that there is no difference at all since the "civil society" upon which an "alien" state is superimposed in the early writings consists of none other than the workers who are oppressed by the state in the "mature" writings, strikes me as little short of

This continuity consists in the fact that *both* the early "radical-democratic" criticisms of the state *and* the "mature" writings seem to be based on a firm belief that some day a society will come into existence in which there will be such a degree of spontaneous harmony between individuals and between the individual and the group, that no special separate institution for the forcible resolution of social conflict will be needed anymore. In the early writings Marx attacks the "false universality" of the state, because he sees it as merely the outgrowth and embodiment of the fact that irreconcilable conflicts and antagonisms remain rampant in "civil society." In the "mature" writings Marx and Engels characterize the state as "nothing but" the instrument of class oppression which temporarily suppresses social conflict. Thus, *both* the early and the "mature" critiques of the contemporary state appear to be based on the anticipation of a harmonious community that will have no further use for the services of the state—"universality" in the early and the "classless" society in the later writings.

Marxists may have some trouble with this continuity because it suggests that the critique of the state is based on a preconceived vision of a future utopia. Marxism, and especially its more "scientific" variant, takes great pride in claiming that it derives the anticipation of a future classless and hence stateless society from the analysis of present-day bourgeois society and not, as utopian socialists would, the other way around. Yet the remarkable similarity between the early and "mature" Marxian critiques of the state strongly suggests that the utopia of the conflictless society *precedes*, and hence must be the basis of, the critique of bourgeois society. As Elster notes, "the ideal of Communist society . . . is constantly present in the background" as the ultimate basis for Marx's "indictment of capitalism" (1985, 51; see also Buchanan 1982, 122; Berki 1983).

Marxism and Utopianism

The suggested connection between the ideal of a future society, free of all conflict, and the critique of "bourgeois" society seems

---

silly. Why not also scrutinize Marx's adolescent poetry for early hints of a nascent theory of surplus value?

worth pursuing, precisely because it is so profoundly at odds with Marx and Engels's own conception of their theory. For if there was one aspect of their theory that to them made it superior to the various socialist doctrines of men like Babeuf, Fourier, Proudhon, Owen, and Weitling, it was the fact that they rejected the latter's "utopianism": the belief that socialism could be realized by the elaboration of detailed blueprints of a "just" society that would convince one and all of its desirability and feasibility (see Gouldner 1980, 193–96; Kolakowski 1978a, ch. 10). Interestingly, this anti-utopianism is perhaps the one other major theme that pervades the writings of Marx and Engels, from their precommunist to their very last works, as much as does the eventual abolition of all politics in the future conflictless community. It is still a source of great pride for Marxists (see, e.g., Cerroni 1978, 241–42, 252; Draper 1977, 101, 104; 1978, 24–28, 83), although it is not entirely clear whose "utopianism" they are still objecting to.

In a letter of 1843, before his "discovery" of either the proletariat or "theoretical communism," Marx already dissociates himself from the confused "reformers" who "anticipate the world dogmatically," and who contrast the real world with some "doctrinaire principle" or other, or "some ready-made system" in the manner of Cabet (Marx 1977, 36–37; cf. Gouldner 1980, 89–90). In *The German Ideology* Marx and Engels declare: "Communism is for us not a state of affairs which is to be established, an ideal to which reality will have to adjust itself" (Marx 1977, 171); in fact, "communists do not preach morality at all" (183). In the *Communist Manifesto* they boast that the "theoretical conclusions of the Communists are in no way based on ideas or principles that have been invented, or discovered, by this or that would-be universal reformer" (231), and they consider the "critical-utopian" socialism of Saint-Simon, Fourier, and Owen as "premature," the typical product of an earlier age when the outlines of the emerging class struggle were still impossible to discern, which forced these theorists to seek refuge in "contrived" and "fantastic pictures of future society" to be realized by seeking support among all classes but especially the ruling class (243–45). Some thirty years later Engels elaborates this argument in his pamphlet "Socialism: Utopian and Scientific"

(Marx and Engels 1959, 68–111).[22] There he argues that the utopian socialists "could, no more than their predecessors, go beyond the limits imposed upon them by their epoch" (70). Since they could not yet observe the economic developments and class struggle that form the real historical foundation for the possibility and necessity of socialism, the whole idea of socialism, Engels claims, could not have appeared as anything but the "accidental discovery of this or that ingenious brain" (89). Thus, the utopian socialists, thinking they were basing themselves on their own individual insights into transhistorical canons of justice and reason, produced a variety of mutually incompatible doctrines and utopias because they were necessarily still largely the product of their own imaginations (68–82). Marx's own "mature" economic writings emphasize the ineluctable "laws of motion" of capitalism which render any hopes of establishing socialism by sheer will or decree hopelessly utopian (see Gouldner 1980, 64–69). But the theme also recurs in his political writings from the famous "Men make their own history, but they do not make it just as they please" in the opening paragraphs of *The Eighteenth Brumaire* (Marx 1963a, 15), to the first draft of *The Civil War in France* in which he describes how the early "utopian founders of sects," in the absence of both the proper "material conditions" and a working class of sufficient "organized power" and "conscience of movement" to point the way to socialism, were hence forced "to compensate for the historical conditions of the movement by fantastic pictures and plans of a new society in whose propaganda they saw the true means of salvation" (Marx 1974, 262), as well as its final draft in which he claims that the Paris Communards "did not expect miracles" and had "no ready-made utopias to introduce *par décret du peuple*" (213), and, finally, his 1874 notes on Bakunin in which he explains once more that the term "scientific socialism" was only intended to distinguish his doctrine from "utopian socialism, which wants to attach the people to new delusions" (337).

The fact that this anti-utopianism is already apparent in

22   This pamphlet is in fact a compilation of passages from *Anti-Dühring* which Engels completed in 1878 (see Engels 1939, 26–33, 282–310).

Marx's earliest writings (see Teeple 1984, 17–45) contradicts the claim that it is an aspect of the increasingly pronounced positivist scientism and economic determinism in Marx and Engels's later writings (e.g., Gouldner 1980, 64–69; Hunt 1974, 116 130–31; B. D. Wolfe 1965, ch. 19).[23] In fact, it is eminently Hegelian. For what Marx and Engels object to most in utopian socialism is not just the fanciful features of its blueprints for the just society which appear contradictory or naive in the light of "scientific" knowledge, nor its tutelary attitude toward the working class and conciliatory attitude toward the ruling class, but, first and foremost, the conception of socialism as a matter of transhistorical Justice or Reason, insight into which is a matter of individual genius and hence historical accident. It is this last misconception that they believed, underlay the others. And underlying it was the essentially Kantian-Humean dichotomy of fact and value, of real and ideal, and of freedom and necessity, which it was Hegel's great merit to have superseded (cf. Stojanovic 1981, 172–76).

According to the Kantian-Humean doctrine there is an unbridgeable logical gulf between "is" and "ought": it is impossible to derive a moral imperative from a factual state of affairs. This does not imply, however, as Marx and Engels sometimes suggest in their criticism of the seemingly "accidental" nature of utopian socialism, that it is impossible to explain the historical emergence of certain norms rather than others or that any norms may emerge at any moment in history. It only means that even when the emergence of such norms can be explained sociohistorically this has no implications whatsoever for the relative "worth" of those norms in comparison to the norms of other epochs. In other words, it means that history has no *intrinsic* meaning, that norms emerging at a later date cannot be said to be, *ipso facto*, superior or inferior to earlier ones. It also means that all human action includes besides a cognitive also a

23   It also renders several other explanations either implausible or at the very least inadequate. Marx and Engels's aversion to utopianism was clearly not just a remnant of the "Jewish *Bilderverbot*" (Von Beyme 1985, 86), nor merely a case of "moral constipation" (Hunt 1984, 179), "a matter of personality" (ibid., 200), a political strategy against rival socialist leaders (Berki 1983, 65–66; Ollman 1977, 8), or tactical subterfuge (Moore 1980, ch. 7).

moral component which is free precisely in the sense that it cannot be justified as "necessary" on any factual (e.g., historical) grounds.[24]

Now, to the Hegelian spirit (no pun intended) all this is profoundly repugnant. Hegel rejects the Kantian dualism of fact and value precisely by claiming that values are "incarnate in history" as Lichtheim (1965, 47) aptly puts it. History *does* have a definite meaning and that meaning is precisely to *overcome* all dualisms of fact and value, will and necessity, real and ideal, without, however, thereby relinquishing the richness and multiplicity created through history and of which these dualisms are a "moment". Thus, knowing that history is the march of Reason toward fulfillment—a fulfillment that will actually be attained some day, not just a regulative ideal never to be actually reached; this is a crucial difference with Kant and Fichte (see Kolakowski 1978a, 69)—philosophical reflection can reveal the difference between essence and appearance, between what is truly real and what is merely actual or empirical. Philosophy can show us what is part of the "will of history" and what is merely ephemeral and thus to be swept aside by history (no matter *how* massively empirical and hence "real" it may appear to the untrained eye). Hegel's famous dictum "the rational is real and the real is rational," then, is neither necessarily a conservative, opportunistic or even cynical acceptance of all that *is* simply because there is no sense in resisting the "will of history," nor an idealistic call to bring reality in line with a preconceived rationality. It means that through philosophical reflection it can be understood what part of the struggles, oppression and suffering that occur is a necessary part of the march of Reason and thus to be accepted and what part is not, and thus to be combatted.[25] Hence, also, the Kantian freedom of the subject to

24   Of course, the differences between Kantian and Hegelian historiosophy raise some very difficult questions about the relation between individual choice and social determination which can hardly be said to have been satisfactorily answered by either philosophy or sociology. For some relatively recent, rather inconclusive thoughts on this perennial issue, see Giddens (1976, 1979).

25   But since neither Hegel nor any of his followers has ever seen fit to disclose the exact method of distinguishing the rational from the irrational, his sys-

choose whatever ideals and norms he or she wishes is only the false freedom of subjective caprice. True freedom consists of the understanding *and thereby* accepting of Reason in history; true freedom consists of the reconciliation of the subjective will with the "General Will," the rational will of history. Any attempts to judge history by some arbitrarily chosen, transhistorical value judgment is thus "dogmatic," "doctrinaire" and "utopian" in the sense that it is futile, sooner or later to be swept aside by the irresistible march of Reason toward reconciliation of freedom and necessity, of reality and reason, of the subjective and the objective (see Kolakowski 1978a, 57–80).

Marx and Engels clearly adopted this Hegelian historiosophy to a large extent. But of greatest interest here is that they adopted its *"immanentism"* (Berki 1983, 94) and the associated ban on any "utopianism," that is, the claim that their theories were based on the analysis of forces *immanent* in the present and *not* on any preconceived, "utopian" ideals of a future society. Although obviously very utopian indeed in the ordinary sense of the word (cf. Lukes 1985, 36, 45–47)—they did clearly believe in the actual attainability and even imminence of the realm of Universal Reason—Marx and Engels insist that the impending "overthrow of capitalism and the . . . inauguration of communism is an historically, scientifically 'necessary' event; communism is not a wished-for, empty, pious dream, a shadowless ideal, a cry of the impotent imagination, something which is merely, and moralistically, *desirable*; it is the actual movement *of existing society*" (Berki 1983, 88). Anything else, any "Kantian" critique based on a *contrast* between factual reality and moral ideals amounts to merely arbitrary, "utopian" whim (cf. Ollman 1971, 47–51).

From very early on Marx dissociates himself from the Young Hegelians whose radical interpretation of Hegel led them back to a Fichtean dualism of "is" and "ought" with its permanent and inevitable conflict between present reality and Reason. Since the Young Hegelians could not ground their critique of reality in a Reason already fully immanent in that reality but

tem is in practice notoriously subject to *either* the conservative *or* the radical interpretation (see Kolakowski 1978a, 67, 77–84).

only on some notion of what ought to be which is necessarily a step "ahead of" that reality, this amounted to a return to pre-Hegelian utopianism (see Giddens 1971, 2–4, 70 ; Kolakowski 1978a, chs. 2, 3). Instead, as Marx puts it in the 1843 letters cited earlier, he wants to "discover the new world by criticism of the old" and "develop out of the actual forms of existing reality the true reality as what it ought to be, that which is its aim." Instead of confronting the world with "some ready-made system," he claims, we "merely show it what it is actually fighting about, and this realization is a thing that it must make its own even though it may not wish to" (Marx 1977, 36–37; cf. Berki 1983, 40). In *The German Ideology* after the "discovery" of the proletariat, communism, and historical materialism, Marx and Engels declare that communism is not some "ideal to which reality will have to adjust," but "the real movement which abolishes the present state of things. The conditions of this movement result from the premisses now in existence" (Marx 1977, 171). In the *Communist Manifesto* they claim that their theoretical conclusions "merely express . . . actual relations springing from an existing class struggle, from an historical movement going on under our very eyes" (231).

Many of the famous passages in the later writings of Marx and Engels, which are often taken as proof of an increasingly anti-voluntarist economic determinism, are in fact no more than restatements, in more narrowly economic terms to be sure, of this Hegelian historiosophy in which the whole question of voluntarism versus determinism is claimed to be "transcended" in a higher conciliation of the two (cf. Kolakowski 1978a, 416; 1978b, 128–29). Thus, in the well-known words of the "1859 Preface,"

> the changes in the economic foundation lead sooner or later to the transformation of the whole immense superstructure. In studying such transformations it is always necessary to distinguish between the material transformation of the economic conditions of production, which can be determined with the precision of natural science, and the legal, political, religious, artistic or philosophic—in short, ideological forms in which men become conscious of this conflict and fight it out. Just as one does not judge an individual by

what he thinks about himself, so one cannot judge such a period of
transformation by its consciousness, but, on the contrary, this consciousness must be explained from the contradictions of material
life, from the conflict existing between the social forces of production and the relations of production. No social order is ever destroyed before all the productive forces for which it is sufficient
have been developed, and new superior relations of production
never replace older ones before the material conditions for their
existence have matured within the framework of the old society.
Mankind thus inevitably sets itself only such tasks as it is able to
solve, since close examination will always show that the problem itself arises only when the material conditions for its solution are already present or at least in the course of formation. (Marx 1974,
426)

As Engels explains it in "Socialism: Utopian and Scientific,"
this does not mean that "socialism" as the ideal of equality and
justice is a simple and automatic reflection of the development
of the forces of production. As the various forms of "utopian
socialism" show, the dream is an old one. But until the forces of
production have been sufficiently developed to actually achieve
it, "socialism" remains just that: a utopian dream. Only when
economic conditions make it *possible* does it also become *necessary* as a result of the proletariat's growing *consciousness* of its
possibility. Thus what was once a utopian dream becomes part
of the "inner law" of history, which is, as Hegel has shown,
nothing but the "process of evolution of man himself" (Marx
and Engels 1959, 66, 82–111 in general). In this process the
dualism of means and ends, of will and necessity, are overcome
(cf. Kolakowski 1978c, 523–25; Lichtheim 1965, 239).

In the passage of *The Civil War in France* immediately following the assertion that the Communards did not expect simply
to realize a "ready-made" utopia *"par décret du peuple,"* Marx
clearly illustrates that in the realization of the historical mission
of the proletariat the distinctions between voluntarism and determinism, means and ends, simply disappear:

They know that in order to work out their own emancipation, and
along with it that higher form to which present society is irresistibly
tending by its own economical agencies, they will have to pass

through long struggles, through a series of historic processes, transforming circumstances and men. They have no ideals to realize, but to set free the elements of the new society with which old collapsing bourgeois society itself is pregnant. In the full consciousness of their historic mission, and with the heroic resolve to act up to it . . . (Marx 1974, 213)

The fact of the matter is that for Marx all questions of voluntarism versus determinism, freedom versus necessity, "is" versus "ought" are simply meaningless as they have been "superseded" by Hegel's historiosophy. But this does not mean, of course, that any of these questions have been effectively settled *in practice*. The Hegelian claim to have "sublated" the Kantian dichotomies remains little more than a purely rhetorical victory (Keat 1981, 199–200; Kolakowski 1978a, 148, 222–24, 304, 416–20). Yet, however meaningless and grotesque such claims, they are what distinguish Marxism from "utopian" socialism as well as from various forms of positivism and Kantianism. Failure to see this has caused a great deal of confusion both among Marxists themselves and among a host of commentators.[26]

But however strongly Marx and subsequent Marxist folklore insist that Marxism's conclusions rest exclusively on the observable ascendancy of the proletariat and not on "the 'application' of an abstract principle" (Cerroni 1978, 241; cf. Stephens 1979, 1), it is surely not entirely irrelevant that the intellectual trajectory by which Marx himself first reached those conclusions was

26 Much of the confusion in the recent, anguished debates about Marxism's (lack of) moral content may stem from the fact that the Hegelian origins of Marx's position are either ignored or misunderstood (see, e.g., Cohen, Nagel, and Scanlon 1980; Elster 1985, 216–33; Geras 1985; Little 1981; Miller 1984, chs. 1, 2; Nielsen 1985; Nielsen and Patten 1981; cf. van der Linden 1984, 133; but cf. Lukes 1985, 38–47, 145–46; McCarthy 1985). Frequently, Marx's often expressed contempt for all forms of "moralism" is taken to be a manifestation of his reaction *against* Hegelian Idealist metaphysics in favor of an empirical, scientific historical materialism, according to which the morals of each historical epoch are the product of, and hence appropriate to, its level of economic development (see, e.g., Nordahl 1985; Wood 1972). But as should be plain by now, Marx's antimoralism, and the historicist relativization of all morality on which it is based, long predate his conversion to historical materialist "science" and are, no less than that "science" itself, profoundly Hegelian in origin.

exactly the other way around. It was not the plight of the proletariat, which, at any rate, hardly existed yet in the Germany
of the early 1840s, that brought Marx to "socialism," but, quite
the contrary, his commitment to the aspirations of German Idealist philosophy, including Hegel's "immanentism," that led him
to go "shopping" for a "historical agent" capable of realizing
them, until he finally found it in the "proletariat"—both the
necessary product and eventual "gravedigger" of the capitalist
order (Berki 1983, 61–62; Gouldner 1985, 22–27; S. W. Moore
1980). As we have seen before in this and the previous section,
Marx was quite sure about the ultimate *telos* of history being a
state of total unity and harmony, and about the futility of anticipating that state by designing fanciful utopias, well before he
showed any interest in the workers (cf. Gouldner 1980, 89–90;
Hunt 1974, 130–31; Lichtheim 1965, 33–40; B. D. Wolfe 1965,
202–3, 317–22).

In fact, at the early age of nineteen Marx consciously adopted
the Hegelian standpoint precisely because it promised to bridge
the intolerable abyss between "is" and "ought" left by Kant and
Fichte, as the well-known letter to his father of November 10,
1837, shows (Marx 1977, 5–10; cf. Avineri 1968, 8–9). It was
then that he started "to seek the idea in the real itself" (Marx
1977, 8), and he would have to struggle for more than six years
before he would finally find it in his "Contribution to the Critique of Hegel's Philosophy of Right, Introduction" (Marx
1964, 43–59), where he discovered the proletariat at last (Bottomore 1975, 9–13).

The argument by which Marx made his discovery very clearly
reveals its philosophical roots. The Young Hegelians, Marx argues, have completed the theoretical task of philosophy by
showing, in their critique of religion as human self-alienation,
that ultimately *"man is the supreme being for man"* (Marx 1964,
52). This having been shown in theory, the next task is to realize
it in practice; that is, theory must become a "material force,"
which it can become only if it is "capable of seizing the masses"
(ibid.). But this requires, particularly in historically (though not
philosophically) backward Germany a *"radical* revolution,"
which, in turn, requires "a *passive* element, a *material* basis" (53).
But a force capable of being such a material basis for the com-

plete and radical humanization shown to be necessary by philosophy will have to be a force shackled in *"radical chains,"* a class with "a universal character because its suffering is universal," a class that has suffered such a *"total loss* of humanity" that it "can only redeem itself by a *total redemption of humanity"* (58). This class can only be the proletariat, Marx concludes, which will universalize its own expropriation by abolishing the private property of all. Thus, "just as philosophy finds its *material* weapons in the proletariat, so the proletariat finds its *intellectual* weapons in philosophy" (59). The *"emancipation of man,"* then, proceeds via the emancipation of the proletariat. Having reached this conclusion, the "Introduction" ends with the following revealing lines: *"Philosophy* is the *head* of this emancipation and the *proletariat* is its *heart*. Philosophy can only be realized by the abolition of the proletariat, and the proletariat can only be abolished by the realization of philosophy (ibid.)."

This crucial work of transition between the early Hegelian Marx and the "mature" Marx demonstrates quite clearly that originally Marx was *not* primarily concerned with the proletariat's rise to power and only secondarily with socialism, as Marxist mythology would have it (see Draper 1978, 24–28, 83), but exactly the reverse: what matters is the ultimate goal of history as revealed by philosophy (cf. S. W. Moore 1980, ch. 2). The proletariat is only of interest because philosophy requires a "material force" that can be shown to be an immanent part of existing reality, and it happens to be a suitable candidate for the job. This fact, however disguised by a later exclusive emphasis on economics and the interests of the working class, has continued to give Marxism its specific character: from the start, it was not primarily interested in devising ways of improving the lot of workers but rather in showing how the workers were destined to take steps, consciously or not, toward what only Marxists knew to be the goal of history (cf. Balbus 1982, 48–49; Lichtheim 1965, 52–56).

One aspect of this "immanentist" legacy is Marxism's virtual taboo on depicting that ultimate goal except in the vaguest and most absurdly bucolic terms, without, however, ever doubting its feasibility and inevitability in the least. Marx's sparse references to communism are formulated in terms that suggest he constantly wanted to remind us of the totally utopian futility of even mentioning it (Berki 1983, 17–19). In the *Economic and Philosophical Manuscripts* of 1844, in which the idea first occurs, Marx contrasts "true communism" with the "crude communism" of the French utopian socialists. The latter merely wish to transfer property from its private owners to a central administration so that the community becomes the capitalist, thus merely universalizing poverty, alienation, and envy (Marx 1964, 152–57).[27] As opposed to this impoverished conception, "true communism" involves "the *positive* abolition of *private property*," which "assimilates all the wealth of previous development" (155). It is thus "the *definitive* resolution of the antagonism between man and nature, and between man and man. It is the true solution of the conflict between existence and essence, between objectification and self-affirmation, between freedom and necessity, between individual and species. It is the solution of the riddle of history and knows itself to be this solution" (ibid.). But Marx is not prepared to go beyond this standard description of the ultimate Hegelian millennium.

In another famous passage, in *The German Ideology*, Marx and Engels claim that ultimately communist society will abolish the division of labor and hence alienation: "In communist society where nobody has one exclusive sphere of activity but each can become accomplished in any branch he wishes, society regulates the general production and thus makes it possible for me to do one thing today and another tomorrow, to hunt in the morning, fish in the afternoon, rear cattle in the evening, criticize after dinner, just as I have a mind, without ever becoming hunter, fisherman, cowherd, or critic" (Marx 1977, 169).

27   Avineri (1968, 220–39; also McLellan 1980, 242), convinced that all Marx's "mature" writings are merely elaborations of themes already present in the early ones, takes this "crude communism" to be a transitional phase similar to the one predicted in the *Critique of the Gotha Programme* (Marx 1974, 339–59), written more than three decades later. This is clearly an overinterpretation, however, since Marx explicitly links "crude communism" to Proudhon, Fourier, Cabet, and Saint-Simon (Marx 1964, 152–55) although there certainly are fascinating parallels between it and the later transitional phase, as Berki (1983, ch. 5; also Elster 1985, 451–52) shows. Inexplicably, Giddens (1971, 60, n. 48) notes the error but then goes on to commit it nonetheless (60–64).

Apart from these two famous quotes there are only a few passing remarks to be found in the entire work of Marx and Engels, in which they refer to "freely associated men" taking control of the means of production and producing "in accordance with a settled plan" (Marx 1967a, 80) and similar statements (e.g., Marx 1974, 213; 1977, 237–38), or claims to the effect that in communist society "accumulated labour is but a means to widen, to enrich, to promote the existence of the labourer" (Marx 1977, 233), so that "the free development of each is the condition for the free development of all" (238). But how and when all this will be achieved must remain speculation and hence futile since it will obviously require a degree of development of the forces of production and change of human nature the extent and outlines of which cannot as yet be discerned in present reality (Avineri 1968, 221; Marx 1967a, 80; 1977, 170–71, 184, 191; see also Balbus 1982, 115–17, 124–25; Chase-Dunn 1980, 509; Israel 1971, 274; McLellan 1980, 240–52).

What *can* be predicted in some detail, however, is the transitional phase that will be necessary between capitalism and the ultimate communist millennium, because this transitional stage is the result of "the dialectical unfolding of the principles of *existing* society" (Avineri 1968, 771). This transitional phase is described in the *Communist Manifesto* and the *Critique of the Gotha Programme*. In the former, it is described as an enormous concentration of control over all spheres of life in the hands of the proletarian state, forced labor for all in industrial armies, and the like, in an intensive and concerted effort to develop the forces of production as rapidly as possible and eradicate all class distinctions (Marx 1977, 237). The *Critique of the Gotha Programme* seems to imply much the same thing. In it Marx warns that at first the transitional society will in every respect still be "stamped with the birth-marks of the old society from whose womb it has emerged" (Marx 1974, 346), that the defects of this first phase are "inevitable . . . given the specific form in which it has emerged after prolonged birth-pangs from capitalist society" (347), and that all these problems will only be resolved once the forces of production have been developed to the point at which the abolition of the division of labor becomes feasible, so that finally the watchword can really be: "From each according to his abilities, to each according to his needs" (ibid.). How long this transitional period is expected to last Marx neglects to say, however (see also Avineri 1968, 220–39; Giddens 1971, 60–64; Rader 1979, 127–29). Engels, finally, in the article "On Authority" maintains that the "despotic" discipline and authority necessitated by large-scale industry and modern technology will have to be retained, perhaps indefinitely (Marx and Engels 1959, 481–85).[28]

Besides the predictions concerning the eventual "withering away" of the state cited in the previous section, this is virtually *all* Marx or Engels were willing to disclose about postrevolutionary society, in whatever phase (see also Fetscher 1961; Hunt 1984, 212–65; McLellan 1969; S. W. Moore 1980; Ollman 1977). Subsequent Marxists have been no less reluctant to go into details (Kolakowski 1978b, 287, 359). They invariably claim that the *eventual* "classless" society will be entirely problemless and conflictless, but at the same time they leave no doubt that this ultimate stage is still far away, awaiting the development of the forces of production to the point at which they can produce an abundance sufficient to permit the abolition of the division of labor (see, e.g., Chang 1931, 125–27, 133–39).[29]

Thus, somewhat strangely, Marxism seems to have nothing

28   Avineri (1968, 235–36) claims that Engels's views could not be representative of those Marx held since for Marx technology was not an externally given datum with unchangeable implications. This may be true, but it should not be forgotten that Engels's article was part of an 1874 polemic to which Marx himself also contributed a piece (see Marx 1974, 327–32) and that he thus must have been aware of Engels's argument and did not object to it. A more likely interpretation is that Engels did not mean to imply that factorylike discipline and authority would last indefinitely, but only for a transitional period of unspecified length, in which case he seems in perfect agreement with Marx.

29   Lenin's *State and Revolution* is a partial and not very credible exception. Another partial exception is Trotsky who was apparently convinced that the era of abundance had already arrived, leading him to make preposterous predictions about the imminent communist paradise which would enable the average man to attain the intellectual level of Goethe or Aristotle (see Knei-Paz 1978, 567–79). His present-day followers, though they have toned down somewhat, still appear to be convinced that if only all production were centrally planned all scarcity could immediately be eliminated with the currently available productive forces (see Mandel 1979, 230–36).

to offer but an utterly cloudy millennium whose credibility can only be sustained, if at all, by postponing its eventual arrival indefinitely for all practical purposes, and an immediate program that hardly appears attractive at all (cf. Berki 1983, 31–42, 142–61).[30] Of course, Marx believed that at a certain point capitalist production relations would become "fetters" upon the forces of production and that further development of those forces would only be possible by means of a transitional state-controlled phase as depicted by him. But today this assumption has become rather dubious, to put it mildly, and even if it had been valid, it is not clear how the workers would be much better off under the transitional regime of uncertain duration than under capitalism. The obvious question arises, How did Marx, and, *a fortiori*, how do today's Marxists expect the working class to rise and overthrow capitalism if its immediate replacement appears far from irresistibly attractive and the eventual goal far from obviously attainable in our lifetime—or ever? What could possibly motivate the workers to attempt a socialist revolution under such circumstances?

Remarkably, it is not very easy to find answers to such obviously central questions in the Marxist literature. This is surely one of the more intriguing paradoxes of Marxism. On the one hand Marxism has nothing but contempt for those who criticize capitalism on the basis of some "fixed" notion of justice, and it never tires of advertising itself as the only theory capable of showing that capitalism *will* be overthrown and replaced by socialism, that capitalism *necessarily* produces "its own grave-diggers" (Marx 1977, 231), the proletariat, the one class whose historical mission it is to abolish all classes at last. Yet, on the other hand, it offers no coherent argument, let alone a convincing one, showing what exactly will motivate these "gravediggers" to do their job, how exactly History communicates Its will to them and equips them to carry it out.

Of course, the writings of Marx and Engels are full of predictions about a variety of "tendencies working with iron necessity

30   Berki (1983) and Moore (1980) provide fascinating discussions of the finally unresolved tension between the more realistic but unappealing "transitional" first phase and the far loftier but utterly ethereal final phase of "communism" throughout Marx's work.

toward inevitable results" (Marx 1967a, 8), which are to help the "gravediggers" in their historical mission (see, e.g., Marx 1967a, 762–64; 1975, 425–26; 1977, 178–81, 226–31; Marx and Engels 1959, 90–111). But upon closer inspection, none of these tendencies constitutes sufficient grounds for expecting the proletariat to rebel against the capitalist system *as such*, let alone conceive of a socialist alternative. At some point, capitalist production relations may become "fetters" on the further development of the forces of production, the "centralization of the means of production and socialization of labour" may become "incompatible with their capitalist integument" (Marx 1967a, 763), in this particular sense, but this does not obviously compel the proletariat to "burst" the integument "asunder," unless it had suddenly come to champion the very technological progress of which it has thus far only been the victim. This seems hardly likely. On the other hand, poverty (whether relative or absolute), economic insecurity, periodic catastrophe, extreme inequality, and the like are as old as class society itself, and it is by no means clear why *only* the modern proletariat would come to find these conditions so intolerable as to rebel against them, to do away with them once and for all.[31]

Peasants may well resent and try to resist being herded into filthy factories, and industrial workers may equally resent and

31   To be sure, there are hints in Marx's writings suggesting why the modern industrial proletariat will be more easily mobilized and organized than peasants living in relative isolation from each other in preceding modes of production. But the factors he suggests—concentration in factories, urban working-class ghettos, homogenization of working conditions and living standards, etc. (see, e.g., Calhoun 1983, 889–92)—are only *facilitating factors*. They may help explain why industrial workers are relatively more likely to organize for the defense of their immediate, material interests than, say, feudal peasants, but they do not provide plausible grounds for expecting them to become implacable opponents of inequality *as such*, the incorruptible and ultimately invincible champions of a radically different, egalitarian society. As we shall see, Marx also sometimes suggests that the very experience of cooperation in the defense of common immediate interests is bound to radicalize the workers into revolutionary socialists, particularly in the final pages of *The Poverty of Philosophy* (see Marx 1963b, 172–75). But, as I argue below, in the absence of some plausible argument showing *why* it is reasonable to expect that the sheer experience of organization will have such an effect on the workers, such suggestions only *add* to the mystery.

try to resist being thrown out of those factories again with every downturn of the business cycle, and, furthermore, modern capitalism may well be unique in allowing and even promoting the organization of its lower classes in the defense of their common economic interests (Draper 1978, 40–48), but none of this necessarily leads to an all-out class war pitting the forces of socialism against those of capitalism (cf. Balbus 1982, 48–54; Boggs 1976, 55; Cottrell 1984, 38–41; Dawe 1978, 390–91; Form 1983; Giddens 1973, 93–94; Gouldner 1980, 202–5; Kolakowski 1978a, 371–75; 1978b, 80–82; Lockwood 1981; Rader 1979, 19–20, 205–9). Yet, to Marx and Engels the feasibility and superiority of the socialist alternative were so utterly self-evident, it seems, that the workers' *every* experience, from the greatest suffering and degradation to the first legislative successes, could *only* serve to rally them to the socialist cause and nothing else (see, e.g., Marx 1967a, ch. 10: 1977, 228–29; Marx and Engels 1959, 90, 107). Not even the bloodiest setbacks could be *anything but* necessary steps in the inevitable process of historical maturation of the proletariat—steps toward its understanding of its revolutionary socialist mission (see, e.g., Marx and Engels 1959, 281–317).

It is only in the earlier writings, before the inexorable "laws of motion" of capitalist accumulation made consideration of the unpredictable whims of mere humans unnecessary, that one finds some hints as to what would eventually motivate the downtrodden working class to rise and perform its noble mission. In *The Holy Family*, Marx claims that

> the class of the proletariat feels annihilated in its self-alienation; it sees in it its own powerlessness and the reality of an inhuman existence. In the words of Hegel, the class of the proletariat is in abasement indignation at that abasement, an indignation to which it is necessarily driven by the contradiction between its human nature and its condition of life, which is the outright, decisive, and comprehensive negation of that nature. . . . Since the abstraction of all humanity, even of the semblance of humanity, is practically complete in the full-grown proletariat, since the conditions of life of the proletariat sum up all the conditions of life of society today in all their inhuman acuity; since man has lost himself in the proletar-

> iat, yet at the same time has not only gained theoretical conscious-
> ness of that loss, but through urgent, no longer disguisable, abso-
> lutely imperative need—that practical expression of necessity—is
> driven directly to revolt against that inhumanity; it follows that the
> proletariat can and must free itself. . . . The question is not what
> this or that proletarian, or even the whole of the proletariat at the
> moment considers as its aim. The question is what the proletariat
> is, and what, consequent on that being, it will be compelled to do.
> Its aim and historical action is irrevocably and obviously demon-
> strated in its own life situation as well as in the whole organization
> of bourgeois society today. (Marx 1977, 134–35)

Thus, there are, on the one hand, the apparently unprecedented conditions of "abasement" in which the proletariat is
forced to live, reminiscent of the "universal suffering" Marx
based his discovery of the proletariat on less than a year before
and, on the other hand, the proletariat's "human nature," of
which its "condition of life" is "the outright, decisive, and comprehensive negation." It is the "contradiction" between these
two, it seems, that inevitably causes the proletariat to be "driven
directly to revolt" by an "urgent, no longer disguisable, absolutely imperative need." Let us examine the two terms of the
"contradiction" separately for a moment.

As for the proletariat's conditions of life, there is some suggestion in the passage cited that Marx expects them to deterio-
rate absolutely to a level of misery far worse than that of any of
the exploited classes of previous modes of production. This, at
least, seems to be meant by the assertions that "the abstraction
. . . even of a semblance of humanity, is practically complete in
the full-grown proletariat," that its "conditions of life . . . sum
up all the conditions of life of society today in all their inhuman
acuity," and that "man has lost himself in the proletariat." Thus,
capitalism could be viewed as the historical breaking point at
which human suffering has finally become completely intolerable.

However, if immiseration in the conventional sense of pauperization, increasing insecurity, and oppression, is meant here,
this would hardly appear to be a tenable explanation for the
coming revolt of the proletariat, even from Marx's own per-

spective, quite apart from the question of whether or not Marx did indeed adhere to an absolute pauperization thesis, which remains unresolved after decades of marxological dispute (cf. Giddens 1971, 55–58; Kolakowski 1978a, 288–91). As Marx himself knew all too well, world history is full of examples of whole populations passively enduring extreme inequality, poverty, and starvation, and a variety of other atrocities without any clear evidence at all of the existence of an absolute point beyond which suffering becomes intolerable (cf. B. Moore 1978). Nor is it obvious why poverty, no matter how intolerable, should lead workers to struggle for communism rather than consumerism, as Balbus (1982, 51–53) rightly points out. Thus, rather than lying in the objective conditions of poverty and inequality, the explanation for the impending workers' revolt must lie in the other side of the equation, their "human nature" (cf. Rader 1979, 23). This is also suggested by the fact that Marx describes even the objective conditions almost exclusively in terms of their inhumanity and not in positive terms, except for a fleeting reference to "powerlessness."

There are some hints in the other early writings, such as "On the Jewish Question," but the only place where Marx tries to expound his views of human nature in any systematic way at all is in the 1844 *Economic and Philosophical Manuscripts* (Marx 1964, 61–219). There he combines elements from Hegel and Feuerbach to argue that man's essential nature as a "species being" entails the individual's awareness of being a member of a species that shares a "human essence," while man expresses his "species-life" through human labor, through the free, conscious, and self-directed creation of a human world in which man freely expresses as well as creates his own nature. History, Marx claims (crediting Hegel for this insight: ibid., 201), is the record of man's exercise and development of his faculties and potentialities in producing his own world and his own nature (see, ibid., esp. 127–29, 152–67, 202–15).

On this basis Marx criticizes capitalism as the sharpest possible negation of man's true "species being." Private ownership of the means of production, commodity exchange, a minute division of labor, all this carries the workers' "alienation" from their product, their labor, themselves, and their masters to an intolerable extreme. It is a world in which workers are treated as commodities, work as merely a means to sheer physical survival, and in which competition and class conflict are rampant. Thus, Marx appears to argue, human nature, man's "species being," objectively demands that man's activities be freely chosen, self-directed and aimed at developing his species powers, and that, since this "is only possible through the co-operative endeavours of mankind" (ibid., 202), this be done in harmony and cooperation only. Man is for Marx first of all a social being, in the sense that he is by his very nature both the product and the producer of himself and his world, but *only in and through* society: "It is above all necessary to avoid postulating "society" once again as an abstraction confronting the individual. The individual *is* the *social being*. The manifestation of his life—even when it does not appear directly in the form of a communal manifestation, accomplished in association with other men—is, therefore, a manifestation and affirmation of *social life*. Individual human life and species-life are not different things" (158).

But while all men partake in man's "species being," the workers clearly suffer most acutely from the extreme and intolerable degree to which capitalism violates the principles of that being. Hence it is the proletariat that will feel the need to assert man's "species being" first. But because it cannot end its own exploitation and alienation without abolishing classes as such, its emancipation will necessarily mean the liberation of all mankind (ibid., 132–33; cf. Marx 1977, 135). Thus the working class will be impelled to replace capitalism by communism, and this "*communism* is the *positive* abolition of *private property*, of human *self-alienation*, and thus the real *appropriation* of *human* nature through and for men. It is, therefore, the return of man himself as a *social*, i.e. really human being, a complete and conscious return which assimilates all the wealth of previous development" (Marx 1964, 155). This is followed by Marx's assertion that, therefore, communism will solve all conflicts between man and man, men and nature, essence and existence, freedom and necessity, individual and species, and so on, which I have quoted already.

We seem to have reached the ultimate ontological grounds for the Marxian critique of capitalism. Capitalism is doomed, in the final analysis, because it is ultimately incompatible with human nature. Egoism, competition, and conflict are not really genuine features of human nature but, at best, the necessary medium through which mankind could create the means to transcend them eventually (cf. ibid., 187). Mankind cannot rest until it has created a society meeting the genuine requirements of human nature, which are perfect solidarity and harmony in a state of unmediated community. This state of total unity, that is, true "communism," is the only and necessary destiny of man because his true nature simply cannot settle for less (cf. Kolakowski 1978a, 40–41; 1978c, 523ff.; Fromm 1961, 25–26, 34, 38; Giddens 1971, 9–16; Lichtheim 1965, 41–50; Ollman 1971, 165; Schacht 1970, 80–82).

This belief that man can only fulfill himself in the complete fusion of individual and community has been identified often enough as the ultimate basis of Marxism, and frequently criticized as inherently totalitarian since any attempt to put it into practice necessarily leads to a glorification of "community" and the *obliteration* of the individual (cf. Hunt 1974, 3–16; Lindblom 1977, 247–60; Schumpeter 1950, 232–68). Moreover, such criticisms are easily supported by quotes from Marx's writings spanning his entire life. Thus, in the "Notes on Bakunin," after first summarily dismissing Bakunin's doubts about the possibility of genuine direct workers' rule, Marx asserts in a remarkably Rousseauian vein: "With collective ownership the so-called people's will vanishes, to make way for the real will of the cooperative" (1974, 336). The would-be totalitarian dictator needs little more by way of legitimation.

However, for Marx, as for Hegel (see Kolakowski 1978a, 70–77), there is nothing inherently totalitarian in the belief that human nature requires the eventual abolition of all conflict and disunity. Marx believed that the elimination of conflict would not lead to the extinction of the individual at all but would instead allow individuals at last to develop their personal capacities in all their variety and fullness, in harmony and peace with other individuals and the community as a whole. The meaning of "socialism" is precisely that it *transcends* the old antithesis of individual and community by uniting them without sacrificing either (see, ibid., 130–131, 168–171; Marx 1977, 190–1; Rader 1979, 128).

But if Marx did not *intend* his ideal of socialism to have total-itarian implications, this does not mean he can simply be re-duced to no more than an unusually consistent democrat, as some have done (Draper 1977, 1978; Hunt 1974, 1984). Or, at least, it should be clear that what Marx envisages is a democracy of a definitely illiberal, Rousseauian type. As opposed to liber-als, Marx does not accept egoism as an ineradicable part of hu-man nature, and hence he does not merely strive, as liberalism does, to organize society in such a way as to restrain this natural egoism where feasible and otherwise guide it into socially con-structive paths by a system of calculated sanctions. To Marx in-dividual egoism itself must be eliminated as it fundamentally violates *genuine* human nature. But, although it may well be possible to envisage in theory a situation in which egoism has been overcome without any coercive restriction of individual liberties, so long as all *practical* attempts to realize that ideal seem to have a way of degenerating into the most abject forms of oppression, this possibility remains little more than a triumph of Hegelian rhetoric over historical experience (cf. Ko-lakowski 1978a, 161–62; 1978c, 409–11).[32]

But whatever its practical implications, the Marxian belief in the possibility and historical imminence of the replacement of capitalism by a socialist society, in which all fundamental con-flicts between individuals, groups, and the community as a whole will be resolved, ultimately rests on the fundamental as-sumptions about human nature as stated in the 1844 *Manu-scripts*. In the last analysis Marxism rests on the belief that hu-man nature simply cannot and will not tolerate inequality, exploitation, and the resulting conflicts forever, and it does so until this very day (cf. Miliband 1977, 17–18, 39). It is true that the terms "human nature" and "alienation" hardly occur in Marx's later writings, but they remain crucial to his arguments nonetheless. Quite probably Marx played down the panhuman

---

32   I find Hunt's (1984) recent attempt to depict Marx and Engels as nothing but lifelong democrats with a deep-seated hatred of bureacracy and the "parasite state," to prove their non-totalitarian sentiments, not only some-what contrived but largely beside the point.

aspects of his argument in favor of a more hard-nosed emphasis on the class struggle in order to dissociate himself as much as possible from the "True Socialists" and other "utopians" who believed they could achieve socialism by universal moral appeals alone (see Kolakowski 1978a, 173–74, 264–65). Not only does Marx continue to use the notions of "species being," "dehumanization," and "alienation" as late as in the *Grundrisse* (Marx 1973), written in 1857–1858, but *Capital* which uses a different terminology, is a critique of dehumanization and alienation in capitalist society which is as much predicated on the assumptions concerning the social character of "genuine" human nature as are the early writings (see esp. Kolakowski 1978a, 263–67: see also, Gouldner 1980, ch. 6; Lichtheim 1965, 41–50; Löwith 1982, 68–99; Mewes 1976, 287–92; Rader 1979, 149–50, 167).

At any rate the Marxian prediction of a working class revolt that will abolish capitalism and establish socialism remains totally inexplicable *without* some such assumptions about human nature. The spectacular *échec* of the Althusserian attempt to stamp out all traces of such "humanism" only serves to reinforce this point (see ch. 4). But this does not make these assumptions any more plausible. It is not at all obvious how the historical record can be used to show that "objectively" the need for harmony and self-development is somehow a more genuine feature of human nature than our obvious talent for strife and oppression. Exactly the opposite argument might be more convincing. Similarly, if past manifestations of "human nature" are any guide, it is not at all clear what would suddenly prompt the dehumanized, downtrodden workers under capitalism to be seized by an irrepressible need to realize the imperatives of "species being" here and now. "Human nature" as it has manifested itself so far hardly provides compelling arguments for such optimism.

But Marx was not unaware of this, of course. In fact, he argued, the "alteration of men on a mass scale," which will be necessary for the "production on a mass scale of this communist consciousness, and for the success of the cause itself," requires an inevitable "revolution." Hence, he reasons, "this revolution is necessary, therefore, not only because the ruling class cannot be overthrown in any other way, but also because the class over-throwing it can only in a revolution succeed in ridding itself of all the muck of ages and become fitted to found society anew" (1977, 179). Thus, Marx does not base his predictions on human nature as it now *is*, but on human nature as he expects it to *become* through the struggle between the classes themselves. After all, human nature is the product of human interaction as much as any other aspect of the human world is, so that "revolutionary praxis" may cause revolutionary change in human nature as well (Marx 1975, 422; cf. Avineri 1968, ch. 3; Fetscher 1961; Giddens 1971, 21–24; Heller 1981; McLellan 1969; Ollman 1977).

Indeed, the expected evolution of the proletariat from a passive class "in itself" to a revolutionary class "for itself" in and through its organization and struggle to defend its interests is another of the recurrent themes in Marx's writings (see, e.g., Marx 1963b, 172–75; 1977, 226–31; Marx and Engels 1959, 281–317; cf. Draper 1978, 77–80). Not only did he believe that under the pressure of the struggle, and out of frustration over the inevitable failure of peaceful reform, the workers would necessarily get better and more widely organized and radicalized, rather than give up, in addition he was convinced that the cooperative effort itself would bring out the latent "species being" in the workers, creating a new "need for society" among them (Marx 1964, 176), which would eventually render present conflict-ridden capitalism intolerable (cf. Avineri 1968, 121–22; B. D. Wolfe 1965, 242–43).

But, of course, the fact that people can and do cooperate in the defense of their common interests does not automatically make them unable to tolerate anything *but* cooperation and solidarity, although this seems to be the assumption underlying much Marxist and para-Marxist theory (cf. Keat 1981, 195–98). Throughout history, people have cooperated with remarkable efficiency in the execution of the most inhuman atrocities, often even committing them in the *name* of human solidarity. Paradoxically, although he expects the last battle of the classes to be perhaps the fiercest yet, Marx expects it somehow to have a profoundly humanizing impact on the participants fighting on the side of the workers.

Thus, Marx's belief in the coming of socialism was in the last analysis based on a Hegelian faith in the ultimate rationality of history (Berki 1983, 69–70). It is a faith that holds that the rational, though often less apparent, is always more real than the irrational—in the sense that it will ultimately prevail. Hegel has already shown this to be the "inner law" of history so that what remains, as Engels puts it, is for "the intellect to follow the gradual march of this process through all its devious ways, and to trace out the inner law running through all its apparently accidental phenomena" (Marx and Engels 1959, 86). The starting point and conclusion of such an inquiry are, however, beyond empirical verification; they are based on a philosophical conviction the proof of which lies in the indefinite future (cf. Lichtheim 1965, 33–40, 238–39, 396–97; Rader 1979, ch. 3).

We seem to have come full circle. The preceding section showed that Marx and Engels's remarks about politics and the state in capitalist society, and by implication their critique of that society as a whole, were ultimately based on a preconceived anticipation of a perfect society in which there would be no more conflict. In the present section I have reviewed their claims that this conception of socialism was by no means "arbitrary" or "utopian" since it rested not on some notion of timeless morality but on trends objectively immanent in history. As part of this "immanentist" perspective they ridiculed any detailed blueprints of the future socialist society as premature, and only vaguely hinted at the probable outline of the transitional phase between it and the present. Instead, they concentrated almost exclusively on trying to document the objective historical trend that would lead the proletariat to rise against the capitalist system and replace it by a system that would eventually grow into a full-fledged socialist society. But as long as the contours and feasibility of that alternative remained so vague, this only raised the question of the grounds on which they expected the proletariat to rebel in the name of the socialist alternative. Economic trends alone, no matter how disastrous, do not appear to be sufficient grounds for expecting a proletarian revolution, let alone a *socialist* proletarian revolution. The ultimate basis for Marx's prediction is, it seems, his belief that eventually human nature will simply not settle for less. But this view of human nature could hardly be said to rest on strong evidence from the past and present. Rather, Marx seems to expect human nature to change drastically in the near future so that it *will* impell the proletariat toward socialism. However, this expectation seems to be based not on present empirically observable trends in the ordinary sense but on the assumption that certain aspects of presently observable reality are more "genuine," more "real" in the Hegelian sense of destined to prevail, than others. In other words, it is ultimately based on the Hegelian claim to be able to distinguish between the genuine and the false, the real and the merely apparent, in observable reality on the basis of preexisting knowledge of the meaning and destiny of history. Thus, in the last analysis, the Marxian forecast of the end of capitalism turns out to rest on something far more utopian (in the ordinary sense) than any fanciful blueprint: it is based on the faith that history has a "rational" aim—without any further justification of that faith.[33]

I am, then, in agreement with those who see Marx's thought as "from first to last inspired by basically Hegelian philosophy" (Collins 1985, 52; Fromm 1961; Giddens 1977, 200; Kolakowski 1978a, 263; cf. Löwith 1982, 68–99; Ollman 1971). There is, no doubt, an important tension between, on the one hand, the more deterministic tone of Marx's "mature" writings, and, on the other, the more activist, Hegelian, and "humanist" flavor of the earlier writings (cf. Bottomore 1975, 9–13; Kolakowski 1978a, 6; B. D. Wolfe 1965, ch. 18). But to some extent this tension runs through Marx's entire work. It is a result of the Hegelian position, apparently never abandoned by Marx,

---

33   To refute such interpretations a passage from *The Holy Family* is often quoted: *"History* does *nothing*; it 'does *not* possess immense riches', it 'does *not* fight battles'. It is *men*, real living men, who do all this, who possess things and fight battles. It is not 'history' which uses men as a means of achieving—as if it were an individual person—*its* own ends. History is *nothing* but the activity of men in pursuit of their ends" (Marx 1961, 76). But as I have just shown, Marx makes very specific predictions about the expected behavior of "real living men" which, it turns out, ultimately rest on a belief that history *will* work its way, although, in true Hegelian fashion, *through* the "free" actions of those "real living men." Once again, we must remind ourselves of Marx's Hegelian standpoint according to which the distinction between voluntarism and determinism is rendered meaningless by history itself (see also Elster 1985, 107–18).

that dismisses the opposition of voluntarism and determinism as entirely meaningless. But although Marx and Hegel could contemptuously rule the issue out of court in the abstract, the lesser mortals among their followers felt compelled to resolve the tension one way or the other. The Second International, under the guidance of Engels and Kautsky, did so in favor of the deterministic side of the Hegelian equation (Lichtheim 1965, 244–88). Until the collapse of the International in 1914, the ruling orthodoxy held that Marxism had uncovered "the law of evolution in human history," which was proclaimed as scientifically valid and inexorable as Darwin's "law of organic evolution" (Chang 1931, 32–33). According to this "law," socialism would be the inevitable result of developments in the economic base that were observable but wholly independent of human will. Human will was, in fact, the wholly determined passive reflection of these economic developments and thus figured only as an intermediate variable without any influence of its own on the inevitable course of social evolution. Matters of justice and morality were thought to be wholly irrelevant, and in fact no more than bourgeois fictions, since whether or not one considered socialism desirable could not affect its historical inevitability (see, e.g., Chang 1931, ch. 2; cf. Kolakowski 1978b, 31–60).

The "nuclear tension" of Marxism (Gouldner 1980, ch. 2) between determinism and voluntarism, science and ideology, necessity and freedom, only became evident with the antideterminist reaction in the theories of Lukács, Korsch, Gramsci, and the Frankfurt School, in the wake of the Bolshevik victory in backward Russia and the defeat of the revolution elsewhere in Europe after World War I. The unexpected turn of events, beginning with the debacle of the International in 1914, severely shook these theorists' confidence in the automatic, economically determined collapse of capitalism and prompted a theoretical return to the seemingly more activist, voluntaristic themes of Hegelian philosophy (see Anderson 1976; Jacoby 1981; Kolakowski 1978c, chs. 7, 8, 10, 11). But their polemics against the mechanical determinism of the Second International, as well as the more recent polemics of the Althusserian variant of "scientific" Marxism against Hegelian voluntarism, have greatly exaggerated the differences and helped to obscure the profoundly Hegelian core of an "immanentist" anti-Kantianism which is shared by all variants of Marxism. The "nuclear tension" between voluntarism and determinism in fact goes back to the Hegelian claims of having "transcended" such Kantian dualisms, claims which *none* of the variants of Marxism has been prepared to give up.[34]

As mentioned before, in neo-Kantian doctrine the dualisms cannot be meaningfully "transcended." Human action always contains two necessary components, one cognitive, the other moral, neither of which can be wholly derived from, or identified with the other. Thus, scientific, that is, empirically verifiable, knowledge will no doubt be needed for the realization of socialism. It will be helpful to know, for instance, what kinds of social arrangements are possible and feasible with currently available resources and in the light of past and present experience, and what the costs of realizing certain arrangements are likely to be. But with all the scientific knowledge in the world it is still impossible to establish the desirability or moral worth of

34   Gouldner, in fact, has a tendency to read recent debates back into older ones and his consequent failure to recognize the common Hegelian core (so vehemently denied by Althusser & Co.) leads him to grossly overemphasize the connection between activism-voluntarism and Hegelianism on the one hand, and quietism and determinism on the other (Gouldner 1980, 32–63, 123–25; 1985, 130–33, 158–62, 168–69, 186–89, 276–79, see also Avineri 1968, 67; Bottomore 1981, 2–5; Jacoby 1981). Thus he is forced to attribute a voluntarist version of "Critical Marxism" to all successful revolutionary leaders which is clearly absurd (Gouldner 1980, 51–53). In fact, Communist leaders, including Lenin, Trotsky, and Mao, have been quite unaware of any "nuclear tension": they firmly uphold the most "scientific" determinism in theory and rhetoric while actually *practicing* voluntarism (see Harding 1977, 273–81; Stojanovic 1981, 177–81), the only partial exception being . . . Stalin (see Rader 1979, 4–5)! On the other hand, one can hardly count such arch-Hegelians as Horkheimer or Adorno among Marxism's more activist theorists. In fact, there appears to be no necessary connection between theory and practice in this respect (cf. Breines 1981, 251–53, 258), and, as we shall see, Hegelianism contains a strong antivoluntaristic element as well. As I have argued elsewhere, these theoretical determinists and practical voluntarists would be better considered as a separate category of "revolutionary" (and Third World) Marxists, in addition to the "scientific" and "Western" and "Critical" varieties distinguished by the authors mentioned. For this and the argument that follows, see van den Berg (1984).

any particular arrangement. This people may freely decide, or impose on each other, but they will never be able to "prove" it scientifically. At most, it might be possible to hazard a scientifically informed, (i.e., based on past and present experience) guess as to the likelihood of people freely choosing or successfully imposing this or that arrangement (and the likely implications of either procedure). But, although norms and values clearly evolve, history does not exactly abound with empirical evidence for the thesis that people are bound to converge spontaneously on any specific ones, or that any such specific norms are bound to prevail for some other reason. And, at any rate, even if this could be shown to be highly probable on empirical grounds, this would *still* not confer any intrinsic worth on such norms, in the absence of any further moral assumptions.

Now, the Hegelian reaction has managed to identify the deterministic Marxism of the Second International with the Kantian conception of science in the sense just described, that is, as a conditional probability statement about the likelihood of capitalist economic breakdown being followed by a socialist revolution. This equation of "scientific Marxism" with the Kantian philosophy of science was helped by the fact that the proponents of the former generally accepted one key Kantian tenet, namely that their "scientific" theory carried no moral implications. But, as opposed to the genuine (neo-)Kantians of the epoch, they also held that, given the "scientifically" proven inevitability of socialism, moral questions were wholly irrelevant (see Kolakowski 1978b, 252–54; Lichtheim 1965, 239–43). "Scientific Marxism," in fact, never was and never *could* be the (neo-)Kantian "positivism" it was made out to be by its Hegelian critics (cf. Berki 1983, 88–95).

For Marx "science" was never the gathering of empirical knowledge to allow people to make more informed choices, in the Kantian sense. On the contrary, he used the term "scientific" exclusively in opposition to precisely those "utopian" socialists who seemed to proceed from the assumption that the realization of socialism was a matter of moral choice. The purpose of "science" for Marx was not simply to gather empirical facts and explain them, nor even to make an empirically based, and hence always provisional and revisable estimate as to the likelihood of this or that occurrence in the near future, as some claim (Avineri 1968, 144; Hunt 1974, 335–36). Its *sole* purpose was to show that history has an ineluctable logic which inevitably leads to the attainment of a perfectly harmonious community, an outcome that in no way depends on merely arbitrary human whim (cf. Lichtheim 1965, 142–43).

As I have tried to show, Marx first adopted the Hegelian belief that history has a destiny in which Reason will coincide with reality and only then set out to show that in the empirical world all the necessary elements were coming together now to consummate the true goal of history at last. However, until early in 1850 Marx's writings were of an extremely voluntaristic and activist cast—calling on philosophers and others to stop interpreting the world and start changing it instead, and on the then barely existing "proletariat" to use every and any occasion that presented itself to provoke a "Revolution in Permanence" (Marx 1975, 423; 1977, 285)—because he was absolutely convinced the expected consummation of history was imminent. It was only after he rather belatedly resigned himself to the fact that the arrival of the revolution might take rather more time than he initially expected that Marx reluctantly began to devote himself to the task of "scientifically" discovering the "natural laws of capitalist production" which would work "with iron necessity toward inevitable results" (Marx 1967a, 8) to eventually produce the long-awaited revolution, despite all temporary setbacks (Alexander 1982b, 164–67; Berki 1983, 83, 93; B. D. Wolfe 1965, 151–64, 176–81, 235–39).

Quite probably the turn to "science" to prove his theory correct "in the long run" helped Marx and his followers keep the faith during the long economic boom of 1850–1873 (cf. Gouldner 1980, 145–46; 1985, 137). At any rate, it certainly did *not* prompt him to subject his faith to a searching confrontation with the empirical facts. If the facts, or even his own arguments, did not support his preconceived conclusions, he simply ignored the former in favor of the latter (see B. D. Wolfe 1965, 186–87, 322–33; but cf. Rowthorn 1980). If and when he *did* confront uncomfortable facts, he sought only to show how they were necessary and inevitable detours in the irresistible march of History (Spencer 1979, 169–76, 178, 184).

The "long depression" of 1873–1896 and the concurrent steady growth of the German Social Democratic party, on the other hand, seemed to confirm at last Marx's "scientific" prognoses. It was during this period that economically deterministic, "scientific" Marxism held most undisputed sway. But even then it was never intended as a truly Kantian science, provisional and revisable in the light of the available empirical evidence, as became quite clear in the violent reactions against Bernstein's "revisionism" a few years later (see ch. 2). Whenever Marxism is invoked as a "science," what is apparently meant is that Marxism is an infallible predictor of the future to which current empirical reality will simply have to adapt, not that Marxism will ever have to adapt to current empirical reality—except insofar as that can hasten the realization of that predicted future (cf. Knei-Paz 1978, 490–94). But from at least 1914 on it became clear that the victory of socialism was not guaranteed by some "law of motion" of the capitalist economy automatically producing the requisite type of class consciousness among the workers, as "scientific" Marxism had assumed. This painful realization prompted a revival of Hegelian elements which allowed greater emphasis on the autonomous role of consciousness in social change. Lukács, Korsch, Gramsci, and the Frankfurt School all rejected the simple base-superstructure model in favor of a more complex "social totality." Thus, socialism is not seen as the automatic outcome of ultimately economic trends, but as the result of the concomitant attainment of the correct consciousness of the proletariat, or at least its "vanguard."

Now, this kind of reasoning might lead to a neo-Kantian perspective, viewing the revolution as a historical *possibility* depending on the choices people make and the resources, including empirically verifiable knowledge, they have at their disposal.[35]

35   Avineri (1968, 124–49) comes close to this by arguing that Marx's activist, Young Hegelian view of consciousness precluded any mechanistic determinism and that, hence, he only claimed that the revolution would occur if the workers, through their struggles, would attain the level of consciousness that would, since praxis and consciousness are inseparable, be identical with a revolution. But either this reduces to an ordinary, testable, Kantian conditional "if-then" statement, which is certainly *not* what Marx had in mind, or Avineri should have added that Marx at the same time insists that the workers *will*, in fact, attain the requisite consciousness, because, whatever

But the remarkable thing is that the Hegelian Marxists chose the exact opposite path. Rather than allowing socialism to be reduced to a mere possibility which the workers are free to choose or reject, they criticize "scientific" Marxism for being *too* empiricist by opening Marxism's insight into the true meaning of history to refutation by means of empiricist and positivist methods.[36] Socialism is not inevitable since it depends on the proletariat's awareness of its historical mission, yet it is not merely desirable as the proletariat chooses, nor is it in some sense the simple sum of both desirability and inevitability: it is the higher, dialectical unity of the two. It is the true meaning of the "objective" historical process as revealed by dialectical insight in the "social totality," irrespective of any merely empirical consciousness prevailing among the workers at any one time (see, e.g., Lukács 1971, 46–82). Thus, rather than questioning the theory in the light of contrary facts, Hegelian Marxists simply declare the "merely empirical" facts irrelevant and the theory valid (ibid., 1), by virtue of some higher, "dialectical reason," to which only they, or the party, are privy (see Bottomore 1975, 47, 56; 1981, 3–5; Kolakowski 1978c, chs. 6, 8, 10–12; cf. also Dubiel 1985).

This brief sketch of the evolution of Marxism is intended to bring out the profoundly antivoluntaristic streak in *all* variants of Marxism, from the most "scientific," determinist to the supposedly most voluntaristic neo-Hegelian versions. Clearly this "antivoluntarism" does *not* necessarily amount to an antimoral economic determinism so often attributed to Marx and Marxism (see, e.g., Alexander 1982b). Only the orthodox Second International espoused that kind of determinist amoralism. For Marx himself, as for the later neo-Hegelian Marxists, the whole question of voluntarism or determinism was simply a non-issue, a false distinction. Their "antivoluntarism" was of a Hegelian kind: their insistence on the need for "immanent" grounds for

---

their present level of consciousness, this is inherent in the "social totality." The latter is Lukács's Hegelian interpretation.

36   Although even Lukács, the very founder of the Hegelian school, is quite prepared to label his particular brand of Marxism a "wholly new science," thus furnishing rather eloquent evidence for my argument that "science" in the Marxist lexicon may not have at all the same connotations as it does in the more conventional (Kantian-Humean) tradition (see Lukács 1971, 27).

criticism was meant to avoid and counter "arbitrary," "dog-matic," "utopian" fancies based on the notorious fickleness of mere human whim. They would reject the charge that they were trying to eliminate free human action from their account of history. Yet, they claimed to have discovered an inner logic *immanent in* the very chaos of the arbitrary, "free" actions by countless actors acting without any consciousness of this "logic." This logic is the objective standard immanent in the current his-torical situation, given by currently observable trends, which provides those capable of separating "essence" from fleeting "appearances" with an objectively valid, nonarbitrary, nonuto-pian, "scientific" basis for criticizing existing social conditions. It is this commitment to Hegelian "immanentism" that *all* var-iants of Marxism share, whether in the guise of "scientific" cer-tainty or neo-Hegelian "totality" (cf. Berki 1983, 71). As Steven Lukes notes, this curious "anti-utopianism [appears to be] dis-tinctive of Marxism" (1985, 37), originating "deep within the structure of Marxist thought itself" (46).

But, again like Hegel, Marxists have never been able to show convincingly *how* they distinguish the essence from mere histor-ical "appearances," the "necessary" from the merely "acciden-tal," without already assuming what needs to be shown in the first place, or, conversely, what there remains of Man and His-tory to interpret once you have eliminated men, their wills, imaginations, and moral convictions as well as the historical "ac-cidents" they cause. As a result, they have by and large failed to convince sufficient numbers of the groups presumably ap-pointed by History of the necessity and urgency of their mis-sion. The resulting repeated default of the expected consum-mation of History, finally, has led successive generations of Marxists to dismiss an ever growing portion of observable real-ity as merely "accidental" and to thereby progressively sever whatever verifiable links there were thought to be between the true meaning of history and its actual course.

There is clearly a process of degeneration going on here, with each successive generation retaining the dogmas in spite of the facts by the eminently Hegelian device of simply dismissing more and more of empirical reality as "mere appearance" (cf. B. D. Wolfe 1965, 334–55). Yet, this is not accomplished on the basis of some appeal to supernatural or suprahistorical truth, but rather, and somewhat paradoxically, in the name of (perhaps some deeper) reality itself. The claim has always remained that the mission of the proletariat is in some sense "immanent" in the here and now, that it can somehow be theoretically derived from historical reality, even when or though the proletariat itself does not acknowledge it. Perhaps this helps to explain the symbiotic relationship that has traditionally existed between Marxism and the intelligentsia, as opposed to its often problematic relations with the actual workers it claims to represent. Or, conversely, the theoretically elaborate constructs by means of which Marxism has repeatedly demonstrated its ability to explain away unpleasant realities seem to be both cause and consequence of its persistent appeal to intellectuals.

This points to a somewhat nastier implication of the above discussion. If, as here suggested, the *differentia specifica* of Marxism is indeed its claim to a higher insight, whether "scientific" or "dialectical," into the goals and requirements of History (cf. also Lichtheim 1965, 8), then it must tend toward authoritarianism in all cases in which the majority does not spontaneously converge upon the single "correct" line. Contrary to the view that tries to present Marx as nothing but a radical democrat, there appears, then, to be an inherently authoritarian streak in Marxism from the start (cf. Elster 1985, 116–118; Gouldner 1980, 47–48; van der Linden 1984, 133; B. D. Wolfe 1965, 202–10, 356–81). In the absence of mass support, the Marxist would be forced to choose *between* Marxism and democracy. Those who refuse to make this choice must remain impotently caught on the horns of what I have elsewhere called the "dilemma of democratic radicalism" (van den Berg 1980). However, it must be added that Marx and Engels so firmly believed that the proletariat would soon be irresistibly drawn toward their brand of socialism and would in the process invent the institutional arrangements allowing it to rule itself, that the problem of implicit authoritarianism simply did not exist for them (cf. B. D. Wolfe 1965, 183–202). For the same reason a related problem of political strategy which was to become the key issue of politics for the next generation—whether or not socialism could be achieved through peaceful reform—hardly appeared problematic at all to them.

Marx and Engels on Revolution and Reform

The emergence and relatively unproblematic persistence of representative democracy in the advanced capitalist countries constitute perhaps the most enduring source of theoretical and organizational schisms among Marxists and of the recurrent depletions of their ranks. As the opponents of reformism charge, there does indeed seem to be some sort of dynamic that leads from the acceptance of the majority principle to the adoption of an exclusively electoralist strategy, to, finally, cautious gradualism and the renunciation of Marxism altogether (see, e.g., Anderson 1980, 196; Lukács 1971, 256–71; Mandel 1978, 19–21, 152, 171, 204–5; Miliband 1969, 88–93, 176–77; Therborn 1978, 108–18). Another such stepwise apostasy may well be occurring right now under the name of "Eurocommunism," as observers of various persuasions have argued (e.g., Mandel 1978, 188–93 and *passim*; Parkin 1979, 193–98; Therborn 1978, 267–71).

Of course, following traditional Marxist practice, all parties to the recurrent disputes claim that their respective positions are fully and unambiguously supported by the writings of the founding fathers. The fact that there are hardly any issues at all on which Marx and Engels can be fairly said to have held a single, unambiguous opinion throughout their writings is one reason why such disputes keep arising and never seem to get settled definitively. In the case of the recurring revolution versus reform dispute, however, there is the additional problem that Marx and Engels simply did not address many of the questions raised by it, let alone provide unambiguous answers, for the simple reason that in their day the rise of democracy had hardly begun (Anderson 1976, 24, 47–48; Hunt 1984, 64–66; Stephens 1979, 13; Therborn 1977).

The usual way to try to solve such doctrinal problems is either to infer the "correct" answers to questions not directly addressed in the Scriptures from answers to related questions that *are*, or to deduce the answers from what one takes to be the general spirit of those Scriptures. The former strategy was generally preferred by Lenin and Trotsky and their followers. They have in fact managed to compress the aforementioned trajectory from acceptance of the majority principle to complete renunciation of Marxism into one single form of heresy, interchangeably called "revisionism" or "reformism." This conveniently permits them to assert such half-truths as: "The very notion of 'reformism', the belief in the possibility of attaining socialism by gradual and peaceful reforms within the framework of a neutral parliamentary State, has no distinct existence in the work of Marx" (Anderson 1980, 176–77). Such statements lump together various aspects of "reformism," some of which Marx and Engels simply did not consider, others of which they took ambiguous positions on, and some of which they rejected unambiguously, so that the first two kinds appear to be discredited by their seemingly necessary association with the third. In fact, so successful has the Bolshevik revolutionary orthodoxy been in confusing the various issues, that even the defenders of reformism have great difficulty disentangling them (see, e.g., Stephens 1979, 11–14; but cf. Miliband 1977, 155–66). At least three questions raised by bourgeois democracy are habitually confused but are analytically quite distinct and hence better dealt with separately: (1) the expected degree of peacefulness and legality of the transition to socialism; (2) its anticipated rapidity; (3) the extent to which explicit majority support is required for a successful revolution.

The first question is whether universal suffrage and the parliamentary system that began to emerge in several Western European countries and North America toward the end of the nineteenth century would make it possible for socialists to gain power and accomplish the transition to socialism by electoral means. Although this question is treated by Leninists as of fundamental doctrinal importance, there is little doubt that Marx and Engels saw it as a secondary tactical matter at best. They always believed a violent insurrection would be necessary in most countries, particularly in those lacking any democratic traditions and institutions, but they were quite willing to entertain the possibility of a peaceful transition by wholly legal means in certain specific cases.

The case for violent insurrection is based on virtually a single passage from *The Civil War in France*, which begins with that Leninist favorite: "The working class cannot simply lay hold of the ready-made state machinery, and wield it for its own purposes" (Marx 1974, 206).[37] This is so, Marx explains, because the centralized state power inherited by the bourgeoisie from the absolute monarchy necessarily assumes, in the course of the intensifying struggles between capital and labor, "more and more the character of the national power of capital over labour, of a public force organized for social enslavement, of an engine of class despotism" (207). Thus, after every "progressive phase in the class struggle, the purely repressive character of the state power stands out in bolder and bolder relief" (ibid.). In this process, Marx continues, the executive branch becomes more and more powerful at the expense of the legislative assembly, culminating, finally, in the Second Empire (207–8). Rather than taking over its vast repressive and bureaucratic apparatus, the working class had to replace it immediately with its "direct antithesis," the Paris Commune (208). Then follows the enumeration of those ultrademocratic features of the Commune (replacement of the army by "the armed people"; all officials elected by universal suffrage, for short terms, under imperative mandate, immediately revocable, and at workingmen's wages; unity of executive and legislative; etc.) which, Marx believed, would allow universal suffrage to really "serve the people," instead of merely letting them decide "once in three or six years which member of the ruling class was to misrepresent the people in parliament" (210).

As usual, Marx's terms suggest he is making a general argument. Moreover, in the 1872 "Preface" to the second edition of the *Communist Manifesto*, Marx and Engels emphasize once again that the Commune had shown that the "working class cannot simply lay hold of the ready-made State machinery" (Marx 1977, 559). Yet, as early as 1852 Marx had hinted at the possibility of the English working class capturing political

37 Marx and Engels's forceful rhetoric of 1848–1852 is neither clearly relevant nor unambiguous evidence for their alleged insurrectionism in the present context since it concerns countries where democracy was either wholly absent or forcibly crushed (see Hunt 1974).

power by means of universal suffrage (Marx 1961, 206–7). Similarly, in the "Inaugural Address to the First International" delivered in 1864, Marx hails the Ten Hours Bill as a true victory for the "political economy of the working class" and calls on the workers to organize into political parties to exploit their numerical advantage and win political power (see Marx 1974, 73–81). He continued to entertain that possibility, including it in an interview he gave shortly after completing *The Civil War in France* (see Avineri 1968, 214–16). A year later, in a famous speech in Amsterdam, he warned that although "in most continental countries the lever of the revolution will have to be force," at the same time "heed must be paid to the institutions, customs and traditions of the various countries, and we do not deny that there are countries, such as America and England, and if I was familiar with its institutions, I might include Holland, where the workers may attain their goal by peaceful means" (Marx 1974, 324).

Again in 1879, Marx declared: "A historical development can only remain 'peaceful' so long as it is not opposed by violence of those who wield power in society at that time. If in England or the United States, for example, the working class were to gain a majority in Parliament or Congress, then it could by legal means set aside the laws and structures that stood in its way" (quoted by McLellan 1980, 228).

In a letter to his British follower H. M. Hyndman, dated December 8, 1880, Marx states clearly "that the party considers an English revolution not necessary but,—according to historic precedents—possible. If the unavoidable evolution turn into a revolution, it would not only be the fault of the ruling classes, but also of the working class. Every pacific concession of the former has been wrung from them by 'pressure from without.' Their action kept pace with that pressure and if the latter has more and more weakened, it is only because the English working class know not how to wield their power and use their liberties, both of which they possess legally" (Marx 1977, 594).

Engels, in his 1886 preface to the English edition of *Capital* (vol. 1), reiterates that Marx's study of "the economic history and condition of England" had led him to conclude "that, at least in Europe, England is the only country where the inevitable social revolution might be effected entirely by peaceful and legal means. He certainly never forgot to add that he hardly expected the English ruling classes to submit, without a 'pro-slavery rebellion', to this peaceful and legal revolution" (Marx 1967a, 6).

Five years later, however, Engels was already beginning to question England's uniqueness. In his critique of the German SDP's (Social Democratic Party) "Erfurt Program" of 1891, although he severely censures the leadership for its naive reformist illusions about authoritarian Germany, he adds: "One can conceive that the old society can grow peacefully into the new in countries where popular representation concentrates all power in itself, where one can do constitutionally what one will as soon as one has the majority of the people behind one; in democratic republics like France and America, and in monarchies like England" (quoted in B. D. Wolfe 1965, 216; cf. Hunt 1974, 332–33). Finally, after four more years of rapid growth of the SDP's membership and electoral support, Engels came to the conclusion that even in authoritarian Germany legality strongly favored the socialists. In the controversial preface to the new 1895 edition of *The Class Struggles in France* (Howe 1976, 102–18), he argues that "rebellion in the old style, the street fight with barricades, which up to 1848 gave everywhere the final decision, was to a considerable extent obsolete" (111) as technological and other developments since then had made such tactics less likely to succeed than they once had been. On the other hand, Engels notes, in spite of all the obstacles the government has attempted to put in its way, the growth of SDP membership and electoral support has been nothing short of spectacular. Thus, "if it continues in this fashion, by the end of the century we shall conquer the greater part of the middle section of society, petty bourgeois and small peasants, and grow into the decisive power in the land, before which all other powers will have to bow, whether they like it or not. To keep this growth going without interruption until of itself it gets beyond the control of the ruling governmental system, not to fritter away this daily increasing shock-force in advance guard fighting, but to keep it intact until the day of the decision, that is our main task" (116–17). Since legality now greatly favors the cause of socialism and harms its enemies, Engels concludes, there is no need for the working class to employ any other means; it only needs to wait for the forces of order "themselves to break through this legality so fatal to them" (117).

Marx and Engels were not dogmatic about the possibility of a peaceful transition by electoral means. They certainly did not consider the need for a violent revolution to be the "iron law" that Leninists have subsequently made it (see, e.g., Chang 1931, 67–87). If they thought violent revolution would remain the rule, they certainly were willing to consider the possibility of a peaceful transition wherever democratic institutions would permit. Their implicit principle seems to have been what Miliband (1977, 162) has aptly called "reciprocal constitutionalism": it is preferable to stick to the electoral strategy so long as that remains legal and the opponents of socialism also stick to it; in some countries those opponents may even allow socialists to come to power in this way (see Avineri 1968, 125–30; Elster 1985, 444–46; Hunt 1974, 144–45; 1984, 200–211, 326–42; Maguire 1978, 168–70; Sowell 1985, 151–56; Stephens 1979, 12–13).

There are a few minor issues in this connection that can be dealt with briefly here. It has been argued that there is a sharp contrast between the views of Marx and Engels before about 1850 and afterward. After that year, it is claimed, they drifted toward a significantly more reformist position as they came to understand better the realities and limitations of labor politics and the possibilities of representative democracy, a position that was also more compatible with their increasingly positivist, "scientific" outlook (see, e.g., Gouldner 1980, 294; Lichtheim 1965, 93–99, 103–5, 222–23; B. D. Wolfe 1965, 211–26). It has also been argued that toward the end of his life Engels went much further than Marx would have in espousing a clearly "reformist" position (Avineri 1968, 217; Lichtheim 1965, 52; Miliband 1977, 79).

Both arguments strike me as highly contrived, however. As for the first, the transition from Marx and Engels's calls for revolutionary insurrection until 1850 to their subsequent growing appreciation of the electoral strategy in some countries with well-established parliamentary traditions, did not necessarily involve a fundamental change of their outlook. They simply did not address the question of a peaceful transition before 1850 for the obvious reason that until then, and for some time thereafter, that possibility was entirely academic (cf. Hunt 1984, 64–66; Sowell 1985, 151). It was only in 1867 that England became the first country to cautiously extend the suffrage to limited strata of the working classes in the context of a truly parliamentary polity (see Therborn 1977, 11–17). Besides, as noted above, Marx anticipated this development, and the possibilities it might open up for a legal electoral strategy, as early as 1852 (Marx 1961, 706–7). Finally, even at their most fanatically chiliastic during the 1848–1850 upheavals, Marx and Engels were first of all concerned with forcibly winning universal suffrage and, once won, with preventing any subsequent retraction or limitation of its effective use by the propertyless classes (see Marx 1977, 277–85; cf. Draper 1978, 259–65, 599–612).

The claim that Engels went further down the road of electoralism than Marx would have is also largely academic since there is no way of knowing for sure what position Marx *would* have taken had he lived as long as Engels. His own rather pragmatic attitude toward the question certainly does not preclude the possibility that he might have agreed. On the other hand, Leninists have charged that the false impression of Engels's growing electoralism is exclusively the result of the "manipulation fraud" (Mandel 1978, 179) of SDP leaders who severely censored and edited the original text of his 1895 preface to *The Class Struggles in France*, so as not to offend German authorities, with the result that Engels appeared to advocate legalism at any price, as he himself complained at the time (Chang 1931, 211–15; Mandel 1978, 178–82). But although it is true that the original was considerably toned down against Engels's wishes and subsequently used to support a perhaps more reformist position than Engels would have actually condoned (Gay 1952, 217–18; Kolakowski 1978a, 361–62), the changes were little more than a propaganda coup with little relevance for the issues at hand. The unabridged original, which I have used above, contains a few remarks in which the need for eventual violent confrontation is not ruled out, but it is otherwise no different from the softened published version in its advocacy of the legalist, electoralist strategy as far as possible (see Chang 1931, 211–15; cf. Lichtheim 1965, 230; Miliband 1977, 79–80; B. D. Wolfe 1965, 219–23).

A somewhat more complex issue has been raised by Lenin, and, of course, faithfully parroted by his followers (but see Avineri 1968, 49), with respect to the *reasons* Marx apparently thought during the 1870s that a peaceful electoral transition was possible in countries like the United States, Great Britain, and Holland, but not in France or Germany. With some textual and contextual justification Lenin interprets Marx's argument to mean that it is the development of a huge bureaucratic and military apparatus for the suppression of the working class that makes it necessary for the latter to begin by "smashing" this "ready-made machinery" and replace it by one that it can "wield for its own purposes" in France, whereas the relative absence of such machinery in Great Britain and the United States still made the seizure of power without such previous destruction of the state possible. This allows Lenin then to argue that since the 1870s even these exceptions to the rule have lost their validity because, thanks to the rise of monopoly capitalism and imperialism, even Great Britain and the United States "have today plunged headlong into the all-European dirty, bloody morass of military bureaucratic institutions to which everything is subordinated and which trample everything under foot" (Lenin 1932, 34). The enormous growth of the repressive military-bureaucratic state machine everywhere as a result of monopoly capitalism and imperialist rivalry has led to a decline of democratic institutions and hence rendered a peaceful transition plainly illusory (ibid., 5, 33–35; Fernbach 1974, 53–56; S. W. Moore 1957, 95–111).

The Leninist argument seems to equate *any* expansion of the state bureaucracy with repression and the decline of democracy. But there is no obvious reason, nor any clear support in Marx's writing, to preclude the possibility that both the degree of democratic control *and* the size of the government bureaucracy may increase simultaneously. Of course, Marx does not clearly distinguish the two or discuss bureaucracy in detail. And he certainly argued that the enormous expansion of the French state apparatus was closely connected with its repeated need to suppress democratic movements. But it does not follow from this that they *must* necessarily be so connected, nor that as bureaucracies and the military expand they cannot be reduced or reformed by legal democratic means anymore and must hence be confronted head-on and destroyed, which sounds like a rather suicidal proposition at any rate. Marx's arguments cannot be used to support such assertions simply because they are not clear enough on these questions (see also Hunt 1984, 330–32). Even less can they be used to lend doctrinal support to the Leninist claims about the rise of monopoly capitalism and decline of democracy which presumably occurred after his death and which he did not foresee. All that can be said, once again, is that Marx and Engels were never in principle opposed to the electoralist strategy, and that they evidently believed it could lead to a peaceful transition to socialism in countries with democratic traditions and institutions strong enough to command the obedience of the enemies of socialism even when they are controlled by legally elected socialists.[38]

Thus, when Marx and Engels call the transition to socialism a "social revolution," they do not *necessarily* mean a violent upheaval. Nor does the term seem to imply anything about the expected rapidity of that transition (Avineri 1968, 217–18; Bottomore 1979, 90; Sowell 1985, 151; Stephens 1979, 12–13)—which brings us to the second question raised by bourgeois democracy. As we have seen above, Marx and Engels envisaged a transitional phase between capitalism and full-fledged socialism—the "dictatorship of the proletariat"—of unspecified duration. At times Marx appears to suggest that it might be a rather protracted process, with the working class having "to pass through long struggles, through a series of historic pro-

---

38   Miller (1984, 114–26) insists Marx and Engels never came to believe that any electoral victory could replace the necessity of open, violent class struggle. Apart from the usual textual exegetics—which the reader will have to compare to that offered here—his main reason seems to be that otherwise, i.e., if Marx and Engels *did* believe it was in some cases possible to effect a legal, peaceful transition to socialism by electoral means alone, their "ruling class" thesis could not be clearly distinguished from today's left-wing versions of pluralism anymore. As we shall see time and time again, the point is quite well-taken, but that hardly suffices to dismiss Marx and Engels's endorsements of electoral reformism for certain countries.

cesses, transforming circumstances and men" (Marx 1974, 213; cf. 346–47). However, the critics of reformism are no doubt right on one point: the kind of gradualism that became the hallmark of "reformism" after Bernstein appears to have been wholly foreign to Marx and Engels.

Marx and Engels supported working-class organizations and activities in defense of their immediate interests, no matter how narrowly conceived, and they hailed every victory won, no matter how partial (see, e.g., Marx 1974, 79; 1977, 228–29). But they entertained no illusions about the significance and permanence of such victories: at best they could last "only for a time" and even then they would necessarily be limited to the workers' "particular interests" only (Marx 1977, 228). Marx and Engels never believed that any lasting concessions could be won short of the final victory, let alone that socialism could be achieved gradually by cumulative, partial reforms under steady working-class pressure. The reason they supported trade unions and limited reform movements such as the Chartists was that they were convinced that *any* kind of workers' organization, whatever its immediate objectives and victories or defeats, would inevitably bring out their "natural" revolutionary consciousness and equip them with the organizational skills and means to execute their historical mission. "The real fruit of their battles lies, not in the immediate result, but in the ever-expanding union of the workers" (Marx 1977, 228; see also Marx 1963b, 172–75; 1977, 226–31; Marx and Engels 1959, 281–317; cf. Draper 1978, 72–80, 95–98, 136–38; Kolakowski 1978a, 348; S. W. Moore 1957, 50–51). As we have seen, even at his most "reformist" Engels advocates legalism and electoralism only so as to keep the "daily increasing shock force . . . intact until the day of the decision" (Howe 1976, 116–117).

Similarly, although they seemed to allow for considerable variation in the length of the transitional period *after* the seizure of political power, nothing could be more foreign to Marx and Engels than the incrementalism of present-day social-democratic and liberal governments, with their reforms and compromises intended to modify "the system" gradually without offending the opposition too much or jeopardizing the support of coalition partners or marginal voters. As I have argued above, by the "dictatorship of the proletariat" Marx and Engels clearly meant something more energetic and purposeful than the compromising, haggling, and electoral maneuvering characteristic of today's social-democratic politics. They clearly saw it as the culmination of the inevitable process by which the proletariat, which, they believed, would soon be the immense majority in the most advanced capitalist countries, had become aware of its historical mission. Once that consciousness had emerged, there would hardly be a point in making any further compromises or postponing things in the interest of bourgeois "civility" or political traditions. If the "dictatorship of the proletariat" meant anything to Marx and Engels, it meant that it was to abolish classes and prepare the conditions for the final abolition of the division of labor as rapidly and ruthlessly as possible (cf. Kolakowski 1978a, 405).[39]

Thus, the Marxist critics of reformism are right on this one point: in the writings of Marx and Engels there is no support for any form of incrementalism, that is, for the belief that socialism can be achieved gradually by piecemeal reforms (see also Hunt 1984, 360–61). Moreover, they *may* well be right to argue that *in practice* acceptance of the majority principle and electoralism inevitably leads to a wholly un-Marxian incrementalism, sooner or later. But they, or many of them, are quite wrong if they argue that there is some necessary *logical* connection between these three aspects of the reformist syndrome, or that Marx or Engels perceived any such logical link. They clearly opposed incrementalism *but not* electoralism.

With respect to the third issue in the disputes about reformism, whether the socialist revolution requires clear majority support, one can make much the same argument. The issue is, of course, inextricably linked with the wider and politically extremely sensitive question of Marx and Engels's attitude toward democracy and the majority principle in general, which I have

39   Gouldner's (1985, 126–37, 171–73, 184–85) suggestion that Marx, being a comfortable intellectual who could, unlike the revolutionary workers of the time, afford to wait for History to run its "inevitable" course, was an incrementalist all along seems to rest on a confusion between determinism (wrongly attributed to Marx in any case) and incrementalism. Obviously one does not necessarily entail the other.

already touched on several times. I have already argued that they always rejected any "educational" dictatorship by an enlightened "elite" à la Babeuf, even at the height of their most revolutionary period, and that their notion of the "dictatorship of the proletariat" is best viewed as a majority tyranny for the speedy eradication of all traces of class society. The same arguments can be—and have been—extended to the revolution itself.

As once again especially Draper (1974; 1977, 36–59, ch. 13; 1978, 115–65, 255–57, 481–572) and Hunt (1974, 84–92, 110–23, 229, 284–336; 1984, 316–24; but see also Bottomore 1979, 23–26; Elster 1985, 443–44; Sowell 1985, 153–55) have most convincingly argued, Marx and Engels also always rejected any kind of minority "putchism" à la Blanqui, as such a notion was completely at odds with their conception of the revolution as the self-emancipation of the proletariat as well as with their Hegelian "immanentism" according to which it is hopeless to attempt to impose solutions upon a society that is not yet ready for them (cf. Avineri 1968, 218; Boggs 1976, 101–2).[40] Thus, Marx and Engels always advocated the most inclusive social movement possible, rejecting all notions of any elite "vanguard," and even in the notorious "March Circular" of 1850, commonly considered to be the high-water mark of their most chiliastic period, they called for universal suffrage as the first aim to be striven for (Marx 1977, 277–85).

But Marx and Engels were not particularly infatuated with parliamentary democracy. In fact, at times they appear to have nothing but contempt for that form of government. Of course, many disparaging remarks about existing regimes had to do with the *limitations* on suffrage or on parliamentary sovereignty that still prevailed almost everywhere during their lifetimes (cf. Avineri 1968, 210; Hunt 1984, ch. 3). This is, I believe, how Marx's assertion in *The Civil War in France* to the effect that be-

40   In a letter quoted by Hunt (1984, 319) Engels dismisses the suggestion of any "vanguard"-made revolution under premature conditions thus: "People who boasted that they had *made* a revolution have always seen the next day that they had no idea what they were doing, that the revolution *made* did not in the least resemble the one they would have liked to make. That is what Hegel calls the irony of history."

fore the Paris Commune the electorate could only decide "once in three or six years which member of the ruling class was to misrepresent the people in parliament" (Marx 1974, 210) should be read: there was universal male suffrage in the Second Empire, but elections were neither free nor of great significance in the absence of parliamentary government (see Therborn 1977, 14).

On the other hand, in his *Critique of the Gotha Programme* Marx ridicules the program's demands for democratic reforms as "the old and generally familiar democratic litany" and asserts that in Bismarckian Germany demands for "these pretty little gewgaws" are hopeless and meaningless. The party leaders, Marx goes on, are worse than "vulgar democrats, who see the millennium in the democratic republic and who have no inkling that it is precisely in this final state form of bourgeois society that the class struggle must be fought to a conclusion" (Marx 1974, 355, 356). Similarly, Engels claims that even "the modern representative state" is ordinarily no more than "an instrument of exploitation of wage labour by capital" (Engels 1972, 160). This is not only the case where property qualifications restrict suffrage to the rich only, but even in the "highest form of state, the democratic republic, which under our modern conditions of society is more and more becoming an inevitable necessity and is the form of state in which alone the last decisive struggle between proletariat and bourgeoisie can be fought out" (161). In this form of state, Engels asserts, "wealth exercises its power indirectly," by "direct corruption of officials," an "alliance between government and Stock Exchange," and, last but not least, "through the medium of universal suffrage" itself (ibid.). For as long as the proletariat remains "not yet ripe to emancipate itself," Engels explains, it will willingly vote for the representatives of capital. Only when it matures sufficiently will the working-class form its own party and cease to "form the tail of the capitalist class." "Thus," he concludes, "universal suffrage is the gauge of the maturity of the working-class. It cannot and never will be anything more in the present-day state" (ibid.).

Passages such as these certainly suggest that Marx and Engels were no great admirers of bourgeois democracy. They have, in any case, provided ample ammunition for the Leninist claims that they loathed everything associated with this type of regime, viewed universal suffrage as nothing but a cynical hoax, and even considered the democratic republic to be "the best possible political shell for capitalism," establishing bourgeois rule "so securely that *no* change, either of persons, or institutions, or parties in the bourgeois republic can shake it" (Lenin 1932, 14; cf. Chang 1931, 55–56; S. W. Moore 1957, 84–94). But if this was really their opinion of bourgeois democracy, one wonders why on earth they so strongly and consistently supported all demands for universal suffrage.

The only reasonable explanation for this apparent paradox is that Marx and Engels did not see universal suffrage as an end in itself, but as a means for achieving another end. They preferred bourgeois democracy to any of its more repressive alternatives not because they saw in it the partial realization of the democratic ideal but because it offered the best environment available for the struggles and organization that would eventually equip the proletariat ideologically and materially to overthrow capitalism and replace it by a system that would render the institutions of bourgeois democracy obsolete. Thus, for Marx and Engels bourgeois democracy was certainly to be preferred, but it would eventually be replaced by a higher form of democracy "in which the so-called people's will vanishes, to make way for the real will of the cooperative" (Marx 1974, 336; see also Draper 1974; 1977, 77–95, 282–310; Harding 1978, 51–55; Hunt 1984, ch. 3, 164–73; Lichtheim 1965, 272–73; Mewes 1976, 281–92; Miliband 1977, 76–78; Mizuta 1984, 18; Sowell 1985, 144–51; Von Beyme 1985, 83–86).

Actually, this rather understates the extent to which Marx and Engels thought universal suffrage would benefit their cause. They called for universal suffrage with such persistence because they believed it to be ultimately incompatible with bourgeois society; they were convinced it would in the long run become profoundly subversive of the existing order, which would necessitate either *its* suppression or the transformation of that order. This belief was already apparent in Marx's earliest, presocialist calls for "true democracy," but it was apparently greatly reinforced by the events of 1848–1849 in France (cf.

Draper 1977, 397–98). About the democratic constitution proclaimed after the February Revolution Marx writes:

> The most comprehensive contradiction of this constitution, however, consists in the following: The classes whose social slavery the constitution is to perpetuate, proletariat, peasantry, petty bourgeoisie, it puts in possession of political power through universal suffrage. And from the class whose old social power it sanctions, the bourgeoisie, it withdraws the political guarantees of this power. It forces the political rule of the bourgeoisie into democratic conditions, which at every moment help the hostile classes to victory and jeopardize the very foundations of bourgeois society. From the former classes it demands that they should not go forward from political to social emancipation; from the others that they should not go back from social to political restoration. (Marx and Engels 1959, 313).

Two years later, in an 1852 article for the *New York Daily Tribune* he comments thus on the Chartists' demand for universal suffrage:

> But Universal Suffrage is the equivalent of political power for the working-class of England, where the proletariat forms the large majority of the population, where in a long, though underground, civil war, it has gained a clear consciousness of its position as a class, and where even the rural districts know no longer any peasants, but only landlords, industrial capitalists (farmers), and hired labourers. The carrying of universal suffrage in England would, therefore, be a far more socialistic measure than anything which has been honoured with that name on the Continent.
>
> Its inevitable result, here, is the *political supremacy of the working class*. (Marx 1961, 206–7)

Almost twenty years after that, finally, Marx claims that the Paris Commune, had it survived, would have inexorably led to "the economical emancipation of labour" because the "political rule of the producer cannot coexist with the perpetuation of his social slavery" (Marx 1974, 212).

Once again, then, we run into Marx's unshakable belief that because of its own experiences and struggles the proletariat will inevitably come to massively support the socialist cause. Hence, universal suffrage and capitalism were in the long run necessarily incompatible. Sooner or later the proletariat would become the majority and become conscious of its cause, and from then on either democracy would have to be suppressed again or capitalism abolished (cf. Avineri 1968, 212–15; Cerroni 1978, 243–49; B. D. Wolfe 1965, 142, 173, 212). It was simply unthinkable to Marx and Engels that the workers would *fail* for any extended period to try to use the vote to realize socialism. When the English proletariat failed to live up to their initial expectations they expressed anger at its "backwardness" and "corruption," surprise at the apparent ease with which it allowed itself to be "bought" by the bourgeoisie, but never any doubt that it would come to its senses fairly soon (see Draper 1978, 61–65; B. D. Wolfe 1965, 186–87).[41] Thus, the Leninist assertion that the democratic republic is "the best possible political shell for capitalism" according to Marx and Engels is plain nonsense—unless they mean a *bomb*shell.

This firm conviction that the working-class would *soon* become the majority of the population *and* aware of its mission to overthrow capitalism explains Marx and Engels's position on majority support and bourgeois democracy in their own day, as well as the fact that their writings offer absolutely no guidance for the problems with which their followers were confronted in the twentieth century. They were not democrats in the sense that they considered the proletariat to be necessarily always the only legitimate judge of its own best interests. Even in the most democratic parliamentary system the workers' votes and chosen representatives may suffer from immaturity and backwardness. However, they never doubted in the least that the working-class, especially in a democratic republic, would inevitably and fairly rapidly attain maturity and would then not hesitate one moment to express its real interests through the ballot box.

Thus, Marx and Engels rejected any minority putschism of the Babouvist or Blanquist variety not because it violated some

41   Marx and Engels were hardly alone in this belief in the incompatibility of capitalism and democracy. As the historian Eric Hobsbawm writes of the 1848–1875 period, "The middle classes of Europe were frightened and remained frightened of the people: 'democracy' was still believed to be the certain and rapid prelude to 'socialism' " (1977, 13).

first principle of majority rule but because they considered such *coup* attempts to be hasty and premature in the absence of clear mass support and thus likely to be defeated right away, or by an eventual Thermidor (cf. Hunt 1974, ch. 7). Similarly, in a "democratic republic" they would counsel restraint until there was a clear majority for fundamental change as shown in the polls, not because they were in some sense morally committed to the principles of bourgeois democracy itself (cf. Mewes 1976, 886–87) but because the vote is a convenient "gauge of the maturity of the working-class," as Engels puts it. Once that gauge indicates the proletariat is ready, there are no intrinsic reasons for sticking to bourgeois legality and, at any rate, by that time the proletariat will have developed its own institutional arrangements for securing the undiluted, unmediated direct rule of the masses.

All this is clearly predicated on the assumption that the proletariat will inevitably attain this level of socialist consciousness and that this "*prise de conscience*" is in fact imminent. Thus, the question that came to haunt Marxism from the turn of the century on, namely, what to do if the expected proletarian revolutionary consciousness did *not* materialize, simply did not occur to Marx and Engels. In fact, they would have considered the possibility that the proletariat might fail to become convinced of the feasibility or desirability of building a socialist millennium on the ruins of capitalism and would, hence, prefer a gradualist strategy of compromises and partial improvements to a radical revolutionary break, as patently absurd and not even worth contemplating. If workers could be swayed by any minor improvements at all, this could only very temporarily slow down the inevitable awakening of revolutionary consciousness (cf. Fernbach 1974, 58–64, 70; Kolakowski 1978b, 25). Thus, also, nothing could be more remote from the thinking of Marx and Engels than the notion that without the leadership and guidance of a well-organized "vanguard" of professional revolutionaries the proletariat could only develop a reformist "trade-union consciousness," a notion that would become the foundation of the Leninist strategy of insurrection (cf. Draper 1978, pt. 3; Hunt 1974, ch. 8).

This does not mean, however, that Lenin somehow grossly

betrayed the Marxian heritage, if only because there *was* no
Marxian heritage to betray with respect to the reality Lenin was
faced with. To Marx and Engels that reality would have been a
plain absurdity, an impossibility, and hence they offer nothing
in the way of a viable answer to the problems Lenin had to deal
with (cf. B. D. Wolfe 1965, 211–29). In fact, if Lenin's estimate
that the working-class would "naturally" tend toward a cautious
incrementalism was correct, his solution may well be the one
that violates the Marxian spirit *the least* among the alternatives
available (cf. Birnbaum 1985, 62–66). If, as I have argued
above, the essence of Marxism in the final analysis consists of a
claim to higher insight into the meaning and goal of history
which will eventually be vindicated by the working-class realizing it, but which cannot be *in*validated by any working-class
thoughts or actions to the contrary, then Lenin had little choice,
under the circumstances as he perceived them, but to either
abandon Marxism, as the social democrats have done after
World War I, or keep the faith and try to arrange for its realization in practice by whatever means available, with or without
the majority support of the working-class. The only other option is to lament the workers' "immaturity" and do nothing
about it (cf. van den Berg 1980), which seems hardly more
"Marxist" than the Leninist option.

In fact, on one of the few occasions on which Marx himself
considers the question of what will happen if the proletariat
were to refuse to fulfill its historical mission, he demonstrates
how easily his position leads to Leninist conclusions. In the passage quoted previously from his letter to Hyndman of December 8, 1880, Marx claims that experience shows that in England
it is possible to wring concessions from the "ruling classes" by
constant "pressure from without" and that, hence, a violent revolution may not be necessary there. If, however, the working-
classes allow the pressure to be "more and more weakened,"
because they "know not how to wield their power," they will in
part have themselves to blame if "the unavoidable evolution
turn into a revolution" (Marx 1977, 594). I do not doubt that
this remarkable passage can be read in many clever ways, but
one obvious one is the Leninist way: the predicted historical evolution is "unavoidable" whether or not the working-class

chooses to play the part assigned to it; if it does not, it will be brought about by some other means, in *spite* of the working-class if necessary.

I am not claiming here that Marx left a "Janus-like" legacy, having abandoned his former Blanquist chiliasm for a more realistic reformism without, however, ever explicitly acknowledging the conversion, as Lichtheim (1965, 103–5, 122–29, 372–73) has argued. If Marx has bequeathed a dualistic heritage it is the dualism that the Hegelian belief that the culmination of History consists of the eventual synthesis of Historical Necessity and (proletarian) Free Will necessarily produces when one of the terms of the synthesis fails to live up to the bargain. One way out of the problem is to ignore the latter term and set out to prove the validity of the former by whatever means are available. Thus practical-political success tends to become the sole criterion of the theory's validity, and all means to this end are justified (cf. Kolakowski 1978c, 523–25). The only other way to deal with uncomfortable reality is to give up the idea of any "necessity" or "meaning" of history altogether.

2 Marxism and Reformism

The presence of errors is one of the marks of any science:
the pretence of their absence has merely discredited the
claim of historical materialism to be one.

(Anderson 1976, 113)

From the late 1890s on, trends and events that Marx and Engels had not foreseen provoked a series of sharp debates among Marxist theorists, particularly among those active in the rapidly growing German Social Democratic party. After initially successful attempts simply to deny the unforeseen trends and thereby the need to revise the theory, in time several tendencies based on competing revisions and reinterpretations of received doctrine emerged. But, although these debates revolved essentially around questions of political strategy, they did not produce much in the way of cogent elaborations of Marxist political theory. Instead, some versions managed to impose themselves as the "correct" orthodoxy whereas others were branded as "revisionist" heresies, usually on grounds other than theoretical strength or even demonstrable fidelity to the Scriptures. In fact, it is often very difficult to determine which of the two constitutes a more drastic revision of the original ideas of Marx and Engels, the arguments of the alleged "revisionists," or those of the self-appointed guardians of orthodoxy, particularly in the case of Leninism (cf. Plotke 1977). There does seem to be a certain logic inherent in the position denounced as "revisionist," however, which leads its adherents progressively to reject more and more of Marxist doctrine, quite apart from the effect of their excommunication from the prevailing orthodoxy. This seems to be the common fate of all "reformist" tendencies, that is, those opting for the legal, electoral, and—it is to be hoped—peaceful road to socialism in parliamentary democracies, starting with the first and only theorist to accept the label of "revisionist," Eduard Bernstein (Parkin 1979, 193–98; Plotke 1977, 80).

Thus, in denouncing various forms of "reformism," "opportunism," and "revisionism" as somehow fundamentally at odds with the true spirit of Marxism, the orthodox do seem to have a point.[1] Whereas orthodox Marxists, whatever their differences in other respects, have generally been united in their rejection of "reformism," "reformists," whatever their initial convictions, have tended to end up renouncing Marxism altogether (see, e.g., Crossman 1950). The question of "reformism" seems to lie at the heart of any Marxist theory of politics. In fact, the recent Marxist literature on the state takes antireformism as its self-evident starting point. It has always been taken for granted—until very recently—that what distinguishes the true Marxist from the mere liberal is the former's rejection of the latter's "reformism." It was not until the late 1970s that this solid basis for identification finally began to crack when the apparently irresistible appeal of bourgeois democracy finally succeeded in eroding the commitment to antireformism of Marxist party leaders and theorists alike. It is, then, of some interest to review the various debates in which Marxism has come to define itself as antireformist, for this should shed some light both on the development of Marxist political theory and on the nature and evolution of Marxist theory in general, particularly in terms of its distinctiveness from "bourgeois" thought.

The Early Debates:
Bernstein and Social Democratic Orthodoxy

In a series of articles published between 1896 and 1898 in the theoretical organ of the German SDP, the *Neue Zeit*, Eduard Bernstein proposed a systematic revision of what had by then become orthodox Marxism, in order to accommodate what he took to be new factual evidence conflicting with many of its predictions. To Bernstein such an undertaking was perfectly legit-

---

1   The terms "reformism," "revisionism," and "opportunism" are often treated as synonymous. But strictly speaking "revisionism" is the more general term referring to any inadmissible deviation from orthodox doctrine (Kolakowski 1978b, 98; Plotke 1977, 79–80), whereas "reformism" denotes only a certain position with respect to political strategy. "Opportunism," finally, is the characteristically abusive term for "reformism" preferred by Lenin and his followers.

imate and there was nothing un-Marxist about it. He took the
orthodox claim that Marxism was "scientific" quite literally, that
is, he took Marxism to be a body of knowledge based exclusively
on empirically verifiable evidence and hence in need of revision
whenever contradicted by such evidence. However, it soon became clear that this was not at all what the orthodox defenders
of "scientific" Marxism had in mind as Bernstein's articles
caused "a raging storm of discussion" in the SDP, leading to
repeated condemnations of his heresies at party congresses and
spreading throughout the Second International after publication (in 1899) of his famous defense, *Die Voraussetzungen des Sozialismus und die Aufgaben der Sozialdemokratie* (Bernstein 1909;
see Gay 1952, 61–66).

The empirical trends that according to Bernstein necessitated
a wholesale revision of received orthodoxy he aptly summed up
in a few notes scribbled on the back of an envelope: "Peasants
do not sink; middle class does not disappear; crises do not grow
larger; misery and serfdom do not increase. There *is* increase
in insecurity, dependence, social distance, social character of
production, functional superfluity of property owners" (quoted
in Gay 1952, 244). The most significant of these were the fact
that the class structure was becoming *more*, not less, complex
because of the persistence of the old middle class, the rise of
the new, white collar middle class and increasing economic and
status differentiation among manual workers, and that, because
of cartellization, technical progress, and the growth of the
world market, the capitalist economy was becoming more and
more regulated so that economic crises became *less* frequent
and *less* serious. On the other hand, Bernstein did believe industrial concentration would continue although at a much
slower pace than Marx had expected (see Cerroni 1978, 250;
Gay 1952, 157–212; Kolakowski 1978b, 105–7; Plotke 1977, 81;
Stephens 1979, 58–59).

It followed, Bernstein argued, that contrary to orthodox
Marxist expectations, an overwhelming majority of uniformly
poor and exploited proletarians forming a natural constituency
for the revolutionary overthrow of capitalism would not
emerge. On the other hand, any attempt to establish socialism
against the will of the majority appeared utterly absurd to Bern-

stein, as it did to most Marxists at the time. Instead, he urged that the SDP moderate its stance so as to attract sufficient electoral support to realize its program by piecemeal reform. The party would have to have the honesty to jettison its revolutionary rhetoric, which had ceased to correspond to its reformist practice anyway, and openly profess its commitment to parliamentary democratic institutions, minority rights, gradual and peaceful reform, and willingness to compromise, and form alliances with like-minded political movements. Only in this way, he felt, could the Social Democrats achieve socialism gradually by realizing more and more of its elements within the existing system (Gay 1952, 213–47; Kolakowski 1978b, 107–9; Pachter 1981; Plotke 1977, 81–82; Stephens 1979, 58).

To Bernstein, democratic institutions, increasing control by those institutions over the economy, expansion of the rights and influence of labor and labor unions, reduction and limitation of the rights of property, greater equality of income and wealth, security of employment, and the like, were all elements of socialism that could be, and in many cases already were being realized in and through democratic parliamentary activity within existing capitalism. Such reforms, he believed, could be realized by careful maneuvering and propaganda to obtain the necessary electoral support, and by compromises with political allies, and they would accumulate within the capitalist system until some day that system would have been, almost imperceptibly, completely transformed. Thus, at least in a parliamentary democracy the transition to socialism would not require a sharpening of the class struggle toward a final confrontation, but public debate and class compromise instead; it would have the character of an "organic evolution" rather than a sudden, violent revolution (Gay 1952, 214–17; Kolakowski 1978b, 108–10; Stephens 1979, 59–60).

Contrary to what his opponents continue to claim, there was never any question of Bernstein giving up the ultimate ideal of socialism, notwithstanding his often-quoted dictum that "the 'final goal of Socialism' " meant "nothing" to him but *the movement everything*" (quoted by Gay 1952, 62). As is quite plain from the passage in which these fateful words occur, and as all observers who at least *try* to maintain a degree of objectivity agree, this did not mean that Bernstein had completely gone over to the bourgeois camp but rather that he believed in the possibility of a piecemeal realization of socialism and was more interested in that than in abstract theoretical declarations about the ultimate aims of the socialist movement (Benson 1978, 163; Gay 1952, 62ff.; Kolakowski 1978b, 109–10; Plotke 1977, 82). Of course, Bernstein did not specify exactly what he meant by "socialism," but then again neither did any of his orthodox opponents—as a matter of Marxist "anti-utopian" principle, as we have seen in the preceding chapter (cf. Gay 1952, 241; Kolakowski 1978b, 110).

Neither did Bernstein reject violent tactics outright as is so often claimed. He did not reject the use of the then much discussed "mass strike" as a weapon of last resort, and he was quite prepared to defend it against the union leaders who were otherwise his staunchest supporters but who fiercely opposed this particular tactic as a dangerous chimera obviously concocted by party theorists who would not have to bear the brunt of it (see Gay 1952, 231–38; cf. Kolakowski 1978b, 108). However, Bernstein *did* insist that such means should only be used when all else failed because of the absence of democratic rights, and *only* in order to obtain and secure those rights. Once these rights were secured, though, Bernstein definitely rejected any illegal extraparliamentary action—and even more so minority violence—as ultimately only harmful to the cause of socialism (Gay 1952, 241–44).

Whether Bernstein could still justifiably claim to be a Marxist, as he did (ibid., 77, 133), is another question. As many observers have pointed out, Bernstein's brand of incrementalism seems rather fundamentally at odds with the Marxian scenario of a constantly sharpening class struggle leading to a final confrontation and clear-cut victory for the proletariat, all preceding reforms having no significance beyond their contribution to helping prepare the way for the final victory (ibid. 135–38; Kolakowski 1978b, 109; Popper 1966b, 153–56, 339 n. 13; Stephens 1979, 59). But Bernstein was in fact prepared to go much further in his apostasy, as is already suggested by his conception of Marxist "science."

Bernstein's definition of "science" as a body of empirically verifiable and hence revisable propositions already betrays his Kantian leanings, which, as I have argued in the preceding chapter, are the complete antithesis of the Hegelianism fundamental to Marxism. Bernstein himself was well aware of this and openly rejected what he saw as the Hegelian elements in Marxism and advocated a return to Kant, although his theoretical grasp of the two perspectives was apparently rather limited (Gay 1952, 150–51; Kolakowski 1978b, 104–5).

The point is not only that Bernstein resurrected the logical gap between "is" and "ought" in the (neo-)Kantian manner. "Scientific" Marxists of the Kautskyan persuasion saw no harm in accepting the idea that one could not infer the desirability or moral worth of a state of affairs from empirical facts. But they simply considered ethics and human will irrelevant since they conceived of Marxist "science" as a completely amoral determinism providing infallible predictions as to the future of capitalist society, quite irrespective of any "morals" or of anyone's arbitrary "will." Insofar as such things had any importance at all in this orthodox perspective, they did only as necessary intervening variables in the wholly predetermined and hence predictable chain of events leading from developments in the economic base to their inevitable repercussions in the superstructures (see Gay 1952, 138–39; Kolakowski 1978b, 31–60). It can be argued that this amoral determinism rests on a lack of understanding of the original Hegelian-Marxian claim to have completely "transcended" all dichotomies of facts and values, necessity and free will, and so on, by an ultimate *fusion* of the two (Kolakowski 1978b, 40–42, 252–54; Lichtheim 1965, 291–300), but at least it upholds the typically Marxist claim that its belief in the coming of socialism is not "utopian," because it does not rest on "arbitrary" moral conceptions or human will but on forces that are "immanent" in capitalism itself.

It is in rejecting this last claim that Bernstein shows the true extent of his apostasy from the Marxism of Marx and his own contemporaries. To Bernstein the advent of socialism could not be guaranteed in advance but had to be fought for with human will and ethical commitment whose emergence and success could not be "scientifically" predicted. This need not entail an arbitrary utopianism, Bernstein claimed, for the commitment to the socialist ideal should be tempered and disciplined by the best available knowledge concerning past and present and the *possible* future. However, this in no way relieves one from the right and duty of making the moral choice to pursue this rather than that possibility which cannot and will not be made for us by "science" or anything "immanent" in "history" (see, e.g., Gay 1952, 131–56; Kolakowski 1978b, 102–3, 108–9). Such views are clearly very different from those of Marx and his orthodox followers. As Gay puts it, Bernstein "relies on voluntarism as Marxism never did, and takes the ground from under Marx's definite predictions. The apodictic certainty of scientific socialism is replaced with the hopefulness of ethical socialism; Marx's monism of being and ought-to-be has been torn in two" (1952, 140).[2] The fact that the great majority of Marxists saw their doctrine as much more than merely the revisable "economic theory of society" that Bernstein took it to be (cf. Connor 1968, xvi), and in particular that they considered its "immanentism"—that is, the unshakable certainty of the historical "necessity" of socialism—to be its indispensable core, became quite clear in the general uproar that Bernstein's arguments caused among them and the degree to which "revisionism," a label Bernstein found quite acceptable at first, became an all-purpose term of abuse.

The revisionism debates, which raged during the years around the turn of the century and largely consisted of a concerted onslaught by virtually all major Marxist theorists on Bernstein's heresies, were to a considerable extent devoted to the question of whether or not he had correctly diagnosed the empirical evidence about socioeconomic trends that presumably contradicted Marx's forecasts. This was, however, not the most significant issue in the debate, nor is it quite clear, even today, who was right (see Plotke 1977, 81; Stephens 1979, 58–59). The more important issue, which was formulated for the first time in these debates and has been a recurring issue ever since, was that of reform versus revolution. Bernstein's reform-

2   Similarly, Przeworski quite correctly points out that Bernstein's return to Kant constituted a return to pre-Marxist, that is pre-"scientific" socialism which "was motivated by moral and thus ahistorical ideals" (1977, 345; cf. also Alexander 1982b, 346).

ism was attacked from two sides, although the differences between them were initially not clearly perceived even by the anti-revisionists themselves (see Plotke 1977, 80). There was the attack from the orthodox "center," led by the "pope" of the Second International, Karl Kautsky, and most forcefully seconded by his Russian "prelate" Georgy Plekhanov, and the attack from the radical left led by Rosa Luxemburg. When in 1910 the differences between the center and left finally came to light in a debate over strategy between Kautsky and Luxemburg it is no small irony that Lenin, always seeking the protective mantle of orthodoxy, strongly supported Kautsky (see Anderson 1977, 65–69).

Long before Lenin, Luxemburg understood quite clearly that Kautsky only objected to certain aspects of Bernstein's reformism and that in other respects he was no less of a reformist himself. This was not mainly a matter of extraordinary perspicacity on Luxemburg's part, however. Kautsky had quite clearly stated his position long before the outbreak of the revisionism debates, and with characteristic rigidity (Kolakowski 1978b, 34–35) he stuck to that position in every respect from then on (see Kautsky 1964, 36–38). Thus, the rather silly distinction between "Kautsky the orthodox Marxist" and "Kautsky the renegade revisionist," drawn by Lenin only when the differences between his own position and Kautsky's "centrism" dawned on him after the outbreak of World War I (Chang 1931, 13n; Lenin 1932, ch. 6), is merely a clumsy attempt to cover up his own rather incredible misreading of Kautsky's perfectly plain position (cf. Parkin 1979, 162–64).

Kautsky objected to Bernstein's relatively conflictless incrementalism, *not* to his advocacy of the parliamentary road to socialism with which he agreed all along. Reforms of whatever kind, Kautsky held, were useful for improving the lot of the workers and necessary to educate and train the workers to achieve socialist class consciousness and effective organization. But they could never, by themselves, cumulatively lead to the realization of socialism. Socialism could *only* be the result of a successful "political revolution," carried out by a proletariat forming the overwhelming majority of the population and having attained a high level of socialist consciousness in the course of the increasing polarization of classes and sharpening class struggle, which would be followed by a relatively lengthy "social revolution." However, in the name of scientific rigor Kautsky refused to specify the exact nature of either "revolution," since this would depend on the historical conditions and circumstances of each individual case (Kolakowski 1978b, 43–47, 55–56).

By "social revolution" Kautsky did not mean a swift, violent event at all, but rather a socioeconomic process of transition from one mode of production to another which might well take several decades to complete and which would be all the more successful the more peacefully it could be carried out, with the strong support of the overwhelming majority of the population. The "political revolution" necessarily preceding such a "social revolution" consisted of a much swifter seizure of political power by the working class. However, it need not necessarily be violent or illegal either. In undemocratic countries it probably would be, but in parliamentary democracies the proletariat might come to power quite peacefully and legally by means of an electoral victory. The latter strategy is preferable by far to the former, Kautsky argues, because such a strategy will enjoy the majority support, moral authority, and peaceful conditions that are most favorable to the realization of socialism. In fact, revolutionary violence should be restricted as much as possible to movements attempting to establish or protect democratic rights only. Once secured, democracy is the most favorable environment for the maturation of the proletariat (see Kautsky 1964, 36–38, 54–58; cf. Cerroni 1978, 254; Kolakowski 1978b, 43–50; Lichtheim 1965, 259–77; Stephens 1979, 57–58).

The difference between revisionism and orthodoxy, then, was *not* necessarily one of revolutionary insurrectionism versus the parliamentary road, as is so often claimed (e.g., Gay 1952, 157; Pachter 1981, 208). Kautsky only objected to Bernstein's incrementalism and his playing down of the class struggle as the necessary preparation for a conscious seizure of power by the proletariat (Stephens 1979, 58–60). In doing so, he remained impeccably "orthodox," in the sense of faithful to the letter and spirit of Marx and Engels's writings on the subject. He firmly believed that the proletariat would inevitably become the huge majority of the population and that its homogeneous character and struggles to improve its living and working conditions would inevitably lead it to adopt the cause of socialism and develop the forms of organization necessary and capable of bringing socialism about. To Kautsky, as to Marx and Engels before him, neither successful reforms nor parliamentary democracy were problematic. On the contrary, they were welcome means that would only hasten the maturation of the proletariat and possibly enable it to take power peacefully. The following could just as well have been written by Marx and Engels: "The proletariat everywhere has the greatest interest in democracy. Where the proletariat represents the majority, democracy will be the machinery for its rule. Where it is in the minority, democracy constitutes its most suitable fighting arena in which to assert itself, via concessions, and develop" (Kautsky 1964, 133). This position was in fact widely taken for granted by nonrevisionist Marxists everywhere until 1917 (cf. Polan 1984, 145–50). They were the last "orthodox" Marxists in that, like Marx and Engels before them, they took it to be self-evident that in the long run capitalism would inevitably be incompatible with any kind of democracy, including the "bourgeois" variety, and that democracy and civil liberties would be automatic features of any socialism worthy of the name. The only issue on which there were significant differences of opinion concerned the expected likelihood of violent bourgeois resistance in formally democratic countries against a working class electoral victory (see Bottomore 1979, 148, 153; Kolakowski 1978b, 4–9, 25, 45–49, 276–82; Lichtheim 1965, 303–14). On this question Kautsky may have been a bit more optimistic than Marx and Engels would have been, although that is by no means certain (see "Marx and Engels on Revolution and Reform," Chapter 1). Luxemburg, on the other hand, certainly was not.

Like Kautsky, Luxemburg was convinced that democracy and capitalism were in the long run incompatible because the proletariat was rapidly becoming the great majority and acquiring socialist class consciousness through its many struggles. However, she argued, to expect the proletariat to seize power peacefully through the electoral process was utterly naive and amounted to a *de facto* abdication of the goal. For, she claimed, "institutions which are formally democratic" remain neverthe-less "in substance instruments of the interests of the dominant class," since there is no doubt that "as soon as democracy tends to deny its class character and to transform itself into an instru-ment of the real interests of the people, these same democratic forms are sacrificed by the bourgeoisie and by its state repre-sentation" (quoted in Cerroni 1978, 259). Thus, Luxemburg ar-gued—or rather simply asserted—that as soon as "democracy" ceases to serve the interests of the bourgeoisie, it will not hesi-tate to suppress all democratic forms, leaving the proletariat no alternative but to seize power through a mass uprising (Gay 1952, 23–24).

Thus, according to Luxemburg, Bernstein's reformism amounted to a *de facto* abandonment of socialism since the only reforms possible before the revolution are those that are ac-ceptable to the bourgeoisie because they fail to affect the system of exploitation seriously. She did not reject agitation for and pursuit of social reform as such, but felt it should only be used to raise the revolutionary consciousness of the proletariat and prepare it for the eventual, inevitable showdown. Any other purpose constituted a *de facto* betrayal of the proletariat (see Gay 1952, 259, 262–63; Kolakowski 1978b, 76–82).

But Luxemburg never did fear that such reforms would dis-tract the proletariat for long. She was totally convinced that capitalism was historically doomed to collapse under its own contradictions. One of her main objections to Bernstein's the-ory was—and she no doubt voiced the deep-seated anxieties of most orthodox Marxists on this point (cf. Kolakowski 1978b, 111)—that it denied the "historical necessity" of socialism, turn-ing it into a mere ideal that could be justified in terms of "jus-tice" only, and thereby abandoning all the achievements of "sci-entific socialism" (Cerroni 1978, 256–57; Gay 1952, 259–60; Gouldner 1980, 137). This certainty was based on Luxemburg's unshakable and almost mystical faith in the proletariat's "natu-ral" propensity and ability to revolt against the capitalist system. In this respect she seems to have stood closer to the original thought of Marx and Engels than any of her orthodox contem-poraries, in that her faith in the spontaneous abilities of the proletariat was least contaminated by any considerations of a practical, organizational, or institutional sort. She allowed for the need for a mass party which should be perfectly democratic and as inclusive as possible but, given the proletariat's revolutionary propensities, she assigned to the party the relatively minor role of keeping abreast of the true consciousness of the masses and refraining from retarding the free development of that consciousness. Triggered by economic crises or wars, a spontaneous rebellion of those masses would soon erupt—which, as the Russian uprising of 1905 convinced her, would take the form of a "mass strike"—automatically leading to an explosion of a higher level of consciousness and the spontaneous creation of all the institutional and organizational arrangements necessary to realize a truly democratic socialism. There was little need for "leadership" in all of this, and any exaggerated emphasis on "organization" and tactical caution could only retard the revolutionary process necessary for the masses to achieve the appropriate level of consciousness (see Kolakowski 1978b, 82–88; Plotke 1977, 80–83; Stephens 1979, 60–61).

Thus, the tenor of Luxemburg's critique of revisionism differed significantly from that of Kautsky. Their differences came to a head in their dispute of 1910 in which Kautsky attacked Luxemburg's advocacy of the "mass strike" as historically obsolete and dangerous. Basing himself on Engels's 1895 preface to *The Class Struggles in France*, Kautsky argued that conditions had changed since 1870 so that the strategy of head-on confrontation seeking the immediate overthrow of the government had, at least in the advanced West, become sheer madness, inevitably leading to bloody defeat, whereas the alternative strategy of a "war of attrition," consisting mostly of electoral campaigning and propaganda, offered the promise of relatively rapid victory. To Luxemburg—though not, at the time, to Lenin—this was an inadmissible concession to reformism which would necessarily lead to a wholesale capitulation to the capitalist system (see Anderson 1977, 61–69).

But the radical left and the orthodox center were united in their as yet unshaken belief that the proletariat would inevitably and naturally become conscious of its revolutionary historical mission, and capable of executing it. They were still being perfectly faithful to Marx and Engels in this respect, and it was in this conviction that they differed most fundamentally from Bernstein's revisionism. *But they were to be the last to base themselves on such a firm belief.* It is one of my major arguments that this loss of the belief in the proletariat's natural inclination toward revolutionary socialism constitutes a fundamental break for Marxism. With it, Marxism has lost its erstwhile democratic "innocence": caught on the horns of the "dilemma of democratic radicalism," it has been forced to choose *between* revolutionary socialism and the workers' more spontaneous tendencies (cf. van den Berg 1980, 453).

Bernstein, of course, did not believe there was any reason to expect the working class to gravitate naturally toward revolutionary socialism, nor that it would reach the numbers necessary to *impose* socialism on the rest of the population. On the contrary, he believed that if the socioeconomic trends he had identified continued, and if parliamentary democracy prevailed, the proletariat's "natural" inclination would be toward *his* brand of incrementalism. The best proof of this, as he repeatedly pointed out, was that the SDP was already committed to such incrementalism in practice, while tenaciously and rather hypocritically holding on to the old revolutionary rhetoric. This was indeed clearly the case even before Bernstein provoked the antirevisionist storm in the party. The party and trade union leadership and rank and file had in practice already come to concentrate heavily on immediate gains and had lost sight of the "ultimate goal." Revolutionary rhetoric and resolutions were left to the party intellectuals and they were apparently allowed to dominate at official gatherings before, during, and after the revisionism debates, mainly because they were considered harmless. Whatever resolutions passed, it was the day-to-day bread-and-butter reformism of the party and union functionaries, who—not always correctly—identified with Bernstein's revisionism, that ultimately won out everywhere in the advanced capitalist world (Gay 1952, 49, 99–105, 251–58, 298–300; Kolakowski 1978b, 99–100, 112–14; Pachter 1981).[3]

3   Gouldner (1985, 181) interprets the rise of Bernsteinian revisionism as a sign of the growing influence of career-oriented *intellectuals* in the German Social Democratic party after the suspension of Bismarck's antisocialist laws,

On this rather crucial point it would seem that Bernstein was entirely right and Marxist orthodoxy entirely wrong. Lenin later attempted to discredit "opportunism" by arguing that it was the ideology of an upper stratum of "working class aristocrats" who had been permitted to enjoy some of the crumbs of imperialist exploitation (see Harding 1977, 291–92; Lenin 1968, 145–48), but this clearly did not correspond to the known facts, especially for German workers, since Germany was not a particularly successful colonial power at the time, nor was it a particularly fortunate explanation from the orthodox Marxist point of view, as it apparently implied that the workers can be diverted from their revolutionary historical mission with remarkably little and remarkable ease (see Gay 1952, 105–30; Kolakowski 1978b, 113–14; Pachter 1981, 214; Polan 1984, 163–76). At any rate for the majority of Western workers incrementalist reformism turned out to be anything but a passing distraction from their "true" interests, and the generation of Kautsky and Luxemburg was the last to be able to hold on to the orthodox faith in the proletariat's "inevitable" embrace of revolutionary socialism. Ironically, on this point Lenin was in fact much closer to Bernstein's position than to that of pre–World War I orthodoxy.

Lenin and the "Renegade" Kautsky

Yet, it was Leninism that eventually became the undisputed orthodoxy of Marxism while the radical left was discredited as an "infantile disorder" akin to anarchism (Lenin 1968, 283–314) and the Kautskyan center, now excommunicated, inevitably drifted toward a social-democratic incrementalism as envisaged by Bernstein and as apparently preferred by the rank and file

---

but presents no evidence to support this claim. Generally, Gouldner assumes gradualism to be typical of middle-class intellectuals who can afford to defer gratification—particularly the gratification of others—and revolutionary impatience to be typical of the proletarian rank and file (185). Logic and what evidence there is suggest just the reverse, however: intellectuals can afford to draft sweeping resolutions calling for heroic actions from the relative comfort of their studies, whereas workers—who already can ill afford to be distracted from the daily concern with more mundane matters—are usually expected to carry them out at *their* risk and peril.

to the elusive guarantees of "scientific" socialism or Hegelian teleology. But there have always been voices, now cautiously, now—especially in recent times—more loudly questioning the fidelity of Leninist conceptions to the original intent and formulations of Marx and Engels—this usually in order to save the founding fathers from the uncomfortably authoritarian reputation attached to the "Marxist-Leninist" orthodoxy (see, e.g., Draper 1977, 1978; Hunt 1974). The issue seems destined to remain unresolved. Lenin was confronted with a situation that Marx and Engels had not foreseen and for which, therefore, they could give no guidance, and, with Bernstein, he was one of the first Marxists to recognize this. Thus he was faced with the choice of either developing a perspective that was *necessarily* somewhat "revisionist" or else sticking to orthodox articles of faith, like Kautsky and Luxemburg, that he *knew* to be out of date. Whether Marx and Engels would have done the same thing is neither an interesting nor an answerable question. On the other hand, there is no doubt that there is *some* basis to be found in their writings for each and every "innovation" of Lenin's, and it could well be argued, as I have done above, that Lenin's solutions remained as faithful to the core of Marxism— its claim to privileged insight into the destiny of history—as was possible under the new circumstances (cf. Birnbaum 1985, 62– 66; Kolakowski 1978b, 381–84; Plotke 1977).

Lenin himself never tired of stressing his unwavering fidelity to the spirit and letter of Marx and Engels's "genuine" thought, and of denouncing any alternative interpretations as more or less deliberate distortions. As a result, his arguments tend to sound more like dogmatic proclamations than coherent analyses to those not already convinced. Lenin's only sustained attempt to deal with the bourgeois state is to be found in his *State and Revolution* (Lenin 1932), written in August 1917, on the very eve of the October Revolution, and a most remarkable pamphlet for what it does *not* say and for how it does *not* correspond *at all* to postrevolutionary practice or to any of Lenin's other writings. Of course, Lenin only claims to "*resuscitate* the real teachings of Marx on the state" which have been "forgotten or opportunistically distorted" by the bourgeoisie and those opportunists of the Second International who have attempted to "omit, obliterate, and distort the revolutionary side of its teaching, its revolutionary soul," the "renegade" Karl Kautsky being "the chief representative of these distorters" (ibid., 6, 7). Thus begins, in typically Leninist fashion, what was to become the basic orthodox text on the bourgeois state and politics, undisputed and unelaborated for decades to come.

Lenin's argument opens with the quote from Engels's *Origin of the Family* in which the state is said to arise from "irreconcilable [class] antagonisms" (Engels 1972, 159). This means, according to Lenin, that the "state is an organ of class *domination*, an organ of *oppression* of one class by another" (Lenin 1932, 9), and nothing else. We have here the *locus classicus* of what I have called the "simple class theory" in Chapter 1. Since the state is "nothing but" an organ of class domination, it will only "wither away" when classes are finally abolished, and conversely, the continued existence of a state, in whatever form, proves invariably and irrefutably that there is still oppression of one class by another. Those suggesting that certain forms of the state may actually be used to "reconcile" class interests thus only provide "the most telling proofs" that they are not real socialists, "but petty-bourgeois democrats with a near-Socialist phraseology" at best (ibid.) The reference here is to the Bolsheviks' main rivals, the Socialist-Revolutionaries and Mensheviks, who were willing to participate in the provisional government established after the February Revolution (see also Chang 1931, 46–62; S. W. Moore 1957, 20–21).

But the principle is meant to have a much wider application. If all states are *by their very nature* forms of class oppression, then so is *any* ostensibly democratically organized state. Since, furthermore, one may treat class oppression and dictatorship practically as synonyms, it follows that dictatorship refers not to a type of government but to a type of state. This, finally, leads to the following conclusion: "The forms of bourgeois states are exceedingly variegated, but their essence is the same: in one way or another, all these states are in the last analysis inevitably a *dictatorship of the bourgeoisie*. The transition from capitalism to Communism will certainly bring a great variety and abundance of political forms, but the essence will inevitably be only one: *the dictatorship of the proletariat*" (Lenin 1932, 31). The difference between the two types of dictatorship is not one of form, which is pretty much irrelevant, but one of content: in the former a small minority oppresses the huge majority, in the latter the overwhelming majority suppresses a resistant but dwindling minority only with the object of doing away with oppression once and for all. Thus, by means of an overinterpretation of one passage by Engels and a simple syllogism approximating plain sophistry (cf. Lichtheim 1965, 344, n. 1), Lenin has in effect equated dictatorship not with a "form" of the state but with the state *as such*, and managed, in the process, to obliterate *any* differences between democracy and dictatorship as merely an irrelevant matter of "form"—a fateful doctrine that remained unquestioned for generations of Marxists (Chang 1931, 112–16; S. W. Moore 1957, 30–33).

But in addition to this doctrinal exegesis, Lenin offers a whole array of more concrete arguments why democracy in a capitalist society is necessarily nothing but a hoax. There is, first of all, Engels's authoritative assertion to the effect that even in a democratic republic, wealth rules indirectly through corruption of officials and an alliance of the government and the stock exchange, methods which since Engels wrote have been developed to "an unusually fine art" with the rise of imperialism and the predominance of the banks (Lenin 1932, 13–14). Furthermore, Lenin claims, Engels's remark about universal suffrage being *nothing but* "an index of the maturity of the working class" means that Engels "quite definitely regards universal suffrage as a means of bourgeois domination," which, contrary to the "petty-bourgeois" illusions of all sorts of "opportunists" is never "really capable of expressing the will of the majority of the toilers and of assuring its realisation" (14). This is so because—and here Lenin hazards some propositions of his own—in capitalism democracy means democracy "only for the rich" (72). "The modern wage-slaves, owing to the conditions of capitalist exploitation, are so much crushed by want and poverty that 'democracy is nothing to them', 'politics is nothing to them'; that, in the ordinary peaceful course of events, the majority of the population is debarred from participating in social and political life" (ibid.) As proof of this statement Lenin notes the fact that in almost half a century of constitutional legality (1871–1914) the German Social Democratic party only managed to enlist 1 million out of 15 million workers as party members and organize only 3 million as union members (ibid.).[4] In addition, Lenin claims, in practice universal suffrage is everywhere hedged in by all kinds of restrictions and requirements (residential requirements, exclusion of women, techniques of representation), limitations to the right of assembly, and capitalist control of the press, all of which serve to "exclude and squeeze out the poor from politics and from an active share in democracy" (ibid.). Hence in practice universal suffrage merely allows the people to "decide once every few years which member of the ruling class is to repress and oppress the people through parliament" (40). Besides, Lenin continues, the "venal and rotten parliamentarism of bourgeois society" (41) ensures that it makes no difference who is elected to parliament anyway. This is so because "the actual work of the 'state' . . . is done behind the scenes and is carried out by the departments, the offices and the staffs. Parliament itself is given up to talk for the special purpose of fooling the 'common people' " (40). These, then, are the arguments justifying Lenin's famous conclusion that the "democratic republic is the best possible political shell for capitalism, and therefore, once capital has gained control . . . of this very best shell, it establishes its power so securely, so firmly that *no* change, either of persons, or institutions, or parties in the bourgeois republic can shake it" (14). They have become the basic arguments for the now standard Marxist dismissal of bourgeois democracy as a "fiction" and of the notion of a democratic parliamentary majority as parliamentalist "fetishism," concealing bourgeois rule and aimed at thwarting the revolutionary movement (see Chang 1931, 55–58; Knei-Paz 1978, 248–57; S. W. Moore, 1957, 92–94).

However, this is a far cry indeed from the confidence of the orthodox, beginning with Marx and Engels themselves, that ul-

4   Lenin's claims are in fact inaccurate. From 1878 to 1890 the SDP was forced underground by Bismarck's "Socialist Law" which declared its organization and organs illegal and its members subject to harassment of all kinds (Gay 1952, 25ff.; B. Moore 1978, 221). Besides, in the present context the electoral support for the SDP would seem at least as relevant a measure of working-class political participation.

timately universal suffrage and capitalism are incompatible. Moreover, the democratic republic as "the best possible shell" seems strangely at odds with Lenin's own declarations elsewhere—this time more in line with the orthodoxy of the time— to the effect that bourgeois democracy is to be favored over more repressive regimes because it allows the proletariat the greatest possibilities for waging the class struggle and developing its strength for the final showdown (Lenin 1932, 18, 59, 66; Knei-Paz 1978, 559; cf. Kolakowski 1978a, 360–67). After all, if bourgeois democracy allows the proletariat to gather sufficient support to be able to win out in a final confrontation with the mighty bourgeoisie, it is not quite clear why a socialist party could not get a sufficient number of workers to commit the much less risky act of voting for it. Conversely, if bourgeois democracy *does* permit socialists to win elections, Lenin's assertions offer no clear reason for rejecting Kautskyan electoralism, which is what the whole argument was intended to counter in the first place.

Perhaps sensing the problem, Lenin offers additional arguments to show that an electoral strategy will never work. He acknowledges that in the 1870s Marx still believed that in countries like Great Britain and the United States the proletariat might come to power legally, and perhaps even peacefully, by means of an electoral victory. At the time this was a possibility because these two countries were still characterized by a relative absence of militarism and bureaucracy. That this was indeed Marx's reason Lenin deduces indirectly, from Marx's comments about France to the effect that the revolution cannot use the "bureaucratic and military machinery" for its own purposes and must instead "*break it up*" (Lenin 1932, 33). As a result of the rise of monopoly capitalism and imperialism since the 1870s, Lenin argues, this has become true for countries such as England and the United States as well. Now they, too, have "plunged headlong into the all-European dirty, bloody morass of military bureaucratic institutions to which everything is subordinated and which trample everything under foot" (34).

Monopoly capitalism and imperialism have, according to Lenin, produced an unprecedented expansion of the military and bureaucratic apparatuses of the state rendering all bourgeois regimes ever more repressive:

Imperialism in particular—the era of banking capital, the era of gigantic capitalist monopolies, the era of the transformation of monopoly capitalism into state monopoly-capitalism—shows an unprecedented strengthening of the "state machinery" and an unprecedented growth of its bureaucratic and military apparatus, side by side with the increase of repressive measures against the proletariat, alike in the monarchical and the freest republican countries. (ibid., 29)

The imperialist war has greatly accelerated and intensified the transformation of capitalism into state-monopoly capitalism. The monstrous oppression of the labouring masses by the state—which connects itself more and more intimately with the all-powerful capitalist combines—is becoming ever more monstrous. The foremost countries are being converted—we speak here of their "rear"—into military convict labour prisons for the workers. (ibid., 5)

It follows from this, according to Lenin, that, as Marx already foresaw as early as 1852, this bourgeois state machinery, which was created and expanded by the bourgeoisie for the sole purpose of repressing the people and which is, hence, "connected by thousands of threads with the bourgeoisie and saturated through and through with routine and inertia" (ibid., 96), cannot be simply taken over by a socialist government and wielded for its own purposes. Instead, as Marx stated quite clearly, it is the task of the proletariat "to crush, to smash to bits, to wipe off the face of the earth the bourgeois state machinery" (83). Moreover, this clearly means, Lenin insists, that the revolution will *have* to be a violent one, as Engels explains when he refers to violence as the "midwife" of historical change (9; 18–20; cf. Chang 1931, 67–75; B. D. Wolfe 1965, 166–67, 292). "This conclusion," he declares, "is the chief and fundamental thesis in the Marxist theory of the state" (Lenin 1932, 25).

The logic underlying this "fundamental thesis" is not entirely clear, however. On the one hand Lenin seems to assert that with the advent of "state monopoly-capitalism" and imperialism the days of liberal bourgeois democracy are numbered, so that the electoral strategy will soon become obsolete simply for lack of liberties and elections (cf. Wirth 1977, 292). The trouble with this interpretation is that it has been so patently falsified as to be of only antiquarian interest today. On the other hand, Lenin can be interpreted as saying that the mighty military and state bureaucracy of state monopoly capitalism is always at the disposal of the bourgeoisie for the forcible suppression of any real threats to its interests, if and when the need should arise. Thus, even *if* a socialist government were legally elected by a majority of the population, the bureaucracy and the army, more beholden to the bourgeoisie than to the legitimate democratic government, would simply refuse to obey it and even turn against it if it dared to attempt any serious incursion on the fundamental interests of the bourgeoisie. This is in fact the same argument Luxemburg raised against reformism: the bourgeoisie will abandon the whole democratic charade as soon as it threatens to go *against* its interests. Lenin only specifies the argument a little further by claiming that the bourgeoisie is at all times able to suppress democracy by virtue of the loyalty of the bureaucracy and military. This is indeed how Lenin's argument has traditionally been interpreted, that is, that bourgeois democracy is essentially a hoax because it will be suspended in favor of some form of right-wing dictatorship as soon as it runs against the interests of (monopoly) capital (see Frankel 1979, 200–201; Knei-Paz 1978, 251, 254–57; Mandel 1978, 182–87; Miliband 1977, 175–76; S. W. Moore 1957, 88–91, 95–97, 104–11; Sweezy 1942, 250–52). Examples usually mentioned to support this argument include the rise of Nazism and fascism in Germany, Italy, and Spain and the overthrow of the Allende regime in Chile (Mandel 1978, 191).

This, then, is the Marxist theory of the state according to Lenin, which presumably demonstrates the futility of all reformist strategies, whether of the Bernsteinian or the Kautskyan variety, and shows the latter to involve (probably deliberate) "distortions" of Marx and Engels (Lenin 1932, esp. 18–20, 40–41, 86–100; Chang 1932; cf. Kolakowski 1978b, 497–501; S. W. Moore 1957). Properly elaborated and codified it became the unquestioned communist orthodoxy under the name of "stamocap" theory.[5]

5   Ironically, during the 1960s this same "stamocap" theory came under fire
     in the nonofficial Marxist literature precisely for its allegedly reformist im-
     plications, in much the same way as the traditional prestamocap Marxist
     theory of the state had; this also closely parallels the developments in Marx-
     ist theorizing on the state discussed in this book (see Fairley 1980; Gersten-

But on closer inspection, Lenin's contribution to the Marxist theory of bourgeois politics and the state is neither terribly coherent and consistent nor terribly convincing. As has already been suggested, the argument that the proletariat cannot effectively express its preferences through universal suffrage is hardly compelling. The various restrictions and qualifications limiting the suffrage that he mentions are not universal in capitalist countries nor do they seem prohibitive obstacles to obtaining a socialist majority. Different living conditions may make for different degrees of political participation between classes, but such differences can, at least with respect to the ballot, be eliminated by compulsory voting and political mobilization of the working class (Korpi 1983, ch. 3; Stephens 1979, 65). But the big unanswered question really is why Lenin expects socialists to be able to mobilize the working class to the point where it will be prepared to engage in a risky final confrontation with the bourgeoisie when they cannot even get those same workers to vote for them in the safety and anonymity of the voting booth!

Moreover, the theory of "state monopoly-capitalism" and imperialism simply contradicts the assertion that the democratic republic is "the best possible political shell for capitalism." If we are to take the latter statement seriously, it would seem downright foolish of monopoly capital to rid itself of this perfect shell in favor of a more blatantly repressive regime, nor is it clear what would prompt it to do so. Conversely, if we take the stamocap-imperialism theory seriously the inescapable conclusion must be that the democratic republic apparently failed to provide the best shell. To argue that it is the best shell except when it is not, amounts to meaningless tautology, of course.

Third, even if one were certain that the bourgeoisie would attempt to destroy democracy the moment it permits a truly socialist government to come to power,[6] this does not, as Kautsky

---

berger 1976, 82–84; Mandel 1975, 513–22; Poulantzas 1973b, 152–53, 271–73; 1975, 156–74; Ross 1978, 169–70; Wirth 1977).

6   It might be noted in passing—this was obviously not one of the major issues at the time—that examples such as the rise of Nazism, fascism, and the Pinochet regime are far from obvious or unproblematic cases of a united bourgeoisie using the armed forces and civil service to suppress a serious threat to its "fundamental" interests (see, e.g., R. F. Hamilton 1982, esp. 400–413). Furthermore, the argument cannot really account for instances

already pointed out in 1918, necessarily prove its uselessness to the proletarian cause but perhaps the opposite, namely that the inviolability of democratic institutions should be defended "with tooth and nail" (Kautsky 1964, 8). After all, if a final, violent confrontation is indeed inevitable, then the moral authority of a legitimate, democratically chosen government on its side may be an invaluable asset for the working class. It would force the bourgeoisie into blatantly illegal acts which might help to win a larger portion of the bureaucracy and military over to the side of the proletariat, being the side of the law, than otherwise. It would seem much more difficult to get them to defect to proletarian counterinstitutions, as Leninists and Trotskyists propose, which would first have to laboriously establish their legitimacy against that of the democratic republic. Yet, without such defectors on a massive scale, the whole thing would appear to be doomed from the start. In short, although Lenin offers several arguments to show that socialists cannot win an electoral majority in bourgeois democracies and that if they do anyway they will not be allowed to rule, he offers none to show that the proletariat's chances of successfully "shattering" the state machinery that supposedly frustrate its rule are any better.

Objections such as these, and many others, were already raised by Kautsky in the wake of the Bolshevik revolution and of the first signs of the suppression of democratic opposition to the new regime. This gave rise to a bitter polemic between Kautsky, Lenin, and Trotsky in which the last two simply failed to respond to Kautsky's criticisms. Instead they tried to drown him out with verbal abuse and invective and the endless repetition of dogmatic formulas, as is quite plain even from accounts that heavily favor Lenin's side (see, e.g., Plotke 1977, 83–87). Consequently, these debates did little to clarify Lenin's arguments. In fact, as even some of his admirers concede, Lenin simply does not provide anything that merits the label of a coherent theory of the state (Anderson 1977, 51; Plotke 1977,

---

of successful significant reforms *over* organized capitalist opposition, except by the rather circular device of declaring such reforms evidently not "really significant." As we shall see, this latter problem was to become a central issue in the debates on the theory of the state that have raged since the late 1960s.

87). But then, this is only a minor paradox of his *State and Revolution*.

The greatest puzzle in his *State and Revolution* is the uncharacteristically anti-authoritarian, almost anarchosyndicalist description of the transitional "dictatorship of the proletariat" that is to replace the "shattered" bourgeois state machinery. Whereas, contrary to anarchists, Lenin *does* insist that the proletariat will still need a state after the revolution—in the sense of an organized body for exercising force in order to suppress the resistance of the former bourgeois oppressors—he claims that this state will already be immeasurably more democratic than bourgeois democracy could ever be. The bourgeois state, no matter how democratic in form, was nevertheless inevitably a machine for the suppression of the vast exploited majority in the interests of a tiny minority. In the revolutionary proletarian dictatorship, on the other hand, the tables will be turned: it will only suppress and exclude a tiny minority of exploiters while constituting the first truly democratic regime in history for the vast majority of the people (Lenin 1932, 21–24, 31, 51–54). Thus, Lenin argues, the state already turns into "something which is no longer really the state in the accepted sense of the word" (37, cf. 56). When the resistance of the bourgeois minority is finally and definitely crushed the state will at last "wither away" completely, as "people will *grow accustomed* to observing the elementary conditions of social existence *without force and without subjection*" (68; also 37, 73–75).

The only form of the state that could be expected to permit this unprecedented expansion of democracy for the exploited masses and prepare the way for its own obsolescence was, naturally, a state run and protected by the masses themselves, "relying directly upon the armed force of the masses" (23). Such a state would have to be, as Marx had shown in *The Civil War in France*, "a democratic republic after the type of the Commune, or a republic of Soviets of Workers' and Soldiers' Deputies, the revolutionary dictatorship of the proletariat" (99). A federation of such Soviets would constitute "the really democratic state" (80), fully under the control of the armed masses. Such control would be guaranteed by the measures Marx had praised so highly in the Paris Commune: replacement of the standing army by "the armed people," election of *all* officials subject to instant recall, remuneration at no more than the average work-ingman's wage, and replacement of the parliamentary "talking shops" of the bourgeois state by representative bodies with *both* legislative and executive responsibility at all levels (35–42, 91–92). Lenin appears quite convinced that in such a state form *"everyone* really takes part in the administration of the state" (83). There is nothing utopian about this, he insists, because the tasks of accounting and control, which form the bulk of such administration, have already been simplified to such an extent by the development of capitalism that they are now "quite within reach of every literate person" (38), and there is, hence, nothing to stop "the whole people in arms" (83) from taking over the entire state and economy and administering them suc-cessfully (38–39, 42–44, 83–85, 96–9).

Thus, according to Lenin, would the "dictatorship of the pro-letariat" emerge out of the spontaneously arisen Workers' and Soldiers' Soviets (see also Chang 1931, 103–24). It would, Lenin insisted, be a true "proletarian democracy," and therefore *"a million times* more democratic than any bourgeois democracy" (quoted in ibid., 115; and Miliband 1977, 18). The feasibility of the official Leninist strategy of "dual power" ultimately rests on the belief that in times of crisis "the masses" are bound to rally to the Soviets organized by a "revolutionary vanguard" because of their incomparably "higher form of democracy," which will successfully challenge the legitimacy and authority of the bour-geois state (see, e.g., Anderson 1980 194–96; Mandel 1978, 172–78; 1979, 1–66; Miliband 1977, 179–82; Parkin 1979, 196).

Unfortunately this ultrademocratic interpretation of the transitional "dictatorship of the proletariat" bears not even the faintest resemblance to the actual dictatorship Lenin himself began to implement within months after completing *State and Revolution*, nor is there anything in any of his other writings that remotely corresponds to it.[7] Thus, whereas the concept of a se-

---

7   Norman Levine (1985) blames the "anarchist and utopian" vision of *State and Revolution* on Lenin's adoption of the "state-as-reflection-of-class para-digm" from Engels which seemed to imply a complete "withering away" of the state under socialism. By contrast, Levine argues, from writings by

cret, exclusive party of professional revolutionaries as the indispensable guide and "vanguard" of the proletariat is perhaps most characteristic of, and certainly most controversial in, his other writings, in *State and Revolution* there is only *one* reference to the party playing a leading role, but even it is highly ambiguous (Lenin 1932, 24–25; see also Kolakowski 1978b, 501; Miliband 1970, 82–83; 1977, 137–38). Yet, when the Bolsheviks overthrew the "bourgeois" provisional government to replace it by the Soviets in October 1917, it soon became clear that it was not the Soviets as depicted in Lenin's pamphlet but the Bolshevik party that had come to power and turned the Soviets into the instruments of its absolute rule (Cerroni 1978, 242; Kolakowski 1978b, 485–89, 501–9; Miliband 1977, 141–44, 167–69). In fact, the discrepancy between Lenin's arguments of August 1917 and his actions beginning almost immediately after the seizure of power in October is so enormous that one can hardly blame critics for questioning his sincerity in *State and Revolution* (Knei-Paz 1978, 568; Lichtheim 1965, 344; see also Polan 1984, 20–27).[8]

Marx that were not available to Lenin, notably the early writings, it is clear that Marx never took such an extreme position. Instead, Marx adopted the "state-as-reflection-of-society thesis" which implied that even under socialism there would still be a need for "governance," a "need of leadership, of consensus, of compromise and accommodation" (96). Levine is plain wrong on several counts, however. First, as we have seen in the previous chapter, Marx's earliest writings were hardly any less "anarchistic and utopian" than Engels's, nor is there any obvious difference between them later on. Second, the two later works by Marx mentioned by Levine, the *Critique of the Gotha Program*, and *Marginal Notes to Bakunin's Anarchy and State* most probably *were* known to Lenin. Third, the depiction of the "dictatorship of the proletariat" in *State and Revolution* was taken, virtually *verbatim*, from *The Civil War in France*, written by Marx, not Engels. Finally, Levine's notion of "governance" is too vague to support any argument one way or the other: it either means ordinary government by consent as advocated by all democrats, but this is clearly far short of what Marx ever had in mind, *or* it is so vague as to be easily reconcilable with the "anarchist and utopian" ideal of a pure "administration of things" as advocated by Lenin and Engels.

8   The discrepancy thesis has been contested from two opposite directions. Polan (1984) argues that despite its apparently democratic libertarianism, *State and Revolution* is based on the same prototypotalitarian assumptions to be found in Lenin's other writings and manifested in his pre- and postrevolutionary political practice: a profoundly antimodern distaste for human diversity, a denial of any authentic, legitimate conflicts of interest, and a resulting desire to put an end to all politics once and for all. As will become

Lenin's conception of the party as a highly disciplined, centrally controlled, and very exclusive "vanguard" of professional revolutionaries has been the subject of controversy ever since he first spelled it out in the 1902 pamphlet *What is to be Done?* (for the main sections, see Lenin 1968, 31–78). The relation be-

---

clear shortly, I agree with much in this diagnosis. Nevertheless, the fact remains that in *State and Revolution* Lenin makes the highly uncharacteristic assumption that the true unity of the masses, the Rousseauian "general will" will emerge spontaneously, without any coercion from above.

Harding, by contrast, strongly argues against the general consensus that *State and Revolution* was "merely a 'pipe-dream', an inexplicable voyage into utopianism and thoroughly inconsistent with Lenin's real Jacobinism" (1978, 323), on the grounds that it was firmly based on Lenin's recently developed theory of imperialism and that after the October Revolution Lenin actually did try to implement the ideal of direct workers' democracy along the lines of his pamphlet (ibid., ch. 8). But it is surely more significant that Lenin's brief spell of confidence in the "masses" lasted only a few months at most, and that, upon realizing that the feeling was not necessarily mutual, he quickly retreated to his old authoritarianism, leading him to seek more and more elitist and coercive solutions to the problems he faced, as Harding himself shows in detail (chs. 9–15).

Wright tries to explain away the discrepancy between Lenin's seemingly hard-nosed critique of bourgeois democracy and his astonishingly naive and uncharacteristic description of "proletarian democracy" by arguing that Lenin, subordinating organizational issues to issues of class domination and possessing information about bourgeois class domination but not about the not yet existing proletarian class domination "is forced to remain quite vague" about the organizational implications of the latter (E. O. Wright 1974, 107 n. 13; 1978, 212 n. 16). Now, to the extent that I understand this it sounds like plain apologetics to me, which is all the more preposterous as it is presented in an article criticizing Max Weber for offering a "one-sided understanding of bureaucracy and the state," ignoring "class domination" (1974, 101–3; 1978, 216–19). After all, it was this "one-sided" theory that permitted Weber to predict with uncanny accuracy what was about to happen in the Soviet Union while Lenin's preoccupation with class domination appears to have been able to produce only silly pipe-dreams. Moreover, when, soon after the Bolshevik seizure of power, the administrative complexities of "proletarian class domination" became painfully obvious, Lenin stubbornly persisted in devising cures of such organizational naiveté that they were *bound* to be worse than the disease (see Harding 1978, chs. 9–15; Polan 1984, ch. 2). Lenin's neglect of organizational issues rather forcefully illustrates the Marxist tendency to assume that if only classes—narrowly conceived—would be abolished *all* (other) problems would be automatically and painlessly resolved. Such an assumption may have been only mildly ridiculous in 1917, but to *still* seek excuses for it in 1974 is quite indefensible. In addition, Lenin's neglect of organizational issues on the very eve of the revolution—which he had been anticipating since *at least* April 1917 (see his famous "April Theses"; Lenin 1968, 158–60)—would appear to have been tween this conception and the dictatorship of the party that emerged after the October Revolution is, of course, one of the most-debated issues arising from that upheaval (see, e.g., Knei-Paz 1978, ch. 5; Kolakowski 1978b, 384–96, 485–91; Lichtheim 1965, 325–51; Miliband 1977, ch. 5). But of greater interest here are Lenin's views of the relation between (his version of) Marxism and the consciousness of the workers, which form the basis of his ideas about the organization of the party, and which furnish the outstanding example of the latent authoritarianism inherent in the conception of Marxism as a "scientific" doctrine providing absolute knowledge concerning the destiny and demands of History, as discussed in Chapter 1.

Of all the defenders of orthodoxy around the turn of the century, none was more convinced of the absolutely "objective" validity of the prophecies of "scientific socialism" than Lenin. Lenin meant this first of all in the traditional, "immanent" sense: "scientific socialism" did not indulge in wishful projections but only in scientific extrapolations of trends and developments already observable and inherent in the present, based on the scientific discovery of the "laws" governing the historical process independently of arbitrary human wishes, opinions, or values (see Kolakowski 1978b, 359). Lenin firmly believed that the Social Democrats—the name of the Russian party until 1918 (see Lane 1982, 9; Popper 1966b, 360, n. 47)—were "blessed with the power of prescience" (Harding 1977, 241; cf. Chang 1931, 33). Thus, in *What Is to Be Done?* his main objections to Bernsteinian revisionism are its denial of "the possibility of putting socialism on a scientific basis and demonstrating its necessity and inevitability," and its rejection of "*the theory of the class struggle*," revolution, and the dictatorship of the proletariat as the *only* possible way of realizing socialism (Lenin 1968, 32).

In addition, Lenin believed—perhaps to a greater degree than most of his orthodox comrades—that "scientific socialism" could not only forecast broad future trends but also occurrences of a quite short-term nature. Having uncovered the "laws" of capitalist development, socialism was able to predict

---

dangerously irresponsible, to say the least. It is a type of irresponsibility to which we will have to return, since it appears to be endemic to Marxism.

scientifically its necessary phases and stages and hence it could provide infallible guidance in all matters of policy and tactics, Lenin claimed. To hasten the advent of the social revolution, then, all issues of policy could be and must be decided with scientific accuracy to correspond with known "objective" trends of history (cf. Harding 1977, 102–3; Kolakowski 1978b, 359–60).

But in calling socialism "scientific" Lenin was equally concerned to distinguish it from the consciousness spontaneously arising out of the conditions of the working class in capitalism. Significantly, the main polemic thrust of *What Is to Be Done?* was aimed at a new faction in Russian Social Democracy called "economism" which had just published its views in a pamphlet entitled *Credo*. "Economism" was an *ouvriériste* reaction against the Russian Marxists' preoccupation with revolutionary theory and politics at the expense of the workers' more immediate needs. In their *Credo* the "economists" advocated a party that would be the instrument of the workers by reflecting and pursuing their immediate demands for improvement of their economic conditions, labor legislation, and the like, and not a group of bourgeois intellectuals pretending to teach the workers about their "real" interests (see Connor 1968, xviii–xix; Kolakowski 1978b, 385).

To this Lenin replied first of all with the standard orthodox argument that it was perfectly legitimate to pursue reforms improving the immediate situation of the workers, but only to the extent that this contributed to the formation of the revolutionary consciousness and organization required for the eventual final assault on capitalism (see Harding 1977, 135–60). However, Lenin goes on to argue, such a policy requires extraordinary political acumen and fine-tuning informed by the most rigorously scientific revolutionary theory. Such a theory clearly does not emerge spontaneously out of the daily economic struggles of the workers with their employers. Rather, the scientific knowledge on which true socialist consciousness is based must be developed by members of the bourgeois intelligentsia, which is, after all, what Marx and Engels themselves were. For this argument Lenin could quote a most unimpeachable source, Karl Kautsky, who was at the time still the universally acknowledged "pope" of the Second International—rather than the despicable renegade he had been all along in secret, as Lenin was to discover only many years later—and who had written that "socialist consciousness is something introduced into the proletarian class struggle from without and not something that arose within it spontaneously" (Lenin 1968, 45).

But, Lenin's insistence on his impeccable orthodoxy notwithstanding (see, e.g., Harding 1977, 187–89, 208–9), he clearly carried the argument further than the orthodox would have. Kautsky and other orthodox Marxists acknowledged the obvious fact that an elaborate theoretical system like Marxism was clearly the product of intellectuals, but, like Marx and Engels, the orthodox were convinced that the workers' material conditions and economic struggles would inevitably lead to their radicalization and eventual adoption of Marxist theory as their own. On this crucial point, however, Lenin was in fact more in agreement with his "revisionist" and "economist" opponents. Like them, Lenin in effect argues that 'the spontaneous, "natural" consciousness which arises from the workers' struggle is not revolutionary at all but reformist: "The history of all countries shows that the working class, exclusively by its own effort, is able to develop only trade union consciousness, that is, the conviction that it is necessary to combine in unions, fight the employers, and strive to compel the government to pass necessary labor legislation, etc." (Lenin 1968, 40). This is clearly much closer to Bernstein and the "economists" than to Marxian-Kautskyan orthodoxy (cf. Fernbach 1974, 58–64; Gouldner 1980, 13–19; Lichtheim 1965, 336–37). The only difference is that where revolutionary "Social Democratic" theory and the workers' actual demands and level of consciousness clash, Lenin unhesitatingly chooses the former as the expression of their "true" interests, whereas the reformists choose the latter as the only reliable evidence of the validity of those interests.

But Lenin is prepared to go much further than this. From Marx's theory that capitalism will inevitably issue in a polarization of classes, pitting the bourgeosie against the proletariat, Lenin deduces what is no doubt the most distinctively Leninist argument in its theoretical as well as its practical implications:

> Since there can be no talk of an independent ideology formulated by the working masses themselves in the process of their movement, the *only* choice is—either bourgeois or socialist ideology.

> There is no middle course (for mankind has not created a "third" ideology, and, moreover, in a society torn by class antagonisms there can never be a non-class or an above-class ideology). Hence, to belittle the socialist ideology *in any way, to turn aside from it in the slightest degree*, means to strengthen bourgeois ideology. There is much talk of spontaneity. But the *spontaneous* development of the working class movement leads to its subordination to bourgeois ideology, *to its development along the lines of the Credo program*; for the spontaneous working class movement is trade unionism, is *Nur-Gewerkschaftlerei*, and trade unionism means the ideological enslavement of the workers by the bourgeoisie. Hence, our task, the task of Social Democracy, is *to combat spontaneity, to divert* the working-class movement from this spontaneous, trade unionist striving to come under the wing of the bourgeoisie, and to bring it under the wing of revolutionary Social Democracy. (Lenin 1968, 45–46)

It follows with unassailable logic that *"all* worship of the spontaneity of the working class movement, all belittling of the role of 'the conscious element,' of the role of Social Democracy, *means, quite independently of whether he who belittles that role desires it or not, a strengthening of the influence of bourgeois ideology upon the workers"* (ibid., 44).

These quotations contain the doctrinal core of Leninism, which has so greatly influenced all subsequent Marxist theory, including, as we shall see, the recent theorizing on the capitalist state. Its main feature is its implacably dichotomous way of thinking: there is no middle ground; every ideology, institution, or organization serves either the true interests of the proletariat or those of the bourgeoisie. Since only the revolutionary theory of social democracy (as "correctly" interpreted by Lenin, of course) represents the proletariat's true interests, *anything* else either is deliberate bourgeois deception or "objectively" serves the interests of the bourgeoisie, irrespective of the express intentions or social origins of its advocates (cf. Harding 1977, 169–70; 1978, 202–5, 272; Kolakowski 1978b, 386–89). Such a doctrine has far-reaching implications for Marxist theory and practice, of course.

For one thing, the relation between theory and the proletariat appears almost reversed. Originally, Marxism proudly proclaimed itself "scientific" because, as opposed to "utopian" so-cialism, it had discovered the "immanent laws" of history that would create the "material force," the proletariat, that would be impelled to realize the theory. With Lenin, on the other hand, the "natural" development of the proletariat leads to *bourgeois* consciousness, and thus the validity of "scientific socialism" comes to depend on its ability to *overcome* the workers' "normal" development which now only appears as an *obstacle* to the rev-olutionary cause (cf. Kolakowski 1978b, 397).

Lenin does not deny that the success of the cause ultimately depends on the support of the working class. He only claims that in "normal" times such support will not be forthcoming since the workers will "spontaneously" gravitate toward the re-formist, that is, "objectively" bourgeois, ideology. Thus, revo-lutionary socialist consciousness is not the irresistible ground-swell that will eventually overtake the overwhelming majority of the proletariat as the orthodox had thought, but rather the ex-ception to the rule of bourgeois consciousness in "normal" times. According to Lenin, revolutionary consciousness erupts suddenly as a result of a sudden "revolutionary situation." Such a situation is triggered by a sudden crisis such as an economic downturn or, more likely, a military defeat which causes an abrupt increase in popular discontent, rendering the suffering of the masses more acute and intolerable than usual. When properly exploited and managed, such a crisis can be turned into a revolutionary situation in which the consciousness of the masses makes a "qualitative leap forward." This leap results from the struggles and confrontations themselves, which dem-onstrate the immanent polarity of capitalist society to the masses with sudden clarity. It is at the height of such a crisis that the legitimate authority of the *ancien régime* crumbles and the masses come to recognize Social Democracy as the repre-sentative of their true interests, enabling it to seize power (Harding 1977, 238–48, 290–91; Kolakowski 1978b, 495).

Thus, in Lenin's version of Marxism the success of the social revolution comes to depend on rare and comparatively elusive moments of popular *prises de conscience* that punctuate the pe-riods of "normal" bourgeois consciousness. Therefore, Lenin argues, Social Democracy must be organized in such a way as to enable it to maintain and develop revolutionary theory and strategy during the long periods when bourgeois ideology holds sway over the toiling masses, while at the same time being able to anticipate accurately impending revolutionary situations and being prepared to exploit them effectively before they pass and the proletariat sinks back to its customary level of bourgeois consciousness again. To fulfill these requirements, Lenin argues, "the organization of the revolutionaries must consist first and foremost of people who make revolutionary activity their profession (for which reason I speak of the organization of *revolutionaries*, meaning revolutionary Social-Democrats). In view of this common characteristic of the members of such an organization, *all distinctions as between workers and intellectuals*, not to speak of distinctions of trade and profession, in both categories, *must be effaced*. Such an organization must perforce not be very extensive and must be as secret as possible" (1968, 62). In addition, such a party cannot afford the luxury of a highly democratic, rank and file controlled decision-making procedure but must be a highly disciplined, centrally controlled organization. This was not just a matter of expediency for Lenin, necessitated by the repressive Russian regime which made a widely based democratic party too dangerous, as some have claimed (Harding 1977, 45–57, 186). Rather it flowed logically from the general principles expounded in *What Is to Be Done?* Since there is no middle road between bourgeois and socialist ideology, to demand greater "openness" and democratic control, Lenin asserts, amounts to demanding "freedom for an opportunist trend in Social-Democracy, freedom to convert Social-Democracy into a democratic party of reform, freedom to introduce bourgeois ideas and bourgeois elements into socialism" (1968, 33).

Thus Lenin's controversial theory of the "vanguard" party of "professional revolutionaries" (see also Harding 1977, 162–76; Kolakowski 1978b, 384–98). Again, the unorthodoxy of the theory can hardly be denied, although Lenin did, of course, forcefully do so. True, the fathers of Russian orthodoxy, Plekhanov and Axelrod, and even Kautsky, did not immediately recognize its heresy (Harding 1977, 187–96, 208–9, 272–73), but that was because they were at first simply unaware of the implications of Lenin's approach and as soon as they became aware of them they became his most vociferous critics. At any rate, soon after the publication of *What Is to Be Done?* and the split in the Russian Social Democratic party during its congress the following year (1903), Lenin was attacked by almost all orthodox theorists, ranging from the center to the far left represented by Luxemburg and Trotsky (Lichtheim 1965, 329–31). Lenin's conception of an authoritarian, exclusive, disciplined "vanguard" party is quite obviously very different from the all-inclusive mass organization that Marx and Engels had in mind and repeatedly tried to organize (cf. Draper 1978, 481–572). But this does not necessarily mean that Lenin's repeated insistence that his approach was nothing but an "adaptation" or "extension" to modern times of the basic principles of Marxism can be simply dismissed as mendacious propaganda. As I have argued before, Lenin's theory differed from Marx and Engels's and Second International orthodoxy and was in fact, *horribile dictu*, closer to Bernstein and the "economists," in that he had little confidence in the workers' ability to grasp the truth of revolutionary "scientific socialism" in other than highly exceptional conditions. It was, indeed, Lenin's lack of faith in the proletariat's free and rational adoption of revolutionary socialism as its own (whoever had formulated it at first), and his consequent reliance on a dedicated, small "vanguard," that was most severely criticized by all as needlessly restrictive and dictatorial (see, e.g., Knei-Paz 1978, ch. 5; Kolakowski 1978b, 50–51, 82–88, 350–53). However, if one accepts the Leninist assumptions about the proletariat's "normal" level of consciousness it is not obvious how he could have adopted a more straightforwardly democratic stance toward the working class without giving up the idea of the ultimate "necessity" of revolution and socialism as both Bernstein and the "economists" had effectively done.

On the other hand, this does little to reduce the fateful implications of Leninism. On the contrary, it only shows more clearly the internal logic by which Marxism can turn into authoritarianism once the comfortable assumption that socialist consciousness is the inevitable, spontaneous result of the workers' struggle to defend their immediate interests through a democratic organization of their own becomes hard to main-

tain. Lenin's suspicion that the workers may under most circumstances be rather more reluctant to make the transition
from the pursuit of immediate, limited objectives to revolutionary socialism forces him to dissociate completely the theory presumably expressing the "true" interests of the proletariat from
that proletariat's actual, empirical state of consciousness—the
more so as his dichotomous model allows for only two alternatives, bourgeois or "true" socialist consciousness. If the proletariat is ordinarily under the influence of bourgeois ideology, then
its support for or opposition to Marxism is entirely irrelevant to
Marxism's validity as the only truly proletarian doctrine.

Marxism thus becomes a wholly self-appointed theory of the
working class, embodied in the party that is "correctly" organized and subscribes to the "correct" interpretation of the theory. Any isolated group of intellectuals claiming to fulfill these
requirements can thus declare itself to be the only "true" representative of the proletariat whether the latter likes it or not,
and before as well as after the revolution. Nothing, least of all
the proletariat that is being "represented," can effectively disprove such a claim (cf. Kolakowski 1978b, 389–91). The only
possible "proof" of the validity of such claims is provided by
History itself, namely by the practical success of the movement
guided by these claims, although such "proof"—that is, success
in creating chaos and obtaining mass support long enough to
seize power, and the means and ruthlessness to retain it—can
always be postponed until the indefinite future. Thus, when the
Bolsheviks enjoyed rising support after 1911 this constituted
"proof positive" according to Lenin of the "correctness of his
political line" (Harding 1977, 283), but the near-disastrous decline in mass support from 1906 to 1911 did nothing to make
him doubt that correctness for one moment (256–60). Similarly,
a variety of Trotskyist grouplets has regularly been predicting
the outbreak of world revolution for more than four decades
now, taking even the slightest disturbance as "proof positive" of
the basic correctness of their "scientific" forecasts, while, much
like what happens in any other apocalyptic sect, the failure of
predictions only seems to strengthen their faith in the validity
of the next one (cf. Festinger, Riecker, and Schachter 1956).

While the party thus becomes the sole embodiment of the

true interests of the proletariat, the latter becomes little more than an adjunct to the party and its "scientific" theory. The only reason for the party to worry about proletarian support at all is because it will enable the party to seize power. But if it could seize power without the support of the proletariat or if it were to lose that support again once in power, this would not in the least affect its status as the only legitimate representative of the proletariat. Thus, more even than in Marx's earliest socialist writings, in Lenin's theory the proletariat is little more than the cannon fodder of history, the "material force" whose only purpose is to "realize philosophy." The true "subject" has become the party, "a party which deems its own interest to be automatically that of the working class and of universal progress, because it possesses the 'scientific knowledge' that entitles it to ignore, except for tactical purposes, the actual wishes and aspirations of the people it has appointed itself to represent" (Kolakowski 1978b, 396).

Moreover, Leninism accentuates other rather dubious tendencies that are more or less latently present in Marxism. The very Hegelian "immanentism" of which Marxism is so proud, its very contempt for merely "arbitrary" ideals, that is, for ideals that lack any historical guarantees that they will be realized, creates an inherent tendency to take the practical success of a social movement as proof of the "scientific" validity of its ideology and as moral justification for whatever it took to achieve it. The belief that the real and the rational must ultimately coincide can lead to *either* an impractical negation of the real because it does not correspond to one's preconceived ideal of the rational *or* a cynical acceptance of whatever is real as thereby "rational" since to resist reality is futile (cf. Kolakowski 1978a, 81–83; 1978c, 523). Thus there seems to be a built-in tendency in Hegelianism and its Marxist offspring to justify the means by the degree to which they contribute to achieving the end, in other words, to view whatever it takes to achieve the end as *ipso facto* "historically necessary" and thus morally justified (cf. Lukes 1985).

But whereas this tendency to justify the means by the end they serve was tempered in pre-Leninist orthodoxy by including certain values as integral parts of the end without which it could not be said to have been successfully achieved (e.g., "formally" democratic institutions, inviolability of civil liberties), Leninism drastically narrows the definition of the end—the criterion of its success, the notion of Reason to be turned into reality. Since the party by definition represents the proletariat and will come to power only through a revolution after an extreme intensification of political conflict, while any other doctrine is necessarily nothing more than bourgeois ideology "objectively" retarding the advent of that revolution, any means that intensify the "class struggle" and help bring the revolutionary party to power are justified. Indeed, any moral scruples limiting the expedients that can be profitably used to help bring the party to power must be rejected as only serving bourgeois interests. Thus Lenin reduces *all* questions of ultimate values, *all* moral choices, and *all* matters of policy and strategy to the single question of their effect on the "class struggle" and the revolution. Everything else is either bourgeois distraction or irrelevant (cf. Kolakowski 1978b, 383).

Lenin frequently shocked his orthodox comrades with his apparently totally unprincipled willingness to sacrifice or ignore theoretical doctrine for political expediency. Thus, his support for the principle of national self-determination greatly upset Luxemburg's doctrinaire internationalism and provoked a bitter polemic. Lenin's position did not rest on any "original and radical principle" (Poulantzas 1978, 94), as his followers would like to believe now that nationalism has become respectable again even in Marxist circles, but purely on tactical considerations, as he himself admitted quite openly. The right to national self-determination would always have to be subordinate to "the interests of the proletarian struggle for socialism," Lenin argued (Harding 1977, 301). Under the czarist empire, advocacy of this right was progressive as it served to unite the opposition to the regime and to intensify political conflict. After the party of the proletariat had come to power, however, the "interests of the proletarian struggle for socialism" might well dictate otherwise (see Harding 1977, 296–302; Kolakowski 1978b, 398–405). As it turned out, they did. Similarly, his advocacy of an alliance with the peasantry, his support for religious freedom, his initial attitude toward the spontaneously formed Soviets of 1905, and his views on war and international aggression were not matters of principle—though he always defended them with the most "theoretical" of arguments—but purely of tactics, depending only on their temporary utility in the struggle for power (see Kolakowski 1978b, 405–19, 459–61, 491–97). Thus, Leninism contains profoundly "instrumentalist" elements which could later be used, despite the arguments in *State and Revolution*, to justify a potentially reformist "capture" theory of the bourgeois state, since all that really matters is who controls it, the Bolsheviks or this or that "objective" representative of the bourgeoisie (cf. Corrigan, Ramsey, and Sayer 1978, 43, 62–63).

But since there can be only one proletarian truth, everything else amounting, wittingly or not, to bourgeois deceit, the struggle for power between the two necessarily extended to the ranks of Social Democracy itself and even Lenin's own Bolshevik faction. Throughout the many controversies that racked the Russian socialist movement, Lenin never displayed even the faintest sign of doubt as to the infallible correctness of his own "scientific" judgments (Harding 1977, 283; Kolakowski 1978b, 393). Furthermore, as he wrote ominously in 1902, "Those who are really convinced that they have made progress in science would not demand freedom for the new views to continue side by side with the old, but the substitution of the new views for the old" (1968, 33). Thus, Lenin also had few scruples when it came to dealing with rivals or with erroneous views among his socialist comrades, as such "bourgeois" scruples could only help to lengthen the dominance of superstition over "science," of bourgeois over proletarian ideology. He was utterly ruthless in his dealings with party activists, viewing them, not excluding himself, purely as either instruments or else obstacles to the achievement of the ultimate goal (Harding 1977, 179–80 193, 234, 265–67, 275–79; Kolakowski 1978b, 520–25; for some examples see: 433, 451–58).

Claims to the contrary (e.g., Althusser 1971; Harding 1977; 1978) notwithstanding, Lenin was first and foremost a practical *Realpolitiker* engaged in a single-minded pursuit of power to which he subordinated everything else, including the "theory" he claimed to uphold (cf. Knei-Paz 1978, 4–5; Kolakowski 1978b, 384, 494). However, this does not mean that he always had an infallible grasp of political reality as the myth has it. On

the contrary, his many miscalculations necessitated frequent re-
versals of policy, although always justified on the best "theoretical" grounds, of course, and presented as perfectly logical extensions of previous, diametrically opposed policies. But all his
miscalculations were in the optimistic direction, overestimating
the revolutionary potential of every disturbance, expecting up-
risings to take place sooner and last longer than they actually
did, and so on. Moreover, his successive "adaptations" of orthodox theory to Russian conditions sound very much like a series
of increasingly explicit rationalizations for seizing power under
what the orthodox would consider "premature" conditions,
from the odd notion of a "bourgeois" revolution being waged
by an alliance of peasants and proletarians *against* the bourgeoisie, developed in the wake of the 1905 uprising (Lenin 1968,
79–110) and to which he stubbornly clung until the very eve of
the October Revolution, to his equally unorthodox theory of
imperialism and its "weakest link" which proved to be so fate-
fully mistaken after the revolution.[9] But these practical miscalculations and odd theoretical constructions are also indicative
of why Lenin finally succeeded. For, as Kolakowski (1978b,
525–26) has noted, it was precisely because Lenin was *always*
prepared for the seizure of power that, when the real opportunity finally came, he was able to use it to the full without hesitation.

But by far the most fateful casualty of Lenin's single-minded
pursuit of "proletarian" power has been "bourgeois" democ-

9   Briefly, Lenin held that since the Russian bourgeoisie under the czar was
    too weak to carry out its revolution against feudalism successfully, this
    "bourgeois" revolution would have to be executed by a coalition of workers
    and peasants who would establish a "revolutionary dictatorship of the pro-
    letariat and peasantry." This dictatorship would merely inaugurate a truly
    bourgeois society and patiently preside over the inevitable development of
    its inherent contradictions until the time would be ripe for another, this
    time truly "proletarian" revolution. The theory of the "weakest link" pre-
    dicted that capitalism would not first be overthrown in the most advanced
    capitalist country but instead in the "weakest link" of the interconnected
    "chain" of imperialist countries. Then, with that link broken, the revolu-
    tions in the other countries would follow very soon (see, e.g., Corrigan,
    Ramsey, and Sayer 1978, 33–37; Harding 1977, 213–38, 291–96; Knei-Paz
    1978, 29–30; Kolakowski 1978b, 405–12, 471–72, 491–94; Lichtheim 1965,
    340–51).

racy. Like everything else, freedom and democracy were merely instruments in the class struggle to Lenin. Under capitalism, freedom and democracy are of great value because they provide the best opportunities for the proletariat to wage an open class struggle and prepare for the final revolutionary confrontation (Lenin 1932, 18, 59, 66, 83; cf. Chang 1931, 79–87; Harding 1977, 51–55; Kolakowski 1978b, 360–61). But he attached no intrinsic value to them. Once the party that represents the true interests of the proletariat is in power there is obviously no more need for the trappings of "bourgeois" democracy. The party, being the self-evident and sole legitimate representative of the masses, provides "a higher type of democracy, a break with the bourgeois distortion of democracy" (Marx, Engels, and Lenin 1967, 323). To permit bourgeois liberties and institutions would only suggest a nonexistent divergence between the party and the masses, and thus allow various bourgeois ideologies free rein (cf. Kolakowski 1978b, 501–9). Thus, Lenin prepared the dispersal of the Constituent Assembly elected right after the October Revolution at the height of the Bolsheviks' popularity, but in which they only received about one-quarter of the seats (ibid., 479), with the argument that one "must not return to the old prejudices, which subordinate the interests of the people to formal democracy" (quoted in ibid., 480). In 1920, at the founding congress of the Comintern, Lenin's views of "bourgeois" democracy as only a useful instrument for preparing the socialist revolution after which it would be abolished with all other bourgeois institutions, were made mandatory for all member parties (Kolakowski 1978c, 106–8).

As all opposition outside the party was silenced relatively rapidly after the October Revolution, whatever freedoms and democratic institutions still existed within the party had to follow soon. It could hardly be otherwise since the "bourgeois" political opposition that had been suppressed outside the party would inevitably reemerge within the party if dissent were permitted there, only more dangerously because it would disguise itself as a "loyal" proletarian opposition (cf. Kolakowski 1978b, 485–89). After all, Lenin had always known that party membership in no way guaranteed immunity to "incorrect" ideas: "In reality, the opportunists' formal membership in workers' parties by no means disproves their objectively being a political detachment of the bourgeoisie, conductors of its influence, and its agents in the labour movement" (Marx, Engels, and Lenin 1967, 493). Lenin did not normally go so far as to accuse dissenting fellow Bolsheviks of such deliberate treason, but he never shied away from pointing out that since they deviated from the one true proletarian "line" they objectively served the interests of the bourgeoisie, whatever their intentions. He habitually dismissed dissent on both the left and the right as forms of "petty-bourgeois instability" (Harding 1977, 276), which was quite logical from his dichotomous point of view (see ibid., 263–81; Kolakowski 1978b, 505).

Thus, after the suppression of democratic freedoms outside the party those still enjoyed within it followed suit with an inexorable logic. At the Comintern Congress of 1920 the infamous "Twenty-One Conditions" of admission subjected all member parties to the strictly Leninist model. They were to purge themselves of all internal dissent, especially "opportunism" (see Kolakowski 1978c, 106–8; Miliband 1977, 167–69; B. D. Wolfe 1965, 312). A year later, during the Tenth Congress of the Russian party in March, while the Kronstadt sailors' rebellion was being bloodily repressed, the left "Workers' Opposition" within the party was effectively eliminated by the adoption of rules prohibiting "fractionalism" of any kind. In the process the trade unions, which had been the major bone of contention between the party leaders and the "Workers' Opposition," underwent a complete *Gleichschaltung*, becoming mere instruments of central party control over the workers (see Kolakowski 1978b, 488–89; 1978c, 20; Miliband 1977, 141–44). The basis for Stalin's one-man despotism was laid. It is not a little ironic that at this time Trotsky was among the most extreme advocates of a complete regimentation of all of society and the party under the strictest dictatorial control of the leadership, as he frankly considered *all* forms of repression and terror fully justified for the great goal of building socialism (see Harding 1978, 256–61; Knei-Paz 1978, 248–52, 262–69, 556–67; Kolakowski 1978b, 509–12; Miliband 1977, 143). In fact, Trotsky was at times too extreme even for Lenin (Kolakowski 1978b, 489). At any rate the argument that Stalinism constituted a "dramatic *break*" with Leninism (Miliband 1977, 144), which is particularly dear to the Trotskyists, seems completely untenable to me. Although it is pointless to debate whether or not Lenin personally would have gone quite as far as Stalin, it is obvious that Lenin not only created the party machine that enabled Stalin to impose his despotic rule but also furnished all the doctrinal arguments to justify such rule. The unprecedented totalitarianism, the complete control and subordination of Communist parties the world over, the apotheosis of the party, all this could easily be justified with Lenin's principle that there can never be any neutral ground between the interests of the bourgeoisie and those of the proletariat as embodied by the party and thus, after October 1917, by the Soviet state (see Harding 1978, chs. 9–15; Kolakowski 1978b, 514–17).

Whether Leninist authoritarianism is a logical outcome of Marxism is another question. Right from the start Lenin never lacked Marxist critics, and they certainly were not only Mensheviks resenting the way he had outmaneuvered them at the famous 1903 party congress. In fact the earliest criticisms came from the radical left and not from the orthodox center, as Kautsky initially did not fully realize the implications of Lenin's views and did not understand the internal squabbles dividing Russian Social Democracy (Harding 1977, 272–73). The most famous attacks on Lenin from the left came from Luxemburg and Trotsky. They objected to Lenin's low estimate of the proletariat's spontaneous abilities and his notion of a highly centralized "vanguard" party (see Knei-Paz 1978, 177–206; Kolakowski 1978b, 82–88, 408; Miliband 1977, 124–25). Such views, they both argued, greatly underestimated the revolutionary potential of the masses. By taking initiative and responsibility for their own emancipation away from them, the party could end up stifling their natural revolutionary energies altogether. Lenin's proposals amounted to substituting the party for the proletariat. Furthermore, as Trotsky wrote prophetically in 1904, "In inner-party politics, these methods lead, as we shall yet see, to this: the party organization substitutes itself for the party, the Central Committee substitutes itself for the organization, and finally, a 'dictator' substitutes himself for the Central Committee" (quoted in Knei-Paz 1978, 199).

The critique of Luxemburg and Trotsky obviously rested on their boundless confidence in the masses' spontaneous inclinations toward socialist revolution, particularly after the "revolution" of 1905 in Russia. They both had such faith in the masses that at times they appeared to think the party might be superfluous altogether (ibid., 53–57, 208–11). This is, of course, the very opposite of what Lenin believed, and in retrospect it does sound rather naive. Trotsky at least seems to have realized this when he joined the Bolsheviks after February 1917 (ibid., 225–33). But Luxemburg stuck to her earlier position. She continued to criticize the Bolsheviks' imposition of one-party rule, although not their "premature" seizure of power. How the Bolsheviks were to maintain power democratically without the support of the majority she never explained. Apparently, the possibility that a Marxist-inspired regime could remain without majority support for long simply did not occur to her (Kolakowski 1978b, 85–88; Lukes 1985, 103–6). Thus, Luxemburg and Trotsky simply did not consider the contingency that Lenin's arguments were designed to meet: what to do if "the masses" *fail* to support the revolution. Kautsky did try to answer this question in his criticisms of the "premature" seizure of power by the Bolsheviks and the dictatorial manner in which they held on to it, but his answer, too, was still based on orthodox assumptions concerning the likely development of the proletariat's consciousness.

Kautsky agreed with Luxemburg and most other Marxists at the time that socialism without democratic freedoms and institutions was an unthinkable absurdity (Kautsky 1964, 6–7, 51; cf. Kolakowski 1978b, 4, 49). However, he did not believe that spontaneous mass action or a successful minority seizure of power would somehow trigger the masses' "true" revolutionary propensities where the power of rational persuasion and electoral propaganda could not, as Luxemburg apparently did. He rejected any capture of state power by a self-appointed vanguard as un-Marxist and doomed to end in a bureaucratic dictatorship or civil war (or both), but not socialism (Kautsky 1964, 17). Thus, to Kautsky the choice was clear: either the revolution enjoys the support of the majority of the population in which case it may be an entirely peaceful and legal "revolution," at least in already democratic countries, *or* it does not have majority support and is therefore premature (42–58).

"Bourgeois" democracy was much more to Kautsky than a mere hoax or a convenient tactical instrument. Democracy allowed the proletariat to be freely organized and enlightened and thus to mature as quickly as possible to the point where it would be ready and able to seize power in order to establish a genuinely democratic socialist society (ibid., 12–24). Moreover, being the most reliable gauge of the proletariat's maturity and strength, democracy, Kautsky argued, would eliminate the need for much violence in the socialist revolution as it discouraged premature attempts and forced the ruling classes to concede on matters where they had already lost the strength to resist (36–38). This was very important to Kautsky since he was convinced that the chances for successfully constructing a genuine socialist society depended in large part on the extent to which violence and upheaval could be kept to a minimum. He did not rule out the need for violence under undemocratic regimes that left one no choice, but such use of violence should always aim at obtaining democratic government only. Once democratic government was in place, he argued, the cause of socialism could only be advanced by patiently working toward a mature majority (54–58).

Kautsky concedes that bourgeois democracy may lead to an excessive preoccupation on the part of the workers and the labor movement with short-term goals and a relative neglect of the ultimate revolutionary goal. But he remains convinced that such lapses of revolutionary consciousness can only be temporary as the practice of organizing and struggling ultimately cannot fail to draw the proletariat as a whole into politics and toward the socialist cause (ibid., 38–41, 96). But in the meantime, Kautsky insists, no party or strategy that does not enjoy the support of the majority can rightfully claim to be the sole representative of the proletariat. Only the proletariat itself can properly judge what is in its own best interests at any one time, and it may well choose to rule through different parties at different times. Any claims to the contrary would necessarily end up making a mockery of the whole notion of democratic socialism (31–32).

Kautsky's attack on the Bolshevik seizure of power and methods of retaining it triggered a fierce exchange between him, Lenin, and Trotsky (see, e.g., Knei-Paz 1978, 247–52). But, as noted earlier, Lenin's and Trotsky's responses hardly qualify as serious attempts to refute Kautsky's criticisms. They consist mostly of repetitions of the arguments attempting to discredit "bourgeois" democracy as a hoax to conceal class oppression; of dogmatic assertions of the obvious identity between the interests of the party and those of "the masses" so that rule by the party, however repressive its "appearance," represents by definition a "higher form" of democracy; of the crudest justification of all forms of terror for the sacred ends, without the least attempt to meet Kautsky's objection that the very nature of some means may render them unsuitable for achieving the end; and, finally, of a flood of verbal abuse decrying the "petty-bourgeois" distortions of the "renegade" Kautsky which only showed he had been an agent of the bourgeoisie all along (Kolakowski 1978b, 501–12; Lenin 1932, 29–31, 87–100; Lukes 1985, 111–14; Plotke 1977, 83–87).

But on one point Lenin may have been right. Kautsky's strategy of faithfully serving the immediate needs of the workers while patiently advocating the larger socialist cause until a firm popular majority had been won depended on the old assumptions of Marxist orthodoxy: that the living conditions of the proletariat in capitalism, and its struggles to improve them, would necessarily lead it to embrace the socialist cause eventually, that is, that organization and struggle for limited reform would naturally issue in support for more fundamental change.[10] If, however, this assumption was mistaken, that is, if under normal conditions the proletariat is much more likely to content itself with limited reforms and partial improvements and progressively to turn away from the socialist ideal unless it is shocked out of its "natural" reformism by economic or political upheaval and guided by a well-prepared organization of

10   As Lukes rightly notes, both Luxemburg and Kautsky still retained a faith in the possibility of a "relatively clean means of realizing socialism," whether by the mass strike or by parliamentary reform (1985, 109).

dedicated revolutionaries, then Kautsky's arguments are likely to become the perfect alibi for Bernsteinian incrementalism. This is, of course, precisely what happened in those parties that refused to join the Comintern: they gradually evolved into social-democratic reform parties whose programs were limited to what the electorate would support. Lenin, on the other hand, clung stubbornly to the orthodox Marxist belief in the inevitable and imminent arrival of "socialism" by means of a sudden, revolutionary rupture, but was forced to abandon the unproblematic faith in the proletariat's spontaneous enthusiasm for the cause of "socialism." As a result, he was forced to come up with a substitute "historical subject": the all-knowing "vanguard" party, with all its authoritarian implications. Thus, with Leninism Marxism has not so much lost its original intent as it has lost its innocence.

But it was not because the Leninist argument was so theoretically convincing that it prevailed as the new orthodoxy, of course. What was far more convincing was the Bolsheviks' success in retaining power in Russia and in gaining complete control over all still genuinely antireformist socialist organizations in the world. Which ironically confirms another of Lenin's— and Marxism's—principles: that the "truth" of the theory is ultimately decided by its success as a movement. But only up to a point: whereas Lenin's successful revolution helped establish his antireformism as the official orthodoxy of Marxism, by one of those typical ironies of history his very success caused Communist parties to drift back toward reformism in practice almost from the start.

Marxism and Politics after Lenin

After Lenin, Marxist thinking about politics and the bourgeois state remained at a standstill until the late 1960s. Once Leninism had managed to claim sole title to Marxist orthodoxy, and turned into Stalinism, it came to be taken for granted that Lenin had already said all there is to know on the subject: "bourgeois" democracy is a fiction and must be overthrown by a violent revolution. Any attempt to add to or modify these dogmas was likely to cost the perpetrator dearly. Hence, Marxist theorizing retreated to the relative calm of academia and the relative safety of philosophy and culture (Anderson 1976; Kolakowski 1978c). The only notable exceptions were Trotsky and Gramsci and, perhaps, Lukács.[11] For different reasons, however, their theories did not, I believe, significantly develop a Marxist theory of the bourgeois state beyond what Lenin had written.

Trotsky is the simplest case because he himself insists, quite rightly in the case of his political theory at least, that he only repeats Lenin's arguments. Indeed, as already mentioned, Trotsky's reiteration of Lenin's dismissal of "bourgeois" democracy as a concealed form of dictatorship, and his defense of repression to maintain power as necessary for the advance of socialism, are noteworthy only for their sheer extremism (Harding 1978, 256–61; Knei-Paz 1978, 248–52, 556–67; Kolakowski 1978b, 509–11). He went so far as to propose the complete militarization of labor and of Russian society in general, purely by force and coercion if necessary, as a legitimate method to keep power and build socialism (Harding 1978, 256–261; Knei-Paz 1978, 262–69; Kolakowski 1978b, 511–12). If it had been up to Trotsky, socialism might have turned into a "huge permanent concentration camp" (Kolakowski 1978b, 512) far surpassing even Stalin's wildest dreams. Clearly, after his sudden and never adequately explained conversion to Leninism in 1917, Trotsky, like Lenin, never entertained even the slightest doubt that the party infallibly represented the "true" interests of the proletariat and the cause of socialism, *whatever* the actual proletariat might happen to believe. Thus, he saw nothing the least bit paradoxical in his defense of the Bolshevik *coup* as expressing the "true" will of the "toiling masses" who themselves were too hesitant and influenced by bourgeois ideology to understand their own interests (Knei-Paz 1978, 239–46). Similarly, and in stark contrast with his former warnings against the Bolshevik organizational model, he argued that the Soviets should leave all major decisions to the party's Central Committee since this was more efficient and guaranteed unity

11   What little other Marxists wrote about bourgeois democracy up until the mid-1960s remained limited to basic repetitions of the Leninist orthodoxy. See, e.g., Chang (1931), Stanley Moore (1957), Sweezy (1942, ch. 13).

of action, it being self-evident that the Central Committee would unfailingly make the "correct" decisions anyway (ibid., 252).

Thus, Trotsky accepted and dogmatically defended every aspect of the Leninist theory of the party as the "vanguard" of the proletariat. He absolutely refused to see any connection between this theory and the rise of Stalinism which caused his own eventual demise. When he belatedly began to demand more freedom of expression and democratic control *within* the party in 1923—only *after* Stalin had begun the campaign against him—he never questioned the party's dictatorship over the rest of society and remained implacably opposed to any form of factionalism inside the party. Even at the 1924 congress, in his very defense against Stalin's attacks he still said: "I know that one cannot be right against the party. One can be right only with and through the party since history has not created any other paths for the realization of that which is right" (quoted in ibid., 379). Unwilling to form his own faction or resist the party until it was too late, Trotsky was an easy prey to Stalin's machine (ibid., 369–80).

But rather than conceding any continuity whatsoever between his own Bolshevik ideas and the regime that had repudiated him, Trotsky explained the rise of Stalinism as the consequence of Russia's backwardness and its postrevolutionary isolation resulting from the failure of the expected world revolution to occur. Being economically poor and socioculturally backward, he argued, Russia did not have the resources to enter socialism at once without material aid from elsewhere. As such aid, in the absence of the world revolution, was not forthcoming, the Soviet Union was forced to struggle with scarcity problems which allowed a new bureaucratic stratum to emerge and monopolize all political power and considerable material privilege. This bureaucracy became more and more preoccupied with maintaining and expanding its own power and less and less with the world revolution which could only spell the end of its comfortable, privileged position—hence the Stalinist slogan of "socialism in one country" which everywhere stifled the revolutionary energies of the masses in the name of the interests of socialism's only fatherland. But Trotsky still consid-

ered the Soviet Union to be a "workers' state," a state some-
where between capitalism and communism, because the
achievements of the Bolshevik revolution on which the bureaucracy itself depended—mainly the abolition of bourgeois property—had not been undone. However, it was a "bureaucratically degenerated workers' state," which meant to Trotsky that
although its socialist achievements must be defended against its
bourgeois enemies, it was at the same time necessary to promote the coming political revolution against its bureaucratic
rulers (see, e.g., Anderson 1983; Corrigan, Ramsey, and Sayer
1978, 76ff.; Knei-Paz 1978, ch. 10; Mandel 1978, 69–78; 1979,
114–161).[12]

However, the great theoretical chasm separating Trotsky's
bolshevism from Stalin's despotism remains rather hard to find
in all this. If the party is always right, if it is entitled to use mass
coercion on any scale necessary to "build socialism," and if the
Soviet Union, despite its "bureaucratic degeneration," remains
the only bastion of socialism in an imperialist world, it is difficult to see what else Trotsky would have done but to begin
building "socialism in one country," or on what grounds he
could possibly object to Stalin's methods of doing so, once the
revolutionary tide in Europe which was to trigger the world
revolution, had definitely turned by about 1921 (cf. Gouldner
1980, 162; Knei-Paz 1978, 298–301). Besides, it was in fact
Lenin who, quite sensibly and always more practical and less
doctrinaire than Trotsky, began to concentrate all his energies

12   Mandel strongly advocates the Trotskyist approach to Stalinism as far superior to the "subjectivism," i.e., reference to individuals' actions and other
"superstructural" phenomena, of alternative approaches (1978, 69–78).
However, he answers the question of whether Leninism laid the structural
and ideological basis for Stalinism in the negative: "No, a thousand times
no" (74), on the basis of the "historical fact" that "to establish his dictatorship, Stalin had to destroy the party of Lenin physically" (ibid.). What is
meant is not entirely clear. If Mandel means that the victims of the Stalinist
terror could not possibly also share the responsibility for its emergence, he
engages in a kind of "subjectivism" himself, and a patently absurd one at
that. On the other hand, Stalin clearly did not destroy the party apparatus
created by Lenin, or at least if this is what Mandel means one would expect
some clarification and relevant evidence. For a Marxist refutation of Anderson's claim that Trotsky's analysis of Stalinism remains "to this day the most
coherent and developed theorization of the phenomenon within the Marxist tradition" (1983, 49), see Gabbert (1985).

on the Soviet Union once he became convinced that the world revolution would still take a while to break out (Knei-Paz 1978, 173, n. 141; Kolakowski 1978b, 476–79). In fact, Trotsky differed from both Lenin and Stalin in that he simply refused to believe the world revolutionary tide had actually turned, in 1921 or at *any* time thereafter. In the final analysis the difference between Stalin and Trotsky, which both had an interest in retrospectively exaggerating out of all proportion, boils down to a difference over tactics based on different estimates of the chances for world revolution: Trotsky always being convinced it was just around the corner if only the Soviet Union would throw all its forces behind it; Stalin being more cautious and hence more willing to subordinate the interests of foreign parties engaged in their remote and uncertain "revolutions" to those of the Soviet Union (see Kolakowski 1978c, 21–25, 183–219).

Trotsky, like Lenin, had an incredible confidence in the strength of "scientific" Marxist analysis which, he firmly believed, allowed him to foretell the future with great precision (Knei-Paz 1978, 359, 490–94). And, again very much like Lenin, Trotsky was armed with an "astonishing belief in his own omniscience"—which helped to cause much irritation and the occasional schism in his already rather diminutive Fourth International (Kolakowski 1978c, 187). Consequently, Trotsky could not keep himself from constantly making the wildest prophecies on the basis of his "scientific" analyses and infallible intuition. In particular, he did not pass up a single opportunity for proclaiming the imminence of the world revolution. When his predictions failed to materialize, which was clearly rather often, this did not in the least shake his confidence in the accuracy of his "science." The persistent failure of the world revolution to break out at the prearranged time was invariably the result of the perfidy and errors of the Soviet leaders and socialist and communist "bureaucrats" the world over (see Knei-Paz 1978, 302–33, 348–66; cf. Mandel 1979, 163–84). Meanwhile, Trotskyism and its Fourth International remained rather more marginal than had been "scientifically" forecast (Knei-Paz 1978, 413–14; Miliband 1977, 171).

Antonio Gramsci, too, believed he was only following and extending Lenin's theories (see Boggs 1976, 12; Genovese 1967, 286). However, his reflections on political strategy in the famous *Prison Notebooks* (Gramsci 1971) contain certain ideas that are quite original and at odds with the Leninist orthodoxy being imposed by Moscow at the time—ideas he was ironically only able to pursue because his imprisonment by the fascists from 1926 until his death in 1937 protected him against Stalinist intrigues and inquisitors (see Anderson 1977, 50). On the other hand, for the very same reason his ideas had little influence and were in fact barely known outside Italy until the late 1960s. But then he suddenly became one of the most discussed and best-liked of the Marxist "classics," being invoked by a bewildering variety of theorists and schools of thought (Anderson 1977, 5; Genovese 1967, 285; Jessop 1980b, 23; 1982, 143, 152–53; cf. Kaye 1981). This sudden popularity is in large part based on the fact that Gramsci appears to offer an alternative to the now discredited Leninist dogmas without succumbing to reformism. As the only major theorist whose thought was considered to be especially relevant to parliamentary democracy in advanced capitalist countries, Gramsci greatly influenced the recent Marxist literature on the state (Anderson 1977, 27, 40; Merrington 1977, 175).

Gramsci's main concern was to explain why the Bolshevik revolution succeeded in Russia in 1917 while similar attempts, and particularly the Italian factory-council movement of 1919–1920 in which he himself played a prominent role, failed in Western Europe (Anderson 1977, 58–61; Buci-Glucksmann 1975, 60–62, 124, 258; Genovese 1967, 291). The Bolshevik "war of manoeuvre" leading to direct confrontation was successful, he reasoned, because at the time the Russian state greatly dominated a weakly developed civil society, so that the downfall of the former dragged the latter along with it. In the West, by contrast, economic crises might shake governments, but civil society was much more developed and resistant to revolutionary change (Anderson 1977, 9–11; Gramsci 1971, 235–38). For in the West the power of the ruling class rests not primarily on the state and coercion but on its "hegemony" exercised through the institutions of civil society, such as trade unions, schools, and the church. Through these institutions,

Gramsci claims, the bourgeoisie is able to rule by a combination of coercion or domination and consent or hegemony (1971, 52–59). Hegemony or "political direction" is organized and maintained by the "organic intellectuals"—by which Gramsci essentially means the officials of the state and various organizations in civil society, especially political parties—who obtain the consent of the subordinate classes by making strategic concessions and disseminating values and beliefs favorable to the maintenance of the existing order (5–23, 148, 161, 182).

Consequently the West does not lend itself to the type of "war of manoeuvre" that was so successful in Russia. Rather, in the West the final assault on the state, and its replacement by a system of workers' councils, would have to be preceded by a long "war of position" in which a convincing "counterhegemony" had to be formulated, capable of uniting the vast majority of the subordinate classes into a "historic bloc" for socialism (Boggs 1976, 36–54; Buci-Glucksmann 1975, 275–334). For this, Gramsci had learned from the failure of the Turin factory-council movement (Boggs 1976, 97–99), it was necessary for the proletariat to produce its own "organic intellectuals" and its own autonomous organizations, particularly a highly disciplined and cohesive party capable of great tactical flexibility (Gramsci 1971, 125–205). Believing the Leninist organization to be such a party, Gramsci became one of the founders and early leaders of the CPI (Communist Party of Italy; Hoare and Nowell Smith 1971, xxxv–xlvi). But unlike Lenin, Gramsci greatly stresses the "organic unity between theory and practice, between intellectual strata and popular masses, between rulers and ruled" (1971, 190), the "dialectic" between "spontaneity" and "conscious leadership" (198–99)—which accounts for his current popularity among Western Marxists, although he nowhere explains by what practical arrangements exactly this "organic" unity is to be secured. Gramsci's admirers, however, appear to be convinced that they can conjure away all dangers of bureaucratization and elitism by ritual incantations of pleasant-sounding terms like "organic," "dialectical," "unity," "fusion," and the like (see, e.g., Boggs 1976, 65–84, 101–18; Buci-Glucksmann 1975, 272–73).

In fact, ambiguity and inconsistency seem to be among the

major reasons for Gramsci's current appeal. The relation and demarcation between state and civil society and between hegemony and domination, for instance, are far from clear. Sometimes domination is equated with the state and coercion, at other times it is equivalent to "hegemony" which, in turn, is sometimes restricted to civil society whereas at other times it is exercised through the state as well. Furthermore, hegemony sometimes includes physical coercion, sometimes not. Finally, the institutions that help secure the hegemony and thereby the rule of the ruling class are sometimes defined as part of the state, no matter how "private" they may appear, precisely *because* they serve that function, whereas at other times they are excluded from the definition of the state for the *exact* same reason (see Gramsci 1971, 210–76 for many examples; cf. Abercrombie, Hill, and Turner 1980, 11–13; Anderson 1977, 8–13, 20–23, 33–39; Boggs 1976, 38, 130 n. 3; Buci-Glucksmann 1975, 114–16, 126–34).

Perhaps more significantly, the strategic implications of Gramsci's analysis are far from unequivocal. On the one hand, Gramsci retains the Leninist doctrine that parliamentary democracy cannot be used to achieve socialism by electoral means but must be destroyed and replaced by a new proletarian state of workers' councils, and he appears to endorse Leninist ideas concerning party organization. Thus, he could be seen as a true Leninist adapting the doctrine in view of the temporary setbacks suffered in Western Europe, as Buci-Glucksmann argues (1975, 24–25, 44–46, 92–93, 117–20, 136, 143–52, 164–80, 185, 187–202, etc.; cf. Pellicani 1981).[13] On the other hand, the notion of a slow, incremental "war of position" in order to obtain majority support is definitely an un-Leninist idea and can easily be turned into a justification for incrementalist reformism. After all, what are the reformist social democratic parties doing, if not trying to win majority support (cf. Anderson 1977,

13   Buci-Glucksmann's (1975) arguments are not all equally convincing, however. In particular, she repeatedly shows similarities between Lenin and Gramsci not by interpreting Gramsci as Leninist but by interpreting Lenin as a Gramscian! In order to do this she frequently takes *State and Revolution* as the point of reference, ignoring the fact that it is totally unrepresentative of Lenin's thought (e.g., ibid., 117–20, 143–52, 187–202).

41, 46, 56, 69–70; Boggs 1984; Clarke 1977, 2–4; Garner and Garner 1981; Gibbon 1983; Pontusson 1980; Stephens 1979, 78–79, 209)?[14]

But, notwithstanding the current Gramsci vogue, his work is today mainly of historical interest. As we shall see, several of his ideas have found their way into the more recent Marxist theories of the state. Interestingly, these theorists display a similar ambivalence toward the question of reformism. Gramsci's popularity is no doubt in part due to this very ambiguity: he offers an attractive combination seemingly avoiding both authoritarian insurrectionism and bland reformism (cf. Kolakowski 1978c, 244–52). But in addition, the major problem facing Marxists today is still the same one that Gramsci tried to grapple with: the failure of the working class to overthrow capitalism. Consequently, his notion of ideological hegemony seems to many current theorists to offer a plausible explanation for the unexpected resilience of advanced capitalist societies. But these theorists *do* seem to have quietly dropped Gramsci's optimism concerning the possibilities of breaking that hegemony by a prolonged "war of position" (cf. Abercrombie, Hill and Turner 1980, 14–15, 29; Buci-Glucksmann 1975, 72–86, 136).

Philosophically, Gramsci belongs with the Hegelian reaction against the economic determinism of the Second International, a reaction that included Lukács, Korsch, and the Frankfurt School (see Kolakowski 1978c). The chief aim of these neo-Hegelians was to reassert the independent causal force of the superstructure, particularly (class) consciousness, in view of the success of the revolution in backward Russia and its failure in the advanced West. Thus, in opposition to the "vulgar" determinism of Bukharin, Gramsci insisted on the reciprocal influence of will and historical necessity and of superstructure and base, which together formed a single "dialectical process" (1971, 366). He saw consciousness and will as indispensable elements in the historical process. The "philosophy of praxis" (i.e.,

---

14 A most ironic demonstration of the ambiguity of Gramsci's conceptions is the fact that Anderson could attack social democratic reformism from a Gramscian perspective in 1966 (Anderson 1966) and then change his mind to attack Gramsci for the reformist implications in his work from a Trotskyist position a decade later (Anderson 1977)!

Marxism) consists of the self-knowledge of the proletariat which permits it to intervene rationally "in so far as it corresponds to objective historical necessities, or in so far as it is universal history itself in the moment of its progressive actualisation" (345). Thus, according to Gramsci, "universal history" has an inherent logic the realization of which depends as much on consciousness of it as on "objective" (e.g., economic) factors. In typically Hegelian fashion knowledge and will, freedom and historical "necessity," consciousness and structure, subject and object, are all fused into one "dialectical" process (see ibid., 323–472; cf. Boggs 1976, 20–36; Carnoy 1984, ch. 3; Kolakowski 1978c, 228–40).

All this is remarkably similar to Lukács's notion of a supraempirical "concrete historical totality," with its inherent "developing tendencies" that depend for their consummation on the proletariat becoming conscious of them. This will lead it, in one single movement, to become the "identical subject-object of history" that the "concrete totality" reveals to be its destiny (Lukács 1971; Kolakowski 1978c, 253–307). Yet Gramsci has been widely interpreted as a near-reformist and democratic Marxist, whereas Lukács's theory amounts to a philosophical justification for Leninist authoritarianism and antireformism (Kolakowski 1978c, 264–69, 280–83; Lichtheim 1965, 368–70). The contrast is instructive because it shows once more the very different implications of virtually the same doctrine depending on one's estimate of the proletariat's "normal" consciousness.

When Lukács refers to "proletarian class consciousness" he does not mean the consciousness of actual proletarians. Far from it, in fact. The actual proletariat only gains "authentic" proletarian consciousness in the very act of revolutionizing the historical totality. Before that great moment, its consciousness lags behind and remains "reified," that is, under the dominant influence of bourgeois ideology. In fact, the fatal flaw of "opportunism" is, according to Lukács, precisely that it *"mistakes the actual, psychological state of consciousness of proletarians for the class consciousness of the proletariat"* (1971, 74; cf. 80, 303–14, 326–29). The *authentic* consciousness of the proletariat, quite to the contrary, can only be *imputed* to it by the theorist:

By relating consciousness to the whole of society it becomes possible to infer the thoughts and feelings which men would have in a particular situation if they were *able* to assess both it and the interests arising from it in their impact on immediate action and on the whole structure of society. That is to say, it would be possible to infer the thoughts and feelings appropriate to their objective situation. . . . Now class consciousness consists in fact of the appropriate and rational reactions "imputed" [*Zugerechnet*] to a particular typical position in the process of production. This consciousness is, therefore, neither the sum nor the average of what is thought or felt by the single individuals who make up the class. . . . This analysis establishes right from the start the distance that separates class consciousness from the empirically given, and from the psychologically describable and explicable ideas which men form about their situation in life. (ibid., 51)

The obvious question is, of course, Who will do the "imputing"? According to Lukács the organization that is structured so that it can infallibly impute the "correct" consciousness to the proletariat is the Leninist party. It alone has full understanding of the "concrete totality" at any one time by virtue of the "dialectical method" of orthodox Marxism which permits the party to determine the "objectively necessary" course of action, the "correctness" of which is constantly tested by the relentless judgment of history (see ibid., esp. 1–26, 295–342). Thus, Lukács proclaims the Communist party to be "the form taken by the class consciousness of the proletariat," which "is assigned the sublime role of *bearer of the class consciousness of the proletariat and the conscience of its historical vocation*" (41). Thereby Lukács provides the philosophical underpinning for the dictatorship of the party and for the doctrine that the party can do no wrong, since whatever is good for the party is *by definition* in the interest of the proletariat and hence of historical progress (cf. Kolakowski 1978c, 281–83). By a single brilliant stroke Lukács has thus produced the perfect Hegelian alibi for the most cynical, amoral *Realpolitik* toward which Leninism was already inclined: whatever works to put and keep the party in power, and whoever manages to grab and hold power *within* the party *must* be "correct" since its very practical success constitutes its benediction by History itself. Thus, Lukács provides "an underpinning, on a high philosophical plane, or at least in inflated philosophical terms" for Leninism (Lukes 1985, 114).

Both Lukács and Gramsci, then, endeavored to reclaim a determining role for human consciousness and will in the historical process. From a remarkably similar Hegelian standpoint both argued that, contrary to the old "vulgar" orthodoxy, consciousness does not automatically "reflect" the development of the economic base and that, hence, the socialist revolution requires a proletarian consciousness *in addition to* economic crises. But, like Kautsky and Luxemburg, Gramsci optimistically believed that the proletariat would readily adopt the proper type of consciousness if only it was properly formulated and developed to correspond to the proletariat's objective situation. Consequently, he argued that the primary task of the party was to build a "counterhegemony" by rallying the masses around a socialist program they could recognize as theirs.

Formally, of course, there is little difference between the Gramscian concept of "hegemony" and the Leninist-Lukácsian notion of "false consciousness" (cf. Calhoun 1983, 903, n.3). Both rest on the implicit claim that the Marxist theorist possesses some sort of higher insight into the "true" interests of the workers than the workers themselves possess. Thus, also, both notions can be used to justify Leninist authoritarianism in the face of prolonged refusal by the proletariat to come to its senses. But Gramsci could still unproblematically refer to the "organic unity" between leaders and masses because he still did not anticipate any such prolonged refusal. Had he been forced to deal with that unsettling possibility, he might have been forced *either* to support the authoritarian solution of Lenin, *or* to accept the apparent judgment of the masses themselves concerning their "true" interests as Kautsky did, and thus drift toward incrementalism. In short, there does not appear to be any good reason for believing that Gramsci might somehow have escaped what I have elsewhere called the "dilemma of democratic radicalism" (see van den Berg 1980, 1983).

Lukács, on the other hand, had no such naive faith in the proletariat. If the revolutionary program is to succeed it must be protected *from* the workers—with their persistent tendency to come under the sway of "reification," bourgeois ideology, and "opportunism"—by a party of professional revolutionaries. Since the proletariat cannot be trusted to do its historical duty without the strict direction and supervision of the revolutionary "vanguard," it can be trusted even less to exercise its own rule during the construction of socialism, which will, hence, also have to be done in its name by the party. Marxism's pre-Leninist "innocence," then, is still quite evident in Gramsci's writing, but it has been irretrievably lost in Lukács's authoritarian "vanguardism."

After World War I, those social democrats who were unwilling to accept Leninist authoritarianism inevitably drifted toward non-Marxist incrementalism—as much because of the exigencies of electoral politics as of their effective excommunication by Lenin (cf. McInnes 1979; Therborn 1978, 247–71). Those who could not wholeheartedly embrace either alternative were forced to retreat in impotent lamentations about the sorry state of proletarian consciousness, without being able to point to a practical alternative except in the most abstract philosophical terms. Such was the fate of the Frankfurt School (Kolakowski 1978c, ch. 11; van den Berg 1980).

Marxism versus Reformism?

The debate between Kautsky and the Bolsheviks proved to be the last one on reformism *within* Marxism. By organizing a separate international—the Comintern—and forcing member parties to purge all "opportunists" from their ranks, Moscow managed to drive a wedge between "orthodox" Marxism as it defined it and all forms of reformism. Henceforth, reformism—that is, the belief that bourgeois democratic institutions can be effectively used to achieve peacefully "fundamental" or "significant" improvements for the majority of the population at the expense of the privileged minority—became the exclusive domain of liberal ("social democratic" or "labor" in Europe) politicians and social theorists.

The reformist perspective as presented by "bourgeois" political scientists and sociologists does not necessarily imply, as many Marxists claim, a denial of the importance of class conflict. In fact, in one of the seminal statements of the perspective, Lipset (1960, 230–300) extensively discusses elections as "the expression of the democratic class struggle," much like an orthodox Marxist might (cf., e.g., Szymanski 1978, 16). The relation between politics and class structure has, of course, long been a primary concern of "bourgeois" political sociology (see, e.g., R. F. Hamilton 1972; Parkin 1971; de Tocqueville 1955; Verba, Nie, and Kim 1978; to mention but a very few at random), although the class concepts used may differ somewhat from the various "correct" ones employed by Marxist purists (see, e.g., E. O. Wright 1980; cf. Parkin 1979). Nor does the "bourgeois" reformist perspective necessarily entail the belief that so-called democratic politics is in fact fully democratic in that it truly allows all to participate equally in communal decisionmaking. On the contrary, Dahl and Lindblom propose to reserve the term "democracy" exclusively for the unachieved ideal of full political equality and to call the actual, imperfect systems whose parliamentary rule, universal suffrage, and civil liberties approximate the ideal somewhat more than other known existing polities, "polyarchies," that is, rule by the many (Dahl 1971b, 7–9; 1982, 4–12; Dahl and Lindblom 1953, ch. 10; Lindblom 1977, 131–32). But relatively closer to the ideal though they may be, inequality of political participation and influence remains enormous in all polyarchies. While some groups, especially business, enjoy political power far beyond what their numbers would warrant, others have so little as to be virtually excluded from the political process altogether, reflecting the enormous differences in resources, tangible as well as intangible, that characterize all advanced capitalist societies (see, e.g., Dahl 1970, 105–40; 1971a, 431–40; 1971a, 81–104; 1982, 207–9; Lindblom 1977, pt. 5).[15] It is not on these matters that Marxism differs from "bourgeois" reformism (see also van den Berg 1981, ch. 4).

15   Similarly, Daniel Bell, hardly known for his Marxist sympathies, agrees that "private property has given a dominant economic class a disproportionate degree of political power" (1976, 231). As Miller rightly notes "it would be hard to find an anti-Marxist social scientist who does not agree that money talks in politics, and says a great deal," which is, after all, little more than a "banal acknowledgment of the relevance of the economic." (1984, 107)

They differ in that reformists insist that bourgeois democratic institutions are nevertheless "worth a great deal more than the paper they are written on" (Lindblom 1977, 133), because they ensure that "the connection between what government does and the interests of the dominant group . . . can be ended by activities that government would encourage, protect, or, in any case, permit" (Miller 1984, 111). If this is the case, Miller continues, "any social bias in government will be a passive reflection of the balance of political influence in society at large," and precisely this "distinction between active and passive bias is the difference between the ruling-class hypothesis and even the most left-wing versions of pluralism, according to which big business is enormously more influential than any other interest group" (111–12). Thus, while in the short run capitalist interests may be virtually able to veto any policy they strongly oppose and even restrict the range of issues publicly debated to those they consider "safe," they are unable to withstand what Lindblom calls a "grand majority," that is, "an unmistakable massive and long-standing majority opinion" (Lindblom 1977, 143). Moreover, business is unable to stop, indeed it is in part the cause of, long-term social trends that tend to create such grand majorities in favor of reformist programs. These long-term trends, which are not unlike those Marx thought would radicalize the working class (e.g., economic concentration, urbanization, unionization), lead to the gradual realization of the natural "demographic superiority of the left" (Wrong 1979, 211). When reformist parties are elected to office they take measures which improve the position of the lower strata and further contribute to mobilizing a grand majority for reform. As a result, there arises a semipermanent electoral majority for reform forcing even the conservative parties to accept past reforms. Those parties have only been able to win elections by agreeing not to undo past reforms and when in office they could only hope to retard further change, not to stop it altogether. Similarly, business interests have tried to intimidate and influence governments of various persuasions, they have forced "radical" governments to make painful compromises, but they have been unable to undo previous losses and they have only retarded future ones. Thus, in the long run capitalist democracies appear to have been subject to an inherent "leftward drift," slowly undermining the position of business and strengthening that of the state and the lower classes (R. F. Hamilton 1972, 9, 534–37; Lindblom 1977, 180; Lipset 1960, 299–300; Wrong 1979, 204–17).

In short, reformists claim that the social reform enacted by governments under electoral pressure in "bourgeois" democracies has in the long run been cumulative. Although conservative forces may have considerable powers of delay and obstruction, they have nevertheless been powerless to prevent the range of "respectable" issues and "acceptable" solutions from slowly shifting leftward, decade after decade, until the system, as well as their own political positions, has changed beyond recognition. Thus, "measures which in the nineteenth century were denounced as rank socialism are today pointed to with pride by conservative orators" (Lipset 1960, 299). Together, these measures have transformed the unrestrained capitalism of Marx's day into an entirely different system of "democratic interventionism" (Popper 1966b, 187). And if present trends continue there is no reason why the capitalist system might not be gradually transformed over the next 100 years into something that today we would consider "rank socialism" (cf. Korpi 1983, 44, 199–200; Lowenthal 1976, 253–60), although such a development is by no means guaranteed or inevitable (Turner 1986).[16]

This reformist perspective offered by "bourgeois" social scientists is obviously closest to that of Eduard Bernstein. The importance of the "economic factor" in history is not denied although class is not treated as quite so exclusively relevant as it is in much of the Marxist literature. Social change is seen as incremental and a matter of trial and error rather than as abrupt and, at least in the case of the transition to socialism, as the product of conscious and determined class will and action resulting from prolonged struggle. Most important of all, per-

16   Turner (1986) provides a particularly sophisticated—in the sense that he does not ignore Marxist objections and views reform as the contingent and always reversible outcome of the often fierce social struggles—defense of reformism based on the work of T. H. Marshall (1964).

haps, "socialism," although not rejected,[17] is not considered to be the inevitable end result of an intensified class struggle, somehow guaranteed by, or at least the culmination of, History. The relative strengths and weaknesses of liberal or social-democratic reformism are not the issue here. In a period of general retrenchment of social programs and determined (neo)conservative attempts to bring back the glory days of unfettered free enterprise, its more optimistic versions may well appear somewhat naive. But the point here is that whatever its merits or flaws, reformism, and particularly the belief in the possibility and desirability (though not necessarily the inevitability) of making significant and potentially cumulative gains for the least privileged strata by effective use of "bourgeois" democratic institutions, became wholly anathema to orthodox Marxism. With the rise of Leninism as the accepted orthodoxy, reformism of any kind automatically became an exclusively "bourgeois" doctrine foreign to Marxism. As we shall see, all subsequent efforts to formulate a distinctly Marxist theory of the state were intended, first and foremost, to prove the reformist position wrong.

There have been some attempts to restore a measure of Marxist respectability to social democracy (Esping-Andersen 1985; Korpi 1978, 1983; Stephens 1979), but these have strayed too far from some of the core tenets of Marxism to have any impact on mainstream orthodoxy. The developments that were, according to Marx, to lead to the transition from capitalism to socialism did in fact occur, Stephens and Korpi argue, but much more slowly and gradually than Marx had expected (Stephens 1979, chs. 1, 2). From the moment workers began to organize effectively to eliminate competition between themselves and wrest concessions from employers and governments, Stephens maintains, the social system began to move "beyond the capitalist model toward socialism" (1979, 11). Therefore, today "nowhere is capitalism found in its pure form. It is always

17   Dahl, in fact, proposes several radical reforms as detailed and as worthy of the name "socialism" as anything Marxists have ever proposed, an egalitarian combination of central planning and workers' self-management not unlike the Yugoslavian model, as a minimum requirement for the truly democratic functioning of any present-day "polyarchy" (1970, ch. 3; 1982).

at some transitional stage" (42). Moreover, in countries where a
strong labor movement has been able to keep social-democratic
governments in power for long periods, Sweden being the
clearest example, reforms redistributing income and economic
power have created a "transitional political economy between
capitalism and socialism" (174), although, Stephens cautions,
there is no historical guarantee that this "transitional" stage will
eventually lead to full-fledged socialism, "the abolition of the
distinction between the state and civil society" (26).

But, although Stephens and Korpi use the Marxist terminology of "class struggle," social "contradictions," and so on, the
actual picture they draw of gradual, limited reform under
union and electoral pressure, which may produce a permanent
"transitional" situation well short of the socialist ideal, seems
quite foreign to the perspective of Marx and Engels and their
more orthodox followers. More tellingly, Stephens and Korpi
make the fundamental assumption of equating the workers'
conscious preferences with their "real" class interests. Since welfare-state reform was introduced by popularly elected, labor-
movement-based governments, Stephens reasons, it *"thus* represents a first step toward socialism" (1979, 72, emphasis
added; also 47, 129). Similarly, Korpi rejects any charges that
reformist labor leaders fail to represent the workers' real interests on the grounds that the rank and file "have daily opportunities to evaluate the consequences of leadership decisions," so
that, if they are "rational actors" one can be reasonably sure
that "the union or party furthers the interests of the actors as
perceived by them," and claims to the contrary remain "rather
absurd" (1983, 24).

It is precisely the categorical rejection of *this* assumption that
has become the defining characteristic of post-Leninist orthodoxy (including neo-Hegelians such as the Frankfurt School
who rejected much else in Leninism; cf. Dubiel 1985). As we
have seen, faced with the choice of accepting the limited "trade
union consciousness" he knew to be the spontaneous state of
mind of most ordinary workers in "normal" times *or* sticking to
the revolutionary strategy of "scientific" Marxism, if necessary
in opposition to the majority of the working class, Lenin resolutely opted for the latter. To him, the reformism based on ac-

ceptance of the workers' majority opinion, as advocated by Bernstein, the later Kautsky, Stephens, and Korpi, could only retard or prevent the socialist revolution and amounted, therefore, to a *de facto* capitulation to "bourgeois ideology." For all their disagreements and polemics, virtually all Marxist theorists of the state solidly agree with the Leninist rejection of all forms of "reformism," "revisionism," or "gradualism" (see, e.g., Anderson 1980, 196–97; Holloway and Picciotto 1978, 15–16; Mandel 1978; Müller and Neusüss 1978, 32–35; Poulantzas 1978, 258–59; Teeple 1972; Therborn 1978, 209–18, 275; Whitaker, 1977, 57–58; E. O. Wright 1978, 227–29). Whatever else separates them, "virtually all Marxist treatments of the state begin with the fundamental observation that the state in capitalist society broadly serves the interests of the capitalist class" (Gold, Clarence, and Wright 1975a, 31), and that this "fundamental observation" is in no way modified by "bourgeois" democracy and the occasional opportunity it provides for social democratic parties to form governments (cf. Ornstein and Stevenson 1981, 748–49). In fact, the recent revival of theorizing on the state began with some explicit attempts to refute the reformist interpretation of the emergence of the welfare state, and was then carried on by theorists attacking these initial attempts as still lending themselves too easily to reformist inferences.

Echoing Lenin's strictly dichotomous perspective, Marxists claim that "fundamental" change is almost by definition an all-or-nothing affair. Lukács, for instance, rejects Kautsky's reformist strategy thus: "To adopt the stance of 'opposition' means that the existing order is *accepted in all essentials as an immutable* foundation and all the efforts of the 'opposition' are restricted to making as many gains as possible for the workers *within* the existing system" (1971, 260). Mandel seems to have something similar in mind when he speaks of the "implacable dialectic of 'partial conquests' " (1978, 205). The very success of reformist labor leaders in obtaining limited improvements for the workers and governmental responsibility for themselves, Mandel argues, inevitably causes reformism to get bogged down well before it affects the capitalist system in any fundamental way. Absorbed by the pressing needs of protecting past gains and of day-to-day management of the economy and easily intimidated by ominous warnings from business leaders and the bourgeois press against any "irresponsible" actions that might affect the "health" of that economy, reformist leaders, handicapped from the start by their lack of long-range vision, gradually come to lose whatever commitment to more fundamental change they still had. In addition, the privileges and recognition reformist officials receive serve to insulate them from their rank-and-file supporters and create "a community of interest between these officials and the bourgeoisie" (ibid., 10) so that the former can be counted upon to administer the *existing* system without attempting to change it substantially (ibid., 19–21, 152, 171, 204–5; cf. Miliband 1969, 88–93, 176–77; Therborn 1978, 108, 209–18).

There is some disagreement over the exact mechanisms through which reformism inevitably becomes the "objective" instrument of bourgeois rule—in fact this is what most of the recent debates have been about. But all participants in those debates are agreed that past reforms, whatever the intentions, have in fact "objectively" served the interests of the bourgeoisie by not only leaving the fundamentals of capitalism untouched but even helping to maintain and strengthen them. Welfare-state reforms, it is widely argued, have done little more than render the system just barely tolerable for enough workers to prevent serious threats to its existence from the working class. Those who have supported "social reform," Miliband, for example, contends, "have not only *not* been concerned to advance toward socialism but have on the contrary seen in social reform an essential prophylactic against it" (1977, 155). Such reform in fact constitutes "an essential moment in social pacification and in keeping class struggles latent" (Hirsch 1978, 84); it is the "relatively low ... price which the dominant classes knew they would have to pay ... for the maintenance of the existing social order" (Miliband 1969, 100); merely "a lubrication of the social mechanism intended to avoid an explosion" (Mandel 1968, 338), and so on and so on. Statements such as these can be quoted *ad nauseam* from the literature (e.g., Armstrong 1977, 290–92; Baran 1957, 96–97; Blanke, Jürgens, and Kastendiek 1978, 142–46; Braverman 1974, 286–87; Mandel 1975, 482–

83; 1978, 142; O'Connor 1973, 138; Poulantzas 1978, 184; Sweezy 1942, 249; Therborn 1978, 72, 234–37; Whitaker 1977, 56–57; E. O. Wright 1978, 91; 1980, 339).

There is, then, a broad consensus among Marxist writers that the timely implementation of welfare reform has only served to prevent a dangerous radicalization of the working class. Rather than substantially transforming the capitalist system, these reforms have actually helped to "reproduce" capitalist social relations by preventing the radical transformation that would most likely have occurred without them (E. O. Wright 1978, 18–19). It is worth emphasizing here that what distinguishes this argument from its "bourgeois" competitors is *not* the assertion that welfare-state reform has helped to reduce social tension. This part of the argument is wholly acceptable not only to liberal reformists (see, e.g., Guest 1980; Wilensky and Lebeaux 1965) but even to arch-freemarketers like Milton Friedman, who advocate dismantling the welfare state now that it has done its job of keeping social strife within acceptable bounds (see Titmuss 1976, 139, 154). Where they differ is in their respective estimates of the alternative. Reformist theorists often appear to suggest that the increased social conflict that might have resulted from the absence of any improvement in the conditions of the workers could easily have escalated and resulted in a repressive, even totalitarian, regime (see, e.g., Dahl 1970, 140–41; 1971a, 27–28). Marxists, on the other hand, appear convinced the alternative would have been a rapid radicalization of the working class resulting in the eventual victory of socialism. Both alternatives are usually only implicit, to be sure, but they *do* represent the crucial difference between the two arguments (see van den Berg 1981, 92–101).

It is somewhat ironic that although Marxist writers frequently raise the possibility of a fascist reaction as an argument *against* naive attempts of reformists to realize "fundamental" change by electoral means (e.g., Mandel 1978, 182–87; Miliband 1969, 242–47; Sweezy 1942, 252), it rarely occurs to them that the *alternative* to seeking limited but tangible improvements might also be some form of totalitarianism, or worse. Among the very few lines by Marx and Engels that has received *less* attention than it deserves is the one at the end of the famous *Communist*

Manifesto passage proclaiming that the "history of all hitherto existing society is the history of class struggles," where they write that those class struggles have ended *either* in "a revolutionary re-constitution of society at large," *or* "in the common ruin of the contending classes" (Marx 1977, 222). In their criticisms of reformism, Marxists have consistently and stubbornly ignored this ominous warning, apparently convinced, against all the available evidence, that a more radical stance and more intense conflict would inevitably have resulted in a better outcome for the workers—an unconscious carry-over of the Hegelian belief in the inherent rationality of History, perhaps.[18]

But in any case, the argument that reform has retarded more radical transformations does not, in itself, refute incremental reformism. It could still be that governments, while merely trying to pacify angry workers with the most limited reforms capable of restoring or maintaining a modicum of social order, unwittingly end up transforming the system quite thoroughly in the long run. It is in unanimously rejecting this possibility that Marxists differ from liberal reformists. Yet, although Marxists routinely dismiss reforms such as social security, unemployment insurance, health care, and the like as not "fundamentally" affecting capitalist social relations, the grounds on which they are dismissed and the criteria of what *would* constitute "fundamental" change remain unclear.

Esping-Andersen, Friedland, and Wright have designed an elaborate typology of "political demands and struggles of the working class" (1976, 198–99) which appears to be intended to answer such questions. They use three criteria of classification. First, demands may be made either at the level of production, concerning "*what* is produced and *how* it is produced," or at the level of circulation, concerning "the *distribution* of what is produced" (199). In Marxist theory questions of production relations are, of course, more fundamental than, and in fact the

18   One of the few to find Marx and Engels's warning "worth noting" is Miliband (1977, 194). Not surprisingly, Miliband is also one of the very few to emphasize (in a discussion of the possible implications of the Leninist "insurrectionary strategy") that *any* dictatorial regime "must be taken to represent a disastrous regression . . . from bourgeois democracy, whatever the economic and social achievements" (189).

foundation of, exchange relations (217, n. 13; cf. Poulantas 1975, 290–94; E. O. Wright 1978, 48–49, 88–91; 1980, 324–26, 399). Second, political demands may take either a "commodified form," that is, demands "for the state to work through and reinforce market mechanisms to accomplish some objective," or a "noncommodified form," pushing the state "to work outside the market or even to directly oppose market mechanisms" (Esping-Andersen, Friedland and Wright 1976, 199). Again, the suggestion seems to be that the latter are inherently more likely to be "fundamentally" subversive of capitalist social relations. However, like demands at the production level, they need not be. Esping-Andersen, Friedland, and Wright introduce the question of whether or not a demand is "reproductive" of capitalist social relations as a third, independent dimension (ibid.). Reproductive demands are those "which, if met, tend to reinforce, stabilize and expand the basic social relationships of capitalism," whereas unreproductive demands "tend to weaken, destabilize, and undermine those social relationships" (ibid.). As the authors themselves point out, this last criterion "is perhaps the least tangible, yet most important" (ibid.). Moreover, they add, "where a particular demand falls . . . cannot be defined abstractly. A demand which is reproductive under certain circumstances may be highly unreproductive in others" (200).

But, as becomes clear from the authors' discussion of the eight cells yielded by their classification, with such vague qualifications the categories become so fluid as to be of no use whatsoever for distinguishing between reforms that *have* and those that *have not* produced "fundamental" modifications of capitalist social relations. In fact, Esping-Andersen, Friedland, and Wright never really go beyond just barely stating the problem. The eight categories of political demands produced by the typology constitute a continuum ranging from "reproductive-commodified-circulation politics," which are least subversive of capitalist social relations, to "unreproductive-noncommodified-production politics," which, if successful, would mean the complete abolition of capitalism. But their classification of specific demands, under any one of these headings only *raises* the issues dividing Marxist and reformist theories; it does nothing to *resolve* them.

Thus, demands for unemployment insurance or minimum wage laws are treated as belonging to the least harmful category because their satisfaction creates only a "minimum disturbance of normal commodity relationships" (ibid., 200). Similarly, demands for state provision of infrastructure, whether through private contractors or directly, as with education and national health services, as well as demands for grants in kind, are all usually reproductive of capitalist social relations (200–202). However, demands for "an *adequate* guaranteed income for all workers" would clearly be unreproductive, as such demands "would seriously undermine the status of labor power itself as a commodity" since "one of the critical elements of capitalist social control, wage discipline, would be undermined" (202). Similarly, when demands for state spending on infrastructure cease to take the state's fiscal capacities into account and thus "attempt to authentically serve working class interests, they will tend to become unreproductive"; demands for free provision of goods and services by the state "become unreproductive beyond a certain point"; finally, demands for workers' control over the labor process and, ultimately, of the entire economy "represent the present form of unreproductive-noncommodified-production politics" (203).

But clearly none of this will help convince those not already convinced. The assertion that unemployment insurance and minimum wage laws do little to disturb capitalist social relations seems highly debatable, to say the least. On the basis of Marx's own discussion of the importance of the disciplining force of the "industrial reserve army" to keep capitalism economically and politically viable (Marx 1967a, 628–40), one *could* argue, as some Marxists have done (Kalecki 1971), that *any* provision of minimum subsistence for the unemployed is bound to undermine capitalism. Of course, as it turns out, most advanced capitalist countries have survived the introduction of unemployment insurance without any serious upheavals. But that does not mean such insurance does not significantly modify "capitalist social relations," possibly providing the basis for future change. Esping-Andersen, Friedland, and Wright in fact seem to admit as much in their rather inconclusive discussion of Sweden's evolution from "commodified-circulation politics" to more fundamental issues of control of production, an evolution that failed to produce the expected politicization of class relations (1976, 210–12).

More seriously, the vagueness of the criteria practically seems *designed* to invite the type of retrospective rationalizations for which Marxism has become infamous (cf. Parkin 1979, 165–73; Van Parijs 1980). Since demands that *would* "fundamentally" affect capitalist social relations are only identified in highly ambiguous terms ("an *adequate* guaranteed income for all workers," to "*authentically* serve working class interests," "workers [must] *authentically* control the apparatus of production," reforms must go "beyond a *certain* point"; Esping-Andersen, Friedland, and Wright 1976, 203), all demands that upon their realization fail to produce the expected results can be retroactively proclaimed to have not been "adequate" or "authentic" after all! Thus, no evidence could possibly refute the theory since it is little more than a tautology: whatever proves to be compatible with the continued existence of some vaguely defined "capitalist social relations" is, *ipso facto*, "inadequate" or "unauthentic."[19]

Other authors have proposed typologies similar to that of Esping-Andersen, Friedland, and Wright. Therborn, for instance, distinguishes between state policies that "further," "maintain," "go against," or even "break" the "relations of economic, political and ideological domination" characteristic of capitalist society (Therborn 1976; 1978, 129–161). This allows

---

19   Cuneo (1980) provides a particularly amusing example of this practice. He bases his proof for "the state's long-term implementation of capitalist class interests" (37) essentially on the fact that in 1935 the Canadian federal government chose to reject proposals by the Communist-inspired Workers' Unity League for a noncontributary unemployment insurance scheme, and favored the contributary plan supported by the majority of the unions instead, while the majority of the capitalist class was solidly opposed to *any* form of unemployment insurance. Cuneo lists a series of relatively radical W.U.L. demands (40) that he hails as "a direct assault on the hegemony of the capitalist class and the foundations of the capitalist state" (43). However, in retrospect those demands do not look all that radical as many of them have in fact been realized since. Are we to conclude, then, that this "direct assault" was successful? Not at all, because "the state's adoption of some of these provisions (although in a modified form) is a measure of its co-optation of the most radical working class elements" (40)!

one to objectively identify the "ruling class" as "the exploiting class of that exploitative system of relations of production . . . by the content and form of the totality of state interventions of a given period" (1976, 12).[20] Similarly, Erik Wright (1978, 15–26) offers a general scheme of six "modes of determination," ranging from "reproduction" to "transformation" with various intermediate forms of "selection," "limitation," and "mediation." Now, such schemes are perhaps useful for taxonomic purposes, but they do little to resolve the issue of incremental reform. The issue is precisely *whether or not* social security, unemployment insurance, and the like "further" or "reproduce" capitalist social relations. On this question Therborn simply ignores his own typology, arguing that all welfare reform and social-democratic government must be merely a form of "bourgeois rule" since they have proved "compatible" with capitalist "relations of domination" (1978, 166–69, 210–11). Wright also abandons his own subtle distinctions, preferring the simpler dichotomy of "fundamental" versus "immediate" working class interests. The first, he asserts, consist of the achievement of "socialism," while the latter consist of limited objectives such as higher wages or welfare legislation. Excessive preoccupation with the latter, he warns, "reflects an incomplete understanding of the nature of capitalist society as a whole, for it fails to grasp the possibility of transcending the entire system of capitalist exploitation through socialism" (E. O. Wright 1978, 90). Thus, the whole issue of incremental change is barely recognized.

The fact is that the whole argument against incremental reformism has never been formulated with sufficient clarity to allow for refutation or corroboration by empirical evidence. Not so long ago the case against incrementalism was generally made

20   Therborn is one of the few Marxists to reject the notion of "objective class interests" as merely providing "a spurious objectivity to essentially ideological evaluations" (1978, 146; also 1976, 16 n. 68). I could not agree more. However, this does not mean his "objectivist" method is any less spurious. I can see no difference of substance between identifying the "ruling class" as that class whose domination is "furthered" by the state and identifying it as that class whose interests are served by the state—unless, of course, Therborn would want to make allowance for the possibility that a class's domination may be against its own interests! For an argument similar to that of Therborn, see Alford and Friedland (1975).

on the basis of evidence presumably showing that the redistributive effects of even the most progressive social democratic reforms were practically negligible (see, e.g., Domhoff 1967, 42–47; 1970, 218, 250, 322–23; 1979, 7–9; Gough 1975, 72–73; Johnson 1979, 153–60; Parkin 1971; Wedderburn 1965; Westergaard 1978). But now that considerable doubt about this evidence has been raised (e.g., Korpi 1978, 1983; Maravall 1979, 268–77; Stephens 1979), it suddenly turns out to be irrelevant since even measures that *do* redistribute income and life chances in general remain within the sphere of "circulation," or within the system as such, or are merely accommodative, and so on (Maravall 1979, 277).

The ultimate evasion of this kind has been offered by some recent reevaluations of the "real existing socialism" practiced in the Soviet Union and its satellites. If one is to argue that social reforms have not affected the "fundamentals" of capitalist social relations it helps, of course, to have a fairly clear-cut idea of what these fundamentals consist of. Although there has always been room for controversy (see Heilbroner 1980, 67), the basic definition of capitalist social relations (of production) used to be fairly clear. They included, at a minimum, private property of the means of production, a formally free labor force compelled to sell its sole possession, labor power, as a commodity on the market, economic competition—in short, the basic relations whose abolition would usher in a socialist millennium after a relatively short transitional stage. But it has recently come to the attention of a few Marxists that the abolition of these capitalist relations of production does not appear to have produced the expected results, and shows no signs that it will very soon, in the countries enjoying "real socialism." But instead of leading to a thorough reexamination of the theory in the light of this remarkable "new" evidence, this has led some Marxists simply to redefine "capitalist" social relations in such a way as to include authority and ideological elements—a process that was luckily already well underway in an effort to accommodate other unexpected developments in capitalist societies (see, e.g., Althusser and Balibar 1970, 212ff.; Poulantzas 1973b; 1975; E. O. Wright 1980)—so that even the Soviet system can now be treated as a variant of "capitalism," namely

"State Capitalism" (see, e.g., Fromm 1961; Israel 1976, 52–53; Poulantzas 1973b, 29; 1975, 188–89; 1978, 60–61, 107–8; Shaw 1974, 441–44; cf. Benhabib 1981, 41; Gouldner 1980, 302; Heilbroner 1970, 142; 1980, 142; Lane 1976, 29–36; 1982, 129ff.; Nove 1983; Parkin 1979, 8–9). It would seem, then, that not even the abolition of private property in the means of production, of the labor market, of the "anarchy" of competition, is "fundamental" enough to affect capitalist relations of production "seriously." Obviously, with the central concepts having become *this* fluid the argument that welfare-state reform does not add up to "fundamental" change of the capitalist system becomes perfectly immune to any counterargument or empirical evidence whatsoever.

In the final analysis all the elaborate classifications of various types of reform and all the learned debates about the "true" nature of production relations seem to have no other purpose but to lend a certain theoretical respectabililty to what can only be described as purely *ad hoc* distinctions between reforms that have manifestly failed to bring on the millennium and those that have not yet been tried. They boil down to little more than the rather trivial observation that none of the typical welfare state reforms has created a socialist paradise. It is trivial since no one would deny it. It is doubly meaningless now that the notion of "socialism" itself has become such an elusive one. Thus, the antireformist argument appears to have deteriorated into a convenient instrument for denouncing any social reform one happens to be dissatisfied with without having to propose a viable alternative, on the simple Leninist principle that anything short of the full-fledged millennium must *therefore* be tantamount to its opposite, the maintenance of capitalist social relations (see, e.g., Clement 1977, 226–28; Finkel 1977, 344–45; Miliband 1969, 71–79; 1977, 39; Offe 1972b; Schecter 1977; Swartz 1977, 331; Teeple 1972; Weiner 1980, 7; E. O. Wright 1978, 249).

The case against incremental reform never was particularly strong (cf. also Bottomore 1975, 74; 1979, 51–52) but it has recently been further and perhaps irreparably damaged by its own strongest adherents. First of all, some of the major Western Communist parties, those erstwhile bastions of Leninist intransigence, seem to have succumbed, at last, to the temptations of reformism. Apparently convinced that they would not be able to overcome "the extremely strong attraction which legality, constitutionalism, electoralism, and representative institutions of the parliamentary type have had for the overwhelming majority of people in the working class movements of capitalist societies" (Miliband 1977, 172), the Italian, Spanish, and to a lesser extent the French, CPs have adopted a new line called "Eurocommunism" which bears a striking resemblance to the "opportunism" advocated by the "renegade" Kautsky against Lenin (Mandel 1978 190–92; Parkin 1979 196–97). Gone are all references to a violent revolution, the "dictatorship of the proletariat" and the CP as the sole "vanguard."[21] Instead of "smashing" the bourgeois state, the Eurocommunists now seek only to win a parliamentary majority, in coalition with whatever social-democratic parties are willing to join them. They now profess to be staunch supporters of "bourgeois" democracy, political liberties, and party pluralism. Even internally, "democratic centralism" is to make way for greater freedom of discussion and rank and file control. They now openly advocate the *gradual* transformation of capitalism involving a long process of transition by way of successive compromises, so as not to antagonize their marginal supporters or even their procapitalist opponents unduly. They have come to accept their countries' memberships in NATO. The CPI has proposed a "historical compromise" with the outright bourgeois Christian Democrats, and the Communist Party of Spain would gladly accept a minor role in a socialist-led government. Moreover, the change of strategy is explicitly based on the belief that insurrectionary politics has become obsolete and would inevitably lead to a bloody disaster (Boggs and Plotke 1980; Filo Della Torre, Mortimer, and Story 1979; Garner and Garner 1981; Mandel 1978, 188–93; Parkin 1979, 193–98; Therborn 1978, 267–71).

Indeed, the distance traveled from Lenin's revolutionary Marxism, and the parallels with the evolution of the Second International, are so obvious as to be downright embarrassing.

---

21   Kautsky actually never went quite so far as to exclude the possibility of violent revolution altogether (see Mandel 1978, 19n, 190–91, 207).

Like Bernstein's and later Kautsky's reformism, Eurocommunism appears to be only a stamp of approval on what had long been daily practice (Anderson 1980, 196; Mandel 1978; Miliband 1977, 170–75; Therborn 1978, 247–71). But any suggestion that they might be headed down the road to social democracy is indignantly rejected by Eurocommunist leaders. As Spanish party leader Santiago Carrillo protests, *"there cannot be any confusion* between *'Eurocommunism'* and social democracy in the ideological sphere. . . .* What is commonly called 'Eurocommunism' proposes to *transform* capitalist society, not to *administer* it; to work out a socialist alternative to the system of state monopoly capitalism, not to integrate in it and become one of its governmental variants" (1978, 103–4).

This fairly accurately echoes the general anti–social-democratic sentiments in the Marxist literature but it remains just as elusive. Any good liberal is committed to "transforming" capitalist society. The trouble is that there has not been sufficient electoral backing nor any well thought-out political programs to support much more radical policies than have actually been implemented. Whatever the reason, it is not immediately obvious that Eurocommunists will somehow be able to mobilize a majority behind anything more than typical, moderate social-democratic reforms, where they and others have previously failed. At any rate, now that they have rejected the Soviet model, they still have to work out the particulars of what exactly they *do* seek electoral support for (Therborn 1978, 260–61). So long as they have failed to do so, claims that Eurocommunists are "essentially 'Kautskyist' " (Salvadori 1979, 13) and that they "seem well on the way to becoming social-democrats who really mean it" (Parkin 1979, 198) can hardly be dismissed as a "cheap cliché" (Therborn 1978, 275).

As if to add to the confusion, the "great majority of the Marxist intelligentsia in the West has rallied to these perspectives" (Anderson 1980, 196–97)—those very theorists, that is, who have tried so hard to demonstrate that the reformism of social-democratic parties in advanced capitalist countries has only helped to maintain capitalism. Thus, Ralph Miliband—best known for his attempt to document the overwhelming obstacles against "fundamental" reform which invariably lead parliamentary reformism to strengthen rather than transform the capitalist system (1969)—now advocates a strategy that he explicitly calls "reformist," although he takes great pains to distinguish it from "social reform" intended to *forestall* more radical change and from elitist gradualism of the Fabian variety (1977, 154–90). Even more puzzlingly, Claus Offe and the late Nicos Poulantzas, after having attacked Miliband for *still* being too much of a latent reformist (Offe 1974; Poulantzas 1972), have come to recommend strategies of transition that are in all essentials identical to Miliband's "reformism" (Offe 1984a, chs. 10–12; Poulantzas 1978, 251–65)!

In fact, in the wake of the debates surrounding Eurocommunism, quite a number of Marxist theorists have recently felt called upon to offer suggestions for a "democratic road to socialism" (Miliband 1977, 182–90; Navarro 1980; Poulantzas 1978, 251–65; Therborn 1978, 272–83; E. O. Wright 1978, 228–52). Remarkably, these suggestions, apparently independently arrived at from different perspectives, are virtually identical, both in what they say and in what they do not say. They all involve the accession to power of a coalition of the left by constitutional means, the subsequent maintenance of civil liberties, multiparty politics, and the like. Such a government would, unlike its social-democratic predecessors, immediately proceed to execute far-reaching reforms, involving nationalization, increased planning, welfare, and redistributive measures. At the same time the strategy must be accompanied by a "flowering of self-management" in the factories, hospitals, and neighborhoods, and the central government is to remain highly sensitive to, and strongly encourage all "mass initiatives" (Poulantzas 1978, 261). This is the only way to create and maintain the "one major resource" (Miliband 1977, 188) of the left: the massive, highly mobilized, and unswerving support of the overwhelming majority of the population. Without such support, it will be impossible to prevent a fatal loss of morale in the initial period of chaos and confusion that will no doubt result from the fierce reaction of the procapitalist forces. To retain such wide and strong support, furthermore, requires the successful maintenance of high living standards and full employment which means that the process of transformation will have to be cautious and slow. In fact, even after the coming to power of a left government committed to a real transformation, the economy is likely to remain "to a certain degree capitalist for a long time to come" (Poulantzas 1978, 197; cf. Carrillo 1978, 77). There is, of course, always a danger of drifting off toward social democratism as the need to retain broad popular support may necessitate a certain degree of moderation (Miliband 1977, 162–64). However, these strategists all appear fairly confident that with a sufficient degree of tactical good sense, perseverance and popular mobilization it will be possible to retain mass support for the radical reforms they envisage. Unlike social democrats, however, they do not foresee a smooth and uncontested process of social reform, but a great deal of "struggle," "sweeping transformations," "radical breaks," and so on.[22]

Yet, none of these recent converts even attempts to answer the question of why such a strategy should work now when it has not in the past. Unyielding critics of social-democratic reformism all, they fail to explain why they expect to find massive support for a strategy of "radical breaks" when social-democratic parties have had trouble getting elected on much more timid platforms or, conversely, how they expect to avoid having to moderate their program to something well short of "sweeping transformations" in order to retain electoral support, maintain living standards and employment, and so on. In the absence of some fairly clear answers to such questions it is hard to see where exactly the difference with social democracy lies, other than in the somewhat more militant rhetoric.

Moreover, these latter-day advocates of the "democratic road" appear to be completely unaware of the fact that the "new" strategy flatly contradicts their own criticisms of social democracy. Only Erik Wright (1978) seems to be dimly aware

22   This scenario reminds one of the "socialist strategy of progressive reforms" proposed by André Gorz some years ago (e.g., Gorz 1968). It, too, involved a series of reforms that were to undermine the "logic of capitalist activity" (118), which, because they involved immediate self-government, would enjoy the support of the highly mobilized masses (124–25). Fully expecting an economic crisis provoked by the bourgeoisie, the government should not hesitate to strike "while the iron is hot" (116), counting on a massive "*prise de conscience*" of its supporters to carry it through the final "sharp trial of strength" (120–21), etc.

that all is not well. In trying to set things straight he produces an argument that easily ranks among the most contrived in the literature. Wright tries to steer a middle course between Leninism and social democracy by claiming that in "advanced monopoly capitalism" one can use "the democratic capitalist state apparatus as a basis for (ultimately) destroying the capitalist state itself" (227, emphasis omitted). This is different from the social-democratic position, he claims, because the latter sees the state as "an essentially neutral instrument" that can be used "as a basis for a transition to socialism," thus failing to recognize the "inherent structural limits to such reforms embedded in the very character of the state" (228). On the other hand, unlike the Leninists, Wright does not believe that those structural limits are at present so narrow as to preclude altogether the possibility of using the state for socialist objectives by constitutional means (228–30).

The argument is a rather curious one. For one thing, Wright fails to specify anywhere what he has in mind when he speaks of "destroying" the capitalist state—other than that the process is bound to be long and gradual (ibid., 238, 240, 249). So it remains completely unclear how he differs from social democracy in this respect. But more important, he criticizes social democrats for believing the capitalist state can be used for "socialist objectives" at any time, maintaining that it could only be so used in recent times, after having undergone some important structural changes. Yet these structural changes, it turns out, are the result of precisely those reforms advocated and implemented by social democrats, namely state intervention in the economy and the welfare state programs (230–32)! In other words Wright is in effect arguing that social democrats, ignorant though they were of the "structural limits" of the capitalist state at the time, have apparently succeeded, by some sort of fluke, in eliminating those very limits. The great flaw of social democracy seems to be that it has confused measures necessary for rendering the state a potential instrument for socialist objectives with those latter objectives themselves. Wright's disagreements with the social democrats are subtle indeed.

But, at any rate, the great majority of Marxists today seems to have adopted some sort of reformist perspective without apparently worrying too much about the inconsistency of that position. In the past reformism was bound to remain limited to adjustments *within* the system in order to maintain its basic stability, but in the future reformism is the only feasible strategy promising successful change *of* the system, they seem to argue, without bothering to explain what makes things so different today. The Trotskyists appear to be the only ones left who still consistently advocate the "storming and destruction of the State machinery" (Anderson 1977, 69) as a necessary part of the Marxist strategy of transition.

According to the Trotskyists only a revolutionary strategy of "dual power" holds the promise of any successful transition to socialism, no less so in advanced capitalist democracies than in czarist Russia. The "vanguard" of the proletariat must form workers' councils on the model of the Russian Soviets and participate in and help extend whatever token organs of self-government may already exist at the level of neighborhoods, factories, the school system, and the like. These are to become "organs of socialist democracy, mobilizing a popular force capable of undermining the unity of the coercive machinery of the established state, and cancelling the legitimacy of its parliamentary machinery" (Anderson 1980, 195). As the conflicts between these organs of proletarian democracy and the central authority of bourgeois "democracy" become sharper, the "immense majority of the population" (Mandel 1978, 172) will become more and more aware of the inherent limitations of the latter and rally to the "higher form of democracy" represented by the former (Anderson 1977, 71; Mandel 1978, 163–65, 172–78; 1979, 14–19, 32–41, 64–65). Such a process takes time, of course, and especially in countries where parliamentary institutions enjoy great traditional prestige, the *"masses must undergo an apprenticeship in new and higher forms of democracy"* (Mandel 1978, 172) which *"may stretch over several years"* (Mandel 1979, 18). During this period of expanding "dual power," the "toiling masses" will become increasingly mobilized and militant while the repressive apparatus of the state on which bourgeois power ultimately rests slowly becomes demoralized and disintegrates. Thus the "inexorable logic of the unfolding class struggle" (ibid., 43) finally culminates in a "revolutionary crisis" that is characterized by a "combination of the impetuous rise of the mass movement with the real inability of the possessing class, the bourgeoisie, to rule" (ibid., 7). It is at this point that the workers' movement must not vacillate, fearing the bloody defeat predicted by all secret reformists from Kautsky to Carrillo, but forge ahead to the inevitable violent confrontation with the bourgeoisie, confident that the "revolutionary crisis can *disintegrate* and progressively *paralyze* the military-repressive apparatus of the bourgeoisie if the proletariat acts resolutely, audaciously, taking the necessary initiatives and mobilizing its enormous strength as a whole (the immense majority of the nation in almost all Western countries) under the leadership of a revolutionary party which is up to its task" (Mandel 1978, 80; in general, 79–81, 140–41, 162–63, 172–78, 193, 188–220). Thus, if the conditions are right, the bourgeois state apparatus may be destroyed and replaced by a federation of workers' councils in a comparatively swift and bloodless insurrection (cf. Anderson 1977, 75–78; 1980 194–96).[23]

The Trotskyist strategy is truly a triumph of consistency over cogency (cf. Polan 1984, 140). Its advocates are quite justified in proudly calling themselves "*revolutionary* Marxists" as they are indeed the only ones left with a consistently revolutionary strategy. On the other hand, that strategy is so utterly implausible as to be almost ludicrous. It seems to be based on an almost mystical faith in the limitless revolutionary energies of the "toiling masses," just waiting to be brought to the surface by a "vanguard" of sufficient determination, and a similarly unshakable faith in the enormous radicalizing effect of any form of "self-government."

Of course, like any good Leninist, Mandel is well aware of the fact that the working class "is 'spontaneously reformist' (trade-unionist) in normal times" (1978, 117) and that the "toiling masses are not capable of spontaneously formulating and real-

---

23   But not even Mandel is willing to predict certain victory: "an *absolute* guarantee of victory obviously being impossible" (1978, 199). Such cavalier treatment of this rather crucial matter is one of the least attractive aspects of the revolutionary Marxist tradition. Somehow its adherents seem to think it very unreasonable of workers to ask for some minimum assurance of success before going out and risking their lives for the cause (cf. Parkin 1979, 199).

izing a coherent project for the conquest of power or the organization of a socialist society" (198). But they have their revolutionary "vanguard" to take care of all that *for* them (186–87,
198–99; 1979, 58–66). In any case, the working class has repeatedly proved to be "spontaneously anti-capitalist during prerevolutionary times" (1979, 61). It is then that it abandons its
reformist illusions and massively adopts the revolutionary line
of the "vanguard."

Now, following their illustrious founder, it takes very little to
convince a Trotskyist that a "prerevolutionary situation" is on
hand. In fact, Trotskyists have made it their specialty to predict
revolutionary upheavals with such regularity as to turn practically the entire post–World War I period into one single "epoch
of revolution" (Mandel 1975, 586), only infrequently interrupted by short bouts of "normality." Thus, Trotskyists seem to
believe that the working class is almost permanently on the
verge of exploding into a revolutionary rage. The only thing
holding it back, they argue time and again when their predictions fail to materialize, is the vacillation and outright sabotage
of reformist labor leaders, including those of the official CPs,
who are either too timid or too corrupt to be up to the task of
leading the masses (see, e.g., Anderson 1980, 176–207; Mandel
1975, 523–61; 1978, 29, 45, 50, 52–56, 59, 61–62, 64–65, 79–
81, 85–86, 115–18, 186–87, 210–11; 1979, 7–14, 53–54).

Trotskyism seems to be the last tendency to retain the old
Marxist faith that history is on the side of the working class no
matter what, so that it only takes a few well-aimed blows to realize the ultimate socialist paradise on earth. But to those who
are not convinced that occasional attendance at the local PTA
meetings, or some other organ of "popular democracy," must
inevitably turn one into a raving revolutionary; to those who
still think that a proletariat that has only hesitantly supported
moderate reformism is not likely to be easily converted into a
revolutionary mass; to those who still wonder what went wrong
in the USSR and find vague formulas like "bureaucratically degenerated workers' state" less than illuminating and assurances
that next time the "vanguard" will graciously allow all rivals to
organize and oppose it, in the midst of revolutionary chaos (see,
e.g., Mandel 1978, 65–67, 85, 122–24, 162–63, 171, 213) less

than comforting; and, finally, to those who wonder how one wins an "overwhelming majority" to "smash" the state if anywhere between 25 and 50 percent of the labor force is *employed* by that state (cf. Frankel 1979, 201–2); in short, to all those who do not share the Trotskyists' unshakable belief in the imminence of the world revolution, their strategy appears as pure utopian fiction.[24]

Conclusion

Thus, the apparently persistent appeal of piecemeal reform among the workers in "bourgeois" democratic countries has produced a situation of widespread theoretical disarray among the Marxist theoreticians with respect to the once so simple issue of reformism. As I tried to show in Chapter 1, the question never arose for Marx and Engels, because they were convinced the working class would soon form an overwhelming majority of the population committed to a complete socialist transformation so that democracy and capitalism would be inherently incompatible. Their immediate followers, such as Kautsky, Plekhanov, Trotsky, and Luxemburg, could still plausibly maintain this untarnished belief in the natural and inevitable convergence of working-class consciousness and radical socialism. Even Gramsci, owing to the peculiar circumstances that insulated him from many of the troublesome experiences and events after the triumph of bolshevism, could still share the innocent optimism of the founding fathers. But by about the turn of the century, it became increasingly clear that the earlier optimism was perhaps not warranted, that the working class might fail to develop the expected revolutionary consciousness and opt for a cautious incrementalism instead.

Among the first to recognize this were Bernstein and Lenin. But they drew diametrically opposed conclusions from this realization. For Bernstein, who saw Marxism as no more than a set of falsifiable propositions about empirical trends, it was merely a matter of modifying the initial propositions to accom-

---

24   For a forceful critique of the Trotskyists' continued adherence to the increasingly implausible "dual power" strategy see Sirianni (1983).

odate the new evidence. The expected class polarization, and the concomitant radicalization of the proletariat, had simply not occurred. Instead, the natural constituents of the SDP, and the union movement, clearly opted for an incrementalist, electoral strategy respecting "bourgeois" democratic legalities, and the party, being a democratic organization, had no choice but to follow suit.

By contrast, Lenin took Marxism to be a "science" in a more Hegelian sense, as a body of profound certainties concerning the forces "immanent" in history and as, therefore, an infallible guide to historically "correct" action, that is, as a "science" that could hardly be disproven by the fickle and notoriously short-sighted opinions of any number of actual workers at any one moment. Thus, Lenin's revolutionary "vanguard" became the sole proprietor and judge of "correct" proletarian class consciousness. The dangerously authoritarian implications of this Leninist fall from innocence were already clear from the start to his critics, especially Trotsky, whose worst predictions have, of course, been amply borne out by the development of Soviet "socialism" since 1917.

The main point of this chapter has been to describe how the rise of Leninism as the sole orthodoxy decisively set the terms for all subsequent Marxist theorizing about politics and the state. Lenin's rejection of all forms of democratic reformism and trade unionism as *de facto* bourgeois ideologies effectively excommunicated all those advocating gradual change "within" the system. Thereby, reformism became in effect a non-Marxist position. As we shall see in the following chapters, in this all Marxist theorists of the state are agreed: democratic social reform, at least in the past, has primarily benefited the capitalist class. They only *dis*agree on the reasons for this. The recent debates and exchanges on the Marxist theory of the state, which began in the 1960s and are still in full swing, can be seen as a series of attempts to produce a progressively more airtight argument to show *how* past reforms have in fact only helped to maintain and strengthen the capitalist system, rather than to transform it fundamentally (cf. Maravall 1979, 277–78).

Yet, at the same time, Marxists, inside the Western Communist parties as well as outside, have recently softened their antireformist stance to such a degree that it has become hard to see in what respect they still differ from the social-democratic reformists they once denounced as traitors to the cause. One reason for this is, no doubt, the persistent support of the majority of the populations in all advanced capitalist countries for gradual, incremental reform and the repeated rejection of more radical options. There are no doubt many reasons for the apparently "natural" reformism of the majority (see Hamilton and Wright 1986, 402–10 for an impressive list). But there is one reason which is widely overlooked that has to do with the nature of Marxism itself. Marxism is prohibited from depicting *in concreto* what kind of eventual state of affairs it expects to achieve by its own "immanentism," which puts a taboo on "utopian blueprints." But this makes it rather difficult for the ordinary worker to weigh rationally the alternative strategies, reformism and revolutionary Marxism, in terms of their likely relative costs and benefits because the likely benefits of the Marxist strategy must be left so vague as to drop out of the equation. What is left, then, for the potential proletarian recruit is to ponder two things: the likely costs of each strategy, and the known outcomes of apparently successful applications of the Marxist strategy, in other words, the Soviet system. Obviously, the great majority of even the most oppressed workers is likely to opt for reformism on both counts. It is something of a tribute to the insulating capacity of the ivory tower that such simple considerations could throw so many talented Marxist professors into such a state of theoretical confusion as now prevails concerning the reformism question (cf. Parkin 1979).

3 The State as the Instrument of the Capitalist Class

The obvious place to begin an account of the past two decades of (neo-)Marxist theorizing about the state is the so-called instrumentalist approach. It is closest to the traditional Marxist views that held sway until recently (see, e.g., Jessop 1982, ch. 2; Sweezy 1942, 239–53). Routinely invoked and taken for granted by both orthodox Marxists and such left-wing critics as the British "Neo-Ricardians" (e.g., Glyn and Sutcliffe 1972; Gough 1975, 1979), the underlying theory was not explicitly formulated until Miliband's *The State in Capitalist Society* (1969), which became the "take-off point for most recent debates" (Skocpol 1980, 160). The theory was an explicit attempt to refute the liberal reformist accounts of capitalist democracy (Domhoff 1967, 2ff, 141ff; 1970, ch. 9; 1972; 1976; 1979, 8–9; Miliband 1969, 6; see also Mankoff 1970). However, it soon came under attack for not being antireformist *enough* and for being too easily refutable. Its major proponents have demonstrated a certain willingness to subject their propositions to "bourgeois" methods of empirical verification and a certain readiness to consider reformism as a political option (Domhoff 1977a, b; Miliband 1977). Consequently, after a series of fatal criticisms by more steadfast Marxist theorists, "instrumentalism" has fallen into general disrepute among the cognoscenti (see, e.g., Plotke 1977; Poulantzas 1972, 1976). The debates can in fact be seen as a series of successive attempts to develop an increasingly sophisticated Marxist theory of the state in response to the apparent defects and lack of sophistication of the original "instrumentalist" position.[1] One of my aims in the

1   Somewhat curiously, however, much of the instrumentalist theory continues

chapters that follow is to assess whether these attempts *do* in fact add up to a progression toward a better Marxist theory of the state.

The State in Capitalist Society: Miliband

Miliband does not dispute the importance of political competition in most advanced capitalist societies, nor of the reforms that result from it (1969, 131, 197, 239; 1977, 189). However, the pluralist inference that the various interests, and especially capital and labor, compete on more or less equal terms he considers to be "in all essentials wrong" (1969, 6, also 131). In fact, he argues, business, and particularly big business, enjoys such a massive and decisive advantage in this formally equal competition as to constitute a ruling class in the Marxist sense, that is, a "class which owns and controls the means of production and which is able, by virtue of the economic power thus conferred upon it, to use the state as its instrument for the domination of society" (23). Thus, it has been able to thwart any attempts to change the system substantially in favor of the subordinate classes and kept reforms limited to those that have merely achieved "a certain humanisation of the *existing* social order" (99).

The decisive advantage enjoyed by business is the result of several concurrent factors. For one thing, the dominant class is far more cohesive and has a far more developed consciousness of its class interests than the subordinate classes (ibid., 43–45; also 1977, 31). Although there is a considerable amount of diversity and disagreement among them, the members of the capitalist class share "a basic political consensus in regard to the crucial issues of economic and political life . . . men of property and wealth have always been fundamentally united, not at all surprisingly, in the defence of the social order which afforded them their privileges" (1969, 44).

The same is true for those politicians "who have generally been able to gain high office" (ibid., 64, emphasis omitted). For

---

to linger in most other approaches, often in a convenient sort of standby capacity (cf. Parkin 1979, 126–29; Skocpol 1979, 160).

all their disagreements, what is remarkable is "the extent of their agreement on truly fundamental issues," that is those concerning " 'the foundations of society', meaning above all the existing economic and social system of private ownership and appropriation" (64). Their disagreements are only over how to run the *same* system, not on whether or not to change it (65–70). This broad consensus is rooted in the fact that these politicians are of overwhelmingly upper- and middle-class background. Although representatives of business are rarely a majority among them, they are certainly overrepresented. The working class, on the other hand, is heavily underrepresented, and those few who reach high office are easily assimilated into the broad conservative or mildly reformist consensus (51–62). Similarly, the top personnel in the civil service, military, and judiciary are almost exclusively drawn from the higher social stratums. Their social origins, education, recruitment, and promotion practices (favoring "moderate conservatives"), as well as their frequent official and informal contacts with business representatives, the prospects of future careers in the private sector, and their present class position whatever their background, ensure a conservative bias that would be hard to overcome by any government attempting fundamental reform (107–30). Thus, "the dominant economic interests in capitalist society can normally count on the active good-will and support of those in whose hands state power lies" (130; cf. Mandel 1968, 498–511; 1975, 480–93; Sweezy 1942, 248; Therborn 1977, 4; 1978, 190–95).

Moreover, business interests dispose of far greater resources than labor to influence government policy from the outside. Their control over economic resources gives them a substantial veto power, since they can refrain from investing in an "unfavorable climate." It also permits them to conduct vast advertising campaigns, which, often as a mere byproduct, never fail to herald the virtues of the free-enterprise system. Business has far easier access to the executive branch of government. It has the ability to launch pressure campaigns of enormous magnitude against any policies it dislikes. It enjoys the support of a powerful international financial "community." It enjoys the substantial advantage of being able to identify *its* interests with the "national interest" in maintaining a "healthy economy." And it greatly benefits from the fact that it is easier to obstruct change than to initiate it. It is no wonder, then, that social-democratic governments have been easily intimidated by these pressures and have generally been eager to moderate their, and their supporters', aspirations and to stick to "sound" policy (Miliband 1969, 88–93, 131–60; for similar arguments see Mandel 1975, 490–92, 1978, 193–97; Sweezy 1942, 251–52; Therborn 1978, 209–18).

Finally, business enjoys such an overwhelming advantage in the formally equal ideological competition that that competition really amounts to "a process of massive *indoctrination*" (Miliband 1969, 164). Conservative political parties enjoy popular support because of heavy financial backing from the business community for campaigning as well as for every conservative cause imaginable, because of the persistence of rural conservatism, the conservative influence of religion, the immaturity of the electorate, and the conservative uses to which notions of "national interest," tradition, the heroic national heritage, and the like can be put (161–95).

The majority of the mass media can also be counted on to help reinforce a conservative consensus, or at least prevent the subordinate classes from conceiving of any radical alternatives. Media content is held within the bounds of the "acceptable" because the mass media are mostly owned by big business interests, because of the potential and real pressures from advertisers, the enormous resources devoted to "public relations" and "news management" by business and governments, and the reluctance of media personnel to stray too far from what is perceived as a broad, popular consensus (ibid., 196–213). Despite their official neutrality, educational institutions, including universities, also contribute to the legitimation of the existing social order. Business representation on boards of trustees, the predominantly conservative influence of hiring and promotion practices, social status, contacts with and dependence on the state and the private sector, all serve to ensure that although criticism emanating from the universities may often be harsh, it will nevertheless remain well short of a "fundamental" critique of the system as a whole (213–33; on ideological indoctrination see also Miliband 1977, 43–65). Most important of all, the very fact of subordination itself tends "to breed its qualified acceptance rather than its total rejection" (1969, 235).

This, then, is Miliband's explanation for the failure of formally democratic regimes in advanced capitalist societies to produce "fundamental" reform of the existing distribution of privilege and power. Because of their superior resources for influencing government policy from the inside as well as from the outside, business representatives are able to prevent or defeat any policy they consider detrimental to their interests. They have been able to block "fundamental" reform because the dominant class is far more class conscious than the subordinate classes, and far more cohesive in the defense of its interests. That is to say, its members are keenly aware of what kinds of reform are "acceptable" because they will not substantially affect their position, and what reforms are "dangerous," and they invariably act in unison to defeat proposals of the latter type. Thus, the dominant class does not merely have a *substantial* measure of political power and influence, "it exercises a much greater degree of power and influence than any other class; . . . it exercises a *decisive* degree of political power; . . . its ownership and control of crucially important areas of economic life also insures its control of the means of political decision-making" (ibid., 45).

These assertions can be tested in a fairly straightforward manner. One would have to investigate a series of "key" issues (i.e., issues considered to be of some importance by the protagonists) on which business and labor were more or less solidly opposed to one another. If it could be shown that on those issues the government has not clearly sided more frequently with business than with labor, the theory would be effectively refuted (see, e.g., Hewitt 1974). It could be objected, of course, that only the issues on which the government complied with business opinion were the ones that "really" mattered, that is, the ones that seriously threatened the interests of the capitalist class. However, a careful comparison of the issues on which business was defeated and those on which it won, and their potential implications, should reveal whether there were any systematic differences between the two sets of issues, or whether the above objection merely serves to render the theory immune to any empirical test whatsoever. But even if one *were* to find such systematic differences, this would not constitute sufficient evidence in support of a Marxist interpretation, as opposed to the pluralist view of an ongoing process of mutual accommodation in which the protagonists respect each other's *temporary* thresholds of tolerance as long as compromise seems preferable to risking a head-on collision. For it could *still* be the case that under the influence of a continuous long-term buildup of pressure for more social reform the bourgeoisie finds itself forced gradually to lower its thresholds of tolerance—that is, redefine those "fundamental" interests on which it will not compromise—in such a way as to allow for a slow but cumulative "leftward drift" toward something worthy of the name "socialism." In addition, then, it should be shown that on those more "fundamental" issues on which business got its way its opinions are *irreversible*, in other words, that the dominant class has a clear conception of what constitutes a serious danger to its interests and what does not, and that this conception is *not* subject to erosion over time.

The "process of legitimation," which figures so prominently in all current Marxist writing,[2] is somewhat more difficult to operationalize and deal with empirically, however. It can be interpreted in two ways. First, the ideological indoctrination might be so complete as virtually to preclude the possibility of any major proposals repugnant to the capitalist class emerging at all. Thus, if it could be shown that in the area of welfare and social security, where business and labor may be expected to clash most often, no measures ever met with significant business opposition, this might be an indication of such a complete "mobilization of bias" (Bachrach and Baratz 1962). But it would be

2 The term "legitimation" has become associated with the "structural" approach to the state advocated by Offe and others (see Chapter 5). However, explicitly or implicitly the underlying notion that all past social reform has been of a "prophylactic" nature only, i.e., that it has done more to "legitimate" the *existing* system in the eyes of the mass of the population than really to *change* the system in any significant way, is part and parcel of *all* Marxist critiques of "bourgeois democracy." They only differ on the question of *who* does the "legitimating": a class-conscious, organized bourgeoisie or a "relatively autonomous" state.

difficult to tell the rulers from the ruled if there were such complete unanimity, and therefore impossible to discriminate between pluralist and Marxist interpretations by means of an empirical test (cf. Dahl 1958).

On the other hand, and this seems to be much closer to what Miliband and others have in mind, the "conservative" consensus reinforced by the media, educational institutions, and the like, might be such as to include a broad range of "legitimately" conflicting opinion, from laissez-faire conservatism to moderate reformism, only excluding "extreme" positions on the far right and the far left. Those members of the subordinate classes and their representatives who subscribe to a position within this broad range would then be victims of "indoctrination" and "false consciousness." However, such judgments seem to be based on rather arbitrary assertions about the nature of "true" consciousness of "objective" class interests. Whether it is at all "unreasonable" for the majority of the subordinate classes to adopt a position within this broad framework cannot even be sensibly discussed before we have some idea of the expected costs and benefits of the alternative, that is, of abandoning the consensus and taking a more radical stance. But even then the ultimate choice would seem to be up to the social actors themselves. Even if they were perfectly informed about the probable results of a less compromising course of action, it is still up to the members of the subordinate classes themselves to decide which alternative they prefer. But at least with some idea of the probabilities involved one could reasonably discuss the relative desirability of the various alternatives in terms of some set of value preferences (e.g., how much more desirable does the probable outcome of a head-on confrontation have to be, compared to the result of compromise, for fierce conflict and possible violence to be preferable to peaceful accommodation?). Yet, although Miliband's critique of "prophylactic" reform clearly rests on his strategic assumption that a more radical stance would surely yield benefits to labor that would exceed the costs (cf. van den Berg 1981, 92–101), one will look in vain for any explicit statement of this crucial presupposition, let alone any discussion of the grounds on which it could appear to be a plausible assumption at all. On the contrary, in fact, Miliband's *explicit* strategic predictions appear so utterly pessimistic that one may well ask how he can possibly expect anyone to be so foolhardy as to attempt the more radical alternative on which his argument is nevertheless implicitly based (see Miliband 1969, ch. 9; cf. Rich 1976, 659).[3]

Once again, Marxism's "immanentism" appears to be at work here. However gloomy his explicit predictions, Miliband still assumes that the more radical resolution is somehow "immanent" in the capitalist system, and easily attainable if only people would shake off their ideological blinders. Otherwise, it would make little sense to say that lesser reforms have served as a "prophylactic" (other than a prophylactic against right-wing dictatorship, which is obviously *not* what Miliband has in mind). But the argument remains beyond rational inspection because the Marxist taboo on utopian speculation precludes any clear description of the more radical alternative, the "real" steps toward "real" socialism, that the lesser reforms are said to have preempted. Therefore, the *crucial* ingredient necessary to make an informed, rational judgment concerning the merits of the "prophylactic" argument is plainly lacking.[4]

"Corporate Liberalism": Domhoff

A more subtle and detailed version of "instrumentalism" is offered by G. William Domhoff.[5] Domhoff's is an impressive at-

3 Although it should be noted that in his more recent work Miliband seems to have become both more optimistic *and* more explicitly reformist at least as far as *future* reform is concerned (see pp. 170–72 above). His critique of *past* reforms as merely "prophylactic" has, however, remained unchanged.

4 In a later work, Miliband views the British political system as an agent for the "containment of pressure from below," and he repeatedly insists that, given the political will, Labour politicians could have obtained far more radical reform than they did. Yet he also recognizes that there were never any "vast forces seething with revolutionary anger, which were only prevented from erupting by the endeavours of labour leaders" (1982, 33). Why, then, the "containment of pressure from below" should have been such an urgent problem for the British state remains unclear.

5 Domhoff (1976) objects to the label "instrumentalist," essentially on the grounds that his approach allows for more influence from the subordinate classes on the process of decision making than pure "instrumentalism" would. However, as I argue below, this qualification mostly has the effect of rendering his theory ambiguous, and not easily distinguishable from so-

tempt to demonstrate in detail that, contrary to pluralist illusions, the political process in the United States is in fact decisively dominated by a self-conscious, cohesive corporate-based "governing class," defined as "a social upper class which owns a disproportionate amount of a country's wealth, receives a disproportionate amount of a country's yearly income, and contributes a disproportionate number of its members to the controlling institutions and key decision-making groups of the country" (Domhoff 1967, 5, also 141–42). However, as it stands, this definition clearly allows for varying *degrees* to which a class can be "governing," "depending upon the percentage of wealth it possesses, the income it receives, and the leaders it contributes" (6, also 145n). Now, this is not necessarily at odds with the pluralist-reformist perspective. It merely states that the unequal distribution of economic resources reflects (as well as causes) an unequal amount of political clout, which few would deny. If one considers the distribution to be sufficiently skewed to call, say, the top 0.5 percent of it a "governing class" by virtue of its disproportionate share alone, then the argument is true by definition. In fact, Domhoff often comes perilously close to making such a circular argument (e.g., ibid., 42; 1970, 218, 322–23; 1979, 7–9, 119). But, of course, this makes any empirical verification of the assertion that there is a "governing class" wholly superfluous, since *any* degree of economic inequality can be taken as incontrovertible proof.

In fact, however, Domhoff has something more specific in mind, and he has come to define the "governing class" more stringently. Thus, he argues that the governing or ruling class does not merely have a disproportionate influence in the political process, it effectively *dominates* that process (1970, 105–9; 1979, 12ff.; 1983, 1; but also 1967, 11). What Domhoff wishes to show is that the ruling class "is able to impose its policies and ideologies in opposition to the leaders of various strata of the non-propertied, wage-earning class" (1979, 16). Like Miliband, he claims that the ruling class has been able to use the state as the instrument of its rule to the extent that it has been able to

---

phisticated versions of liberal pluralism like Dahl's and Lindblom's, except for the more radical rhetoric.

hold off or divert any measures that would "seriously" upset the existing "structure of the corporate system" (1970, 249, also 185, 218).

Thus, Domhoff, too, points out the vast advantages enjoyed by the major corporate interests and their representatives over the rest of the population in the struggle to influence public policy. The richest of the corporate rich and persons closely linked to the many institutions under their control are very heavily overrepresented in the executive branch of the U.S. government, advisory commissions, ad hoc task forces, regulatory agencies, and the like. The members of the judiciary and politicians tend to be of upper- or upper-middle-class origin (1967, 97–114; 1970, 331–38, 345–55; 1979, 129–67; 1983, 126–29). By virtue of their indispensability in raising campaign funds, the corporate rich virtually control the candidate selection process of both major political parties (1967, 87–96; 1979, 143–49; 1983, 117–29). Corporate interests have lobbying organizations at their disposal far superior to those of any other interest group (1967, 111–14; 1979, 25–60; 1983, 117–29). Frequent formal and informal contacts and exchanging of personnel between top government offices and the corporate sector ensure governmental good will toward corporate views and interests (1979, 25–60). Furthermore, the ruling class controls the major universities through their boards of trustees and their control of a large portion of research funding (1967, 77–79), as well as the major media of mass communication through ownership and the indirect influence of major advertisers (1967, 79–83; 1983, 107–9). Finally, it employs vastly superior resources to mount advertising and propaganda campaigns to get its views across or at least preempt the field so that "dangerous" ideas are unable to gain wide exposure (1979, 169–200).

However, according to Domhoff, none of this necessarily implies the notion of a ruling class, in the sense of a self-conscious class actively pursuing the overall, long-term interests of the class as a whole. It might simply indicate, as pluralists would have it, that various corporate groups, whose interests often clash, possess greater resources than other groups to pursue their short-term, special interests, but that those corporate groups are not sufficiently united to determine long-term public policy and to prevent other interests from having an effective voice in it. Hence, unlike Miliband who takes the unity of interest of the dominant class more or less for granted, Domhoff attempts to show in detail that a great variety of major corporate interests and their representatives actively and self-consciously cooperates through a nationwide network of commonly controlled institutions to formulate their common, long-term interests and to dominate broad public policy to such an extent as to be able to secure the maintenance of the existing distribution of power and privilege in the long run against any attempts to modify it seriously (1979, 53–60).

First, Domhoff documents the existence of a nationwide social upper class, consisting of perhaps 0.5 percent of the population, of extremely wealthy individuals and their families who can be identified through social registers, blue books, exclusive clubs, private preparatory educations, and exclusive life styles. Through such socializing institutions, the members of this upper class both interact intensively and intermarry among themselves and maintain an extreme degree of exclusivity with respect to the lesser classes of the population. Such shared experience, interaction, and exclusivity could hardly fail to breed a high degree of cohesiveness and consciousness of common, separate interests among the members of the upper class (1967, 12–37; 1970, 9–32, 71–99; 1974; 1983, ch. 2).

As might be expected, the members of this social upper class own a grossly disproportionate share of the nation's wealth and receive an only slightly less disproportionate share of the nation's annual income (1967, 40–47; 1983, 41–44). However, they not only own an enormous share of the country's corporate stock, they also effectively control the country's major economic institutions directly. A majority, or close to it, of the corporate directors of all the biggest banks, insurance companies, industrial companies, and other large businesses, as well as about one-third of the directors of the most important corporate law firms, turns out to be members of the social upper class by Domhoff's criteria (1967, 50–62; 1983, ch. 3; for the criteria, such as listings in social registers, private-school attendance, etc., see 1967, 33–37; 1970, 21–29; 1983, 44–49). The remainder of the corporate boards consists mainly of career executives, "experts," college and foundation presidents, corporate lawyers, and the like, who are not themselves members of the social upper class (1967, 50–52). Domhoff rejects the "managerial revolution" hypothesis as unfounded, on the grounds that it does not offer any reason to believe that there exist any conflicts of interest between the upper-class and non-upper-class top corporate executives (1967, 57–58; 1979, 18–21; 1983, 76–77). These executives should be viewed as the trusted employees of the upper class serving the interests of that class. In addition, the sprinkling of college and foundation presidents and corporate lawyers should be seen in the same light since the institutions from which they come are also controlled by the upper class (1967, 51–52, 77–79). Thus, in Domhoff's view, there is in fact a "power elite," which serves the interests of the upper class, and which consists of members of the upper class actively engaged in the direction of the major economic institutions and other upper-class-controlled organizations plus the occupants of command positions in those same upper-class-controlled organizations who are not themselves of upper-class origins (8–11; 1970, 106–7; 1979, 13–15). Now, if it can be shown that the members of this power elite are systematically and self-consciously seeking a broad consensus *among themselves* on their common, long-term interests and hence on broad policy issues, and that they are, furthermore, capable of regularly having these interests incorporated in government policy even when opposed by other interest groups, the country may be said to be run by a ruling class.

Domhoff's major preoccupation is to show this. He has tried to demonstrate the existence of an impressive network of closely interlocked organizations and institutions through which the power elite reaches a broad consensus on major issues, in which detailed policy proposals that correspond to its overall interests are conceived, which serves as a transmission belt communicating these proposals to the government and the general public, and which provides the government with expert advice and personnel to execute the policies favored by the ruling class (for an overview, see the charts in 1972, 34 and 1979, 63). All the noise of political conflict and competition so dear to pluralists notwithstanding, through this powerful policy network the ruling class as a whole is able to define the broad issues, limit the range of acceptable solutions, in short, fully shape the framework within which governmental decision making must take place (e.g., 1970, 105–6).

The institutions in the network that are most obviously controlled by the upper class are the many tax-exempt foundations funded by the big corporations and private wealth, such as the Ford and Rockefeller foundations and the Carnegie Corporation. These foundations are entirely funded by the upper class, and their trustees are overwhelmingly upper class, supplemented by a few non-upper-class members of the power elite. They spend huge amounts of money on scientific, cultural, and educational ventures and thus provide the upper class with the extremely important power to influence the country's implicit values and sociopolitical climate by encouraging those projects of which it approves and discouraging those it considers "harmful" (1967, 64–71; 1983, 92–95).

A second set of institutions consists of the elite universities with a virtual monopoly on the best scientific and administrative talent. They, too, are controlled by the upper class through power-elite trustees, foundation funding, private endowments, corporate gifts, and the like. Although the upper class may not be able to exercise day-to-day control on the ideas produced in these universities, it certainly has "control of the broad framework, the long-run goals, and the general atmosphere of the university" (1967, 77). These universities provide a large part of the expertise of the policy network (77–79).

But the core of the network consists of a set of associations concerned with broad policy issues, which were formed to influence government and public opinion in the various issue areas. Some of these associations are openly business oriented, such as the National Association of Manufacturers (NAM) or the Business Advisory Council (BAC), whereas others are more careful to cultivate an image of "neutral expertise," such as the Council on Foreign Relations (CFR) or the National Planning Association (NPA). However, all of them have an overwhelmingly upper-class, or at least power-elite, membership. The associations are tightly interlocked with one another as well as with the major exclusive businessmen's clubs (e.g., 1974, 103–9). They are heavily dependent on the foundations for funding. These associations are surrounded by a host of more specialized satellite organizations, "think tanks" and policy research organizations (e.g., the Brookings Institution, the Rand Corporation), which provide them with the necessary information and expert advice. These organizations, too, are heavily dependent on foundation money.

It is primarily in these associations that the members of the national power elite meet to hammer out a consensus on broad policy issues. Here they work out detailed policy proposals with the help of the best available research and the most prominent experts commissioned from their satellite organizations and research institutions. In these associations the members of the power elite are also able to meet with government officials in a relatively shielded and "neutral" atmosphere to promote the policies they favor. Furthermore, these associations provide the government with expert personnel and prestigious personalities to man presidential commissions and special task forces that serve to legitimize the proposed policies for the general public. Finally, these organizations actively provide funds and information to be disseminated by the media to convince public opinion of the "sensibleness" of the proposed policies (1967, 63–83; 1970, 111–95, 251–75; 1974, 91–109; 1979, 61–92, 120–27, 169–200; 1983, ch. 4, 131–36). Thus, a ruling class has been able to dominate the broad policy formation process in the United States because upper-class-controlled policy associations have "outresearched, outplanned and outworked any of its potential class or governmental rivals" (1979, 108, referring to the CFR in particular).

The ruling-class policy network is not entirely united, however. In fact, there appear to be two more or less separate networks which represent two major factions within the power elite. On one hand there is a group of organizations representing the ultraconservative tendency, of which Domhoff most frequently mentions the NAM and the Chamber of Commerce of the United States. These organizations tend to be isolationist on foreign policy and implacably opposed to any state intervention, social legislation, or concessions to organized labor. They represent "interests within the upper class which have failed to come to terms with the New Deal and the governmental needs of internationally oriented corporations" (1967, 77). They represent the smaller of the big corporations, although some of the very biggest also support the ultraconservative network (153–55; 1970, 225–27, 325–27; 1979, 82–87; 1983, 91). Their political representatives are conservative Republicans and Southern Democrats and their power base is Congress (1970, 252–53; 1979, 117–19).

On the other hand, there is the more powerful moderate conservative wing of the power elite represented by such "liberal" organizations as the Council on Foreign Relations, the Committee for Economic Development (CED), and the now-defunct National Civic Federation (NCF). It is based on the biggest of the big corporations, and promotes internationalist foreign policies and takes a more conciliatory and farsighted attitude in welfare and labor issues. It has great influence with the centrist forces in both major parties, and its major strength is with the executive branch of government (1970, 215–16, 225; 1979, 117–19).

Now, these two wings of the power elite have often found themselves in bitter conflict over highly visible policy issues. Moreover, it has usually been the ultraconservative NAM–Chamber of Commerce wing that has lost out in such conflicts. Pluralists have taken this as evidence against the ruling-class thesis. However, the pluralist view is based on the mistaken belief that those ultraconservative organizations were *the* representatives of big business. "What is not understood is that those setbacks are usually at the hands of their more moderate and soft-spoken brethren within the policy network and the corporate community" (1979, 82; cf. 1983, 90). What are often considered to have been popular victories over "big business" on closer inspection turn out to be reform measures worked out by the more farsighted and class-conscious moderate wing of the power elite, intended to *maintain* the existing corporate system by preempting more radical attacks on it. Thus, most policy disputes concern differences of opinion *within* the power elite, with little or no interference from the underlying population (1970, 107–8). These differences may have been real enough. "However, from a larger perspective, looking down at the foci of power within the overall system, these differences were primarily technical conflicts within the power elite over means to agreed ends, those ends being the maintenance of the wealth distribution and a private property system in which a very small percentage of the population enjoys great prestige, privilege and authority" (1970, 185).

The loose coalition of labor and liberals based on the unions, middle-class reform organizations, university communities, and liberal Democrats has no governmental stronghold of its own, nor any significant clout in the policy formation process. It is almost entirely dependent on the benevolence and resources of the moderate faction of the power elite to achieve any reform at all. The ultraconservatives have at their disposal considerable independent power to delay or modify policies through Congress. The moderate power elite seems to hold the balance because of superior economic leverage, organization, and access to the dominant executive branch of government, and it has thus been able to determine the content of major policy and set the limits of reform. The evidence shows, Domhoff claims, that "moderate leaders within the upper class, somewhat restrained by their more conservative brethren, have made the key decisions of the twentieth century" (ibid., 1970, 108).

Of greatest interest here is Domhoff's explanation for the emergence of social-reform measures such as social security or regulation of industry, which are often hailed as popular victories over the united opposition of big business. In fact, Domhoff argues, they were nothing of the sort. Every one of these reforms has been almost exclusively inspired, carefully planned, and deftly orchestrated by the moderate wing of the power elite to suit its own long-run purposes, often with some backing from conservative labor leaders and over the opposition of ultraconservative forces in the power elite (see ibid., 1970, 196–250; 1979, 93–100, 109–17).

The usual scenario, according to Domhoff, runs along the following lines. The moderate wing of the power elite consists mainly of the representatives of the biggest and most powerful corporations, whose oligopolistic position enables them to make concessions at little or no cost to themselves in exchange for social peace, which naturally predisposes them to take a relatively conciliatory attitude toward popular demands for social reform. Thus, when faced with economic crisis and rising social unrest, these more powerful and farsighted elements of the power elite are the first to realize that some concessions are in order to head off more serious threats to the corporate system. Through the resources and expertise of their moderate policy network they work out and launch detailed plans and model legislation for modest social reform, to preempt more radical proposals. These plans usually meet with fierce opposition in Congress, the bulwark of the ultraconservative forces representing the smaller corporate interests. Either the moderates are able to overcome this opposition by virtue of their more powerful economic position, better organization, and easier access to the executive branch, or some kind of compromise is worked out, producing even more modest reform than the moderates had proposed. Meanwhile, liberals and labor leaders have little choice but to accept the watered-down version, for lack of any feasible alternatives. Thus, in the end the moderate wing of the power elite gets reform on its own terms or better, the corporate system is restabilized, the existing distribution of privilege, power, and wealth remains untouched (for summaries, see 1970, 217–18, 223, 249–50; 1983, 143–46).

This "revisionist" view of the origins of social reform has come to be known as the theory of "corporate liberalism." It is based on the New Left historiography of the 1960s (e.g., Kolko 1963; Radosh 1972; Weinstein 1968; see also Mankoff 1970, 420–25; Silva 1978), and has been very influential among some Marxists (e.g., O'Connor 1973). It also has some obvious affinities with the orthodox communist "stamocap" theories mentioned in the previous chapter. It amounts to a well-specified, empirically testable, straightforward version of "instrumentalism." However, on closer inspection, the theory turns out to suffer from several serious defects.

For one thing, there is some doubt as to the accuracy of the "corporate liberal" account of reform. According to one critic it is in fact "highly misleading" since it rests on "a purely illustrative and selective citing of facts" (Skocpol 1980, 162). If put to a more rigorous empirical test, Skocpol argues, the theory is not supported by the available evidence. Taking the New Deal as a test case, Skocpol claims that: (1) precisely the one piece of reform that was most obviously inspired by corporate interests (the National Industrial Recovery Act) failed to achieve its goal because corporate interests *were unable* to take the long-run, overall perspective needed to make it work (163–66);[6] (2) the other New Deal reforms Domhoff analyzes (the Wagner Act, 1934, and the Social Security Act, 1935) were *in fact* forced through by politicians and government officials sympathetic to labor *against* virtually solid opposition from the business community (166–69); (3) the ultraconservative National Association of Manufacturers, on whose presumably small(er) business constituency Domhoff leans heavily in his argument, had *in fact* been transformed into a vehicle for big-business interests by the early 1930s (168). Thus, Domhoff's case for the big-business origin of New Deal reforms is not supported by the evidence (see also Finegold and Skocpol 1980, 77–86; Noble 1985; Piven and Cloward 1971, 84 ff.; Quadagno 1984; 1985; Skocpol and Amenta 1985; Stephens 1979, 151).

Second, Domhoff never makes it quite clear why it is that moderate elements of the power elite so regularly prevail over the ultraconservatives. Is it a matter of the largest corporations, with their superior resources, overpowering the smaller ones? Although this is what Domhoff seems to have in mind, instead of any systematic evidence (e.g., how many of, say, the Fortune 500 favored reform? What was the percentage of corporate assets commanded by these companies as compared with those that were opposed? Is the ultraconservative policy network really funded by lesser corporate interests, and less generously

6   In my view Skocpol specifies the corporate liberalism theory perhaps a little *too* rigorously, however. I do not think the theory necessarily implies that *all* policies promoted by corporate liberals are so farsighted as to always be successful. Nevertheless, the point about the corporate world lacking any vehicle to develop an overall economic perspective at the time, if it is in fact historically correct, remains a very damaging one for the theory. Also, I do not think the theory requires that the benefits of corporate liberal reform (almost) exclusively accrue to its advocates, the biggest of the corporations, as Skocpol seems to argue (1980, 162). Domhoff would no doubt claim that all corporate interests, including those initially vehemently opposed to any reform, ultimately benefit from the stabilizing effects of such reform (see, e.g., 1970, 249).

than the moderate network?), Domhoff only offers vague allusions, and rather ambiguous ones at that.

We are told about the "most powerful and forward-looking
segment of the corporate community" (Domhoff 1970, 161),
without any indication how it compared to the presumably less
powerful and more reactionary segment. He claims that "some
of the most powerful bankers and industrialists in the country"
supported social security (216), but it is never clear whether
their numbers were sufficient or their companies sufficiently
powerful to overrule the remaining most powerful bankers and
industrialists who were apparently opposed. In fact, the supporters seem to be the same ones who, according to Skocpol,
were no more than isolated exceptions to the rule of business
opposition. Although Domhoff claims, without any evidence,
that "bigness seemed to dispose a company toward more moderate views," he adds that in addition to "some" U.S. Steel executives and Morgan bankers, "the DuPont–General Motors
clique was to be a very large exception" (225). A very large exception indeed! How many more were there, and what portion
of the corporate community did they represent?

Moreover, although his argument that pluralists, concentrat-
ing on the many defeats suffered by the ultraconservative NAM
and Chamber of Commerce, ignore "the more powerful moderate element within the big business community" is essential to
Domhoff's theory, he presents little systematic evidence to show
that the NAM *is* in fact the effective vehicle of smaller business
interests, rather than simply representing reactionary corporations just as large as the biggest among the moderates, while
counting more smaller businesses among its members than organizations of a more exclusive nature and purpose, such as the
CED or the CFR. By all accounts, the "very largest corporations"
(Domhoff 1979, 86) are quite well represented in the NAM leadership, and Domhoff even concedes at one point that the organization "continues to be dominated by very large corporations" (1967, 77).

On one occasion Domhoff *does* offer some indications on the
balance between pro- and contrareform forces, and it is worth
examining this in some detail. It concerns the not exactly insignificant case of the congressional hearings on the second at-

tempt to get the Wagner Act passed. Domhoff gives a list of those who testified in favor of the bill, and those who testified against it (1970, 243). Those in favor were "Garrison, Biddle, Leiserson, Dennison, labor leaders, and one or two little-known, middle-sized businessmen." Presumably, the intimate links between the first four men and the biggest of the giant corporations have been sufficiently established elsewhere in the book to require no further comment. In addition, Domhoff reports, Senator Wagner submitted a favorable report by a committee of the Twentieth Century Fund (TCF), an organization Domhoff had previously identified as part of the moderate policy network. The committee that wrote the report consisted of the aforementioned Dennison and Leiserson, in addition to its chairman, William H. Davis, "a New York corporation lawyer," "economist" Sumner Slichter, and John G. Winant, who had previously been shown to have been "one of the most prominent and respected leaders within the upper class" (all ibid.).

Now, since the bill eventually passed, and since, according to the theory, this must have been the result of the powerful big corporation–moderate power elite backing it enjoyed, while being opposed by smaller corporate reactionaries, one would expect the above gentlemen to have been very closely tied to the biggest corporate interests in the land, especially since the lineup that showed up to testify *against* the bill was rather formidable indeed (see below). Hence it will be useful to trace how Domhoff describes these men elsewhere.

Davis is not mentioned anywhere else, so he remains simply a "New York corporation lawyer." Garrison, it turns out, was of rather prominent old Bostonian stock, son of a lawyer, and married to a descendant of first Chief Justice of the Supreme Court John Jay. Definitely social upper class. Furthermore, he had been a very prominent Wall Street lawyer in his own right, dean of the University of Wisconsin Law School, investigator of bankruptcy frauds under President Hoover, and the first head of the short-lived and ineffectual National Labor Relations Board (Domhoff 1970, 239). His *social* upper-class credentials are certainly impressive, but there is not a word about any connections with big (or small, for that matter) corporate interests, and his heading of the NLRB would seem to give him sufficient motive to desire a bill on labor relations with teeth, quite apart from his origins.

Francis Biddle was one of the most prominent New Dealers. He was "an even more eminent member of the upper class" than Garrison, a former corporation lawyer who had been "counsel to the anti-union Pennsylvania Railroad" (ibid., 239) and a director of the TCF. He succeeded Garrison as head of the NLRB, which convinced him of the need for stronger legislation (239ff., also 182). Again, impeccably upper class, but, apart from the railroad, no obvious ties to corporate business, at least not the biggest ones. Dennison is described as a "liberal big businessman" who cofounded and helped finance the TCF (180, 182). He was also a member of the Business Advisory Council (237), about whose business orientation there is no doubt (189– 90), but which also happens to be the *only* business organization to have endorsed the Roosevelt administration while the rest of the business community was becoming increasingly opposed to the New Deal, according to Skocpol (1980, 168). At any rate, if he had any close ties with the Rockefellers or the Morgans, Domhoff doesn't mention them. Leiserson had been executive secretary to the National Labor Board, which had been as in- effectual as the NLRB, under Senator Wagner's chairmanship. He is only identified as "a long-time AALL [American Associa- tion for Labor Legislation] member who had served under Commons on the Commission on Industrial Relations from 1914 to 1915" (236). John R. Commons was the famous Wis- consin labor economist, founder of the Wisconsin or "institu- tionalist" school of labor economics, who drafted much of the Wisconsin reform legislation that was to serve as a model for federal legislation on regulation and social security. However, Commons's involvement in such organizations as the NCF and the AALL shows beyond a shadow of a doubt that this "middle- class economist" (Domhoff 1970, 164) was merely the willing tool of the moderate power elite (162, 166, 172, 203, 208ff., 219, 230), which must of course have rubbed off on Leiserson, his subordinate in 1914–1915. At any rate, Leiserson is already compromised by his "long-time" membership in the AALL, an organization obviously controlled by the moderate power elite (170–79), which was instrumental in the passage of a whole series of reforms (174–78, 207–18). To what extent this organization was really "controlled" by the power elite is itself open to question (see below), however. In any case, if Leiserson's *only* link with the biggest corporate interests consists of his AALL membership—from Domhoff's list of AALL financial backers (172–73) it is not even clear whether they really *are* representatives of the biggest corporations, rather than a mixed bunch including some run-of-the-mill multimillionaires—it is rather a tenuous link indeed!

Sumner Slichter was a Harvard economist who had helped the CED (whose big business orientation I do not doubt) in its early years. Besides, "two of his brothers were corporate directors in their native Wisconsin" (ibid., 190). Again, *some* business ties, but not clearly a spokesman for the biggest corporations.

Winant, finally, was an AALL and Brookings Institution trustee (ibid., 216). The "great prominence and respect Winant commanded within the upper class" (216, n. 105) has been "stressed" by E. Digby Baltzell, the well-known sociologist and observer of the *social* upper class (ibid.).

As for the TCF, whose favorable report apparently helped the Wagner Act pass, Domhoff has little to say about it. Apparently, it was dominated by New Dealers, and its only financial backers mentioned are the aforementioned "industrialist" Dennison and its other founder, NCF and AALL member Edward E. Filene (ibid., 182). Filene is identified as "a department store owner who was an important business leader into the New Deal years" (166, also 172, 209, 233). Leader of what business interests exactly is not quite clear, but his department stores hardly rank him among the Fortune top ten, nor would they enable him to overwhelm the NAM forces.

The TCF was not just strongly pro New Deal, it seems to have been rather a maverick among the power-elite-controlled organizations in general. After A. A. Berle took over the chairmanship from Filene in 1951, it "remained the most liberal of the power elite research groups" (ibid., 194). It counted "many well-known Democrats (some upper class, some middle-class)" among its trustees. "The presence of J. Robert Oppenheimer and Robert Lynd on its board, along with its sponsorship of several critical liberals, even led to an investigation of that group by an ultra-conservative congressional committee" (ibid.).

This, then, was the lineup in favor of the Wagner Act: besides unidentified "labor leaders" and "one or two little-known, middle-sized businessmen," we have four patrician New Dealers, frustrated by their experiences with former labor boards that lacked enforcement powers, and with but the most tenuous connections with the really big corporate interests. Furthermore we have a favorable report by *one* research organization which also happens to be run mostly by the very same frustrated New Dealers. Finally, we have a bill submitted and drafted almost single-handedly by Senator Wagner (with help from Biddle, two other unidentified lawyers, and an economist; ibid., 240–41). There is no evidence whatsoever of *any* active backing from really big business apart from the fact that *some* business members of the NCF had been relatively moderate toward unionism earlier in the century, and had backed the previous attempts to set up labor relations boards without any teeth, which leads Domhoff to argue that these were "precedents" for the act (241). This is *it* as far as the pro-Wagner forces are concerned.

Now for the opposition. There were the NAM "and its affiliates." "However, there was more than the NAM, for representatives of steel, autos, newspapers, and textiles also spoke against it. Henry I. Harriman of the United States Chamber of Commerce, a moderate on some New Deal matters, was very much opposed. So was Alfred P. Sloan of General Motors" (ibid., 243). Notice that this may well mean that some of the corporate giants that are behind the country's biggest nonprofit foundations, which, in turn, supposedly finance and control such policy organizations as the AALL and the NCF, were among the opponents. At least the vague reference to "autos," which might include Ford, suggests as much.

Domhoff is deceptively cautious in drawing any conclusions from the above evidence. It indicates "a deep and serious split within the power-elite on how to deal with organized labor," he claims (ibid., 243), suggesting that if a poll had been taken among all power-elite members "many probably would have disapproved of the Wagner Act" (244). This is worse than misleading. Domhoff's own evidence allows for only one interpretation: the proponents of the bill consisted of a grand total of one Senator, four patrician New Dealers without obvious connections with big business, one liberal research outfit largely run and financed by the same men, and an undisclosed number of labor leaders representing an undisclosed number of organized workers. Practically the *entire* corporate community was opposed, including corporate interests that backed organizations the four proponents were members of. Yet it is precisely that financial backing that Domhoff uses as evidence to discredit those proponents—and a wide assortment of scholars, such as John R. Commons—labeling them lackeys of the moderate power elite.

Undaunted by his own evidence, Domhoff continues to treat the passing of the Wagner Act as an unambiguous victory for the moderate wing of the power elite. Despite the formidable opposition "the moderate clique within the power elite" succeeded because it "held the political reins at that crucial juncture . . . and it was this clique which chose a moderate course, appealing over the heads of their conservative brethren to the laborer, the farmer and the middle-class liberal" (ibid., 244). After listing the rather unfavorable balance of forces just discussed, this is Domhoff's *entire* explanation for the passing through Congress of the act after it had been defeated once before by an apparently less formidable opposition (238, 243)! He then goes on to discuss how Roosevelt got the act through the Supreme Court by putting "a fine set of lawyers" and a new solicitor general on the case (a grand total of one corporation lawyer, one upper-class and one middle-class lawyer, and one middle-class law professor), and making his famous threat to "pack" the Court (245).

Now, who did the moderate clique of the power elite, supposedly holding the "political reins" consist of? Since Domhoff does not further identify them, we must assume that they were Francis Biddle and his allies and the president, obviously himself a member of the power elite, albeit the moderate wing, by virtue of his one-time membership in the NCF (ibid., 169, 240–42). (F.D.R., incidentally, did nothing to encourage Senator Wagner to draft his bill, preferring to remain neutral; 240.)

Again, this is the "moderate clique within the power elite" *not* because its members entertained close links with the most powerful corporate interests, but *only* because of their one-time membership in associations that are in part funded by the foundations that were set up by those interests (and/or their patrician origins). But, I have tried to suggest, it is reasonable to suspect that the Wagner Act was in fact strongly opposed by those same corporate interests. This suspicion is confirmed by the fact that when Roosevelt set out to "mend the rift within the power elite" (246), the business interests that needed to be placated included U.S. Steel, Morgan, and even, at this time, Rockefeller, though not, as far as I can tell, the Ford Motor Company. Clearly, then, there was a conflict of opinion between the corporate financiers of those policy associations and some of the (ex-)members of the associations.

This raises some very disturbing questions about Domhoff's whole theory. Members (or at least the prominent ones) of associations funded and hence controlled by the major corporations, Domhoff has argued, can, *ipso facto*, be taken to be members of the (moderate) power elite voicing the interests and opinions of those major corporations. But here we have a significant case in which they apparently did not. Thus, either those corporations simply do not sufficiently control the associations to ensure that their members reflect the corporations' opinions, in which case membership in the associations becomes meaningless as evidence of power-elite membership, *or* Biddle and the others suddenly ceased to be members of the power elite when they began to promote causes disliked by their associations' corporate backers. In either case the passing of the Wagner Act cannot possibly be interpreted as a triumph of the "moderate clique within the power elite" over "their conservative brethren." Thus, the reason the act passed remains a mystery. However, Domhoff's passing references to "labor leaders" *tout court* and to the moderate clique's appeal to the liberal electorate over the heads of its conservative brethren, raises an awesome possibility: might the bill have passed, against the express will of virtually the entire corporate community, simply because it enjoyed the massive support of organized labor and made good electoral sense? If these were indeed the major reasons this would be a mortal blow to the entire "corporate liberalism" theory, of course.[7]

This raises further issues about Domhoff's general approach. What he does is the exact inverse of what he accuses pluralists of. The pluralists take every NAM–Chamber of Commerce defeat for a defeat of "business in general." Domhoff, by contrast, takes every piece of reform that enjoys the support of *some* wealthy individuals, however few they may be, as an unequivocal *victory* for "business in general," irrespective of the amount of business opposition or labor support. Moreover, these reforms invariably constitute a *complete* defeat for labor, because it did not get everything its more radical wing wanted, or, worse, because what it got was less than what it *ought* to have gotten (ibid., 198, 200–201, 216–18). By the same procedure, one could take even the slightest encroachment on the nineteenth-century laissez-faire ideal as incontrovertible proof of the diabolical powers of a cabal of liberals and "big labor," which is of course precisely what the ultraconservatives do. One can always find at least a few labor leaders willing to support even the most shamefully inadequate "reforms" to back up such a claim, and never mind that some of the biggest businessmen in the country wholeheartedly backed the more modest reforms—they are simply misguided or worse. This is no caricature; it is in fact a quite accurate mirror image of how Domhoff treats the labor leaders who were willing to work with the supposedly corporate-controlled reform organizations (e.g., 186, 224–25, 230, 232).

What is so sorely lacking in Domhoff's accounts is *any* systematic evidence as to what portion of the corporate community

7   In light of the rather strong evidence to the contrary (corroborated by similar evidence on the political battles fought over union rights in other countries; see, e.g., A. Wolfe, 1977, 140–45), Domhoff has now reversed his initial "corporate liberal" interpretation of the passage of the Wagner Act (see 1983, 145–46, 151). But if he concedes this hardly minor episode as a defeat of the united forces of business, it is not entirely clear how his approach can be said to differ significantly from that of the more sophisticated reformist pluralists, who also argue that business usually, *but not always* gets its way, which is precisely why they raise the possibility of a gradual "leftward drift" (see, e.g., Lindblom 1977, 143, 180). At any rate, all this only reinforces the more fundamental criticisms of Domhoff's approach that follow.

favored a particular reform and what portion was opposed, what the balance of resources was between the two camps, what the position of labor was, whether it was split, and in approximately what proportions, or united, what the electoral salience of the issues was, and so on. Only with this kind of evidence could one verify the hypothesis that big business has imposed reform on not-so-big business while the position of labor and the electorate was of little consequence. Moreover, Domhoff's case is weaker still if he wishes to show "how the ruling class, through the power elite, is able to impose its policies and ideologies *in opposition to* the leaders of various strata of the non-propertied, wage-earning class" (1979, 16, emphasis added), since he has no evidence to show that there ever *was* such opposition. In fact, although he is never very clear about it, all his case studies suggest that labor leaders were generally in agreement with the moderate proposals (even though they no doubt would have liked farther-going reform even better) because they thought they were settling for the best they could get, given ultraconservative opposition.

All Domhoff has shown, then, is that even those reforms most repugnant to business did enjoy the support of at least *some* wealthy individuals, some of whom were of distinctly patrician background. By such criteria, as Skocpol (1980, 163) pointedly remarks, even Marxism could be discredited as merely a capitalist ploy, since Friedrich Engels was, after all, a very wealthy textile manufacturer from a very wealthy family![8] Of course, Biddle and the others were not exactly a bunch of raving socialists, and it is reasonable to suppose that their wealth and background might predispose them to a relatively

8   In this connection, consider the following bit of curiosa which accidentally came to my attention: John R. Commons, the Wisconsin labor economist and reformer whom Domhoff repeatedly mentions as a servant of the moderate power elite because of his links with the NCF and AALL, also happens to have been the "respected teacher" of S.H.M. Chang, author of the most blatantly Leninist text purporting to expound the "Marxist theory of the state" I know of (Chang 1931). Commons even wrote an approving *introduction* to that work (ibid., v–x)! Does this mean Leninism, too, is really a corporate liberal ploy to preempt even more radical change, or does it mean that Commons was really a Bolshevik agent who had deviously won the confidence of some unsuspecting misguided businessmen?

conservative stance. But for all we know they might just have been a few wealthy mavericks (perhaps precisely because of their contacts with labor leaders in those infamous policy associations!) who happened to play a role in what otherwise amounts to a resounding political victory for labor over business.

So far, I have mostly criticized Domhoff from the point of view of the "decision-making approach." I have argued that it is not enough to establish the upper-class credentials of some of those who have tried to influence political decision makers, and those of the decision makers themselves. One must also establish that these were, in fact, the salient factors that led to the decision, that is, that those upper-class credentials led and enabled the decision makers to impose decisions over the express opposition of, say, the labor movement or the electorate, on several significant occasions (see, e.g., Dahl 1958). But it is notoriously difficult to find satisfactory evidence for this approach (Domhoff 1967, 143–46; 1972, 30–31), although, to my mind, it remains ultimately indispensable nonetheless (and Domhoff has apparently come to agree: 1970, 1979, 1983). However, even Domhoff's "sociology of leadership approach" suffers from some fatal flaws.

Domhoff considers all top-level officials of institutions controlled by the upper class to be members of the power elite, "the operating arm of the upper class" (1970, 107). In practice, as we have seen, even ordinary members of certain upper-class-controlled organizations are suspected of being at least spokesmen for the upper class. This can lead to some curious results however. Many of the organizations he mentions count a significant number of scholars, experts, college presidents, and even labor leaders among their members and officers. Significantly, these happen to be exactly those organizations that figure most prominently in Domhoff's accounts of how the ruling class "shapes" social legislation. For instance, the NPA vice-chairman was an AFL official and its secretary a CIO leader (187). AFL president Samuel Gompers was the first vice-president of the NCF (224). Should Gompers be seen as a member of the power elite serving the interests of the upper class and its big corporations, too? Obviously, as Domhoff himself realizes (1979, 16), this would be stretching the notion of a power elite to the point of making it meaningless. But if labor leaders who occupy top positions in these organizations are not members of the power elite, why should scholars or college presidents, including the ones from the presumably upper-class-controlled elite universities, be?

This raises the all-important question of what Domhoff means by "control." He defines it unambiguously enough: "I will use the term 'control' to mean legal authority over non-governmental organizations and institutions. 'Control' will refer to what various members of the upper class have over most major corporations, foundations, and private universities" (ibid., 104). However, in practice there can be a whole variety of degrees of "control," which renders the term far more ambiguous than it might seem at first glance. Members of the upper class and corporate executives may sit on the boards of all kinds of organizations, and hence exercise *some* legal authority, but this authority is usually hedged in by all kinds of guarantees and safeguards protecting those over whom the authority is exercised. It is also limited to the extent that it must be shared with others, and these members of the "power elite" may often choose not to exercise their authority to the fullest to avoid open conflict with those others or to maintain the viability of the organization, especially in the case of voluntary associations. "Control," then, is a matter of degree, and in Domhoff's account it looks as though in many cases the amount of "control" exercised by the upper class over the various organizations is inversely related to the organizations' proximity to the political process (cf. Heilbroner 1970, 247–57).

In the case of the major corporations, power-elite control is not much of a problem. The majority of directors of major corporations are members of Domhoff's *social* upper class, anyway, and most of the remainder are corporate executives, supplemented by a handful of experts, college presidents, and the like. At any rate, one can safely assume that being a corporate director would tend to dispose one to be sympathetic to corporate interests, and it hence seems somewhat circular of Domhoff to insist that many of the college and foundation presidents on corporate boards are members of the power elite because the institutions they *come* from are also upper-class controlled (1967, 51–52).

The case of the major foundations seems pretty straightforward, too. Two-thirds of their trustees are either upper class (51%) or corporate executives (15%), while the rest are college presidents, media people, and professors, for the most part (ibid., 1967, 65). Besides, according to Domhoff, they are obviously dependent on the major corporations and wealthy families and individuals for funding. Thus "their independence from their rich donors cannot be underemphasized" (64). As a consequence, "sponsorship of a project by one of these foundations implies that it meets with the approval of at least some members of the upper class" (71). This conclusion is not necessarily warranted, though. For instance, a famous and avowedly Marxist study of the educational system in "capitalist America" seems to have been funded almost entirely by the Ford Foundation (Bowles and Gintis 1976). The member of the upper class who approved of this particular study would have to be rather a maverick indeed! One wonders how many other examples like this one could be found.[9]

The same goes *a fortiori* for the elite universities on whose boards of trustees members of the upper class sit and which are dependent on wealthy donors and the foundations. Domhoff is careful to point out that tenure "makes it difficult for members of the upper class to quash any but the most extreme of opinions with which they disagree" (ibid., 77), but he does insist that they have "control of the broad framework, the long-run goals, and the general atmosphere" (ibid.). One wonders what Domhoff means by "the most extreme of opinions." Again, it would no doubt be easy to come up with a long list of renowned Marx-

9   A recent study purporting to demonstrate how the Rockefeller Foundation's policies toward the social sciences between 1910 and 1940 were a key element in the "reproduction and production of cultural hegemony" serving "the interests of the ruling class" was partly funded by . . . the Rockefeller Archive Center (Fisher 1983, 206, 224, 225)! It could be argued, of course, that occasional funding of Marxist research is merely a ploy to conceal the real bias of the granting agency (see Berman 1983, 105, 121, 142, 159), but Domhoff sensibly rejects such absurdly conspiratorial interpretations (1986, 132) which would end up discrediting all radical scholarship except what was done without *any* support from anybody.

ist scholars, tenured and not-yet-tenured, teaching at the prestigious universities he lists (78; in fact, Domhoff himself is employed by one of them, the University of California). No doubt there have been many attempts to silence radical professors over the years, and the successful ones, by their very nature, we do not know about. But anyone in touch with the academic world knows that this has become very much more difficult in recent years, to the point where such attempts are so sure to raise a scandal that it may even be suspected that some professors whose jobs are insecure for reasons of incompetence have found a "radical" reputation to be quite useful. Under these circumstances, the upper-class control of the "broad framework, the long-run goals, and the general atmosphere" would seem to have diminished considerably. Similar arguments apply to the media of mass communication, despite the fact that they are largely or completely privately owned (see Hamilton and Wright 1986, 414–16).

Now for the policy associations that constitute the centerpiece of Domhoff's analysis: three business organizations are, according to Domhoff (1979, 73, n. 20), "at the heart of the national power structure" by virtue of their centrality in the network of social clubs and policy groups (72–73)—the Business Council (BC), the CED, and the Conference Board (CB). Of the three, the BC is clearly the first among equals, pretty much "the unofficial board of directors within the power elite" (72). The Business Advisory Council (BAC) was founded in 1933 as *the* vehicle of the moderate power elite. "Essentially a discussion committee of thirty to sixty leading businessmen who were sympathetic to the attempts being made by President Roosevelt to deal with the Depression" (Domhoff 1970, 190), it was intended to advise the Department of Commerce. After a minor row with the Kennedy administration over the council's exclusiveness and secretiveness, the BAC severed its semiofficial ties with the Department of Commerce and became the "independent" BC in 1962 (1979, 70–71). Membership is by invitation only, and in 1971 its 197 members were, "with few exceptions, the chairmen or presidents of the largest corporations in the United States" (Domhoff 1974, 100). Its members regularly meet with government officials, and although the precise amount of influence it exerts is hard to gauge since its activities are shrouded in secrecy, Domhoff maintains that although it may have had little impact in its early years (1979, 74), it has become extremely influential since the Eisenhower years (1967, 75–76; 1970, 189–90; 1974, 98–103; 1979, 70–75; 1983, 133–35).

Having been created in 1942 as the research branch of the BAC, the CED has a membership almost identical to that of the BAC, except that the CED now admits "a handful of university presidents" (Domhoff 1970, 124; 1979, 67) and makes use of "leading economists" as "research advisors" (Domhoff 1979, 67–68). The CED is mainly funded by the Ford Foundation. The apparently excellent work done by the CED's "hired economists" (Domhoff 1970, 190) has given the organization great influence on matters of foreign and domestic economic and fiscal policy, and it has supplied the government with considerable numbers of personnel for the departments and presidential commissions dealing with these issues (Domhoff 1967, 74–75; 1970, 123–24, 144–45, 189–91, 192–94; 1979, 67–69, 75–78, 83–85, 89–91, 105).

On the membership and influence of the CB, finally, Domhoff has little evidence (1979, 69–70). It was originally a rather narrowly oriented business organization which drifted to an extremely right-wing position in the 1930s and 1940s, but "by 1977," Domhoff asserts, "when its president was selected by President Carter to chair the Federal Reserve Board, it was one of the most central and important of the policy groups" (69).

The other organizations mentioned by Domhoff are, by and large, irrelevant to the "corporate liberalism" thesis. They are policy groups exclusively concerned with foreign policy; the National Advertising Council (NAC), which promotes public interest causes such as Smokey the Bear, the Red Cross, the Peace Corps, the U.N., traffic safety, and Radio Free Europe (RFE),[10]

10   Significantly, Domhoff focuses exclusively on Radio Free Europe, and an assortment of upper-class members and generals involved in it, thus completely ignoring the other rather harmless-sounding causes promoted by the NAC. At any rate, even the significance of RFE for maintaining the corporate order *in the United States* is far from clear, unless one wished to argue that the USSR is in any way a threat to that corporate order. The very opposite seems more likely, not only because Soviet leaders have shown little reluctance to deal with U.S. corporate giants for mutual benefit, but even

and which has a majority of non-upper-class, noncorporate members on its directing committee (Domhoff 1967, 76); the Business Roundtable, a lobbying-coordinating organization mainly concerned with *blocking* reform legislation (Domhoff 1979, 79–81; 1983, 135–36), even though, according to Domhoff, it "is in many ways the lobbying counterpart of the Business Council" (1979, 79); finally, there are the organizations of the ultraconservative network, such as the NAM.

The B(A)C, CED, and CB, then, appear to be *the* major vehicles of the moderate power elite. There is no doubt that they are business oriented, avowedly so, in fact. They seem to be dominated by the nation's biggest corporations (although this is not clear for the CB), and they are no doubt quite influential. Thus, one would expect these organizations to have played a central role in the shaping of reform policy, as the "corporate liberalism" thesis predicts. In fact, however, they seem to have been rather unimportant judging by Domhoff's own accounts.

The BAC's "only real domestic success throughout the New Deal was its supportive involvement in the Social Security Act" (Domhoff 1979, 74; 1983, 134). However, Domhoff's use of this as a major piece of evidence for the "corporate liberalism" thesis seems rather dubious (1970, 213–15; 1974, 99). Again, he presents no evidence as to the *proportions* of the corporate community that favored and opposed Social Security, and there is reason to believe that the BAC represented a small minority at the time (Skocpol 1980, 167–68), while Domhoff himself admits "it had little impact on government policy during its early years" (1979, 74), and in fact mostly credits *other* organizations with the passage of the Social Security Act of 1935 (1970, 207–18). It should also be noted that the BAC, those "thirty to sixty leading businessmen" who were "sympathetic" to Roosevelt, was opposed to the Wagner Act (1979, 74–75, n. 23), which supports my suspicion that, in fact, virtually the entire corporate world was against it. Apart from these two instances, how-

more because the existence of an extremely oppressive but nominally "socialist" regime in the Soviet Union may have done much to discredit "fundamental" opposition in advanced capitalist countries (cf. Parkin 1979, 198–203).

ever, the B(A)C played no part in shaping the reform policies treated by Domhoff.

Similarly, the CED only figures once in connection with social-reform legislation. After a liberal-labor attempt to commit the federal government firmly to a Keynesian full employment policy after World War II had suffered a resounding defeat in Congress—even though it enjoyed "the qualified endorsement of two big business people from the CED" (Domhoff 1979, 111) which, had the bill passed, would no doubt have been sufficient evidence to discredit it as a product of the moderate power elite in Domhoff's eyes—the CED is credited with having inspired a more moderate proposal which passed as the Employment Act of 1946 (111–15). However, here too it is not clear whether this really supports the "corporate liberalism" thesis which maintains that the moderate power elite pushes through modest reforms to *preempt* more radical reform. It seems more likely that at the time no proposal more radical than that of the CED stood the slightest chance of being passed by Congress, judging from the "reluctant" liberal-labor support that it enjoyed (115) and the fact that Domhoff himself admits that the CED "*salvaged* the Employment Act of 1946 from its conservative NAM opponents" (1970, 191, my emphasis).

The CB, finally, does not appear at all in Domhoff's accounts of social policy formation, which is not so surprising since he only covers such legislation in a period when the CB was on the extreme right wing. Thus, *none* of the powerhouses of the moderate power elite, the B(A)C, the CED, and the CB, played a significant role in the formation of social-reform policy, at least as far as Domhoff's *own* accounts are concerned. The areas in which they appear to be most influential are foreign (economic), fiscal, budgeting, and other more narrowly economic domestic policies (1970, 123–24, 144–45, 190–91, 193–94; 1974, 100–02; 1979, 68, 89, 90–91). Although the BC *does* concern itself with labor, housing, and urban development (1974, 101), its influence in these areas is unknown, perhaps because of its secretiveness.

Which, then, *were* the power-elite-controlled organizations that in Domhoff's accounts were in large measure responsible for the passage of social-reform legislation? Three organizations get most of the credit: the NCF, the AALL, and the NPA. The passage of workmen's compensation legislation by most states between 1911 and 1920 is credited to the efforts of the NCF and the AALL (1970, 196–201). The NCF seems to have been the driving force behind the Federal Trade Commission Act of 1914, which set up the regulation of industry (201–6; 1979, 93–100). The AALL was deeply involved in the passage of the Social Security Act of 1935 and a whole series of (campaigns for) social and industrial legislation besides (1970, 174–76, 207–18). Domhoff depicts the Wagner Act as the culmination of a business-labor alliance that had been gradually worked out over the years by the NCF (218–49). The NPA, finally, was, together with the CED, a major force behind the Employment Act of 1946 (188–89; 1979, 109–15).

Now, on the basis of Domhoff's evidence I see no reason to doubt that these organizations were indeed instrumental in these reforms, except for one case. The relation between the NCF and the Wagner Act appears to be rather tenuous. For one thing, by the early 1930s the NCF had drifted "into right-wing hysteria and anti-communism" (1970, 169), and, in fact, "there is no evidence that the NCF had any effect on events in the 1930's" (ibid.). But Domhoff is arguing that the successful role the NCF played in mediating labor disputes and the generally cordial relations between labor and business leaders fostered by the organization *before* its drift into right-wing oblivion helped convince the moderate power elite to accept the terms of the Wagner Act (e.g., 242, 249). However, although the "ideological bargain" the NCF businessmen were willing to strike (224–25) apparently did include recognition of unions (where they were strong enough) and acceptance of collective bargaining on a *voluntary basis*, government-*enforced* recognition and bargaining as stipulated by the Wagner Act clearly went too far in the eyes of even the most liberal businessmen. Domhoff himself attributes the demise of the NCF partly to the fact that "following certain of the reforms of the Wilson Administration [!], NCF leaders had gone just about as far as they were willing to go with organized labor" (168). Besides, as was seen earlier, virtually the entire power elite was opposed to the Wagner Act, including the liberal BAC which had supported the preceding ineffective attempts to promote voluntary recognition and bargaining (Domhoff 1979, 74–75, n. 23). Thus, Domhoff's claim that the NCF had any relation to the passage of the Wagner Act appears to be unfounded, and the act does not stand up as a case supporting the "corporate liberalism" theory. Either it was a "fundamental" victory over business, or else not even the class-conscious "vanguard" of the capitalist class was able to recognize the eventual prophylactic effect the act was to have (Domhoff 1970, 249). In the other cases, however, the organizations identified by Domhoff no doubt played a significant role, although it is hard to say *how* significant in the absence of any evidence on the importance of other forces, notably labor.

What *is* in doubt, however, is the extent to which "they are organizations of the power elite" (ibid., 184). For on closer inspection the NCF, AALL, and NPA turn out to be somewhat different from the exclusively and avowedly business-oriented organizations of the CED-BC type. Thus, although the NCF (1900–1939) was "one of the first self-conscious, nationwide responses by big businessmen as a group to domestic unrest" (163), and although by 1903 its members included "one or more persons from almost one-third of the then largest 300 corporations, excluding railroads" (ibid.), it *also* included "many of the leading academic reformers of the era" (1979, 96), who are elsewhere identified as "liberal and socialist professors" (1970, 158),[11] and "many of the major union leaders of the day" (1979, 96; also 1970, 166, 224), among whom was, as already mentioned, the NCF's vice-president, Samuel Gompers. The organization clearly served as a *meetingground* to resolve business-labor differences by *compromise* (1970, 163–70). To what extent the big businessmen and wealthy backers could be said to have "controlled" the NCF in the sense that they clearly got a better deal out of the "ideological bargain" than the liberal professors and the labor

11   As elsewhere, Domhoff does not fail to point out that some of these professors had upper-class backgrounds (1970, 159–60, 171). This seems to me to be as irrelevant as Engels's antecedents, however. Although they were apparently not considered raving lunatics by some of the more moderate businessmen at the time, it is not at all obvious that they faithfully reflected moderate business opinion *ab initio*, i.e., there is no reason to reject the possibility that in the subsequent interactions they influenced moderate business opinion as much as they were influenced by it.

leaders, is far from clear. At any rate, there are no indications that the professors and labor leaders ever resigned in disgust because the NCF did not adequately represent *their* points of view.

Similarly, the AALL (1906–1945), although it had some membership overlap with the NCF and counted some big businessmen and foundations among its members and backers (ibid., 170–73), was hardly a mere front for business interests. In fact, the organization seems to have been initiated and pretty well dominated not by big businessmen, but by those same academic reformers, with "even a few socialists" among them (170; see, in general, 170–79). Again, there are no signs of liberal and socialist professors disgustedly leaving the AALL because of its probusiness bias.

The NPA (1941–), finally, is made up of "progressive business people, labor leaders and farm spokesmen" (1979, 110). It also must have included many academic reformers, however, since it was in fact the outgrowth of a decidedly avant-garde New Deal discussion group consisting mostly of "social science experts who worked for labor organizations and corporate research groups" (1970, 187), although "few of its members advocated socialist planning" [!] (ibid.). While the chairman was a big corporate executive, the vice-chairman and the secretary were from the AFL and the CIO respectively (ibid.). Although the NPA's relationships with the major foundations are apparently "close" and with the CED even "very close" (192), this does not seem to have so alarmed the few advocates of "socialist planning" and the AFL-CIO to withdraw from it. Domhoff himself seems to have some doubts as to the degree to which the NPA really *is* a power-elite organization. At one point he claims that the originally proposed full employment bill which was largely inspired by the NPA and the National Farmers Union, and which was defeated in Congress, "would have been a major victory for liberals and labor if it had passed in anything close to its original form" (1979, 109). It is somewhat hard to imagine why an organization of the power elite would propose such a bill, unless the corporate system was about to collapse under the assault of the militant masses, which apparently was far from the case since "labor and its liberal allies" finally accepted the very much watered-down CED-inspired Employment Act of 1946, albeit "reluctantly" (115). It is considerably *less* difficult to imagine whose victory it would have been, according to Domhoff, had the *original* bill passed, though.

Nor were the labor leaders and academic reformers merely passive onlookers in these organizations, deploring their pro-business bias, but staying in just to keep the "lines of communication" open. In fact, Domhoff's treatments of reform legislation abound with indications that the liberal professors and labor leaders were very actively involved in the NCF-AALL-NPA drives for social legislation, even including apparently significant labor participation in the campaign leading up to the Federal Trade Commission of 1914 (1970, 203–4; 1979, 98).

There are further scattered indications that these organizations are qualitatively different from the "pure" business groups. In 1957 the NPA and the CED actually considered the possibility of a merger. However, the idea was finally rejected by both: the NPA wanted to retain its mixed character and the CED its pure business character for fear of antagonizing its more conservative members (1970, 192; 1979, 75–76). Although Domhoff presents this as evidence for the closeness between the organizations, it could just as well mean the opposite: the presence of noncorporate members means that concessions must be made. Similarly, Domhoff attributes the eventual decline of the NCF partly to disenchantment on the part of its business members, because "many felt constrained in an organization which could make pronouncements as a group only when labor and business members agreed" (1970, 168). In the AALL, finally, it was partly "the disagreement among its members over details as to the financing of the Social Security Act" (178) that weakened it and helped hasten its decline.

On the basis of *this* evidence, then, it is not obvious that noncorporate members participated in these organizations "on the ideological terms set by the corporate leaders" (ibid., 186). In fact, the picture that emerges is remarkably easy to interpret in pluralist-reformist terms. The NCF, AALL, and NPA appear to be precisely the sites where the process of "peaceful accommodation" between the moderate representatives of labor and business took place. When they reached a compromise behind which they could unite, they were able to overcome the resistance of the ultraconservatives in the business camp. In fact, they appear to have been effective only when, and insofar as, their positions could clearly be seen to represent significant portions of the labor movement and the business community. Otherwise, labor could, under certain conditions, win even against a united business elite (the Wagner Act), but it also often loses such contests. Generally, labor appears to be most influential on issues on which business is not firmly united, and it has helped to maintain such disunity among the capitalist class by regularly compromising with the more moderate elements of that class. The government appears to actively encourage this process of mutual accommodation by appointing the most moderate business and labor leaders to boards and committees that deal with business-labor relations (e.g., 230, 232, 236). The general picture on presidential commissions is also remarkably pluralistic. Members of the corporate community clearly dominate in certain issue areas, notably foreign and military policy and the more narrowly economic domestic matters on which labor does not appear to have expressed any clear-cut position or distinctive interest. Commissions on other issues are "more likely to be headed by specialists in the specific field" (1979, 89; 1983, 133), including labor leaders (1979, 87–93). Thus, while the influence of the corporate "power elite" may be grossly disproportionate in matters closest at heart, its degree of "control" is progressively diluted as issues move closer to those of greatest concern to other powerful interests such as labor.

Domhoff has attempted to deal with some of these points, but his answers are not, it seems to me, satisfactory. Thus, he argues that conflict within the upper class by no means warrants pluralist conclusions, because such conclusions would ignore a "prior and more fundamental ... function" of the state, namely, "the protection of private property as a system" (1967, 150). This appears to be a retreat to a functionalist position, now very popular among Marxists, but, as I try to show in the following chapters, wholly devoid of operational meaning. Also, Domhoff acknowledges various "restraints from below" on the power elite, but replies that the potential for unity is much greater in the upper class than in the rest of society. But since his entire theory is based on the assumption of persistent disunity within that class it is not quite clear what to make of this (151–52). At any rate, as Domhoff himself has begun to recognize (1983, 209–10), it mostly seems to be a matter of whether the restraints from below are seen as relatively significant or as grossly inadequate. And this, in turn, involves a value judgment as well as some evidence concerning the available options, which Domhoff nowhere supplies.

Once again, we encounter the "immanent" assumptions on which the argument seems to be based. Although by no means a doctrinaire Marxist himself, Domhoff, like his more orthodox colleagues, *assumes a priori* that more radical reforms would surely have been successfully imposed on the upper class if the clever preemptive maneuvers of the moderate power elite had failed. Only *this* tacit assumption allows him to treat reformist labor leaders, academics, and others as virtual conduits for and collaborators with the corporate ruling class rather than as responsible representatives of nonbusiness constituencies seeking to obtain the best policies they consider feasible in a less than ideal world. Yet not even Domhoff, who is obviously not consciously bound by any Hegelian ban on "utopianism," finds it necessary to discuss the alternative scenarios on the feasibility of which his judgment nevertheless unavoidably rests.

In conclusion, then, I have tried to show that Domhoff's evidence is simply inadequate to sustain convincingly the "corporate liberalism" thesis. This does not mean, however, that the theory is untestable, as is the case with many of the theories I discuss below. It is, however, necessary to apply more stringent criteria of proof than Domhoff has done. First, one would have to identify those institutions that can be expected to reflect the opinions of the biggest corporations *only*. With organizations that only count the biggest corporations among their members this is no problem of course. With "mixed" organizations it might be a matter of degree. If the members not representing the largest corporations are clearly a small minority within it, or do not assist in the formulation of policy, or represent only small fractions of their respective social groups (small business, farmers, labor), it might reasonably be argued that the organization probably represents big-business interests, but all this has to be *shown*, not *assumed*. If none of the above holds, one would need additional evidence to show that big business effectively "controls" the organization, for example, cases in which big-business members clashed with others and regularly managed to impose their views as the official position of the organization. Then one would have to establish what percentage (assets, number of companies, strategic importance) of the corporate community could be said to be represented by these organizations.

When all this is done, one would have to trace the positions on reform legislation taken by these organizations. If the big-business organizations consistently take positions more liberal than organizations representing smaller business interests, this might be considered partial validation of Domhoff's theory. However, at this point it is crucial to take the potential influence of liberal politicians and labor into account. Situations in which corporate-backed reforms pass with heavy and united support from liberals and labor (and the electorate in general, if its preferences can be determined) would not adequately discriminate between the "corporate liberalism" thesis and more pluralist views. Hence, it is *crucial* to find cases in which an (almost) united liberal-labor coalition (supported by public opinion, if possible) was opposed to proposals emanating from the moderate corporate elite. Of course, in such cases the moderate corporate elite is most likely backed by its more conservative brethren, making it difficult for the evidence to discriminate between Domhoff's theory and Miliband's broader "instrumentalism." Therefore, the ideal case would be one in which the ultraconservatives, the moderates, and labor each made clearly distinguishable proposals, which could then be compared with the final outcome to see which had the greatest clout. Of course, if the outcome was closest to the moderate position one could still interpret this according to the pluralist perspective, but a careful analysis of the economic strength, position taken, and credible threats made by each of the three parties would certainly help to determine whether the case better fits this perspective or Domhoff's. Again it would most likely be a matter of degree.

These are very stringent criteria of verification indeed, and no doubt they cannot be fully met, but the attempt must be made if one wishes to convince those who are not already convinced, which is clearly Domhoff's intention (see Domhoff 1972). On the strength of the evidence presented so far by Domhoff and others (e.g., Hewitt 1974; Skocpol 1980), one can only conclude that business interests are indeed better organized and better endowed with crucial resources than any other groups, that they are hence, no doubt, disproportionately influential in the public policy-making process, especially in areas with which they are most concerned, but that they are by no means always united nor all-powerful and that other interest groups, especially well-organized ones like labor, farm, and professional groups, do have some significant influence of their own, albeit by no means enough in terms of the ideals of equal democratic participation (not to speak of the grossly under-represented interests that are not well organized to begin with). Thus, if it is merely claimed that "governments are inserted in a structure of power in which capital plays a major part" (Miliband 1982, 99), then this is hardly earthshaking, or at least it would not be denied by a sophisticated pluralist like Dahl or Lindblom (see, e.g., Dahl 1956, 1970, 1971b, 1982; Dahl and Lindblom 1953; Lindblom 1977). Thus, the instrumentalist critique of pluralism may well amount to little more than an angry restatement of the fact that business enjoys a greater degree of influence than any other group, which is not all that different from reformist pluralism. The main difference between the two positions would seem to lie in the degree to which they are implicitly (dis)satisfied with the amount of reform that nonbusiness groups have so far been able to obtain. And this, in turn, is largely, as noted earlier, a matter of personal judgment and implicit assumptions as to the most likely alternatives (see van den Berg 1981). But other than this rather elusive difference of degree, there does not seem to be all that much of a doctrinal gulf between liberal reformism and "instrumentalism." It is perhaps primarily because they sensed this that Marxist theorists have sought to formulate an alternative theory of the state.

Marxist Criticisms of "Instrumentalism"

As noted, nowadays instrumentalism is relegated to "the prehistory of theoretical formalisation" (Laclau 1975, 96; see also Carnoy 1984, 128; Holloway and Picciotto 1978, 4; Jessop 1977,

357; 1982, 12–16; Poulantzas 1976, 64–68), having been made obsolete by the development of far more sophisticated Marxist theories of the state. The demise of instrumentalism has been surprisingly rapid. A little over a decade ago it was still the only respectable Marxist theory around. Today it is routinely dismissed as hopelessly outdated. Such is the speed with which Marxist theory has advanced in recent years.[12]

To appreciate fully the extent of these advances, it is useful to review briefly some of the arguments that have presumably rendered instrumentalism obsolete in such a short time. First, it is often argued that instrumentalism fails to refute reformism conclusively because it essentially conceives of the state as a neutral, passive instrument which happens to be at the disposal of the bourgeoisie. This conception, it is argued, implies that, given the electoral support and appropriate leadership, the state or certain parts of it could in principle be "captured" and effectively used to obtain anticapitalist reforms that undermined rather than strengthened the system. Such a reformist conclusion is simply un-Marxist (Clarke 1977, 2–4; Müller and Neusüss 1978; Offe 1974, 32–33; Poulantzas 1972, 245, 250; 1973b, 256–57, 263–74; 1975, 153–54; 1978, 163; E. O. Wright 1974, 80–81, 106, n. 8; 1978, 194–95).[13]

However, in the absence of any *additional* argument or evidence showing that *in fact* the state or any of its branches cannot

12   Chase-Dunn clearly demonstrates how deeply "instrumentalism" has fallen into disrepute by protesting: "I am not a vulgar instrumentalist" (1980, 506, n. 3). It is somewhat ironic, given its etymology, that the word "vulgar" should be reserved by so many Marxists to express their most heartfelt detestations! In this connection, see also Poulantzas (1973b, 257). Alford and Friedland (1985), in their presumably exhaustive survey, do not even *mention* the instrumentalist approach.

13   Block (1977b, 12) claims that Marxist critiques of instrumentalism are intended to *justify*, not to attack, "reformist socialist politics." Since these critics usually base themselves on the presumed lack of class consciousness and sophistication of the ruling class, he reasons, this implies that the ruling class cannot effectively control the state, and hence the state can be used against it. However, this is certainly not an implication drawn by the authors discussed here. Block does not seem to have fully grasped the "logic of structural necessity," which, according to the critics of instrumentalism, irresistibly forces the state to do whatever serves the long-run interests of the ruling class, irrespective of *who* happens to "control" the state (see Chapters 4, 5). The error is understandable.

be used for anticapitalist purposes, this sort of objection to instrumentalism will convince only those wishing to be considered "true Marxists." But some *do* offer additional arguments. Poulantzas, for instance, discovered a "flagrant theoretical inconsistency" inherent in the "simplistic and vulgarized conception which sees in the state the tool or instrument of the dominant class" (1973b, 256, 257). This flagrant inconsistency is that "the capitalist state is at once the simple 'clerk' of the dominant class and also a conglomeration of lots which are waiting only to become the prey of the working class" (257), or, as he puts it elsewhere, "an 'instrument' is at the same time totally manipulable by the person who wields it and entirely independent of him, in the sense that it can be used, just as it is, by someone else (the working class)" (1975, 163). But it is not entirely obvious where the logical inconsistency lies. The idea that the state can be, and generally is, used by one class as an instrument for the protection of its interests would seem to be entirely compatible with the possibility that some day *another* class might be able to seize control of this instrument and use it to protect *its* interests. Rhetoric aside ("simple 'clerk,' " "conglomeration of lots," "just waiting"), the point is, it seems to me, about as flagrantly inconsistent as it is to say that my typewriter, which I am obviously "manipulating" in the service of "bourgeois" interests as I write this, may someday be "wielded" for a quite different purpose, say, to write revolutionary tracts!

Unpleasant political implications and inconsistencies aside, the main objection seems to be that instrumentalism cannot adequately demonstrate the theoretical *necessity* of the fact that the capitalist state must serve the interests of the capitalist class. This is because of its essential voluntarism or "subjectivism" (Gold, Lo, and Wright 1975a, 35; Poulantzas 1972, 242–44; Therborn 1976, 1978, 129–61). Like pluralists, "instrumentalist writers tend to see social causes simply in terms of the strategies and actions of individuals and groups" without paying any attention to "how the strategies and actions of ruling class groups are limited by impersonal, structural causes" (Gold, Lo, and Wright 1975a, 35). In all advanced capitalist countries there has been a *persistent* pattern of social reforms ultimately benefiting the capitalist class as a whole by helping to maintain the existing social relations, regardless of how radical those reforms may have seemed when they were implemented. Such a systematic pattern just cannot be plausibly "reduced to a kind of voluntarism on the part of powerful people" (ibid.). To explain the pattern as a result of the disproportionate influence of the capitalist class on policy formation, one would have to attribute a wholly unrealistic degree of omniscience and omnipotence to the members of this class (E. O. Wright 1978, 231, n. 8; also Block 1977a, b; Esping-Andersen, Friedland, and Wright 1976).

As a matter of fact, the critics claim, the short-term pressures of competition, conflicts of interest, and the like render the capitalist bourgeoisie extremely divided and fragmented, generally incapable of articulating the long-term interests of the *class as a whole*. In addition, instrumentalism is unable to show that such consensus as is occasionally reached by the members of the class, or a powerful fraction thereof, actually does reflect such *class* interests, rather than merely their short-term, parochial group interests. If such interest groups were regularly able to impose *their* short-term interests over and against the interests of the class as a whole, this would probably end up wrecking the system rather than helping to maintain it. Thus, the capitalist class, since it cannot be counted on regularly to recognize its own long-term interests, needs an outside force that it cannot completely control to secure the preservation of the system: the capitalist state—hence the frequent phenomenon of the state imposing reform despite the united opposition of business or its most powerful fractions, which instrumentalism is unable to explain (Cuneo 1980, 44–45; Flacks and Turkel 1978, 101; Lindsey 1980, 21, 27; Mollenkopf 1975; Müller and Neusüss 1978; Offe 1974, 33–35, 55, n. 9, 11; Poulantzas 1973b, 284–85; 1978, 11–14, 180–89; Therborn 1976, 12; 1978, 148).

The demise of instrumentalism began with the widely noted polemic between Ralph Miliband and Nicos Poulantzas in the pages of the *New Left Review*, starting with a critical review of Miliband's *The State in Capitalist Society* by Poulantzas in 1969 (Poulantzas 1972, originally in *NLR* 58, November-December 1969). According to Poulantzas, Miliband's procedure of simply confronting bourgeois ideologies with "the facts" may serve as a healthy antidote to those ideologies, but it remains fundamentally and dangerously flawed if it is not explicitly grounded in a theoretical, scientific Marxist perspective replacing the conceptual framework of bourgeois theory. Failing to develop such a theoretical foundation, Miliband cannot transcend the bourgeois "problematic," which leads him "to attack bourgeois ideologies of the State whilst placing himself on their own terrain" (Poulantzas 1972, 241).

Miliband's approach, Poulantzas tells us, suffers from a serious lack of epistemological sophistication, for "the analyses of modern epistemology show that it is never possible simply to oppose 'concrete facts' to concepts, but that these must be attacked by other parallel concepts situated in a different problematic. For it is only by means of these new concepts that the old notions can be confronted with 'concrete reality' " (ibid., 241). Thus, it is necessary to subject the ideological notions of one's adversary to a thorough preliminary critique before one can usefully appeal to "the facts." One can only ignore these precepts of "modern epistemology" at the risk of "floundering in the swamp" of the adversary's "ideological imagination, thus missing a scientific explanation of the 'facts' " (ibid.). In fact, "in the extreme case, one can be unconsciously and surreptitiously contaminated by the very epistemological principles of the adversary" (241–42).

Miliband, it seems, is such an extreme case. He constantly attempts to reduce the concepts of scientific Marxism to matters of motivation of conduct and interpersonal relations of "subjects," apparently unaware that scientific Marxism sees "social classes and the State as *objective structures*, and their relations as an *objective system of regular connections*, a structure and a system whose agents, 'men', are in the words of Marx, 'bearers' of it— *träger*" (ibid., 242). Thus, also, Miliband fails to convey that "the relation between the bourgeois class and the State is an *objective relation*. This means that if the *function* of the State in a determinate social formation and the *interests* of the dominant class in this formation *coincide*, it is by reason of the system itself: the direct participation of the members of the ruling class in the State apparatus is not the *cause* but the *effect*, and moreover a chance and contingent one, of this objective coincidence" (245). Furthermore, and very much contrary to Miliband's argument, "it can be said that the capitalist State best serves the interests of the capitalist class only when the members of this class do not participate directly in the State apparatus, that is to say when the *ruling class* is not the *politically governing class*" (246). Finally, Poulantzas goes on to expound his celebrated notion of the "relative autonomy" of the capitalist state, which results from the fact that "this State can only truly serve the ruling class in so far as it is relatively autonomous from the diverse fractions of this class, precisely in order to be able to organize the hegemony of the whole of this class" (247).

Poulantzas's own "problematic" is further explained in the next chapter, but the above quotations should at least convey the enormous "scientific rigour" Miliband was up against. Nevertheless, in his reply (Miliband 1972, originally in *NLR* 59, January-February 1970), Miliband stubbornly maintains that "there *are* concepts of bourgeois social science which can be used for critical as well as for apologetic purposes" (Miliband 1972, 255), and that he was concerned to show the deficiencies of the democratic-pluralist view "in the only way in which this seems to me to be possible, namely in empirical terms" (254). As if this was not enough, he also launched a counterattack against Poulantzas's "structural super-determinism" (259).

Almost two years later the counterattack continued with Miliband's review of Poulantzas's *Political Power and Social Classes*, which had just appeared in English. He now accused Poulantzas of "structuralist abstractionism" and of "an absurdly exaggerated fear of empiricist contamination" (Miliband 1973, 84), among other things. However, it was already apparent that Miliband's original position was starting to crumble, for in the same article he acknowledges the legitimacy of the notion of the "relative autonomy" of the capitalist state, although he insists that this is only the beginning of a valid Marxist approach. In a much-quoted passage, he argues that the famous formula from the *Communist Manifesto* about the state being "but a committee for managing the *common* affairs of the *whole* bourgeoisie" should be interpreted to mean that "the state acts *on behalf* of the dominant 'ruling' class," but not necessarily "*at the behest* of that class" (85, n. 4; also Miliband 1975, 316; 1977, 74).[14]

14   Overwhelmed by the anti-instrumentalist tidal wave Miliband is apparently forced to ignore temporarily his own stricture that "there is a limit to what

Perhaps encouraged by this partial victory as well as by endorsements from other Marxists for his defense of the principles of "modern epistemology" against Miliband's inability to vacate "the positivistic terrain of the pluralists" (Kesselman 1983, 830; see also Laclau 1975),[15] Poulantzas endeavored for one last time to warn against the "absence of any theoretical problematic" in Miliband's writings (Poulantzas 1976, 64), and to expose the latter's "demagogy of common sense," and that of the "dominant 'Anglo-Saxon culture' " in general, which "is constitutively imbued, and not by accident, with a prodigious degree of empiricism" (65). Miliband's "empirical and neo-positivist approach" only yields "narrative descriptions, along the lines of 'that is the way it is', recalling powerfully to mind the kind of 'abstractionist empiricism' that Wright Mills spoke of" (67). Paradoxically, Poulantzas emphasizes, it is *his* position that has been significantly developed and modified as a result of the *empirical* developments since 1968, while Miliband's position has apparently remained unaffected by "the facts." But then again, this is not so surprising, Poulantzas claims, for "it is this noisy illusion of the evident that gives rise to immutable dogmas" (68).

This last judgment is perhaps a bit too harsh, though. In fact, by 1977 Miliband had come to realize that to depict the state as "the 'instrument' of the 'ruling' class" is clearly "misleading" because it obscures "what has come to be seen as a crucial property of the state, namely its *relative autonomy* from the 'ruling class' and from civil society at large" (1977, 74). His position now seems to be that his own earlier instrumentalist arguments *and* the "structural" view *together* constitute the Marxist answer to the question of why the state serves the long-term interests of the bourgeoisie (66–74), although taken separately neither has yet been "adequately theorized" (68). Apparently, the capitalist class is able to impose its views on the state except when it is too shortsighted to recognize its own long-term interests. In

can properly be squeezed out of a paragraph, a phrase, an allusion or a metaphor"(1977, 2).

15 It has now become routine to credit Poulantzas with having been right in his debate with Miliband even, or perhaps especially, by those who show little understanding of what exactly the debate was about (see, e.g., Alford and Friedland 1985, 278; Carnoy 1984, 104–7, 214).

such cases the state temporarily becomes "relatively autonomous" from bourgeois influence so that it can impose the necessary reforms. However, to ensure that the state does not
abuse this temporarily enlarged space to maneuver, there is an
undisclosed number of " 'structural constraints' which . . . beset
any government working within the context of a particular
mode of production" (73). Regrettably, Miliband does not further specify the nature of these "structural constraints," however. Nevertheless, he seems to have come a long way toward
meeting Poulantzas's objections (see also Miliband 1983).[16] Although Domhoff, too, has been criticized along similar lines
(e.g., Block 1977a, 1978b; Esping-Andersen, Friedland, and
Wright 1976; Gold, Lo, and Wright 1975a; Mollenkopf 1975),
he has shown no such theoretical flexibility, stubbornly sticking
to his blatantly empiricist ways (Domhoff 1972, 1976, 1978,
140–45; 1979, 57–58, 122–24; 1983, 211–16).[17]

Another influential critic of instrumentalism, particularly
among American Marxists (see, e.g., Gold, Lo, and Wright
1975b; O'Connor 1973; Weiner 1980; A. Wolfe 1977; E. O.
Wright 1978), is Claus Offe. Offe takes it for granted that the
"objective complementary relationship between economic and
political power" in capitalist societies justifies Engels's description of the state as the "ideal collective capitalist" (1974, 31). He

16   However, in a more recent work, depicting British "capitalist democracy" as
a system for "the containment of pressure from below" and "the management of class conflict," Miliband seems to have returned to his old instrumentalist ways. Although he does accept the idea that, in order to "maintain the stability of the social system" governments may occasionally have to
do things "which are not to the liking of large sections or even the whole of
the capitalist class" (1982, 7), and he does make some passing references to
the "relative autonomy" of the state (95, 99), there is no mention of Poulantzas or any of the other Marxist "structural" theorists of the state, and his
main explanations for the coincidence of government policy and capitalist-
class interests are once again such things as the upper-class origins of civil
servants and politicians, the control of capital over the economy and mass
media, and so on (ibid. and *passim*).

17   Although even Domhoff has apparently been somewhat intimidated by the
onslaught of highly "theorized" attacks on instrumentalism. After—quite
rightly as will be seen in the chapters below—criticizing the critics of the instrumentalist approach for simply equating capitalist-class rule with the
continued existence of capitalism, and for equating working-class consciousness with Marxism by definition, he hastens to add that this "is not meant as
a criticism of Marxist theoretical work" since the authors of that work "explore other questions" than he (Domhoff 1983, 212).

is concerned to show "that the State, although not itself a capitalist, nevertheless must be understood as a capitalist State—and not, for example, merely as a 'State in capitalist society' " (ibid.), as suggested in "the significantly watered down title of the book by R. Miliband, which evades the problems" that Offe wishes to tackle (55, n. 3). These problems concern the "mechanisms which guarantee" the class character of the capitalist state (31).

There are, according to Offe, "two false, or at least inadequate, interpretations" (31) which he calls "Influence Theories" and their reverse, namely "Constraint Theories." The former are clearly identical to what is referred to here as instrumentalism (32). What Offe means by "Constraint Theories," however, is less clear. Apparently, this group of theories "emphasizes practically only the reverse side of the basic argument employed by the Influence Theories. They insist that there is factual evidence of a structural limitation to the possible courses of action, of the lack of sovereignty of political institutions and processes, and they point to the ineffectiveness of possible regulation and intervention measures" (32). Thus, it appears that "Constraint Theories are based on the assumption that the institutions of the political system cannot effectively become the instrument of *any non-capitalist interest* whatsoever" (ibid.). However, only a few lines after that Offe claims that *both* kinds of theory "imply the assumption of the neutrality of the State apparatus as an instrument which, according to its internal structure, could in principle also be used to implement other interests" (32–33). Since Offe also does not provide any references to literature presenting Constraint Theories, it is somewhat difficult to fathom what he has in mind. I can only guess that he is referring to theories that emphasize the separation of the economic and political realms as a characteristic feature of capitalist societies, rendering it impossible for the state to intervene "fundamentally" in the economy (e.g., Giddens 1973; Holloway and Picciotto, eds. 1978; Parkin 1971), or more orthodox economic determinism as advocated by some of the contributors to the German "state derivation" debate (cf. Jessop 1982, 107).[18]

18   At least this is what the only slightly less obscure original German text, which contains a fleeting reference to the notion of a "welfare-state illusion" ("*Sozial-Staatsillusion*") (Offe 1972c, 68), criticized by Müller and Neusüss

In any case, although Offe grants the empirical validity of these theories, he claims that they cannot "be made use of to prove the *class-character* of the State" because they "stick themselves to a pluralistic model of policy-analysis," which only enables them "to state that within the plurality of political forces there is an enormous empirical preponderance of those which represent and implement interests oriented toward the process of accumulation" (1974, 33). What they are unable to do is "to demonstrate the *structural necessity* of this state of affairs" (ibid.).

This inability is, according to Offe, the result of two major flaws in instrumentalist theories. First, there is a "confusion of *empirical* interest-*groups* and the concept of *class-interest*" (ibid.). Even if it can be shown that certain policies were implemented largely because of successful pressures from certain capitalist interests, it must be demonstrated that they "really do have a *class-interest* quality, i.e. that they are more than simply the expression of particular and situation-bound *special interests*" (ibid.). Class interest, as opposed to special interest or "false consciousness," Offe argues, "clearly presupposes that the definition of interests possesses a degree of 'rationality' cleansed of situational and particular coincidences and divergencies" (ibid.). However, market competition, the short-term strategic orientation dictated by the need for economic survival, and the broad scope of many political issues, which all severely limit the relative "scope of action and interest" of the "individual accumulating unit," render it "extremely unlikely that such a standardized concept of capitalist class-interest would emerge" (ibid.). Even when the capitalist class is upon occasion able to present a united position, this still "says nothing about its *long term* rationality, i.e. its permanent consistency with the interest of the ruling class" (34).

In addition, there are many empirical cases that are inexplicable within the instrumentalist framework. On the one hand, there are state activities "which in their *function* can plausibly be interpreted as being highly significant for the maintenance and the development of collective capital's conditions of accumula-

---

(1978), suggests. See also Carnoy (1984, 131–32), Keane (1978, 85, n. 54) and Sardei-Biermann, Christiansen, and Dohse (1973, 61).

tion," but that "frequently cannot be *genetically* traced back to the interest-orientated influence of groups or authorities advocating them" (ibid.). On the other hand, there are instances "where the content of political decisions and processes is manifestly contrary to the definitions of capitalist interests encountered empirically" (ibid.). In such cases policies "can be associated with the interests of the ruling class only very *indirectly*, namely via the roundabout way of *ex post* interpretations" (35). Here Offe seems to refer to policies that are unambiguously opposed by the "ruling class," yet turn out to be to its benefit in the long run. For instance, he mentions the legalization of unions which, he claims, was unanimously opposed by employers, at least in Germany, even though "there can be little doubt that the trade-unions have a stabilizing effect, that they are a functional necessity for the relatively conflict-free maintaining of capitalist production relationships" (55, n. 11).[19]

All this, Offe maintains, suggests an alternative hypothesis, "namely that the common interests of the ruling class are most accurately expressed in those legislative and administrative strategies of the State apparatus which are *not* initiated by articulated interests, that is 'from outside', but which arise from the State organizations' own routines and structures" (ibid., 35). Given the expected inability of individual capitalist interests to articulate regularly their common, long-term, "rational" class interest, the maintenance of the capitalist mode of production would seem to require a state that is structured in such a way as to present "itself to the particular and narrow interests of individual capitalists and their political organizations as a supervisory, tutelary force—at all events one which is an alien and sovereign authority—since it is only through the State's becoming relatively autonomous in this way that the multiplicity of partic-

19 Like so many other Marxist theorists, Offe apparently does not see the need for distinguishing between reforms that have failed to seriously *destabilize* "capitalist production relationships," those that have helped to *stabilize* them, and those that have been a *"functional necessity"* for their "relatively conflict-free" maintenance. Thus, *anything* short of the complete overthrow of capitalism, i.e., anything *not entirely* incompatible with its continued existence, can, *ipso facto*, be retrospectively "associated with the interests of the ruling class." The unquestioned assumption of an "immanent" alternative is once again clearly at work here.

ular and situation-bound special interests can be integrated into a class-interest" (ibid.).

The second objection Offe raises against instrumentalism has to do with the inadequacy of its concept of power. The concept rests essentially on "physical analogies," viewing political power "as a mechanically operating force" (ibid.). However, Offe argues, "even the repeated observation of an influence relationship does not allow an analytical concept to be derived regarding power relationships but at most makes it possible to generalize empirically. No proof of their necessity is gained in this way" (ibid.). For the concept of power to be meaningful in social systems, one must first recognize that it is a "relationship-category," that is, "one can only have power over something which according to its own structure *allows power to be exercised on it* and responds to it, which for its part so to speak authorizes the exercise of power" (ibid.). This, in turn, "means that a power relationship can exist between two social sub-systems only when their structures display a minimum of reciprocity or complementarity. Any proof of the 'capitalist' class-bound character of a State governance organization therefore stands or falls by whether it can uncover structural analogies between the State and the capitalist economy" (ibid.).

Now, the previously demonstrated necessity for the state to confront the individual capitalists and their political organizations as an "alien force" renders it difficult to uncover such structural analogies. This leads Offe to conclude that "one must ask which *internal structures* within the political system guarantee the implementability of initiatives and interests arising from the process of accumulation" (ibid., 35–36). Thus, "one can speak of a 'capitalist State' or an 'ideal collective capitalist' only when it has been successfully proved that the *system of political institutions displays its own class-specific selectivity corresponding to the interests of the accumulation of capital*" (36).

If I understand this second point correctly (the German original is of little help here; see Offe 1972c, 72–74), it appears to me to be plainly nonsensical. Offe seems to point out, no doubt correctly, that subject A can only influence the behavior of subject B if A is in a position to give or withhold something that is of value to B. This is hardly a brilliant new discovery (see, e.g.,

Crozier 1964, 61–142). In addition, Offe seems to be saying that for such a power relationship to "gain necessity" there must be elements in the "structural" makeup of B that make B value the things that A is in a position to give or withhold. If this is all Offe means by "a minimum of reciprocity and complementarity" between the "structures" of the "social sub-systems," I can see no reason to object, except for the superfluous and unnecessarily obscure "systemic" jargon and the somewhat strange notion of "necessity."

But this conception of power is exactly the one employed in the instrumentalist approach. It is based precisely on some such "structural complementarity": because of the very "structure" of the political system (governmental dependence on the favor of the electorate; dependence of top officials on the favorable attitude of the corporate world for effective policy execution and future career possibilities in the private sector, etc.), political decision makers highly value certain outcomes (economic prosperity and electoral success), the occurrence of which is strongly dependent on the actions and attitudes of the capitalist class (which finances electoral campaigns, controls the media, can cause economic havoc by refusing to invest, etc.). Such are the "structural analogies between the State and the capitalist economy,"[20] which according to the instrumentalist view ensure that public policy remains within the range acceptable to the capitalist class. Thus, Offe's second objection to instrumentalism is quite simply misconceived.

Moreover, it is not at all clear why the fact that the short-sighted bourgeoisie needs an "alien force" to take care of its long-term interests necessarily precludes any "structural analogies" between it and that "alien force," and why it is therefore necessary to look at the state's *internal* structures to find the "mechanisms that guarantee" the "class-character of the State." But this obscure argument seems to be somewhat beside the

20   Offe's switch from structural "reciprocity or complementarity" to "structural analogies" seems a bit deceptive. The term "structural analogies" appears to imply that the state and the economy should somehow *resemble* each other rather than complementing or mutually influencing each other, although nothing in his argument suggests the necessity for such a resemblance.

point with respect to instrumentalist theories of the state anyway. The fact that the capitalist class cannot figure out what its own long-term interests consist of in the first place effectively precludes the possibility of any structurally anchored power relationship between it and the state that would guarantee that the state will act according to the wishes of the capitalist class *and* serve its long-term interests at the same time. So, leaving this whole nebulous point aside, Offe's principal objections to the instrumentalist theory of the state remain that it is unlikely that the members of the capitalist class can be counted upon to perceive their own long-term class interests regularly and that empirically there are many instances of policies that were either not initiated by capitalists or even fiercely opposed by them, but that nevertheless turned out to be necessary in the long run to safeguard their general class interests.

Another critic of instrumentalism, from a more orthodox Marxist standpoint, is Göran Therborn (1976, and a more elaborate version, 1978, 129–61). Many of his arguments are similar to those of Poulantzas and Offe. He accuses instrumentalists of remaining "within the framework of liberal political ideology and liberal political theory," thus "accepting battle on the terrain chosen by the enemy" (1976, 3). He points out that frequently "a certain intervention may very well go against prevailing ruling-class opinion, while objectively furthering or maintaining its mode of exploitation and domination" (1978, 148). Contrary to those approaches that seek to identify the ruling class by documenting interpersonal relations and ruling-class cohesiveness, this "frequent phenomenon" implies that "the bourgeoisie as a class, and its interests, are not identical with the identity or ideas of a particular group of business leaders at a particular point in time" (1976, 12). However, Therborn rejects the notion of "objective" class interests employed by Poulantzas and, despite vigorous efforts, not entirely transcended by Offe (ibid., 16, n. 68), as providing no more than "a spurious objectivity to essentially ideological evaluations" (1978, 146, but see note 20, Chapter 2). At any rate, the notion is "dispensable for most scientific purposes" (ibid.).

Therborn's main criticism, however, is aimed at what he calls the "subjectivist" approach to power: the approach that focuses on *who* holds power, that is, the subject of power. Pluralism and elitism as well as Marxist instrumentalism take this approach (1976, 3; 1978, 130–31). Against this he poses a "structural-processual approach" focusing on "society as an objective structured totality and on contradiction, motion, and change," in short, "the *dialectical-materialist approach*, embodied in the new scientific study of history and society founded by Marx, historical materialism" (1976, 4). In this approach, "the primary focus is on the historical social contexts and modalities of power, and the first question is: *What kind of society is it?* Then: *What are the effects of the state upon this society*, upon its reproduction and change?" (ibid.).

The first question is concerned with whether or not a given society is a class society. "If immediate production . . . and the appropriation and control of the surplus produced are separated among different role incumbents, and are not united in an individual or in a collective, there are classes" (ibid., 4–5). Once it has been determined whether a society is characterized by exploitative relations of production and is, hence, a class society, the next step is to inquire into the processes of reproduction of these relations, particularly as they are affected by state intervention. These processes may occur in a variety of ways. The basic flaw of subjectivism is that it focuses "on only a single possible form of the patterning of power—one, moreover, which is hardly the most important form in complex modern societies" (1978, 135; also 1976, 6). Alternatively, Therborn claims,

> the analysis of reproduction makes possible an answer to the question of how the different moments of the exercise of power in society are interrelated, even if there is no conscious, interpersonal interrelation. They are interrelated by their reproductive effects. A given kind of relations of production may be reproduced without the exploiting (dominant) class defined by them being in "control" of the government in any usual and reasonable sense of the word, even though the interventions of the state further and/or allow these relations of production to be reproduced. And yet the fact that a specific form of exploitation and domination is being repro-

duced, *is* an example of class rule and is an important aspect of
power in society. (1976, 6; also 1978, 138)

Thus, according to Therborn, rather than looking into the
interpersonal relations between elites, social backgrounds, issues, and decisions, as "subjectivists" do, the primary object of
investigation should be the objective effects that state intervention has on the reproduction of the relations of production and
domination. He proposes a typology of state interventions according to the effects they may have: state intervention may *further* (increase, extend, intensify), *allow* (maintain through actively solving crises and conflicts), *go against* (restrict a mode of
production, alleviate domination and exploitation, go against
the logic of capital accumulation without breaking it; this may
be necessary for the ultimate preservation of the system, but it
does indicate weakness on the part of the ruling class), or, finally,
break (help create new relations benefiting a new class) the existing relations of production (1976, 11; 1978, 145–48, 160–61).

By means of this typology one can objectively locate the ruling class in any given class society, without having recourse to
"subjective intentions and actions" or "objective class interests"
(1976, 12). "*The ruling class* of a given society is the exploiting
class of that exploitative system of relations of production furthered . . . by the content and form of the totality of state interventions during a given period" (ibid.; for a similar argument
see Alford and Friedland 1975). What we have here is "an objective social process," since "the rule of the ruling class is not
necessarily, and is usually not, expressed in conscious collective
decisions and actions by the class as a whole" (1976, 12). Thus,
the ruling class rules if it manages to reproduce the relations of
its domination through state measures, whether or not it directly controls them (1978, 161).

However, this raises the obvious question, If not through direct control of the state how *does* the ruling class pull it off?
Therborn's answer resembles that of Offe: the organizational
structures of the state have a (varying) degree of "class character" compelling them to produce policies that help to further
certain relations of production over others, although, at the
same time, these same policies may have different effects on the
class character of the state structures themselves (increase,

maintain, etc; 1976, 11; 1978, 144, 147). Similarly, his reasons for seeking the explanation in the class character of state structures are no less obscure than Offe's. At one point the argument amounts to no more than the flat assertion that to ask "*how* things are done that are done through the state" is to identify "broad types of state structures . . . in terms of their class character" (1976, 11). This seems hardly satisfactory. Elsewhere, Therborn essentially bases himself on the doctrinal authority of Lenin (1932), who interpreted the notion of a "dictatorship of the proletariat" to mean that a "proletarian state" would have to be organized in a way radically different from the "bourgeois state" (Therborn 1978, 25, 122–24).[21] Unless one is willing simply to take Lenin's word for it, this is, of course, not terribly impressive either.[22]

But a few points about Therborn's argument as presented so far seem to be in order: for one thing, Therborn's rejection of the notion of "objective" class interests is little more than a terminological subtlety. As I have argued before (see note 20, Chapter 2), whether it is "exploitative relations" or "class interests" that are "furthered" by the state makes little difference. The point is that one has to show in what sense government policy can be said to enhance them. With respect to this question, Therborn's typology of a variety of possible effects of state intervention might appear to be a step in the right direction. His use of it turns out to be somewhat disappointing, however.

Although the specifications of the various effects (further, maintain, etc.) remain rather vague (the descriptions with parentheses above summarize virtually all Therborn has to say by way of specification; see Therborn 1978, 160–61), they *do* suggest a more subtle interpretation of the position of the "ruling class" in advanced capitalist countries than is usually found in the Marxist literature. As we have seen, Therborn explicitly defines the ruling class as that class whose exploitation relations

21   As is so often the case in doctrinal disputes, Lenin (who, in turn, bases himself on Engels, whose authority, he claims [1932, 19–20], has been falsely invoked by the Kautskyan "opportunists"!) can be used to authorize the "instrumental" as well as Therborn's "structural-organizational" approach.

22   However, it must be added that Therborn is one of the few current Marxist theorists who has actually tried to identify the organizational features of the capitalist state that exhibit a capitalist-class character, rather than being content with a few unsubstantiated assertions (1978).

are *furthered* by state policy. The question, then, is whether, according to Therborn's own criteria, government policy has indeed furthered capitalist relations of production.

Therborn mentions a few examples of what he considers to be "furthering" capitalist relations of exploitation (1978, 160), and indeed some of them appear to fit the bill. Thus, governments in capitalist societies do usually pursue employment and economic policies that "open up new areas and labor resources for capitalist exploitation," and that aim at "actively promoting capital accumulation." However, these happen to be precisely those policies whose unambiguous class character remains a matter of dispute. "Bourgeois" economists prefer to call them "economic growth" policies, which do not differ in principle from similar policies pursued in the "socialist" countries. This may be another ideological ploy intended to deceive the proletarian masses, but the plain assertion, now very much the vogue among Marxists, that accumulation in general is clearly in the exclusive interest of the bourgeoisie does not seem to be based on much more than rhetoric either and is, in any case, rather odd, given the fact that governments are regularly voted out of office for *failing* to produce policies that promote "accumulation" (see Chapter 5).

As for Therborn's other examples, either they are not clear, or they have clearly *not* occurred. Thus, it is not obvious whether the "relevant class-specific apparatuses" in "the state and ideological system" have been expanded, nor whether the "national-bureaucratic or national-technocratic character of the state, as well as its pro-capitalist repressive functions" have been augmented in most countries so as to intensify "the exploitation or domination of the ruling class." Furthermore, arguments such as that of Braverman (1974) notwithstanding, *governments* have hardly been "actively promoting . . . capitalist 'factory despotism' " in recent years, and the evidence on "the surplus-value extracted from the workers" suggests it has *clearly not* "augmented" (see van den Berg and Smith 1981). I may be wrong on these matters (particularly in the ambiguous cases: it all depends on what you mean by "class-specific," "national-bureaucratic," etc.), but then one would like to hear some *arguments*, not just rhetorical allusions.

As for the *bulk* of public (or at least domestic) policy that has been pursued by governments in advanced capitalist countries at least since the Great Depression, a fairly strong case could be made for viewing them as mostly *maintaining* (solving conflicts and crises), and often *going against* (social reforms alleviating exploitation and domination, implemented against the opposition of the bourgeoisie) the prevailing relations of exploitation, not furthering them. Strictly following Therborn's own argument, one might conclude from this that in fact there *is* no ruling class in these countries, or at least that its position has been rather ambiguous for some time now, as the very pluralists and reformists he claims to refute would argue.

But Therborn, not entirely unexpectedly, is not inclined to draw such a disturbing conclusion. In fact, the whole preceding discussion is irrelevant because after establishing his fine typologies Therborn simply proceeds to ignore them. Like so many other Marxists, in practice Therborn considers *any* policy that has not clearly precipitated the overthrow of capitalism as *hence* serving the interests of *only* the bourgeoisie (e.g., 1978, 72, 220–40), and he merrily describes social democracy as just another form of "bourgeois rule" (209–18), oblivious to his own earlier distinctions. Thus, what we have is another of those rather unsatisfactory dismissals of reformism discussed in Chapter 2, which seem to be saying little more than that capitalist countries are indeed still capitalist. And once again, this appears to be based on an unelucidated assumption about the "immanent" alternative. Unlike instrumentalists, however, Therborn apparently finds this enough to designate the capitalist class a "ruling class," *whether or not* it actually controls the state. For the state can apparently contribute to the preservation and reproduction of capitalist production relations, and thereby serve the interests of the capitalist class, for reasons other than capitalist influence and pressure and sometimes even *in spite of* such pressure.

To conclude this section, then, whatever the deficiencies of the various particular arguments raised against instrumentalism, there is a common thread that runs through all of them.[23]

23   For a useful summary of all the supposedly fatal flaws attributed to "instrumentalism" see Balbus (1982, 89–93).

They all claim that the capitalist class is inherently incapable of consistently and accurately formulating its own long-term interests, that is, policies that are indispensable for the relatively peaceful preservation of the capitalist mode of production. In fact, policies that in retrospect turn out to have been highly beneficial to the capitalist class frequently could only be carried through over capitalist-class opposition. Nevertheless, the state appears to have consistently produced just such policies, the "proof" usually being simply the sheer endurance of the system. The question, then, is what causes the state to generate just these policies, rather than policies that cater to noncapitalist (majority) interests or to the narrow self-interests of the capitalist class as its members see them. The relentless criticism of the "instrumentalist" answer to this question triggered a succession of presumably increasingly sophisticated answers which I discuss in the following chapters in more or less chronological order.

4 Structural Functionalism Revisited (1): Structuralism

If "the decade of the theory of the state" has produced any major theoretical advance at all, it would be the widespread adoption of structural-functional approaches by Marxist theorists who have come to view instrumentalism as theoretically inadequate and empirically invalid. The central tenet of these approaches is that the state is compelled to fulfill certain "functions" in capitalist societies that objectively serve the common, long-run interests of the capitalist class, irrespective of the composition of state and governmental personnel and of attempts by capitalists to influence its policies. As Miliband puts it, "the argument is simply that the state is the 'instrument' of the 'ruling class' because, *given its insertion in the capitalist mode of production*, it cannot be anything else" (1977, 72).

It should be noted, though, that this approach is only *analytically* distinct from the other explanations since few authors employ an exclusively functionalist model. As we shall see in this and the following chapter, even the "purest" structural-functional approaches are at times contaminated by elements of other explanations. In addition, there are now several theorists who conveniently alternate between functionalist and instrumentalist explanations, thus easily "explaining" whatever the evidence may happen to be in any one particular case (e.g., Miliband 1977; O'Connor 1973; Weiner 1980). Advocates of the newly emerging "class struggle" approach (see Chapter 6) also display a tendency to fall back on the ironclad logic of structural functionalism when the argument so requires (e.g., Gough 1975; Whitt 1979a; cf. Potter 1981). Finally, there are those who, just to be sure, adopt all approaches at once (e.g., Mandel 1975, 474–99; 1978, 150–87). Such theoretical strategies would seem to amount to a bit of overkill, however, since, as we shall see, the structural-functional arguments are already perfectly suited to account for *any* empirical state of affairs and meet *any* contingency.

At first sight this wholesale adoption by contemporary Marxists of elements of structural-functional reasoning might seem a little surprising. After all, has not this type of argument been discredited once and for all as inherently, inescapably conservative (e.g., Gouldner 1971)? But perhaps Robert Merton was right after all when he wrote: "The fact that functional analysis can be seen by some as inherently conservative and by others as inherently radical suggests that it may be *inherently* neither one nor the other" (1957, 39). Whether this is a virtue or weakness remains to be seen. It is clear, however, that the original Marxian base-superstructure model—with its impersonal causal forces and a superstructure "arising from" and "corresponding to" the "requirements of the economic base"—may have some affinities with structural functionalism, as many authors have noted (e.g., Cohen 1978; Collins 1975, 22–23, 201–22; Elster 1985, esp. 27–37; Giddens 1981; Gouldner 1971, 354–70; Heilbroner 1970, 61–89; Stinchcombe 1968; Van Den Berghe 1963; see also Rader 1979, 179–83). Engels's view of the state as an "ideal collective capitalist" whose function consists of providing the preconditions for capital accumulation that the economic base cannot itself produce (above all the regulation and suppression of class conflict), which was later adopted by Lenin (1932, 8–9), is a clear precursor of present Marxist functionalism (cf. Offe 1974). Gramsci, although from a more Hegelian-dialectical perspective, argued that the function of the state was to safeguard the "hegemony" of the ruling classes by maintaining an "unstable equilibrium" in "civil society" through a combination of "coercion and consent" (1971, 5–23, 52–59, 148, 161, 182, e.g.; cf. Genovese 1967, 300–303). Gramsci's ideas have been particularly influential in the current functionalist literature.[1] Obviously, this type of reasoning has a long and re-

1 It seems rather far-fetched, though, to trace Althusser's decidedly antivoluntaristic and anti-Hegelian "structuralism" to Gramsci's "dialectical" conception of the relation between base and superstructure, which was clearly an attempt to introduce an element of voluntarism of neo-Hegelian inspiration into "scientific" Marxism (see, e.g., Gramsci 1971, 323–77), as Merring-

spectable history in the Marxist literature (for another example see Baran 1957, 93; see also Jessop 1977, 355–56; 1982, ch. 4).

No name has been associated more closely with the meteoric rise of the postinstrumentalist, structural-functional Marxist theory of the state than that of the late Nicos Poulantzas, viewed by many as "the most seminal postwar Marxist political theorist" (Kesselman 1983, 831) and certainly "the single most influential" one (Jessop 1982, 153; 1985, 5). His approach, it is claimed, "disposes of the simplistic notion that capital is an indivisible entity and that 'the ruling class' exists as the coherent agent of this entity" (Caplan 1977, 86). Unlike the old orthodox instrumentalists, Poulantzas "was able to tackle the pluralists on their own terrain, arguing that a class is not a group or monolithic entity, but expresses structural relations constituting a social formation as a whole. Thereby he was able to acknowledge that certain elements of the pluralists' arguments are correct— for example, that there are diverse, and often conflicting, 'class fractions' in all capitalist societies—without compromising the significance of class analysis" (Giddens 1981, 216). The primary purpose of this chapter is to examine the merits of this assessment.

For several reasons, however, my discussion and criticisms of Poulantzas's approach will have to be more extensive, more detailed, more tortuous, and more tedious than those dealing with any of the other theories treated here. For one thing, his approach, and particularly his widely adopted notion of the "relative autonomy" of the capitalist state, are, of course, based on Althusser's "reading" of Marx.[2] Althusserian "structuralism"[3]

---

ton attempts to do (1977, 143–44). Poulantzas, who has adopted some of Gramsci's terminology, is quite clear about the need to "purge" these terms of any Gramscian connotations before they can be fruitfully applied in a "scientific" (i.e., Althusserian "structuralist") analysis (1973b, 137–41, 197–201). Even Jessop, who is concerned to show Poulantzas was as much a Gramscian as an Althusserian concedes the tension between the two influences in his work (1982, 152–58; 1985).

2   Whether or not Poulantzas ever "subscribed fully to the Althusserian position" may be open to question (Jessop 1985, 81), but there is no doubt that his theory of the state, especially the earlier and most influential version, is entirely incomprehensible without some acquaintance with Althusserian terminology and style of reasoning, as will become abundantly clear shortly.

3   Althusser and his followers object to the label "structuralism" on the grounds that their approach does not consider *only* the relations between

is, in turn, a most ambitious and obscurantist attempt to recast Marxism in wholly structural-functional terms.[4] Thus, in order to be able to understand and assess Poulantzas's arguments at all, it is necessary to discuss their Althusserian origins at least briefly. Second, Poulantzas himself came to abandon some of his own erstwhile Althusserian doctrines for something more closely resembling the "class struggle" approach discussed in Chapter 6. This necessitates some consideration of the relation between the "early" and the "late" Poulantzas, especially with respect to those arguments and concepts for which he has become widely known and invoked. Third, it is worth examining Poulantzas's arguments in some detail because they exhibit in an extreme form some of the basic tendencies of all "postinstrumentalist" Marxist theories of the state. Finally, their sheer obscurity requires a lengthy and perhaps at times rather complex exposition, just to be able to follow and criticize what is easily one of the "most complex theoretical systems in contemporary Marxism" (Jessop 1982, 190).

But in order to guide the weary reader through the sometimes labyrinthine journey that follows, I briefly present an overview of the chapter here. First, it is necessary to establish what exactly the arguments are, so as to clear the way for closer scrutiny. This I try to do in the first three sections that follow. In the first section I have tried to present the basic outlines of Althusser's peculiar brand of "scientific" Marxism as clearly and succinctly as I can. The next section is a more detailed exposition of Poulantzas's application of this approach to construct his famous theory of the capitalist state. In the third section I review some of the criticisms by fellow Marxists of Poulantzas's

---

unchanging elements, or "*combinatories*" as they are called by "true" structuralists, but that it also views the elements of a structure in various "*combinations*" that affect the very nature of the elements themselves (Althusser and Balibar 1970, 7, 176, 216, 226; Poulantzas 1973b, 25–26). Nevertheless, their approach has become widely known by the label "structuralism" so I will continue to use it. At any rate, as we shall see, the above objection is a little "pedantic" (Craib 1984, 136) and of dubious validity at best (cf. Appelbaum 1979, 31, n. 23).

4   For some surprisingly intelligible summaries, see Appelbaum (1979), Benton (1984), Burris (1979), Callinicos (1976), Geras (1977), and Smith (1984).

initial, most rigidly "structuralist" position and consider his later modifications of that position in response to those criticisms. I argue in that section that those "modifications," Poulantzas's own claims to the contrary notwithstanding, are in fact so sweeping in nature that they amount to a complete renunciation of the initial argument. Therefore, to assess his most celebrated contributions to the recent Marxist theory of the state, especially his notion of the "relative autonomy" of the capitalist state, we must confine ourselves to the earlier version, leaving the further examination of the later, "modified" theory for Chapter 6, in which other similar approaches are discussed. Before doing so, however, I review some of the most basic weaknesses of the Althusserian approach in the fourth section, once again as briefly as possible. Then, finally, in the fifth section I set out to do what is the main purpose of this chapter, namely to examine and criticize Poulantzas's original theory of the capitalist state in order to assess the claims that have been made on its behalf, in particular the claim that it offers a Marxist theory that provides a better explanation for why and how the state serves the interests of the capitalist class than does the old "instrumentalist" approach. This is by far the lengthiest and most difficult section of the chapter so I preface it, too, with a brief overview of its main points. The last section of the chapter, finally, summarizes the overall argument and briefly discusses some attempts to test Poulantzas's theory of the state empirically.

Althusserian "Structuralism"

Althusser credits Marx with "the greatest discovery of human history" (Althusser 1971, 7), comparable in importance only to the discovery of mathematics by the ancient Greeks and the foundation of physics by Galileo (Althusser 1969, 14; 1971, 15, 38–39; Althusser and Balibar 1970, 153). What Marx did was to establish "a new *science*: the science of the history of 'social formations' " (Althusser 1969, 13). But it seems that Marx had considerable difficulty in extricating himself from all kinds of "ideological problematics"—especially Hegelianism—so that only his mature works (from about 1857 on) can be considered "completely scientific" (Althusser 1969, 34–35; 1971, 9).[5] Thus, Althusser has taken it upon himself to extract the "theoretical problematic" that implicitly and unconsciously guides Marx's mature works, by means of a "symptomatic reading" of Marx's texts, identifying the "silences," "lapses," and "lacunae," in the explicit discourse that indicate the concepts it needs, but as yet lacks (Althusser and Balibar 1970, 13–33, 50, 86, 143–44). Paradoxically, Althusser's technique of "symptomatic reading" consists of applying the very "theoretical problematic" to Marx's works that it is supposed to extract from them (ibid.).

Luckily, however, Althusser's profound epistemological breakthrough need not detain us here. It consists mostly of flat denunciations of anything Althusser does not like as "ideological" and of endlessly repeated proclamations of his own theory as "rigorous" and "scientific" (see, e.g., Althusser 1969, 183–84, 190–91, 228–29; Althusser and Balibar 1970, 35–41, 43, 87, 117–18, 132, 138, 161, 183). Since it has been quite adequately exposed by his critics as little more than dogmatic posturing there is no need to criticize it further here (see, e.g., Glucksmann 1977; Kolakowski 1971; Pedraza-Bailey 1982, 11; Schorsch 1983, 106; Smith 1984, ch. 4; Thompson 1978).[6] At any rate, Althusser himself has since repudiated much of it as a "theoreticist deviation" (Althusser 1976, 142, 161), and Poulantzas, too, has taken his distance from the "over-rigid epistemological position" in his early writings (Poulantzas 1976, 6).

Be that as it may, Althusser's principal aim is to refute, once and for all, any kind of reductionist interpretation of the relation between base and superstructure, whether it be economism-mechanism which views the superstructure as merely the

5   And not even all of *them* meet the rigorous criteria of Althusserian "scientificity." Subsequently, Althusser has come to claim that only two of Marx's later pamphlets (the *Critique of the Gotha Programme* of 1875 and the *Comments on Adolph Wagner* of 1880; see Marx 1977, 564, 581) "are *totally and definitely exempt* from *any* trace of Hegelian influence" (Althusser 1971, 94), which understandably causes Kolakowski (1978c, 486) "to wonder if Marxism existed at all in Marx's day, or whether it was left to Althusser to invent it."

6   Sica's description of Alexander's (1982a) position is an apt summary of Althusser's epistemology which consists of nothing but "the fond belief that science is science, ideology is ideology, and *real* scientists know the difference" (Sica 1983, 213).

passive "expression" of the economic base, or voluntarism-humanism which sees conscious human (or class) "praxis" as the ultimate source of all social change, or, finally, "historicism"— the Althusserian shorthand for all reductionist sins (Geras 1977, 254)—which reduces the separate evolutions of the base and superstructure to one single development of the social totality in "a single ideological base time" (Althusser and Balibar 1970, 105), subject to some single developmental principle or other.[7] As opposed to all these ideological distortions, what Althusser claims to have found in the writings of the mature "scientific" Marx is an entirely *"new conception* of the relation between *determinant instances* in the structure-superstructure complex" (1969, 111). This new conception unambiguously establishes that both the base and the superstructures possess *"their own essence and effectivity"* (100, see also 99–101, 106).

Although the "specific *relations* between structure and superstructure still deserve theoretical elaboration and investigation," Althusser claims that "Marx has at least given us the 'two ends of the chain,' " namely "on the one hand, *determination in the last instance by the (economic) mode of production*; on the other, *the relative autonomy of the superstructures and their specific effectivity"* (ibid., 111). Althusser's investigation of the links connecting these "two ends of the chain" starts by conceiving of the base and superstructure as so many "practices," which all exhibit formally analogous "structures" but remain nevertheless irreducibly distinct. A "practice" refers to any process in which a "raw material" is transformed by means of a particular combination of "agents" and "means of production" into a "product." But whereas all "practices," whether economic, political, ideological,

---

7   Kolakowski (1978c, 484) takes Althusser's term "historicism" to refer to any theory that would view culture, and thus also knowledge, as historically relative and would, hence, belittle the special dignity and infallible "scientificity" of Althusser's own "theoretical practice" as well. This is certainly not an unreasonable interpretation since Althusser does indeed use the term quite indiscriminately to denounce any theory that might possibly be used to question his own. Moreover, since Althusser does not bother to define the term anymore than he does any of his other key (i.e., endlessly repeated) "concepts," the two interpretations of it need not be incompatible. It should be noted, however, that at least in this one case the general confusion surrounding the term is not entirely of Althusser's making (cf. Nisbet 1978, 103–4; Rader 1979, 86–88).

or theoretical, are *formally* similar in this sense, they are distinguished not only by their respective "raw materials" and "products," but more importantly by the procedures and mechanisms of transformation they employ. Thus, the social totality consists of a system of structures that are all homologous "practices" characterized by distinct mechanisms of transformation: the economic, political, theoretical, and ideological "regional structures" (see Althusser 1969, 166–67; Althusser and Balibar 1970, 41, 58).

The notion of "structure" should not be confused, however, with observable social relations or institutions. Structures are, rather, thought constructs by means of which observable reality can be grasped scientifically, much as Newton's law of gravity is the intangible explanation for the falling of tangible bodies (Althusser and Balibar 1970, 181). In Godelier's words, structures "constitute a *level of reality* invisible but present behind the visible social relations. The logic of the latter, and the laws of social practice more generally, depend on the functioning of these hidden structures and the discovery of these last should allow us to 'account for all the facts observed' " (quoted by Bridges 1974, 163). Or as Althusser puts it, a structure "is not a thing, but the concept of a relationship, the concept of an existing social structure of production, of an existence visible and measurable only in its 'effects' " (Althusser and Balibar 1970, 180). But, he adds, this "does not mean that it can be grasped completely in any one of its determinate effects: for that it would have to be *completely present* in that effect, whereas it is only present there, as a structure, in its *determinate* absence. It is only present in the totality, in the total movement of its effects" (180–81). On the other hand, the structure is wholly immanent in the totality of its effects, which means "that *the whole existence of the structure consists of its effects*, in short that the structure, which is merely a specific combination of its peculiar elements, is nothing outside its effects" (189). But these structures *do* determine the whole of observable reality "down to the visible detail of the empirical phenomena—while remaining *invisible* even in their blinding obviousness" (181; see also Poulantzas 1973b, 115, n. 24).

Thus, Althusser conceives of base and superstructure as what he calls relatively autonomous "levels," "instances," or "regional structures": the economic, political, ideological, and theoretical. These constantly interact, each being determinant and determined at the same time, each enjoying an "effective presence" in all the others, constituting, in fact, each other's very conditions of existence. The overall configuration of mutually interacting instances is itself a "structure of structures," or a "global structure," with a "specific effectivity" of its own on the regional structures of which it is the complex articulation. This means that the regional structures can ultimately only be defined by their respective roles and functions within the global structure. Although each instance is autonomous in the sense that it is governed by its own structure, which cannot be completely reduced to any one of the other instances, this autonomy is only *relative* since it is in part determined by every one of the other instances and most of all by the complex whole that assigns it its function. This complex system of mutual determination is what Althusser means with his celebrated notion of "overdetermination" (1969, 101, 106, 205–6, 209; Althusser and Balibar 1970, 17, 42, 177–80). Thus, he claims, in contrast to all reductionist distortions, "the unity discussed by Marxism is *the unity of the complexity itself.* . . . the mode of organization and articulation of the complexity is precisely what constitutes its unity" (1969, 202).

Moreover, this in no way implies some kind of methodological pluralism in which the relations between instances are simply considered to be theoretically random or contingent. For the complex totality is "an *organic* hierarchized whole" (Althusser and Balibar 1970, 98), which means that one instance or another has dominance, in other words has the greatest degree of autonomy and hence the greatest "effectivity" on the others. This is a crucial point for Althusser: "Domination is not just an indifferent *fact*, it is a fact *essential* to the complexity itself. That is why complexity implies domination as one of its essentials: it is inscribed in its structure" (1969, 201). Thus, instead of being merely an indeterminate collection of instances, *"the complex whole has the unity of a structure articulated in dominance"* (202, see also 110–11, 113, 199–202, 205–6, 209–11; Althusser and Balibar, 1970, 97–100).

The economy may be the "determinant in the last instance" but it is not necessarily the *dominant* "level," and the basic flaw of economism is, according to Althusser, that it does not make this crucial distinction. Actually, he claims, "from the first moment to the last, the lonely hour of the 'last instance' never comes" (1969, 201). "Determination in the last instance" means that it is ultimately the economy that *assigns* dominance to one instance or another, possibly but not necessarily to itself. Hence, displacements of dominance between the instances, or changes in the "index of effectivity" of the global structure, are also not random but governed by the economy, "giving these displacements the necessity of a function" (Althusser and Balibar 1970, 99, also 220–24; Althusser 1969, 213). For instance, in laissez-faire capitalism the economy assigned the dominant role to itself, thus being *both* dominant and determinant, whereas in modern monopoly capitalism, characterized by massive state intervention, it assigns dominance to the state (Poulantzas 1973b, 54–56; 1975, 165–68).[8]

This whole complex of relatively autonomous, overdetermined instances constituting a global structure articulated in dominance, enables us, according to Althusser, "to think the effectivity of the whole on each of its elements" (Althusser and Balibar 1970, 187) without having to fall back on the reductionist Leibnizian-Hegelian totality which can only "think" this causality by reducing all "phenomena" to a single "essence," thereby forfeiting a full grasp of the complexity of the structured whole (166–67). "Structural causality" represents a whole new concept of causality, he maintains, which is "*contained* 'in the practical state' in Marx's scientific discovery," although Marx himself was unable to produce "*the concept* of it" (486). "Structural causality"

8   At the same time, however, following Balibar (Althusser and Balibar 1970, 224), Poulantzas repeatedly claims that the economic instance is determinant in all modes of production, the distinctive feature of *capitalism* being that the economy *also* holds the *dominant* place (1973b, 14–15, 21, 27–29, 33; cf. Jessop 1982, 173–77). Thus one might be tempted to conclude that the current dominance of the interventionist state has put an end to the capitalist mode of production! To make matters worse, Poulantzas also came to view "real socialism" (i.e., Soviet-type socialism), in which the state seems rather dominant indeed, as a form of capitalism (1973a, 29; 1975, 188–89; 1978, 60–61, 107–8)!

can "think" the "effectivity" of the whole without having re-course to some additional "essence," that is, without claiming that the whole is somehow fundamentally different from the sum of its parts. The individual elements ("agents," "means," and "raw materials") are combined in specific ways to constitute practices articulated in a regional structure and these regional structures together form the complex articulation that is the global structure: all this in the "real" sense that the higher-order structures *only* exist in and through the elements constituting them by their combinations. Yet, the order of determination is the exact reverse: the global structure assigns to the instances their exact function and effectivity with respect to one another, defining their very nature, while the instances do the same to the elements ("agents," "means of production") of which *they* are made up. Only this new concept of causality is capable of grasping reality in all its complexity without disintegrating into an atheoretical causal pluralism, according to Althusser (182–93, 241–53).

Thus, as opposed to economism, Althusser's position is that the economy need not necessarily be the dominant instance and that the superstructures always possess a certain degree of relative autonomy from it. As opposed to "historicism," his claim is that in view of his conception of a complex articulation of relatively autonomous levels "it is no longer possible to think the process of development of the different levels of the whole *in the same historical time*" (ibid., 99). Each instance has its own "rhythm," "meter," or temporality which causes constant "uneven development" among the instances and hence displacements within the hierarchy of effectivity. Each "conjuncture" (i.e., current situation) is therefore a unique and highly complex *"intertwining of different times"* (104), characterized by "the peculiar relations of correspondence, non-correspondence, articulation, dislocation and torsion which obtain, between the different 'levels' of the whole in accordance with its general structure" (108, in general 97–108; cf. Althusser 1969, 106–8, 179, 212–14; Poulantzas 1967, 1973b, 153–67).

Voluntarism-humanism, finally, is perhaps the worst form of reductionism. It tends to obliterate the very specificity and autonomy of theoretical practice itself, turning it into a mere byproduct of subjective proletarian consciousness and political "praxis." Thus it commits the unspeakable sin of ignoring the basic thesis of Lenin and Kautsky "that Marxist theory is produced by a specific theoretical practice, *outside* the proletariat, and that Marxist theory must be 'imported' into the proletariat" (Althusser and Balibar 1970, 141; cf. Poulantzas 1973b, 206). Voluntarism-Humanism suffers from the ideological "problematic of the subject," which erroneously considers "men" or social classes as conscious subjects, the creators of social structures. Indeed, as Balibar puts it with characteristic eloquence, "the 'obviousness', the 'transparency' of the word 'men' (here charged with every carnal opacity) and its anodyne appearance are the most dangerous traps" (Althusser and Balibar 1970, 207). For, rather than being the conscious subjects, "men" are no more than the *effects* of the structures, they are no more than "bearers" or "supports" of the places and functions assigned to them by the structures. If anything, the structures are the "subjects," or, as Althusser puts it, "history is a *process without a subject*" (1971, 122; in general see Althusser 1969, 36–37, 219–47; Althusser and Balibar 1970, 111–12, 119–44, 174–75, 180, 250–53; Poulantzas 1973b, 37–40, 66–77, 195–201).

Poulantzas's Theory of the Capitalist State

Althusser's nonreductionist "reading" of Marx at last "permits us to constitute the political into an autonomous and specific object of science" (Poulantzas 1973b, 29).[9] Poulantzas's procedure consists once again of a "symptomatic reading" of Marx's texts to uncover the concepts they contain in the "practical state." But because of the mostly circumstantial nature of Marx's political writings Poulantzas has also had to draw on certain "contemporary texts in political science," some of them non-Marxist, which, he finds, "sometimes contain, as scientific elements within an ideological discourse, authentic concepts," so long as these are "purified" by thoroughly "critical study," to be sure (19, see, in general, 16–23).

9   To check the accuracy of the following summary, please see the alternative expositions by Jessop (1982, 153–81; 1985, ch. 3) and Carnoy (1984, ch. 4).

Like other instances, the political must be conceived, according to Poulantzas, as an Althusserian "practice." The "specific object" that is "transformed" is in this case the "conjuncture," the historically unique "present moment." This "is the place where relations of different contradictions finally fuse, relations which specify the unity of the structure" (ibid., 41). But in addition, the *objective* of political practice is the political structure, that is, *"the institutionalized power of the state"* (42). This gives us the *"general definition of politics"* that is implicitly contained in the Marxist classics: "it is precisely the above-mentioned conception of political practice, which has as its object the present moment and which either transforms (or else maintains) the unity of a formation. But in this case only to the extent that political practice has the political structures of the state as its point of impact and specific strategic 'objective' " (43).

The reason the practice that is concerned with the maintenance or transformation of the unity of the social formation should be aimed specifically at the state is to be found in "the scientific Marxist conception of the state superstructure" (ibid., 44). According to this conception, "inside the structure of the several levels dislocated by uneven development, *the state has the particular function of constituting the factor of cohesion between the levels of a social formation . . . and . . . the regulating factor of its global equilibrium as a system"* (44–45). In other words, the state "prevents the social formation from bursting apart" (50). But since the state is the factor of unity of a social formation it is obviously also the *"place in which its transformations occur"* (45). This enables us to understand, according to Poulantzas, the two "basic propositions in the *Communist Manifesto*" concerning political practice: "(a) *'Every class struggle is a political struggle'*, and (b) *'The class struggle is the motive force of history'* " (37).[10]

The state's "global role" of cohesion, Poulantzas maintains, is intrinsically political because "the state is related to a 'society

10   The second of these "quotations," also quoted by Althusser (1969, 215), is
     nowhere to be found in the *Communist Manifesto*, nor, in this form, any-
     where else in Marx's or Engels's writings (see Thompson 1978, 103). It may
     be a minor point, but it is still an odd inaccuracy in what is otherwise easily
     one of the most "Talmudic approaches" ever to the "classics" (A. Wolfe
     1974, 141).

divided into classes' and to political domination, precisely insofar as it maintains, in the ensemble of structures, that place and
role which have the *effect* (in their unity) of dividing a formation
into classes and producing class domination" (ibid., 51; cf. Poulantzas 1972, 246). The specific economic, ideological, "social,"
and political (in the narrow sense of maintaining political order
in class conflict) activities of the state are all "overdetermined"
by its global function (Poulantzas 1973b, 53–54). That is to say,
"these functions are political functions to the extent that they
aim primarily at the maintenance of the unity of a social formation based in the last analysis on political class domination"
(54). Therefore, "these functions correspond *in this manner* to
the political interests of the dominant class" (ibid., also 287).

Although the global function of the state is always crucial for
the maintenance of the unity of the social formation, the state
need not necessarily be the dominant instance in the hierarchy
that constitutes the global structure. In current monopoly capitalism, with the conditions for reproduction becoming increasingly political and ideological, the global role of cohesion necessitates an increasing latitude for the state to intervene and
modify the other instances, that is, play the dominant role,
which is reflected in the state's massive intervention in the economy. In liberal laissez-faire capitalism, on the other hand, the
economy was both dominant and determinant "in the last instance" and this was reflected "by a specific *non-intervention* of
the state in the economic" (ibid., 55). The state's strictly political
function was dominant among its various functions (the "night
watchman" state). Thus, the state's function as cohesive factor
is neither synonymous with intervention nor with dominance,
which may or may not be required for the successful maintenance of the unity of the social formation (54–56; Poulantzas
1975, 81, 101–2, 165–68; but cf. note 8, this chapter).

Before examining the relation, as seen by Poulantzas, between the state and class domination it is necessary to say a few
words about his somewhat idiosyncratic conception of social
class and class practices as distinct from structures, without
which the rest of his argument would be completely unintelli-
gible. First, according to Poulantzas, social classes cannot be
conceived in purely economic terms. A "correct reading" of

Marx's political writings reveals the equal "importance of political and ideological determination in the construction of the concept of class," he claims (1973b, 58). Thus, "social class is a concept which shows the effects of the *ensemble* of structures, of the matrix of a mode of production or of a social formation on the agents which constitute its supports" (67–68, emphasis added),[11] that is, it is the *"global effect"* of the structures (63–66, 69, 75).[12]

However, social classes are not themselves part of the structures. Instead, they are located in what Poulantzas interchangeably refers to as "the field of class practices," "social relations," or "the class struggle." This "field" consists of a whole hierarchical system of "levels" parallel to that of the structures, that is, of economic, political, and ideological class struggles. Thus, according to Poulantzas, social classes "do not manifest themselves in the structures, but entirely as the *global effect of the structures in the field of social relations*" (ibid., 64). Being the effect of the matrix of structures, "the levels of class struggle are related in the same kind of way as the instances of the matrix" (69),

11   Poulantzas, like Althusser, makes much of the distinction between a mode of production, which "constitutes an abstract-formal object which does not exist in the strong sense in reality," and a social formation, the "real-concrete object" which always contains "a particular combination, a specific overlapping of several 'pure' modes of production," one of which is dominant (1973b, 15–16, also 47, 70–73, 77–84; 1973a, 32–34; 1975, 21–23). The distinction is not of great importance for present purposes, however, since "the dominance of one mode of production over the others in a social formation causes the matrix of this mode of production (i.e. the particular reflection of determination by the economic element in the last instance by which it is specified) to mark the whole of the formation. In this way a historically determined social formation is specified by a particular articulation (through an index of dominance and overdetermination) of its different economic, political, ideological and theoretical levels or instances" (1973b, 15), which is all we are interested in here. The term "social formation" refers, of course, to what is ordinarily called "society." But instead of that vague term Poulantzas prefers "the rigorously defined concept of a social formation as a complex unity of instances" (49).

12   Poulantzas's multiple criteria (economic, political, and ideological) of class determination have caused a considerable polemic in the Marxist literature, particularly when he added the distinction between "productive" and "unproductive labor" as an additional criterion (1973a, 1975), which tended to reduce the working class to a tiny minority in modern capitalist societies (see Lindsey 1980; E. O. Wright 1976, 1978, ch. 2; 1980).

meaning that they are relatively autonomous from one another and that one is dominant, determined, "in the last instance," by the economic class struggle (or "socioeconomic relations"), and so on.

But the relations between the matrix of structures and the field of class practices are extraordinarily complex, at times causing Poulantzas to apparently contradict himself. Thus, although he sometimes suggests that the relations between the levels of class practices are "as a general rule" identical to those between the regional structures (ibid., 66–67, 75, 85–86), he also claims that "the relations between these two series of relations are themselves relations of dislocation characterized by an unambiguous non-correspondence between the terms of the respective levels of these systems" (90, also 113). Monopoly capitalism presents a primary example of such dislocation in which the state is the dominant instance, but the political class struggle is (unfortunately) not necessarily dominant in the field of class practices (90–91).

Similarly, although class practices appear to have *some* autonomous effects on the structures (ibid., 95, 188), it is not clear to what extent they can really modify them. Class practices, according to Poulantzas, cannot be conceived as conscious behavior of "men," but only as the "effects" of the structures which impose strict "limits of variation" on them (95, 187–88, 230, 261).[13] "The concept of practice covers not behavior but an operation carried on within the limits imposed by the structure," he claims (111). But in any case, the main point here is that classes and their conflicting practices (the class struggle) produce relations of power and domination. "They define *at every level* fundamental connections of *domination* and *subordination* of classes (class practices)" (86, also 99).

Poulantzas defines power as "*the capacity of* a social class to realize its specific objective *interests*" (ibid., 104; see also Poulantzas 1978, 36, 147). This definition avoids the "various misinterpretations" (Poulantzas 1973b, 100) that are current in the literature (99–105, 109–11). First, "capacity" need not imply that

13   In his later writings, following Althusser's *volte-face* (Althusser 1976), Poulantzas completely reversed his position, now repeating *ad nauseam* that the class struggle has primacy over the structures (1973a, 1975, 1978).

a class must have an organization "of its own" to realize its objective interests. Since "power is obtained in the limits (*qua* effects) of the structures" (108), its "organization" can take on a variety of forms, sometimes hidden, sometimes "declared" (107–8). At the same time, the capacity of one class to realize its interests depends on the capacity of other classes to realize *their* interests. "In this sense," Poulantzas states, "power reveals relations not directly determined by the structure, and depends on the exact relation of the social forces present in the class struggle" (108).

However, this does not imply some sort of "zero-sum" conception of power which is "the basis of several contemporary forms of reformism" (ibid., 118). Being an effect of the structures, one class's loss in power is not necessarily another class's gain. Nor need the loss of power at one level of the class struggle be reflected in a similar loss at the other levels. Furthermore, the two-class model implicit in the zero-sum conception must ignore the fact that any concrete social formation always contains several classes and class fractions because of "the overlapping of several modes of production" (119; see note 11, this chapter). But most important, the zero-sum conception implies that the working class could conquer a "portion" of power from the bourgeoisie, which is a dangerous misconception (117–19).

Second, by the "objective interests" of a class Poulantzas means those effects of the structures that "are reflected . . . as an *extension of the ground* which this class can cover according to the stages of specific organization attainable by it," since "this ground extends as far as its objective interests" (ibid., 111). The objective interests of a class "appear . . . as the *horizon* of its action as a social force" (112). But objective interests also indicate "the *extension of the field* of the practice of one class in relation to those of the other classes" (111). This permits Poulantzas to make a distinction between "*long-term interests*" consisting of the "limits-effects of the structure" and "*short-term interests*" which are "limits-effects at one remove, imposed by the intervention of the practices of different classes (class struggle)" (112).

Freely translated, Poulantzas seems to define the objective interests of a class as the maximum that that class can get away with given the prevailing "relation of forces." These interests are objective, according to Poulantzas, in the sense that they are in no way affected by the "imaginery interests" that agents and even classes often fabricate out of the "numerous forms of illusion" produced by ideology (ibid., 113). Yet, such imagined interests cannot be simply dismissed as " 'subjective' limits" either since the ideological is as much a regional structure as the state or the economy (the relations of production), performing the functions assigned to it within the global structure, that is, imposing objective limits on the thought and discourse of the agents who are no more than "bearers" of the structures (112–13, 206–21).

The "specificity" of the objective interests refers to the relative autonomy of the levels of class struggle and hence of interests and power. These give rise to *"economic power, political power, ideological power,* etc."[14] The relations between these various powers "relate to the articulation of the various class practices (class interests) which, in a dislocated manner, reflect the articulation of the various structures of a social formation" (ibid., 113). This means that there is always the possibility of "decentration": a class or fraction may be dominant at one level yet subordinate at another (113–14; also Poulantzas 1975, 93, 110, 132).

But despite these complications Poulantzas "rigorously" defines "the dominant class(es) in a formation" as "in the last analysis, that which occupies the dominant place(s) at that level of the class struggle which maintains the dominant role in the complex whole of that formation" (1973b, 114). However, he does not make it clear whether it is the dominant role of that level with respect to the other levels in the field of the class struggle that matters *or* the dominant role of the corresponding structural instance in the global structure. As just mentioned, the former "reflects" the latter "in a dislocated manner," that is, they are not necessarily the same level. The examples that Poulantzas gives (ibid.) suggest that he is referring to the dominant *instance* among the structures. This would seem to imply that, as a result of the dominance of the political instance in contemporary monopoly capitalism, the dominant class is now the one

14   What the "etc." refers to is not entirely clear; "theoretical" power perhaps?

that "occupies the dominant place" in the *political* class struggle, in other words, is *politically* dominant. As we shall see, this is in fact what Poulantzas seems to be saying.

Finally, Poulantzas clearly intends the concept of power to refer to *class* relations only (ibid., 105–7). For classless societies he proposes the term *"authority"* (105–6).[15] Thus, also, although power is organized through such institutions as the state, these institutions cannot themselves possess power, they "can be related only to *social classes which hold power*" (115). Institutions function only as *"power centres,"* the state being *"the centre of the exercise of political power"* (ibid.). On the other hand, this does not mean that these institutions "are mere instruments, organs or appendices of the power of social classes" because they retain their autonomy and specificity by virtue of "their relation to the structures" (ibid.). Therefore, Poulantzas argues, one must strictly distinguish, as Lenin has done, between the *"state apparatus,"* which consists of its functions in the ensemble of structures, its organizational structure and its personnel, on the one hand, and *"state power,"* referring to "the social class . . . which holds power," on the other (116–17).

That a class holds state power does not necessarily mean, however, that other classes are precluded from being "social forces" at the political level. They can have a significant impact in the sense that their *"economic existence . . . is reflected on the other levels by a specific presence"* (ibid., 78), which qualifies them as *"a distinct and autonomous class"* (ibid.). By a "specific presence" Poulantzas means that the class has *"pertinent effects"* at those levels, consisting of "a *new element* which cannot be inserted in the typical framework which these levels would present without this element" (79). Whether or not any one such element can be considered "new" in this sense "always depends on the concrete conjuncture of a concrete situation" (81).

"Pertinent effects" must be clearly distinguished from power.

15   He also wonders whether "authority" would not be more appropriate than "power" to describe "non-antagonistic class relations in the transition from socialism to communism" (1973b, 105). If this is a reference to "real socialist" countries of the Soviet type one cannot help but wonder whether such a fine terminological distinction would appear very meaningful to, e.g., the Polish workers!

Thus, for instance, in the case of Bonapartism the election of Louis Bonaparte, who ended up abolishing parliamentary democracy, was clearly the "pertinent effect" of the small-holding peasants who elected him. Yet, although he was their "representative," he catered exclusively to the interests of the bourgeoisie, merely taking "measures of a *compromise* sort" to feed the "ideological illusion" (ibid., 244) of the peasant masses, as Marx demonstrated in *The Eighteenth Brumaire of Louis Bonaparte* (Marx 1963a; see Poulantzas 1973b, 79–81, 243–45). Another example consists of current cases in which the working class lacks any significant "revolutionary political organization and ideology," yet manifests itself at the political level by means of social-democratic and reformist organizations and ideologies (Poulantzas 1976, 69). In many such cases the effects clearly "amounted to quite considerable ones," enough, at any rate, to qualify as "pertinent effects" (ibid.). However they definitely do *not* qualify as manifestations of real power because "this economist/reformist policy is ineffectual from the point of view of the long-term strategic interests of the working class, from the class viewpoint of the working class: in other words . . . this policy cannot lead to socialism" (70).[16]

The crucial difference between "pertinent effects" and power can be expressed by means of the same spatial metaphor Poulantzas uses to explain his notion of "objective interests." Whereas the latter can be viewed as the "far side" or "horizon" of the field of action of a social class, "pertinent effects" can be visualized as the "near side" of this field. Whereas objective interests refer to the "extension of the ground" of this field, "pertinent effects" are "the effects of the structures on the field of

16   Even complete abstention from political action, as, for instance, advocated by the "trade-unionist" tendency that Lenin polemicized against, does not prevent the working class from having "pertinent effects" at the political level, according to Poulantzas. "To confine itself to the strictly economic struggle alone may produce wholly positive 'pertinent effects', namely *noninterference* in the opponent's policy," he argues (1973b, 92). This appears to be plain nonsense, even from Poulantzas's own perspective, however. If both interference and noninterference qualify as "pertinent effects," then the working class, and *any* other class for that matter, *always* has "pertinent effects," no matter what it does, and hence there is no need for the concept. A temporary lapse of "rigor," perhaps (see also the scathing critique on this point by Miliband 1973, 86–87)?

the class struggle [which] are reflected here as a class's *threshold of existence* as a distinct class" (ibid., 111–12). Thus, it appears that objective interests are the maximum a class can get away with given the prevailing structures and balance of social forces, whereas "pertinent effects" are the minimum impact necessary for a class to qualify as a "social force" in Poulantzas's lexicon.

The possibility of permitting the working class to obtain "pertinent effects" at the political level *without* granting it any real political power appears to be a specifically capitalist phenomenon. It is the result of certain "fundamental characteristic" features of the capitalist type of state (ibid., 123) which are the product of the type of articulation of instances characteristic of the capitalist mode of production (relative autonomy, etc.). As opposed to the political instances in other modes of production (e.g., feudalism), the capitalist state denies social classes access to its institutions *as social classes*. The capitalist type of state, Poulantzas maintains, "contains no determination of subjects (fixed in this state as 'individuals', 'citizens', 'political persons') as *agents of production*" (ibid.).[17] This is ultimately the result of capitalist relations of production (the "determinant in the last instance"). Whereas in all modes of production, the dominant class owns the means of production, determines to which uses they shall be put, and extracts a surplus (the "relation of property"), in capitalism the workers are in addition deprived of any control of the immediate labor process (relation of "possession"), and progressively so as expanded reproduction proceeds. It is this total dispossession of the workers that allows the capitalist type of state to remain relatively aloof, that is, relatively autonomous, from the relations of production since, unlike the feudal state, it need not intervene directly in the labor process to ensure surplus extraction. This determines the structures and functions of the capitalist type of state (Poulantzas 1973a, 28–30; 1973b, 25–33, 124–29, 275; 1975, 18–19, 98; 1978, 18–19,

17   Quite a few Marxist theorists have recently argued that the capitalist state does not clearly acknowledge the class character of the interests of its "citizens," allowing them access to its institutions as "isolated, atomized" individuals only (Mandel 1975, 496), and that this is in itself an indication of class domination (Gerstenberger 1976, 82; Mandel 1979, 15; Offe 1985, ch. 7; Therborn 1978, 63–73; E. O. Wright 1978, 241–42).

25–6, 49–50, 63–69; also Althusser and Balibar 1970, 212–24).[18]

Being thus relieved of the need to intervene directly in the labor process, the state and the regional structure of the ideological have a very peculiar effect on the economic class struggles of the agents of production in capitalist social formations: the "effect of isolation." This effect consists of "concealing from these agents in a particular way the fact that their relations are class relations. . . . This effect of isolation is *terrifyingly real*: it has a name: *competition* between the wage-earning workers and between the capitalist owners of private property" (1973b, 130, also 275). The state and the ideological instance set the agents up as "juridico-ideological subjects," which causes them to perceive their relations as a competition of all against all rather than as *class* relations (ibid.). This effect of isolation simply expresses the fact that the economic and the political class struggles in capitalist social formations tend to be relatively autonomous, that is, isolated from one another (135–36, 275). It is important to note that, according to Poulantzas, this effect applies to workers and capitalists alike (131, 275).

Largely because of this isolation effect, the state can effectively play its global role as the factor of cohesion of the social formation. After having "set up" the agents of production as a mere aggregation of "private individuals" with a multitude of isolated "competing and divergent economic interests," the state can present *itself* as the only possible "representative of the 'general interest,' " as the "strictly *political* unity" of the people

18   However, somewhat oddly, because of relations of "non-correspondence and dislocation" it is possible for the state to be equipped with capitalist structures and functions even *before* the dispossession of workers has been realized, according to Poulantzas. This was the case, for instance, with the absolutist state whose function it was "precisely not to operate within the limits fixed by an *already given* mode of production, *but to produce not-yet-given relations* of production (i.e. capitalist relations) and to put an end to feudal relations of production" (1973b, 160–61), for which it obviously needed the type of unity and relative autonomy characteristic of the capitalist state (1967, 1973b, 157–67). Thus, the transition state already possessed the structure necessary to create the very preconditions for those structures! One is reminded of Althusser's procedure of applying his "theoretical problematic" to Marx's writings precisely to uncover that very problematic in the first place.

or nation as a whole (ibid., 133, 135, 188). Thus the state presents itself not as "the power of one or several determinate classes," but as "the power of the political unity of private agents, given over to economic antagonisms which the state claims to have the function of surmounting by unifying these agents within a 'popular-national' body" (276). This role of unity, Poulantzas claims, produces the characteristic "*institutional unity*" of the capitalist state and the unity of state power (277–79). And, finally, precisely this "unitary institutional framework . . . allows the state to function, in its relations to the class struggle, as the *unambiguous* (*univoque*) political power *of the dominant classes or fractions*" (279).[19]

Although both capitalists and workers are affected by the isolation effect, it "clearly does not appear in the same way in the socio-economic relations of these two classes" (ibid., 275). It is most effective with respect to *the capitalist class*. Because of the isolation effect capitalists are so hopelessly divided and fragmented in rival fractions, cliques, and interests as to render the class as a whole permanently unable "to achieve its own unity" (284). Obsessed by their competing short-term economic inter-

19 The isolation effect and the state as the sole embodiment of the unity of an atomized "people-nation" help explain "the so-called phenomenon of totalitarianism," according to Poulantzas (1973b, 290). Since the capitalist state and ideology produce this effect and contain no inherent limits on their possible encroachments on the "private" sphere, he argues, totalitarianism is merely "a particular reinforcement" of the capitalist type of state, i.e., an exclusively capitalist phenomenon (294, see also 216–21, 290–95; 1978, 69–75). Contemporary "socialist" countries, then, cannot be scientifically understood as "totalitarian," it would seem (cf. note 15, this chapter). However, in his later writings Poulantzas does explicitly refer to these countries as totalitarian (1978, 24, 51, 60–61, 72–74, 120, 207–8), but this does not invalidate the argument since "the hidden roots of certain totalitarian features of the East lie essentially, though not exclusively (since capitalism is not the source of all evil), in . . . *capitalist aspects* of this State, and of the relations of production and social division of labour that underlie it" (1978, 24). In fact, since the workers in "socialist" countries do not really own the means of production nor control the labor process or the surplus, the mode of production remains essentially capitalist: "state capitalism" with a "state bourgeoisie" exploiting the mass of the workers, according to Poulantzas (1973a, 29; 1975, 188–89). With this kind of reasoning (cf. note 8, this chapter) it is actually becoming rather difficult to think of any evil capitalism is *not* the source of, despite Poulantzas's rather disingenuous disclaimer (cf. Jessop 1980a, 126).

ests capitalists are incapable of translating these into common class interests by their own devices. "Left to themselves," Poulantzas claims, they are "exhausted by internal conflicts" and hence they "founder in contradictions which make them incapable of governing politically" (298).

Not so for the working class: although Poulantzas is unfortunately much less explicit on this point, this is, I believe, a crucial link in his argument without which his theory of the capitalist state would make very little sense (cf. Gold, Lo, and Wright 1975a, 37; E. O. Wright 1978, 102). From scattered remarks one can infer that he believes that the isolation effect on the working class, causing it to be "constantly ravaged by 'individual', 'local', 'partial', 'isolated' economic struggle" (Poulantzas 1973b, 275), is nevertheless counteracted by powerful forces pressing toward its unification as a class and toward the coalescence of the economic and the political class struggle. Thus, although the state and ideology impose competition on the workers, Poulantzas argues, "nonetheless, the real structure of the relations of production . . . leads to a remarkable *socialization* of the labour process" (275; also 127–28). Elsewhere he states that the isolation effect on the capitalists "is not compensated by anything, as it is by 'collective labour' on the side of the wage-earning workers" (289). Moreover, the political parties of the bourgeoisie are "unable to play an autonomous organizational role, let alone one analogous to the role of the working class's parties" (299). Thus, Poulantzas clearly assumes that the "collectivization of the labour process" (127) in capitalism constitutes a powerful force pushing toward "the rise and organized political struggle of the working class" (284). Poulantzas's argument here seems in accordance with what is generally held to be the original Marxian doctrine (for a useful discussion see, e.g., Bottomore 1965, 17–28).

Consequently, the cohesion and unity of a capitalist social formation are threatened from two sides: the capitalist class is too shortsighted and divided to assert and maintain its dominance on its own, and the working class is constantly on the verge of uniting against this dominance. Hence, the capitalist state is faced with two major tasks if it is to maintain unity and cohesion: "With regard to the dominated classes, the function of the capitalist state is to prevent their political organization which would overcome their economic isolation. . . . On the other hand, with regard to the dominant classes, the capitalist state is permanently working on their organization at the political level, by cancelling out their economic isolation" (1973b, 188–89, also 136–37, 287–88). To accomplish this complex feat, the state needs to be relatively autonomous, not only from the relations of production (the economic regional structure) but especially, and somewhat paradoxically, from the pressures of the politically dominant classes, that is, from the very classes whose "*unambiguous* and *exclusive* power" (288) it exercises.

Poulantzas is at great pains to show that this notion of relative autonomy as an inherent feature of the capitalist state—his main contribution to the "Marxist science of the state"—is in fact the only authentic Marxian conception to be found in "a practical state" in the political writings of Marx and Engels, especially those on Bonapartism. A correct "reading" of these texts reveals, according to Poulantzas, that Marx and Engels never succumbed to the "simplistic and vulgarized conception which sees in the state the tool or instrument of the dominant class" (ibid., 256).

On the contrary, those texts clearly show that "*the relative autonomy of the state vis-à-vis the dominant classes or fractions*" was "one of the essential characteristics of Bonapartism" (ibid., 259). However, lacking the rigorous concepts to "think" this relative autonomy scientifically, Marx and Engels mistakenly attributed it to a temporary "equilibrium of social forces," when, as they put it, "the bourgeoisie had already lost, [but] the working class had not yet gained, the ability to govern the nation" (ibid., also 166, 256, 289, 302–3, 351–52). But obviously, Poulantzas argues, to attribute "a constituent characteristic of the capitalist type of state" to a historically contingent equilibrium of social forces is "*totally insufficient*" (260). A "deeper reading of the texts" (ibid.) shows that this is really an unwitting "attempt at the *theoretical construction of the concept* of the capitalist state" in which relative autonomy is systematically conceived "*as a constitutive theoretical characteristic of the very type of capitalist state*" (258).

For one thing, it turns out that not even in the concrete his-

torical case of Bonapartism was there anything like an equilibrium of forces between the working class and the bourgeoisie
(ibid., 260). Second, there is a symptomatic ambivalence in
Marx's treatment of Bonapartism: he frequently refers to "an
opposition between state and society" yet insists that the state
exclusively served the interests of the bourgeoisie (279–83). Finally—and Poulantzas apparently considers this to be the
strongest evidence for his "reading" of Marx and Engels, judging by the frequency and emphasis with which he mentions it—
in a letter to Marx, Engels refers to Bonapartism as *"the real
religion of the modern bourgeoisie"* (258; see also, e.g., 260, 281,
283, 299, 302), "in other words as characteristic of *all* forms of
the capitalist state" (Poulantzas 1972, 247).[20] Therefore, Poulantzas concludes, "the French Bonapartist state's relative autonomy vis-à-vis the dominant classes or fractions can be understood only from the fact that this concrete form belongs to the
capitalist type of state—a state which presents this relative autonomy as a constitutive feature of its concept" (1973b, 261).

However, these "very principles of the Marxist theory of the
State" merely "lay down the general negative limits of this autonomy," Poulantzas concedes (1976, 72). Within these limits,
"the degree, the extent, the forms, etc. (*how* relative, and *how is
it* relative) of the relative autonomy of the State" can vary considerably depending on the "precise *conjuncture*" (ibid.), "which
reflects the always-original (because singular) historical individ-
uality of a formation" (1973b, 93, also 192, 262, 286, 301–3,
317–21). As a result of the varying balance of forces in the concrete conjuncture, the state sometimes seems to cater to the
wishes of the dominant classes while at other times it may respond to the demands of the dominated classes, seemingly *at
the expense of* the dominant classes. Such variations have given
rise to a variety of "ideological currents" (269), which view the
state as either a neutral power broker or an independent power
with its own interests (266–69). Marxist theory, too, has been
contaminated by these currents, "which have caused it to move
away from the scientific standard of the Marxist theory of the

20   Somewhat curiously, Poulantzas also attributes this quote to Marx himself
(1972, 247). See note 10, this chapter.

state" (265), as can be seen in various instrumentalist theories as well as in the naive social-democratic belief in the state as potentially an impartial arbiter between classes (see, e.g., Poulantzas 1973a, 44–47; 1973b, 269–74, 297–301; 1975, 103–6, 158–61; 1976, 74–75; 1978, 11–14, 131–32). What all these "distortions" (1973b, 265) have in common, according to Poulantzas, is that they fail to see that all the observed variations in the degree and kind of relative autonomy taken on by the capitalist state are always "variations within the limits fixed by its structures" (303, also 274, 286–87). And about these limits Marxist theory is quite clear: "The (capitalist) State, in the long run, can only correspond to the political interests of the dominant class or classes" (Poulantzas 1976, 72).

The reason the capitalist state must at all times possess some (albeit variable) degree of relative autonomy from the capitalist class stems from the differential impact of the "isolation effect" on the working class and the capitalist class, a concept that Marx and Engels did not have at their disposal, of course. As noted earlier, the dynamics of capitalist relations of production (the "collectivization of the labour process") exert a powerful pressure on the working class to overcome the effect of isolation, thus posing a permanent threat to the unity and cohesion of the system as a whole. This situation is aggravated by "the institutions of the capitalist state (for example, universal suffrage), which hurl all the classes or fractions of society on to the political scene," and also by "the continued existence of the classes of the small producers in capitalist formations and their complex reflection at the political level" (1973b, 284). Under these precarious circumstances, Poulantzas argues, the capitalist class "can dominate effectively only if it sets up its economic interests as political interests. In holding state power it can perpetuate existing social relations only through a whole series of compromises which maintain the unstable equilibrium of the classes present" (283). This requires a clear and unfailing understanding of what compromises and concessions are necessary for the long-term maintenance of the general conditions (political interests) that permit individual capitalists to continue to exploit and subordinate labor (economic interests).

But as a result of the isolation effect the capitalist class is or-

dinarily far too divided and fragmented into competing fractions wholly preoccupied with their own short-term, parochial
economic interests to achieve any consensus on its common,
long-term class interests, let alone one that is guaranteed to represent its *objective* interests (i.e., one that *will*, in fact, "perpetuate existing social relations"). The capitalist class has never been
capable of this (ibid., 168–84), and it probably never will be
(297–99; 1975, 108–55). This is why the state, in its capacity as
factor of cohesion of the social formation, has to step in:

> It takes charge, as it were, of the bourgeoisie's political interests
> and realizes the function of political hegemony which the
> bourgeoisie is unable to achieve. But *in order to do this, the capitalist
> state assumes a relative autonomy with regard to the bourgeoisie.* . . . For
> this relative autonomy allows the state to intervene not only in or-
> der to arrange compromises vis-à-vis the dominated classes, which,
> in the long run, are useful for the actual economic interests of the
> dominant classes or fractions; but also (depending on the concrete
> conjuncture) to intervene against the long-term economic interests
> of *one or other* fraction of the dominant class: for such compromises
> and sacrifices are sometimes necessary for the realization of their
> political class interests. (1973b, 284–85).

Thus, "the state's so-called 'social functions' " are, according
to Poulantzas, "a good example." They may well have been "*imposed* on the dominant classes by the state, through the pressure
of the dominated classes," and sometimes even "by *social democratic* governments." But, he argues, "strictly speaking, this does
not alter the situation. These governments used the state and
its relative autonomy to function as the political organisers of
the dominant classes" (ibid., 285).

The capitalist state politically unifies the various competing
fractions of the bourgeoisie by uniting them in what Poulantzas
calls a "power bloc," which involves "*the particular participation of
several classes and class fractions in political domination*" (ibid., 234).
This should not be interpreted as an effective *sharing* of power
among these classes and fractions, however. For, according to
Poulantzas, the relative autonomy of the capitalist state is com-
plemented by another basic, characteristic feature which consists of "the *unity proper to* institutionalized political power" pre-

cluding any " 'parcellization', *division* or *sharing* of the institutionalized power of the state" (255, also 288–89).

The class fractions that are united in the "power bloc" are not unified in the sense that they have truly surmounted their differences. On the contrary, "the class struggle, the rivalry between the interests of these social forces, is *constantly present*, since these interests retain their specific character of antagonism," Poulantzas claims (ibid., 239). The "power bloc" is thus "a complex contradictory unity," and what lends it unity is the fact that it is a "unity *in dominance*" (ibid., emphasis added). Its unity derives from the fact that within the "power bloc" there is always *one* "hegemonic" fraction that is "the *dominant* element" among the "politically *'dominant'* classes or fractions" (237, also 141).[21] This hegemonic fraction, Poulantzas asserts, "*polarizes* the specific contradictory interests of the various classes or fractions in the power bloc by making its own economic interests into political interests and by representing the general common interest of the classes or fractions in the power bloc: this general interest consists of economic exploitation and political domination" (239).

In addition, this fraction is usually also "hegemonic" in a more Gramscian sense in that it manages to present its own specific interests as "the 'general interest' of the body politic" (ibid., 140, 303–5), that is, of "the ensemble of society" (240). Usually, Poulantzas claims, these two functions are united within one and the same fraction, although, depending on "the conjunc-

---

21 Throughout, Poulantzas stubbornly persists in referring to *several* politically dominant classes and fractions and to one *class* or fraction being "hegemonic" among them (see below). But rather than demonstrating his much-vaunted "rigor" this amounts to little more than a bit of redundant pedantry. The only class other than the capitalist class that could ever have been a candidate for participation in political dominance was the large landholding nobility (1973b, 230–34), which may have played an important role in the absolutist state of transition (157–67; 1967), but hardly, one must assume, in today's "monopoly capitalism," its members presumably having been absorbed into the capitalist class. Other classes such as the peasants or the "petty bourgeoisie" are never more than "supporting classes" at best, according to Poulantzas (1973b, 243–45; 1975, 287–99). Hence, for all practical purposes there can be only *one* dominant class, namely the capitalist class (and then only when *none* of its fractions is excluded from the "power bloc"), and there can only be a hegemonic *fraction*, not a class.

ture of the social forces," there is always "the possibility of dislocation, dissociation and displacement of these functions of hegemony to different classes or fractions, one representing the
hegemonic fraction of the ensemble of society, the other representing the specific hegemonic fraction of the power bloc"
(ibid.).

The dominance of the hegemonic fraction in the power bloc
strictly precludes *any* sharing of power, according to Poulantzas. The hegemonic fraction does not merely possess a greater
share of power than the others, it holds *"state power in its unity"*
(ibid., 297). The *"unity proper to* institutionalized political power"
and the "unity in dominance" of the power bloc appear to be
inextricably intertwined in Poulantzas's argument so it is worth
quoting him at length on this difficult but crucial point:

> With regard to the dominant classes and fractions, the capitalist
> state *presents an intrinsic unity* . . . precisely because it is the *unifying
> factor* of the power bloc. Social forces, therefore, do not *share* insti-
> tutionalized power; what we have here is a case of several classes
> and fractions present on the terrain of political domination, which
> are able to assure this domination only to the extent that they are
> politically unified. The state derives its own unity from this plural-
> ity of dominant classes and fractions, in so far as their relation is
> incapable of functioning by means of a share-out of power and
> needs the state as the organizational factor for their strictly political
> unity. This unity is realized under the protection of the hegemonic
> class or fraction and thus corresponds to the unity of the state as
> the organizational factor of this class or fraction. In this sense the
> unity of state power is, in the last analysis, to be found in the state's
> particular relation to the hegemonic class or fraction, i.e. in the fact
> of the *univocal correspondence of the state to the specific* interests of that
> class or fraction. (ibid., 300–301; see also 297–99)

Yet, although in the last analysis the state exclusively serves
the interests of the hegemonic fraction, which is the result (or
the cause?) of its own very unity, it nevertheless maintains a relative autonomy even from *this* fraction. For even this fraction is
generally too preoccupied with its own parochial interests to
recognize the real and mutual political sacrifices that are often
necessary to maintain its hegemony within the power bloc.

Thus, Poulantzas argues, "the state may, for example, present itself as the political guarantor of the interests of various classes and fractions of the power bloc against the interests of the hegemonic class or fraction, and it may sometimes play off those classes and fractions against the latter. But it does this in its function of political organizer of the hegemonic class or fraction and forces it to admit the sacrifices necessary for its hegemony" (ibid., 301, also 1975, 97–98; 1978, 180–89).[22]

Moreover, the politically hegemonic fraction is not necessarily also the economically dominant class or fraction. Because of the relative autonomy of structural instances and levels of class struggle, the hegemonic fraction "can in no way be identified with that which holds the preponderant position in economic domination" (1975, 93). Although, as he repeatedly states (1973a, 44–47; 1973b, 308–17; 1975, 157–74), it so happens that in the current phase of monopoly capitalism "the economic domination and political hegemony of monopoly capital are being overwhelmingly asserted" (1975, 168), this by no means implies that one can equate economic domination and political hegemony "in a necessary and mechanical fashion" (1973a, 44). Which class or fraction is able to achieve political hegemony always depends "on the concrete stages and turns of the class struggle" (1975, 93, also 132).

The "complex contradictory unity in dominance" of the power bloc is reflected, according to Poulantzas, in the institutional separation of powers (legislative, executive, judiciary) characteristic of the capitalist type of state. This separation of powers contributes to the state's relative autonomy with respect to the dominant classes by allowing the various branches to function as "power centers" of different fractions of the power bloc without, however, undermining the unity of state power (1973b, 303–7). When these branches are controlled by rival

---

22   Perhaps this is what Poulantzas means by the "degree" of hegemony within the power bloc in connection with his argument about the variability of the degree of relative autonomy within limits, discussed earlier (1976, 72). Given the absolute unity of state power it is not clear what else he could possibly mean by it. And even this interpretation of a variable "degree" of hegemony (i.e., as a measure of the sacrifices the hegemonic fraction must make to *maintain* its hegemony) would seem to get Poulantzas into serious difficulties, as we shall see.

fractions of the power bloc this still does not imply an *"effective sharing"* of political power since these branches, too, constitute a unity in dominance. The unity of institutionalized power is at all times maintained "by being concentrated around the dominant place where the hegemonic class or fraction is reflected" (305). Rather than becoming effective countervailing powers, the other branches "function more especially as *resistances* to the dominant power: inserted into the unitary function of the state, they contribute to the organization of the hegemony of the class or fraction which is reflected as a political force in the dominant power" (ibid.).

This also demonstrates, in Poulantzas's view, why the " 'parliamentarist' deformation" of social democrats who seek to obtain a share of political power by conquering a majority in the legislature ultimately boils down to *"a myth"* (ibid., 312–13). If they were ever to succeed, he argues, "the centre of gravity of the unity of power" would simply shift to another branch of the state (313; 1978, 138–39). The current predominance of the executive, reflecting the rise to hegemony of monopoly capital, is a clear case in point, he claims (1973b, 308–17).

But this "deformation" is in fact a double illusion in view of Poulantzas's principal claim that the functioning of the state and its various branches in the service of the power bloc, and more particularly its hegemonic fraction, has nothing to do with the composition of its personnel or any direct attempts by the dominant classes to exert pressure on it, as the instrumentalist view has it. The political parties that dominate the "political scene" may, in fact, draw upon and "represent" entirely different classes (which Poulantzas calls "ruling classes"), and the same goes for the state bureaucracy ("classes in charge of the state"). They may be, and often are, of mainly petty bourgeois or reformist working-class affiliation, yet they objectively serve the interests of the power bloc (ibid., 245–52, 317–21; 1972, 246–48; 1973a, 45–47; 1975, 148, 183–89). In fact, Poulantzas maintains the very *opposite* of the instrumentalist position: given that the state is structurally compelled to serve the interests of the dominant class, and more specifically those of its hegemonic fraction, and since this involves presenting the latter's interests as the "general interest" of the "people-nation," "it can be said that the capitalist state best serves the interests of the capitalist class only when the members of this class do not participate directly in the state apparatus, that is to say when the *ruling class* is not the *politically governing class*" (1972, 246).[23]

Thus, according to Poulantzas, the objective function of the state apparatus to serve the interests of the dominant classes is unaffected by the class origins of its personnel. That function is entirely determined by the state's "relation to the structures" (1973b, 115), which ensures its unity (i.e., indivisibility of its power) and relative autonomy, whether its members are mainly recruited from the bourgeoisie or not (335–37). The bureaucracy is merely "the specific effect of the state's regional structure" (332); it is not a social class but a "social category," usually drawn from several classes. Therefore, it may possess the unity and relative autonomy characteristic of the capitalist state, but it cannot have power of its own.

Nevertheless, Poulantzas does not deny that the bureaucracy may affect the functioning of the state "to some extent" (ibid., 337), namely by certain "additional limits and barriers posed by the class affiliation of the heights of the bureaucracy to the hegemonic class or fraction" (ibid.), and in transition states (e.g., the absolutist state) these limits and barriers may even take "the form of *hindrances* and *resistances*" (338). Thus, although the bureaucracy cannot possess any power of its own, it *can* manifest itself in a concrete conjuncture as a "social force" (357–58), playing "a role of its own in political action, *but this does not confer on it a power of its own*" (358, 325–59 in general).

As noted above, Poulantzas contends that while the state organizes the dominant classes in the power bloc, it simultaneously *dis*organizes the dominated classes whose potential or-

---

23 Poulantzas's terminology is not entirely consistent. In the last quote "ruling class" is, in accordance with more conventional usage, equivalent to his "dominant class," whereas he refers to the "ruling classes" (i.e., those whose parties dominate the "political scene") and "classes in charge" (i.e., those from whose ranks the individuals occupying the "heights of the bureaucracy" are recruited) of the preceding quote *together* as "politically governing classes." Elsewhere the last two are called "reigning classes" (1973a, 45; 1975, 148). The point, however, remains the same; the "reigning classes" need not include either the hegemonic class or fraction or any of the classes or fractions of the power bloc.

ganization permanently threatens the system. It does this by presenting itself as the unity of the "national-popular ensemble" (ibid., 192), that is, by presenting the specific interests of the hegemonic fraction as "representative of the people's general interest, as the materialization of popular sovereignty" (304). However, Poulantzas argues, this function of the capitalist state should not be reduced to "simply a mendacious mystification" (192, also 1978, 184). The "normative institutional ensemble of *political democracy*" that permits the state to fulfill this function and the concessions to the dominated classes that result from it are real enough (1973b, 123–24, 133, 276–77). Poulantzas resolves this apparent paradox by drawing a strict distinction between *economic* and *political* class interests.

The capitalist state, he claims, "does not *directly* represent the dominant classes' economic interests, but their *political interests*" (ibid., 190). To protect these interests, this state "has inscribed in its very structures a flexibility which concedes a certain guarantee to the economic interests of certain dominated classes, within the limits of the system" (ibid.). Such guarantees may actually "cut into the dominant classes' economic power" (193), while reinforcing their political power, since "such compromises and sacrifices are sometimes necessary for the realization of their political interests" (285). Thus, "in making this guarantee, the state aims precisely at the political disorganization of the dominated classes; in a formation where the strictly political struggle of the dominated classes is possible, it is the sometimes indispensable means of maintaining the dominant classes' hegemony. In other words, according to the concrete conjuncture, a *line of demarcation* can always be drawn within which the guarantee given by the capitalist state to the dominated classes' economic interests not only fails to threaten the political relation of class domination but even constitutes an element of this relation" (191).

From his subsequent argument it appears that this "line of demarcation" for Poulantzas consists of the maintenance of the structures of the capitalist state that compel it to serve the exclusive political interests of the dominant classes. Since these structures constitute the unambiguous political power of the dominant classes, he argues, their remaining intact constitutes the *"limit within which the restrictions of the economic power of these classes has no effect"* (ibid., 192). The capitalist state has the possibility "inscribed within the limits of its structures" (193), of making economic concessions to the dominated classes, Poulantzas explains, but such a policy, "though it may happen to contain real economic sacrifices *imposed on* the dominant class *by the struggle of the dominated classes*, cannot under any circumstances call into question the capitalist type of state, so long as it operates within these *limits*" (194; see also 1975, 167–68; 1978, 184–89). But, of course, the precise location of these limits depends at all times on the manifold social forces and struggles present in the concrete conjuncture (1973b, 192).

In addition, the struggles of the dominated classes help the state to achieve the very relative autonomy it needs to serve the political interests of the dominant classes (ibid., 289). The state encourages the dominated classes "in various ways, to work against the dominant class or classes, but to the political advantage of the latter" (285). The support of the dominated classes allows the state to enforce decisions that are opposed by the dominant classes, too shortsighted to recognize their own *political* interest, as, once again, the example of Bonapartism demonstrates, according to Poulantzas (285–86). However, all this remains within the limits imposed by the structures of the state, and "within these precise limits, the capitalist state does not take even one step away from the political interests of the bourgeoisie" (286). This relative autonomy is "inscribed in the institutional play of the capitalist state," so that "the political struggles of the dominated classes can be expressed there" while at the same time it "neither authorizes the dominated classes *effectively to participate* in political power nor cedes 'parcels' of institutionalized power to them" (288–89). Thus, according to Poulantzas, the "ensemble of structures" of the state paradoxically enables it to assume a relative autonomy from the dominant classes "precisely in so far as it constitutes their *unambiguous* and *exclusive* political power" (ibid., 288).

However, although the process whereby the state manages to elicit support from the dominated classes for measures serving the political interests of the dominant classes is not merely a matter of "straightforward ideological mystification" (1978,

184), the ideological "level" nevertheless *does* play a crucial role. But rather than conceiving of ideology in the "historicist" manner as simply the spontaneous consciousness of a historical class subject (1973b, 195–206), Poulantzas treats the ideological as another regional structure, which is, like the state, "fixed in its limits by the global structure of a mode of production and social formation" (209). This means that the ideological instance, too, has certain objective functions to perform quite irrespective of the wills of the "men" who are merely its "bearers." In fact, its structure and functions are remarkably similar to those of the capitalist state.

For one thing, ideology "has the particular function of cohesion" (ibid., 207, also 208–9, 214). In addition, it has the isolation effect on economic class practices (213), and the concomitant "political role of the dominant bourgeois ideology" is to impose a "way of life" on "the ensemble of society" which allows the state to present itself as the guardian of the "general interest" (214). Like the state it does this by concealing class exploitation *"to the extent that all trace of class domination is systematically absent from its language"* (ibid.). Again like the state, the dominant ideology corresponds to the interests of the politically dominant class by virtue of the fact that it aims at the maintenance (the cohesion) of a social structure of a class-divided society, "and this means *above all* class domination and exploitation" (209). Finally, the dominant ideology possesses the same combination of unity (i.e., unambiguous correspondence to the interests of the dominant classes) and relative autonomy as the state. Since the dominant ideology could hardly be expected to be effective if it were too obviously linked to the dominant classes, it must also enjoy a "specific autonomy" from them (203). The relation is "always masked" as shown by the fact that the dominant ideology is always permeated by elements stemming from the "way of life" of the dominated classes, sometimes to such an extent that it may *appear* closer as a whole to their interests than to those of the dominant classes (ibid.; 1967, 66–67). On the other hand, the dominance of the dominant ideology is shown by the fact that the dominated classes spontaneously adopt its terms as theirs, even when they revolt against the system itself, which can be seen in such demands as " 'social justice', 'equality', etc." (1973b, 213, also 205, 223).

Given this remarkable structural-functional similarity between the ideological instance and the state, it is not suprising, then, that, according to Poulantzas, there is a considerable overlap between the two, despite their irreducible "specificity," in the form of institutions that "belong to the system of the state whilst depending principally on the ideological level" (1972, 251). These "Ideological State Apparatuses," as Althusser has called them (Althusser 1971, 127–86), include institutions "such as the Church, the political parties, the unions (with the exception of course, of the *revolutionary* party or trade union organizations), the schools, the mass media (newspapers, radio, television), and, from a certain point of view, the family. This is so whether they are *public* or *private*—the distinction having a purely juridical, that is largely ideological character, which changes nothing fundamental" (Poulantzas 1972, 251, also 1973a, 47).[24] In fact, their "privateness" merely expresses the relatively high degree of relative autonomy these apparatuses require to fulfill their ideological functions, which often demands a high degree of responsiveness to the needs of the dominated classes (Poulantzas 1972, 251; 1973a, 48; also Althusser 1971, 146–47, 185–86).

Yet, according to Poulantzas, they *do* belong to the state since they perform the same function of factor of cohesion of a social formation characterized by class domination. In addition their functioning ultimately depends on the repressive apparatus of the state which "is always present behind them" (Poulantzas 1972, 252). Moreover, their relations with one another and with the repressive apparatus are strongly affected by "every important modification of the form of the State" (ibid.). And finally,

24   Elsewhere, Poulantzas also includes "the cultural apparatus (cinema, theatre, publishing)" (1975, 25) among the "Ideological State Apparatuses," although in a more recent lineup the family and nonrevolutionary parties and unions are absent (1978, 289). The notion goes back to Gramsci, by the way, who repeatedly argues that "hegemony" is "exercised through the so-called private organizations, like the Church, the trade unions, the schools, etc." (1971, 56n, also, e.g., 221, 258–59, 261), although he, of course, did not "sufficiently found and develop" the concept (Poulantzas 1972, 251; cf. note 1, this chapter).

their designation as *state* apparatuses reminds one of the need for a socialist revolution to "break" not only the represssive apparatus of the state but also the church, parties, unions, schools, media, and the family (ibid.).

This, then, is Poulantzas's theory of the capitalist state, based on Althusser's "reading" of Marx. As opposed to the instrumentalists, Poulantzas holds that the capitalist state constitutes a "regional structure," which performs the objective function of maintaining the unity and cohesion of the "global structure" of a social formation characterized by class domination and exploitation, irrespective of the class allegiances of its personnel and of any direct pressures from the bourgeoisie. In conjunction with the dominant ideology the state has the "effect of isolation" on the socioeconomic relations between the agents of production which means that it conceals from them the fact that these relations are ultimately *class* relations, that is, that they are ultimately struggles over the maintenance or abolition of class domination and exploitation *as such*. But the ongoing collectivization of the labor process constantly pushes the working class toward overcoming this isolation effect, while this same effect renders the capitalist class too fragmented and short-sighted to realize what concessions are necessary to prevent this threat from becoming reality. Hence the state, in its capacity of factor of cohesion of the social formation, performs the function of making and enforcing the concessions and compromises necessary to maintain the acquiescence of the working class, that is, necessary to maintain the cohesion of the structures that permit the continued domination of the capitalist class, often against its declared opposition. To do this effectively the state must enjoy a relative autonomy from the capitalist class so that it can present itself as the embodiment of the "general interest" to convince the dominated classes to accept those concessions as in *their* interest. Moreover, the state is structurally constrained to make such concessions *only* to the extent that they are necessary for maintaining cohesion and unity, that is, in the *political* interests of the capitalist class, never more than that. So, in contrast to instrumentalism, Poulantzas's theory implies that "while the apparent determinants of state action may involve the political defeat of the bourgeoisie, the consequences of that state action reproduce and reinforce that class's domination" (Esping-Andersen, Friedland, and Wright 1976, 189).

From "Cohesion" to "Class Struggle"

However, it would not be entirely fair to judge Poulantzas's theory of the capitalist state by its original formulation only. In his later writings he considerably modified this earlier version, presumably in response to some stiff criticisms from fellow Marxists.[25] For one thing, his claim that Marx and Engels's analyses of Bonapartism were actually a subconscious "attempt at the *theoretical construction of the concept* of the capitalist state" (Poulantzas 1973b, 258) is little more than "a careless and unfounded over-interpretation" (Keane 1978, 52; see also Draper 1977, chs. 14–19; Hunt 1984, 47–63; Laclau 1975, 98–99; Miliband 1972, 260; 1973, 89–92; but cf. Perez-Diaz 1978). Poulantzas's procedure for validating his contention is somewhat curious, to say the least. He never provides the "deeper reading" (1973b, 260) on which his textual interpretation supposedly rests. The quotation he *does* provide (259) lends no support to his case whatsoever, no matter how "deeply" one "reads" it (cf. Miliband 1973, 91). His additional arguments are either irrelevant (the alleged inadequacy of the explanation given by Marx and Engels to account for the emergence of the historical phenomenon of Bonapartism) or assume what needs to be demonstrated in the first place (that, since this relative autonomy is characteristic of *all* capitalist states, it cannot possibly be explained by a historically contingent equilibrium of social forces). His *only* remaining piece of evidence is the fact that, in a letter (!), Engels once referred to Bonapartism as "the true religion of the bourgeoisie," a quotation Poulantzas repeats *ad nauseam*. And even this is hardly much of an argument since Engels was clearly referring to Bonapartism's *dictatorial* features, which seemed necessary for the protection of the bourgeoisie against the restive lower classes, and *not* to the re-

25 For an alternative summary of Poulantzas's later views of the capitalist state, see Jessop (1982, 181–91; 1985, chs. 4, 5, 10).

gime's "relative autonomy" *from* the bourgeoisie (see Marx and Engels 1965, 177)!

So far as I know, however, Poulantzas never openly retracted this claim, although references to Bonapartism and *The Eighteenth Brumaire* are conspicuously absent from his last book (Poulantzas 1978). The one time he does mention Bonapartism, he lumps it together with fascism and military dictatorships as *"exceptional forms of State"* (74)! He also appears to have lost some of his earlier confidence in the unsurpassed explanatory powers of the Marxist "science" of social formations (*"the break between science and ideology is far from possessing the radical character that we assigned to it some years ago"* 1978, 111, also 23, 53, 74), and has belatedly rejected anyone's right to claim to be "the keeper of the holy dogmas and texts" (8, 22–3). Taken together, I suppose, these could be interpreted as a tacit admission that his strenuous attempts to establish the Marxian pedigree of his notion of the relative autonomy of the capitalist state may have been somewhat misplaced. Of course, one could question the relevance of it all for the notion's validity, but, not surprisingly, few of Poulantzas's Marxist critics have dared to go *that* far.[26]

Althusser's concept of "Ideological State Apparatuses" has not found much favor among fellow Marxists either. This notion, which practically incorporates *all* social institutions into the capitalist state (with the significant exception of "revolutionary" organizations), it is argued, turns the state into an "all-pervasive *quality*" (Laclau 1975, 100), thus totally obliterating the state's "peculiar apartness" in capitalist societies (Therborn 1978, 172; also Miliband, 1973 88, n. 16; Weiner 1980, 6). In addition, the critics claim, the notion leads to the politically catastrophic conclusion that there are no real differences between bourgeois democracy and more repressive forms of class domination (Miliband 1972, 261–62; 1977, 54–57, 74–90).[27]

26   Alan Wolfe is a rare but notable exception. In a scathing critique he takes the Althusserians to task for their "Talmudic approach," "excessive dogmatism," and "Scholasticism," and for their curious insistence on trying to solve twentieth-century problems "through a rigorous understanding of nineteenth century writings" (1974, 140–42).

27   Poulantzas indignantly rejects Miliband's (1973) charge that his "structuralist abstractionism" leads to a dangerous equation of fascism and bourgeois democracy as "pure mythology" (1976, 76). Poulantzas's book on German

Again, Poulantzas did not find this criticism worthy of a direct reply, nor did he even tacitly concede the point, although he *does* seem to have softened his initial stance to some extent. Thus, neither "the trade-union apparatus of class collaboration and the bourgeois and petty bourgeois political parties" (1975, 25), nor the family appear to belong to the "Ideological State Apparatuses" in Poulantzas's later writings (1978, 28). Also, he came to accept the idea that the capitalist state performs other functions besides outright represssion and ideological manipulation (28–34, 78–79, 84, 170), and he came to put greater emphasis on "the momentous difference between the parliamentary-democratic State and the exceptional State" (125). But he apparently continued to consider the concept of "Ideological State Apparatuses" to be a useful one, and, as we shall see, it does indeed fit remarkably well in his overall approach.

But the main objection of Marxist critics to Althusser's and Poulantzas's structuralism is that the theory cannot explain social change, particularly the kind of prospective revolutionary change that no self-respecting Marxist theory can do without (Bridges 1974, 178–80; Jessop 1977, 355–56). From the humanist-voluntarist perspective "structuralism" has been criticized for its "implacable determinism" (Anderson 1976, 65) which leaves no room whatsoever for conscious human agency and hence no "motive force for political action" at all (Appelbaum 1979, 26; Benton 1984; Best and Connolly 1979; Burris 1979, 13–16; Esping-Andersen, Friedland, and Wright 1976, 188; Giddens 1981, 171; Gold, Lo, and Wright 1975a, 39; Smith 1984; Thompson 1978, 75–84; Wolfe 1974, 140).

Similarly, Poulantzas has been criticized from a more ortho-

---

and Italian fascism (1974) should be sufficient proof of his respect for the "concrete facts" and his concern to distinguish between different types of bourgeois political domination, he claims. However, in a devastating critique, Caplan (1977; see also Jessop 1985, ch. 8) has shown that Poulantzas's historical analysis of Nazism is principally based on ignorance of the historical facts, a grim determination to make the facts fit into preconceived theoretical models, total confusion of his own theoretical categories, leaving crucial concepts completely undefined, and, of all things, such a naive confidence in the factual evidence available at the time that subsequent research rendered his "analyses" entirely obsolete in no time at all! How Caplan can still praise Poulantzas for his "theoretical rigour," "conceptual precision," and "subtle differentiations" (1977, 85) is a great mystery.

dox point of view for his apparent "politicism," that is, for failing to give his theory of the capitalist state a "scientific footing" (Clarke 1977, 14) in the economic base, the general laws of motion of capital accumulation, the tendency of the rate of profit to fall, economic crises, and the class struggle. Thus, it is argued, Poulantzas's theory lacks any internal contradictions and systematic limitations on the efficacy of state policy. It merely reproduces bourgeois structural functionalism with a quasi-Marxist rhetorical veneer. Since his system lacks any internal contradictions, the critics argue, Poulantzas's assertion that the capitalist state is a class state because the social formation it holds together happens to be divided into classes is no more than "an arbitrary moral claim" (ibid., 19; also Holloway and Picciotto 1978, 3–10; Jessop 1977, 367–69; 1982, 181–91).

Of course, these are serious allegations which not even an Althusserian Marxist can afford to ignore. Hence Poulantzas found it necessary to reply to them in some detail (1976). The "humanist" claim that his "structuralism" did not assign sufficient importance to the role of free will and human agency did not really faze him, though. This "is nothing more, in the final analysis, than a reiteration in modern terms of the kind of objections that bourgeois idealism has always opposed to Marxism of whatever stripe," he maintains (70). Case closed. It would be a far more serious matter, however, if by "structuralism" the critics meant "a theoretical conception that neglects the importance and the weight of the class struggle in history." But, even when applied to his early work only, this criticism is still "utterly inappropriate," Poulantzas believes (71).

The charge applies to the earlier works of other Althusserians, especially that of Balibar, but not to his own which has always stressed the importance of the specific social formation and the concrete conjuncture, which, Poulantzas maintains, "clearly shows . . . that I attributed the highest importance to the class struggle" (ibid., 79, also 77–82; 1975, 13, n. 1, 49, n. 4). Elsewhere, he dissociates himself once and for all from "the whole institutionalist tradition" according to which the "state apparatuses . . . command the class struggle" (1973a, 49). This kind of structuralism, which attributes independent powers to structures and institutions, thereby overlooking "the primordial role of classes and the class struggle by comparison with structures—institutions and organs, including the State organs," is precisely what he was trying to avoid: "by comprehending the relations of power as class relations, I have attempted to break definitely with structuralism, which is the modern form of bourgeois idealism," Poulantzas argues (1976, 73).

Nevertheless, only one page later he concedes that his earlier formulations (esp. in 1973b) may have failed to "sufficiently emphasize the primacy of the class struggle as compared with the State apparatus" (1976, 74). But this error has since been rectified in his subsequent writings, he asserts, although definitely not in the direction desired by the victims of "the force of the dominant ideology," such as Miliband (70). Instead, the modifications have gone "in the direction already inherent" in his early work (74). His early distinction between structures and class practices, Poulantzas claims, was already "patently anti-structuralist" since it allowed him to advance the "fundamental proposition . . . that social classes, although objectively determined (structures), are not ontological and nominalist entities, but only exist within and through the class struggle (practices)" (82). Yet he *does* admit that his early formulations suffered from "a certain degree of formalism" which may have given the reader the false impression that he was "according pride of place to 'structures' that were said to be external to or outside the class struggle" (ibid.). Since then, however, Poulantzas claims to have cleared up such ambiguities.

This does not mean that Poulantzas finally gave in to humanist-voluntarist ideology in his treatment of social classes, though. He still insists on the objective "structural determination" of classes and class interests: "class determination . . . designates certain objective places occupied by the social agents in the social division of labour: places which are independent of the will of these agents" (1975, 14). Thus, a social class and its objective interests are still "defined by its [the class's] *place* in the ensemble of social practices," that is, in the relations of production and of political and ideological domination or subordination (1973a, 27–28; 1975, 14–17).

But the *practices* (struggles) of these classes are no longer merely the "effects" of the "structures," as Poulantzas had formerly maintained. Moreover, the direction of determination between practices and structures now appears to be reversed: Poulantzas now firmly (and in endless repetition) upholds "*the primacy of the class struggle over the apparatuses*" (1973a, 30; 1975, 34; 1978, 38, 45, 53, 126, 149, 151).[28] He now frequently stresses the "historical, dynamic dimension" of the class struggle which "governs the functioning and the role of the apparatuses" (1973a, 50, also 48–49; 1975, 23, 27–29), and insists that "institutional modifications do not lead to social movements, as a whole series of institutionalist sociologists believe: it is the class struggle which determines how the apparatuses are modified" (1973a, 48; 1975, 27). Thus, in Poulantzas's revised theory the class struggle, far from merely being "an operation carried out within the limits imposed by the structure" (1973b, 111), now "goes beyond the apparatuses, generally escapes their control and in fact assigns *them* their limits" (1973a, 50, emphasis added; 1975, 29). This new conception of the relation between class practices and structures has, naturally, also necessitated a different conception of the state, since Poulantzas now holds that "the apparatuses are never anything other than the materialization and condensation of class relations" (1975, 23).

According to the "new" Poulantzas, the state must be seen "as a relation or more precisely as the condensate of a relation of power between struggling classes" (1976, 74). This conception, he claims, avoids the false dilemma between the instrumentalist view of the state as a thing, that is, a passive tool in the hands of the dominant class, and the view of the state as a subject with interests and power of its own (ibid.; 1975, 158–61; 1978, 131–32). The state is not "a monolithic, fissureless bloc," but is, instead, "structurally shot through and constituted with and by class contradictions" (1976, 75). Its apparatus consists of competing organs and branches that are the seats of power of rival

28   Once he began "rectifying" his earlier mistakes (starting with Poulantzas 1973a), Poulantzas hardly used the term "structure" anymore, preferring the notion of "apparatuses" instead. Because he did not explain the conversion anywhere it is hard to tell whether he still adhered to the strict distinction between institutions and the structures that constitute the "*organizing matrix*" hidden *behind* the institutions, as he once did (1973b, 115, n. 24), or whether he gave up on the notion of invisible yet all-determining "structures" altogether.

fractions of the power bloc. The divisions and contradictions internal to the state are further intensified by the fact that "popular struggles traverse the State" (1978, 141), by means of which the dominated classes can create "centres of opposition to the power of the dominant classes" within the state itself, although they cannot obtain any real power of their own, of course (142). Thus, Poulantzas argues, state policy is established through a process that in the short term often "appears to be phenomenally incoherent and chaotic" (135). Yet, "a certain coherence arrives with the conclusion of the process" (ibid.), which permits the state to serve "the general, long-term political interests of the power bloc" (134). For the state is a "fissiparous *unity*" (136) since it is still dominated by that organ or branch that is the seat of power of the hegemonic fraction (136–37; also 1973a, 48). Thus, the role of the state as the guardian of the interests of the dominant classes and guarantor of "the reproduction of the overall system" is viewed by Poulantzas "as a resultant of inter-organ and inter-branch contradictions" (1976, 75; see also 1973a, 47–48; 1975, 98, 158–64, 168–70, 183–89; 1978, 73, 119, 127–45, 151).

Since he now conceives of the "role of the state and its interventions" as "the contradictory condensation of a balance of forces" (1975, 170), Poulantzas can no longer be accused of depicting the state as a unitary monolith flawlessly maintaining the cohesion of the social formation to the exclusive benefit of the dominant classes. Because of the manifold contradictions at the very heart of the state apparatus, "the organizational role of the State is quite clearly marked by structural limitations," he now argues (1978, 135). Instead of constituting a single apparatus "united and cemented around a univocal political will," the state bureaucracy is divided in "fiefs, clans and factions" (ibid.), which pursue contradictory interests and policies. As a result, "the policy of the State essentially consists in the outcome of their collision, rather than in the (more or less successful) application of the global objective of the state apex" (135–36). Instead of being coherent and "rational," then, state policy is characterized by frequent contradictions, conflicts, turnabouts, hesitations, and nondecisions (185–86; 1975, 168–70). For this reason, Poulantzas argues, "capitalist planning, in the sense of an effective control of the contradictions of capitalist reproduc-tion, is actually unthinkable (the myth of organized capitalism)" (1975, 169).

In addition, Poulantzas turned increasingly to what in the Al-thusserian jargon would be called "conjunctural" analysis. He also returned to more orthodox Marxist economics, invoking Marx's law of the tendency of the rate of profit to fall (see Marx 1967b, pt. 3) to explain current transformations of the role of the capitalist state (Poulantzas 1975, 42, 62–63, 107, 111–12, 117–18, 123, 136, 142, 166, 171–72, 241; 1978, 143, 166ff., 212).[29] The tendency of the rate of profit to fall as a result of a secular rise in the organic composition of capital, which is un-avoidable under capitalism, may not be empirically observable at any time, according to Poulantzas, particularly because of the countertendencies mobilized by the state (1978, 173–74). Nevertheless, he argues, the tendency "still remains active and explains the introduction of *counter-tendencies* which thwart this tendency by preventing it from concretely manifesting itself," and therefore "it is not only legitimate, but absolutely indispen-sable, to take the tendency of the falling rate of profit as the central reference-point" (174).

Thus, the enormous growth of the socioeconomic functions of the state under monopoly capitalism is explained by Poulan-tzas as an attempt by the state to offset the tendency of the profit rate to fall by raising the productivity of labor and hence the amount of relative surplus value that can be extracted from the working class. The means include monetary management, subsidies, industrial planning and restructuring, research and development, increased reproduction of labor power by means of collective consumption (welfare measures), and the like, all of which causes the state to become ever more directly involved in the process of capital accumulation itself, an involvement that becomes ever more *"incompressible"* (ibid., 169). This, in turn, tends to "overpoliticize" the actions of the state which must now take increasing responsibility for economic growth and stability, thus sharpening the contradictions within the

29   For some clear expositions of this "law," and its rather dubious status, see
        Heilbroner (1980, 119 ff.), Hodgson (1974), Steedman (1975), E. O. Wright
        (1975, 1978, ch. 3), and especially Van Parijs (1980).

power bloc, as well as those between it and the dominated classes, while simultaneously undermining the state's room to maneuver in order to maintain hegemony (166–79).

This state is confronted with increasing popular struggles against its measures to improve capital accumulation, which produce a rising rate of exploitation; deterioration of the position of the elderly, women, youth, the petty bourgeoisie, and the environment; rising regional inequality; sharpening conflicts between fractions of the power bloc over which of them is to be favored by state intervention; additional tensions between the state's top personnel and lower-level bureaucrats who are increasingly affected by proletarianization and consequently by the popular struggles just mentioned; and, finally, by recurring "fiscal crises" caused by the fluctuations in tax revenues. At the same time the resources necessary to fulfill its growing functions continue to rise (ibid., 154–56, 190–94, 210–16, 241–47). Yet, because of the relative separation of state and economy and the state's internal contradictions (190–94), the state is structurally incapable of removing the ultimate cause of these problems, namely "the 'hard core' of capitalist relations of production" (191). Therefore, Poulantzas maintains, the capitalist state is confined to chaotic, ultimately ineffective "*ad hoc* tinkering" (ibid.) which only aggravates the problems in the long run. The result is that the capitalist state suffers an ever-deepening "*crisis of legitimation*" (245) from which it cannot extricate itself (see also 1975, 171–74).

This dilemma has given rise in Western capitalist societies to what Poulantzas calls "authoritarian statism": "intensified state control over every sphere of socio-economic life *combined with* radical decline of the institutions of political democracy and with draconian and multiform curtailment of so-called 'formal' liberties, whose reality is being discovered now that they are going overboard" (1978, 203–4). The discovery appears to be mostly Poulantzas's own, however, and has led to a radical change in his evaluation of bourgeois democracy (see below).

Poulantzas's thinking about the correct strategy for achieving socialism also appears to have been drastically revised under the influence of his newly found appreciation of "bourgeois" liberties and democracy. In a direct (but unacknowledged) contradiction of his earlier statements (1973b, 59, 74, 78, 275, 287, 299, 300n; cf. Jessop 1980a, 123; 1982, 177–80) he now totally disavows Leninist vanguardism, holding it partly responsible for the brutal repression of Stalinism (1978, 251–55; see also Hall and Hunt 1979, 65–66). Instead, Poulantzas proposes a "democratic road to socialism" which combines the preservation of civil liberties, political and ideological pluralism, and the institutions of representative democracy with *"the unfurling of forms of direct democracy and the mushrooming of self-management bodies"* (1978, 256), so as to avoid both social democratization and authoritarian dictatorships of the Stalinist variety (see also Hall and Hunt 1979; Jessop 1985, ch. 10; H. Weber 1978).

Yet, although Poulantzas advocates preservation of the institutions of "bourgeois" democracy, which, he now claims, were truly "a conquest of the masses" (1978, 256), he still maintains that "truly profound breaks are required, rather than secondary modifications of the state apparatus" (263). But the "sweeping transformation of the State" (261, 263) he seeks is to lead only to the "extension and deepening" (256, 261) of these institutions, not to their destruction. Yet exactly how "sweeping" a transformation Poulantzas envisions is not entirely clear. He repeatedly cautions against rash action and warns that the transition is likely to be "a long process" (197, 257, 258, 263). In fact, the process as envisaged by Poulantzas appears to be a very gradual one indeed. To prevent economic collapse, and presumably also to maintain the broadest possible popular support as the only possible defense against bourgeois reaction if civil liberties are to be maintained (263–64), Poulantzas recommends a long and gradual transformation of the various state apparatuses at different speeds, depending on their proximity to the hegemonic fraction, the extent to which they already correspond to "the needs of the masses" (198), their economic role, and their "exact political content" (197–99 generally). However, as to the precise nature of the desired transformation Poulantzas has little to say. He confines himself to a few rather vague indications: "the long process of taking power essentially consists in the spreading, development, reinforcement, coordination and direction of those diffuse centres of resistance which the masses always possess within the State networks, in such a way that they become the real centres of power on the strategic terrain of the State" (258).

Nor does he offer any further specifications as to the exact nature of these "new forms of direct, rank-and-file democracy" and "self-management networks and centres" (ibid., 261–62), other than that they should be "mushrooming," "flowering," "unfurling," and so on (256, 260–63). Quite rightly, it seems to me, Poulantzas identifies the problem of how exactly such a "flowering" of self-management bodies should be "articulated" with an "extension and deepening" of representative democracy, as the crucial question in his scenario (256, 262, 264). But unfortunately he does not even *attempt* to answer it, apparently content with the rather lame observation that "the answer to such questions does not yet exist" (265; cf. Hall and Hunt 1979, 71–74; Jessop 1980a, 124–25; H. Weber 1978, 24–28). All that history has given us so far, Poulantzas claims, are negative examples to be avoided. Perhaps democratic socialism is unattainable, he ponders, and any attempts to achieve it are certainly fraught with the risks of either social democratization or fascist repression. However, Poulantzas nevertheless boldly concludes, "if we weigh up the risks, that is in any case preferable to massacring other people only to end up ourselves beneath the blade of a Committee of Public Safety or some Dictator of the proletariat. There is only one sure way of avoiding the risks of democratic socialism, and that is to keep quiet and march ahead under the tutelage and the rod of advanced liberal democracy" (1978, 265).

These are brave words indeed, but they hardly suffice to conceal the fact that Poulantzas's own strategy has become virtually indistinguishable from that of the very advanced liberal democracy whose tutelage and rod he seeks to escape. He admits that his democratic road to socialism is not as clearly distinct from reformism as was the Leninist dual-power strategy and that, consequently, the danger of social democratization is correspondingly greater (Hall and Hunt 1979, 61; H. Weber 1978, 18). Yet, he claims, unlike the reformists' "successive reforms in an unbroken chain," *his* democratic road to socialism "denotes nothing other than a *stage of real breaks*, the climax of which— and there has to be one—is reached when the relationship of forces on the strategic terrain of the State swings over to the side of the popular masses" (1978, 258–59). This distinguishes his "left wing" Eurocommunism from the reformist "right wing" variety, he now claims (Hall and Hunt 1979, 61–62; Jessop 1985, 297–98). But if *this* is the crucial difference between Poulantzas's strategy and reformism it is one of mere rhetoric, not substance, since, according to Poulantzas himself, the expected "swing" is likely to take a long time and he nowhere saw fit to specify further those "real breaks" he anticipates. In fact, Poulantzas's suggestions are so vague and so elaborately qualified that they need not offend even the most timid of social democrats, despite the militant-sounding rhetoric. One can always claim—and this is precisely the usual argument to justify social-democratic restraint—that any reforms more radical than those presently attempted would not enjoy sufficiently broad and active popular support to overcome the expected opposition from the capitalist class, or that they would seriously endanger the stability of the economy and thus provoke a serious loss of popular support (see also Jessop 1985, 299–310). In other words, Poulantzas has moved "light-years away" (ibid., 295) from his original theory of the capitalist state which was intended to demonstrate that the capitalist state *must* unambiguously and exclusively serve the interests of the capitalist class so long as all its institutions (which included, as "Ideological State Apparatuses," virtually *all* social institutions other than outright revolutionary organizations) are not completely "broken" by a socialist revolution.[30]

The question is, however, whether, with these later "rectifications" Poulantzas "ably addresses many of the questions that critics raised" (Kesselman 1983, 832), that is, without fundamentally affecting the central tenets of his original theory as he claimed. The answer, I would argue, is a definite no: the "revised" theory is in reality a completely different one, quite incompatible with the much acclaimed initial formulations.

To begin with, despite the interminable references to class

30   In fact, Poulantzas's "democratic road to socialism" reminds one most vividly of Gorz's "socialist strategy of progressive reforms" which, as I have noted above (see note 22, Chapter 2) differed from run-of-the-mill social democracy only by its militant-sounding rhetoric.

"practices" and "struggles" it is simply not true that the notion of the "primacy" of the class struggle over the structures was "already inherent" in Poulantzas's early work. To be sure, as noted above (pp. 254–56), his distinction between structures and practices *did* lead to some ambiguous assertions about the causal relation between the two. But they are no more than ambiguities that are either trivial or completely contradict the overall theory—not just minor qualifications.

In fact, if Poulantzas's later declarations on the primordial role of the class struggle, which "governs" and "limits" the "functions" of the apparatuses, are taken seriously, his whole original theory of the "structural" determination of the functions, unity, and relative autonomy of the capitalist state goes *completely* by the board. If the class struggle, with its "historical, dynamic dimension" independent of the structures, determines the functions and structure of the state, then these structures and functions can clearly not at the same time be the result of the role assigned to the state by its place in the "global structure." We are left, after Poulantzas's revisions, with the rather commonplace "theory" that what the state will or will not do depends on the historically contingent ups and downs of the class struggle, a "theory" with rather uncomfortably "instrumentalist" implications. For if the "balance of forces" *really* determines the functioning of the apparatuses this could only mean that the state will serve whatever class happens to have the upper hand at any particular "conjuncture." Any other interpretation of the "primacy" of the class struggle is either absurd (the state systematically serving the losing side?) or deprives it of all substance. If the state always serves the long-term interests of the capitalist class, either that class must always be winning the class struggle or else the class struggle is as irrelevant as Poulantzas's earlier "structuralist" theory suggests. In either case we can do quite well without the vacuous rhetoric about its "primacy."

But Poulantzas denies that his new conception of the state as a "contradictory condensation of a balance of forces" carries the instrumentalist implication that the state is the prize that accrues to the winner of a class struggle taking place outside the state (the state as a "thing"). The class struggle goes on inside

the state, with different branches representing different fractions of the power bloc, and "centres of opposition" conquered
by the "popular masses," constantly competing with one another, counteracting each other's policies, and so on. But he
never explains how and in what sense these branches and centers ever come to "represent" these various fractions and classes
in the first place. Have they become direct class instruments (by
virtue, e.g., of the class sympathies of their personnel, or close
contacts with the members of certain fractions and classes), or
is this "representation" a matter of "structural" necessity, the
various branches still enjoying the relative autonomy they possessed in Poulantzas's earlier formulations? And if so, what
could the misty metaphor of "*condensate* of a relation of power
between struggling classes" possibly mean?

Similarly, it may sound vaguely plausible that an institution
that is "structurally shot through and constituted with and by
class contradictions" cannot be expected to produce any coherent planning policies capable of effectively controlling the "contradictions of capitalist reproduction," but neither would one
expect such an institutional mess to be able to produce any coherent policies that serve the long-term political interests of the
dominant class. Why it can do one but not the other is never
explained by Poulantzas. He merely asserts that policies that advance "the general, long-term political interests of the power
bloc" are the long-term "resultant" of the incoherent and chaotic rivalries between branches—not a word about how this mysterious metamorphosis takes place.

This is rather odd in view of his earlier theory according to
which the capitalist class is so hopelessly divided and shortsighted that it badly needs a state with an extraordinary degree
of coherence and institutional unity to produce a coherent policy safeguarding that class's overall, long-term political interests. Of course, Poulantzas still maintains that the coherence of
state policy is ultimately guaranteed by the dominance of the
hegemonic fraction and *its* power center within the state. But
either this dominance is absolute, as it seemed in his initial theory, and then one is forced to ask why the petty bickering between rival branches matters at all, or it is not, but then there is
no obvious reason why short-term chaos should produce long-

term coherence (cf. Alford and Friedland 1985, 277–78; Jessop 1982, 183; 1985, 192–94).

Clearly, moreover, if the state is really the "condensate" of the balance of forces of the class struggle, there can be no "structural" guarantee of the state invariably constituting the "unambiguous power" of the capitalist class, as Poulantzas used to claim, unless that balance of forces is itself "structurally" fixed or unless it is only the balance *within* the power bloc that matters. But then the "primacy" of the class struggle would be totally meaningless. Thus, short of a retreat to the earlier "structuralism," Poulantzas's new theory necessarily implies that the state will, in times of great working-class strength and militance, make concessions that are truly in that class's interest, in other words, that do not merely serve to reinforce the hegemony of the dominant classes. But this would seem to lead to blatantly reformist conclusions which directly contradict Poulantzas's earlier formulations, as his newly found appreciation for "bourgeois" democracy and his rather reformist "democratic road to socialism" vividly illustrate.

Those very institutions of public, democratic control (parliament, universal suffrage, the competitive party system), whose supposed decline he now bemoans, used to be the very institutions that permitted the capitalist state to "*dis*organize" the dominated classes by providing the state with just the degree of relative autonomy from the dominant classes to make precisely those concessions—and *only those* concessions—required to maintain the hegemony of the dominant classes. Whereas Poulantzas had previously depicted parliamentary deputies as doing little more than contributing to the masquerade of presenting the interests of the power bloc as the "general interest," he now deplores their loss of power as representatives of "the people . . . in relation to every level of the state bureaucracy . . . appearing before the administration in their capacity of people's delegates who legitimately represented such interests as components of the national interest" (1978, 222). Executive decision making, he now claims, has replaced "striking political compromises on the political arena" (224), and now the executive branch exclusively represents "monopoly interests as the 'general' or 'national' interests" (225). Yet, according to his earlier analyses such compromises were *always* exclusively to the advantage of the dominant classes, and the executive branch (or whichever branch happened to be the dominant one in the state apparatus) was virtually by definition the one that had the function of converting the interests of the hegemonic fraction into the interests of the "people-nation." He once claimed that the bureaucracy, irrespective of its class composition and formal subjection to other branches of government, was "structurally" compelled to execute the objective functions of the capitalist state, which partly explained its cohesion, pathological secretiveness, "distance from the masses," and the like as typically capitalist phenomena (see, e.g., 1975, 54–62). Now we suddenly hear of the decline of "the principle of public knowledge" and the consequent loss of public democratic control of the bureaucratic apparatus (1978, 226). The formal separation of powers, Poulantzas used to argue, was little more than a sham because the branch that represents the hegemonic fraction always obtains complete dominance. This was one of his major arguments against the " 'parliamentarist' deformation." Now he mourns the loss of the "limited distribution of powers" that once prevailed between the branches of government (ibid., 227). Political parties, he notes regretfully, are ceasing to be the "crucial networks in the formation of political ideology and a social consensus," of reciprocal vertical influence, and of citizen's control, that they used to be (229). But his whole former argument was intended to show the utter irrelevance of the vicissitudes of the "political scene" and its political parties, for they (with the exception of "revolutionary" parties, of course) belong by definition to the "Ideological State Apparatuses" and are doomed to serve the interests of the dominant classes, no matter what class they claim to "represent." There was never any question of "reciprocal vertical influence" or "citizens' control." Finally, Poulantzas's lamentation about the undermining of the dissociation between public and private spheres, that "cornerstone of traditional representative democracy" (238), is most curious of all. He used to consider the whole distinction as a purely ideological one that only served to buttress the "isolation effect," allowing the state to exercise class rule under the banner of classlessness ("citizens-subjects"), and one, moreover, that contained the very seeds of totalitarianism (see pp. 261–63 and note 19, this chapter; cf. Panitch 1979, 6).

All this implies that, contrary to Poulantzas's former claims, the institutions of representative democracy render parliamentarism *anything but* "a myth," that the dominated classes can successfully employ the electoral strategy to force the state to attend to some of their real interests and hence to cease being "the unambiguous and exclusive power of the bourgeoisie." His "democratic road to socialism" further confirms this. But Poulantzas is not quite prepared to face up to these blatantly reformist and gradualist implications of his own "revised" theory. When confronted with the apparent possibility for the working class to wrest real concessions from, and hence gain a piece of real power in, the state by means of a "class struggle" consisting of electoral politics, he simply retreats to the old structuralist formulas. Incrementalism by partial conquests is still flatly dismissed on the grounds that the unity, functions, and class domination characteristic of the capitalist state are *"inscribed in the institutional materiality and organizational framework of the state apparatus"* (1978, 189, also 14, 126, 143; 1975, 25–26, 163–64; 1976, 73). The capitalist state is structurally incapable of affecting the "hard core" of capitalist production relations, and it can therefore never serve the true interests of the working class (1978, 190–91). Whatever concessions are made to the working class serve either to facilitate the reproduction of labor power to allow more intensive exploitation or to maintain political cohesion and hence hegemony (180–89).

But Poulantzas cannot have it both ways. Either democratic institutions make a real difference *or* they do not. If they do not, his lamentations about the decline of representative democracy make little sense; if they do, then the capitalist state's "institutional materiality" does not preclude its incremental conquest by the dominated classes. Perhaps Poulantzas means that the capitalist state cannot be used, as it now exists, to abolish capitalist relations of production outright, but that it *does* allow for significant reform, short of such outright abolition, that favors the dominated classes at the expense of the dominant classes. But this is either a not very informative truism or it *still* contradicts the earlier argument. It is rather obvious, of course, that presently existing states would need additional departments, powers, and personnel to enable them to abolish and replace capitalist production relations, just as the liberal "laissez faire" state, to the extent that it ever really existed anywhere, had to be equipped with additional taxing powers and departments before it could begin issuing social security checks. The point is whether this could be achieved by an incrementalist electoral strategy or not. But even if it could not, for some deeper "structural" reason, this still leaves the possibility of *significant* reform short of complete abolition of capitalism. Now, again, either these reforms *are* significant or they are not. If they are, that is, if they do not merely maintain the hegemony of the capitalist class but instead constitute significant curtailments of its (political) power, then the state is not the *unambiguous* power of the bourgeoisie anymore, of course, and therefore the old theory must be discarded. If they are not significant, the old theory still holds, but then the "rectifications" concerning the primacy of the class struggle, the "condensation" of a balance of forces, and the significance of representative democracy are totally redundant, little more than irrelevant window dressing.

In conclusion, then, if one wishes to evaluate the theory that made Poulantzas "the most influential Marxist political theorist of the postwar period" (Jessop 1982, 153), and in particular its central claim that the capitalist state is compelled to promote the interests of the capitalist class even when it is opposed by the members of this class, one is forced to confine oneself to his earlier "structuralist" formulations. His later "revisions" are in fact completely incompatible with the original theory. They amount to an entirely different theory with implications that are wholly at odds with that very central claim.[31]

---

31   Poulantzas's "conjunctural" analyses of the rise of "authoritarian statism" ultimately caused by the tendency of the rate of profit to fall does not seem to fit very well with his earlier, much more static theory either, but it need not detain us here. It is altogether too fragmentary, ad hoc, and undocumented to add up to a theoretical statement worthy of detailed examination; it is largely borrowed from other theorists (cf. Hirsch 1978; Holloway and Picciotto, eds. 1978); and the basic premise, the tendency of the rate of profit to fall, is plainly untenable (see Elster 1985, 155–61; Fine and Harris 1976; Robinson 1966, 35–42; Sweezy 1942, 96–108; Van Parijs 1980; Yaffe

Althusser's "Orrery"

For[32] all the reservations expressed by fellow Marxists about Althusserian structuralism, few would have dared to deny its "indubitable rigour and theoretical sophistication" (Laclau 1975, 87). It is still billed as "a remarkably sophisticated and stimulating interpretation of Marxism" (Craib 1984, 124). Many have praised Althusser and Poulantzas for finally casting off the Marxist propensity toward simplistic reductionism by emphasizing the complex interactions between the base and superstructures (see, e.g., Anderson 1980, 59–79; Caplan 1977, 85–86; Geras 1977, 258–62; McNall 1983, 477; Mann 1973, 16–18). In particular the idea that the capitalist state promotes the interests of the dominant classes while maintaining a degree of "relative autonomy" from these classes has been an appealing one, even for some explicit critics of Poulantzas (see, e.g., Holloway and Picciotto 1977, 1978, 3–10; Lindsey 1980; Miliband 1973, 85; 1977, 66–90; Weiner 1980, 7–8). But Althusserianism's heyday already seems to have passed. Its decline has been as stunningly rapid as its meteoric rise to prominence. Now that a growing number of critics have exposed its splendid vacuity, adding yet another extensive critique would be like flogging a dead horse (see note 34, this chapter). Rather, in the brief remarks that follow I merely wish to establish that the *only possible* merit of this approach is that it may have helped persuade orthodox Marxists such as Poulantzas of the legitimacy of considering politics as a realm with some degree of autonomy from the economic "base." Thus, Poulantzas's theory will have to be judged on its own and cannot, after my criticisms of it below, be rescued by appeals to its "scientific" Althusserian origins.

To put it bluntly, Althusser's "science of the history of social formations" turns out, on closer inspection, to have none of the rigor, specificity, or originality he claims for it. His notion of people being the mere "bearers" of roles imposed upon them

---

1973; for a Canadian debate see Cuneo 1978, 1982, 1984; van den Berg and Smith, 1982, 1984).

32   I take the term "orrery" from E. P. Thompson's (1978, 1–210) magnificently witty attack on Althusser which was one of the first to expose the utter hollowness of his so-called structuralism. For commentaries and summaries see Anderson (1980) and Porpora (1985).

by the "structures" is, as DiTomaso has convincingly shown (1982; cf. Pedraza-Bailey 1982), virtually indistinguishable from the structural functionalism of Talcott Parsons, including its basic flaw of "sociological reductionism." In addition, the key concepts of Althusser's structuralism, and the relations between them, remain so fundamentally ill defined, that his arguments—if they can be called that—boil down to little more than endlessly repeated, obscurely formulated platitudes of the most embarrassing kind.

Consider, first, Althusser's conception of various social activities (political, ideological, economic, theoretical) as formally similar "practices" in the sense that they can be said to involve processes of transformation by specific combinations of analogous "elements" ("raw materials," "agents," "means," and "procedures" of "production"), although they are differently structured and different in nature for each distinct "practice." Now, the utility of such a vaguely plausible-sounding metaphor depends, of course, on whether it provides any new insights into the *substantive* similarities, differences, and relations between the social activities so described. As it is, the notion of structured "practices" means little more than "the way things are done," which is claimed to have some sort of theoretical primacy over the people who do them. In addition one has to specify what makes these "practices" distinct, what it is in the structure and elements of, say, *economic* practices that distinguish them from *political* ones, and how and why such differences and distinctions matter. On this crucial point Althusser is completely (and rather symptomatically, one might add) silent, however. He simply never bothers to explain by what "mechanism" economic "practice" produces economic products or political "practice" political "products."[33]

Thus, the various "levels," "instances," or "regional structures" Althusser is at such pains to distinguish (economic, political, ideological, theoretical) remain purely formal categories

33 Althusser *does* identify the mechanism by which "theoretical practice" transforms its "raw materials" into scientific "knowledges": the mechanism producing *"knowledge effects"* consists of "the action of particular *forms* which ensure the *presence* of scientificity in the production of knowledge, in other words, by specific forms that confer on a knowledge its character as a ('true') knowledge" (Althusser and Balibar 1970, 62, 66). Q.E.D.

without any substance whatsoever. Althusser simply does not provide any criteria by which we might be able to distinguish among them nor even any justification for distinguishing between *these* specific "levels" rather than some other ones (cf. Giddens 1981, 46). All we are left with, in fact, is the incredible banality that the rather conventional distinction between political, economic, ideological, and scientific activities points to the fact that these activities do indeed differ although, since they are all social activities, they naturally exhibit some similarities, too—without any but the vaguest metaphorical clue as to the nature of *either* the differences *or* the similarities. Unbelievable as it may seem, the *entire* remainder of Althusser's version of the "science of history" consists of nothing but endless repetitions of this one profound insight: the activities people engage in are in some ways similar and in some ways not.

Thus, Althusser's notion of the relative autonomy and "specific effectivity" of the various "instances," which he grandiloquently presents as a "*new conception* of the relation between *determinate instances* in the structure-superstructure complex" (1969, 111), turns out to amount to nothing more than the commonplace assertion that the economy and the superstructure affect one another but neither fully determines the other, an assertion that has for some time been rather obvious to all but the most "vulgar" of Marxists. The rather grandiose notions of "overdetermination" and "structural causality" simply repeat the same banality once again, namely that the "instances" are related to one another in a complex articulation of mutual influences, or as Kolakowski aptly puts it, that "particular . . . phenomena are generally due to a variety of circumstances" (1978c, 485). Nor is the rather obscure notion of a "global structure" that is no more than the complex articulation itself but that has causal effects of its own of much help, since Althusser never gets around to explaining what these effects are and how they operate.

Of course Althusser claims that his theory differs from mere indeterminate causal pluralism because the global structure is always a "structure articulated in dominance," that is, one of the instances is always dominant and hence gives the structure its unity, and this is determined, "in the last instance," by the economy. But he nowhere specifies what he *means* by "dominance" and "determination 'in the last instance' " or how these modes of "effectivity" actually work. Hence "structure in dominance" boils down to the rather uninteresting assertion that one "instance" is generally at least a little bit more prominent than the others, in some sense, without giving us a single clue as to how this can be observed or how it matters. The determination by the economy of displacements of dominance between instances may give these displacements "the necessity of a function," but this necessity remains largely rhetorical so long as Althusser refuses to disclose the terms and mechanisms of that function. Things are not helped much by the obscure claim that "from the first moment to the last, the lonely hour of the 'last instance' never comes" (1969, 201). Besides, this determination by the economy would seem to contradict Althusser's claim that it is the *global* structure that assigns the instances their places and functions. Finally, Althusser's famous use of the concept of "uneven development" is just as theoretically vacuous as the rest of his arguments. Since we have no idea what *even* development— or "corresponding," "articulated," or "related" development, to use Althusser's other favorite vacuities—between the economy and, for example, the "political instance" would look like, we have no way of knowing when it is "*un*even." In fact it can quite literally be *anything*, since as a result of "uneven development" any concrete conjuncture can be characterized by "peculiar relations of correspondence, non-correspondence, articulation, dislocation and torsion which obtain, between the different 'levels' of the whole in accordance with its general structure" (Althusser and Balibar 1970, 108). For all its self-proclaimed "rigor" and "scientificity," Althusserian "theoretical practice" apparently does not know the difference between vague physical-spatial metaphors or allusions and coherent, logical argumentation.

In short, because Althusser refuses to define and specify his central concepts his "theoretical practice" yields nothing but the common-sense banality that all things are related, yet not identical.[34] But, while the "knowledge effect" of Althusser's "science

34   For similar criticisms of the theoretical emptiness of some of Althusser's key concepts because they remain unspecified, see Appelbaum (1979, 26–28), Benton (1984), Burris (1979, 11), Clarke et al. (1980), Connell (1982), Gi-

of history" may be perfectly nil, it does not immediately follow that the same is also true of the theory of the state of his disciple Poulantzas. It still can be, and has been argued (e.g., Anderson 1980, 59–79; Burris 1979, 9–11; Giddens 1980, 885–86), that Althusser at least provided a set of principles justifying the study of the various "instances" in their own right by the practitioners of Marxist "science," thereby liberating Marxism from its longstanding economic-reductionist straightjacket. Of course, that it took the unequaled verbal contortionism of an Althusser to do this should at the very least be "mildly alarming" (Parkin 1980, 894), and certainly no cause for self-congratulation. Nevertheless, it can be argued that Althusser formally established the study of the *inter*action between "instances" without reducing any of them to epiphenomena of the economic base as a legitimate enterprise for orthodox Marxists, thus allowing Poulantzas to develop a substantive Marxist theory of the capitalist state capable of doing full justice to the complex interactions that take place in real "social formations." In short, whatever one may think of Althusser's "science," Poulantzas's theory of the capitalist state will have to be judged on its own terms. The rest of this chapter is an attempt to do that.

"Theoretical Practice," Scientific Explanation, and Dogma: A Critique of Poulantzas

As noted earlier, Poulantzas's theory of the state is widely regarded as a defense of Marxist orthodoxy against "bourgeois" reformist doctrines that is both theoretically and empirically more sophisticated than the "instrumentalist" critiques of pluralism. Unlike "instrumentalism," Poulantzas's approach is said to be "able to tackle the pluralists on their own terrain" (Giddens 1981, 216). This is primarily attributable to Poulantzas's famous conception of the "relative autonomy" characteristic of the capitalist type of state. This notion allows Poulantzas to con-

---

rardin (1974, 198), Glucksmann (1977, 308), Gold, Lo, and Wright (1975a, 38–39), Jessop (1980a, 116–19), Kolakowski (1971, 119–21), Laclau (1975, 101–19), Shapiro (1981, 11–12), Smith (1984), Thompson (1978, 1–210), and E. O. Wright (1983).

cede the empirical validity of some of the claims made by pluralists, while denying that this in any way disproves the orthodox Marxist theory of the state. Simply put, Poulantzas agrees
that the state in capitalist "social formations" *does* enjoy a certain
degree of autonomy from the capitalist class which enables governments to act *against* the preferences and even the active resistance of the members of this class, as can from time to time
be observed to happen empirically. However, he argues, this
autonomy nevertheless always remains *relative*, which means
that it can *only* be used to implement policies that are in the
long-term interest of the capitalist class anyway, even though
the members of this class may themselves fail to recognize this.
Thus, while governments *do* occasionally defy the capitalist
class, this does not necessarily disprove the Marxist doctrine
that the state acts in the (ultimate) interests of the capitalist
class.

But when compared to liberal pluralism or Marxist "instrumentalism" this general argument immediately raises questions: how and in what sense can such cases be said to be in the
interest of the capitalist class *despite* the apparent evidence to
the contrary? Although pluralists and "instrumentalists" may
disagree on whether or not government policy in the "democratic" capitalist countries reflects (only or primarily) the interests of the capitalist class, they do share two key assumptions:
first they agree that the conscious preferences of the members
of the capitalist class are necessary and sufficient indicators of
their "true" interests, especially when they are united; second,
they view government policy as in large part the result of pressures from societal interest groups. Poulantzas's argument contradicts both of these assumptions. Therefore, if we are to evaluate the alleged superiority of his approach, we will have to ask
whether it offers anything that could plausibly take their place.
In examining Poulantzas's theory, then, I am looking for the
answers to two crucial questions without which the theory cannot reasonably claim to offer something better than the theories
it seeks to replace: (1) if not by consulting the preferences of
the members of the capitalist class themselves, on what grounds
can we establish what sort of policy is and what is not in their
("true") interest? (2) if not the overt and covert pressures and

manipulation by (representatives of) the capitalist class, what constrains the state nevertheless to pursue only the ("true") interests of this class, even when resisted by it? In short, to be a credible alternative to its theoretical rivals, Poulantzas's approach will have to provide some alternative method for determining the "true" interests of the bourgeoisie, *and* it will have to explain the causal mechanism by which the capitalist state's autonomy is kept "relative."

In what follows I seek out Poulantzas's answers to these questions by scrutinizing his whole elaborate argument point for point. However, primarily to give myself and the reader a fighting chance of finding our way through the dense thicket of definitions, taxonomies, and interdependent propositions, I have divided the section into three subsections, which group together three more or less distinct sets of arguments. In the first subsection I discuss some of the major conceptual issues and distinctions to which Poulantzas devoted so much of his attention. Of primary interest here is Poulantzas's concept of power and related concepts, including his discussions of the "dominant class," "hegemony," and the crucial notion of the indivisible "unity" of capitalist state power. As we shall see, there is much of substantive consequence in these ostensibly purely formal, definitional discussions with respect to the two central questions just posed. Presumably true to the canons of "modern epistemology," Poulantzas does not appear to recognize any difference between conceptual and substantive issues. In the next subsection I am primarily concerned to try and find some answer to the first question raised, How do we know what really *is* in the interest of the capitalist class if not by the conscious preferences of its members? I examine Poulantzas's distinction between "economic" and "political" interests here, as well as his much-quoted definition of the capitalist state as the "factor of cohesion" of the "social formation," and some related arguments. Finally, in the third subsection I at last examine Poulantzas's central and most famous argument, the one concerning the "relative autonomy" of the capitalist state. There, naturally, I am mostly interested in the answer to the second question: what causal mechanism, if not the direct influence of the bourgeoisie itself, keeps the state's autonomy "relative," that is, in line with the "true" class interests of that bourgeoisie?

It would probably be helpful to summarize my main conclusions here, so as to keep an eye on the overall forest while we stumble through the thick foliage. These conclusions, which emerge time and again from the closer examination of Poulantzas's arguments below, can be summed up as follows. On the empirical side, Poulantzas certainly *does* grant a great deal to the pluralists. In fact, his depiction of the real world of modern capitalist politics might even seem to exaggerate the degree and frequency of bourgeois defeats and popular victories as compared to the more sophisticated pluralists. On the other hand, his reassertion and defense of the antireformist Marxist orthodoxy that the state *never* serves *any* but the interests of the capitalist class remain categorical and utterly uncompromising. The way he manages to reconcile these apparently contradictory strands in his argument is *not* by offering clear answers to the questions I have posed, however, but by carrying out a radical separation between the empirical facts as he perceives them and his theoretical propositions. He does this essentially by rendering the "propositions" compatible with *any* empirical evidence, that is, in principle unfalsifiable. As we shall see again and again, Poulantzas, much like his onetime mentor Althusser, methodically redefines the terms of the orthodox propositions so that they come to cover *all* possibilities imaginable; in other words, they become completely devoid of distinct content or empirical referents. As a result, the "propositions" still *sound* like the orthodox Marxist doctrines, but in reality they have become perfectly vacuous tautologies which, by their very nature, are compatible with *any* empirical state of affairs, including the exaggeratedly pluralist world actually depicted by Poulantzas and the more complacently conservative of the pluralists. At the same time, while thus emptying Marxist theory of its substantive content, Poulantzas's arguments interestingly continue to display some of the traits typical of Marxist theorizing after the loss of the uncomplicated faith in the obvious long-term incompatibility of capitalism and democracy as described in Chapters 1 and 2. The Leninist claim that the members of a class are not necessarily themselves the best judges of their own "true" class interests, and its corollary that only "scientific" Marxist theory can determine the "objective" interests of a class, are extended by Poulantzas to apply not only to the working class but to the capitalist class as well. Moreover, Poulantzas also appears to have adopted the strictly dichotomous perspective of Lenin: whatever is not entirely "socialist" is, *ipso facto*, entirely capitalist. Thus, the "objective" interest of the working class is, obviously, the attainment of "socialism," whereas *anything* short of this automatically amounts to maintaining capitalism which is, of course, in the "objective" interest of the capitalist class. Once again, moreover, we encounter the implicit assumption that these "objective" interests are wholly "immanent" in the system as it is, that is, they in no way depend on what exactly is meant by "socialism" and, by implication, its absence. This considerably facilitates Poulantzas's argument that all government policy is necessarily in the interest of the capitalist class, since he, like a good "anti-utopian" Marxist, need not clearly identify what *would* be "socialist," or conducive to "socialism," to begin with. Finally, again like much of post-Kautskyan Marxism in general, there is an odd tension in the argument between the recurring implicit guiding assumption that capitalism is perpetually on the verge of collapse and the whole drift of his theory which seems to be nothing so much as a long testimony to capitalism's infinite capacity for survival.

Power, "Hegemony," and the State: Twirls of the Conceptual Barrel

Given Poulantzas's own emphasis on "rigor" in defining and developing concepts suitable for his "problematic," it seems appropriate to start by examining his key concepts.[35] No doubt the most basic of these is his concept of "power," as it presumably underlies his entire theory. This is, at any rate, what one would conclude from the amount of effort and attention Poulantzas devotes to clarifying the terms of his definition and establishing the most subtle distinctions from related concepts (1973b, 100).

The concept of power accepted by both pluralists and "in-

35   I have taken part of the title of this section from a phrase by Connell which describes the Althusserian approach rather well: "History becomes a kaleidoscope, whose pieces can be re-arranged by a twirl of the conceptual barrel" (1982, 135).

strumentalist" Marxists is the traditional, Weberian one: an actor's ability to "carry out his own will despite resistance" (M. Weber 1947, 152). Thus, one can in principle objectively determine the amount of power that an actor or group possesses by observing the frequency with which the actor or group is able to have his or its preference prevail as a result of his or its conscious actions. As we have seen at the end of the last chapter, the Marxist critics of the "instrumental" view of the state have been especially critical of this "mechanical" conception of power. Therefore, one might expect *their* conceptualizations to offer some alternative way of measuring the power of an actor or group. This is, of course, directly relevant to the two major questions I raised in the introduction to this section.

As we have seen, Poulantzas defines power as "the capacity of a social class to realize its specific objective interests."[36] There are several obvious differences between this definition and the more conventional conception outlined above, but clearly the most important of these is that in Poulantzas's definition not the conscious will but the "objective interests" of the subject have to be realized. Here, if anywhere, we should be able to find some indication as to how Poulantzas intends to identify the "objective interests" of actors, if not by their own conscious preferences.

Interests are "objective," Poulantzas tells us, in the sense that they are in no way to be confused with the actors' subjective "imaginary interests" which are the product of "numerous forms of illusion." Rather, objective interests are objective limits imposed by the structures: they should be conceived as "an *extension of the ground* which this class can cover according to the stages of specific organization attainable by it," and they appear "as the *horizon* of its action as a social force." Whereas these limits-effects constitute the objective "long-term interests" of a class, its "short-term interests" consist of "limits-effects at one remove, imposed by the intervention of the practices of different classes (class struggle)."

---

36   To avoid tedious repetition, the reader should consult pp. 256–61, where I explain Poulantzas's concept of power in more detail, for the exact references for all direct quotations of Poulantzas in this subsection, unless indicated otherwise.

This, then, is how Poulantzas defines the crucial notion of "objective interests." It "is not any kind of metaphorical play on the terms of limits and field," he insists, "but a result of the complexity of the relations covered by these terms" (1973b, 111). Yet, rather ironically, this attempt to preempt criticism only makes it perfectly clear what *is* the matter with his "definition." Indeed, Poulantzas offers *nothing more* than a spatial metaphor, one that does not even *begin* to answer the question I have raised. All he says is that objective interests consist of the maximum a class can get away with (the "ground" it can "cover"), given the prevailing "objective" circumstances, such as the existing procedures and institutions ("structures"), the (organizational) resources a class happens to have available ("stages of specific organization attainable"), and the momentary strength of other classes.[37] Thus, Poulantzas defines objective class interests as the maximum a class could get away with given the prevailing circumstances, if only its members were sufficiently aware of it.

This boils down to a standard definition of "objective interests." At a minimum, the attribution by an observer of "objective interests" to (a group of) actors always means that the observer claims to know what the actors can "objectively" expect to obtain even though the actors may not be aware of this or even consciously want it. But such claims raise some notoriously tricky questions. By virtue of what special competence can the observer claim to know better than the actors? What right does the observer have to dictate his or her *own* preferences to the actors? On these questions Poulantzas remains entirely silent, not unlike most other proponents of "objective interests." Nor do the few instances in which he actually imputes specific objective interests to actors reveal much about the method by which

37 As I have argued above (pp. 257–58), the exclusion of ideological illusions from the "objective" circumstances determining what a class can get away with seems somewhat questionable since in the Althusserian model ideology is as much an objective "structure" imposing itself irresistibly on its "bearers" as any other structure. But then again, to *include* ideology would mean that the objective interests simply reduce to the "imaginary interests" pursued by the members of a class, since these are generally below what they could achieve given the other "objective" conditions, which would render the whole notion of *objective* interests meaningless.

Poulantzas arrives at his "objective" judgments, as we shall see. Once again, they appear to be based on the implicit assumption of class interests arising "immanently" from capitalism itself. In the meantime, those who honestly believe that under the present "objective" circumstances gradual reform through electoral politics is the best the working class can "objectively" hope for, will simply have to take Poulantzas's word for it that they suffer from the " 'parliamentarist' deformation." On the basis of undisclosed credentials Poulantzas is able to grasp "objectively" "the complexity of the relations covered" where the poor, deluded reformists, alas, are not.

This is not necessarily to say that imputations of "objective" interests must always be wholly arbitrary—although the dangers of arbitrariness are very real indeed and overcoming them presents formidable methodological problems. In a widely noted book, Lukes (1974) proposes a "three-dimensional" concept of power based precisely on nonarbitrary attribution of "real" interests. Although difficult, he argues, it *is* possible to determine these interests by asking how people *would* have acted if they had felt they had a choice in the matter. Through careful examination of all relevant evidence, Lukes concludes, it is possible to make a convincing, nonarbitrary argument, "though by nature of the case, such evidence will never be conclusive" (50). Thus, Lukes explicitly charges the observer with the task of identifying the conditions under which and the reasons for which it is hypothesized that the actors would choose the course of action imputed to be in their "real" interest. *This* is what opens the observer's reasoning to public scrutiny and thereby gives it its potentially nonarbitrary character. And it is precisely on this point that Poulantzas's orthodox Marxism, with its assumption of the "immanence" of objective class interests in capitalism as such and its refusal to accept the specific nature of the implicit alternative option ("socialism") as in any way relevant, prevents him from making a nonarbitrary, convincing case, as we shall see below.

Moreover, by firmly linking the concept of power to "objective" interests, that is, to interests the power holders themselves may not even be aware of, Poulantzas necessarily deprives it of the crucial ingredient of intentionality that is implied in the conventional definition of power as the ability to realize one's *will*. Thus, "power" becomes identical with having one's "objective" interests, the nature of which can only be determined by Marxist "science," realized by whatever means or for whatever reason, whether one knows it or not. This is very similar to the definitions of power advocated by Therborn and others (see pp. 234–36). Its basic flaw is that it simply reduces the notion of power to an alternative and largely redundant way of describing the "objective interests" of the actors, as decreed by the theorist.[38] Thus, it makes the concept of power even *more* dependent on the elusive notion of "objective" interests, since no behavior, or absence thereof, on the part of the alleged possessors of power can serve as evidence of that power. As a result, the arbitrariness of Poulantzas's definition of power, as compared to the more conventional one, is only further accentuated.[39]

But let us briefly turn to the other distinctive terms in Poulantzas's definition. The "specificity" of class interests refers to the distinction between economic, political, and ideological interests and the corresponding distinct levels of power. However, the distinction remains a purely formal one since these respective "levels" are merely formal labels, the substantive differences between them remaining completely unspecified in the Althusserian literature (cf. Glucksmann 1977). Thus, it is impossible to tell which are typically economic, which are political, and which are ideological "interests" except in a vague, intuitive sense. Moreover, Poulantzas leaves the relations that obtain between these respective powers completely open. They "relate to the articulation of the various class practices (class interests) which, in a dislocated manner, reflect the articulation of the various structures of a social formation" (1973b, 113). They do indeed.

38   Even Lukes (1974, 55–56), who, as just noted, proposes a concept of power that *does* rest on a concept of "objective" interests attributable to actors, feels compelled to reject Poulantzas's structural definition of power because it obliterates the crucial distinction between purely structural determination and the willful exercise of power.

39   For more detailed criticisms of this tendency to confuse the concept of power or "domination" with the effects it was supposed to help explain in the first place, see van den Berg (1981, 75–76) and especially Wrong (1979, 252–54).

Moreover, Poulantzas claims, this "explains" the possibility of "decentration" between the various powers. Thus, all bases are nicely covered. Whatever the actual evidence may be, it will necessarily support the "theory" since the "theory" simply tells us, quite literally, that *anything* is possible. As we shall see, this distinction between purely nominal "levels" of power allows Poulantzas to argue that however powerless to realize its interests the "dominant class" may seem to be, this is in reality only proof of its omnipotence at *another* level (see the next subsection).

By definition, Poulantzas restricts the concept of power to *classes only*. Other social strata and institutions cannot possess power. They can only *exercise* the power that belongs to a class. Thus, the state does not have any power of its own, it is merely the "centre of the exercise of political power," which belongs to the politically dominant class.[40] This is far from innocent. It is, in fact, a way of conveniently sidestepping some of the most disturbing implications of his own theory of the capitalist state. Poulantzas wishes to account for all possible conflicts between the capitalist class and the state and for all possible outcomes of such conflicts, particularly those in which the state prevails, yet he also wishes to demonstrate that the capitalist class possesses exclusive *political* dominance at all times. In the process he is forced to attribute *such* a degree of autonomy and unity of purpose to the state that he may appear to endow the state and bureaucracy with purposes and a great deal of power of their own, which would bring him closer to Weber than to Marx. Thus, restricting the definition of the concept of power so that it applies exclusively to social classes *by definition* looks an awful lot like a device to close off the "path that leads to the forbidden land of bureaucratic theory" (Parkin 1979, 128). The fact that virtually everything else Poulantzas has to say about political power seems to be specifically designed to reserve that concept

40   In his later writings Poulantzas seems to have retreated somewhat from this extreme position. "We now know," he concedes, "that class division is not the exclusive terrain of the constitution of power" (1978, 43), specifically mentioning the relations between men and women (ibid.) and the independent significance of nationality (115–20). Yet he still insists that such relations always bear "a class pertinency" (43) and that class power is still "the cornerstone of power" in class-divided social formations (44), and he still retains the same definition of power (147).

exclusively for the capitalist class, or, more precisely, for *one* fraction of that class, seems only to confirm this suspicion.

In short, this "definition" of power does not provide us with clear criteria for identifying the phenomenon in empirical reality or for distinguishing it from other phenomena. Instead, it offers only two things: (1) the rather arrogant and wholly arbitrary assertion that Marxist "science" as practiced by Poulantzas shall be the sole judge of the "objective" interests of social classes, and (2) the no less arbitrary decision that, by definition, only social classes can possess power. Neither is very likely to persuade anyone who has not already done so to adopt Poulantzas's concept of power.

It hardly comes as a surprise, then, that his definition of the "dominant class," presumably the class that wields the greatest amount of power (or rather has it wielded on its behalf), has none of the rigor Poulantzas claims for it. The "dominant class(es) in a formation," we are told, is "in the last analysis, that which occupies the dominant place(s) at that level of the class struggle which maintains the dominant role in the complex whole of that formation." How does this definition help us to discover the dominant class in any particular "social formation"? It simply does not. First, since it is never explained what is meant by "dominant" we have no way of determining which "level" is dominant at any particular time. All we know is that this is somehow "determined 'in the last instance' " by the economy. We will simply have to take Poulantzas's word for it that in liberal laissez-faire capitalism the economy bestowed "dominance" upon itself whereas under modern monopoly capitalism it has seen fit to yield "dominance" to the political level (cf. Jessop 1982, 173–77). As I have already noted (pp. 258–59), this would seem to imply a rather awkwardly un-Marxist definition of the dominant class in monopoly capitalism, namely, as the one that is *politically* dominant.

But this would cause the whole theory to become entirely circular, at least with respect to current monopoly capitalism. The whole point of Poulantzas's theory of the capitalist state was, after all, to demonstrate that the capitalist state is "structurally" constrained to serve the interests of the "dominant class." But if the "dominant class" is *defined* by its occupancy of the "dominant place" at the "dominant level" in the social formation, and if in monopoly capitalism this dominant level happens to be the political, then whichever class holds the politically "dominant place" is *by definition* the "dominant class." In other words, at least for modern twentieth-century capitalism, Poulantzas's famed theory of the state is simply true by definition and hence as irrefutable as it is empirically indifferent: whichever class turns out to be politically dominant at any one time is, *ipso facto*, the overall dominant class, and vice versa. But this does not preclude, of course, the possibility that some class *other* than the bourgeoisie might obtain overall dominance by means of a successful conquest of the politically "dominant place."

The last point, however, still assumes that Poulantzas actually provides some way of ascertaining who "occupies" the "dominant place." One can only surmise that such "occupancy" is equivalent to possessing the greatest amount of power, but this is not of much help either. After all, a class's power is defined by its "objective interests" which, as we have seen, only Poulantzas himself appears to be competent to determine. Thus, it is absolutely impossible to identify the "dominant class" with Poulantzas's definition unless one happens to be endowed with this special ability to determine the "true" interests of social classes. Once again, these are hardly compelling grounds for preferring this to more conventional (instrumentalist and pluralist) approaches.[41]

Poulantzas does not deny, moreover, that the "dominated classes" often appear to have a quite considerable impact at the political level. Reformist working-class organizations have been quite successful at obtaining welfare and social security pro-

---

41   The definition of the "dominant class" does tell us *one* thing, however: that it is not the *amount* but the *kind* (economic, political, ideological) of power that matters. But this information is rather superfluous since the whole thrust of Poulantzas's theory of the capitalist state is that, at the political "level" at least, power is strictly an all-or-nothing affair. The dominant class holds *all* power "in its unity"; the other classes have none. If this holds for the other "levels" as well, or if, as Poulantzas actually seems to believe, only the political level really matters, then, indeed, the dominant class would be the one that holds *all* power at the dominant "level," irrespective of whether it possess any power at any of the other levels. Other classes may have power and even be "dominant" at other "levels," but where it counts, at the "dominant" level, they are powerless by definition.

grams, nationalization and the like, which cannot be simply dismissed as insignificant or as not "really" in the interest of the working class. Thus the "dominated classes" would often appear to possess something that looks remarkably like an ability to realize their interests, in other words, power. But to concede this would raise some troublesome questions. If the dominated classes are able to realize *some* of their interests does this mean that there can be *degrees* of domination? If so, what stops the dominated classes from realizing even *more* of their interests, that is, from increasing their power? And if they can increase their power, at what point would they cease to be dominated? What *specific* interests would need to be realized to indicate an equal distribution of power between the classes, or even a reversal of the previous positions of dominance and subordination?

Instead of squarely confronting such basic issues, Poulantzas once again tries to "resolve" them with another barrage of neologisms, definitions, and classifications. Certainly, he concedes, reformist policies show the working class to be a "social force" whose "economic existence is reflected on the other levels by a specific presence."[42] This "specific presence," moreover, manifests itself by "pertinent effects," that is, by "a new element which cannot be inserted in the typical framework which these levels would present without this element," although whether or not any particular element can be said to be "new" in this sense, Poulantzas cautions, "always depends on the concrete conjuncture of a concrete situation." But "pertinent" though these "effects" may be, they are to be strictly distinguished from "power" in the full sense of the word, because such reformist policies are ultimately "ineffectual from the point of view of the

---

42   Although he does not elaborate further on the matter, Poulantzas seems to suggest here that "social forces" can manifest themselves at the ideological as well as at the political "level." It matters little, however, since in the end Poulantzas completely obliterates the "specificity" of these two "levels" with respect to one another by effectively merging them in the "Ideological State Apparatuses" which include absolutely everything other than certifiably "revolutionary" organizations and ideologies (see pp. 277–78). In what sense the "pertinent effects" of reformist working class organizations still retain any significance at all if they are *by definition* part of the "ideological apparatuses" of the *capitalist* state is another matter (cf. Panitch 1979, 6–7).

long-term strategic interests of the working class"; in other words, "this policy cannot lead to socialism." Thus, although Poulantzas characterizes the objective interests of a class as the "horizon" of its action, he presents "pertinent effects," by the same spatial metaphor, as "a class's threshold of existence as a distinct class." "Pertinent effects," then, qualify a class as something more than a merely passive, subordinate collectivity, they qualify it as a "distinct autonomous class" that acts as a "social force."

Obviously, the first question raised by all this is, How does one distinguish insignificant "effects" from those that are "pertinent"? How can one determine whether any particular class is an autonomous "social force" or merely a subordinate class? Once again, Poulantzas's "definitions" are of little use. To say that "pertinent effects" are "a new element which cannot be inserted in the typical framework which these levels would present without this element," is to say no more than that in some unspecified way the "levels" would not be quite the same without the element in question and that the element is hence *in this sense* significant, which is not saying very much, really. Moreover, it all depends on the "concrete conjuncture." Finally, even *none*vents qualify as "pertinent effects," since, of course, the "framework" would not be quite the same without them (i.e., if something *had* occurred; cf. note 16, this chapter)! So the definition includes, in principle, *anything* as a potential "pertinent effect." One imagines, with some distaste, the endless debates about whether any particular (non)occurrence is really "new," whether it can be "inserted in the typical framework," what is "typical" in the present "concrete situation" to begin with, whether the class in question has reached the "threshold," and so on.

But more important, it is by no means clear on what grounds Poulantzas distinguishes between mere "pertinent effects" and power. Both apparently involve the ability to realize class interests. But "pertinent effects," it seems, are "ineffectual" for the realization of "long-term strategic interests," whereas power, one must assume, *does* realize those interests. As we have seen before, Poulantzas distinguishes between long-term and short-term interests in his definition of power, but these seemed to be coexistent elements in the definition of a single concept of power. Now we suddenly seem to have a distinction between some kind of "short-term power" (the ability to realize "pertinent effects") and "long-term power" (the ability to realize "long-term strategic interests"). But this obviously raises the difficult question of how the two are related. If "pertinent effects" cannot eventually add up to the achievement of long-term strategic interests (if they could, the distinction would not make much sense), why not?

In addition, power now seems to be the ability to realize a fixed strategic interest rather than (presumably changing) objective interests that are limits-effects of the structures. This is suggested by the claim that in the case of the working class the interest is the realization of "socialism." But then the definition of power as the ability to "cover the ground" that a class can "cover," given the specific circumstances, is quite redundant. For the working class that "ground" is by definition synonymous with "socialism," and any achievements short of that ultimate state of affairs automatically mean that the working class has no power, merely "pertinent effects." Anything short of socialism also seems automatically to mean that the capitalist class still has *all* the power. It is starting to sound very familiar. All we learn from this is that in Poulantzas's private vocabulary, classes whose political or ideological "effects" are for some reason "significant" in *his* view, yet short of achieving their ultimate interests as decreed by *him*, deserve the distinction of being called "social forces." I am sure the classes in question are grateful for being so rewarded for their efforts, but to anyone else this is hardly very exciting news. Once again, then, *all* Poulantzas offers is a restatement of the Marxist dogma that reformism cannot lead to "socialism." It remains sheer dogma because, in lieu of an argument, Poulantzas offers nothing but "a definitional grid for classifying things" (Connell 1982, 138).

The *effect* of the obscure notion of "pertinent effects" is, however, perfectly clear. It allows Poulantzas to disqualify any phenomena that bear an uncanny resemblance to the exercise of power by or on behalf of (it makes no difference which according to Poulantzas's own definition of power) the "dominated classes," without opening himself to the charge of ignoring the gains made by the working class, by the simple expedient of calling it by another name. He uses the same convenient device to explain away other instances in which it might appear that groups other than the "dominant class" are able to realize some of their interests, that is, possess *some* "power." Thus, he does concede that branches of government other than the one that "reflects" the apparently omnipotent "hegemonic" fraction of the dominant class may function as the "power centers" of other classes and fractions. At first sight, and particularly in view of his earlier assertion that the state cannot itself possess power but can only function as the "power center" of the dominant class, one might be tempted to conclude that Poulantzas allows for the possibility of several classes and fractions *sharing* power. But then he quickly retreats from this dangerous implication by arguing that these other "power centers" do not really exercise any power: at best they "function more especially as *resistances* to the dominant power." This is apparently also true for the legislature and the executive if they ever come to be controlled by working-class parties, for Poulantzas also discusses the " 'parliamentarist' deformation" in this connection (see p. 272).

Similarly, Poulantzas does not wish to deny that the class composition and particular interests of the state bureaucracy may affect the functioning of the state "to some extent," but this does not confer any "power" at all on the "social category" of bureaucrats. Instead, their influence remains confined to mere "additional limits and barriers posed . . . to the hegemonic class or fraction" which under exceptional circumstances may even manifest themselves in "the form of *hindrances* and *barriers*." The bureaucracy may play a "role of its own in political action," but power—no (see p. 273).

This whole business about "hindrances," "resistances," and "barriers"—which is rather redundant in the case of the bureaucracy anyway since, by definition, only *classes* can have power[43]—is somewhat curious, to say the least. First of all, with

43   As Draper points out (1977, 497–510), Marx himself was never particularly finicky about whether or not bureaucrats could be called a "class." He had no trouble with that label at all, particularly in cases where they clearly *did* pursue their own interests. But then again, Marx was not (yet?) engaged in

rigorous consistency, Poulantzas does not bother to explain what these "resistances" and "hindrances" might consist of. But whatever they are, one must assume that they are in some sense in accordance with the wishes and interests of the classes, fractions, and bureaucrats in question; otherwise it would hardly be worth the trouble of activating "power centers" and taking to "political action." Therefore, if power means the *extent* to which one is able to realize objectively (given the particular "conjuncture") attainable interests, the ability to put up "resistances," even if it only amounts to the ability to stall temporarily the "dominant power," indicates *some* degree of power. Conversely, such "hindrances" and "barriers," if they mean anything at all, *must* mean that the "hegemonic" fraction or class is *prevented*, however temporarily, from realizing those interests it could otherwise have realized, and thus it implies a reduction of *its* power. Poulantzas cannot have it both ways: he must either admit that nonhegemonic, and nondominant, classes and fractions, and "social categories" like the state bureaucracy, may exert *some* power, in which case his entire theory about the *unambiguous* "correspondence" between state policy and the interests of the hegemonic fraction goes by the board, *or* he will have to drastically modify his own definition of power. The mysterious talk of "resistances" and "hindrances" is merely a rather transparent attempt to paper over this dilemma.[44]

However, Poulantzas *does* implicitly attempt a resolution of sorts of this dilemma with his argument concerning the "*unity proper to* institutionalized political power," which, he claims, constitutes an essential feature of the capitalist state. By this he means that the very nature of the capitalist state unconditionally precludes any " 'parcellization', *division*, or *sharing* of the institutional power of the state" between several classes or fractions. Thus, in the final analysis only one fraction, the "hegemonic" fraction, possesses "*state power in its unity*" while all

---

a wholesale attempt to shield received dogma against all criticism or evidence (cf. Connell 1982, 135–36, 138).

44 As Flew (1985, 119) rightly remarks in this connection, Poulantzas "was . . . trying, no doubt unconsciously, to ensure that neither he nor his readers should be forced to attend to the falsity of the contention that wielders of political and military and bureaucratic power are always and everywhere completely the creatures of class interests outside the state machine."

other classes and fractions, whether "dominant" or "dominated," are necessarily excluded from having any political power at all (see pp. 268–70). This sounds a lot like an attempt to answer my second question, What is it that keeps the state from serving interests *other* than those of the capitalist class? Curiously, however, this argument renders Poulantzas's own definition of (political) power entirely inoperative. If *all* political power *necessarily* accrues to one single fraction of the "dominant class," it makes little sense to speak of power as the *extent* to which this fraction is capable of realizing its objective interests since it is necessarily always at the very maximum the "structures" will allow. Moreover, the capacity of *other* classes and fractions to realize *their* interests is totally irrelevant since that capacity is *necessarily* nil. This amounts to a resolution of the aforementioned dilemma all right, but at the price of rendering his whole elaborate conceptualization of power completely superfluous. This may not be a great loss in view of the fact that that conceptualization was not very illuminating anyway, but unfortunately it is being replaced by an argument that, if anything, is even *less* illuminating.

Poulantzas offers two arguments to explain *why* the capitalist state exhibits this peculiar "unity" that precludes any sharing of its power. First, he claims, in its capacity as the "factor of cohesion" of the "social formation" the capitalist state presents itself as the "representative of the 'general interest,' " that is, as the "strictly *political* unity" of the ensemble of private agents who, because of the "isolation effect," are wholly "given over to economic antagonisms." This presumably explains the "unitary institutional framework" so typical of the capitalist state,[45] which "allows the state to function . . . as the *unambiguous (univoque)* political power *of the dominant classes or fractions*" (see p. 263).

---

45   As we have seen (pp. 284–86), Poulantzas came to emphasize the disunity of the "institutional framework" of the capitalist state in his later writings, arguing that state policy is the result of a chaos of contradictions, rivalries, inconsistencies, etc., between its branches and the classes and fractions they "represent." Yet at the same time he continues to invoke the "unity" of the state which somehow guarantees that the end result of this confused hodgepodge is always in strict accordance with the exclusive long-term interests of the "hegemonic" fraction. For a fine sample of this curious logic see Poulantzas (1975, 163–64).

The second reason is essentially the same, except that it involves the relations between the various "dominant" classes and fractions only. Since these are as hopelessly divided as the above "private agents," the state has the function of unifying them in a "power bloc." This permits "the particular participation of several classes and class fractions in political domination," enabling them to be "present on the terrain of political domination." But to "be present" and to "participate" does *not* mean that they actually *share* political power, Poulantzas tells us, for the "power bloc" can only be unified to the extent that it is exclusively subject to one "dominant element," namely the "hegemonic" fraction that always holds "state power in its unity." Hence, Poulantzas maintains, "with regard to the dominant classes and fractions, the capitalist state *presents an intrinsic unity* . . . precisely because it is the *unifying factor* of the power bloc." From the fact that the unity of the power bloc can only be realized "under the protection of the hegemonic class or fraction" *it follows* that this unity "corresponds to the unity of the state as the organizational factor of this class or fraction," according to Poulantzas. "In this sense," he continues, "the unity of state power is, in the last analysis, to be found in the state's particular relation to the hegemonic class or fraction, i.e. in the fact of the *univocal correspondence of the state to the specific* interests of that class or fraction" (see p. 270).

Leaving the apparently teleological causation aside for the moment, we are left with an argument that sounds vaguely convincing. It is indeed commonly held that one of the primary tasks of the state consists of "unifying" a variety of disparate individuals and groups, with a multitude of conflicting interests, if only in the sense of keeping them from going at each other's throats. This would seem to require an ability to "resolve" various conflicts in one way or another, and obviously a state that is consumed and paralyzed by its own internal divisions and rivalries could hardly be expected to do so effectively. So in order to perform this task adequately there would have to be *some* degree of coordination between the various state agencies and their activities. Moreover, this probably also necessitates *some* sort of hierarchical authority structure, with the final authority accruing to a single agency or office at the top, in order to settle conflicts between agencies that endanger the minimum amount of coordination deemed necessary. In this sense one can even legitimately speak of a certain necessary "unity of state power." If this is all Poulantzas means by "unity," he may be quite right, albeit only trivially so, since the *degree* of unity seems to be capable of quite considerable variation and, so broadly conceived, it is hardly confined to capitalist states (see Badie and Birnbaum 1983; Huntington 1968, ch. 2).

But Poulantzas claims *more* than this. The "unity of state power" for him means that only *one* fraction can be its beneficiary. He appears to believe that "unity" in this sense somehow follows logically from the "unity" discussed in the previous paragraph. But this is by no means obvious. Poulantzas in fact confuses the "unity" of the *source* of state policy (ultimate responsibility resting with a single agency or office) with the "unity" of its *consequences* (it can only benefit one class fraction), between which there is no necessary relation at all. There is no reason why a policy that emanates from a single or "unitary" source must, *for that reason*, also have a single beneficiary. Yet Poulantzas does not offer any other reasons why the beneficiary can only be a single fraction.

This whole nebulous non sequitur only obscures the fact that it would seem much more plausible to draw the *exact opposite* conclusion from the state's role as the "representative of the 'general interest'" and "unifying factor of the power bloc." It seems, rather, that the state would have to make compromises regularly and concede to the demands of classes and fractions *other* than the "hegemonic fraction" in order to play an effective unifying role, which is, of course, precisely the argument of the "bourgeois" pluralists. Poulantzas even *appears* to acknowledge this by allowing other classes or fractions to be "present on the terrain of political domination," but then denies it again by simply declaring this to be entirely different from "sharing" political power! But whatever idiosyncratic terminology Poulantzas may wish to employ, the fact of the matter is that *if* such concessions and compromises do indeed form an integral part of the state's "unifying" function, then this *does* look an awful lot like *some* sharing of power in any reasonable sense of that term.

This raises some troubling questions as to what exactly Poulantzas means when he proclaims a "univocal correspondence of the State to the specific interests" of the hegemonic fraction. The position of the hegemonic fraction, both in the social formation as a whole and within the power bloc, turns out to be far from "univocal," to put it mildly. The hegemonic fraction, Poulantzas informs us, "*polarizes* the specific contradictory interests of the various classes or fractions in the power bloc by making its own economic interests into political interests and by representing the general common interest of the classes or fractions in the power bloc: this general interest consists of economic exploitation and political domination." At the same time, he claims, it generally also "represents" the " 'general interest' of the body politic," or of the "ensemble of society" (see p. 269).[46]

This does *not* necessarily mean that the hegemonic fraction always gets its way. On the contrary, the relatively autonomous state "may, for example, present itself as the political guarantor of the interests of various classes and fractions of the power bloc against the interests of the hegemonic class or fraction, and it may sometimes play off those classes and fractions against the latter. But it does this in its function of political organizer of the hegemonic class or fraction and forces it to admit the sacrifices necessary for its hegemony" (see p. 271). It also does not necessarily mean that the hegemonic fraction is capable of realizing its own specific economic interests since it need not necessarily also be the economically dominant class. It all depends on the "concrete stages and turns of the class struggle" (see p. 271).

Thus, there is nothing particularly "univocal" nor very "spe-

46 To "represent" the "general common interest" in "economic exploitation and political domination" of the power bloc *and* the "general interest of the ensemble of society" simultaneously sounds like an extraordinary feat. The audience(s) to whom the hegemonic fraction manages to "represent" these two rather conflicting interests would have to be pretty gullible indeed! But instead of explaining how the hegemonic fraction realizes this remarkable achievement, Poulantzas only tells us that "the conjuncture of social forces" may cause "dislocation, dissociation and displacement of these functions" so that the fraction "representing" the interest in "domination" and "exploitation" may not be the same as the one "representing" the "general interest." Thus, as usual, all bases are covered, because in the "concrete conjuncture" anything is possible. As Maravall quite rightly points out, these are "concepts whose main consequence is to avoid generalizations, predictions and refutations" (1979, 281).

cific" about the way the state produces policies that are in "univocal correspondence" with the "specific interests" of the hegemonic fraction. If the state may realize the interests of other
classes and fractions of the power bloc *against* the interests of
the hegemonic fraction and even "play off" the former against
the latter, one wonders how the hegemonic fraction can at the
same time also "polarize the specific contradictory interests of
the various classes and fractions in the power bloc." If the hegemonic fraction is not necessarily economically dominant, one
wonders how it can make "its own economic interests into political interests." All we know is that whatever apparent defeats
the hegemonic fraction may suffer they are never more than
"the sacrifices necessary for its hegemony." Once again, we encounter the dogmatic assertion that whatever losses the hegemonic fraction may have to endure they are always the best it
could possibly hope for because the state is somehow compelled
to perform "its function of political organizer of the hegemonic
class or fraction."

One *really* wonders what to make of the whole notion of "hegemony" under these circumstances. In his desire to immunize
received doctrine against any conceivable empirical evidence
Poulantzas ends up depriving his concept of "hegemony" of all
substance. What good is it to a fraction to know that it is "hegemonic" and that it holds *all* political power "in its unity," if it is
totally at the mercy of the unpredictable "concrete stages and
turns of the class struggle" which may force it to make any
number of political and economic sacrifices? The notion of "hegemony" reduces to little more than a meaningless label bestowed on some "fraction" or other by Poulantzas on grounds
known only to him. The claim that there is a "univocal correspondence" between the state and the interests of the "hegemonic fraction" boils down either to tautology or to dogmatic
assertion of Marxist orthodoxy. It could simply be true by definition that the "hegemonic" fraction is the exclusive holder of
"state power in its unity," but if so, this tells us little about the
real world. For all we know, the unemployed might well be the
current "hegemonic fraction," their sufferings merely being the
"sacrifices necessary" for their hegemony. Or there might not
even *be* any "hegemonic fraction" at all in the present "conjunc-

ture"! Alternatively, the claim might mean that some identifiable "fraction" of the capitalist class, say "monopoly capital," is
getting about as favorable a deal from the state as it can expect
under present conditions, however strongly its members may
disagree with that assessment. But in the absence of *any* arguments to support such a statement, this reduces to purely dogmatic postulation. In either case, there is no conceivable way to
measure it against "bourgeois" liberal arguments to the contrary, and thus it can hardly be said to be much of an improvement over the "instrumentalist" theory, even by Marxist standards.

This, in fact, fairly sums up the general conclusion that can
be drawn from our examination of Poulantzas's key concepts so
far. Poulantzas tries to reconcile his acceptance of an empirical
reality as described by pluralists and reformists with his antireformist doctrine by means of an elaborate "network of definitional arguments" (Connell 1982, 137), purportedly demonstrating that that empirical reality does not *really* contradict the
doctrine. But he can only accomplish this by doing one of two
things. On the one hand, his conceptual discussions may be
taken as purely arbitrary definitional exercises which simply re-
name commonplace phenomena without affecting their substantive meaning in any way. But then the Marxist-sounding
doctrines are rendered compatible with *any* empirical reality
whatsoever simply because they have been reduced to a set of
tautologies, emptied of any distinctively Marxist *content*. Thus,
the "dominant class" is *whichever* class, if any, happens to "occupy the dominant place"; the "hegemonic fraction" is *whichever*
fraction, if any, happens to be designated the sole beneficiary
of state power; the interests of the "dominated classes" that receive state attention are simply *called* "pertinent effects"; for bureaucrats it is, by definition, "resistances," and so on. If these
are really all purely definitional matters, then they have no empirical implications at all, of course: reformists may still be quite
right in claiming that there *is* no dominant class or hegemonic
fraction, that past "pertinent effects" and "resistances" *are*
proof of the viability of a reformist political strategy, and so on.
On the other hand, however, Poulantzas's conceptual discussions could all be interpreted as substantive statements meaning

that the capitalist class has "objectively" gained as much as was possible even from policies its members opposed. But this remains arbitrary, dogmatic postulation as long as Poulantzas systematically refuses to discuss the grounds on which such a judgment could be based and leaves the terms of these assertions so utterly undefined that they could not possibly be empirically verified anyway ("objective interests," "unity of state power," "dominant class," "hegemonic fraction," etc.). The slippery quality of many of Poulantzas's arguments, which appears to make it so hard to pin them down on any definite meaning, is partly the result, no doubt, of the fact that he never really makes it clear whether he *is* dealing with purely definitional or with substantive questions. But, at any rate, these conceptual exercises yield no answers whatsoever to the crucial questions we began with. Poulantzas categorically claims to be able to assess the "objective" interests of social classes but will not say how, and he maintains equally categorically that the state can only serve the interests of the capitalist class but will not say why.

The "True" Interests of the Dominant Class

These conclusions only serve to underline once more the absolute indispensability of an answer to the first question I posed at the beginning of this section, If not on the basis of the preferences of the members of the capitalist class itself, how do we know whether government policy actually serves their best (class) interests? Clearly, without *some* answer to this question, Poulantzas's "theory" would simply collapse into an empirical description of an essentially pluralist political world and a purely dogmatic—because unsupported—assertion that government policy nevertheless *still* serves only the interests of the capitalist class. Although, as we have just seen, his definition of power and of "objective" interests does not even give us a *hint* as to what Poulantzas's answer might be, perhaps we can glean some clues from his discussions of what these "true" interests of the bourgeoisie that are supposedly served by the state in fact *consist of*.

One such discussion seems particularly promising, namely the one in which Poulantzas distinguishes the economic from the political interests of the capitalist class. The capitalist state, Poulantzas claims, "does not *directly* represent the dominant classes' economic interests, but their *political interests*," it functions "as the organizational factor of their strictly political unity."[47] The state may sacrifice the economic interests of this or that fraction of the dominant class but only to the extent that this is necessary "for the realization of their political class interests." Similarly, the state may exact (presumably strictly economic) concessions from the hegemonic fraction, but "it does this in its function of *political* organizer of the hegemonic class or fraction and forces it to admit the sacrifices necessary for its hegemony" (see p. 271, emphasis added). For the state "has inscribed in its very structures a flexibility which concedes a certain guarantee to the economic interests of certain dominated classes, within the limits of the system." Thus, the capitalist state "gives to the economic interests of certain dominated classes guarantees which may even be contrary to the short-term economic interests of the dominant classes, but which are compatible with their political interests and their hegemonic domination" (1973b, 190–91). "In other words," Poulantzas continues, "according to the concrete conjuncture, a *line of demarcation* can always be drawn within which the guarantee given by the capitalist state to the dominated classes' economic interests not only fails to threaten the political relation of class domination but even constitutes an element of this relation." Thus, it would seem that the state imposes strategic *economic* concessions on the dominant class in order to safeguard its *political* interests.

All this is rather vague and qualified, to be sure,[48] but it *does* seem to give us something to go on. The key question obviously is, What distinguishes *political* from *economic* interests? Thus, we need to know what, in Althusserian parlance, the "specificity" of the economic and political "instances" consists of. As we have already seen, however, it is not much use to consult Althusser

47 Unless otherwise indicated, references for the direct quotations in this subsection can be found on pp. 253–54, 274–79.

48 In almost every case the wording implicitly *suggests* that there are limits to the size of the concessions and the possible number of victims and beneficiaries, but these are never spelled out: "certain" guarantees, "certain" dominated classes, "this or that" fraction, "short-term economic" interests.

on the matter since he refuses to provide even the slightest clue as to what distinguishes the economic from the political "instance" beyond stating the obvious, namely, that they are in some ways similar and in some ways not. But Poulantzas might be expected to pay more attention to the "specificity" of politics since it is, after all, primarily the "political instance" that he seeks to "theorize," to stick with the jargon.

"Political practice," Poulantzas declares, takes the "conjuncture" as its "object" and the "political structures of the state as its point of impact and specific strategic 'objective.' " It therefore "either transforms (or else maintains) the unity of a formation." One wonders, however, how this helps us much to distinguish political from other "practices." It is difficult to see how any economic "practice," or *any* "practice" for that matter, could *fail* to affect the "unity of a social formation" in some way or another (either transform or maintain it), except for "practices" that are entirely irrelevant to the "social formation" and hence of little interest from a sociological point of view. Perhaps "transforming" or "maintaining" is meant to refer to something more significant than merely "affecting" the "unity of a formation," but this hardly makes it a useful criterion for distinguishing between economic and political phenomena. A great deal of "practice" that is strictly economic by *any* standard has very profound effects on the "unity" of the "social formation"—indeed by far the most profound ones, according to conventional Marxist theory. Nor is it of much help to know that the "political structures of the state" are the "point of impact and specific strategic 'objective' " of political practice. At first sight this might appear to mean that political practice aims at influencing and "using" the state apparatus, which is commonplace enough as a definition, albeit not necessarily terribly fruitful (cf. Bachrach 1967). However, Poulantzas's entire argument is intended precisely to show that it is in the best political interest of the "dominant class" to stay as far away from the state apparatus as possible. Thus "political" seems to refer to whatever is in some ill-defined way related to the actions of the state. But this does not clarify the distinction between political and economic interests either since it is precisely the state that decides what "economic" interests are to be sacrificed to safeguard the "political" interests of the dominant class!

Nor does defining political practice as having the "conjuncture" as its "specific object" illuminate the distinction between economic and political interests. The conjuncture, according to Poulantzas, is "the *nodal point where the contradictions* of the various levels of a formation *are condensed* in the complex relations governed by over-determination and by their dislocation and uneven development." It is "the 'present moment' (as Lenin said)" in which "relations of different contradictions finally fuse" (1973b, 41), where in some sense all things come together. Thus, Poulantzas argues, political practice "bears at once on the *economic, ideological, theoretical* and (in the strict sense) *political*, which in their interrelation, make up a conjuncture" (41–42). This would seem to suggest that political interests are in some sense more inclusive than economic interests, although it is totally unclear then what political interests "in the strict sense" could possibly consist of. Besides, it is not clear either in what sense they are more inclusive. If political interests refer to those of a class as a whole, as opposed to economic interests which are narrowly fractional, then one wonders how Poulantzas can speak of economic *class* interests in his discussion of the "specificity" of power, or of economic concessions made by the dominant class as a whole as opposed to the sacrifices imposed on this or that fraction of it. If, on the other hand, Poulantzas means to say that both fractions and classes have political interests that are distinguished from their economic interests in that they are more inclusive, then the question remains *in what sense* the former are more inclusive.

In Poulantzas's arguments about the economic sacrifices the dominant class must make to maintain its political dominance there is some suggestion that political interests refer to *long-term* interests. The function of the state within the social formation is *inherently* political and corresponds "*in this manner* to the political interests of the dominant class," Poulantzas claims. Conversely, for all the possible variations in the degree of relative autonomy "the (capitalist) State, in the long run, can only correspond to the political interests of the dominant class or classes" (see p. 267). Furthermore, the capitalist class "can dom-

inate effectively only if it sets up its economic interests as political interests," and more particularly only if its hegemonic fraction "*polarizes* the specific contradictory interests of the various
classes or fractions in the power bloc by making its own economic interests into political interests and by representing the
general common interest of the classes or fractions in the power
bloc: this general interest consists of economic exploitation and
political domination" (see pp. 267, 269). None of this is terribly
lucid to be sure, but such passages *do* appear to suggest that
the *political* interests of the dominant class consist essentially of
preserving the system of "economic exploitation" as much as
possible in the long run, and its *economic* interests are those
short-term benefits that it must occasionally forgo to maintain
the system's long-run viability.[49]

But then again, Poulantzas also speaks of the "long-term *economic* interests of *one or other* fraction of the dominant class"
(first emphasis added). Are we to understand that fractions can
have both short- and long-term economic interests whereas
classes can only have short-term economic and long-term political interests? If so, can fractions have political interests at all?
This would seem to imply that political interests are peculiar to
a class as a whole and that economic interests pertain to either
a class or a fraction. Things are getting rather murky at this
point, and since Poulantzas does not address *any* of these questions, it does not seem sensible to pursue the matter any further. Suffice it to say that Poulantzas's *separate* treatment of the
distinction between various "specific" powers (economic, political, ideological) and the distinction between long-term and
short-term interests (see pp. 257–58), although neither is particularly illuminating, would seem to contradict the equation of
political with long-term and economic with short-term interests.

Finally, if we were nevertheless to accept the interpretation
that political interests are in some sense more inclusive than
economic interests, this could easily render the whole theory

49   If this interpretation is correct, however, it is not clear how "political domi-
      nation" can at the same time be singled out as a distinct component of the
      "general common interest" of the dominant class since *both* presumably re-
      fer to the long-run capacity of maintaining the system of "economic exploi-
      tation."

entirely circular once again. Since Poulantzas does not bother to tell us anything about the nature of "economic" interests *except* that they are the ones that are occasionally sacrificed to protect "political" interests, his whole argument may simply be true by definition. The overall argument is, let us recall, that the state may make certain concessions to the "dominated classes" at the apparent expense of the "dominant class," but that these concessions are "really" in the latter's interest. Now we are told that the concessions are always of a less inclusive nature ("economic") than the ("political") interests that are being protected by them. This is hardly surprising: the interests of the "dominant class" would be rather badly served if it were the other way around!

But there is another, much more famous argument that might give us some idea of what these interests are. I am referring to Poulantzas's celebrated and much-quoted "scientific Marxist conception of the state superstructure," according to which "the state has the particular function of constituting the factor of cohesion between the levels of a social formation . . . and . . . the regulating factor of its equilibrium as a system." In a class-divided social formation the successful performance of this function is *ipso facto* in the political interest of the dominant class, Poulantzas argues, since it amounts to maintaining "the unity of a social formation based in the last analysis on political class domination." This widely used passage is clearly in keeping with received antireformist doctrine: the state serves the interests of the capitalist class by maintaining the social system of which that class is the main beneficiary. Whether it is much of an improvement over the "instrumentalist" arguments to the same effect, however, is another matter.

There are two distinct claims here: (1) that it is the function of the state to maintain the "cohesion" or "unity" of the "social formation"; and (2) that the maintenance of this "cohesion" or "unity" is in the interest of the capitalist class. Let us begin with the first of these. On the one hand—and this is, believe it or not, by no means the least plausible interpretation—it could simply be true by definition: whatever contributes to maintaining "cohesion" is *by definition* part of the "state superstructure" as defined by this "scientific conception," and whatever does not, is not. But like any other definition this tells us nothing about the real world, of course. It could well be that *none* of those institutions we ordinary mortals conventionally refer to as "the state" has *anything* to do with maintaining the "cohesion" of the "social formation." If so, they simply do *not* belong to the "state" as "scientifically" conceived by Poulantzas, and that is that. On this interpretation the proposition that the "state superstructure" is the "factor of cohesion" of the "social formation" reduces to a pure tautology which cannot possibly serve to counter pluralist or "instrumentalist" arguments. Governments, and the institutions under their jurisdiction, may well be engaged in a continuous process of *transforming* the "unity of the social formation" beyond recognition in order to satisfy persistent demands by the electorate, as some pluralists would argue, but this would naturally leave Poulantzas's "scientific" definition of the "state superstructure" completely unaffected—it simply excludes such governments and institutions *from* that definition.

Alternatively, if maintaining "cohesion" means nothing more than maintaining a tolerable degree of order and continuity, as Poulantzas's definition of the state's "political" function in the narrow sense ("maintaining political order in class conflict") suggests, he is not saying much more than that states, or rather governments,[50] do not ordinarily seek to create havoc. Few people would deny such a truism (see Schott 1984), and, at any rate, it would seem rather difficult to come up with historical examples of governments deliberately pursuing chaos (although, of course, many may have created disruption inadvertently, which is not the issue here). To attribute this rather widespread phenomenon—hardly confined to capitalist "social formations"—to the "function" assigned by a mysterious "global structure" to the "state structures" does not in the least advance our understanding of it. But the point is that "reformists" would argue that precisely in order to maintain some "order" (i.e., the sort of "stability" that produces and maintains electoral

50   Poulantzas, like most other Marxist theorists of bourgeois politics, refers exclusively to the state and does not distinguish between (temporary) governments and (more enduring) states. After all, the whole purpose of their arguments is to show that even in bourgeois democracy it makes little difference *who* is temporarily in charge of the state apparatus.

support) democratic governments have been forced to carry out quite considerable transformations of the "unity of the social formation" and that there is no guarantee that the process might not ultimately lead to a social formation whose "unity" has nothing in common anymore with those we call capitalist.

It is precisely *this* argument that Poulantzas wishes to refute, of course. But to do that convincingly, he must explain what constitutes the minimum "unity" of the present "social formation," so that one may determine what sorts of reforms would merely "maintain" and what would truly "transform" that "unity." Yet this is exactly what Poulantzas, in keeping with the common practice among his fellow antireformist Marxists (see Chapter 2), does *not* do. He does, of course, equate maintaining the "unity" of the present "social formation" with maintaining class-divided society *tout court*, and we also know that the transition to "socialism"—that is, presumably the true "transformation" of the present "unity"—involves "sweeping transformations," but this hardly serves to clarify matters. As Poulantzas appears to allow for only two possibilities, moreover, anything short of such "sweeping transformations" seems to amount automatically to "maintaining" the "unity" of the present, class-divided "social formation" (cf. Jessop 1982, 184). Thus, Poulantzas's argument becomes unfalsifiable: we have no way of knowing what "transformation" of the "unity of the social formation" would *in*validate it while anything short of such an undefined "transformation" qualifies as evidence to support it. It simply boils down to the wholly arbitrary assertion that nothing that merits the label "socialism" by Poulantzas's own, undisclosed criteria has yet been the aim or outcome of government policy in any capitalist country. As long as Poulantzas's criteria remain unknown, we simply do not know what this means.

Thus, Poulantzas's famous assertion that the state is the "factor of cohesion" of the "social formation," which became an instant hit among Marxist authors, cannot tell us much about what Poulantzas considered to be in the interest of the capitalist class either. This is so because he fails to make clear what he means by the "cohesion" or "unity" of the "social formation." It can be interpreted in such a way that the assertion turns into either a tautology or a common-sense banality. Or else it re-

mains effectively undefined as anything short of some unidentified "transformation." But in any case the meaning of Poulantzas's claim remains indistinguishable from alternative views of
the state, bourgeois or otherwise, and it hence also remains useless for determining what, according to Poulantzas, the "true"
interests of the "dominant class" consist of.[51]

Yet, the second part of the "factor of cohesion" argument,
namely that the sheer maintenance of a "unity" that seems to
include everything short of its complete "transformation" is *intrinsically* in the interest of the capitalist class, reveals something
of the underlying presuppositions of Poulantzas's theory. Like
other orthodox, antireformist Marxists, Poulantzas claims that
all policies that appear to support the case for reformism have
not in fact really "transformed" the "unity" of the present, class-
divided "social formation" at all, but merely "maintained" it,
and that they have, therefore, been primarily of benefit to the
capitalist class. The underlying assumption clearly is that the
capitalist class should count itself lucky to have gotten away with
so little change of the "unity" of the "social formation," while
the working class is really being duped if it rests content with
anything short of a total "transformation" of that "unity." As

51 By arguing that the state's function of "cohesion" need not imply that it
    must always be interventionist nor that it is necessarily the dominant "in-
    stance" in the "ensemble of structures," Poulantzas provides another fine
    example of the utter vacancy of the central concepts of Althusserian struc-
    turalism. Althusser's *only* defense against the charge of indeterminate causal
    pluralism, it will be remembered, was that his "global structure" of mutually
    determining "instances" is given unity and direction by the fact that it is a
    "structure in dominance," i.e., that one instance is the dominant one. But if
    this is so, one would expect that the "factor of unity" par excellence, the
    state, would therefore *always* be the dominant instance, although such a
    conclusion has a rather un-Marxist ring to it of course. Only by leaving no-
    tions like "factor of unity" and "dominance" totally undefined is it possible
    to escape this rather embarrassing conclusion. Since the terms do not have
    any meaning, Poulantzas can in effect argue that the "factor of unity" of
    the "social formation" is not necessarily the "instance" that gives the "global
    structure" its unity! Nevertheless, as we shall see, there is an odd "politi-
    cism" in Poulantzas's *exclusive* preoccupation with the role of politics and
    the state in maintaining or transforming the "unity of the social formation,"
    which sits rather uneasily with classical Marxism according to which, after
    all, the sources of fundamental social change are to be sought in the dy-
    namic between the forces and relations of production and the class strug-
    gles produced by it.

Poulantzas himself declares in precisely this context, the state "prevents the social formation from bursting apart" (1973b, 50). Thus, the Marxist guiding assumption that capitalism must be permanently teetering on the brink of collapse is apparently still retained, *even though* the proletariat itself, the gravedigger-designate who was to be the very *cause* of that teetering in the first place, may not be aware of it! If (quite literally) nothing else, Poulantzas's celebrated formula of the state as "factor of cohesion" does at least have the merit of clearly bringing out this curious tension between the explicit argument and its implicit presuppositions.

Moreover, this points once again to that curious "immanentism" in Marxist theorizing. The above tension could only go unnoticed because the workers' "objective" interest in "socialism," and the capitalists' equally "objective" interest in its prevention, are assumed to be based on forces "immanent" in the capitalist system. Thus, neither the "immanent" pressures toward "socialism," nor theories based on the *assumption* of their immanence such as Poulantzas's, are taken to require any specific conception of what "socialism" might conceivably look like. In the absence of the taboo on "utopian" speculation, it would have been immediately obvious that the imputation of "real" interests to workers and capitalists with respect to "socialism," and, *a fortiori*, arguments whose key concept, "cohesion," is effectively *defined* as the *absence* of "socialism," depend crucially on what exactly is meant by that. The resulting need to clarify the minimal meaning of "socialism," in turn, would have brought out the odd tension in Poulantzas's argument quite clearly.

Our search for clues to Poulantzas's conception of the "true" interests of the "dominant class" is not turning out to be very fruitful. There is one remaining argument distinct from, though closely related to those already examined that might be worth exploring. At times it appears as though Poulantzas were arguing that the "line of demarcation" that the state cannot overstep without seriously jeopardizing class domination consists of the integrity of the state structures themselves. For example, Poulantzas argues that the state may limit the economic power of the dominant classes, "but on the one condition . . . that their political power and the state apparatus remain intact.

Hence, in every concrete conjuncture, the dominant classes' political power, which has become autonomous, represents in its relations with the capitalist state *a limit within which the restrictions of the economic power of these classes has no effect*" (1973b, 192). This passage is admittedly a bit confusing. It is not clear how one can speak of relations *between* the political power of the dominant classes, on the one hand, and the capitalist state, on the other, if the capitalist state *is* the "*unambiguous* and *exclusive* political power" of the dominant class to begin with, as Poulantzas repeats *ad nauseam*. That they are indeed one and the same and that the unsurpassable limit beyond which concessions to the dominated classes may not go does indeed consist of the integrity of the state itself, is, however, confirmed by the following quotes. The "type of capitalist state," Poulantzas tells us, "involves the possibility inscribed within the limits of its structures" of making major concessions to the dominated classes, such as those characteristic of "the so-called 'Welfare State,' " but such policies "cannot under any circumstances call into question the capitalist type of state, so long as it operates within these *limits*" (193–94). This is ultimately in the long-run interest of the dominant class because "within these precise limits, the capitalist state does not take even one step away from the political interests of the bourgeoisie." Thus, "the political struggles of the dominated classes can be expressed" in the "institutional play of the capitalist state," but this "neither authorizes the dominated classes *effectively to participate* in political power nor cedes 'parcels' of institutionalized power to them." The capitalist state is after all "an ensemble of structures" which is only autonomous from the dominant classes "precisely in so far as it constitutes their *unambiguous* and *exclusive* political power."

This, then, is Poulantzas's final indication of what he believes the "true" interests of the capitalist class to be. As long as the state maintains *its own* structures, he appears to be saying, its policies will necessarily "correspond to the political interests of the dominant class or classes," no matter what apparent concessions to the dominated classes they may involve. After all, these are the structures that produce that peculiar "unity" which "corresponds precisely to the fact that it constitutes an unambiguous power for the dominant classes or fractions" and hence necessarily excludes the dominated classes from sharing that power (ibid., 283). Thus, the supreme political interest of the capitalist class lies in keeping these structures intact, so that they will continue to limit the possible actions of the state to those that are in the objective interest of the capitalist class.

This amounts to a rather curious twist in the overall argument, however. First, it is predicated on the *prior* acceptance of Poulantzas's general claim that the state *does* serve the interests of the capitalist class and none other. Otherwise, the argument that the maintenance of its "structures" is in its interest is nonsense, of course. Yet, we have only come this far precisely because we were unable to find any clear indication as to what the "true" interests of the capitalist class *are* to begin with, let alone whether or how they are being served by the state, in the absence of deliberate pressure from that class.

Moreover, even if we *did* accept the prior argument that the state serves only the interests of the bourgeoisie, this merely renders the subsequent assertion that the maintenance of the structures that cause it to act in such a way is, therefore, also in the bourgeoisie's interest, perfectly tautological. The statement that the bourgeoisie's interests are protected as long as the "structures" that protect these interests remain intact, is, of course, true by definition. But, equally obviously, such a statement cannot tell us *anything* about what is happening in the real world out there: *are* any real states "structured" to promote only the "true" interests of capital? What do these "structures" look like? And—the question we are *still* seeking the answer to in this subsection—*what* do these "true" interests *consist of*? Thus, the present "argument" is entirely superfluous. It will not do anything to persuade anyone who is not persuaded already of the validity of the theory, and it boils down to another tautology for those who *are* already so persuaded.

In the meantime, however, our quest for some hint of the "true" interests of the capitalist class is only leading us away from those interests themselves and toward the state "structures" that allegedly promote them. This is not exactly making things much clearer, but if we could only get some idea of what these *structures* consist of we could at least have *some* empirical referent for Poulantzas's idea of the "objective" interests of the capitalist class. So let us look a little more closely at the state structures within whose "precise limits," according to Poulantzas, "the capitalist state does not take even one step away from the political interests of the bourgeoisie." These limits, Poulantzas informs us, depend "equally on the relation between the forces in the class struggle, on the forms of the state, on the articulation of its functions, on the relations of economic power to political power and on the functioning of the state apparatus" (ibid., 192).

But unfortunately, this does not get us much further. First, we have already been unable to establish what the difference is between "economic" and "political" interests, *let alone* the "relations" between them.[52] Second, we are, of course, asking precisely what the "forms of state," the "articulation of its functions," and the "functioning of the state apparatus" consist of. Clearly, these are *exactly* those "structures" whose "precise limits" we are trying to establish. Third, the dependence of these "limits" on the "relation of forces in the class struggle" once again renders Poulantzas's argument effectively indistinguishable from its pluralist and "instrumentalist" rivals. The rivals are saying the *exact same thing*, the only differences being that pluralists maintain that that relation is such as to allow for a gradual but indefinite shift of the "precise limits" until they have come to incorporate the interests of the "dominated classes," whereas "instrumentalists" deny that this is so. At any rate, if we accept that these "limits" depend on all the factors mentioned, they are obviously anything *but* "precise."

But Poulantzas goes even further in blurring the "limits" of the state's "structures" that constrain it to serve the interests of the "dominant class." As noted on several occasions, neither Althusser nor Poulantzas really establishes the much-touted "specifity" of his "instances" except in the most abstract and formal manner, that is, by effectively leaving them undefined and hence indistinct. Moreover, when Poulantzas discusses the ideological "instance," and particularly the "dominant ideology," he ascribes the exact same functions to it as he does to the state

52   As we have seen in the previous subsection, "power" is virtually defined by the notion of "objective interests" in Poulantzas's lexicon.

(cf. Abercrombie, Hill, and Turner 1980, 63–65; Lewis 1981, 39–42). In particular, the "dominant ideology" displays the same combination of "relative autonomy" and "unity" as the capitalist state, implying that it, like the state, is somehow intrinsically "capitalist" no matter *how* remote its contents may appear from the interests of the capitalist class. However, as with the state, Poulantzas fails to disclose what it is, exactly, in the nature of this ideology that makes it "correspond" to the interests of the "dominant class," except for the flat assertion that its "unity" makes this correspondence necessary, which is simply true by definition, as we have seen with respect to the "unity" of state power. Thus, again as with the policies of the state, Poulantzas can literally proclaim *any* ideology to be merely a variant of the "dominant ideology," no matter how hostile it may seem to capitalism.

But Poulantzas does not stop there. Having enabled himself to declare any state policy and any "ideology" intrinsically "capitalist" simply by blurring the distinction between "capitalist" and everything else, he then proceeds to carry this kind of reasoning to the ultimate absurdity with his (and Althusser's) notion of "Ideological State Apparatuses." These apparatuses include the churches, political parties, unions, schools, mass media, cultural institutions, and the family, "with the exception, of course, of the *revolutionary* party or trade union organizations." Not only has Poulantzas succeeded in totally blurring the "specificities" of the political and the ideological, now he in fact merges the state with the social system as a whole. It is difficult to think of any social institutions that are *not* by definition part of the "Ideological State Apparatuses" (cf. Polan 1984, 34–35)! The exception of "revolutionary" organizations would appear to be a minor one, although, as Connell rightly notes, "the naiveté of this, in a world where 57 different sects each proclaim themselves *the* revolutionary party, is charming" (1982, 142). But in most advanced countries these sects are tiny at best, and where the "revolutionary" organizations are large (Italy, France, Spain) they have by all accounts ceased to be terribly revolutionary. The exception is only significant for revealing once again the underlying Leninist dichotomy: what is not entirely "socialist" is therefore entirely "capitalist."

If taken seriously this complete fusion of state and society does reduce Poulantzas's contention that to serve the dominant class the state merely has to maintain its own structures with their built-in "limits," to his earlier claim that the function of the state is to be the "factor of cohesion" of the "social formation." Since to all intents and purposes the state *is* the "social formation," to maintain itself *is* to secure the "cohesion" of the social formation. But in the meantime, of course, the "precise" limits of the structures of the state have become about as imprecise as they can possibly get. If Poulantzas refuses to indicate in any way what "limits" and "structures" of the state (in the more limited sense) exactly must be maintained for the state to remain the "unambiguous and exclusive power of the dominant class," he is even *more* reluctant to disclose what distinguishes the "maintenance" of the "unity of the social formation" from its "transformation," as I have noted earlier. The "cohesion" of the "social formation" which is said to be to the exclusive benefit of the capitalist class appears to include *everything* short of its complete "transformation" into "socialism." Hence the fusion of state and society implies that *whatever* happens inside this society-become-state that does not immediately bring on the socialist millennium is *therefore* exclusively in the interest of the bourgeoisie. Moreover, since, for lack of any definite conception of "socialism," there is no telling what kinds of events will hasten the "transformation" and what kinds will not, we are left with the arbitrary assertion that everything is always in the exclusive interest of the bourgeoisie—until further notice. In addition, having effectively reduced his entire theory to his initial claim that the state is the "factor of cohesion," *all* Poulantzas's other arguments beyond this initial claim, that is, the overwhelming bulk of his celebrated theory of the capitalist state, turn out to be little more than window dressing.

Furthermore, the fusion of state and society renders "any distinction between a set of independent and dependent variables largely inappropriate," as Frank Parkin sarcastically observes with respect to the related recent practice among Marxists of merging the "mode of production" with society as a whole (1979, 6). If the entire social system becomes part of the state and hence presumably partakes in its efforts at maintaining "cohesion" it is a little difficult to see *who* is maintaining *what* exactly.[53] Society simply maintains itself for "structural," that is to say unknown, reasons. Nor is it very clear *why* any efforts should be expended to "maintain" anything at all, since all social institutions, except for a tiny fringe of bona fide but ineffective "revolutionaries," are already intrinsically "capitalist" and hence hardly likely to pose any serious threats to the system. In fact, one wonders why the dominant class should have to make any concessions at all and how there could be *any* change "within," let alone "of" the system. The close affinity between structuralist Marxism and Parsonsian functionalism is becoming embarrassingly obvious here (cf. DiTomaso 1982; Pedraza-Bailey 1982; Thompson 1978).

But let us return, for a moment, to Poulantzas's claims that the political interests of the dominant class take precedence over its economic interests and that its ultimate political interest consists in the preservation of the structures of the "capitalist" type of state. Once again this betrays the curiously *"étatiste"* strain in his theory. One would expect a true Marxist to argue that economic interests are primordial and that, although the state may be important in helping to safeguard the economic interests of the capitalist class, this is secondary to the economic power of that class itself which permits it to retain and increase its privileges. For all we know Poulantzas might be saying exactly the same thing, of course, since his distinction between economic and political interests remains utterly obscure. But he *seems* to be saying that the ultimate source of capitalist dominance is not private property and the market, or the "relations of production," but rather the state. In a characteristically tau-

53   As Bernstein once wisely remarked apropos the excessively abstract debates about "the state" raging in his day: "Was aber ist überhaupt der Staat? Soviel ist jedenfalls klar, wenn wir vom Staat sprechen, müssen wir uns zunächst darüber verständigen, was wir unter ihm verstehen. Das ist nun auch keine ganz einfache Sache" (1922, 76), which translates roughly to this: "But what, after all, is the state? One thing at least is clear, when we speak of the state we have to first come to some mutual understanding of what we mean by it. But that is not exactly a simple matter either." Apparently, things have not changed much since then.

tological formulation Poulantzas declares that "the state is related to a 'society divided into classes' and to political domination, precisely in so far as it maintains, in the ensemble of structures, that place and role which have the *effect* (in their unity) of dividing a formation into classes and producing class domination." Thus, class division and domination appear to be the direct "effect" of the "place and role" maintained in the "ensemble of structures" by the state. Such a statement would seem to belong in the tradition of Pareto and Mosca (see, e.g., Dahrendorf 1959; Lenski 1966) but hardly in that of Marx.[54]

But the contention that in serving the exclusive interests of the "dominant" class the state may virtually grant *anything* to the "dominated" classes as long as it does not "call into question the capitalist type of state," has stranger implications. For one thing, it makes a complete mockery of the whole notion of a "dominant" class. If the only *sure* benefit that accrues to the "dominant" class by virtue of its "dominance" consists of the sheer maintenance of the "structures" of the state, "dominance" becomes an elusive notion indeed. One could imagine a state that expropriated all means of production, put all former owners behind bars, and turned over the economy to workers' councils, without changing its own "structure" one bit. Yet, according to Poulantzas this would still be in the best interest of the former capitalists!

Of course, Poulantzas would claim that such a thing would be impossible without an equally profound transformation of the "structures" of the state. And, at least in a trivial sense, he would be right: such drastic social change would no doubt be accompanied by some modification of the "structure" of the state. But so long as Poulantzas refuses to disclose what *other* interests of the dominant class the "capitalist" state must serve, over and above maintaining its own "structures," the above *reductio ad absurdum* remains at least formally consistent with his argument. By implication, anything short of the patently absurd may be taken as positive "proof" for the theory.

With this, we have finally reached the end of our tortuous

---

54   For Poulantzas's persistent tendency toward a rather un-Marxist "politicism," see Jessop (1985, 72–74, 333–34).

search for Poulantzas's conception of the nature of the interests of the bourgeoisie which, he claims, are protected by the state *against* the resistance of the often shortsighted bourgeoisie itself, if necessary. We have come up with exactly nothing. As I have argued at the outset, the fact that Poulantzas concedes that the state does occasionally face and surmount capitalist opposition makes it absolutely necessary for him to distinguish his theory from both pluralism and "instrumentalism" by, first, clearly stating his reasons for considering such cases to be in the bourgeoisie's "objective" interests nonetheless and second, providing an alternative causal mechanism that constrains the state to act as the guardian of those interests. It is on the first of these issues that I have tried to shed some light in this subsection. My scrutiny of Poulantzas's remarks about the nature of these "objective" interests, however, inescapably leads to the following conclusion: instead of showing in what sense Poulantzas's argument differs from that of its theoretical rivals, these remarks only serve to systematically *blur* the distinction. In his discussions of "political" versus "economic" interests, the state's function as the "factor of cohesion," and the "precise limits" of its structures, we found an abundance of near tautologies and trivia but *nothing* that any pluralist or "instrumentalist" would (or could) feel moved to dispute. Thus, although Poulantzas's conception of the "true" interests of the bourgeoisie is evidently not based on the opinions of the capitalists themselves, we simply haven't a clue as to what it *is* based on, or even what these interests *are*.

But then again, as we have seen in Chapter 2, Poulantzas is hardly alone among Marxists in failing to specify the interests of the bourgeoisie beyond the sheer avoidance of "socialism." However, in this case the failing is more serious since it renders his entire "theory" incapable of being usefully measured against bourgeois pluralist theories that have much the same empirical implications. Be that as it may, it is the notion of "relative autonomy" that is the most distinctive and widely acclaimed contribution Poulantzas has made to the Marxist theory of the capitalist state, and thus it presumably should give us *some* idea of how his approach differs from both pluralism and "instrumentalism."

The Autonomy of the Capitalist State: What's So Relative?

The argument that the capitalist state is characterized by a "relative autonomy" from the capitalist class is unquestionably the *pièce de résistance* of Poulantzas's theory of the state. It is *this* argument that supposedly enabled him to "tackle the pluralists on their own terrain . . . without compromising the significance of class analysis" (Giddens 1981, 216). It permitted Poulantzas simultaneously to "acknowledge that certain elements of the pluralists' arguments are correct" *and* reassert the validity of the orthodox Marxist doctrine that the state serves the interests of the capitalist class. Unlike "instrumentalist" Marxists, Poulantzas accepts pluralist claims that clashes between governments and (fractions of) the bourgeoisie do occur and that in such cases governments do regularly prevail, often appearing to give in to working-class demands. However, unlike the pluralists, Poulantzas maintains that this does not refute the Marxist theory of the state *at all*. On the contrary, such cases merely confirm the theory that in capitalist society the state possesses that "relative autonomy" from the ruling class that enables it to act *"on behalf* of the 'ruling class,' " without acting *"at its behest,"* as Miliband aptly puts it (Miliband 1977, 74; also 1973, 85, n. 4; 1975, 316). This argument is now widely acknowledged, even by former "instrumentalists" such as Miliband, as undoubtedly the single most important theoretical breakthrough produced by almost two decades of Marxist theorizing. It constitutes nothing less than "a 'Copernican revolution' in the Marxist study of politics" (Kesselman 1983, 832).

Simply put, the "relative autonomy" argument runs something like this. Since the dominant class is usually too divided and preoccupied with its short-term pursuits to take the long-term strategic view, it is by itself unable to develop those policies that can secure the conditions necessary to maintain its dominance in the long run. Thus, in its own long-term interest this class needs a relatively autonomous state capable of forcing through the required policies, against strong capitalist opposition if necessary. Moreover, one primary condition for continued dominance is the acquiescence of the working class which is continuously in danger of being undermined by the daily experience of exploitation and domination. A relatively autonomous state, it is claimed, can win the allegiance of the working class, and thereby secure the acquiescence necessary for continued capitalist hegemony, by making strategic concessions at the apparent expense, and hence often over the strong opposition, of the capitalist class. This is why Poulantzas argues that the capitalist state serves the interests of the capitalist class best when it is *least* visibly linked to that class.

Thus, according to Poulantzas the state's relative autonomy permits it to force the dominant class and its various fractions to accept all kinds of compromises and sacrifices whenever these are necessary for the maintenance of their overall domination. As he repeatedly insists, "a whole series of compromises which maintain the unstable equilibrium of the classes present" is necessary in order to "perpetuate existing social relations."[55] Moreover such compromises and sacrifices should *not* be seen as the product of unilateral planning and action by civil servants and governments that are for some reason deeply committed to the interests of business, but better able to grasp the "objective" interests of the capitalist class than most businessmen themselves. Policies that end up benefiting the bourgeoisie may very well be *"imposed* on the dominant classes by the state, through the pressure of the dominated classes," or even more directly *"imposed on* the dominant class *by the struggle of the dominated classes."* A "good example" of this are "the state's so-called 'social functions,' " Poulantzas maintains. In fact, even policies originated by social-democratic governments determined to alter the "existing social relations" fundamentally invariably end up "perpetuating" them instead.

All these are merely instances in which the capitalist state uses its relative autonomy to present the long-run interests of the capitalist class as "representative of the people's general interest, as the materialization of popular sovereignty." The "normative institutional ensemble of *political democracy*" allows the state to do this as well as to obtain the necessary autonomy from the dominant class to impose the policies on it that are required for the perpetuation of "existing social relations." For it permits the

55 Unless indicated otherwise, full references for the direct quotes in this subsection can be found on pp. 261–68, 273–76.

state to gather the popular support necessary to overcome shortsighted dominant-class opposition. The state may even encourage such "supporting" classes "in various ways, to work against the dominant class or classes, but to the political advantage of these latter. In this way it succeeds precisely in *making* the dominated classes *accept* a whole series of compromises which appear to be to *their* political interest" (Poulantzas 1973b, 285).

In a similar manner, the state intervenes in the relations between the fractions of the power bloc itself to engineer compromises and to exact sacrifices in their common interest. Its relative autonomy allows it "(depending on the concrete conjuncture) to intervene against the long-term economic interests of *one or other* fraction of the dominant class: for such compromises are sometimes necessary for the realization of their political class interests." Nor does the state necessarily always intervene on the immediate behalf of the hegemonic fraction, although such interventions do, of course, ultimately benefit that fraction alone. Thus, "the state may, for example, present itself as the political guarantor of the interests of various classes and fractions of the power bloc against the interests of the hegemonic class or fraction, and it may sometimes play off those classes and fractions against the latter," but it does this only "in its function of political organizer of the hegemonic class or fraction," forcing it "to admit the sacrifices necessary for its hegemony."

None of this implies, however, that these compromises and sacrifices are in some sense merely illusory, although Poulantzas does sometimes come close to suggesting as much. Thus he claims that the state's relative autonomy allows it "to arrange compromises vis-à-vis the dominated classes, which, in the long run, are useful for the actual economic interests of the dominant classes or fractions" while it also allows the state "to intervene against the long-term economic interests of *one or other* fraction of the dominant class." This would seem to suggest that concessions to the dominated classes never amount to much in comparison to the important, because long-run, sacrifices specific fractions of the dominant class sometimes have to make for the good of the class as a whole. Yet elsewhere he insists that concessions to the dominated classes may "contain real economic sacrifices" and even significantly "cut into the dominant classes' economic power," that is, reduce their very *capacity* to realize their economic interests. Thus, the compromises and sacrifices imposed on the dominant class by the state are often considerably more than merely symbolic concessions, and, indeed, if this were not the case the stubborn opposition of the dominant class and the consequent "need" for a relatively autonomous state would not make much sense.

Poulantzas certainly *does* grant "certain elements of the pluralists' arguments"! In fact, with all these considerable concessions and sacrifices being *imposed* on the dominant class, and even on its "hegemonic" fraction, by the very "struggle of the dominated classes" and by a state that even "encourages" these latter classes and uses its own "normative institutional ensemble of political democracy" to bring the "dominant" class to heel, and so on and so on, it is hard to see in what respect Poulantzas *differs* from the most complacent "bourgeois" pluralism. In short, the crucial question now becomes, If the state and the "dominated" classes can actually do all this, what keeps the state from becoming the instrument of a determined and skillful labor government in the pursuit of the long-term interests of the working class and, therefore, *against* the long-term interests of capital? It is, of course, precisely on such evidence of "concessions" and the like, which Poulantzas accepts, that pluralists and reformists base their case. So, if Poulantzas's argument is *not* to be completely indistinguishable from the pluralist theory it was supposed to "tackle on its own terrain," it *must* provide an answer to this question: what keeps the state's autonomy "relative"; what keeps it from becoming "absolute" in the sense suggested by liberal reformists? In short, by what causal mechanism is a state that appears to be able to systematically overcome bourgeois opposition to its policies *nevertheless* ultimately constrained to serve only the long-term interests of that class? This clearly is the acid test for Poulantzas's theory of the state. If the theory provides a convincing answer to this question, Poulantzas's admirers can rightly claim that it represents a "Copernican revolution" in the Marxist theory of the state, by offering firm grounds at last for Lenin's assertion that the "democratic republic is the best possible political shell for capitalism." On the other hand, if it fails to provide such an answer, we will be forced to conclude that the alleged difference between Poulantzas's "Marxist" theory of the state and the conventional "bourgeois" pluralism it was supposed to have "tackled" is, in fact, entirely illusory.

The logical place to look for an answer to this question is Poulantzas's account of what causes the capitalist state to take on this peculiarly truncated autonomy. We can leave Poulantzas's Scriptural exercises aside here. The claim that the idea can be found in Marx and Engels—unconvincing anyway—hardly constitutes a sufficient reason for capitalist states to behave accordingly, although Poulantzas often seems to think it does (see pp. 265–66, 279–80). Hence the discussion can be confined to the *sociohistorical* causes to which Poulantzas attributes the relative autonomy peculiar to the capitalist type of state.

Ultimately, Poulantzas claims, the relative autonomy of the capitalist state rests on the capitalist relations of production which are, after all, determinant "in the last instance." In addition to the "relation of property" (private ownership of the means of production), which is common to all class-divided modes of production, capitalist production relations are characterized by a progressive "dispossession" of the worker which means that the workers are progressively deprived of whatever control over the immediate labor process they may still enjoy in other modes of production (e.g., feudalism). This eliminates the need for the state to intervene directly in order to ensure surplus value extraction, as was necessary in the feudal mode, and this explains, according to Poulantzas, the relative independence of the economic and political "instances" from one another in capitalism (see pp. 261–62).

This relative independence of the various structures enables the capitalist state, in conjunction with the ideological "instance," to produce the "isolation effect" on the agents of production. This "terrifyingly real" effect, according to Poulantzas, "sets" the agents "up" as "juridico-ideological subjects," pitted against one another in a relentless economic competition of all against all, thereby "concealing from these agents in a particular way the fact that their relations are class relations." The isolation effect, in turn, permits the state to present itself as the only "representative of the 'general interest,' " that is, "as a state which does not represent the power of one or several determinate classes, but which represents the power of the political unity of private agents, given over to economic antagonisms which the state claims to have the function of surmounting by unifying these agents within a 'popular-national' body."

But the working class is not as easily fooled by the "isolation effect" as the capitalist class. Because of the inexorable "collectivization of the labour process" brought on by capitalist development, the working class is constantly reminded of the fact that its relations with the capitalist class *are*, in fact, class relations, and as a result there is a continuous danger of a "rise and organized political struggle of the working class," which would seriously endanger capitalist domination. In addition there are the "institutions of the capitalist state (for example, universal suffrage), which hurl all the classes or fractions of society on to the political scene," as well as the "continued existence of the classes of the small producers" with their "complex reflection at the political level," which further complicate that domination. As a result, the dominant class can "dominate effectively," that is to say "perpetuate existing social relations," "only through a whole series of compromises which maintain the unstable equilibrium of the classes present." For, Poulantzas claims, "in a formation where the strictly political struggle of the dominated classes is possible, it is the sometimes indispensable means of maintaining the dominant classes' hegemony."

But unfortunately, the members of the capitalist class appear to be the primary victims of the debilitating "effect of isolation." They are so preoccupied with their parochial, conflicting interests that "left to themselves" they would be "exhausted by internal conflicts." As a result they cannot be counted on to develop the shrewd and intricate strategic planning, which would frequently include accepting painful short-term losses, necessary to maintain their precarious dominance. Therefore, the bourgeoisie needs the state to do the job *for it*. It needs the state to organize it politically, that is, to formulate and defend its long-term interests, which includes *dis*organizing the workers "to prevent their political organization which would overcome their economic isolation" by timely concessions, which are, however, ultimately in the long-term interest of the dominant class only.

Since the bourgeoisie is too shortsighted to accept willingly the concessions that are necessary to maintain its hegemony in the long run, the state *must* be relatively autonomous from the bourgeoisie to enable it to perform effectively the double function of organizing the capitalist class and disorganizing the working class. Thus, he declares, *"in order to do this, the capitalist state assumes a relative autonomy with regard to the bourgeoisie. . . . For this relative autonomy allows the state to intervene . . . in order to arrange compromises vis-à-vis the dominated classes, which, in the long run, are useful for the mutual economic interests of the dominant classes or fractions."*

This is how Poulantzas explains the emergence of a relatively autonomous state in capitalism. The argument is less than compelling on several grounds. Take, first, Poulantzas's explanation of the relative autonomy of the state from the economy as a consequence of the progressive "dispossession" of the workers. Presumably, here Poulantzas is referring to something like the gradual extension of managerial control over the immediate labor process, which Braverman and others (Braverman 1974; Edwards 1979; Marglin 1974; Stone 1974) have subsequently sought to document. According to this literature, the capitalist development of the labor process has been characterized by a continuous intensification of the division of labor. This has resulted in the reduction of skill requirements, closer supervision, and more detailed managerial control over all planning aspects of production, culminating in large-scale mechanization and the adoption of "scientific management" techniques around the turn of the century.[56] This is indeed widely considered to be a typically capitalist phenomenon, although it is hardly confined to capitalist societies anymore, as even Poulantzas has had to concede (see notes 8, 19, this chapter).

But it is not at all obvious how *this* particular process eliminates the need for the state to intervene directly with force to

56   What has happened since, especially with respect to clerical work, is the subject of much controversy (see, e.g., Braverman 1974, pt. 4; Gagliani 1981; Glenn and Feldberg 1977; Stewart, Prandy, and Blackburn 1980).

secure surplus value extraction from the workers and thus explains the relative autonomy of the state from the economy in capitalist society. For one thing, by most accounts the process has hardly been a very smooth one, involving frequent and rather forceful interventions by the state to put down rebellious craftsmen whose skills were rendered obsolete (see, e.g., Moore 1978, ch. 5; B. Stone 1974; Tilly 1978, 184–88; but cf. Stearns 1975). Furthermore, it appears that the state interfered *least* in the economy precisely when the process of "dispossession" was just starting, that is, in the laissez-faire era, whereas modern monopoly capitalism, in which, according to Poulantzas himself (1975, 224–81), the "dispossession" of the worker has reached unprecedented heights, apparently requires a dominant and aggressively interventionist state because "the political and ideological 'conditions' of production" have become "the very forms of . . . existence" of "the process of capital's extended reproduction" (168).[57] To make matters worse, Poulantzas also insists that the absolutist state was *already* relatively autonomous from the economy even *before* capitalism, let alone "dispossession," came into existence (cf. Giddens 1973, 45ff., 139–43)! In fact, he claims that this relatively autonomous absolutist state largely *created* capitalism to begin with (see note 18, this chapter), which would seem to be an oddly "*étatiste*" deviation from Marxist orthodoxy according to which new modes of production are born out of the contradiction between the forces and relations of production of the preceding one.

This is not to deny that capitalism may well be characterized by a relative "separation of economy and polity" (Giddens 1973, 202) as compared to other modes of production. But rather than attributing this to a process of "dispossession" which was not in full swing until the end of the nineteenth century, one could far more plausibly account for it by the fact that the re-

57 To take the English nineteenth-century "laissez-faire" state as a model of *all* states in early capitalism is clearly nonsense (see, e.g., Giddens 1973, 143–48), but not the issue here. Modern interventionism and the welfare state are surely relatively recent phenomena (partial exceptions such as Bismarck's Prussia and Meiji Japan notwithstanding), whereas the "dispossession" referred to here had barely begun during the period of early manufacture, according to the Althusserian theory itself (see, e.g., Pedraza-Bailey 1982, 215).

lations between owners of the means of production and non-owners are not regulated by physical coercion but by an economic mechanism: market exchange. Among Marxists, but not among them alone, it is accepted as a matter of course that "the *differentia specifica* of capitalistic production" (Marx 1967a, 618) consists of a market for labor in which a formally free labor force is compelled to sell its labor power just like any other commodity, or else starve (see, e.g., Cottrell 1984, 34; Giddens 1971, 232–33; Giddens and Held 1982, 82; Harding 1977, 87; Heilbroner 1980, 100–101; Kaye 1983, 168; Kolakowski 1978a, 276, 279; Marx 1967a, 167–76; S. W. Moore 1957, 75n; Offe 1985, 52; Sweezy 1942, 56; M. Weber 1958, 21–22).[58] The state was probably deeply and often rather forcefully implicated in the creation of such a "free" market for labor (see, e.g., Dobb 1964; Marx 1967a, pt. 8; Polanyi 1957), but, once created, the existence of such a market explains the relative absence of direct coercive intervention by the state in the production process much better than the barely begun process of "dispossession" (cf. Meiksins Wood 1981). Since the threat of unemployment was by itself quite enough to force labor to comply with the directives of management, the state only needed to uphold the rights of property and create and maintain the institutions of the "free" labor market. Thus, it is the fact that in capitalism "labor power" has been turned into a "commodity," to use the Marxian terminology, that explains the "relative autonomy" of the capitalist state with respect to the economy. And it is only on this basis that "dispossession," which, according to Marxist theory, is only one possible way of raising surplus value (viz., "relative" surplus value by way of intensifying labor and reducing wages relative to the total produced value; see Marx 1967a, pt. 5), can take place to begin with.[59]

58   This conventional interpretation has, of course, been challenged by Wallerstein (1974a and esp. 1974b) and his school. The issues they raise, however, do not bear directly on the argument at hand.

59   I only wish to argue here that the "classical" (Marxian) view that in capitalism the labor market, i.e., the threat of unemployment, has replaced direct coercion as a mechanism to discipline the labor force, provides a far more plausible explanation of why the role of physical coercion and the state in capital-labor relations has become more indirect than in other modes of production, than does Poulantzas's curious argument involving "disposses-

Oddly enough, Poulantzas does not attribute economic competition to the elimination of "feudal" constraints on free exchange and the resulting emergence of a market economy, but
to the "isolation effect" produced by the state and bourgeois
ideology, which "conceals" from the "agents of production" that
their relations are in reality class relations and which thereby
pits worker against worker and capitalist against capitalist in a
relentless competition for jobs and markets. Here is another example of Poulantzas's "*étatisme*." Certainly, the state was deeply
implicated in the forcible creation of a formally free labor
force, from the enclosure movements to the Poor Law Reform
of 1834, as well as in the elimination of other traditional barriers to free trade. But this was hardly achieved by anything as
gentle as an "isolation effect." And once the market system was
established, the sheer need to survive would appear to have
been quite sufficient to pit worker against worker and capitalist
against capitalist, quite apart from any "concealment" of class
relations and any "setting up" of the "agents of production" as
"juridico-ideological subjects." It is true, of course, that the
emergence of notions like equality before the law was intimately
linked to the breakdown of feudal ties, but to claim that such
notions are the *cause* of economic competition, rather than a
concomitant of the creation of the capitalist market system, is
little short of ludicrous (cf. Bridges 1974, 173–74).

At best, this whole notion of an "isolation effect" that "conceals" from the agents of production that "their relations are
class relations," so that the state can present itself as the only
possible "representative of the 'general interest'" appears to be
yet another way of sidestepping the central points at issue. *Of
course* states, or rather governments, whether capitalist, feudal,
or socialist, claim that they represent the "general interest."
But, as I have pointed out already in connection with the very
similar assertion that states seek to maintain "cohesion" (i.e.,
some semblance of social order), this has nothing to do with any

---

sion." This is not to deny, however, that the direct role of the state in those
relations has subsequently increased dramatically again, nor to argue that
such interventions, as some have claimed (e.g., Piven and Cloward 1971),
necessarily still serve the main purpose of disciplining the labor force to allow for maximum exploitation.

"isolation effect," which noncapitalist states presumably do not have to begin with. Governments claim to represent the "general interest" for the very simple reason that they would be creating completely unnecessary problems for themselves if they did *not*. The issue is not whether governments make such claims or not, but whether in "bourgeois democracies," where all citizens are, as far as the political realm is concerned at least, indeed formally "set up" as equal juridical subjects, irrespective of race, creed, gender, *or* class membership, such claims are in fact to some extent justified. Liberal pluralists argue that they are, instrumentalists claim that they are not. Poulantzas, characteristically, argues nothing. He merely describes the obvious in a manner that tries to *insinuate* where others would prefer rational argument ("conceal," " 'general interest,' " " 'popular-national' body," "juridico-ideological subjects").

Moreover, the claim that the members of the capitalist class are in some sense more easily fooled into failing to recognize their own class interests than the working class would appear to fly in the face of all the available empirical evidence.[60] There is a vast empirical literature suggesting quite the reverse, namely that generally the upper class exhibits a far greater degree of "class consciousness," however measured, than the working class, which is, of course, precisely the sort of evidence used by "instrumentalists" to support their case (in addition to the "instrumentalist" literature see, e.g., Bottomore 1965, 66ff.; Bridges 1974, 174–78; Collins 1975, 64–69, ch. 3; R. F. Hamilton 1972; Mann 1970; Parkin 1971, ch. 3; Runciman 1966). But Poulantzas's assertion of the contrary is, of course, in line with the assumption that seems to underlie most antireformist Marxist arguments, namely that if it had not been for whatever concessions, the workers would surely not have hesitated to destroy the entire system as they were supposed to to begin with.

At the very least, then, we are forced to conclude that Poulan-

60   It is also a little curious that the state, which is in other respects so remarkably well equipped and fine-tuned as to be able always to serve unambiguously the long-term interests of the capitalist class, even when nobody else seems to be aware of those interests, would have to do this by way of the rather clumsy detour of an "isolation effect," which reduces the capitalist class to a state of chronic debilitation, while apparently being of little use for keeping the working class under control.

tzas's "isolation effect" falls somewhat short of being "terrifyingly real." But let us not lose sight of the question we are trying to answer here: what keeps the state's autonomy "relative"? So far we have only encountered arguments—rather unsatisfactory ones, to be sure—for the capitalist state's autonomy, but *none* for its "relativity"! We have an "isolation effect" that leaves the members of the capitalist class in such a state of chronic debility that, as Connell puts it, "they can't organize their way out of a paper bag, it seems" (1982, 137), while apparently doing little to restrain the natural inclination of the workers to unite in the struggle for socialism. In addition, there is the troublesome "continued existence" of the small producers with their "complex reflection at the political level" (but not "power," of course!), and also the "institutions of the capitalist state (for example, universal suffrage), which hurl all the classes or fractions of society on to the political scene." As a result, the perpetuation of "existing social relations" requires "a whole series of compromises" without which the entire system, and thereby the rule of capital, would be in serious jeopardy. But unfortunately the members of the capitalist class are too severely handicapped by their own shortsightedness to be able to orchestrate the subtle and farsighted strategies capable of producing this "whole series of compromises." In fact, they are so blinded by the "isolation effect" that they would not even recognize the concessions required for their own long-term benefit if these were presented *to* them by the state!

So what does all this add up to? Nothing short of a pluralist paradise: strong, apparently well-organized workers and "small producers," a fragmented bourgeoisie, and an electoral system that forces the capitalists to put up with government policies that satisfy the workers' and "small producers'" demands at least to *some* extent *some* of the time. What, then, ensures that such policies always correspond to the long-term interests of the capitalist class nonetheless?

The *only* answer to this question that I have been able to find in Poulantzas's *entire opus*—other than the assertion that the capitalist state's power is afflicted by the peculiar "unity" that I discussed in the first subsection above ("Power, 'Hegemony,' and the State")—seems to be the following. Since the "isolation effect" renders the bourgeoisie too divided and short sighted to accept voluntarily the concessions and sacrifices necessary to keep the workers sufficiently docile for the maintenance of capitalist hegemony, the bourgeoisie *needs* the state to impose those sacrifices *on it*. Thus, "*in order to do this, the capitalist state assumes a relative autonomy with regard to the bourgeoisie.*" "In order to do this" is the operative phrase here. The argument plainly seems to be that the capitalist state possesses a relative autonomy from the capitalist class, that is, the ability to impose policies on it against the will of its members but *only* insofar as these policies are necessary for the long-term maintenance of their class domination, because the capitalist class "needs" it to do so.

But the causal connection between the existence of the "need" of the bourgeoisie and its fulfillment by the state still remains to be established. From the above argument it is hardly immediately obvious *why* the state should be moved to provide the services the bourgeoisie allegedly "needs." Presumably the other classes have no less "need" to have *their* interests looked after than the capitalist class, but this is apparently not a sufficient reason for the state to serve *them*. The question is, *Why?* Clearly not because the bourgeoisie has perceived its "needs" and has subsequently authorized the state to act accordingly. If it could recognize those "needs" it would not "need" a relatively autonomous state to impose them on it to begin with. On the contrary, seeing no need at all for the compromises imposed by the state, the bourgeoisie is presumably not a little annoyed by the way the state serves its "needs."

In fact, everything in Poulantzas's account suggests that the state should have all the reason in the world to serve the "needs" of the other classes and ignore those of the capitalist class. The "isolation effect" has the capitalist class so fragmented that the state could get away with just about *anything*, it seems. Furthermore, for whatever reason, it has made room for "the strictly political struggle of the dominated classes" and even gone to the point of "hurling" all classes on to the political scene. Why would the state, under these circumstances, so doggedly pursue the thankless task of serving the "needs" of precisely the class that shows the least appreciation, at the same time running the risk of provoking the wrath of the other classes? The state would get a far better bargain by simply satisfying the real needs of the "dominated classes": the capitalists would, of course, be annoyed as usual, but at least the state would earn the enduring gratitude and support of the working class in return.

But none of this seems to even *occur* to Poulantzas, who is apparently content to assume, without giving it any further thought, that what the bourgeoisie "needs" the bourgeoisie gets. Hence, I am forced to conclude that the present search has failed spectacularly. I have simply *not* been able to locate anywhere in Poulantzas's arguments an answer, let alone a convincing one, to the all-important question—an answer on which his whole theory necessarily stands or falls—if not the bourgeoisie itself, who or what compels the state to pursue exclusively the long-term interests of the bourgeoisie? As I said earlier, this means that in effect there remains *no real difference of any substance* between Poulantzas's account of "bourgeois" democratic politics and that given by the liberal pluralists who reject the Marxist assertion that those politics necessarily end up serving the interests of the capitalist minority. Thus, Poulantzas's celebrated theory of the capitalist state, if it can be called that, turns out to have been an unstable compound consisting of two disparate elements that lack any force to bind them. On the one hand, there is an empirical description, of sorts, of bourgeois democratic politics which, apart from the Marxist-sounding terminology, could have been taken *verbatim* out of any conventional, even somewhat conservative pluralist school text. On the other hand, there is the constantly reiterated orthodox Marxist assertion that no reform policies have ever done anything but barely "perpetuate existing social relations" which, presumably, would have been in serious jeopardy without those policies, so that the capitalist class has in all cases been their "true" beneficiary. However, the theoretical argument that would somehow render these contradictory strands compatible with each other *is simply lacking*. Poulantzas does not just fail to provide such an argument, he does not even *consider* it. Indeed there *is* no theory here in any reasonable sense of the term. There is only a descriptive account of a pluralist world combined with an utterly dogmatic reassertion of Marxist orthodoxy by means of "sheer postulation" (Connell 1982, 135). Poulantzas appears to have proceeded on to the pluralist "terrain" all right, but it was hardly he who did the "tackling."

Summary and Conclusions

To spend this much time and effort laboriously wading through the Althusserian jungle only to end up with nothing at all may seem a trifle excessive. I have, no doubt, taxed the reader's patience beyond reason. Yet I would argue that the extreme detail in which I have criticized Poulantzas's theory of the capitalist state was necessary, for two reasons. First, Poulantzas's conception of the capitalist state as "relatively autonomous" from the capitalist class has been widely celebrated among Marxists as the single most important breakthrough to come out of the "decade of the theory of the state." It is said to have rendered the older "instrumentalist" Marxist theory obsolete once and for all, and it has virtually become the new orthodoxy. Second, Poulantzas's theory and the "structuralism" of Althusser on which it is based are of such abstruseness and turgidity that only a blow-by-blow confrontation will convince the uninitiated reader that there *really is* nothing there.

Let me briefly recapitulate my argument. Poulantzas's principal claim is that the capitalist state is not the willing instrument of the capitalist class, as the "instrumentalists" appear to argue, but that it is "relatively autonomous": it is structured in such a way that it can and does on occasion impose policies over the opposition of the capitalist class but only insofar as these are to the long-term benefit of that class, although its members may not be aware of this. Thus the theory has in common with "bourgeois" pluralism that it concedes the possibility that the state may act against the expressed preferences and active resistance of the capitalist class, but it is Marxist in that it maintains that in such cases the state serves the interests of that class *nevertheless*. Hence, if it is to persuade a pluralist or an "instrumentalist," the theory will have to provide convincing answers to two questions: (1) in what sense are the policies imposed on the capitalist class against its will nevertheless in its long-term interest? (2) if the state has the ability to override the opposition and resistance of the capitalist class, why and how is it *nevertheless* constrained to serve only the long-term interests of that class?

With these questions in mind I have scrutinized Poulantzas's arguments point for point. As it turns out, they do not offer a plausible answer to either question. Poulantzas's arguments remain so vague, and his key concepts so ill defined, that the "theory" ends up being compatible with any evidence whatsoever; in other words, it is wholly unfalsifiable. Yet Poulantzas remains faithful to Marxist orthodoxy by taking refuge in tautologies, circular reasoning, dogmatic assertions, and *non sequiturs*. In the end, Poulantzas does not really offer a theory but rather a description of "capitalist" politics that is in all essentials identical to the one offered by "bourgeois" pluralism combined with unsupported proclamations of Marxist dogma and appropriately militant rhetoric.

As we saw in the first subsection of our critique, Poulantzas defines the basic concept of power as the capacity to realize objective class interests. The effect of this definition is to deprive the concept of any of the clear empirical referents the more conventional concept may have had *without replacing them*. Thus, classes may possess power whether they know it or not; it all depends on whether their "objective" interests are being realized. However, Poulantzas does not bother to disclose how it can be "objectively" determined what these interests are. He only offers a vague spatial metaphor which amounts simply to the standard Leninist–Lukácsian definition of "objective" interests as that which, given prevailing conditions, the subject can "objectively," that is, whether he or she knows it or not, get away with. In addition, Poulantzas's definition arbitrarily restricts "power" to classes alone. Thus, his definition simply allows anyone who claims to be privy to the secret technique of determining "objective" interests arbitrarily to attribute power to whichever class he or she wishes, without the least fear of possible refutation.

Similarly, his definition of the overall "dominant class" as the class that "occupies the dominant place" at the "dominant level" of the social formation remains vacuous as long as the "dominance" of either a class or a "level" remains completely undefined. In the case of current "monopoly" capitalism, moreover, it renders his whole theory that the state serves the interests of the "dominant" class true *by definition*, since here the political "level" (the state) is "dominant," according to Poulantzas.

Although his definition of power leaves little to be desired in terms of unfalsifiability, Poulantzas nevertheless proceeds to define away all possible cases in which any but the "dominant class" might appear to be capable of realizing its interests. The "dominated" classes may obtain considerable concessions, he acknowledges, but this does not mean that they have power: these are merely "pertinent effects." This is so because such concessions cannot lead to "socialism." Again, Poulantzas does not offer any arguments, he simply *asserts* Marxist orthodoxy. Similarly, various fractions and classes may realize their interests through their own "power centers" within the state, and even the bureaucracy may do so, but this is not power: it is merely a matter of "hindrances" and "resistances" to the absolute power of the "hegemonic" fraction of the capitalist class.

Poulantzas asserts that the "institutionalized power of the state" is characterized by a peculiar "unity": it cannot be shared. Only the "hegemonic" fraction holds political power "in its unity." Thus the state is necessarily the *"unambiguous* and *exclusive* political power" of the "hegemonic" fraction and, through it, of the "dominant" class as a whole. This would appear to be one of Poulantzas's principal answers to the second question above, What forces the state to serve *only* the dominant class? But Poulantzas's explanation for this "unity" turns out to consist of the obvious *non sequitur* that the "unity" of the state apparatus that is required for the state to fulfill its tasks adequately implies the "unity" of the consequences of its policy, that is, that it can only serve *one* class fraction. Moreover, this "unity" appears to necessitate numerous compromises, sacrifices, and concessions by the "hegemonic" fraction and the "dominant" class so that Poulantzas ends up with a remarkably pluralistic picture but without any convincing rationale for claiming that it is all nevertheless in the exclusive interests of the "dominant" class. Poulantzas simply asserts dogmatically that the two are not contradictory—hardly a promising strategy for persuading those who think that perhaps they might be.

Then, having been unable to identify Poulantzas's procedure for determining "objective" class interests, in the next subsection I reviewed his remarks on what the "objective" interests of the "dominant class" consist of, in the hope of shedding at least *some* light on the first question, In what sense are the "sacrifices" imposed on this "dominant class" nevertheless ultimately to its benefit? First, we encountered Poulantzas's repeated claim that the state may sacrifice the "economic" interests of the "dominant class" or "hegemonic fraction," but *only* to safeguard its "political" interests. The distinction between "economic" and "political" interests turned out to be totally meaningless, however, because Poulantzas simply fails to provide any criteria for making it. His definition of "political practice," that is, the very "practice" he sought to "theorize" comprehensively, is in fact so utterly devoid of any distinctive, unambiguous referents that it completely fails to distinguish this "practice" from any other. Moreover, if we are to interpret the distinction to mean that "economic" interests are by definition in some sense short-term, narrower, less important interests, whereas "political" interests refer to long-term, more inclusive, more important interests, as many of Poulantzas's passages suggest, this simply turns his whole theory into one grand tautology. For it reduces the theory to the claim that whatever the "dominant class" sacrifices is *by definition* narrower, less important, more short term ("economic") than what it gains from these sacrifices ("political interests").

Poulantzas's much-quoted designation of the capitalist state as the "factor of cohesion" that maintains the "unity of the social formation" and *thereby* serves the interests of its "dominant class," did not turn out to be of much help for specifying the "true" interests of that class either. If taken as a pure definition it would, once again, reduce the argument to sheer tautology. If "cohesion" and "unity" simply refer to the fact that states do not usually deliberately pursue chaos, the designation turns into a banality, rendering the argument undistinguishable from conventional bourgeois pluralism. If, finally, it means that government policy has somehow prevented or postponed the arrival of "socialism," the argument reduces to unfalsifiable dogma because, as a good Marxist, Poulantzas cannot disclose what the arrival of "socialism" *would* look like.

Finally, I have considered one last possible interpretation of the "true" interests of the dominant class: that they consist of the sheer maintenance of the "structures" of the "capitalist" state, since these, after all, force the state to serve the interests of the "dominant" class. But this simply turns the whole theory into a self-sufficient tautology once more: a "capitalist" state is defined by its "structures," which force it to serve the interests of the dominant class, and as long as it retains those "structures" it will, naturally, continue to do so. Whether any actual, observable states in any capitalist societies are "capitalist" in this sense cannot be determined. Alternatively, the argument *presupposes* the validity of the assertion that existing states are afflicted by a peculiar "unity of power," which, as we have seen, was plain nonsense. To top it all off, Poulantzas finally so broadens his concept of the "capitalist" state that it ends up merging with the entire "capitalist" social system. As a result, explanations as to who "maintains" what become largely redundant.

In the third subsection, finally, I examined the very pinnacle of Poulantzas's contributions to the Marxist theory of the state: the notion of the "relative autonomy" of the capitalist state which supposedly enabled Poulantzas to "tackle the pluralists on their own terrain." Here, if anywhere, we should have found some sort of answer to our second question, What, if not the bourgeoisie itself, keeps the state from acting *against* its interests? As I noted, Poulantzas certainly does present an almost exaggeratedly pluralistic picture when describing the sorts of things the state's "relative autonomy" permits it to do. The "dominant" class has to make "real economic sacrifices," often under direct pressure from the "dominated" classes which are even "encouraged" by the state to "work against" the "dominant" class, and so on. But by what mysterious mechanism all this is somehow constrained to "univocally correspond" to the "exclusive" interests of the capitalist class at all times remains totally obscure. In explaining the origins of this "relative autonomy" Poulantzas gives many complicated reasons (although none of them is even remotely plausible) for the state's autonomy but *none* for that autonomy's "relativity." The only reason, in the final analysis, the state will not impinge on the fundamental interests of the bourgeoisie seems to be an unexplained "need" of the bourgeoisie for the state not to do so. Apparently, other classes have no such "needs." In the meantime, however, Poulantzas unwittingly provides ample grounds for believing that the state has no reason at all to confine itself to satisfying the "needs" of the bourgeoisie. Again we have a description of pluralism disguised in a dogmatic assertion of Marxist orthodoxy.

Poulantzas's famous theory of the capitalist state turns out not to be a theory at all. What it amounts to is no more than a curious mix of descriptive statements that are indistinguishable from bourgeois pluralism, on one hand, and Marxist-sounding rhetoric, on the other. The way Poulantzas manages to leave the impression that the former does *not* contradict the latter is by formulating the rhetoric in such a way that it can be interpreted as *either* pure tautology which is, by its very nature, completely unrelated to *any* empirical reality, *or* as the simple reassertion of the orthodox claim that gradual reform does not lead to "socialism," which *might* be a falsifiable statement if we had some minimal idea of what "socialism" *would* amount to. In the absence of such a minimal idea, Poulantzas's "theory" simply boils down to an odd juxtaposition of pluralist reality and plainly dogmatic proclamations to the effect that this reality in no way detracts from the validity of orthodox Marxist doctrine regarding the capitalist state. Thus, I can only agree with Balbus's final verdict: "It would appear, then, that the structuralist approach is able to sustain the basic Marxist thesis that the state serves the interest of the capitalist class only by transforming this thesis into a nonfalsifiable statement that is true by definition" (1982, 97).

Yet the fundamental unfalsifiability of this "theory" has not deterred some researchers from attempting to "test" it empirically. Such attempts, however, only serve to demonstrate its inherent untestability. Skocpol (1980), for instance, has derived the following empirical implication from Poulantzas's theory of the capitalist state: policy is initiated by the state, not by the representatives of the capitalist class; the capitalist class is initially divided and subsequently united by the state; state interventions are always immediately functional for the system as a whole; they quickly reestablish the "global equilibrium," order, "cohesion," and economic prosperity. She then proceeds to show that the case of the New Deal provides a decisive empirical refutation of these claims (see ibid., 169–81).

A true follower of Poulantzas could easily dismiss such disproof as being based on incorrect specifications of the theory. All the theory implies is that the state *may* act against the capitalist class when necessary. Who "initiates" the policy is irrelevant. If the policies proposed by representatives of the capitalist class do not seriously endanger the "cohesion" of the social formation, the state may well agree to implement them; if they do endanger it, the state will act autonomously to maintain cohesion. Thus if a policy can be observed to be clearly the result of business "initiative," this merely provides retrospective proof that the "cohesion" of the "social formation" was not at stake. The capitalist class is indeed *usually* divided but it need not always be. At any rate, whether or not it is divided has no bearing on the actions of the "relatively autonomous" state. Moreover, the fact that government policies have on occasion exacerbated the divisions within the capitalist class by no means refutes the claim that the state "unifies" that class. The state may well "unify" the capitalist class by "playing off" its fractions against one another! Finally, the theory does not stipulate that the stabilizing effects of government policy be immediate, only that they maintain "cohesion" *in the long run*, which of course can be put off forever. Thus, both business initiatives and their absence, both divisions and unity (in the conventional sense) of the capitalist class, and both order and chaos may serve as evidence supporting the "theory." In fact, as Skocpol herself seems to realize (ibid., 181), only a state that would spontaneously self-destruct and establish "socialism" in one single movement would constitute definite disproof of the theory.[61]

Mollenkopf (1975), in another example, criticizes the "instrumentalist" approach for remaining too close to the pluralist methods and conceptions of interest-group politics and for con-

61   Incredibly, even Poulantzas himself apparently conceded at a conference in 1973 that only a successful socialist revolution initiated by the existing state could possibly *dis*confirm his theory (see Balbus 1982, 96)!

sequently being unable to distinguish between the narrow interests of various business groups and the interests of the capitalist class as a whole. Furthermore, he argues, "instrumentalism" seriously overestimates the ease with which business can manipulate government and public opinion and thus underestimates the independent influence of politics and political culture. He claims that the "structuralist" approach is better equipped to deal with these problems. Then he calls for a "careful specification of the alternative explanations" (257), so that they may be evaluated in the light of empirical evidence. Mollenkopf specifies four empirical implications of the "structuralist" approach: policy originates with the state, not with business; business acts out of narrow interest-group motives, not class interests; state bureaucracies are relatively insulated from outside control; political culture is not homogeneous but contains "contradictions" and "dysfunctional values" (257–58).

The first implication we have already seen to be beside the point. The other three merely illustrate how "structuralism" accepts a pluralist reality while *assuming without argument* that this reality corresponds to the interests of the capitalist class. Internal divisions and a preoccupation with narrow interests among business leaders, the claim that the state is not controlled by any one group or class, and a diversity of political interests and opinions are virtually the stock in trade of pluralist theory, and, whatever the "methods" or "concepts," such empirical evidence would support the pluralist view while not providing the slightest grounds for claiming that the state serves the "class" interests of business. Such grounds must be provided *in addition* to the above evidence for the "structuralist" approach to be distinct from "bourgeois" pluralism. As we have seen, the "structuralism" of Poulantzas simply does not provide them.

Finally, Cuneo (1979, 1980) offers an attempt to demonstrate the superiority of "structuralism" in the spirit of Mollenkopf.[62]

---

62   Although Cuneo, especially in the second article (1980), lumps together Poulantzas's early "structuralist" position with the later "class struggle" approach as if they formed a coherent "structuralist" theory. This is not terribly important, however, since the "class struggle" approach suffers from *exactly* the same ambiguity with respect to empirical implications as "structuralism" (see Chapter 6).

Cuneo uses evidence showing that the Canadian government, after a decade of rising working-class pressure, finally adopted an Unemployment Insurance Act in 1941 which was virtually unanimously opposed by business but strongly supported by the moderate wing of the labor movement. This shows, Cuneo claims, how "the state ensures its own relative autonomy and at the same time reproduces the economic dominance of the capitalist class over the working class" (1980, 57). His sole reason for claiming that the act helped reproduce the "dominance of the capitalist class" appears to be that it did not fully meet the extreme demands of a more radical, communist-inspired working-class movement of the period. But in the meantime many of the "revolutionary" demands Cuneo mentions have been met, which would seem to cast some doubt on their "revolutionary" nature (see note 19, chapter 2). Wholly preoccupied with "demonstrating" the superiority of structuralism over instrumentalism, Cuneo is apparently totally unaware of the fact that he has confirmed liberal pluralism and the "leftward drift" thesis![63]

But what would seem to be much more in need of explanation is the rather embarrassing fact that such a totally vacuous "theory" as this could be so widely and swiftly adopted by so many contemporary Marxists. Some of the reasons are, however, not hard to see. There were good grounds for doubts about the adequacy of the old instrumentalist view. When confronted with empirical evidence of compromises and even the occasional defeat of a seemingly united capitalist class, instrumentalism tends to degenerate into no more than an angry version of liberalism. It offers no certain theoretical guarantees against the viability of gradualism and the possibility of a long-term "leftward drift." Even the members of the capitalist class are only human and hence the correspondence between their opinions and actions and their true, long-term interests is tenuous at best.

63   Another amusing example of the confusion that besets the admirers of "structuralism" is provided by Weiner (1980). While he claims that Miliband's instrumentalism "evades the underlying 'structural' issues" (1), he presents Domhoff's theory of "corporate liberalism" as proof of the existence of a "hegemonic power bloc" that maintains the existing "structure of dominance" (12–13)!

By contrast, Poulantzas's structural theory does account for all the facts observed and yet offers a theoretical guarantee that state policy *necessarily* corresponds to the long-term interests of the capitalist·class. Its unsurpassed obscurity and pretentiousness no doubt only heighten the fascination. But more important, they give the comforting impression that it is indeed a *theory*. The endless typologies and definitions, the omnipresent qualifications and caveats, the systems of mutually reinforcing postulates, the repetitive denunciations of "ideology," the constant boasting about "scientificity" and "rigor," and the sheer obscurity of it all, seem to have conveniently concealed the fact that Poulantzas offers no more than an incoherent mixture of "bourgeois" pluralism and unsubstantiated assertions of Marxist articles of faith.

Interestingly, these assertions rather faithfully capture much of what became orthodox Marxism after it lost its pre-Leninist innocence. The failure of the proletariat to perform its historically appointed duty is accepted as an empirical reality, but not as in any way affecting the initial theory that it would or should have. Instead, the working class has simply failed to recognize its "objective" interests, which, as only Marxists know, consist of the realization of an as yet indescribable state of affairs called "socialism." Thus, like Marx and Lenin before him, Poulantzas continues to judge current political realities from the exclusive vantage point of that rather elusive future condition. The "objective" interest of the "dominated classes" consists of the realization of socialism. Anything short of this is, therefore, at best a "pertinent effect" since it is tantamount to maintaining the "cohesion" and "unity" of the "social formation." The guiding assumption in all this is clearly that capitalism has indeed, as Marx predicted, continuously teetered on the brink of total collapse. Workers are *assumed* to be permanently on the very verge of grasping their "true" interests and taking to the streets behind the banner of "socialism," while capitalists are *assumed* to be hopelessly constricted by their own narrow preoccupations, fragmented interests, and the like. Once again, we see the "immanence" principle at work. Both the working class's natural predisposition toward "socialism" *and* the theory explaining the failure of "socialism" to arrive are exclusively based on forces intrinsic to capitalism. The specific nature and outlines of "socialism" itself are entirely irrelevant to all this. To the extent that the massive amount of empirical evidence to the contrary is acknowledged, this becomes the thing to be explained: how are the workers kept from forming a revolutionary mass and how are the capitalists kept from destroying their own system through their internecine squabbling? The entire "theory" is an attempt to resolve this self-imposed puzzle: the state and the dominant ideology must have persistently operated in such a way as to pull the system back from the brink of disaster just in time. In the process, however, while attempting to explain away what are implicitly assumed to be extremely powerful centrifugal forces, Poulantzas ends up depicting capitalism as a mighty many-tentacled machine whose capacities for self-regeneration seem absolutely infinite. Intriguingly, the very same can be said of the *other* functionalist Marxist theories of the state that claim to have superseded "instrumentalism," as we shall see in the next chapter.

5 Structural Functionalism Revisited (2): Accumulation versus Legitimation

The perceived shortcomings of the old "instrumentalist" theory of the state have prompted the formulation of a second structural-functional approach, which, though apparently developed quite independently from Poulantzas's structuralism, exhibits some striking similarities with it. This is all the more remarkable as the origins of these two approaches could, within Marxism, hardly have been further apart. The second approach originates with the German theorist Claus Offe, a former student of the critical theorist Jürgen Habermas who himself has adopted major elements of his former pupil's theory (see, e.g., Habermas 1968, 73–79; 1971, 260–64; 1973a, 14–20, 44–50; 1973b, 9–60, 85–87, 128–30; 1976, 287–90, 306–10, 316; cf. Frankel 1979; Friedrichs 1980; Keane 1984; Offe 1984a, 252, 255–56; Schroyer 1975; van den Berg 1980, 454–59, 453–69; 1981, 27–39); that is, this approach originates with the very Hegelian tradition in Marxism that the Althusserians have sought to eradicate. Moreover, this theory of the state does not rest on a radical rethinking of basic epistemological presuppositions as the Althusserian approach allegedly does, but on fairly conventional "systems theory." Intriguingly, whereas Poulantzas's structuralist theory of the state was initially favorably received primarily in Britain, Offe's systems-theoretic version seems to have captured an audience mainly in North America.[1] Furthermore, whereas Poulantzas has been criticized

---

1 This has not, to my knowledge, been widely noted. Yet it can easily be documented. For some examples of the preference of North American writers for Offe as compared to Poulantzas, see, e.g., Bridges (1974), Deaton (1973), Esping-Andersen, Friedland, and Wright (1976), Flacks and Turkel (1978, 219), Frankel (1979), Gold, Lo, and Wright (1975a, b), Keane

by many for the profoundly static implications of his theory of
the capitalist state, Offe is praised by his admirers precisely for
"restoring dialectics" (Gold, Lo, and Wright 1975b, 45), that is,
for providing a *dynamic* theory of the state, one that allows and
accounts for social change based on the still fundamentally contradictory nature of the capitalist mode of production (Esping-
Andersen, Friedland, and Wright 1976, 190–91; Frankel 1979,
225ff., 235ff.; Giddens 1981, 219–20; Mollenkopf 1975, 256;
Pierson 1984; Weiner 1980, 1, 6).

Nevertheless, the two theories are remarkably similar not
only in their criticisms of the instrumentalist view of the state
but also in the solutions they propose to the riddle of how the
formally democratic bourgeois state manages to serve and defend the class interests of the capitalist minority. In fact, in this
chapter I argue that the two approaches are virtually interchangeable in all but terminology.[2] Of particular interest is the
fact that Offe's theory suffers from the exact same flaws as the
structuralist approach does. It remains worthwhile treating
them separately, however, for two reasons. First, their virtual
identity is not widely acknowledged and in fact often denied.[3]
Second, the very terms in which Offe and his followers cast
their theory reveal more clearly than anything else the implicit,
unexamined "domain assumptions" (Gouldner 1971) that continue to underlie the recent theoretical Marxist literature on the
state and, by implication, Marxist theory in general.[4]

(1978), Mollenkopf (1975), Panitch, ed. (1977), Sardei-Biermann, Christiansen, and Dohse (1973), Weiner (1980), D. A. Wolfe (1981), and E. O.
Wright (1978). Castells (1980) adopts a virtually identical approach, but
bases himself on Habermas (1973b) instead. In the United States Offe has
been associated with the group behind the journal *Kapitalistate*, in which he
himself has published (1973a, b), and his ideas have been widely discussed
(see many of the previous references). Poulantzas, on the other hand, was
favorably received in Britain by the editors of the *New Left Review* in which
he first published several of his articles (1967, 1972, 1973a, 1976).

2   One reason for Offe's greater popularity in North America may be the relatively greater receptivity to his Parsonsian systems-theory terminology
there.

3   Particularly amusing are Gold, Lo, and Wright (1975a, b) and Esping-Andersen, Friedland, and Wright (1976), who, after first criticizing Poulantzas
and extolling Offe for providing a superior alternative then go on to criticize the latter for the very same flaws!

4   Offe's Marxist pedigree is not entirely unproblematic. Pierson (1984) refers

State Functions and System (In)Stability

As we have seen in Chapter 3, Offe criticizes "instrumentalism" as an inadequate refutation of reformism on grounds similar to Poulantzas's.[5] It may be able to document the regular and overwhelming preponderance of capitalist interests and interest groups in the policy-making process of the formally democratic bourgeois state, Offe concedes, but it cannot "demonstrate the *structural necessity* of this state of affairs" nor can it "be made use of to prove the *class-character* of the State" (1974, 33). Not unlike Poulantzas, Offe blames the "pluralistic model of policy-analysis" (ibid.) accepted by proponents of the instrumentalist model, which essentially presents the state as a passive reflector of the balance of class forces in civil society, for the ultimate failure to establish "the class character of political governance, its structural complicity with an interest of capital as a whole" (46).

Since I have already extensively examined Offe's critique of instrumentalism in Chapter 3, I will not repeat his arguments in detail here. Simply summarized, Offe argues, again much like Poulantzas, that capitalists are generally so consumed by the short-term pressures of economic survival and their diverse interests that they are unable to achieve the consensus necessary to impose policy on the state or if and when they do there is no guarantee such consensus actually represents the bourgeoisie's objective, long-term *class* interest. Furthermore, empirically, policies that definitely *do* serve those long-term interests fre-

---

to Offe as a "post-marxist" analyst of the state, Jessop (1982, 106) questions his "relationship to orthodox Marxism," and Offe's own response to the question of his fidelity to Marxism has become rather evasive: he concedes that he thought of himself as a Marxist *"in the past"* (Offe 1984a, 254, emphasis added), yet he also contests "anybody's right to monopolize definitions of Marxism and its limits" (ibid.). As we shall see, although he does indeed deviate greatly from some of the basic tenets of "orthodoxy," he still retains some of the assumptions that are emerging as the doctrinal "core" of (at least Western) Marxism in this book.

5   For alternative summaries of the main arguments by Offe and others discussed in this chapter, see Jessop (1982, 106–12) and Carnoy (1984, chs. 5, 8), who are both far more sympathetic to these views than I. My summary is based primarily on Offe's earlier writings which contain the most coherent version of the theory of the capitalist state for which he has become known internationally. His more recent writings contain some significant shifts in emphasis and substance which will be noted where relevant.

quently are *not* initiated by bourgeois representatives at all, and sometimes they are even imposed *in opposition to* the explicit preferences of the capitalist class.

Hence, the task for an adequate Marxist theory of the state is, according to Offe, to lay bare "the mechanisms which *guarantee* . . . the establishment of an objective complementarity relationship between economic and political power" (ibid., 31, emphasis added), while taking into account the fact that the state need not, and in fact *cannot* be "the lackey or the junior partner of the capitalists" (Macpherson 1977a, 233). Thus Offe's critique of instrumentalism leads to a conclusion that is almost identical to that of Poulantzas: "The common interests of the ruling class are most accurately expressed in those legislative and administrative strategies of the State apparatus which are *not* initiated by articulated interests, that is 'from outside,' but which arise from the State organizations' own routines and structures" (Offe 1974, 35). Therefore, "one must ask which *internal structures* within the political system guarantee the implementability of initiatives and interests arising from the process of accumulation" (35–36), since "one can speak of a 'capitalist State' or an 'ideal collective capitalist' only when it has been successfully proved that the *system of political institutions displays its own class-specific selectivity corresponding to the interests of the accumulation of capital*" (36). But whereas Poulantzas's arguments are supposedly derived from Althusserian "structuralism," Offe's approach purports to be based on a "systems theoretical" analysis of advanced, or "late" capitalism.[6]

Offe views capitalist society as a social system consisting of three subsystems each with its own distinct "organizational principle": the economic subsystem is based on *"exchange relationships,"* that is, its "organizational principle" consists of the exchange of marketable commodities; the political subsystem comprises those processes involving *"coercive relationships"* based

6   As should be abundantly clear from my criticisms in this and the previous
      chapter, I am not at all sure that this "structuralism" and "systems theory"
      are anything more than vacuous exercises in relabeling and reclassifying
      things with the evident effect or purpose of sidestepping the basic problems
      facing Marxist dogma. Nor am I, consequently, convinced that there is any
      substantial difference between them.

on power; the normative subsystem, finally, is based on specifically *"normative structures"* (1976a, 33–34; cf. Haas 1979, 26–27). What characterizes the social system as capitalist is the fact that in it "the organizational principle of exchange (of equivalents) is *universalized*, i.e., also extended to apply to labor power—which is in the process of becoming a commodity—and becomes *dominant*, i.e., is freed from normative and coercive restraints" (Offe 1976a, 33). The defining characteristic of capitalism, then, is that all elements of the social structure are determined by the exchange relationships between private owners of commodities, including capital and labor power, seeking private gain (1972c, 8, 10; cf. van den Berg 1980, 456; 1981, 28). The function of the other two subsystems is primarily of a supportive, subordinate nature: the normative system is supposed to provide the "normative structures," and the state provides the framework of "sanctioned rules" that are necessary to sustain the dominance of the organizational principle of exchange in the overall system. They are what Offe calls the "flanking subsystems" required to maintain the viability and identity of the system as a whole (1976a, 33–35).

But, although it is a defining feature of the capitalist system as a whole that the normative and political subsystems and their respective organizational principles remain subordinate, they are at the same time indispensable to its very survival. For, as Marx had shown, accumulation through commodity exchange, that is, capitalist economic growth, is a profoundly contradictory process as it constantly tends to undermine and destroy the conditions of its own existence and continuity. The contradiction referred to here is, of course, in formal Marxist terms, that between the forces and the relations of production or, in Offe's own words, the "disproportion that exists between the unconscious (unintentional, merely factual) expansion of relations of interdependence in the *process of socialization*, on the one hand, and the absence of conscious organization and planning of this process, which is structurally blocked by the intransigence of privatized investment strategies and appropriation relations (i.e., *production relations*), on the other" (1972c, 11–12, my translation). Concretely, this contradiction means that the capitalist accumulation process, because it follows the dictates of the uncoordinated search for private gain, constantly tends to throw capital and labor out of the commodity form. That is, it renders them unprofitable and hence not readily exchangeable on the market, as a result of economic crises and rapid, unplanned technological change, while systematically leaving unsatisfied those urgent needs of various groups and classes that for one reason or another are not easily turned into *effective* demand that can be profitably met through the marketplace. The results can be seen in the continuously self-destructive character of the process of accumulation, the creation of social wealth based on scarcity, of capital based on its destruction, persistent and re-current imbalances, conflicts, repression, want, and alienation (11–17; Offe and Ronge 1975, 141–44).

Hence, the role of the "flanking subsystems," especially the state,[7] is vital for the survival of the system as a whole, as it consists of counteracting the self-destructive tendencies of the capitalist accumulation process by correcting its dysfunctional effects, while violating as little as possible the dominant organizational principle of commodity exchange. Thus, much of state policy can be seen as adaptive mechanisms produced by the political subsystem to maintain or restore the necessary conditions of profitable capital accumulation whenever and wherever these are impaired by the self-destructive tendencies of capital. This is how Offe interprets the massive transformation of capitalism from the nineteenth-century liberal laissez-faire model to the "organized" capitalism of today: as the result of a cumulative series of mainly state-initiated "adaptive mechanisms" ("*Auffang-Mechanismen*"; see, e.g., 1972c, 23). In its efforts to alleviate and preferably even prevent major crises caused by the inherently contradictory process of capitalist accumulation, the state has become increasingly involved, however reluctantly, in the regulation of markets and of competition generally; in the provision of more and more of the

7   The normative subsystem does not really play a prominent role in Offe's argument—at least not explicitly—an omission for which he has been criticized by Keane (1978). In fact, until a relatively late piece (1976a) Offe hardly ever discussed the normative order as a separately significant subsystem at all, and even then his treatment of it is very cursory indeed (see Haas 1979, 27).

"infrastructure" that is needed but cannot be profitably supplied by private capital; in massive efforts at what might be called "*administrative recommodification*" (Offe and Ronge 1975, 143), like labor-retraining programs, regional development plans, the underwriting of massive research and development efforts to provide profitable investment opportunities for the long run, subsidized and planned dismantling of technologically obsolete industries and their replacement by advanced ones, and the like. Thus state intervention in the economy is the result of the recurrent need for the state to counteract the crises provoked by the process of private capitalist accumulation. Similarly, many welfare-state provisions and programs are best seen as efforts by the state to avoid or resolve crises and conflicts that might otherwise have threatened the very foundations of the capitalist system, rather than as fundamental changes *of* that system. They are all part and parcel of the state's effort to *maintain* and *restore* the conditions of profitable capital accumulation (Offe 1972a; 1972c, 21–25; Offe and Ronge 1975, 141–43; also Habermas 1973b, 50–60; van den Berg 1981, 29–31).

"In the most general sense," as Offe himself puts it, "the capitalist state has the responsibility of compensating the processes of socialization triggered by capital, and which constitute a threat to the capital relation, in such a way that neither a self-obstruction of market-regulated accumulation nor an abolition of relationships of private appropriation of socialized production takes place" (1976a, 49). The capitalist state, to put it slightly differently, is subject to "the imperative to universalize the commodity form" (1975a, 251), it has the general assignment of "securing the commodity form of both labor and capital" (252) by maintaining the conditions that allow both to find remunerative employment through the market mechanism. "In this sense full employment of all units of value under the exploitative conditions of the capitalist mode of production is in fact the supreme purpose of the capitalist state and the substance of its observable activity" (251; see also Haas 1979, 28; Keane 1978, 56, 63; Macpherson 1977a, 233).

That the activity of a *capitalist* state cannot transcend this "supreme purpose" is implied by the very definition of such a state as located in and hence circumscribed by the overall system of which it is a major constitutive part. The capitalist state is defined by Offe by "the way it is functionally related to and dependent upon the accumulation process" (1975b, 126, 144). At the same time, however—and this is the second major defining characteristic—the power of the state, and its very ability to act for that matter, depend fundamentally on the rate and the continuity of private accumulation as it provides the state with the resources it needs to carry out policy (via taxation and borrowing on the capital market). This means, third, that any holder of state power has, *ipso facto*, a strong interest "in promoting those conditions most conducive to accumulation" (Offe and Ronge 1975, 140). In fact, "the state does not only have the authority, but the *mandate* to create and sustain *conditions* of accumulation" (Offe 1975b, 126). As a result, and because in formally democratic regimes governments also need to placate the electorate (127; Offe and Ronge 1975, 140),[8] it follows, according to Offe, that the "commodity form is the general point of equilibrium of the capitalist state" (Offe and Ronge 1975, 140–41). Thus, Offe concludes that "there is no need to equate the capitalist state, either empirically or theoretically with a political alliance of the personnel of the state apparatus on the one side and the class of owners of capital (or certain segments of this class) on the other side. For the abstract principle of making a subject of permanent market exchange relationships out of every citizen does more to keep state policies in tune with the class interests of the agents of accumulation than any supposed 'conspiracy' between 'overlapping directorates' of state and industry could possibly achieve" (1975a, 251).

In the first instance, then, for Offe the class character of the capitalist state resides in the fact that its primary function consists of maintaining or restoring the long-term conditions of profitable capital accumulation because it thereby serves the long-term, collective interests of the members of the capitalist class. It must therefore suppress any anticapitalist interests that in any way threaten to impede this (1972c, 74–78; 1974, 36–

8   I discuss this fourth characteristic of the capitalist state more extensively below since it is part of the state's "legitimation" function, not the accumulation function discussed here.

38). But as we have already seen, the state cannot necessarily count on the support of the bourgeoisie and it may well have to face its strong opposition, since the members of this class often lack the foresight and perspective to grasp the long-term significance of state policies for their own class interests. Consequently, the state must be able to present "itself to the particular and narrow interests of individual capitalists and their political organizations as a supervisory, tutelary force—at all events one which is an alien and sovereign authority—since it is only through the State's becoming relatively autonomous in this way that the multiplicity of particular and situation-bound special interests can be integrated into a class-interest" (1974, 35). Elsewhere, in a passage that is again remarkably reminiscent of Poulantzas, Offe argues that both the normative system and state power must be relatively autonomous in discharging their increasingly important functions of counteracting the problems resulting from the accumulation process: "In order for them to be able to deal with these resultant problems compensatorily, it becomes functionally necessary for them to partially emancipate themselves from the relationship of positive subordination, i.e., gain the *relative autonomy* they require for the performance of their specific regulatory services . . . since capital as a whole exists only in an ideal sense, i.e., is incapable of articulating and perceiving a unitary and common class interest, it requires special guidance and supervision by a *fully differentiated* political-administrative system" (1976a, 48).

To gain this relative autonomy, Offe continues, the state "must procure for itself a basis for overall legitimation" (49). Paradoxically, the capitalist state has been able to gain the required autonomy from the bourgeoisie in the latter's own long-term interest only by making use of the "formal structures of bourgeois democracy" (1974, 54). It is through these that the capitalist state has been able to acquire the basis of independent legitimacy needed to overrule capitalist opposition to its long-term system-maintaining policies (1972c, 33–36, 184–85). In this way, however, the "political-administrative system" has become "dependent on 'mass loyalty' ('diffuse support'), upon whose extent its autonomy and capacity to act depend" (1976a, 53). This may well cause as many new problems for the capitalist state as it solves since it imposes a second function on it, in addition to its accumulation function, namely the need to maintain its legitimacy so as to retain the mass loyalty it needs to carry out the accumulation function.

Now, this need to retain mass loyalty, Offe argues, "obliges the State apparatus to execute its *class-bound functions under the pretext of class-neutrality* and to provide its particular exercise of power with the alibi of the general interest," since "an openly practiced class character of political governance which is apparent as such involves the risk of class-polarization and a politicization of the class struggle" (1974, 47). In other words, in addition to securing the long-term conditions favorable to profitable accumulation the capitalist state must systematically deny and conceal this function lest it lose the mass legitimacy it needs to perform it in the first place (cf. Offe 1975b, 127; Offe and Ronge 1975, 140). And for this, too, the "formal structures of bourgeois democracy" appear quite serviceable as they provide "an ideological mechanism . . . to make it possible to deny the objective complicity of collective-capitalist accumulation interests and the functions of the State" (1974, 54). But these structures can only operate as "the most important instruments for maintaining the mass loyalty necessary for stability" (1972b, 105) if they effectively help convey the image of the state as a class-neutral institution that encourages universal participation in the process of consensus formation; offers equal access for all to the benefits of its services, interventions, and regulations; and only serves the general interest of society as a whole. This is done through the whole complex of concessions, programs, and interventions collectively known as the welfare state. These fulfill the legitimation function of retaining the necessary mass acquiescence, which allows the state to perform its functions favoring the long-term interests of the capitalist class (1972a; 1972b, 81).

Thus, for Offe, the capitalist state's ability to conceal its own class character becomes an integral part of that very class character itself. "In a simplified form, we can say, that State power in capitalist industrial societies is the method of class rule which *does not disclose its identity as such*" (1974, 46). But here we seem to run up against a methodological dilemma resulting from the very success of the capitalist state in concealing its class character: if one sticks to a narrow, behaviorist empiricism one is not likely to find any evidence of the state's class character at all, only evidence of the ability of the masses or at least noncapitalist groups to use the institutions of bourgeois democracy to wrest benefits and concessions from the state, even over capitalist-class opposition; on the other hand, the only available alternative seems to be to base one's case on some attribution of "objective" interests which is likely to strike those whom the intended proof is supposed to convince as arbitrary. After examining several possible strategies for empirically demonstrating the class nature of the capitalist state, Offe is forced to conclude with "the paradoxical observation that the class character of the State can only be empirically deciphered in situations in which the State apparatus fails in one of the three functions which make up its class character (namely, the 'co-ordination' of a 'capitalist collective interest', repression and control of revolutionary class-conflicts, and *disguising of these functions*) and 'distorts itself to recognizability' by this failure" (ibid., 56, n. 32). This means, in effect, that empirical proof cannot be obtained *until political practice* forces a breakdown of the state's ability to perform its functions. "The class character of the State becomes evident analytically only in an *ex post* perspective, namely when the limitation of its functions becomes apparent in class conflict" (45).

But Offe does not despair at this paradoxical conclusion. The contradictions of capitalist accumulation are such that they cannot but carry over into the very mechanisms called forth to counteract them (1972c, 7–25; 1975a, 246–47; 1976b, 7–10). There is something inherently paradoxical about a "private" mode of production whose essential features can only be maintained by such pervasive public intervention in all spheres of life that one can reasonably only speak of "state-regulated capitalist systems" (1972b, 78–79). From the systems-theoretical point of view, the steady expansion of the political subsystem, with its own peculiar organizational principle, *in order to* maintain the dominance of the economic subsystem and *its* organizational principle of market exchange, may be expected to lead, sooner or later, to a clash *between* those two systems, that is, to an "intensifying incompatibility between component structures" (1972c, 12, my translation). There is a basic "contradiction between form and content" here: "By their origin and functional content, such organizations are designed to create options of exchange for both labor and capital. By their formal administrative mode of operation they are exempt from commodity relationships: use values are produced and distributed without being controlled and dominated by exchange values" (1975a, 255; cf. Offe and Ronge 1975, 140). More concretely, state policies are by their very nature *political*, that is, unlike the purely economic decisions of private commodity owners they are not automatically dictated and hence justified by the blind compulsion of "market forces." Consequently, they require explicit justification. But as the maintenance of the commodity form becomes increasingly visibly dependent on the intervention and expansion of state agencies and programs and since the latter "are—by their form and according to the image they project of themselves—a model of social relations that is liberated from the commodity form" (1975a, 256), it becomes increasingly difficult to justify further state activities to prop up the private enterprise system. Thus, the very state policies that are supposed to help maintain conditions of profitable capital accumulation turn out to "contain the seeds of noncapitalist organizational forms" (1976a, 38) which increasingly will tend to subvert their very purpose (see also Offe 1972c, 44–58; 1973a, b; Todd, 1982, 360).

Moreover, the very policies of legitimation that were intended precisely to *prevent* such a dangerous politicization of the state's accumulation function, eventually also end up *raising* the likelihood of greater class conflict. For the effect of such legitimation policies as welfare programs is to cause a relative growth of "groups whose lives are organized in decommodified forms of socialization according to politically administratively determined criteria" (1972c, 44, my translation). These include students, draftees, women, the disabled and aged, welfare recipients, and to only a slightly lesser extent civil servants themselves, as all of them are not directly dependent on market exchange for their livelihoods. In relative terms, this "decommodified" sector has grown rapidly as compared to those still fully dependent on the commodity form. If one divides the economy into four sectors, in order of decreasing degree of commodification of labor, a monopolistic (M), a competitive (C), a public (P), and a residual-labor (R) sector, it is immediately apparent that the relative growth rates of labor time spent in them is inversely related to the degree of commodification (1976a, 39–47). This leads Offe to draw the "paradoxical conclusion" that "in late capitalist societies the processes of exchange-regulated accumulation or capitalist growth are simultaneously dominant *and* 'recessive'; in other words, although they are decisive for the stability of the system as a whole, they have at the same time been reduced in their potential to organize the vital activity of society to a small core area and have become increasingly obsolete" (46–47).

Thus, for growing sectors of the population the exchange-value and achievement orientation is losing its relevance to their life situations and hence their potential for legitimating state policies to maintain commodity exchange opportunities (1972c, 27–63; 1973a, b, 1976b). Conflicting norms (hedonism vs. the Protestant ethic, solidarism vs. individualism, etc.) become superimposed until their coexistence "can no longer be accommodated within the limits of tolerance of social identity" (1976a, 62). Thus, the very policies that should have legitimated state policy and the capitalist mode of production only lead to the "structural weakening of the moral fiber of a capitalist society" (Offe and Ronge 1975, 147). The result is that the state will encounter more and more "legitimation deficits," more and more opposition to its policies to uphold the commodity form, and more and more demands that tend to question their validity, or are wholly outside of the commodity form altogether (Offe 1980).

So the capitalist state may produce effective mechanisms to counteract the "classical" symptoms of the fundamental contradiction of capitalism, but only at the cost of eventually reproducing such symptoms within the political sphere itself. Although the relatively successful performance by the capitalist state of its accumulation and legitimation functions has gotten the most system-threatening forms of economic crises and class struggles under control—by economic interventionism and the organization of what amounts to a virtual class compromise in the most vital industries, especially the monopolistic sector (see, e.g., Offe, 1972c, 112–14; 1976a, 46)—it merely ends up re-creating them in the form of crises of legitimation and new political struggles waged on the growing decommodified periphery of the process of commodity production and exchange (1972c, 169–88). The "classical" proletariat may have been successfully pacified by economic stability and social benefits, but only at the cost of creating new groups of contestants to question the foundations of the system as such. Their new "class" struggle constitutes proof that the capitalist system is still as contradictory as ever, that is, it is still subject to an inherent tendency "to destroy those very preconditions on which its survival depends" (1975a, 246). Instead of *resolving* the contradictions of the capitalist mode of production, the capitalist state can only *displace* them within the overall system (246–47; 1976b, 6–9).

Offe claims that his approach avoids *both* the flaws of pluralism and instrumentalism, which seek to explain government policy as the result of demands and pressures from interest groups, *and* the pitfalls of those "hyperfunctionalist constructions," which view policy as the product of the " 'objective' imperatives of the process of valorization of capital" (1984a, 102, emphasis omitted). Unlike the latter " 'harmonistic' interpretations" (103), Offe's theory explains policies as attempts to reconcile "the political processing of both class conflict and the crises of the accumulation process" (ibid.), which requires solutions that "are mutually contradictory" (104) in the long run. Such a theory can be empirically verified by its predictions for the near future. If the theory is valid, then it is to be expected that the growing legitimation efforts that must accompany the state's growing involvement in accumulation-related tasks will come to cause more tension and conflict than they resolve and will eventually conflict directly with the accumulation policies by undermining their necessary popular support and competing with them for scarce governmental resources. In attempts to resolve these problems, governments may be expected to try to extricate themselves from "excessive" legitimacy commitments, for example, through social-spending cuts and more reliance on repression, but such "solutions" are likely to be short-lived and only cause more tension and legitimacy problems, because legitimation programs are not readily reversible: they are a bit like a physiological addiction in that their stabilizing and legitimating potential is rapidly exhausted, only producing demands for more of the same while they can nevertheless not be cut back without the danger of severe losses of legitimacy (Offe 1976a, 59; cf. E. O. Wright 1975, 28; 1978, 157). Thus, Offe's theory predicts an increasingly uncontrollable conflict between the requirements of the state's accumulation function and its legitimation function, manifesting itself in intensifying struggles over state policies spilling over into conflicts involving the foundations of the mode of production itself (Offe 1972c, 96–102; 1974, 49–52; cf. Sardei-Biermann, Christiansen, and Dohse 1973, 63–64). But, even though the process appears to be irreversible and the *types* of adaptive mechanisms available to the capitalist state seem to have been exhausted (hence the designation "late" capitalism, see Offe 1972c, 19, 24–25),[9] Offe does not in any way wish to "prejudge the question of the existence and effectiveness of 'counteracting tendencies', nor that of the If and When of the 'collapse,' " since "the question of

9   In addition, Offe predicts that the capitalist state may suffer crises of "administrative rationality" as its organizational structure becomes technically inadequate to deal with the increasingly complex *economic* functions it is expected to perform. However, the exact status of this point in the overall argument remains unclear. Sometimes it appears to be merely a subvariant of it, as when Offe claims that the "logics" of policy formation available to the capitalist state are incapable of producing the appropriate substantive policy decisions required by its "productive" (as opposed to merely "allocative") functions: bureaucratic and technocratic modes of decision making lack substantive guidelines while the consensus or conflict mode threatens to politicize the decision-making process dangerously (Offe 1975b, 133–34, 143). But elsewhere he seems to suggest that the state is somehow necessarily ill equipped to do the coordinating, information gathering, and forecasting required of it in advanced capitalism (1976a, 60–61; see also 1985, ch. 10). This would appear to flatly contradict the original theory, however, which was based on the very assumption that the capitalist state *was* structurally equipped to deal with accumulation problems—albeit only in such a way as to create new, "legitimation" problems. At any rate, in either version Offe fails to disclose *how* exactly "administrative rationality crises" would manifest themselves: the ubiquitous appeals to governments "to get the economy going again" in times of economic recession by themselves hardly add up to anything worthy of the term "crisis."

whether it will result in the establishment of a socialist society or in the perpetuation of a historically unproductive process of decay" must remain "a question of political practice" (1976a, 67, n. 10). But his theory *does* point to the basic dilemma facing the modern capitalist state: "If, accordingly, the capitalist system is *not* able to survive *without* bourgeois-democratic forms of organizations of political power, the contradiction between the economic and the legitimation functions of the capitalist State points on the other hand to an irreversible politicization of class-conflicts, that is, to the fact that it cannot live *with* them either" (1974, 54).

The idea of a basic contradiction between the accumulation and legitimation functions of the capitalist state found wide currency among North American (neo-)Marxists, in part, no doubt, via the much-discussed book *The Fiscal Crisis of the State* (1973) by James O'Connor (see, e.g., Armstrong 1977, 292–94; Craven 1980, 158–62; Flacks and Turkel 1978, 218–19, 225; Frankel 1979; Gold, Lo, and Wright 1975b, 41–43; Swartz 1977, 312–15). The extent to which O'Connor is directly indebted to Offe's formulations is unclear as he does not refer to him, but there certainly are some (mutual) influences, and, at any rate, the similarity between the two arguments is unmistakable.[10]

O'Connor starts from the "premise ... that the capitalistic state must try to fulfill two basic and often mutually contradictory functions—*accumulation* and *legitimation*" (1973, 6). He further explains this "premise" as follows:

> This means that the state must try to maintain or create the conditions in which profitable capital accumulation is possible. However, the state also must try to maintain or create the conditions for social harmony. A capitalist state that openly uses its coercive forces to help one class accumulate capital at the expense of other classes

10 Both Offe and O'Connor have been associated with *Kapitalistate*, the main vehicle through which many of their ideas became known to a wider public (see Woodiwiss 1978, 186; the exchange of letters between O'Connor and Domhoff in the *Insurgent Sociologist* [Domhoff 1980; O'Connor 1980]; and note 1, this chapter). Carnoy (1984, 223) claims that O'Connor developed his theory independently but fails to document this highly implausible claim.

loses its legitimacy and hence undermines the basis of its loyalty and support. But a state that ignores the necessity of assisting the process of capital accumulation risks drying up the source of its own power, the economy's surplus production capacity and the taxes drawn from this surplus. (ibid.)

This "contradiction" (ibid.) is the basis for O'Connor's theory of the "fiscal crisis" of the state.

State expenditures, O'Connor claims, can be subdivided into those that primarily serve the *accumulation* function, or "social capital," and those that primarily serve the legitimation function, or "social expenses." The former include *both* state-provided infrastructure, research and development, and the like, *and* services and programs such as social security that essentially serve to reduce labor costs by expanding labor's reproductive power. The latter includes, for example, welfare programs, which, O'Connor argues, are "designed chiefly to keep social peace among unemployed workers" (ibid., 7). However, since social security also "contributes to social and political stability by conservatizing unemployed and retired workers" (138), the distinction between the two types of expenditure is not always clear-cut: "Because of the dual and contradictory character of the capitalist state, nearly every state agency is involved in the accumulation and legitimation functions, and nearly every state expenditure has this twofold character" (7). O'Connor then goes on to argue that (1) there is a basic mutual reinforcement between government spending and the relatively rapid growth of the monopoly sector which forces up state expenditures on both accumulation and legitimation, and (2) because "the social surplus (including profits) continues to be appropriated privately" (9), most of it in that very same monopoly sector, this will lead to a "fiscal crisis," eventually creating "tendencies toward economic, social, and political crises" (ibid.), as the monopoly sector corporations and labor unions become increasingly reluctant to finance further increases in state expenditures out of their "rightful" share of the economic surplus (7–10).

O'Connor's argument was not primarily intended as a contribution to the Marxist theory of the capitalist state but rather as an essay in the "political economy" of advanced ("monopoly") capitalism.[11] Hence, his theoretical treatment of the state remains largely limited to the above "premises," which add little to the Offean argument. Nevertheless, his formulation has become very influential, and it is worth mentioning because it provides a perhaps clearer statement of the argument than Offe's rather involved "systems theory" approach does. It may be summarized thus: "The state attempts to support the accumulation of private capital while trying to maintain social peace and harmony. Since accumulation is crucial to the reproduction of the class structure, legitimation necessarily involves attempts to mystify the process and to repress or manage discontent" (Gold, Lo, and Wright 1975b, 41). As Fred Block remarks, this "contradiction" ultimately boils down to the "basic contradiction between democracy and capitalism" (1981, 2). Offe concurs in formulating "the dilemma of the *capitalist* state" in a more recent essay: "The political and economic structures of advanced capitalism are not in harmony. What the state is *required* to do becomes evidently *impossible* to accomplish unless either the private character of accumulation or the liberal democratic character of the polity are suspended" (1984a, 243–44).

Another American writer, Alan Wolfe, who very definitely *has* been strongly influenced by both Offe and O'Connor (A. Wolfe 1974, 155; 1977, 6, 250–51, 263–70), draws much the same conclusion. The political expression of the contradiction between accumulation and legitimation, Wolfe contends, is to be found in the contradictory hybrid called "liberal democracy." It has sought to combine "liberalism," which Wolfe defines as "the marketplace ideology" used to justify political arrangements that "facilitate the accumulation of capital" (1977, 4), with "democracy," defined as "a political ideal that advocates the maximum participation of all citizens in order to create a community based upon the mutual and respectful interaction of all toward commonly agreed-upon goals" (6). Since "the logic of participation and equality leads as surely to socialism as the logic of individualism and appropriation leads to capitalism"

11   The Marxist pedigree of O'Connor's economics has been controversial; see Mosley (1978) and O'Connor (1978).

(ibid.), the two are obviously antithetical. And the antithesis is the very same as that between accumulation and legitimation emphasized by Habermas, Offe, and O'Connor, Wolfe argues: "The symbolic political expression of this duality is liberal democracy, for liberalism becomes the ideology of and the justification for accumulation while democracy upholds the importance of legitimation, of some kind of popular participation and some equality of results" (7; see also 247).

Wolfe extensively reviews the history of Western polities since the rise of capitalism, interpreting their various forms and transformations as so many temporarily successful but eventually doomed attempts to meet "both liberal requirements (capital accumulation) and democratic expectations (legitimation)" (ibid., 85). But in "late capitalism" the capitalist state seems to have run out of options for concealing its inherent contradictions. It finally gets caught in the "devastating contradiction" between its own noncapitalist logic of operation and its function of propping up the capitalist mode of production, as Offe has shown (ibid., 264). In the face of ever-mounting problems of "disaccumulation" (250–51), persistently contradictory pressures, bureaucratic immobilism, and decreasing options, the capitalist state faces acute legitimacy problems, as it simply cannot continue to perform the conflicting services expected of it. "The legitimacy crisis is produced by the inability of the late capitalist state to maintain its democratic rhetoric if it is to preserve the accumulation function, or the inability to spur further accumulation if it is to be true to its democratic ideology" (329). Late capitalism is characterized by a peculiarly "alienated politics" in which politicians are forced toward a sort of schizophrenic frenzy, alternating between active and passive stances, between pragmatism and utopianism, between democracy and capitalism, and in which politics, political parties, and interest groups become increasingly "depoliticized," at least as measured by the standards of the ancient Greek "conception of politics as the common quest of equals for the just and happy society" (312, also 289; in general see ch. 9; also 1974, 144–59). Since "without politics there can be no legitimacy" (1977, 295), "the inherent tensions within liberal democracy will increasingly come to the surface. *In late capitalism, in other words, the major political issues will not take place within the parameters of liberal democracy but over them"* (252).

But, like Offe, Wolfe is reluctant to make any definite predictions as to the time frame involved: "Contradictory systems can continue to exist for some time, and this one may (or may not) do so as well" (ibid., 253). Political leaders in late capitalism may be tempted by more authoritarian solutions or they may simply continue to muddle through for some time, as, according to Wolfe, the "most distinguishing characteristic of late capitalist political elites may be their ability to live with contradictions that nonleaders would find intolerable" (315). But eventually "capitalism and democracy do face each other as real alternatives, and at some point in the near future—one cannot tell when—one or the other will come to dominate" (329), as the immortal "democratic dreams" that have provided the pressure for change in the past will reemerge time and again, because "even though they may be suppressed momentarily, their existence can never be discounted, for the desire to be part of a meaningful community is a human urge that no historical event has yet completely overcome" (342).

State "Functions" as Marxist Dogma

In summary, then, Offe's theory of the capitalist state, much like its structuralist counterpart, seeks to demonstrate, in contrast to the discredited "instrumentalist" approach, that the class character of the capitalist state is a matter of *"structural necessity"* (Offe 1974, 33) which in no way depends on the direct influence or interference of the capitalist class itself. Liberal-reformist claims that democratic pressures can and on occasion do force the capitalist class to accept policies to which it is strongly opposed are by no means denied. What Offe, like Poulantzas, denies is that such instances detract in any way from the class character of the state. On the contrary, they claim that these are only proof that the capitalist state has a "relative autonomy" from the capitalist class which precisely "makes it *possible* for the state to play its class role in an appropriately flexible manner" (Miliband 1977, 87). Thus, in very much the same manner as Poulantzas has done, Offe turns what used to be taken as empirical evidence *refuting* the Marxist thesis that the state serves the interests of the bourgeoisie into evidence apparently *supporting* that thesis. The question, then, is whether Offe's systems theory provides a more satisfactory alternative than the "structuralism" of Poulantzas.

First, as in the case of Poulantzas we must ask, If not the power of the capitalist class itself, what compels the state to realize only *those* interests? If the capitalist state is capable of confronting the capitalist class "as a supervisory, tutelary force . . . an alien and sovereign authority" (Offe 1974, 35), and get away with it, what keeps it from acting *against* the common, long-term interests of that class? Why does it keep on fumbling about, perpetuating a "historically unproductive process of decay" (1976a, 67, n. 10), so obviously without any hope whatever of extricating itself? It certainly appears *capable* of solving its problem by means of a few well-aimed blows to the source of its predicament, the bourgeoisie. Why does the state insist on remaining caught between the requirements of profitable capital accumulation and the masses' clamoring for "legitimation" when it would appear so much easier simply to opt for the latter at the expense of the former and get it all over with? In short, what keeps the state's autonomy *relative*, what keeps it from obtaining *absolute* autonomy from the (interests of) the capitalist class?

Although Offe dismisses this as "an obviously absurd idea" (1972c, 179), his reasons for finding it absurd remain as obscure and unconvincing as Poulantzas's. In fact, it is hard to tell *what* his answer to this crucial question really is. Sometimes he appears to argue that the ultimate force keeping the state in line consists of the threat of retaliation by a united capitalist class. Thus, he claims that the capitalist state must protect the capital relation "without being able to affect the status of this relationship *as* the dominant relationship—because otherwise sanction mechanisms of the type represented by the 'investment strike' . . . would set in" (1976a, 49; also 1972c, 12; 1975b, 143). But the deceptively impersonal, "structural"-sounding formulation of "mechanisms" which "set in" hardly suffices to obfuscate the blatant inconsistency for, as Offe himself acknowledges quite explicitly elsewhere (1972c, 67; 1974, 32), the "investment strike" argument is of course typically "instrumentalist," presupposing the very omniscience and capacity for consensus and concerted action on the part of the bourgeoisie that he considers so improbable as to render the whole "instrumentalist" approach ("influence theory") futile.[12] Clearly, if the class character of the capitalist state *does* in the final analysis depend on the (economic) power of the bourgeoisie, the whole problem becomes once again the reverse: why would the bourgeoisie allow the state any autonomy at all? If the capitalist class is capable of forcing the state into submission whenever it threatens to "affect" the dominance of the "capital relation," why can it not unite on other issues as well? Is there some automatic mechanism that brings the members of the capitalist class together whenever the threat to their long-term interests is "serious"? What then of those policies serving these long-term interests but not traceable to class-conscious capitalist influence, and those implemented *despite* united opposition from the bourgeoisie? Clearly, Offe must either retract his criticisms of the "instrumentalist" theory of the state *or* he will have to come up with some mechanism other than the threat of capitalist retaliation to keep the capitalist state's autonomy relative—he cannot have it both ways.[13]

12   The theme of the possibility of an "investment strike" enabling the capitalist class to "blackmail" democratic governments has become increasingly prominent in Offe's more recent work (see, e.g., 1983, 740–41; 1984a, 223, 244, 246–47; 1985, 191–92, 198). Yet Offe has nowhere retracted his earlier critique of "instrumentalism" or his influential "systemic" alternative. Thus, it is not entirely clear whether his approach to the capitalist state is still a coherent one. With such equivocations—which I have deliberately left out of my exposition of Offe's approach to render it initially as coherently as possible—it is no wonder that some observers have simply been unable to detect *any* real differences between "instrumentalism" and the "relative autonomy" argument, as both ultimately seem to rely on the same class-conscious ruling class being able to keep the state from infringing on its class interests (Block 1977b, 9; Holloway 1983, 327–29; cf. note 13, Chapter 3). This would, however, reduce many years of celebrated theoretical advances in the Marxist theory of the state to little more than a pointless squabble—a conclusion that even the most severe critics have been understandably reluctant to draw.

13   It is worth noting that neither O'Connor nor Alan Wolfe is quite as guilty of inconsistency on this point as Offe is, mainly because they are not as concerned to formulate a full-fledged alternative to "crude instrumentalism" in the first place. O'Connor's argument is in fact replete with unabashedly in-

A second reason Offe sometimes gives is the state's dependence on the accumulation process for its resources. The state's "extensive reliance on resources created in the accumulation process and derived through taxation from wages and profits," he argues (1975b, 126), explains why "every occupant of state power is basically interested in promoting those conditions most conducive to accumulation" (Offe and Ronge 1975, 140), since "every interest the state (or the personnel of the state apparatus, its various branches and agencies) may have in their own stability and development can only be pursued if it is in accordance with the imperative of maintaining accumulation" (1975b, 126). The point seems to be that no matter what the intentions of the elected government in power, "the holders of state office must in their own interest maintain and support the accumulation process because the state's revenue, and hence the power of the state's officers, depends on it" (Macpherson 1977a, 233). However, although this may be plausible enough to explain what motivates governments to try and maintain a "healthy" economy, it offers no explanation whatsoever for why governments should wish to maintain a healthy *capitalist* economy, which is the issue here. Obviously, states to a great extent depend for their effective power on the strength of the economies within their territories and their ability to extract resources from those economies, not just in capitalist societies but in all societies, at all times, *whatever* the mode of production. By itself this truism hardly motivates any state to nurture and maintain a specifically *capitalist* economy. On the contrary, in fact, it

---

strumentalist explanations for the occurrence of specific government policies and programs such as social security, various "social investment" expenditures, and so on, in the best tradition of "corporate liberalism" (see Chapter 3), as he himself freely admits (see, e.g., O'Connor 1973, 41–42, 64–70, 97–124, 137–42; 1980). However, both he and Wolfe also freely employ the functionalist-sounding *terminology* of accumulation and legitimation "functions," thereby contributing to the overall state of convenient confusion in which Marxists can appeal to the old "instrumentalist" explanations when there is any evidence of blatant government-capitalist collusion while switching to the more theoretically "sophisticated" functionalist terminology whenever the evidence won't support the straightforwardly instrumentalist line (the most blatant example is Mandel 1975, 474–99; 1978, 150–87; cf. Frankel 1979, 205; for another case, see van den Berg and Smith 1981, 1983).

would seem to give the state a strong incentive to obtain greater control over the economy than would be compatible with the "dominance" of the "capital relation" so it will not have to beg and bargain with shortsighted capitalists for much-needed revenue and constantly run the risk of fiscal crisis or worse (cf. Levi 1981). In fact, if one were to assume, as Marxists presumably do, that a socialist economy would be far superior in terms of productivity and hence state revenue, it would seem to follow from Offe's own line of argument that the state has a built-in interest in *abolishing* capitalism and replacing it with a healthy *socialist* economy. And even without the assumption of socialist superiority this line of argument can easily be used to suggest an intrinsic "socialist" bias in all states as the right-wing defenders of individual liberty and free enterprise do (e.g., Hayek 1944).

But then, Offe might argue, the state obviously ceases to be a capitalist state as defined. It often seems as if Offe, like Poulantzas, wishes to settle the argument on purely definitional grounds. He *defines* the capitalist state as a state that "*depends* on a process of accumulation which is beyond its power to *organize*" (Offe and Ronge 1975, 140), since the capitalist state has, *by definition*, "no authority *to order production* or *to control* it" (1975b, 126). Thus, the *capitalist* state must support and maintain private capital accumulation simply because it is so defined—it would cease to be capitalist by this definition from the moment it did otherwise. But this is, of course, as incontestable as it is trivial: it is simply true by definition without providing the least bit of information or argument about any real states. In fact, it could rather easily be argued that, *according to this definition*, there now exist hardly any truly capitalist states, since virtually all governments are nowadays deeply implicated in the "organizing, ordering and controlling" of huge sectors of production, by means of state-owned corporations, regulatory agencies, marketing boards, planning agencies, fiscal instruments, and the like. During periods of war or economic crisis such regulation and control often even become economywide. In fact, perhaps no "capitalist state" meeting Offe's specifications has *ever* existed! If there are or have been any, on the other hand, a purely definitional argument like Offe's does not even *try* to answer the question posed here, namely, what forces those states to *remain* capitalist as here defined—surely not the arbitrary definitions produced by Marxist theorists.

Thus, as was the case with Poulantzas, all we have so far are good reasons for the state to establish full autonomy from (the interests of) the capitalist class and none for keeping that autonomy relative, that is, within the limits of the long-term interests of the capitalist class. Nor are there any other such arguments to be found anywhere in Offe's writings. All that is left are a few obscure passages suggesting the sort of inadmissible teleological reasoning that "bourgeois" functionalists have long been effectively criticized for but that is gaining a great deal of currency among contemporary Marxists.[14] As we have seen above, Offe argues that the state must be able to confront capitalists as a "supervisory, tutelary force," "*since* it is only through the State's becoming relatively autonomous in this way that the multiplicity of particular and situation-bound special interests can be integrated into a class-interest" (1974, 35, emphasis added), and that "*in order for*" the state and the normative subsystem to be able to perform their functions properly, "it becomes *functionally necessary* for them" to gain the relative autonomy "*they require* for the performance of their specific regulatory services," because capital, "incapable of articulating and perceiving a unitary and common class interest . . . *requires* special guidance and supervision" from a relatively autonomous state (1976a, 48, emphasis added). But obviously, the claim that a relatively autonomous state is "functionally necessary" for upholding the interests of the bourgeoisie does not explain why and how such a relatively autonomous state ever *came about*, and even less how its autonomy is *kept* relative. In exactly the same way as Poulantzas did, Offe appears to assume that although the bourgeoisie does not always get what it wants, it *does* always get what it needs, even when it does *not* want it! But, again like Poulantzas, he completely fails to explain how this remarkable feat is accomplished.[15]

14   The use of functionalist teleological reasoning among Marxists is also coming under sustained criticism, at last. See, e.g., Elster (1979, 34–35; 1982, 1983), Halfpenny (1983), and Koch (1980).
15   Small wonder, once again, that some commentators have detected a dan-

Finally, there is that superbly obscure passage in which Offe asserts that "the abstract principle of making a subject of permanent market exchange relationships out of every citizen does more to keep state policies in tune with the class interests of the agents of accumulation than any supposed 'conspiracy' between 'overlapping directorates' of state and industry could ever achieve" (1975a, 251). An abstract principle indeed! If not through some sort of conscious propaganda effort by the mighty free-enterprise forces, it is very hard to see how such a "principle" could ever come to get such a stranglehold on the state as to render it capable of beating down capitalist opposition but incapable of doing anything at variance with long-term capitalist interests. In fact, one is simply at a loss to understand what Offe could possibly mean in this mysterious passage.

But it is no less mysterious than the rest of Offe's "systems theory" of capitalism. Like Poulantzas, Offe arbitrarily subdivides his "system" into three "subsystems" (cf. Haas 1979, 36), which, apparently simply as a result of their being that, are compelled to perform "flanking" functions for the system as a whole. And what an odd "system" it is! On the one hand, the system produces a subsystem, the state, which is so remarkably equipped and fine-tuned that it has an infallible grasp of the common, rational, long-term interests of the bourgeoisie even when the members of that class are unable to determine what those interests are. One may well ask what wondrous equipment and resources the state has at its disposal that allow it to succeed where the capitalists, controlling practically all of society's resources, regularly fail (Domhoff 1979, 57–58, 124–25). Offe refers vaguely to the *"internal structures"* of the state which ensure *"class-specific selectivity"* (1974, 35–36), but he never specifies what exactly these "structures" consist of (Haas 1979, 44–45).[16] But although the system is apparently capable of produc-

---

gerous tendency toward reformism here, since this sort of "argument" simply does not specify why the state could *not* become fully autonomous and defect to the side of the working class instead (see Block 1977b, 12; Holloway 1983, 329), whereas others view it as an *antidote* to functionalism since it does not posit a simple one-to-one "functional" relation between state policy and the wishes of the dominant class (Shapiro 1981, 8–10)!

16   Offe does occasionally discuss what might appear to be such "selection mechanisms." Thus, he argues that the realities of mass party electoral com-

ing, in the form of the state, an apparatus endowed with almost miraculous powers of conception and execution which, more-over, it can—even more miraculously—*only* employ to the long-term benefit of the capitalist class as a whole, at the same time it has been unable to design this perfect instrument in such a way that its "organizational principle" would be more or less compatible with that dominant in the system as a whole. His own declarations to the contrary notwithstanding, Offe in fact

petition, pressure and interest group politics, unequal distribution of mobi-lization and organizational resources, and executive ascendancy over the legislature all conspire to favor easily identifiable and hence organizable groups with comparatively large resources and disruptive potential, as well as political moderation and "realistic" bargaining, all at the expense of the less well endowed, less easily organized, less potentially disruptive groups and of internal democracy within the large representative organizations that do the bargaining, as well as at the expense of "general needs" (1972b, 82–93). Moreover, these conditions heavily and systematically favor clear and effective interest formulation and representation on the capitalist side while no less systematically interfering with and distorting the collective in-terest formation process on the side of labor. This is not only because of capital's far superior resources, its control over crucial investment decisions, its ability to elicit favorable government responses by invoking the need for a "healthy investment climate," its control of the major media of mass com-munication and sundry other "mechanisms of bourgeois hegemony" (1985, 199), and so on, but also because there are no difficult conflicts between in-dividual and collective interests to overcome for capitalists as there are for the workers. Thus, whereas the latter must rely on the arduous and uncer-tain "dialogical process of collective interest articulation" (212), the "mono-logical," individualistic "logic of collective action" encouraged by liberal de-mocracy suffices for the capitalist class to promote its interests (ibid, ch. 7; see also 1983, 726–28, 742; 1984a, ch. 8). This line of argument is open to several objections, however. First, none of this is exactly new to non-Marx-ists (see, e.g., Collins 1975; Dahl 1970, 1971b; R. F. Hamilton 1975, ch. 7; Lindblom 1977; Olson 1965, 1982). Second, as an explanation of why the state specifically selects out those alternatives that favor capitalist interests at the expense of others this argument is, once again, patently "instrumental-ist"; that is, it depends entirely on the equation of what capitalists *conceive* to be their interests with their "true," collective, long-term interests, thus com-pletely abandoning Offe's earlier criticisms of this central assumption of "instrumentalism." Finally, it appears to rely on the attribution of "objective interests," whether as "general needs" (1972a, 92–93), as a "socialist trans-formation" (1985, 206), or simply as the implicit assumption that workers *do* have a single, shared, collective class interest whatever it may be, which Offe rejected as arbitrary and which led him to argue for the empirical identification of "selection mechanisms" in the first place (1972c, 86–87; 1974, 43), Offe's protestations to the contrary notwithstanding (1985, 337, n. 22, 26; see also note 32, this chapter).

does initially attribute "fine-tuning and balance mechanisms of colossal complexity and unerring accuracy" to the capitalist state apparatus, no less so than is done in the "hyperfunctionalist constructions" he ridicules (1984a, 103). He only manages to avoid drawing the same " 'harmonistic' " (ibid.) conclusions by an entirely arbitrary and obscure proclamation of the incompatibility of two "organizational principles" that are nonetheless mutually indispensable. This is hardly much of an advance on "hyperfunctionalism." As we shall see below, the "incompatibility" thesis, which is seemingly based on "systems analysis," is in fact merely a disguised version of a basic unexamined domain assumption that has underlain Marxism from the earliest writings of Marx himself on (see also van den Berg 1980, 464–65; 1981, 82–84).

But to return to our question, we must conclude that Offe's theory of the capitalist state has failed its first major test: it does *not* provide a coherent or even intelligible—let alone convincing—account of what keeps the state from straying from the interests of the capitalist class, if not the political pressures from the members of that class. This is a crucial failing. Since, as I have tried to show in the preceding chapter, Poulantzas *also* fails to answer this central question satisfactorily, this means that in *either* of its major variants the much-celebrated theory of the "relative autonomy" of the capitalist state lacks a crucial ingredient for a Marxist theory: while allowing for the possibility of capitalist defeat at the hands of the state, it quite simply *lacks* any argument explaining how state policy is nevertheless kept to correspond to the interests of the bourgeoisie. In this respect, this supposedly much more "sophisticated" approach is decidedly and, it seems, fatally inferior to the "instrumentalism" it seeks to replace (cf. E. O. Wright 1978, 231, n. 8).

But if we cannot get a straight answer to the question of *how* exactly, or even approximately, the policies of the capitalist state are made to correspond to the interests of the capitalist class (other than in instrumentalist terms), perhaps we can at least get an answer to the question *why* such policies as are produced are judged to be in the capitalists' interests despite all appearances to the contrary. In other words, as I have tried to do in vain in the preceding chapter, I am inquiring into *the grounds on which* state policies are judged to be wholly or primarily in the interests of the capitalist class.[17] I am not primarily concerned here with policies classified under the state's "accumulation function," such as the provision of infrastructure, subsidies, research and development support, retraining programs, and the like. Although it is by no means self-evident that such policies benefit the capitalists *exclusively* (see below), there is little doubt that they *do* benefit some of them, as the active support from some capitalists for such policies clearly indicates. The problem only arises—it is worth reminding ourselves—because "relative autonomy" theories *deny* the validity of evidence of capitalist-class support or opposition as a criterion for the class character of state policy. Therefore, these theories must answer the obvious question, On what grounds are state policies that have been implemented over bourgeois opposition—policies, in other words, that by all conventional criteria would be seen by liberal pluralists as well as Marxist "instrumentalists" as proof of (the possibility of) gradual, cumulative reform by means of democratic institutions—on what grounds are such policies nevertheless claimed to be in the interest of the capitalists who opposed them? In short, what is the justification for calling such policies as social security, welfare, and union support legislation, "legitimation" rather than "reform," even when (or in some cases especially when) they are strongly and unanimously opposed by the bourgeoisie?

As a first approximation, to label a government policy "legitimation" is obviously meant to suggest that it is intended, (or has in fact succeeded in so doing) to obtain or maintain "legitimacy" for some agent or institution that was or would have been lacking in the absence of that policy. But it is not obvious exactly who or what are the intended recipients of this "legitimacy," nor what exactly the term itself means (see Friedrichs 1980, 545–46; Mayntz 1975). Clearly, "legitimacy" must refer to something more serious than simply popular support for the

17 But, as the perceptive reader will have noticed immediately, I have reversed the order of treatment of the two questions here, beginning with an examination of the causal mechanisms keeping the autonomy of the state "relative" and now proceeding to the question of the grounds for judging state policy in the (exclusive) interest of the bourgeoisie.

government in power. When Offe and his followers speak of an impending "legitimation crisis" they are obviously not referring to such routine matters as slipping popularity ratings accompanied by the inevitable calls for early elections. If "legitimation" was merely a matter of retaining, or preventing the impending loss of, electoral support for the party in office, the argument would not differ materially from that of liberal pluralists. After all, according to the pluralists it is precisely by means of the threat of electoral defeat that democratic government is supposed to guarantee that reforms that are desired by a determined and persistent majority are sooner or later implemented. If this is all that is meant, then the use of the term "legitimation" rather than "democratic reform" amounts to nothing but a rather disingenuous "semantic trick" (Mayntz 1975, 262) to conceal the otherwise embarassing lack of difference between this kind of "Marxism" and perfectly "bourgeois" pluralism.

But rather than just raising the government's popularity rating, we are told, "legitimation" involves the effort that the state must make "to maintain and create the conditions for social harmony" (O'Connor 1973, 6), it is "designed chiefly to keep social peace" and to promote "social and political stability" (7, 138), and so on. But again, this cannot be merely a reference to the commonplace that governments usually try to keep a semblance of social order within the borders they control. As noted in the previous chapter, governments that deliberately seek to wreak havoc are something of a rarity in *any* place, time, or mode of production. Moreover, there is no indication whatsoever as to *how much* "social harmony" is needed for "stability" or at what point the amount of "legitimation" would fall short of the quantity required for "stability." As these values appear to be capable of rather large variation within and between countries, it is hard to see how this could be a reliable measure of a single phenomenon called "legitimation." At any rate, once again the argument would be indistinguishable from liberal pluralism since the latter argues precisely that in democratic countries governments must rely more on persuasion, compromise, and reform, and less on naked repression to maintain social order than in other types of political systems (see, e.g., Bell

1976, 230–31; Dahl 1956, 131–34; 1971a, 43–45; 1971b, 17–32, 88–94; Lowenthal 1976, 258).

Clearly, the notion of "legitimation" is intended to suggest something much less banal than governments seeking popular support or choosing the path of least resistance. The very survival of the capitalist system itself depends on it. To perform its indispensable system-maintaining function, the capitalist state "*must* procure for itself a basis for overall legitimation" (Offe 1976a, 49, emphasis added); it simply *has* to obtain the requisite amount of "mass loyalty" (53). But it is self-evident that this involves systematic concealment of "its *class-bound functions under the pretext of class-neutrality* . . . the alibi of the general interest" (1974, 47). *This* is what "legitimation" means: the mystification of the class character of the state by means of concessions and benefits to noncapitalist groups through the state so as to maintain the fiction that at least the state is equally accessible to all and hence available for redressing and compensating for the imbalances and inequities produced by the capitalist process of accumulation. If the state does not discharge this crucial task successfully, it courts disaster (1972a, 485), since "an openly practised class character of political governance which is apparent as such involves the risk of class-polarization and a politicization of the class struggle" (1974, 47; cf. Macpherson 1977a, 234; O'Connor 1973, 5).[18]

Thus, the fundamental assumption underlying the use of the term "legitimation" to describe welfare legislation, union protection, and the like is that *without* such policies the working class, the "masses," or a whole assortment of noncapitalist groups would, first, have withdrawn their support for the exist-

---

18   The need to "legitimate" the state, then, is an absolute functional imperative whose failure poses a direct threat to the system's very survival. The reasoning here appears unmistakably and relentlessly functionalist: the occurrence of a policy is explained by the system's "need" for it (cf. Koch 1980). It has nothing to do with the explicit intentions of the policy makers who, as in every other type of state or society, naturally see themselves as impartial umpires. A good deal of the appeal of this variety of Marxist theory of the state, however, may well stem from its extreme ambiguity on points like these, conveniently allowing its adherents to work both sides of the street, now emphasizing the subjective intent of policy, now its presumed "objective" effects. For an example and critique of this practice, see Craven (1980, 1983) and van den Berg and Smith (1981, 1983).

ing political system (which is, I take it, the institution receiving "legitimacy"— not the "state apparatus" in the sense of the bureaucracy, which in most places neither needs nor seems to enjoy a great deal of popularity) for not fulfilling its promise of acting as a neutral arbitrator and protector of the weak in the dog-eat-dog world of capitalism. This would then, second, paralyze the state's capacity to mediate between conflicting demands, which would, in turn, with the "legitimating" buffer of the state now out of order, likely cause a further dangerous radicalization of the populace, posing a serious threat to the system at its very foundations. All this is more or less implicitly suggested in the argument that the state must "legitimate" *itself* as a neutral mediator to prevent a potentially dangerous politicization of the relations of production.

Here we encounter, once again, that unexamined presupposition that also underlay Poulantzas's argument: it is simply *assumed* that the working class, the "masses," or the noncapitalist populace, is and has been almost constantly on the verge of breaking out in open rebellion, of tearing down the whole hated system of exploitation once and for all. For the argument is clearly that without the policies designated as "legitimation"— which includes virtually everything other than purely economic policy or direct subsidies to the capitalist class (see Panitch 1977, 19; Stevenson 1977, 74)—the state and eventually "the system" would have been in very serious trouble indeed, having to fend off furious mobs of dangerously politicized workers (Pemberton 1983, 300–301). Otherwise, the designation of "legitimation" remains entirely meaningless.

But the empirical evidence for claiming that social legislation has served this crucial preventive function anywhere in the advanced capitalist world is very slim indeed. Although certainly not for lack of trying to find it (see, e.g., for Canada: Chorney and Hansen 1980; Cuneo 1979, 1980; Panitch, ed. 1977; Walters 1982), there is *very* little evidence of any link between dangerous upsurges in working-class radicalism and the dramatic reduction of such radicalism after the passage of welfare-state legislation anywhere, not even during the worst of the Great Depression (see Finegold and Skocpol 1980; Skocpol 1980). In fact, instances of any dangerous upsurges of working-class radicalism themselves are hard enough to come by (see B. Moore 1978). Some attempts have been made to link temporary increases in welfare expenditures in the United States to urban (race) rioting in the 1960s (Isaac and Kelly 1981; O'Connor 1973, 162–68; Piven and Cloward 1971), but that hardly amounted to a serious threat to *capitalism,* nor is there any evidence showing the rioters were particularly pacified by those short-lived increases in Aid for Dependent Children spending.

In a later essay, Offe predicts that any serious attempts to dismantle the welfare state will inevitably "leave the system in a state of exploding conflict and anarchy" (1984a, 153; cf. ibid., 288; 1984b, 240). But after the years of budget restraints, cutbacks, and monetarism that began in the late 1970s in virtually all advanced capitalist countries, there is still precious little evidence of any mass assault on the capitalist system as such (cf. Schmidt 1983). One can, of course, dispute the "seriousness" of cutbacks so far ad infinitum, but Offe's prediction seems rather implausible to begin with. For one thing, in *all* countries concerned, the overwhelming share of social expenditures goes to the elderly (50% or more), the disabled, widows, and war veterans, who can hardly be expected to mount a massive attack on the capitalist mode of production (see Armour and Coughlin 1985, 782; Pemberton 1983, 297). Moreover, the complexities of public opinion with respect to welfare-state policies are such that no dramatic polarization is likely in response to any cutbacks, no matter how drastic (see Beedle and Taylor-Gooby 1983; Taylor-Gooby 1982, 1983). If anything, the citizenry is more likely to wearily turn away from politics altogether than to erupt in open rebellion when "the state" fails to live up to its promises (cf. J. D. Wright 1976).

Nevertheless, a whole range of reformists, from liberals to "Eurocommunists," would agree that social reform through "bourgeois" democracy has contributed significantly to the moderation of sociopolitical conflict. But they would accept evidence of successful democratic reform, even over solid capitalist opposition,[19] as proof that it is possible to achieve significant

19 Whether or not there really *is* evidence of such opposition is not the issue here, of course, since liberal reformists and "relative autonomy" theorists agree that there is.

change by means of a democratic reformist strategy (see, e.g,
Lowenthal 1976, 253–60). Relabeling all such reform "legitimation" is, quite obviously, intended precisely to put the validity of this reformism into doubt. The clear suggestion is that the
apparent beneficiaries of the reforms have in some sense been
fooled, that the popular victories that seem to validate the reformist position are—however much unity and bitterness the
bourgeois opposition may have displayed—in some sense more
apparent than real. The reforms, so the implicit argument
seems to go, do not add up to fundamental change of the system but only to just enough change within the system to give
the false impression that fundamental change has occurred or
at least is possible. Thus, the state's *real* class functions are effectively obscured.

Here we have another version of the "no fundamental
change" or "change within, not change of" argument which is
as popular as it is elusive—and the two are obviously related
(see, e.g., Halfpenny 1983, 78; Lowenthal 1976, 253–56; van
den Berg 1981, 77–91). At the very least, such arguments raise
questions like, On what grounds are the changes judged to be
any less "real" than what has remained unchanged? Why is a
society that offers social security benefits and union protection
to its workers not "really" different from one that does not?
What level or rate of change *would* qualify as "real," "fundamental" change "of" the system, rather than merely "legitimation" of a "basically" unchanged system?

But, although many have eagerly adopted the suggestive "legitimation" idiom to discredit social-reform policies, none has
even *attempted* to answer such crucial underlying questions.
Once again, this may be a consequence of Marxism's commitment to "immanent" critique. For to indicate exactly where the
dividing line between mere "legitimation" and "real" or "fundamental" change is located would require some fairly clear information about the nature of the aim of "real" change, that is,
of "socialism."[20]

20   In a recent critique of neoconservative attacks on the welfare state, Offe de-
      clares: "Every political theory worth its name has to answer two questions.
      First, what is the desirable form of the organization of society and state and
      how can we demonstrate that it is at all 'workable', i.e., consistent with our

As a result, the whole notion of "legitimation" constitutes little more than a standing invitation to theoretical abuse and confusion. It can, for instance, be used as a device for discrediting *any* reform by implicitly suggesting that it was the bare minimum that could have been obtained, while conveniently relieving the user of the arduous task of actually considering and examining the strategic alternatives open to the actors in the political arena. From the point of view of the workers whose interests such theorists claim to have at heart, however, such practices can only be called callously irresponsible since it is the workers, not the theorists, who generally run the risks and pay the costs of any errors of strategy.[21] Moreover, in the absence of any clear meaning of the term not only policies presumably benefiting mainly the workers, the poor, and other disadvantaged groups, but *any* governmental activity that is not blatantly intended to line the pockets of the capitalists can be, *ipso facto*, classified as "legitimation," including such seemingly innocent activities as the protection of civil rights or "the solemnization of marriage" (Stevenson 1977, 75), since, after all, they all serve to distract from the state's "true" function of serving the long-term interests of the bourgeoisie (see also Panitch 1977, 19). In this manner there is literally nothing that the state *could* do without serving the interests of the capitalist class! Moreover, by the same "logic" one could argue that the more radical the reform the better it serves those interests as it will only more effectively "conceal" the state's "real" nature, while conversely,

---

basic normative and factual assumptions about social life? This is the problem of defining a consistent *model* or goal of transformation. Second, how do we get there? This is the problem of identifying the dynamic forces and *strategies* that could bring about the transformation" (1984a, 152). While neoconservatives, Offe claims, fail on both counts, he concedes that "it is not perfectly evident that the situation is much better on the Left where one could possibly speak of a consistent theory of socialism but certainly not of an agreed-upon and realistic strategy for its construction" (157). The self-criticism is commendable, but unfortunately Offe fails to provide further details of the "consistent theory of socialism" alluded to.

21   With regard to the long Liberal reign under Prime Minister Mackenzie King in Canada we are told that "the Liberal state [*sic*] would be moved just so far as popular demands forced it, and never a step further. Minimal legitimation was always the maximal program" (Whitaker 1977, 60). One hesitates to ask what sort of "democratic" paternalism that would do *more* than this is the implicit alternative here!

the more conservative the policy, the *more* the workers gain, in the "long run" at least. The argument can be carried on indefinitely as there are no criteria by which to recognize "really significant" change. Incredible as it may seem, this is not a *reductio ad absurdum* but an implication that *has* actually been drawn by at least one author (Craven 1980, 307; see van den Berg and Smith 1981, 514). Conversely, however, this very same equation of more reform with *more* legitimation can also easily lead to the very opposite conclusion, namely to identifying it with the interests of the working class after all since it ultimately points to a complete transformation of the system. Thus, Wolfe repeatedly uses democracy, which, as we have seen, for him ultimately means "socialism," and "legitimation" as if the two were completely interchangeable terms, arguing, for instance, that "democracy upholds the importance of legitimation, of some kind of popular participation and some equality of results" (A. Wolfe 1977, 7; cf. 85, 145, 247, 329). Here the term "legitimation" seems to have finally lost all content whatsoever, simply becoming a synonym for democratic reform.[22]

Clearly, the term "legitimation" is so utterly fluid that it can safely be applied to any reform one wishes to discredit without the least fear of ever being refuted. Exactly as was the case with Poulantzas's "theory," the *only* governmental act that could ever invalidate the claim that democratic reform merely amounts to "legitimation" would be the establishment of a completely socialist society in one single stroke, as anything short of this complete transformation can be interpreted as "legitimation," that is, as partial reform intended to convey the *false* impression that "real" change by democratic means is possible. The final proof of the "falseness" of this impression, for those not yet fully convinced, will only be given when the state finally refuses to allow any further reform in favor of the working class, *in spite of* persistent democratic majority support for such policies, that is,

22   It is a fitting tribute to the great versatility of a term so devoid of content as this that Craven has managed to use it in *both*, obviously contradictory senses, namely as meaning that the more radical the reform the more it benefits the bourgeoisie *and* as containing a "logic" of its own which would ultimately lead to "an array of equitable social relations" obviously incompatible with the continued existence of capitalism (1980, 160)!

when the state, having run out of any further "legitimation" ploys, is finally forced to resort to naked repression in order to keep on fulfilling its class function, and is thus unable to continue concealing its "true" nature. Perhaps this is what Offe means when he says that the class character of the capitalist state can only be demonstrated empirically when it finally breaks down. But this *does* mean that the use of the "legitimation" label renders the theory of the class character of the state entirely unfalsifiable. For the state really only has two alternatives, both of which can only confirm the theory: either it effectively conceals its "true" nature by "legitimatory" reform, *or* it reveals that nature by resorting to plain repression. The third alternative, that of undertaking an immediate transition to "socialism," would in principle refute the theory but is, as I have noted before, impossible to observe as long as "socialism" itself remains an unknown quantity. So once again, what we have here is not so much an explicit argument but rather a convenient device *in lieu of* an argument that serves to discredit anything beyond naked oppression but short of an undefined millennium. It is a convenient way of giving short shrift to liberals and reformists without having to confront the tough issues that they raise. No doubt the welfare state *"bears no resemblance to what Marxist theorists would call a revolutionary process, that is, basic structural change"* (Offe 1972a, 481), but as long as those Marxist theorists refuse to disclose what they *would* consider "basic structural change," such pronouncements tell us more about the state of Marxist theory than about the nature of the welfare state.

Thus, this Marxist "structural functionalism" consists of much the same exercise in theoretical evasion as Poulantzas's "structuralist" approach. It originates in an apparently fundamentalist rejection of the old "instrumentalist" theory of the state in capitalism as insufficiently ironclad because its failure to transcend the "bourgeois" pluralist framework renders it vulnerable to reformist criticisms (cf. Gold, Lo, and Wright 1975a, 34–35). Instead, it is argued, Marxist theory must produce a more "structural" proof of its claim that the capitalist state is still "but a committee for managing the common affairs of the whole bourgeoisie." The alternative proof is ironclad all right, but only at the cost of making it unfalsifiable in principle. This is the exact same result as was obtained after examining Poulantzas's theory more closely in the previous chapter.

Precisely like Poulantzas, Offe and his followers concede far more to "bourgeois" theory than any instrumentalist ever could. In fact, the *substance* of their depiction of politics and the state in advanced capitalist society is for all intents and purposes indistinguishable from the most complacent of "bourgeois" perspectives. The idea that the polity has the "function" of counteracting and compensating for the "dysfunctions" of the capitalist economy can easily be traced back as far as Adam Smith and has certainly been commonplace in "bourgeois" accounts, both functionalist and nonfunctionalist, of the rise of the welfare state (see, e.g., Armitage 1975; Guest 1980; T. H. Marshall 1964; Polanyi 1957; Titmuss 1976; Wilensky and Lebeaux 1965). Nor are the claims that governments have a strong interest in maintaining a "healthy economy" while also seeking to prevent unnecessary social disorder by helping to resolve social conflicts where possible particularly shocking to "bourgeois" ears. The corollary claim that in formally democratic countries governments must regularly take into account the demands of large nonelite sections of the population is, of course, the very stock in trade of the liberal pluralist. If anything, some of the more "sophisticated" bourgeois observers would probably be *more* cautious than Offe and his followers in claiming that there is a great deal of evidence to show that working-class or electoral pressure can induce formally democratic governments to adopt policies that meet with strong capitalist-class opposition (see, e.g., Lindblom 1977; Turner 1986; cf. Block 1981, 8–9).

Instead of denying any of the "bourgeois" empirical claims, the "structural" Marxists *incorporate* them by suggesting that they are not at all incompatible with the orthodox Marxist proposition concerning the inescapable class nature of the state, and that they even *support* that proposition. This is accomplished by the simple device of relabeling the various state activities, thus replacing the conventional, perfectly innocent-sounding designations with terms that *sound* far less innocent and more in keeping with a Marxist perspective. Thus, economic policy becomes the "accumulation function," and social policy and virtually everything else is reclassified as "legitimation." As we have seen, this is a purely formal operation because the concept of "legitimation" is effectively left undefined. But the term *does* nicely suggest that there is something discreditable about the policies so designated without disclosing exactly what it is. In this way, the impression is created that the empirical evidence of government policy supports the theoretical proposition concerning the class nature of the state since the "concepts" that have presumably been derived from that proposition can be successfully applied to those policies. The proposition is that the state is compelled to serve the long-term interests of the bourgeoisie. This means that it must maintain the conditions of profitable capital accumulation and conceal this by appropriate "legitimating" gestures. The activities of any actual state can be classified as either one or the other of these two categories without much difficulty. Therefore, the state appears to be fulfilling its functions which, as the theory postulates, serve the long-term interests of the bourgeoisie. Q.E.D.

But these "concepts" are applicable to the empirical world not as a result of their theoretical soundness but, on the contrary, because they are either trivial or perfectly meaningless. "Accumulation" simply refers to keeping the economy going: that it is a capitalist economy that is kept going is hardly news. The meaning of the term "legitimation," on the other hand, is left so unclear that it virtually amounts to an all-purpose residual category. Thus, there are indeed no empirical cases imaginable that could not be classified as either one or the other: any particular policy is *necessarily* either a case of economic policy ("accumulation"), or not ("legitimation"). Such an effectively exhaustive classification is obviously compatible with *any* empirical state of affairs and hence so, presumably, is the underlying theory. But this can only be achieved, of course, by dissolving the "theory" into a vacuous tautology. What is left is the Marxist dogma of the class nature of the state which is kept intact by simply immunizing it against any empirical evidence or rational argument. The cherished dogma can thus be safely maintained without having to debate any of the arguments advanced by "bourgeois" reformists, as the latter have been rendered totally irrelevant to the former. Thus, complete theoretical closure has indeed been achieved, but the victory seems rather an illusory one. For instead of refuting the position of opponents this amounts to abandoning the debate altogether, in favor of the comforts of dogmatic certainty. One cannot help but suspect that the many who remain to be convinced, particularly those workers who invariably end up paying the price for the mistakes of would-be saviors, need something more substantial than mere word juggling to abandon the relatively tried course of "reformism."

The Unexamined Presuppositions of Marxism and the Appeal of Structural Functionalism

So far, I have had little to say about what appears to be the capitalist state's primary task, according to the theory, namely its "accumulation" function—other than that it does not seem to refer to anything more shocking than the fact that governments generally seek to maintain a healthy growth rate in their economies, which in capitalist countries means, naturally, *capitalist* economies. This is hardly earthshaking. But it raises an intriguing and, as it turns out, quite revealing question: why would any government even *bother* to try and conceal this? For it is a basic premise of the theory that in addition to performing its "accumulation" function the state must "conceal," "deny," or "mystify" this very fact by means of "legitimatory" policies. But, quite apart from the fact that such an attempt to deny the obvious would seem doomed from the start, why *should* the state need to conceal its involvement in maintaining economic growth to begin with?

In fact, at first glance the very opposite assumption would appear far more plausible. Does not practically everybody benefit from "accumulation"? Perhaps capitalists benefit more than any other group, but that hardly reduces the importance of a "healthy" economy to all the others who depend on it for employment, rising living standards, and indeed those very benefits that are, according to these Marxist theorists, intended to *conceal* the state's efforts to keep the economy going. More than that, high levels of economic growth make many of the so-called legitimation policies (e.g., unemployment insurance, welfare) *less* needed! The more one thinks about it the harder it is to imagine any other policy objective that could rally such unanimous support from all quarters as economic growth![23] If anything, governmental efforts to promote economic growth, it would seem, are perfectly self-legitimating, and possibly the most potent *"source of legitimation"* (Feher and Heller 1983, 233) available to the "capitalist state." Consequently, one would not expect governments to conceal such efforts at all but, quite the opposite, to advertise them as loudly and frequently as possible.[24]

Moreover, the available empirical evidence would seem to offer a degree of support for this hypothesis rarely found in the social sciences. In times of rapid economic growth and prosperity governments may gain some electoral support by using some of the growing resources to finance widely desired social programs, but as soon as such programs, and public expenditures generally, even *appear* to hold back "accumulation" they are in big trouble. In economic hard times social-democratic governments, no matter *how* much "legitimating" they do, are as surely swept out of office as conservative parties are swept in if the latter manage to convey the impression that they are more competent to get the economy "working again," even if this means

23 The only group that might have to be excluded from the virtually unanimous consensus on the desirability of economic growth is active environmentalists. But the environmentalists hardly form a credible threat to the capitalist system as such—in fact, they object to all rapid economic growth, whether capitalist or socialist—nor are they either the major beneficiaries of, or likely to be placated by, the capitalist state's "legitimation" policies.

24 Some authors appear to acknowledge the truth of this rather obvious point but do not seem to realize how fundamentally it undermines the whole basic assumption that the state must "legitimate" its involvement with "accumulation" (see, e.g., Bridges 1974, 173; E. O. Wright 1978, 122–23). The same can be said of Offe's remark that "the state does not only have the authority, but the *mandate* to create and sustain *conditions* of accumulation" (1975b, 126), and of Wolfe's claim that the coming "crisis of legitimacy" results from the state's inability to stop *"dis*accumulation" (A. Wolfe 1977, 250–51, emphasis added). A grudging acceptance of the obvious may also have inspired Offe and Ronge's rather obscure assertion, aimed primarily at "instrumentalism" to be sure, that the "state does not defend the interests of one class, but the *common* interest of all members of a *capitalist class society"* (1975, 139). If so, one is forced to wonder from *whom* the capitalist state "needs" to conceal its "true" nature. From the members of *non*capitalist societies?

severe cutbacks of so-called legitimation programs. If recent experience is any guide, the relationship between "legitimation" and "accumulation" is, if anything, the very opposite of that postulated by the theory: the electorate will tolerate the former *only so long as* the government can be seen to be doing all it can to promote the latter! Burstein surely understates the case when he concludes that "a growing weight of data and theory suggests that democratic governments, realizing the central importance of the state of the economy for most people, devote great effort to trying to satisfy public opinion on economic growth and economic policy" (1981, 295).

Nor are there any signs of major stirrings in the "decommodified" sectors which, according to Offe, should be the first to question the state's role in propping up a capitalist economy. The most devastating evidence refuting that particular proposition is the fact that in recent years governments have embarked on unprecedented bail-out programs for big capital (Chrysler, Massey-Ferguson), *while* cutting back drastically on social programs of all kinds without so much as a peep from the "decommodified" sector! The few protests there were did not come from the unions, the civil servants, pensioners, welfare clients, social workers, or students, but, of all people, from the arch-free-marketers of the Milton Friedman school, and a few business representatives who cried favoritism. But as long as those "decommodified" sectors do in fact quite visibly depend on the state's ability to raise the necessary revenue which, in turn, quite visibly depends on a strong economy, it does not really make a great deal of sense for them to *oppose* the state's performance of its "accumulation function." It remains, in fact, far from clear *what* exactly in those "decommodified" sectors Offe finds so subversive of support for economic growth (cf. Haas 1979, 38–43; Keane 1978, 69–75; Macpherson 1977a, 237ff.).

Both plain, everyday logic and the overwhelming evidence suggest, then, that the vast majority of the population in advanced capitalist countries both *expects* and *wants* the state to perform its "accumulation" function to the best of its ability, simply because virtually everyone reaps *some* benefits from it. But even if "accumulation" had no noticeable effects whatso-

ever on the well-being of the proverbial "man in the street," it
is *still* not obvious why he should necessarily demand compensation for it from his government in the form of "legitimation"
policies.[25] Given the overwhelming weight of argument and evidence to the contrary, then, why do so many Marxists treat the
supposed tension between "legitimation" and "accumulation" as
"a truism never questioned or tested" (Domhoff 1986, 132)?
The apparent reasons for this turn out to be very instructive
indeed.[26]

The reason the capitalist state must engage in legitimatory
gestures toward the masses, we are told, is because it must
"deny the objective complicity of collective-capitalist accumulation interests and the functions of the State" (Offe 1974, 54). It
must hide the fact that it helps "one class accumulate capital at
the expense of other classes" (O'Connor 1973, 6). The state
must "mystify" its support of the "accumulation of private capital" because "accumulation is crucial to the reproduction of the
class structure" (Gold, Lo, and Wright 1975b, 41). The state
must apparently conceal the fact that it is the capitalist class that
benefits *more* than others from its policies in support of accu-

25   Offe in fact does seem to argue in one place that the workers have not
     "really" received any net benefits from economic growth, since their stand-
     ard of living is still at the "subsistence level" as it has merely and barely kept
     pace with the (partly culturally determined) rising costs of the "reproduc-
     tion of labour power," meaning that even the "affluent" workers in ad-
     vanced capitalist countries are paid *just* enough to maintain the minimum
     of acquiescence and social order to keep profitable capital accumulation
     possible (1972c, 153–68). This argument, however, suffers from all the
     basic flaws I am criticizing here: it turns the notion of "subsistence level"
     into a meaningless tautology; it is based once again on the unsubstantiated
     assumption that the Western working class is virtually permanently on the
     verge of rising up against the capitalist system; and it implies a curious the-
     ory indeed of how workers perceive things, although it is common enough
     among Marxists, as I am trying to show in this section.
26   In his more recent work Offe seems to have moved increasingly toward a
     version of the "accumulation vs. legitimation" thesis not unlike that of neo-
     conservative critics of the supposed "excesses" of the welfare state. Like the
     latter, Offe now emphasizes how Keynesian welfare-state spending tends to
     stifle economic growth (see, e.g., Offe 1984a, chs. 2, 6, 8; 1985, ch. 8), while
     continuing to insist, contrary to the neoconservatives, that it remains indis-
     pensable for the maintenance of social order. As we have seen, this latter
     claim is highly questionable, while the anti-welfare-state argument is hardly
     very Marxist.

mulation (Bridges 1974, 183, 186; Deaton 1973, 18–37) "for fear of exposing latent class conflict" (Todd 1982, 361). In a more idealist vein, Wolfe ultimately derives the capitalist state's need to engage in "legitimation" activities from the basic human "desire to be part of a meaningful community" which he declares to be an irrepressible "human urge that no historical event has yet completely overcome" (A. Wolfe 1977, 342). According to Offe, finally, the capitalist state is caught in a "contradiction, which is a basic characteristic of every capitalist society," namely "the coexistence of the logic of industrial production for profit and the logic of human need" (1972a, 480).

Here we have, I think, finally arrived at the crux of the matter. As far as I can see, there are two claims being made here, although they may be different versions of a single claim. On the one hand, it is asserted that the state must produce "legitimatory" policies to compensate for or conceal the fact that the capitalist minority benefits *more than* the huge majority of the population from policies promoting "capital accumulation." Presumably, if this fact were not so concealed or compensated for, the majority or a significant section thereof (e.g., the working class) would withdraw its support for the government first, for the political system ("the state") next, and finally for the capitalist system as a whole, thus seriously jeopardizing its survival. In other words, it is claimed here that the majority will not tolerate the state helping to perpetuate the inequalities characteristic of a capitalist economy unless the majority is suitably compensated or kept ignorant of such help. On the other hand, "legitimation" appears to be the necessary response to the majority's irrepressible desire to be part of a "meaningful community" that obeys "the logic of human need," a desire that renders policies that promote capital accumulation deeply offensive to that majority. The latter claim probably underlies the former, so that it is the majority's desire for a "meaningful community," that motivates it to reject any unconcealed state support for an economy as unequal as a capitalist one. The question now becomes, What is so particularly repulsive about the inequalities produced in a capitalist economy and where does this irrepressible yearning for a "meaningful community" come from?

I can think of two possible answers—one that is as un-Marxist as it is unconvincing and one that may be more orthodox but is hardly any more compelling today than it was over a century ago. First the "un-Marxist" answer: it might, as Wolfe seems to suggest, simply be a matter of basic human nature—the perennial quest for "meaningful community" expresses a fundamental "human urge" which will remain unsatisfied until it has been realized, that is, until the arrival of "socialism."[27] Much like the young Marx, from whom he explicitly borrows in some of his formulations (see esp. A. Wolfe 1974), Wolfe argues that the state is nothing but "the illusory community arising out of alienated social relations," as Ollman aptly puts it (1982, 41; cf. Gold, Lo, and Wright 1975a, 40–41). As it is in the nature of man's "species being" to conquer all alienation, there is an inherent tension that will only be resolved when man has finally fulfilled his destiny. But Marx the Hegelian knew full well, as I have tried to show in Chapter 1, that history does not exactly abound with evidence of the reality of this benevolent, harmonious "species being." If anything, history is one long testimony to man's apparently infinite capacity to both inflict *and* endure exploitation, injustice, oppression, misery, and strife (see B. Moore 1978). Therefore, Marx would argue, to base one's argument on a supposedly fixed human nature is to fall prey to "utopianism" in the specific sense of a moralism that cannot be firmly grounded in any material reality and that cannot explain why "true human nature" should come to the surface just now and not before, or why there ever was any inequality, oppression, and the like to begin with, which the proponents of such an argument must assume to have been nothing but a nasty ac-

---

27   Wolfe's rather facile equation of democracy, "meaningful community," "socialism," and even "politics" (in the original Greek sense of "the common quest of equals for the just and happy society," A. Wolfe 1977, 312) is too obvious to merit a great deal of comment. At the very least it renders his central thesis of an inherent contradiction between any one of the above and "liberalism" (defined as "the marketplace ideology;" ibid., 4) true by definition or tautological, since "socialism" is, of course, by definition the very opposite of "liberalism" and so are, therefore, "democracy," "meaningful community," and "politics."

cident that can be remedied by sheer human (good) will. In the main this criticism is clearly applicable to Wolfe's argument. If the quest for meaningful community is really a basic human urge, then it will hardly do as an explanation for the rise of the welfare state in twentieth-century capitalism. If human nature really does not tolerate inequality or "nonmeaningful" community, whatever that means, then one must wonder how it has managed to tolerate them so far and why it is *just now* that it will not tolerate them any longer.

It was precisely in order to meet such objections that Marx found it necessary to look for a "material force" that would "realize philosophy" and discovered it in the nascent proletariat. And this also constitutes the second possible answer to the questions raised above. If an unchanging "human nature" cannot explain why the capitalist state should have to hide its complicity in the process of capital accumulation from the mass of the population, perhaps that complicity can be explained as a result of capitalism's fateful production of its own "gravediggers," whose working and living conditions turn them into a radical, revolutionary class unable to tolerate any further exploitation and debasement.[28] As we have seen several times now, this is indeed the assumption that still seems to underlie much of the recent Marxist theorizing on the capitalist state: the notion of "legitimation" as used by Offe and others, much like Poulantzas's "cohesion," only has any meaning at all if one assumes that since the late nineteenth century the working class in advanced capitalist society has been continuously just about to launch the socialist revolution, just as Marx had predicted, only to be held back, again and again if only just barely, by well-timed "legitimation" policies of the state.

But even in Marx's day the prediction was not particularly compelling, actually boiling down, as I have tried to show in Chapter 1, to a mystical belief in the rationality of History which had appointed the proletariat Grand Redeemer of the species. Today, more than a hundred years later, it is consider-

28 Thus, as Offe puts it, "the Marxist anthropology of labour and theory of alienation" imply that there is a "deep-seated problem of the 'social integration' of wage labour [which] must be dealt with by mechanisms of social control" (1984a, 96).

ably less so. In fact, the theories reviewed here are all designed to explain why the proletariat has thus far *failed* to live up to its appointed mission. Poulantzas does so with such "rigor" that it is hard to see how there ever could have been a possibility of *anyone* rising up against the system, while Offe writes the working class off as hopelessly pacified by various "system-conform" benefits and puts his hopes instead on the "decommodified" sectors.[29] But now it turns out that these very same theories still fundamentally rest on the assumption that Marx's original prediction was true after all! Or at least they implicitly assume its basic logic, namely that capitalism constantly creates groups whose inability to tolerate its inequalities and injustices constitute a real threat to the survival of the system as a whole—only they are somewhat vague about the precise identity of the successors to the now-pacified proletariat. This in contradistinction to Marx who at least identified the class that was to be the Historical Subject and tried, however unsuccessfully, to explain why.

Thus, the whole theory that the capitalist state must somehow conceal its complicity with capitalist accumulation is no more than the reformulation of what is undoubtedly Marxism's most basic "domain assumption" (Gouldner 1971), namely, that capitalism is bound to become unbearably repugnant to large enough sections of the population living under its sway as to create a serious threat to its survival sooner or later.[30] It is

29   Yet Offe still confidently predicts, even as he presents a catalogue of reasons why the working class has failed to rise up against capitalism, that if the "dialogical," collectivist "logic of collective action" appropriate to the working class were allowed full rein the outcome would involve "nothing less than a model of socialist transformation" (1985, 206).

30   According to Gouldner, everyone operates with certain tacit "background assumptions" of a very general nature of which one may not even be aware, but which *do* determine whether one finds a particular sociological theory *"intuitively* convincing" (1971, 30). Background assumptions that apply to some limited domain of experience, e.g., the relation between individual and society, Gouldner calls "domain assumptions." "Domain assumptions about man and society," he writes, "might include, for example, dispositions to believe that men are rational or irrational; that society is precarious or fundamentally stable; that social problems will correct themselves without planned intervention; that human behavior is unpredictable; that man's true humanity resides in his feelings and sentiments" (31). It is precisely this sort of "domain assumption"—an unspoken assumption about the "nat-

clearly *this* basic but unclarified and unexamined assumption
that underlies the substitution of the term "legitimation" for
what liberal pluralists would simply call "social reform," without
any change whatsoever in the description or substantive interpretation of the policies so renamed. The *only* difference between otherwise apparently identical accounts of the emergence of social-reform legislation seems to be that Marxists
tacitly continue to assume that without such legislation the proletariat would have revolted and replaced capitalism by "socialism" whereas liberal pluralists appear to agree that political relations would have been more strained and probably more
violent but are not so sure this necessarily would have resolved
itself to the benefit of all and tacitly fear it might lead to the
ruin of all (see van den Berg 1981, 92–102). Perhaps this also
explains how Offe can so easily assume that the living conditions in "noncommodified" sectors are such as to lead to open
questioning of the capitalist system as a whole. Sheer exposure
to any "organizational principle" other than that of exchange is
bound to render the latter intolerable. It seems to be impossible
for Offe to entertain the thought that perhaps the *alternative*
"organizational principles" to which civil servants, welfare recipients, draftees, pensioners, the disabled, and the like are subject in their respective "decommodified" sectors are neither so
wonderfully benevolent nor so superbly efficient as to inspire
them with great confidence or a burning desire to apply those
principles to the capitalist economy as well. Having been thoroughly exposed to those fine principles they may well find
Offe's hopes that their imposition on the economy will turn
"the private mode of production for profit into public work directed to the solution of human need" (Offe 1972a, 481) a trifle
naive (cf. Keane 1978, 72).[31]

---

ural" relations between man and society (and history) that renders the theories I have been criticizing "intuitively convincing" to their adherents—that
I have in mind here.

31   In a recent interview Offe concedes that his earlier formulations "tend to
create the impression that non-market forms of life are harbingers of socialism" (1984a, 264). Instead, he would now argue that "areas of social life
that have been decommodified by welfare state interventions can be developed, through struggle, into relatively autonomous subsystems of life oriented to the production and distribution of use-values" (265). However,

The contrasting assessments of the available options that implicitly underlie the otherwise identical accounts of "legitimation" or "social reform" by Marxists and liberal pluralists respectively are worth exploring a little further. What is so puzzling, from a non-Marxist perspective, is not just this unshakable faith in the workers' natural inclination toward the overthrow of capitalism, despite all the evidence to the contrary, but even more the fact that the actual strategic options open to the workers, and particularly the anticipated features and feasibility of "socialism," are treated as of little or no significance in all this. Once again, Marxism's "immanentism" and the concomitant taboo on "utopianism" are no doubt in part to blame.

Again, a comparison with Lukes's "three-dimensional" concept of power proves instructive. Power can be said to have been exercised not only when actors are in conflict and one side prevails, as Dahl (1958) requires, nor when one side can be seen to manipulate the public agenda, as Bachrach and Baratz (1962) add, but also when one side's "real interests" have been violated, Lukes (1974) argues. The imputation of such "real" interests need not be wholly arbitrary, he contends,[32] since it

---

without some further explanation as to what exactly is the difference between "socialism" and "production for use-value," it is not clear whether and how this significantly modifies the earlier formulations.

32   In a widely noted critique of the "hidden cynicism of the liberal equation" of the workers' *perceived* and *real* interests (Offe 1985, 202), Offe argues that workers "experience greater difficulties in finding out what their 'true' interest is" than the members of the capitalist class. This is because their consciousness is much more affected by "ambiguity, alienation, mystification and fetishism" (197), which in turn results from the great difficulty experienced by workers in liberal democratic capitalist societies in resolving the "objective and subjective ambiguities" (199) of individual vs. collective, political vs. economic, consumer vs. producer, etc. interests (ch.7). Yet Offe insists that this argument in no way rests on imputing any *a priori* "true" interests to the workers (337, n. 22, 26). This is plainly unconvincing, however. At the very least, Offe's argument clearly *pre*supposes that the members of the working class *do* have *one*, common, collective interest. Otherwise there would be no grounds for claiming that the above "ambiguities" are due to "mystification," "fetishism," etc., rather than being real dilemmas involving possibly equally "rational" alternatives, which is how many "bourgeois" theorists view them. Moreover, Offe himself cannot help but disclose the "true" interest of the working class *malgré soi*. The outcome of an entirely undistorted process of "dialogical" interest articulation among work-

requires making a persuasive counterfactual case to the effect
that the victim of the exercise of power would most likely have
acted or chosen differently in the *absence* of the alleged exercise
of power. In other words, Lukes's argument rests on a counterfactual claim concerning "what it is that people would have
done otherwise" (ibid., 50).

Now, Offe's argument, too, rests, albeit implicitly, on such a
counterfactual assumption, namely that, in the absence of effective "legitimation" the workers in capitalist societies would have
rebelled, overthrown the capitalist system, and replaced it with
an infinitely better "socialism." Without such counterfactual beliefs the label of "legitimation" is entirely pointless. Offe clearly
means to suggest much more than that the workers might have
gotten away with a slightly better deal at this or that juncture if
they had played their cards better, which would amount to a
quibble over tactics, *not* a refutation of "reformism."

The crucial difference between Lukes and Offe and his followers is, however, that Lukes is quite explicit about the pivotal
role of the counterfactual assumption in the argument and em-
phatically calls for "evidence . . . which supports the relevant
counterfactual" (ibid., 50), whereas Offe's assumption remains
implicit and without any empirical or theoretical support whatsoever.[33] This is at least in part because the Marxian prohibition
on discussing the nature and feasibility of an as yet nonexistent
"socialist" utopia deprives Offe of a crucial argument. Without
this argument his counterfactual assumption does not stand
much of a chance of persuading anyone but the already converted. For, as we have seen in the previous section, to be able
to assess the claim that "socialism" was at any time, or is now, a
desirable and feasible option one would *have* to know something about what "socialism" would look like.[34] Yet, the taboo

---

ers would, he confidently predicts, lead to "nothing less than a model of socialist transformation" (206).

33   I am not here taking any position on the relative merits of Lukes's concept
of power. At the very least, it would seem to me to be very hard to substan-
tiate any imputation of "real" interests *across ideological lines*. But Lukes's argument certainly has the merit of clearly bringing out the hard-to-docu-
ment counterfactual assumptions that underlie such ideological dividing
lines (see also van den Berg 1981, 92–101).

34   Offe actually seems to recognize the problem at times. "No one in the tradi-

on "utopian blueprints" withdraws precisely this crucial piece of information from discussion and analysis. As a result, the putatively available strategic options on which the basic differences between Marxist and reformist interpretations rest cannot be rationally discussed and compared, and the Marxist interpretation therefore fails to persuade either reformist theorists or the workers who, inexplicably, would like to know something about their options and chances before running to the barricades.

But to return to the earlier point, if Marxist theorists have simply taken over the basic assumption of the inevitable repugnance of capitalism unexamined from Marx on down, it is not very surprising that they should also end up with virtually the same conclusion as Marx concerning bourgeois democracy. That conclusion was, it will be remembered from Chapter 1, simply that capitalism and democracy were ultimately inherently incompatible: sooner or later one of the two has got to go. Offe explicitly takes "the Marxist thesis that bourgeois democracy and the capitalist mode of production stand in a precarious and immanently indissoluble relation of tension" (1984a, 66), a thesis shared by nineteenth-century liberals such as John Stuart Mill, as his point of departure. The matter to be explained is how "these two partial principles of social organization" could have coexisted for so long (180). "To pose these questions at all is to presuppose, in accordance with both Marx and Mill, that there *is* some real tension between the two respective organiz-

tion of Marxist theory has talked about socialism *as such*," he writes at one point, "but only about the present reality as a history out of which socialist social formations are *real* (as opposed to merely imagined) *possibilities*—if only one among a number of possibilities, as Rosa Luxemburg's formulation of 'socialism *or* barbarism' reminds us" (1984a, 239). Although Marxists have been successful enough in demonstrating "the self-annihilating nature of the capitalist mode of production" (ibid.), he continues, "one would have to demonstrate that the crisis of capitalism is *not* a total crisis (a crisis of *history*, as it were), but a crisis that *contributes to* and *prepares* a socialist transformation rather than chaos, stagnation or barbarism" (240). However, after such a promising start, Offe does not talk "about socialism *as such*" either but proceeds to some inconclusive reflections on the prospects of a more pluralist, participatory Eurocommunist strategy instead. The shift of focus and consequent failure to address his own question are significant in themselves.

ing principles of social power and political power, market society and political democracy, a tension that must be (and possibly cannot indefinitely be) bridged, mediated and stabilized"
(180–81). Compare this to Wolfe's conclusion that "capitalism
and democracy do face each other as real alternatives, and at
some time in the near future—one cannot tell when—one or
the other will come to dominate" (A. Wolfe 1977, 329). This
remarkable similarity to Marx's conclusion is not so surprising
since it is already presupposed by the assumption of the inevitable repugnancy of capitalism: if the majority of the population is sooner or later bound to find the capitalist system intolerable then, obviously, it will either seek to abolish the system
by means of democratically decided state action or democracy
itself will have to be abolished to stop the majority.[35]

But if the initial assumption has not become any more plausible since Marx's day, neither has the conclusion derived from
it. Marx's original claim about the incompatibility of capitalism
and democracy could not be verified at the time since there
hardly *were* any democracies to speak of. But since then, virtually every advanced capitalist country has adopted formally
democratic political institutions, and the two have proved to be
capable of relatively unproblematic coexistence now for close to
a century in some cases. And this, too, was one of the puzzles
the recent Marxist theorizations of the capitalist state set out to
unravel. But instead of explaining it, these theories only offer a
reassertion of the old "ultimate" incompatibility thesis—which
was already presupposed anyway—either almost verbatim, as in
the cases just quoted, or in the guise of a theory of an impending "legitimation crisis." All that has been added to Marx's original, rather rudimentary "theory" is the somewhat lame observation that the "legitimation crisis" originally predicted by Marx
has been held off until now because of the success of the state's
"legitimation" policies. Also, the predictions of the impending

35   A good illustration of the fact that such an assumption directly implies the
     conclusion that capitalism and democracy are fundamentally incompatible
     is the fact that Macpherson, more a liberal than a Marxist (see Macpherson
     1977a, 230), arrives at exactly the same conclusion from virtually the same
     premises *without any* elaborate "theorization" of capitalist "state functions"
     (see Macpherson 1977b, 64–71)! As noted in note 27, this chapter, Wolfe
     comes close to doing the same, as his "theory" is virtually true by definition.

crisis are now couched in such cautious terms and with so many qualifications as to render them effectively indeterminate— leaving the "theories" even less vulnerable to disproof than they were already.[36] But that really seems to be all that has been added to Marx's original remarks about the democratic state whose very incompleteness today's theories were supposed to remedy. It is hardly a sign of great theoretical vitality that after more than a hundred years of Marxist theorizing and some two decades of intense concentration on politics and the state all that these theorists have been able to come up with is the original "domain assumption" left completely unexamined, the literal repetition of its logical implication that capitalism and democracy simply cannot go on together forever, and an argument that is as laborious as it is diffuse to the effect that everything that happened since Marx first reached that conclusion was just an unfortunate detour. Such startlingly meager results after so much apparent effort can only mean one thing: the effort was not directed at developing a theory of the capitalist state in the first place but rather at finding ways to avoid having to question the cherished "domain assumption."

This also casts a curious light on the remarkable conversion of so many Marxist theorists to structural-functionalist-sounding terminology and forms of argument, as seen in this and the preceding chapter. There is, no doubt, a certain natural affinity between Marxism and the "structural" tradition in "bourgeois" social theory in that they both prefer the more "structural," "systemic" types of explanation for social behavior to the more voluntaristic, methodologically individualistic approach of the Weberian, "liberal" school. Marx may well have been a "systems theorist" *avant la lettre* in this sense (see McQuarie and Amburgey 1978), but the current Marxist infatuation with "systemic" theorizing as exemplified by the theories of the state of Poulantzas and Offe goes *much* further than this. As I have already mentioned, their "explanation" of the emergence of the welfare

36   For my criticism of this practice in the arguments of Offe and Habermas, see van den Berg (1980, 466–69; 1983, 1269; cf. Magnussen 1981, 572, n. 42). Once again, Wolfe is exemplary with his somewhat sheepish remark that "contradictory systems can continue to exist for some time, and this one may (or may not) do so as well" (A. Wolfe 1977, 253).

state as an apparently automatic response of the state to the "dysfunctions" of the economy is virtually indistinguishable from orthodox "bourgeois" accounts which also tend to take such a response by the "political system" to the obvious "social problems" resulting from "industrialization" completely for granted (compare, e.g., Wilensky and Lebeaux 1965 to Offe 1972a; cf. Gerstenberger 1976, 87; Wedderburn 1965, 137). In fact, in their strong preoccupation with the seemingly automatic self-stabilizing properties that guarantee the "reproduction" over time of the capitalist system, at the expense of the original Marxist concern with the system's inherent tendency toward instability and collapse, theorists like Poulantzas, Offe, and their admirers, appear to be closer to the tradition of Comte, Durkheim, and Parsons than to that of Marx (cf. Connell 1982, 139; Giddens 1981, 215).[37] But this may not be as strange as it seems: formally at least, there is a remarkable similarity between the original "domain assumption" that prompted Parsons to construct his elaborate theoretical edifice and the rather more implicit, and consequently safely unexamined, presuppositions that appear to inspire the theoretical efforts of these Marxist functionalists. The parallels that can be drawn are in fact quite startling.

The basic theoretical problem that both Parsons and modern "Western Marxism" (Anderson 1976) set out to resolve is, formally at least, one and the same: the fundamental irrationality, in terms of their own domain assumptions, of social *order*. Parsons explicitly states this in his discussion of the "Hobbesian problem of order" as the starting point for his theoretical labors (1937, 89–94). Briefly, Parsons argues that if Hobbes's assumption that human nature is basically selfish and calculative-rational and his famous inference that the "state of nature" was hence a "war of all against all" in which life would be "solitary, poor, nasty, brutish, and short" were correct, then this would create the problem of having to explain the existence and even the possibility of any social order at all. Parsons rejects what he takes to be Hobbes's own solution of a rational social contract by which all coercive powers are transferred to a central au-

---

37 For an early critique of Marcuse along these lines, see Macintyre (1967).

thority and thenceforth used to maintain social order, stability, and security by the threat of force, as both inconsistent with the initial utilitarian assumptions about individual rationality and insufficient as an explanation for durable, stable social order.[38] Thus, in the words of one of his recent champions, "Parsons begins his own argument with the claim that social order *does* exist, even if in an always incompletely realized form, and that our task should be to try to explain how this is possible" (Münch 1981, 722).

Now compare this to the revealingly similar terms in which Offe expresses *his* theoretical starting point: "For Marx the point was to examine the 'laws of movement' of capital in order to prove that capitalism as a social formation is—contrary to the belief in harmony characteristic of vulgar economics—in fact a 'moved,' a historical and transitory social formation; *today*, on the other hand, the tantalizing and baffling riddle (in a political as well as a theoretical sense) lies in the proven capacity of capitalist systems to guarantee their ability to exist—in spite of all existing contradictions and conflicts—up to the present day" (1976a, 30–31). This could easily stand as a programmatic statement for most of Western Marxism, which has, understandably enough, become more and more preoccupied since the early 1920s with trying to explain why the revolution did *not* occur in the advanced capitalist countries as Marx had predicted (see Anderson 1976). But, at any rate, it is strikingly analogous to Parsons's "Hobbesian problem" as a presupposed "problematic," to use the catchy Althusserian term, which determines in advance what requires theoretical explanation.[39] Both start out with certain unexamined assumptions about what constitutes "rational" or "sensible" behavior—that is, behavior that does not require much additional explanatory effort to be understood—that would lead one to expect that if people behaved accordingly the social order would be highly unstable and chaotic. For Parsons those assumptions are the Hobbesian view of

38   The accuracy of Parsons's presentation of Hobbes's own solution to the problem of order is controversial (see, e.g., Barry 1978, 77), but this is not the issue here.

39   For an early suggestion concerning the basic similarity between the "Hobbesian Question" and the "Marxist Question" see Wrong (1961).

human nature, for the Marxists they are the firm conviction that it is not only the historical duty but also in the objective interest of the working class to overthrow the capitalist system and establish "socialism" in its stead. Accordingly, the fact that (capitalist) society has, on the whole, proved to be quite stable and fairly orderly is a "tantalizing and baffling riddle" for *both*, a riddle all theoretical efforts must aim at solving. Significantly, both Parsons and Western Marxists also reject sheer coercion as an acceptable answer. For Parsons this could only account for very short periods of fragile stability (see Münch 1981, 721; 1983, 62), whereas Marxists simply assume that the workers not only *should* have risen in revolt but also that they *could* easily have overthrown their exploiters by the sheer force of their overwhelming numbers. Thus, given the initial assumptions about what *would* have constituted "rational" behavior on the part of the working class, it is not so surprising that, much like Comte, Durkheim, and Parsons, Marxists have come to rely more and more on forces of a symbolic, normative, that is, plainly nonrational, nature, such as "ideology," "reification," "false consciousness," "legitimation," and "hegemony" for an answer to the "tantalizing and baffling riddle" of capitalism's apparent staying power. This is, however, characteristic of all brands of Western Marxism, not just of the functionalist varieties discussed in this and the preceding chapter (cf. Abercrombie, Hill, and Turner 1980). But for now I limit my discussion to those who have adopted not only the normative consensus view of the social order, but *also* functionalist or "systemic" arguments similar to Parsons's. In view of the striking similarities between their initial assumptions, it would seem understandable, too, that at least *some* Marxists might be tempted to travel the whole road with Parsons to the final, highly abstract "systems theory."[40]

40   Carnoy's (1984, 149, 222, 251) claim that Offe, unlike Poulantzas, pays little attention to the Gramscian, ideological function of the state in (re)producing "hegemony" and that he focuses on the accumulation function instead, is clearly mistaken. Offe's "legitimation" is every bit as ideological as Poulantzas's "hegemony." Carnoy seems to have gotten this erroneous impression from the fact that Jessop (1982, ch. 3) discusses Offe in connection with the German "state derivation" school, which *does* on the whole stress the capitalist state's economic functions.

It is a commonplace that not only Parsons's early emphasis on normative consensus as the basis for social order, but his whole subsequent theoretical development through structural functionalism and systems theory was essentially one long "attempt to account satisfactorily for social order" (P. Hamilton 1983, 93). But the resort to "systemic" logic can also be seen as perhaps not an inexorable but then at least an understandable consequence of the initial presuppositions. After all, to reliably and durably keep everyone from behaving as they "naturally" would would seem to require a force that was not only quite massive and pervasive, but that also put *external* constraints on human action, one, in other words, that is independent of the wills of the very people—which, of course, includes everyone—whose behavior it is supposed to modify. Thus, the search for apparently suprahuman, "systemic" processes and "functions" also flows quite naturally from the initial assumptions (cf. Dawe 1978, 381–84, 402–8).[41]

The reasons Marxists, too, find the conceptual apparatus of "structures" and "functions" appealing are, I suspect, quite similar. They, too, start with the assumption that rational behavior by all social actors, workers and capitalists alike, can only serve to jeopardize the stability and viability of the capitalist system. Thus, the system's ability to survive can only be explained by its apparent ability to prevent *all* actors from doing the "rational" thing, from what would otherwise come naturally to them. Obviously, to obtain such a massive modification of expected social behavior you need a force of exceptional strength and perva-

41   Offe has come to recognize the "implicitly Parsonian bias" (1984a, 268) in his earlier emphasis on the importance of legitimation and normative integration. He now offers an alternative approach in which it is accepted that questions of legitimacy can be relegated to the background in "a régime of power that confirms itself, as Marcuse puts it, by delivering the goods" (ibid.). However, he adds, whenever the system fails to do so, it is likely that more fundamental questions about the legitimacy of basic social and political arrangements resurface, as is the case, Offe maintains, in the current period (268–70). It is not quite clear, however, in what way this new approach alters much in the original formulations in which "legitimation" might well be based on "delivering the goods" in some sense (e.g., by way of various welfare-state support systems), while the stability of the social order seems to rest, now as before, on the unquestioned "legitimacy" of existing social arrangements.

siveness, but above all you need a force that operates autonomously, independently of the wills of the actors whose behavior
it is supposed to modify. Thus one can understand how theorists like Poulantzas and Offe, deeply puzzled by capitalism's
unanticipated longevity, would come to depict it as a self-stabilizing system of interdependent structures, with the state as the
principal, self-guided homeostatic device. Anything short of
such massive, suprahuman processes could only once again
raise the question of how on earth whole social classes, including the supposedly invincible proletariat, could have been prevented from doing the obviously rational thing. That, in turn,
would almost inevitably lead to uncomfortable questions as to
whether that "thing" was as obviously rational to begin with as
heretofore assumed.[42] What is remarkable here is how what was
initially an explicit, though not necessarily very convincing theory predicting the great proletarian revolution could, after having been refuted time and again, so easily be converted into the
"domain assumption" of the new theory explaining the failure
of that revolution to occur, *without any apparent attempt at all to
reexamine the original theory*. Once again, Marxism's "immanentism" may have played a role. It is obviously much easier to retain one's belief that the "socialist" option was and is the only
"rational" one for the working class if one can successfully ban-
ish all disturbing worries concerning the features and feasibility
of that option from one's mind.

But the comfort of not having to raise such awkward questions is bought only at the price of compromising the original
theory to such an extent that eventually even *more* awkward
questions about its tenability arise. As we have seen in the previous chapter, Poulantzas, following Althusser, ends up depicting the capitalist system as such an awesomely powerful and

42   At the normative level as well, there are some remarkable parallels beween
the Durkheimian tradition in sociology and Marxism. Offe rejects neoconservative proposals for subordinating more areas of social life to the imperatives of market exchange thus: "In fact it is the potency of these imperatives themselves that must be curbed and rendered capable of
subordination to political-normative rules" (1984a, 84). One could hardly
ask for a clearer illustration of the oft-noted fact that both the Durkheimian
and the Marxist traditions were born out of a reaction against the supposedly corrosive amoralism and individualism of modern capitalism.

versatile self-maintaining machine that it can even turn the class struggle itself into a device for *maintaining* stability, and the working class into the system's strongest (albeit unwitting) supporter. As Poulantzas himself eventually came to realize, under such circumstances it is hard to imagine how the system could *ever* have been threatened by anybody or anything and, by implication, it is hard to see how *any* form of Marxism could still remain tenable or even how it could ever have *been* plausible in the first place.

Offe and other advocates of the "systemic" approach in Marxism would deny that the same applies to their theories too. They claim that their "systems theoretical" approach remains fundamentally different from the static Parsonsian variant because it retains the crucial elements of contradictoriness, conflict, and social change which are the hallmarks of any truly Marxist perspective (cf. Bottomore 1979, 13; Panitch 1977, 9). But although Offe does uphold the fundamental contradictoriness of capitalism in some sense, his argument is neither very convincing or forceful nor is it, for that matter, recognizably Marxist. To begin with, like Poulantzas, Offe appears to view the traditional class struggle between the industrial working class and the bourgeoisie as having become a completely functional element in the *maintenance* of the system as it provides the state with the necessary maneuvering room to serve the long-term interests of the bourgeoisie in relative autonomy and simultaneously masquerade as the protector of the interests of the masses. But this only raises the question of where and how the "contradictoriness" of capitalism *does* manifest itself if not in the traditional class struggle. Offe's answer to this rather crucial question, however, remains something short of compelling.

First, instead of seeking a new "material force" to replace the proletariat as the designated gravediggers of the capitalist system—which was, after all, the basis for claiming that Marxism had transcended "utopian" socialism—Offe's conception of the "contradictions" of capitalism seems to return entirely to the realm of disembodied moral principles. The impending irreconcilable conflict between classes is replaced by the supposedly irresolvable clash of "organizational principles," of "form" and "content," of "use value" versus "exchange value orientations," of "commodification" versus "decommodification," and so on. Such conflicting norms, we are told, can sooner or later "no longer be accommodated within the limits of tolerance of social identity" (Offe 1976a, 62) and must, therefore, inevitably lead to the "structural weakening of the moral fiber of . . . capitalist society" (Offe and Ronge 1975, 147). As Offe himself explicitly states, *who* exactly the social carriers of these conflicting principles and, presumably, the historical actors whose conflict will make the latent contradictions manifest are going to be is a secondary, empirical matter (1972c, 13–14). This seems a far cry indeed from Marx's original search for the "historical subject" to "realize philosophy" in real life. As the rather loose talk of "moral fiber" indicates, this is a clear instance of the general drift toward the Parsonsian moral consensus model alluded to above.

But the argument gets more curious still. Where Offe *does* try to identify the social groups that will most likely be involved in the anticipated conflicts over capitalism's "organizational principles," he seems to apply a logic that is the exact reverse of Marx's. For it is not in the sectors where labor is most "commodified" that Offe expects the opposition to the "organizational principle" of capitalism to emerge but, quite to the contrary, in the *least* "commodified" public and "residual" sectors, that is, in the relatively rapidly growing sectors where labor is being "*de*commodified" as a result of government intervention. The monopolistic sector, Offe claims, is characterized by the highest degree of commodification of labor, little price competition, a high organic composition of capital, strong trade unions, and relatively high wages. "As a consequence," he states, "it is most likely that a picture of society which views all social relations, all determinants of the individual's chances in life as mediated by *exchange relationships* can be maintained within this sector" (1976a, 40). For a Marxist, this is an odd argument indeed. Is not the whole Marxist theory of the contradictions and eventual collapse of capitalism based, first and foremost, on the commodification of labor which is its very defining feature? Did not Marx himself argue throughout that the fundamental cause of capitalism's eventual downfall would be the fact that it treats labor power, and hence its owners, as a mere dispensable commodity, resulting in the workers becoming entirely dependent on the insecurities and vagaries of the market, a dependence that would eventually become intolerable?[43] It is not easy to see what Offe's theory, apparently arguing the very opposite of this, can still be said to have in common with Marxism.[44]

43   To make matters worse, in his more recent writings Offe continues to emphasize the "commodification of labour" as the central feature of capitalism (1984a, ch. 3, 282–84; 1985, ch. 1), at the same time arguing that its importance, both as an "organizing principle" and as a factor motivating collective (class) action, has declined dramatically (1985, chs. 5, 7, 20–21, 30–35). He now questions "the grandiose scenario of a bipolar struggle between social classes" as "a model of the structure and dynamic of relations within civil society" because, given the availability of a wide variety of compensatory measures for the basically exploitative relations of production, it is by no means necessarily "the rational response" of workers to engage "in a class-wide collective conflict centering on the abolition of the commodity form of labour power" (ibid., 2). "Indeed, there are good reasons why it may be rational for individual actors in a class society *not* to act in reference to classes or in accordance with their class interests" (ibid.). At this point Offe's project seems to have lost the last traces of both its Marxism and its coherence. The contrast between individual "rationality" and "class interests" belongs to the "bourgeois" theory of collective goods (Olson 1965) rather than Marxism and undermines, if we are to take the term "rationality" seriously, the entire rationale for his earlier theory of the state. If it is "rational" for workers to accept rather than combat government "legitimation" as well as "accumulation" policies, in what sense are workers' and capitalists' interests still opposed and does the capitalist state serve the latter rather than the former? Nor does it seem to make much sense to continue to harp on the theme of labor commodification if the phenomenon itself is of little and decreasing consequence anyway.

44   Actually, Offe's notion of "commodification" of labor is itself rather obscure. It is not at all clear how he can claim that labor is in any sense more "commodified" in the monopoly sector than in the competitive sector. Obviously, monopoly sector workers are, if anything *less* subject to the vagaries of the market, and *better* protected against the harsh consequences of the commodification of labor, precisely for the reasons Offe mentions. Offe seems to confuse degree of commodification with being relatively privileged. It is, in fact, precisely *because* the monopoly sector is better sheltered from the uncertainties of the competitive market that its workers enjoy relatively higher wages. Thus, they may well be relatively less dissatisfied and less likely to rebel against "the system," as Offe claims, but hardly because they suffer a higher degree of "commodification." But even then, this is still rather different from claiming, as Offe appears to be doing, that monopoly sector workers are likely to be a bunch of raving free enterprisers! This seems no more likely for these workers, whose relatively privileged position

If the answer is not the class struggle or the commodification of labor, it is not the focus on "contradictions" and social change either, all pretentions to the contrary notwithstanding. Quite apart from Offe's reluctance to identify the likely social actors and conflicts that are to verify, in the near future, the assertion that capitalism remains as "contradictory" a system as ever, to the extent that he (and Wolfe) are willing to draw any verifiable implications at all these are so cautiously qualified as to render them utterly meaningless. Conflicts will erupt again, we are informed, but it is impossible to predict at this point where and when, and they may well result in the indefinite "perpetuation of a historically unproductive process of decay" (Offe 1976a, 67, n. 10), since "contradictory systems can continue for some time" (A. Wolfe 1977, 253). With such marvels of evasion (What would be "historically productive"? When will "some time" have elapsed?), it is difficult to tell *what* exactly is being predicted here, if anything. As I have argued elsewhere (van den Berg 1980, 466–69) this deprives the notion of "contradiction" of all meaning. All we are told is that in the future we are likely to see social tensions and conflicts again as we have in the past. No "bourgeois" social scientist, whether of the Parsonsian persuasion or otherwise, could possibly deny such a platitude. The only difference is that the "bourgeois" social scientist would not consider *any* sign of tension or conflict to be conclusive proof of the existence of a profound "contradiction." Thus, Offe's model of the "social system" is no more or less "contradictory" or "dialectical" than Parsons's—except in empty rhetoric.[45]

In conclusion, then, both Poulantzas and Offe have had to

---

is so obviously the result of the willful organization of both markets and labor, than it does for the competitive sector workers whose being left at the mercy of the market would hardly endear them to its principles (of "exchange relationships")! It should be noted, however, that the prediction that the working class's consciousness will become *more*, not less, "reified"— i.e., accepting of total commodification as "natural"—as capitalism develops, does go back to Lukács, who seems to have wanted to out-Lenin Lenin himself (see Israel 1971, 60).

45   For a trenchant criticism of the loose application of the term "contradiction" by Marxists, particularly in connection with the welfare state, see Pemberton (1983).

pay a very high price indeed for the luxury of adopting the "structural" or "systemic" model of society on the basis of their unexamined presuppositions. In their preoccupation with explaining capitalism's remarkable reproductive capacity—instead of questioning whether it really ever was as much in danger of collapse as previously assumed—they have ended up with a completely static and rather un-Marxist theory of modern capitalism as a self-stabilizing machine with about as many endogenous sources of strain and social change as have been attributed to it by the most conservative schools of "bourgeois" sociology.[46] Ultimately, of course, this fateful theoretical turn cannot but raise that troublesome question again, If capitalism is so well equipped to maintain its own identity and stability over time, in what sense can the Marxist theory of its transitory nature and its impending demise be said *ever* to have been plausible to begin with?

46 Actually Poulantzas and Offe view capitalism as far *less* subject to strain than the conservative tradition in sociology which, from Burke and de Bonald to Parsons and Schelsky, is practically defined by its deep concern over the supposedly disruptive effects of capitalist development on the fragile social order (see, e.g., Nisbet 1967, 1978).

6 The State
and the Class Struggle:
Dynamics Restored?

"Structural" theories of the capitalist state such as those of Offe and Poulantzas were so well received by Marxists that they soon produced a "new orthodoxy of the relative autonomy 'school' " (Krieger and Held 1978, 191). But the story of recent Marxist theorizing on the state does not end there. Although most Marxists seem to agree that the old "instrumentalist" theory's main flaw was that it "remained on the positivist terrain of the pluralists" (Kesselman 1983, 830), several of them have grown increasingly uncomfortable with the "implacable determinism" (Anderson 1976, 65) inherent in "structural" attempts "to establish theoretical *guarantees* that the state in a capitalist society necessarily functions on behalf of capital" (Jessop 1977, 357, emphasis added). As a result, the most recent trend in Marxist theorizing seems to be the search for an alternative to *both* "instrumentalism" *and* functionalism. Both approaches, it is felt, tend to ignore the class struggle, the pressures from below which are neither initiated nor controlled by either the state *or* the bourgeoisie and which, consequently, pose real limits and constraints on the latter's hegemony. As a result, neither can adequately deal with, and take account of "historically dynamic class conflict as a motor of structural change" (Esping-Andersen, Friedland, and Wright 1976, 188; cf. Block 1977a; Bridges 1974, 178–80; Clarke 1977; Gough 1975, 53–58; Jessop 1977, 367–69; Stephens 1979, 77–78; Whitt 1979b, 83–85).

These critics appear to be groping for what may be called a "class struggle" or "class dialectical" perspective, that is, a perspective that considers state power and government policy "as a complex, contradictory effect of class (and popular-democratic) struggles, mediated through and conditioned by the institutional system of the state" (Jessop 1977, 370; cf. Isaac and Kelly 1981, 1380; Skocpol 1979, 28). The basic idea and, indeed, the very way it is formulated here, are strikingly reminiscent of (and no doubt partly inspired by; cf. Jessop 1980a, 1982) Poulantzas's own conversion to a more dynamic, "class struggle" oriented conception of the state, in response to critics who had argued that his earlier formulations left no room or "motive force for political action" (Appelbaum 1979, 26). As we have seen, although Poulantzas has continued to dismiss such criticisms of his earlier work as "utterly inappropriate" (1976, 71), he did in fact, and in stark contrast to the earlier work, come to put *such* a heavy and frequent emphasis on the "historical, dynamic dimension," which now presumably "governs the functioning and the role of the apparatuses" (1973a, 50), that one cannot but conclude that he in effect adopted an entirely new and different approach—or else was not really serious about this new-found "dynamic" dimension. But whatever the sincerity or depth of his conversion, in his later work Poulantzas left no opportunity unused to proclaim boldly *"the primacy of the class struggle over the apparatuses"* (1973a, 30; cf., e.g., 1975, 34; 1978, 38, 45, 53, 126, 149, 151). He came to conceive of the capitalist state "as the condensate of a relation of power between struggling classes," which is, thus, "structurally shot through and constituted with and by class contradictions" (1976, 74, 75). Since "it is the class struggle which determines how the apparatuses are modified" (1973a, 48), it would seem to follow that these "apparatuses are never anything other than the materialization and condensation of class relations" (1975, 23; see also, e.g., 1973a, 48–49; 1975, 27–29), and so on and so forth, *ad nauseam.*

In less convoluted language and a somewhat less dogmatic tone, others have come to similar conclusions. Thus, after a critical review of the theoretical stalemate between the old, discredited "instrumentalist" approach and the new, excessively static and abstract structural-systemic theories, Gold, Lo, and Wright set out to preserve the best of both in an attempt to "define the contours within which . . . a general theory of the capitalist state might be developed" (1975b, 46). As one of those contours they offer the proposition that *"the internal structures of the state, as well as the concrete state policies shaped within those structures, are the objects of class struggle"* (ibid.). This means, according to Gold et al., that "the state is seen not merely as helping to reproduce the capitalist system in contradictory ways, but as being itself shaped by the class struggle which results from those contradictions" (47). At the same time they concede that for the moment this "remains a somewhat ad hoc argument . . . only a starting point" since it "is further necessary to develop a proper theory of such political class struggle itself" (ibid.).

In an article that according to Domhoff "nicely transcends the 'instrumentalist-structuralist' distinction" (1976, 221), Esping-Andersen, Friedland, and Wright (1976) appear to offer the beginnings of such a theory of the political class struggle. Like Gold, Lo, and Wright (1975a, b) they start by briefly reviewing the available alternative perspectives. Although they criticize the "instrumentalist" position—including Domhoff's "corporate liberalism" thesis (see Esping-Andersen, Friedland, and Wright 1976, 187)—for tending "to be somewhat situational and voluntaristic," relying too heavily "on observable class input into, and control of, policy formation" and hence ignoring "the extent to which the demands and interests of the dominant class must take into account the limits of direct manipulation imposed by a historical social formation" (ibid., 189), they chide the structuralist approaches for not being "situational" *enough,* as they are "unable to locate specific actors and historically dynamic class conflict as a motor of structural change" (188) and tend "to view class originated inputs and demands as 'passive' responses to stimuli born out of the structure" (189). They also mention, albeit almost in passing, "pluralism," the "liberal perspective, long dominant in American social science" (186), but they do not appear to find it worthy of an in-depth critique. They merely summarize it as the perspective that views "the state as a political market place . . . a pluralist, aggregating mechanism in which agencies, programs and legislation are substantive responses to the demands and interests of competing groups" (187), a position they attribute to Lipset (1960) and Dahl (1961) among others.

Instead, Esping-Andersen, Friedland, and Wright offer an alternative view of the state which they call the "political class struggle" approach. Rather than depicting the state as either "a neutral instrument or a functionalist thermostat for capitalist society" (1976, 197), they propose to elaborate what they see as the theory of the state implicit in the work of Offe and O'Connor "by arguing that the internal structure of the state is simultaneously a *product*, an *object*, and a *determinant* of class conflict" (191).[1] Thus, "in order to assess the contradictory ways by which state structure reproduces capitalist political domination" (197), one must take into account *both* the challenges posed to the rule of capital by the demands of the working class, *and* the more or less successful maneuvers by the capitalist class to use or restructure the state to neutralize those challenges. Esping-Andersen et al. emphasize that "the critical point in the present discussion is that political challenge by the working class shapes the historical development of state structure. The actual structures of the state are thus not a simple reflection of capitalist interests, but a contradictory reflection of the class struggle between workers and capitalists" (192). They summarize their basic approach as follows:

> The political struggles of the working class thus gain analytical importance absent from the "instrumental corporate liberal" and "structuralist" approaches. Political class struggle becomes the central determinant both of the restructuring of the state itself and of the contradictory consequences of that restructuring. To para-

1 It is unclear on what grounds Esping-Andersen, Friedland, and Wright believe their "political class struggle" approach is really "implicit in O'Connor's and Offe's work" (1976, 191). They themselves present Offe's arguments as unabashedly structural-functional or "systemic" and criticize them—quite correctly in my mind, as I have tried to show in the previous chapter—on basically the same grounds as they criticized other "structuralist" approaches (187–91). At the same time, in his more recent work Offe does seem to have shifted toward an approach quite similar to that of Esping-Andersen et al., now viewing "the state of democratic politics . . . as both determined by, and a potential determinant of social power" (1984a, 161; cf. Keane 1984, 26). But, as with Poulantzas's conversion to the "class struggle" approach, if taken seriously this simply contradicts Offe's earlier "systemic" theory of the state. As for O'Connor, there does not really appear to be *any* coherent theory of the state implicit in his arguments concerning the "fiscal crisis." If anything, he combines functionalist-sounding phraseology in the more general statements that I have mentioned in the previous chapter with purely *ad hoc* instrumentalist explanations for concrete, empirical occurrences (for references, see note 13, Chapter 5).

phrase Marx, capitalists may manipulate the state, but they do not
do so just as they please. The instrumental domination of the capitalist class is constrained by the structures of the state formed out
of past class struggles, by the exigencies of current class struggles
and by the contradictory consequences of state activity for future
class struggle. (197–98)

Thus, the "political class struggle" approach of Esping-Andersen, Friedland, and Wright asserts that the structures of the
state are the result of struggles between *two* classes, the capitalist
class and the working class, and not the unilateral creation of
the former class or of the capitalist "system" alone. Consequently, the policies produced by those structures are also the
result of two clashing forces and hence not *necessarily* exclusively
in the interests of the capitalist class. In fact, it is only when
"successfully shaped by the capitalist class" alone that the state
structures can be expected to accomplish their "two critical
tasks: a) . . . limit state interventions within bounds compatible
with the imperatives of capital accumulation; b) . . . politically
neutralize the working class in the sense of making its political
demands congruent with the reproduction of capitalist social
relations" (ibid., 198). However, the capitalist class is never completely successful in this. The process is "inevitably contradictory," because the "working class can never be perfectly incorporated, totally neutralized" (ibid.). Thus, whether the state
serves the interests of the bourgeoisie is a matter of degree, to
be established separately in each case by means of empirical investigation.

It is to this end that Esping-Andersen, Friedland, and Wright
develop their eightfold typology of different forms of political
class struggle according to criteria dichotomizing working-class
demands by whether they are production or merely circulation
oriented, whether they are commodified or not, and whether
they are reproductive of capitalist social relations or not (ibid.,
198–203). The typology ranges from those policies and demands that "represent the purest form of capitalist politics" because they presumably are most compatible with capital accumulation and help neutralize the working-class threat, to
demands that "represent the purest form of class conscious

working class politics" because they presumably are most subversive of capitalist social relations (206). The typology and its peculiarities have been discussed in Chapter 2 (see pp. 162–64); the only additional point worth mentioning is that this typology leads Esping-Andersen et al. to reconceptualize the political class struggle

> as a struggle over which of these types of political demands will dominate, that is over the content of class conflict itself. The capitalist class tries to push demands towards commodified forms and away from the production level, and tries to exclude unreproductive demands altogether; the working class, on the other hand, moves toward noncommodified politics, production politics and, ultimately unreproductive politics. Needless to say, the movement towards this revolutionary pole has often been thwarted, and in periods of relatively uncontested capitalist hegemony, may remain only a latent possibility. (207)

Yet Esping-Andersen, Friedland, and Wright appear to entertain little doubt that the working class's "natural" tendency to gravitate toward this "revolutionary pole" cannot be successfully suppressed or neutralized for long, as is clear from the following rousing passage:

> If reproductive-commodified-circulation policies represent the purest form of capitalist politics, unreproductive-noncommodified-production demands represent the purest form of class conscious working class politics. When the working class is organized around these kinds of demands it challenges the very premises of capitalist society. The working class becomes a class "for itself", and class politics must involve conflict for generalized power, involving ever larger segments of state power and state apparatus, calling into question not only the structure and legitimation of private production, but also the structure of the state. Political demands around social needs can no longer be reduced to the better commodification of labor power, and these demands can no longer be satisfied through consumption and non-work alone. In short, working class political struggle around noncommodified, unreproductive production demands naturally moves toward political struggle for socialism. (206)

Finally, in a fairly widely discussed article, Fred Block (1977b; cf. Block 1978a; Hammond 1978; Krieger and Held 1978; Skocpol 1980, 182ff.) presents yet another "class struggle" approach of sorts.[2] Like the other authors discussed in this chapter, Block rejects the "instrumentalist" or "corporate liberal" approach because it "exaggerates the capacity of corporate capitalism to rationalize itself through the use of the state" (1977a, 357), and it has a "tendency to ignore how much reforms are forced on capitalism from below" (ibid.). Moreover, Block argues, this type of theory operates on the "problematic assumption that the relationship between the state and the corporations is clear" (358). The simplistic assumption that the corporations can simply use the state for whatever purposes they see fit "obscures the continuing tensions between government and big business which serve to regenerate business distrust of government" (ibid.). Rather, Block asserts, much like Esping-Andersen, Friedland, and Wright, "specific reforms are a result of demands from below, combined with the efforts of the powerful to shape and control the process of change" (357; see also Block 1978a, b; Silva 1978).

Block's treatment of structural-systemic "relative autonomy" arguments is a little more eccentric, however. Ultimately, he claims, such arguments must inevitably collapse "back into a slightly more sophisticated version of instrumentalism" (1977b, 9). For, after all, what would seem to keep the state's autonomy relative, Block reasons, is the fact that "the ruling class will respond effectively to the state's abuse of that autonomy" (ibid.). But if that is so, then these arguments rely on the very same exaggerated assumptions of "consciousness, consensus, and political capacity of the capitalist class or its most important fractions" that they rightly criticize the "instrumentalist" approach for (Block 1980, 228; also 1977b, 9). The only other alternative,

2   Burris (1979, 11) presents Block's argument as an attempt "to concretize Poulantzas' notion of the relative autonomy of the state." This obvious misinterpretation is perhaps attributable to Poulantzas's own theoretical vacillations as well as to Burris's apparent desire to find at least *something* worth salvaging from the Althusserian theoretical quagmire. As we shall see, however, Block's "concretization" of the autonomy of the state leads him, predictably, in exactly the direction that Poulantzas so persistently tried to avoid.

it appears, is to claim that there are "concrete structural mechanisms that prevent the state from exceeding its normal authority" without specifying what those mechanisms are (1980, 228).[3] Furthermore, Block continues, the relative autonomy approach appears to be little more than "a cosmetic modification of Marxism's tendency to reduce state power to class power," forcibly and implausibly seeking "to explain all *major* state initiatives as the products of specific class interests" (229). Instead, Block intends to take the idea of the (relative) autonomy of the state seriously, that is, to treat the state as an institution pursuing interests and exercising power in its own right.

Thus, Block adds a third party, the state itself, to the two classes whose "struggle" is considered to be the determinant of government policy by other "class struggle" theorists.[4] The policies of the state, then, are to be viewed as "the outcome of a conflict among three sets of agents—the capitalist class, the managers of the state apparatus, and the working class" (1977b, 8). The "key idea" of Block's approach is that there is "a division of labor between those who accumulate capital and those who manage the state apparatus" (10). The former may be "conscious of their interests as capitalists, but in general, they are not conscious of what is necessary to reproduce the social order in changing circumstances" (ibid.). On the other hand, those who wield the powers of the state, the "state managers," who include "the leading figures of both the legislative and executive branches" (8), "collectively are self-interested maximisers, interested in maximising their power, prestige, and wealth" (1980, 229). What requires explanation is how such a "division of la-

---

3   Block seems to have the mistaken impression that "relative autonomy" theorists such as Poulantzas or Offe *do* in fact argue that in the last resort the relativity of the state's autonomy depends on the willingness and ability of the capitalist class to "act to bring the state back into line" (Block 1980, 228). As I have, I believe, amply documented by now, however, these theorists have *indeed* been quite content to claim that some unspecified "structural" mechanism keeps the state in line, and leave it at that (see also note 13, Chapter 3, notes 12, 15, Chapter 5).

4   Although Esping-Andersen, Friedland, and Wright pay lip service to the idea that the "internal structures" of the state are not only "a *product*" but also "a *determinant*" (1976, 191), they then go on to ignore their determining influence and focus exclusively on how they are on the receiving end of the class struggle.

bor" can help account for capitalism's "remarkable capacity to rationalize itself in response to the twin dangers of economic crisis and radical working-class movements" (1977b, 7).[5] By "rationalization" Block means "the use of the state in new ways to overcome economic contradictions and to facilitate the integration of the working class" (ibid.). In other words, "the central theoretical task is to explain how it is that despite this division of labor, the state tends to serve the interests of the capitalist class" (10). Since, however, the capitalist class does not know "what is necessary to preserve and reproduce capitalist social relations," and the state managers do not have an obvious motive to pursue policies toward that end, even if they *did* know how, one must assume that "such policies emerge out of the structural relationships among state managers, capitalists, and workers" (12).

The major "structural mechanisms" that, according to Block, explain "why the state avoids anti-capitalist policies" and why it "has served to rationalize capitalism" (ibid., 15) arise from the interaction between two factors: the existing political institutions within which the state managers operate, on the one hand, and the broad context of capitalist class relations on the other (see Block 1977b, 14–15; 1980, 229–30).[6] Under the assumptions made by Block, it follows that "those who manage the state apparatus—regardless of their own political ideology—are dependent on the maintenance of some reasonable level of economic activity" (1977b, 15). This is so both because the revenues needed to finance the state's activities are dependent on a healthy economy and because the state managers need the support of an electorate that holds them responsible for the health of the economy (ibid.; 1980, 230–31). Yet, in a capitalist economy the level of economic activity and "health" depends pri-

5   In recent work Miliband (1983) seems to be edging toward an argument similar to Block's, describing the relationship between those in charge of the state and the capitalist class as a "partnership" in which each side has its own concerns and responsibilities. Whether this allows for an explanation of the procapitalist nature of government policy *without* falling back on basically "instrumentalist" arguments remains to be seen.

6   Block does not, in fact, pay much attention to the first of these—which is, I would argue, a reason for one of the major flaws in his approach—but it is clearly an indispensable part of the argument.

marily on private investment decisions. This implies, according to Block, "that capitalists, in their collective role as investors, have a veto over state policies in that their failure to invest at adequate levels can create major political problems for the state managers" (1977b, 15). Thus, since state managers have a direct interest in promoting and facilitating private investment, they have a strong incentive to pursue only the policies that are generally viewed by capitalists as either favoring general profitability or else not threatening it, which, in turn, "increases the likelihood that such policies will be in the general interest of capital" (ibid.).

This is not, Block insists, simply another version of the instrumentalist argument, because it does not involve the problematic assumption of a united capitalist class, or its most powerful fraction, that is improbably conscious of its own, common, long-term interests. Instead, it merely claims that capitalists will evaluate government policies exclusively from the perspective of their own narrow self-interest, that is, in terms of how they will affect the profitability of investments. The notion of "business confidence," "rooted in the narrow self-interest of the individual capitalist who is worried about profit" (ibid., 16), is ordinarily sufficient to prevent governments from attempting to impose any policies that are strongly opposed by business. Block tries to demonstrate this by tracing out the likely sequence of events when democratically elected left-of-center governments try to implement major reforms. Invariably, he claims, the result is inflation caused by business raising prices to regain some of the lost ground. This leads to a drop in the value of the country's currency, balance of trade and payments problems, and an acute decline in business confidence insofar as it had not fallen already in response to the initial attempts at reform, which, in turn, leads to a new drop in investment and, hence, to a recession, unemployment, shortages, and so on. This, finally, produces a collapse of popular support for the reforms and for the government that proposed them. Since there is no popular support for the only alternative to capitulation, namely, a radical move to take control of the economy, because leaders of gradualist, reformist movements generally have not prepared their electoral supporters for such drastic options, the government is forced to repeal the reforms most offensive to the capitalist class or face removal from power by either the ballot box or the military. This also shows the futility of the reformist strategy, but to Block the "key point in elaborating this scenario is that the chain of events can unfold without any members of the ruling class consciously deciding to act 'politically' against the régime in power" (19).

However, this does not yet explain "the dynamic through which reforms that increase the rationality of capitalism come about" (ibid., 20). Such reforms almost always involve the extension of the role of the state in the economy and society, he claims, an extension that should ordinarily, under the assumption that the capitalists are as shortsighted as the model suggests, meet with declines in business confidence. But this is where "another structural mechanism" comes into play, namely "class struggle" (21). "In its struggles to protect itself from the ravages of a market economy, the working class has played a key role in the steady expansion of the state's role in capitalist societies," Block asserts (22). But in addition, the state managers have been more than willing to extend the state's powers as this meant increasing their own power. Thus, "the major impetus for the extension of the state's role has come from the working class and from the managers of the state apparatus, whose own powers expand with a growing state" (ibid.). But given their interest in maintaining and facilitating "a smooth flow of investment" (ibid.), these state managers can be counted on to try and find that way to implement the reforms demanded by working-class pressure that most aids or least impedes the accumulation process, that is to say, the way that is least harmful to "business confidence." This is how the demands emanating from the class struggle usually end up rationalizing the capitalist system by enlarging the role of the state without slowing down the process of accumulation. However, the process by which state managers try to expand their own powers while offending "business confidence" as little as possible, without losing popular support or risking an escalation of class antagonisms, is always a delicate balancing act, involving a lot of potential problems and friction, whose successful outcome is never guaranteed (22–24).

Nevertheless, major, dramatic reforms, especially in the form of great extensions of government intervention, do occur from time to time. But this always happens during exceptional periods when the force of a possible decline of business confidence as a veto is temporarily suspended, as in major wartime mobilizations, economic depressions, and postwar reconstruction periods. During the last two types of periods, business activity is already so low that the threat of a further decline in business confidence loses much of its force, and during periods of war the state has an unassailable justification for extending its powers far beyond what business would ordinarily tolerate. These are periods, then, in which state managers "can concentrate on responding to the popular pressure, while acting to expand their own power" (ibid., 25). It is for this reason "that such periods have seen the most dramatic qualitative growth in state activity and the most serious efforts to rationalize capitalism" (1980, 233). But when the war or the depression is over, and business activity returns, partly because of successful government intervention, to "normal" levels, the capitalists regain their former veto through the threat of a loss of business confidence. To avert such a loss in business confidence state managers are likely to repeal some of the more offensive reforms, but they will "also want to avoid the elimination of certain reforms important for the stabilization of the economy and the integration of the working class" (1977b, 26). Thus, a selection process takes place in which "reforms that are most beneficial for capitalism will be retained, while those whose effects are more questionable will be eliminated" (ibid.).

These, then, are the major "structural mechanisms" through which the state comes to play the central part in the process of self-rationalization of capitalism, according to Block. In addition he mentions some "subsidiary mechanisms," such as techniques by which capitalists can exert direct pressure on the state apparatus in the pursuit of their special interests, which tend to make governments more receptive to capitalist wishes generally, but these remain of secondary importance, "really more like the icing on the cake of class rule" (ibid., 14). A more important subsidiary mechanism is "bourgeois cultural hegemony," which consists of "widespread acceptance of certain unwritten rules" whose violation is likely to cost any government dearly in terms of popular support. This acts as "a powerful constraint in discouraging certain types of state action that might conflict with the interests of capital," Block claims (ibid., 14). However, the way in which such rules emerge and are made consistent with the interests of capital, and how they change over time are other matters which are "beyond the scope" of Block's present discussion (ibid.). That discussion was first of all intended to show how the interplay between capitalists who are exclusively interested in their balance sheets, workers who are engaged in a struggle to protect themselves "from the ravages of a market economy," and state managers who seek to maintain and expand their own power, results in the recurrent "use of the state in new ways to overcome economic contradictions and to facilitate the integration of the working class."[7]

There have been a few efforts to apply variants of the "class struggle" approach to empirical cases of policy formation and social reform. Skocpol (1980) compares "corporate liberalism," Poulantzas's structuralist "functionalism," and Block's "class struggle" approach as three alternative neo-Marxist explanations of the New Deal. After examining the historical evidence, she concludes that Block's model fares much better than either of the other two (199). However, she also notes that in its present formulation the "theory" is hardly more than "a general 'explanation sketch' " (185) identifying some of the factors likely to be necessary for an adequate explanation but without providing any clues as to the relative importance of, and interrelations between, those factors (185–86). Moreover, although a clear improvement over its neo-Marxist rivals, Block's "class struggle" approach still has not "arrived at the point of taking state structures and party organizations *seriously enough*" (199–200).

Using empirical data on five political campaigns concerning public transportation issues in California between 1962 and 1974, Whitt (1979a, b, 1982) attempts to demonstrate the superiority of the "class dialectic" model over alternative theories

7   For an argument fairly similar to Block's, but based on a detailed critique of Poulantzas's approach, see Bridges (1974, 171–73).

in making sense of the evidence. Whitt recommends his "class-dialectic" model as *both* a resolution to the longstanding theoretical stalemate between pluralists and elitists in American mainstream political science (1979b) *and* "a theoretical synthesis . . . based on the most powerful explanatory features of existing instrumentalist and structuralist models" (1979a, 59). It is interesting to note, in view of my argument in the preceding two chapters, that the pluralism of Dahl (1961) and the "structuralism" of Poulantzas and Offe on the one hand, and Millsean elitism (Mills 1956) and neo-Marxist instrumentalism on the other, turn out to be virtually interchangeable for the purposes of Whitt's argument (see Whitt 1979b, 84–85, n. 5). Thus, on one hand Whitt finds evidence of a high degree of unity and conscious coordination among corporate interests, even on potentially very divisive issues, in two of the five cases studied—the two cases with the greatest degree of business involvement in terms of campaign funding in fact (see 1979a, 54; 1979b, 86)—which contradicts the pluralist and structuralist claims that the capitalist class is usually divided and fragmented into conflicting interest groups. On the other hand, he finds that the proposals backed virtually unanimously by big business were actually defeated at the ballot box, which would appear to demonstrate that, "in contrast to the elite [instrumentalist] model, dominant classes do not always win each battle" (1979b, 96). This evidence suggests, Whitt concludes, "that the situation is more complex than either of these models would lead us to believe" (98).

Whitt's own "class dialectic" model, based on a "rejection of the assumption of capitalist class disunity—and equally of the opposite assumption of unvarying cohesion," is presumably better suited to deal with the complexities of the situation since it "would recognize the historical contingency of such factors as capitalist class cohesion, working class opposition, and accumulation crises" (1979a, 59). To begin with, the "class-dialectic model holds that political processes must be understood in terms of the institutional structure of society and in terms of the relation of social classes to each other" (1979b, 83). Institutions shape and restrain the behavior of classes, but classes, and especially the dominant class, also shape the social institutions

(84). More specifically, dominant-class control of the means of production gives that class "the ability to shape the more super-structural institutions of society, including the ability to carry out ideological hegemony . . . and generally to manipulate the societal context in which political contests are waged" (ibid.). As a result, the state generally "functions to serve the interests of the dominant class by preserving the bases of class hegemony" (ibid.). However, since "the degree of class-consciousness and extent of class political organization" constitute "resources for power" as well, power is also "potentially available to the sub-ordinate classes if they become sufficiently class-conscious and politically organized" (ibid.). Therefore, "the power of the dominant class is not absolute." Its power is further limited, moreover, to the extent that the dominant class's ability to act is impeded by intraclass conflict among capitalists themselves re-sulting from "disruptions" produced by "contradictions within the economic and class structure" (ibid.). As opposed to the elit-ist or instrumentalist model, then, this amounts to a *"dialectical* conception of power" (ibid.).

According to Whitt, this "class dialectical" model better ac-counts for the complexities of his empirical cases than either the pluralist or the power-elite model. The pluralist model, he concedes, "is fairly accurate as far as it goes" (ibid., 98), but "it does not dig deeply enough beneath the surface of events" (90). The elite model is already an improvement because it fits with the evidence of more or less successful, conscious attempts to coordinate and unify corporate interests, but it cannot account for the two defeats that those interests suffered nonetheless at the hands of a recalcitrant electorate (90–94, 98). The "class di-alectical" model, on the other hand, can account for such de-feats, according to Whitt, because it accepts the fact that "mass persuasion does not always work, just as structural contradic-tions cannot always be overcome" (96). Moreover, it "can see these political events in the context of the contradictions which the dominant class must face" (97). Among the "contradictions" uncovered by applying the "class dialectical" model to his evi-dence, Whitt includes

> (1) the market economy vs. the need for some planning, (2) the
> selling of transportation as a private good vs. the requirement for

public services, (3) the competition among cities and among capitalists for growth-generating developments vs. coherent structure and regularity in urban development, (4) the need to construct new urban transit systems vs. the budget crisis and occasional mass resistance, (5) the desire for class hegemony vs. the requirements of legitimacy and mass persuasion, and (6) the desire for class unity vs. the divisive tendencies of intracapitalist class differences and conflicts. (97–98)

Primarily because "the class-dialectic model sensitizes us . . . to . . . an appreciation of these six factors," Whitt finds it superior to the other theoretical approaches, which do "not envisage the complexity of the structural contradictions to which the dominant class must respond" and which do "not recognize the inherent dialectical nature of power" (98).

In Canada, Cuneo has attempted to explain the genesis of the Federal Unemployment Insurance plan by means of what he calls a "structuralist" approach (1979, 1980). This approach explains "the state's long-term implementation of capitalist class interests, not through a direct manipulation of the state by the capitalist class, but through the state's mediation of contradictions, rooted in a capitalist economy, between the working and capitalist classes" (1980, 37). Unlike the instrumentalist perspective, Cuneo asserts, this "structuralist" approach implies that "state action may occur in spite of substantial business opposition because militant working class pressure is also taken into account" (45). He then goes on to recount how the Canadian federal government was finally persuaded to opt for the contributory unemployment insurance scheme, which was backed by what appears to have been a majority of organized labor and a minority of business, against a backdrop of agitation for a noncontributory scheme by the more radical Workers' Unity League and solid opposition to *any* scheme from a large majority of business. This, according to Cuneo, constitutes evidence supporting his "structuralist" approach, as opposed to instrumentalism.[8] However, as he appears to be exclu-

8   Similarly, an examination of the genesis of the Social Security Act of 1935 in the United States purportedly confirms Poulantzas's theory that the "state mediates between various interest groups who have unequal access to power, negotiating compromises between class factions and incorporating

sively concerned with disproving instrumentalism, he does not make any distinction between the "structural" approaches of Poulantzas and Offe and the "class struggle" approach discussed in this chapter, and, in fact, he does not even appear to grasp the differences between them as he indiscriminately cites both types of arguments as his sources (1979, 148, n. 1; 1980, 61, n. 1). Since, like Poulantzas and Offe, Cuneo also totally fails to specify by what mechanism the state is so persistently compelled to pursue "the long-term implementation of capitalist class interests" in the midst of the "class contradictions" it is supposed to "mediate," in opposition *to* that capitalist class if necessary, it is not quite clear exactly *what* theory Cuneo believes is supported by his evidence.

Of the other attempts to apply some version of a "class struggle" approach to government policy (e.g., Devine 1985; Griffin, Devine, and Wallace 1981; Isaac and Kelly 1981; R. F. Levine 1981; Quadagno 1984; Swank 1981), Ian Gough's (1975, 1979) are perhaps worth separate mention as representative of the British "Neo-Ricardian" approach (see also, e.g., Glyn and Sutcliffe 1972). Gough seeks to explain the ups and downs of British public expenditures in general since World War II (1975) and of the welfare state in particular (1979) as the outcome of the interaction of two sets of factors: "the 'demands' of contemporary capitalism and the state of the class struggle" (1975, 73). Thus, he traces the steady rise in state expenditures from the early postwar settlement between capital and labor, through the prolonged economic boom of the fifties and sixties, to the period of "slumpflation" of the seventies, attributing it to long-term trends in British industry and the economy in general, attempts by the state to maintain an adequate profit level, and increasingly effective pressures from organized labor strengthened by a long period of near-full employment (71–92). The reason this sort of analysis is often labeled, somewhat dispar-

working-class demands into legislation on capitalist terms" (Quadagno 1984, 646). According to Skocpol and Amenta (1985, 572), however, Quadagno "vastly exaggerates big business's influence on framing" the legislation, as "virtually all politically active business leaders and organizations strongly opposed" it. Thus it is not entirely clear what "capitalist terms" were met in the Act.

agingly, "Neo-Ricardian" is that it is viewed as too heavily reliant on the "class struggle" as an unexplained *deus ex machina* and too narrowly concerned with distributive matters only. In fact, the critics argue, this approach is virtually indistinguishable from conventional bourgeois theories concerning wages, profits, and state expenditures, except for some "radical overtones" (Jessop 1977, 359; cf. Holloway and Picciotto 1977, 82–83; 1978, 10–12; E. O. Wright 1975, 24–26; 1978, 147–54).

This criticism of "Neo-Ricardianism" raises some uncomfortable questions about the "class struggle" approaches generally. One has only to examine briefly the kinds of empirical evidence presented in support of the "class struggle" theory to discover that virtually the same evidence could be used to corroborate the conventional liberal-reformist position outlined in Chapter 2. Indeed, what evidence have Skocpol, Cuneo, or Whitt uncovered that could *not* be easily accommodated by that "bourgeois" model? That government policies are usually the result of complex interactions between organized groups such as business, labor, consumer groups, and environmental groups; government officials; and electoral pressures? That governments generally try to find compromises that offend the various participating groups the least? That such compromises will tend to reflect the relative strengths of such groups in terms of their ability and willingness to cause serious problems for those governments? That, hence, (big) business is in a very strong position to extract favorable policies from governments? That, in "formally" democratic systems at least, the electorate or labor nevertheless *does* occasionally succeed in forcing its will on governments *even* in the face of united, well-organized, and well-financed business opposition? That "state managers" do not act as they do out of the sheer goodness of their hearts, but because it serves their own purposes, first among which is usually the retention of their public offices? Dahl, Lipset, and the other pluralists would be positively delighted with such evidence. It supports *their* "bourgeois" accounts of the functioning of pluralist democracy (or "polyarchy"; see, e.g., Dahl 1971b; Lindblom 1977) perfectly, and, indeed, such evidence has been routinely *used* to support that position (see, e.g., Hewitt 1974; Schmidt 1983).

Yet, this uncanny resemblance between their own and the pluralists' evidence seems to have entirely escaped the notice of the proponents of the "class struggle" approach. This may be because they simply have not taken the "bourgeois" alternative seriously enough to pay much critical attention to it—those who mention that alternative at all only reinforce this impression. Thus, Esping-Andersen, Friedland, and Wright briefly summarize what they take to be the "liberal perspective, long dominant in American social science" (1976, 186), and they even do so fairly accurately, but they do not bother to subject it to the type of criticism they apply to the other theories they mention. Similarly, Whitt, after first explicitly introducing the "pluralist" model as one of the alternative models to be tested, and showing its fit to the evidence to be rather close indeed, then proceeds to dismiss the model nevertheless, simply because it "does not dig deeply enough underneath the surface of events" (1979b, 90). In the wake of the proliferation of Marxist theories of the state in the past two decades Marxists apparently assume that "bourgeois" theories can now be confidently treated as obsolete.

This was already apparent among the "relative autonomy" theorists discussed in Chapters 4 and 5. They, too, seem to be totally oblivious of the fact that their description of empirical reality does not necessarily differ in the least from standard "bourgeois" accounts. However, the "class struggle" approach goes considerably further down the road of "embourgeoisement." While "relative autonomy" theory is *compatible with* empirical evidence generally thought to support the "bourgeois" position—albeit merely because it is compatible with *any* empirical evidence whatsoever—the "class struggle" approach specifically *calls* for just such evidence. Whitt and Esping-Andersen seem to be dimly aware that there might be something of a problem here. After showing the pluralist model to be "a plausible argument" (Whitt 1979b, 90) and "fairly accurate as far as it goes" (98), Whitt may dismiss the model out of hand, but he *does* devote the greater part of his efforts to showing the superiority of his "class dialectic" model in probing deeply beneath the surface of events to uncover the "contradictions" that escape the attention of pluralists (95–98). In a footnote, Esping-

Andersen, Friedland, and Wright have this to say about the difference between their "political class struggle" approach and pluralism: "The general approach we have outlined allows us to understand how politics in advanced capitalist states has appeared pluralist despite the reality of capitalist domination of the state. Pluralism, as the phenomenal form of political conflict in capitalist societies, can be understood as one manifestation of the political neutralization of the working class. The empirical data of pluralist theory are thus saved, but raised to a higher analytic level" (1976, 217, n. 12).

Yet it is precisely in raising the empirical data of pluralist theory to "a higher analytic level" that the contributions of the various "class struggle" approaches become somewhat elusive. To put it bluntly, these "class struggle" approaches are not only empirically virtually identical to plain "bourgeois" pluralism, they are equally indistinguishable in their *theoretical* arguments, aside from radical-sounding terminology. The "bourgeois reformist" argument, it is worth recalling, was that government policy is the resultant of competing pressures from various organized interests, which include, of course, corporate interests and organizations representing working-class constituencies (unions, labor parties). There are, clearly, vast differences in the resources various groups and potential groups have at their disposal for effectively organizing themselves into interests with political clout; in this respect corporate interests possess by far the greatest organizational resources of any of the groups that might or do participate in the political arena, including organized labor; however, in formally democratic polities the nonprivileged majority has one crucial resource, universal suffrage; through its ability to elect a new government, the majority can in principle, and occasionally does in practice when it is sufficiently united and determined, impose its will even over united opposition from corporate interests; thus, in principle at least, the majority may use its formal democratic power to counter and gradually reduce the power of the privileged minority.[9]

9   This is obviously a relatively sophisticated and liberal version of the "pluralist" position, but it is certainly not far from the arguments of some of the major figures associated with that label (see, e.g., Dahl 1956, 1970, 1971a, b, 1982; Dahl and Lindblom 1953; Lindblom 1977; Lipset 1960; Turner

It is not clear how the Marxist "class struggle" approach raises this argument to "a higher analytic level." In fact, it is not clear in what respect the "class struggle" theory differs at all from the theory just outlined or that it has anything particularly Marxist to add to this rather "bourgeois" perspective, other than the militant-sounding terminology of "class struggle." If it is to be taken seriously, that is, if government policy is to be viewed as genuinely contingent upon a "struggle" between competing groups that is neither so lopsided that one group invariably wins out, as "instrumentalists" claim, nor so "structurally" rigged as invariably to yield outcomes favorable to the long-term interests of one group even when it ostensibly does *not* win out, as "relative autonomy" theorists argue, then it is hard to maintain that "the state in capitalist society broadly serves the interests of the capitalist class" (Gold, Lo, and Wright 1975a, 31). Yet, this is the "fundamental observation" (ibid.) that has always been the hallmark of the distinctly *Marxist* theory of politics and the state in capitalist society. If there are indeed cases in which governments pursue policies strongly opposed by the corporate world because of effective pressures from other quarters, and if such policies are not somehow "structurally" guaranteed to serve long-term capitalist interests anyway, then these must be genuine instances of the state acting *against* the interests of capital and *in favor of* the interests of the aforementioned other quarters. In other words, the class character of the state is a matter of degree, just as "bourgeois" pluralists would have it (see, e.g., Dahl 1958, 464–66; 1963, 53–54; 1971a, 33–34). This would also seem to imply that, given a sufficient degree of unity of purpose and organization ("consciousness"),

---

1986; cf. van den Berg 1981, 50–69). Moreover, it is compatible with Esping-Andersen, Friedland, and Wright's description of pluralism as a doctrine that views "the state as a pluralist, aggregating mechanism in which agencies, programs and legislation are substantive responses to the demands and interests of competing groups" (1976, 187). At any rate, no useful purpose other than reinforcing one's own prejudices is served by setting up implausible theories as straw-men alternatives to one's own—in this case the more complacent and conservative versions of pluralism—as Whitt sometimes appears to do (1979b, 82–83; also Carnoy 1984, 33–43). It should be clear, finally, that my following argument about the indistinguishability of the "class struggle" from "pluralist" theories is wholly independent of my (or anyone else's) assessment of the latter's merits or flaws.

the working class can compel the state regularly, and perhaps cumulatively, to cater to *its* interests (cf. Kesselman 1983, 834). Formulated in this way, the differences between the "class struggle" theory and reformist pluralism become rather elusive indeed.[10] Besides some minor differences of emphasis, in fact, there is no clear difference at all.[11]

Yet the "class struggle" theorists themselves have been reluctant to draw such disturbing conclusions from their own theoretical premises. On the contrary, none of them abandons the orthodox doctrine that the state *does* serve the interests of the capitalist class after all, even while insisting its actions reflect a struggle *between* the capitalist and the working classes, the outcome of which is by no means predetermined. The resulting theoretical inconsistency manifests itself in the fact that whenever these theorists choose to reassert the old orthodoxy they are forced to abandon their own "class struggle" principles in favor of either the instrumentalist or the structuralist accounts they had previously rejected.

I have made this point already with respect to Poulantzas's somewhat half-hearted conversion to the "class struggle" model. Although Poulantzas seems to have drifted toward a

---

10   This has not been lost on the authors who seek some support for a reformist position in the recent Marxist literature. Both Korpi (1983, 19, 245, n. 20) and Stephens (1979, 215, n. 5) invoke Esping-Andersen, Friedland, and Wright (1976) as evidence for the Marxist pedigree of their own approaches. As Miller (1984, 152–57) rightly notes, although the conservative, complacent pluralism of the 1950s has long been *passé*, a more subtle version is today even more widespread as an unstated assumption.

11   Two differences in particular are more apparent than real. The fact that the "class struggle" approach seems to be concerned exclusively with classes, rather than organized interest groups of all kinds, does not render it incompatible with pluralism, only more narrow in focus. Besides, some have, like Whitt—and wisely, it seems—in practice broadened the focus to include a variety of "popular-democratic" struggles (Jessop 1977, 370; cf. Mizruchi 1983, 647). Second, as noted before (see note 4, this chapter), there is much talk about the state and its "internal structures" as determinants in their own right, but the commitment to this view appears to be mostly rhetorical. In practice, none of the authors discussed here pays much attention to this aspect, nor would that be a particularly Marxist contribution to make. As Pal (1986) shows in a criticism of Cunco's (1979, 1980) "class reductionism," when one broadens the approach to incorporate the "internal dynamics of state action," one quickly ends up with an approach that is not recognizably Marxist anymore (see also Palmer 1985).

rather reformist position, whenever he is faced with the uncomfortably "bourgeois" implications of his new arguments he retreats to the old orthodox structuralist formulas again. The state may have become the "condensate of a relation of power between struggling classes" (Poulantzas 1975, 74), but it still serves "the general, long-term political interests of the power bloc" (1978, 134) since it remains a "fissiparous *unity*" (136), as exclusive class domination remains *"inscribed in the institutional materiality and organizational framework of the state apparatus"* (189). But in this way the "primacy" of the class struggle over the "apparatuses" is of little consequence, of course (cf. Jessop 1980a, 115–16, 119–23).

Similarly, in a discussion of the notion of the relative autonomy of the state which they think "needs further theoretical development," Gold, Lo, and Wright (1975b, 47), go so far as to suggest the possibility that the state might "develop a much greater degree of autonomy than is understood by the conventional Marxist notion of 'relative autonomy,' " but they hasten to add that "there is no implication that the capitalist state can ever be emancipated from the constraints of a capitalist social formation" (48). Whether these "constraints" are primarily of an "instrumental" or of a "structural" kind is hard to say since Gold et al., although they wish to salvage unspecified elements of both approaches in an unspecified synthesis of some sort (46), do not elaborate any further. But if the state is subject to such crucial constraints, whatever their origins, one is forced to wonder what difference the "class struggle" can still make in "shaping" that state, as Gold et al. *also* claim. If that "shaping" takes place only within the limits imposed on the state by "the constraints of a capitalist social formation," then this whole "class struggle" argument boils down to little more than a footnote to a broader (instrumentalist? structuralist? not yet developed?) theory of the capitalist state, a theory that explains the origins and operation of those "constraints."

Esping-Andersen, Friedland, and Wright repeatedly insist that "political challenge by the working class shapes the historical development of state structure," that the "actual structures of the state are thus not a simple reflection of capitalist interests, but a contradictory reflection of the class struggle between workers and capitalists" (1976, 192), that "the instrumental domination of the capitalist class is constrained" by past, current, and future class struggles (198), and so on. Yet, at the same time they appear to have few doubts that the "state structure reproduces capitalist political domination," albeit in "contradictory ways" (197). How exactly the "state structure" manages to convert the input of a "political class struggle" into an output that "reproduces capitalist political domination" is, however, not entirely clear. Esping-Andersen et al. provide only a few clues. Thus, they argue that when "successfully shaped by the capitalist class" the structures of the state "accomplish two critical tasks: a) they limit state interventions within bounds compatible with the imperatives of capital accumulation; b) they politically neutralize the working class in the sense of making its political demands congruent with the reproduction of capitalist social relations" (198). Yet they also insist that the process is "inevitably contradictory," since "the working class can never be perfectly incorporated, totally neutralized" (ibid.). Elsewhere, they describe the class struggle as a struggle between the capitalist class seeking to limit the content of class conflict to demands compatible with its dominance and the working class pushing toward demands of an "unreproductive" nature, although they admit that "movement toward this revolutionary pole has often been thwarted, and in periods of relatively uncontested capitalist hegemony, may remain only a latent possibility" (207). In addition, they briefly discuss three "historical examples of neutralization of politically organized and challenging segments of the working class through state structural change" (192), all of which seem to revolve around farsighted, well-organized actions on the part of the capitalist class (192–97).

Although it is far from clear in what "contradictory ways" capitalist political domination is "reproduced" and what exactly a "contradictory reflection of the class struggle" might look like, it *is* fairly obvious *why*, according to Esping-Andersen, Friedland, and Wright, the state reproduces the political domination of the capitalist class to the extent that it does: the state does so because, and to the extent that, it is "successfully shaped by the capitalist class." Moreover, the state clearly does so to a very large extent since otherwise it would not make much sense to call the state's tasks "critical" in this connection. Furthermore, the capitalist class also seems to have been rather spectacularly successful at "thwarting" any movements toward the "revolutionary pole" on the part of the working class, as the kinds of demands Esping-Andersen et al. consider to be "unreproductive" have not exactly been prominent in the "class struggles" of the recent or even distant past (see, e.g., Bauman 1983; Calhoun 1982; B. Moore 1978). Clearly we have come full circle to a straightforwardly instrumentalist explanation of why the state serves the interests of the capitalist class. But if the net effect of the "political struggles of the working class" is virtually nil, as is clearly, albeit implicitly, suggested here, in what sense can Esping-Andersen et al. still claim to have raised it to an "analytical importance absent from the 'instrumental corporate liberal' and 'structuralist' approaches" (1976, 197)? To the extent that they retain the Marxist doctrine that the state serves the interests of the capitalist class, they obviously rely just as much "on observable class input into, and control of, policy formation" as they accuse the "instrumentalist" approach of doing (189). To the extent that they explore the implications of their own theoretical stance at all, and are thus forced to depart from orthodox doctrine, they do so only in terms of the vaguest generalities possible, alluding to "contradictory" processes and "reflections" without ever clarifying such terms. This hardly adds up to a theoretical advance on the approaches they criticize.

Of the theorists discussed in this chapter, Block offers by far the most intricate and curious blend of pluralist theory and Marxist doctrine. To begin with the former, Block's attempt to explain the sources of social reform and of the long-term tendency of government intervention in the economy to expand, brief as it is, could have been taken almost verbatim from any standard pluralist text on "democratic government." Social reform and growing government regulation, Block argues, are the result of a combination of "class struggle" by the working class and the inherent interest of state managers in the expansion of their powers. This may sound slightly leftish, but by "class struggle" Block does not appear to have anything more

subversive in mind than plain electoral politics, and the reference to the interests of state managers is more likely to offend
the sensibilities of a Marxist than those of a mainstream (let
alone conservative) pluralist, of course. Moreover, Block goes
on to argue, governments will seek to implement reform and
impose regulation in such a way as to upset "business confidence" no more than absolutely necessary to satisfy the demands of labor or the electorate. Such behavior on the part of
formally democratic governments may be a constant source of
amazement for Marxists, but to a pluralist nothing could be
more obvious: governments will not ordinarily seek to antagonize powerful interests just for the fun of it.

But Block insists that reform and expansion of the state,
whatever their origins and initial purpose, do end up serving
"the interests of the capitalist class" in the long run because they
serve to "rationalize capitalism" by using "the state in new ways
to overcome economic contradictions and to facilitate the integration of the working class" (1977b, 15, 10, 7n). This is the
result, Block argues, of certain "structural mechanisms" that
characterize "the structural relationships among state managers, capitalists, and workers" (15, 12). But once again, on
closer examination these "structural mechanisms" take on an
uncanny resemblance to what pluralists would simply refer to
as the ordinary politics of "pluralist democracy." Government
policies end up rationalizing capitalism, according to Block, essentially because policies that don't will undermine "business
confidence" which is not in the interest of state managers. But
why is it not in the interest of state managers? Primarily because
the electorate at large will not put up with the consequences of
a loss of "business confidence," and state managers depend on
the support of the electorate for their very jobs.[12] Thus, Block's
"Marxist" argument turns out to be that the state does not upset

12   The other reason Block mentions is that the state managers are dependent
on a "healthy" economy as a source of public revenues. This would seem to
be of secondary importance, however, since there are other ways for states
to raise revenue, at least in the short term, and no amount of public revenue can compensate for the loss of public office. Moreover, as I have argued in the previous chapter in connection with similar assertions by Offe,
this hardly provides the state managers with an adequate motivation to wish
to "rationalize" a specifically *capitalist* economy (see pp. 389–90).

"business confidence" because the electorate does not want it to and because state managers have no choice but to comply with the wishes of the electorate if they are to stay in office. Not even the most complacent of "bourgeois" pluralists could possibly disagree with such an argument.

If only Block had paid a little more attention to the *political* mechanisms on which his argument relies so heavily, rather than taking them virtually for granted, he would have quickly realized how indistinguishable his argument is from liberal pluralism. The core of the liberal pluralist argument is, after all, that in formally democratic polities the vote constitutes a crucial resource through which the otherwise nonprivileged majority can make its preferences count. Now, according to Block's hypothetical scenario, the reason any attempts by left-wing governments at "serious" reform invariably end in retreat or defeat is *not* because capitalists have some way of sabotaging such attempts directly, *nor* because there is some invisible "structural" force holding the state in check, but simply because no electorate has thus far been willing to take the risk of economic chaos for the sake of achieving an uncertain "socialism" (see ibid., 17–19). This may well result from the reformist leaders' failure to prepare their electoral supporters properly (19) (although one may wonder why they would make such a fateful mistake more than once), or it may be an example of "bourgeois cultural hegemony" (14), but those are separate issues, which Block is not prepared to discuss in this context at any rate. The main point here is that if it is indeed primarily the electorate's insistence on maintaining a "healthy" economy that makes governments reluctant to upset "business confidence," then the implication clearly is that if the electorate *were* willing to pay the price, governments might well have to *ignore* "business confidence," "regardless of their own ideology" (15), which is, of course, precisely what liberal pluralists have been saying all along.

But even if one were to ignore this rather oddly pluralist "refutation" of reformism, the rest of his argument—and here we switch to the apparently more "Marxist" part—as to how and why reform turns into "rationalization" is not much more satisfactory. Because the strength of the economy depends on "business confidence," that is, the expectations of business concerning the likely profitability of current investments, Block argues, "capitalists, in their collective role as investors, have a veto over state policies" (ibid.). As a result it is likely that "such policies will be in the general interest of capital" (ibid.).[13] Similarly, when capitalists finally regain their collective veto power after "exceptional periods," governments will repeal those reforms most harmful to "business confidence" so that only "reforms that are most beneficial for capitalism will be retained" (26).

Such statements have a strangely "instrumentalist" ring to them. The term "business confidence" here simply seems to have taken the place of "farsighted class consciousness" in instrumentalist accounts, but otherwise the two theories are identical: the main deterrent to "fundamental" reform is the collective wrath of the capitalist class which knows exactly which reforms will end up "rationalizing" the system and which are simply too dangerous to be tolerated (cf. Hammond 1978). Block categorically rejects such an interpretation, however, insisting that "there is a huge difference between awareness of common interests, or even willingness to act on those interests, and a fully developed strategic class consciousness" (1978a, 213). But either "business confidence" includes a rather accurate sense of what will and what will not end up "rationalizing" capitalism in the long run, in which case it is indeed synonymous with the "fully developed strategic class consciousness" attributed to the capitalist class by instrumentalist theories, *or* it does not, in which case Block *still* has to explain why policies that maintain "business confidence" also happen to end up "rationalizing" capitalism. To attribute the coincidence to some sort of fluke is hardly satisfactory, and to attribute it to the foresight of state managers, as Block sometimes appears to do (see also Krieger and Held 1978, 194–95), would seem to contradict the rest of his theory or at least render it superfluous.

Finally, it is not even clear from his own argument that what Block calls "rationalization" of capitalism is necessarily in the "general interest of the capitalist class" at all. When business

13   I am skipping an intermediate step in the argument here in which Block (1977b, 15) appears to be attributing a "broader perspective" to state managers than to capitalists, which simply contradicts his other statements (23, 25–26). For a critique of these inconsistencies, see Skocpol (1980, 189–91).

regains its veto power after exceptional periods of dramatic reform made possible by the temporary weakening of that veto
power, Block maintains, governments will repeal those reforms
that are most strongly opposed by the capitalist class, but they
will "also want to avoid the elimination of certain reforms important for the stabilization of the economy and the integration
of the working class" (1977b, 26). But there is nothing within
the theory that suggests that measures necessary to stabilize the
economy (other than those necessary to bolster "business confidence") and to integrate the working class are necessarily in the
interest of the capitalist class or "beneficial to capitalism" (ibid.).
Such measures might well necessitate a gradual but drastic curtailment of the rights and privileges of capitalists, as reformists
have always argued. Block seems to be aware of the problem,
and he has subsequently come to argue that because of the continuing expansion of state control over the economy a "tipping
point" may eventually be reached beyond which governmental
control is so pervasive as to suspend the capitalists' power to
determine the level of investment unilaterally (1978a, 218–19;
1980, 234–36). Moreover, he claims, this "tipping point" may
well be imminent since "only another quantum leap in the extent of state intervention . . . will produce the conditions under
which a new period of capitalist accumulation can take place"
(1978a, 219; 1980, 238–39). But Block has by no means suddenly capitulated to a naive reformism. Rather, he warns, the
more likely result of such a fusion of economic and political
power in the hands of state managers is a highly centralized
authoritarianism, as there would be no more independent interests strong enough to oppose the state (1980, 236).

This is quite remarkable, not only because the claim that another "quantum leap" in state intervention is "necessary" for
economic recovery already sounds quaintly outdated after a few
years of Reaganism and Thatcherism, but even more so because it suggests Block has become a pluralist *pur sang*. For it is
precisely the pluralists' implicit fears that excessive concentration of economic and political power is more likely to lead to
authoritarianism than to "socialism" that most deeply divides
pluralists and Marxists (for an extended argument to this effect, see van den Berg 1981, ch. 5)! Clearly, Block continually

wavers between a vague "instrumentalism" and plain "bourgeois" pluralism, with the latter rather more prevalent. He may
have set out "to construct a critique of socialist *reformism* that is
far more powerful than the critiques derived from the instrumentalist tradition" (1977b, 12, emphasis added), but the most
he ends up with, after a great deal of incoherence and obscurity, appears to be an implicit critique of *socialist* reformism!

Whitt's "class struggle" approach suffers from a similar form
of theoretical instability. As noted, he concedes that his data appear to support the pluralist model fairly well but then goes on
to dismiss it nonetheless because it "does not dig deeply enough
underneath the surface of events." The implications and merits
of his own "class dialectic" model, which presumably *does* dig
deeply enough, are not entirely clear, however. On the one
hand it apparently holds that the capitalist class, by virtue of its
control over the means of production, has "the ability to shape
the more superstructural institutions of society, including the
ability to carry out ideological hegemony . . . and generally to
manipulate the societal context in which political contests are
waged," which explains why the "state functions to serve the
interests of the dominant class by preserving the bases of class
hegemony" (1979b, 84). But this sounds like plain instrumentalism of the most orthodox kind, of course. The only problem
is that in two out of Whitt's five test cases the dominant class's
"ability to carry out ideological hegemony" was not exactly evident as proposals that were heavily and virtually unanimously
backed by big corporate money, without much evidence of a
well-organized opposition, met with defeat at the ballot box
nonetheless. This prompts Whitt to observe that "dominant
classes do not always win each battle," apparently because "mass
persuasion does not always work, just as structural contradictions cannot always be overcome" (96).

The reason for this is that power is also "potentially available
to the subordinate classes if they become sufficiently class-conscious and politically organized" (ibid., 84), as well as the fact
that capitalists have to cope with intraclass conflict and various
"disruptions" resulting from "contradictions within the economic and class structure" (ibid.). But this is of course precisely
what a "bourgeois" pluralist would argue, albeit in slightly dif-

ferent language, and, moreover, it clearly contradicts the preceding apparently instrumentalist claims about the ability of the
capitalist class "to shape the more superstructural institutions of
society." But in this way all possible bases are certainly effectively covered: the "class dialectical" model predicts that the
capitalist class wins all political contests, except when it does
not. This is in fact precisely what the empirical hypotheses
Whitt derives from his model predict.[14]

With such a "theory" one cannot go wrong, of course, no
matter *what* the evidence may show. But this hardly demonstrates its superiority, nor does it refute the validity of its competitors.[15] Whitt appears to be vaguely aware of this for instead
of systematically discussing his evidence in the light of the hypotheses presumably derived from the "class dialectical" theory,
as he does with respect to the other two models, he embarks on
a rambling discussion of all the varied "contradictions" the
dominant classes encounter in their efforts to "manipulate the
societal contexts" of transportation politics in California. I have
already quoted the list of six "contradictions" that concludes
this discussion, which the "class-dialectic" model apparently

14   These hypotheses are as follows: "If the class-dialectic model is correct, the
      study of an important political issue should reveal (1) biases of social insti-
      tutions that favor outcomes beneficial to dominant classes; (2) evidence of
      latent class conflict (divergent interests) or observable class conflict over the
      issue, perhaps including intraclass conflict among the dominant class, but
      accompanied by attempts to achieve class unity and cohesion; (3) political
      alliances and stability of power relations that are historically contingent, re-
      flecting the need to respond to inter-and intraclass conflicts and structural
      crisis; and (4) outcomes that usually favor dominant class interest, but may
      also reflect the power of opposing classes and the limitations imposed by
      structural contradictions" (Whitt 1979b, 85). Point 4 is particularly notewor-
      thy in this context, but given Whitt's rather loose definition of "class" (see
      Mizruchi 1983, 647), they are all marvels of inclusiveness.
15   Whitt seems to think that the fact that in three of the five cases he studied
      the business-backed alternative prevailed constitutes disproof of the plural-
      ist model (1979b, 90). He provides little evidence of any opposition to these
      business-backed options, though, and, as Dahl pointed out long ago, victo-
      ries without much opposition are hardly proof of great power, unless of
      course these are examples of complete "ideological hegemony" in which
      case, however, ruler and ruled become somewhat difficult to distinguish
      from one another (1958, 468–69), and then one would like some explana-
      tion of why this hegemony was suddenly so completely absent in Whitt's
      other two cases.

helps us uncover and "appreciate." The most charitable thing that can be said about it is that it lists a rather incongruous set of what can at best be described as *possible* "issues" or "problems," the meaning of which or the connections between which are not entirely obvious.

I trust I do not have to elaborate the point further: the "class struggle" approach is not, in fact, a real Marxist alternative to the existing "instrumentalist" and "relative autonomy" theories. In their search for a more dynamic, historically contingent theoretical alternative to the excessively abstract formulations and static implications of he recently emerged "relative autonomy" orthodoxy, these "class struggle" theorists have inadvertently produced almost perfect replicas of the old, mainstream "bourgeois" pluralism.[16] The fact that none of them has noticed this rather uncomfortable similarity suggests that the flood of literature on "the Marxist theory of the state" since the late 1960s may have done little more than serve as an excuse for ignoring everything that was written on the topic, before that time or since, by non-Marxists.[17] But whenever these theorists are confronted with the rather un-Marxist implications of their approach they quickly retreat into the old security of the alternative Marxist theories they had criticized at the outset. That this kind of theoretical impasse should be the end result is not so surprising, however, for these "class struggle" theorists seem to wish to accomplish the unaccomplishable: they wish to have a theory that allows for change and historical contingency, *yet* they also want theoretical guarantees concerning the class character of the capitalist state. Obviously they cannot have it both ways (see also Balbus 1982, 104–9; Koch 1980; Potter 1981).[18]

16   Even Lipset, who is perhaps the greatest of the old pluralist villains for having somewhat prematurely declared that in Western democratic countries "the fundamental political problems . . . have been solved" (1960, 442), explicitly discusses elections as "the expression of the democratic class struggle" (ibid., ch. 7).

17   Had they bothered to take note of some earlier literature, they might have noticed the virtual identity between their formulations and what Paul Sweezy criticized as the "class-mediation conception of the state" propounded by "modern liberal theorists" more than forty years ago (1942, 240–42).

18   It is rather interesting to note that in the early seventies a widely publicized debate took place among Marxist theorists in West Germany concerning the

There remains, finally, one more point worth making about these somewhat abortive attempts to revive the dynamic element in the Marxist theory of the state. "Class struggle" theorists may have inadvertently replicated bourgeois theory almost to perfection, but there is one revealing respect in which they still remain, even at their most "pluralistic," distinct from their bourgeois counterparts and closer to their fellow Marxists. As we have seen, they are essentially forced to agree with "bourgeois" pluralists that governments in capitalist countries have generally not sought to overthrow the capitalist system and replace it by socialism primarily because, thus far, no electorate has ever demanded such a thing. But, whereas this fact is taken as unproblematic by pluralists, it remains in need of special explanation to the "class struggle" theorists. Thus, even though they are well aware that this movement has in fact rarely if ever really occurred, Esping-Andersen, Friedland, and Wright continue to treat the "revolutionary pole" as the one to which the working class would "naturally" gravitate if it weren't for "capitalist hegemony" constantly "thwarting" that movement, since they remain firmly convinced that the working class "naturally moves toward political struggle for socialism" (1976, 206). Similarly, Block blames the electorate's repeated reluctance to support radical measures that endanger economic prosperity in the short run in the name of a "socialism" to be achieved in the long run, on reformist politicians' neglect to prepare their supporters properly for an all-out battle with capital and (probably) on

"true" nature of the capitalist state, known as the "state-derivation debate" (*Staatsableitungsdebatte*) which followed an almost identical trajectory as the one depicted here: from rejections of "instrumentalism" to "functionalist" formulations of an obscurity and abstractness as to make Poulantzas look like a model of Anglo-Saxon simplicity, to calls for a more "dynamic," "historically contingent" approach taking the "class struggle" into account, to, finally, the exact same wavering impasse the "class struggle" theorists discussed here have managed to create for themselves (see Gerstenberger 1976, 1978; Holloway and Picciotto, eds. 1978; Jessop 1977, 364–67; 1982, ch. 3; Offe 1984a, 261–62). The similarities are really too strong to be coincidental! In fact, Poulantzas's "conversion" to the "class struggle" approach may have been inspired in part by his reading of the German debate, as his highly favorable references to it suggest (see, e.g., Poulantzas 1975, 169–70, 173; 1976, 75–76, 81; 1978, 135). Debates concerning the "dependent" (i.e., Third World) state seem to have followed a similar path as well (see Carnoy 1984, ch. 7).

the strength of "bourgeois cultural hegemony." The meaning or purpose of Whitt's list of "contradictions" may not be perfectly clear, finally, but one thing *is* clear, and that is that he assumes that there are certain "obvious" social needs whose satisfaction is thwarted by the dominant classes with their ability, however limited by "contradictions," to "carry out ideological hegemony" and what not. What all this shows is that even the "class struggle" theorists, for all their similarity to pluralism, share what appears to be the one domain assumption common to all Marxist theories: *that there is a cause called "socialism" to which the workers' objective position in capitalist society naturally compels them to rally*, banning exceptional circumstances which may temporarily distract their attention from this "natural" cause of theirs. The fact that these "exceptional circumstances" have obtained almost without interruption for the past century and a half or more does not appear to have shaken the basic domain assumption at all. As I have argued before, this "immanentism", that is, the assumption that the workers' natural proclivity toward "socialism" results exclusively from their objective position in the *present* capitalist system and *not at all* from any appealing but necessarily fanciful depictions of the *future* socialist utopia, may have spared Marxists the unpleasantness of having to reexamine that domain assumption. The absence of any serious questioning about the exact nature and feasibility of "socialism"—indeed the explicit *prohibition* of such questioning—has enabled them to take for granted *precisely* what non-Marxists find highly implausible: that the "revolutionary pole" has anything worthwhile to offer to workers and other noncapitalists.

7 Conclusion:
From the Marxist Theory
of the State
to the State of Marxist Theory

> We do not know whether democratic socialism would be a
> system in which resources would be rationally allocated to
> satisfy human needs. I will go as far as to say that we do not
> know whether any form of social organization can rationally
> allocate resources to satisfy needs. Certainly, we do not have
> a blueprint for one. We do not even know whether a society
> in which all institutions—including the economic ones—were
> democratic would be necessarily a society free of inequalities,
> privileges and prejudices. (Przeworski 1981, 48)

In the preceding chapters I have considered the different theoretical approaches mostly in isolation. I have discussed some
of the debates that have taken place between the proponents of
the various perspectives, particularly the objections that have
been raised against the now virtually defunct "instrumentalist"
theory of the state,[1] but I have had few occasions to compare
the perspectives to one another in order to establish broad differences, similarities, and trends. I have had even fewer occasions to comment on the nature of Marxist theorizing in general, although there are fairly obvious indications as to what
some of these comments would be in some of the preceding
chapters (especially Chapters 1, 2, and 5). This chapter is intended to draw such more general conclusions about the Marxist theory of the state and from this to arrive at a more systematic perspective on the state of Marxism in general.

First, let me briefly comment on the significance and representativeness of the theories I have examined. In a tradition as
racked by dispute and division and as preoccupied with sectar-
ian concerns and schisms as Marxism is, a would-be critic is always open to the charge of using some weak point, tradition, or
debate of Marxism as a straw man for Marxism in general and
ignoring the other infinitely stronger points, traditions, or

1   As noted in Chapter 3, G. William Domhoff remains a major but somewhat
     lonely defender of "instrumentalism" although even he does not wish to be
     identified by that now clearly abusive label (see Domhoff 1976).

whatever, which tend to include or even be coextensive with the objector's own preferred point or tradition, of course. With respect to the issues and theories I have discussed I think such charges would be quite unjustified, however, although I have few illusions as to my ability to preempt them here. The theory of the state and of the superstructure in general may have been the traditional weak spot of "historical materialism" in the past, but since the late 1960s the theory of the state has been the area in which Marxist theorists have been far and away the most active and productive (in a purely quantitative sense, that is). Surely, after such a period of feverish activity and debate it must have ceased to be one of Marxism's "weak spots"! But even if it had not, this too would be highly significant for the general state of Marxist theorizing. As for the representativeness of the arguments I have included in my review, I have certainly dealt with *all* the most widely discussed approaches that have determined the character of the recent debates. Moreover, as for those few whose disciples may be expected to raise objections on this score,[2] the arguments that follow would not, I believe, be affected in any way whatsoever by considering any other purportedly Marxist theories or theorists of the state. On the contrary, I believe that my argument and conclusions could be replicated quite closely in an analysis of recent debates in areas of more traditional Marxist concern such as Marxist economic theory and class theory, as I have already noted in the introduction.

The arguments in this chapter are divided into three sections,

2   My relative neglect of Gramsci, Trotsky, and a group of German theorists associated with the so-called state-derivation debate of the early 1970s, and sometimes referred to as the "capital logic" school, is bound to provoke criticisms of the representativeness of my "sample." As for the first two, I have tried to justify my summary treatment of both of them, despite their near-sainthood in some circles, in Chapter 2. Gramsci's appeal has widened enormously in recent years, it is true, but, as I have argued, more for reasons of his convenient ambiguities and resonance with the current ambivalence about "reformism" among Marxists than for his compelling contributions to the Marxist theory of the state. Moreover, his introduction of a strong normative, superstructural element into Marxist theory (cf. Alexander 1982b, 354-57) closely parallels similar tendencies discussed in Chapter 5 and would, hence, not noticably affect my general argument. For the "state derivation" debate, see my remarks in note 18, Chapter 6 (also, Holloway and Picciotto, eds. 1978; Jessop 1982, ch. 3).

each of which deals with more or less distinct sets of questions. In the first of these sections ("Marxism: Creeping Embourgeoisment") I compare the Marxist theories of the state, especially the recent variants, to their "bourgeois," particularly their "reformist" counterparts. How do these Marxist theories measure up to their "bourgeois" rivals in terms of explanatory power, coherence, and empirical verifiability? Are there any signs of convergence or divergence between the two traditions? In the next section ("Marx and the Marxist Theory of the State: Some Continuities") I try to assess whether all this theoretical activity has produced a Marxist theory of the state more coherent and systematic than the few fragmentary remarks to be found in the Marxist "classics" discussed in Chapters 1 and 2. Do the current theories constitute an advance upon the "classics," and if so, in what respect? Are there, conversely, any noteworthy continuities between Marx's own remarks on the state and the recent contributions? This naturally leads into the question I try to answer in the final section ("Marxism: The 'Immanentist' Core"): given the enormous proliferation of "Marxisms," all heavily borrowing from various "bourgeois" disciplines, what, if anything, do they still have in common? Is there some common core of propositions or presuppositions that still characterizes a theory as distinctively Marxist? In other words, does Marxism still constitute a distinct, more or less coherent body of thought? My answer to this question and some of its implications are explored in this final section. But before embarking on my concluding remarks, I first, in the following section, summarize the arguments of the preceding chapters, which constitutes the material on which my conclusions are, after all, based.

Marxist Theories of the State: A Summary

Any study that claims to be an assessment of the current state of Marxist theorizing on capitalist politics and the state and even of Marxist theorizing in general, must, naturally, begin with an examination of Marx's own writings on bourgeois politics if only to provide a baseline against which the great advances—or lack thereof—made by later Marxist theorists can be measured.[3] This was my major purpose in Chapter 1. In the first section of that chapter ("Marx and Engels on the State") I analyzed Marx and Engels's major writings on politics and the state in order to determine whether they contained any consistent and coherent theory of the state at all. I reached two major conclusions from this analysis. First, I concluded that the only fairly coherent theory of the state that can reasonably be attributed to Marx and Engels is what I have called the "simple class theory." According to this "simple class theory," the state is "nothing but" a purely repressive agency created and employed by the dominant class for the purpose of forcibly suppressing the dominated class. By implication, the state will "wither away" with the abolition of class society since without classes there will be no further need for a special agency of class repression. It is true that hints of a more complex perspective on the state are scattered through the writings of Marx and Engels, particularly in their political commentaries on developments in France and in Engels's brief speculations about the origins of the state, but, I have argued, it is plainly impossible to reconcile them with the "simple class theory" evident in their more general and more frequent remarks on the state to produce some overall coherent approach. A brief examination of Marx and Engels's apparently unproblematic conviction that after a transitional period of a "dictatorship of the proletariat" to root out the remnants of class society, the state would simply "wither away" by itself confirms my interpretation, since that conviction clearly rests on the assumption that the *only raison d'être* of the state is the existence of class division, the abolition of which will, therefore, also automatically render the state totally obsolete.

I also made a second, somewhat more intriguing finding from a comparison of Marx's early "radical-democratic" criticisms of the state to his "mature" writings on the subject. Despite the intervening radical transition from Left Hegelianism to "historical materialism" there appears to be a remarkable

3   The following summary of my arguments is not intended as a comprehensive recapitulation of every major point made. I am deliberately limiting myself here primarily to those points that are important to the general arguments I make in the subsequent sections. More detailed summaries can be found at the appropriate places in the chapters themselves.

continuity between the early and the "mature" critiques of the
state. *Both* critiques are similarly based on the *presupposition* that
there will some day be a state of complete, natural harmony and
bliss, of unforced reconciliation between man and man, individual and collective, and so on, in which there will, therefore, be
no more need for a separate institutition to forcibly resolve conflicts between groups and individuals in the name of some
falsely proclaimed "general interest." The only apparent difference is that in the early, "pre-Marxist" writings the implicit utopia that serves as a yardstick with which to criticize the shortcomings of the current state is conceived as the realization of
the philosophical ideal of unmediated Universality or True Humanity, whereas in the "mature" writings the implicit utopia
has, of course, become the classless society created by the proletarian struggle for emancipation. In either case, however,
Marx's criticisms appear clearly based on a *pre*conceived utopia-
to-be, a finding that is totally at odds with the traditional self-
conception of Marxism as a completely "scientific," "anti-utopian" form of socialism, based on a purely "immanent" critique
of capitalism.

As discussed in the second section of Chapter 1, ("Marxism
and Utopianism"), Marx and Engels consistently derided the
"utopian" socialists for believing they could realize their ideals
by designing detailed blueprints for a future society supposedly
based on timeless notions of Justice and Humanity whose moral
appeal will prove irresistible to rich and poor alike. Instead,
Marx and Engels insist, "scientific" socialism must be firmly
rooted in present historical, empirical realities; it must be able
to show that its ideals are not just the futile fancies of some
isolated visionary but that they are inexorably immanent in
present historical conditions, in contemporary social forces in
the process of changing the world through their current struggles. This "immanentism" can be directly traced to Hegel's philosophy of history. Hegel had claimed to have "transcended"
the Kantian antinomies of fact and value, choice and necessity,
voluntarism and determinism, by conceiving of history as the
necessary *fusion* of both sides by which History works its Will.
Thus, according to Hegel, it was not the task of the philosopher
to try and impose his own arbitrary notions on History (which

was, anyhow, futile and in that sense "utopian") but to penetrate the thicket of contradictory "appearances" in order to grasp the "essence" immanent in his own historical epoch; that is, to reveal what the true Will of History currently is, so that he may accept this Will rather than resist it in the vain belief that he can arbitrarily change it.

This is clearly at the origin of Marx and Engels's ban on any "utopianism," as can be seen from the fact that this ban remained in force from Marx's earliest Hegelian writings to his last most hard-nosed "scientific" materialism. In fact, from his discovery of the as yet nonexistent "proletariat" as the "material basis" for the realization of the ideals of philosophy in the "Contribution to the Critique of Hegel's Philosophy of Right, Introduction" of 1843 to his post-1850 drift toward an ever more "scientific" determinism, Marx's work can be seen as an attempt to practice Hegel's "immanentism" more thoroughly than Hegel or any of his followers had done. Yet somewhat ironically, by thus depriving himself of a more detailed conception of the future socialist society as an important weapon in the struggle for its realization, Marx in effect was unable to provide a plausible theory to show why workers should feel compelled to move from their "natural" struggles over bread-and-butter issues toward the wholesale adoption of the cause of revolutionary "scientific socialism." The few hints Marx gave about the rather grim transitional phase he anticipated certainly did little to promote such a mass conversion, nor did Marx the "anti-utopian" intend them to. As a matter of fact, he seems to have tacitly assumed that "human nature" is somehow compelled to seek absolute redemption once exploitation and dehumanization have finally gone beyond the point of endurance. Yet, as Marx realized full well, that point would itself seem to be historically and culturally variable, so that his faith in the proletariat as the eventual carrier of the socialist cause must have been based, in the final analysis, on a belief in the ultimate rationality of history itself, that is, on a form of what Popper (1957) has called "historicism."

Significantly, however, as Marxist movements were defeated and Marxist predictions vitiated by successful repression and the reluctance on the part of large numbers of workers to execute "historical laws" the outcomes of which remained uncertain at best, "Western Marxism" did *not* return to a Kantian voluntarism, which would have involved at least *some* "utopian" specification of the "socialist" society to be created, but instead to a Hegelian "voluntarism," which turns out to be more of an *escape from* voluntarism in the ordinary sense. While accepting the idea that the arrival of socialism is not simply the inevitable mechanical result of economic trends and crises but that it requires, in addition, that the proletariat achieve true consciousness of the historical task that lies before it, Hegelian Marxists such as Lukács, Korsch, and the members of the Frankfurt School categorically deny that the *absence* of such consciousness among the workers in any way affects the validity of the original theory. Rather, they dismiss this absence as a matter of temporary (sometimes even not so temporary) "false consciousness," which only shows that the workers have yet to grasp the full significance of the "historical totality" and their own "objective" interests and role therein. In other words, although evidence contradicting the original thesis of the proletariat as the Historical Subject appointed by history itself—the thesis that was to be the proof of Marxism's scientific character in the first place—is now simply dismissed as irrelevant, the "objective" validity of Marxism is maintained on the basis of an even *less* verifiable superior insight into the requirements of the "historical totality," *irrespective* of the delusions that may have beset the supposed "gravediggers" of capitalism. Rather than opting for a Kantian voluntarism, "Western Marxists" have taken a Hegelian, increasingly anti-empiricist, and implicitly rather authoritarian route.

Marx and Engels themselves, standing as they thought they did at the very beginning of the rise of the socialist labor movement whose eventual victory they prophesied, obviously did not have to struggle with such a painful choice between Kantian "utopianism" and Hegelian elitism, as is evident from their views, discussed in the third section of Chapter 1 ("Marx and Engels on Revolution and Reform"), on what was to become the most burning political issue among their followers: the possibility of a democratic reformist road to socialism. Although Marx and Engels did not exclude the possibility of a legal, noninsurrectionary transition to socialism by means of electoral victory in countries with strong parliamentary traditions, they were *not* incrementalists or gradualists. They firmly believed the transition would be a relatively rapid and decisive one, once the proletariat, soon to be the overwhelming majority, had come to suppport socialism. As a result, they also rejected any revolutionary minority vanguardism, not out of some overriding commitment to "bourgeois" majoritarianism or civil liberties but because the idea that the relatively rapid emergence of an overwhelming prosocialist majority could *fail* to materialize simply never occurred to Marx or Engels. Convinced as they were that the working class, that is, the majority, would inevitably be compelled by its own misery and struggles to adopt the socialist cause, they considered the possibility of a prolonged coexistence of capitalism and parliamentary democracy a patent absurdity. Ultimately, they firmly believed, capitalism and (even merely formal) democracy were necessarily incompatible. Either one or the other would have to go. Thus, although it is true that there is little support in Marx and Engels's writings for Lenin's vanguardism, this is primarily because Marx and Engels simply did not have to deal with the possibility that the proletariat might *fail* to more or less automatically adopt "scientific socialism" as its own.

In Chapter 2 I have tried to trace the major debates and theories that were responsible for the complete divorce between reformism and Marxism, in which antireformist vanguardism became the Marxist orthodoxy and reformism the exclusive domain of "bourgeois" liberals. The first section ("The Early Debates: Bernstein and Social-Democratic Orthodoxy") deals with Eduard Bernstein's revisionism and the orthodox reaction it provoked. Bernstein gave up two key assumptions of Marxism: that there was, or soon would be, a "natural" majority constituency for full-fledged socialism, and that the achievement of "socialism" was somehow historically guaranteed or at least "objectively necessary." Instead, he assumed it would be necessary to convince potential constituents by means of appeals to their sense of justice and equity and rational arguments as to the feasibility of proposed reforms, and he advocated a cautiously reformist strategy that would gradually change the existing system without pressing beyond what an electoral majority could support. These heresies provoked an outrage among the more orthodox and radical Marxists. Karl Kautsky, representing the orthodox center, simply but with impeccable accuracy repeated the position of Marx and Engels. There was no doubt in Kautsky's mind that there would soon be a staunchly socialist working-class majority. Rosa Luxemburg, speaking for the radical left wing, also attacked Bernstein for the fatal heresy of questioning the "historical necessity" of socialism but was at the same time deeply suspicious of Kautsky's legalism and electoralism, as became clear in the later debates between them. She simply did not believe the bourgeoisie would merely stand by and watch as the working class used its electoral majority in parliament to abolish capitalism. But, whatever the differences between them may have been, Kautsky and Luxemburg still shared with Marx and Engels the unshakable faith that an overwhelming prosocialist majority would soon emerge, and that, therefore, capitalism and democracy *had* to be incompatible in the long run. They were the last Marxists to enjoy the innocent faith both in history and in the proletariat as the destined "historical subject." With Lenin this "innocence" was lost once and for all.

In the chapter's second section ("Lenin and the 'Renegade' Kautsky") I briefly describe Lenin's antireformist vanguardism. Contrary to those contemporary writers who have tried to dissociate "genuine" Marxism from the embarrassingly authoritarian reputation of bolshevism, I have argued that Lenin remained about as faithful to the spirit of Marxism as he could under what he (consciously or not) perceived as radically new circumstances. Ironically, Lenin was closer to Bernstein than to the orthodox "innocence" of Kautsky and Luxemburg in that he, too, had reached the conclusion that the workers would spontaneously ("left to themselves") support cautious economic reform rather than an uncertain socialist "revolution." But having dropped one crucial ingredient of the old innocence, Lenin had only two options: he could either proceed to abandon the rest of Marxism's characteristic doctrines, particularly its Hegelian, historicist belief in the "immanence" of socialism as Bernstein had done, *or* he could try to retain as much of the original doctrine as possible *without* a spontaneously revolutionary proletariat. Lenin opted for the latter and in the process brought out some of the uglier implications of this historicist "anti-utopianism" with exemplary clarity.

Lenin's theory of the state is a good example of this. Given the proletariat's spontaneous tendency toward reformist "economism" he cannot simply assume that capitalism and parliamentary democracy are inevitably incompatible in the long run. Instead, he dismisses "bourgeois democracy" as nothing but a hoax which, to the extent that it succeeds in fooling the masses, is in fact "the best possible political shell for capitalism," to be "shattered" by the socialist revolution and replaced by the "higher democracy" of the "revolutionary dictatorship of the proletariat." It is one of the great ironies in the history of Marxism that the one time Lenin deviated from Marxism's strict ban on "utopianism" he described this "higher democracy" in his *State and Revolution* as a form of direct democracy of the "armed masses," which in sheer simple-mindedness and naiveté easily surpassed any of the bucolic utopias derided by Marx and Engels—only *months* before his successful *coup d'état* suddenly made it a very urgent issue indeed. Not very surprisingly, this naive blueprint bore not even the faintest resemblance to the "higher form of democracy" Lenin was actually to implement after coming to power, nor to any of his other pronouncements and practices, for that matter. Clearly, Lenin's Marxism had failed to prepare him for what to do *after* a successful seizure of power so that all he had to work with was his own vanguard of professional revolutionaries organized along strictly authoritarian lines—the product of his distrust of the workers' spontaneous tendencies—and his unshakable faith in "scientific Marxism."

Combining that distrust and elements of the faith, particularly the strict dichotomization of all thought into *either* bourgeois or "genuinely" socialist and the claim that only the "true" initiates into "scientific Marxism" can be its guardians, Lenin entirely reverses the old relationship between Marxist theory and the proletariat. Now only a small vanguard of professional revolutionaries can be trusted to sustain and protect the correct, "scientific" line while the workers, customarily caught up in their essentially bourgeois consciousness, have become obstacles to or cannon fodder in the socialist revolution. Moreover, having thus dismissed the support of the workers themselves as a necessary and sufficient criterion for the validity of Marxist "scientific" doctrines and strategies, Lenin also accentuated the tendency toward cynical historical opportunism in Hegelian historicism. Since not the proletariat but History will be the judge of the "scientific" correctness of strategies and tactics, plain success at grabbing and holding on to power, *by whatever means*, becomes a sufficient justification for any policy, as only such success *proves* that one has History on one's side. Whatever the additional historical causes may have been, these doctrines of Lenin's and the correspondingly authoritarian practices could hardly have produced anything but the repressive regime he helped create. Yet, short of abandoning Marxism altogether, it is not easy to see what else Lenin could have done once he had given up faith in the proletariat's inevitable conversion to revolutionary socialism. Significantly, Lenin's orthodox critics merely clung to that faith a little longer, continuing to believe that with overwhelming majority support being imminent a minority dictatorship simply was not necessary.

Trotsky, Lukács, and Gramsci, most often mentioned as important precursors of modern Marxist theories of the state, did not really go much beyond Leninist orthodoxy, I argue in the third section of Chapter 2 ("Marxism and Politics after Lenin"). Trotsky and his followers combine a rigid adherence to the Leninist "best shell" theory and the related vanguardism with a mystical faith in the profoundly revolutionary energies of the "toiling masses," belatedly developed in opposition to Stalin's anti-spontaneism, which is a bit of a throwback to Luxemburgian "innocence." The resulting mixture—*State and Revolution* Leninism frozen in time—is more notable for its insurrectionary consistency than its theoretical cogency. Lukács, although he did provide Leninism with a fine Hegelian-historicist philosophical foundation, simply was not a theorist of the state. Gramsci, finally, did have some things to say about the state and political strategy but they were rather ambiguous and vague, reflecting the fact that—perhaps because of his long incarceration—he was a bit of a transitional figure who recognized some of the superstructural obstacles to be overcome in the struggle to win over the proletarian majority to the revolutionary cause but did not, on the other hand, have any doubts as to the eventual success of that struggle if the appropriate mass organization and strategy were pursued. Thus he has won a prominent place in the hearts of those who wish to rid Marxism of its rigid antireformism and authoritarianism perhaps precisely because he did *not* offer a coherent theory of the state.

In the fourth section of Chapter 2 ("Marxism versus Reformism?"), I describe the current state of confusion in the Marxist camp with respect to the reformism issue. On the one hand, reformism has become the exclusive domain of "bourgeois" liberals who argue that through the numerical strength and political organization of the less privileged socioeconomic strata in the democratic capitalist countries it may be possible to achieve something even many Marxists might consider worthy of the name "socialism" by means of a slow incremental "leftward drift." Ever since Lenin, Marxists have categorically rejected this reformist position. Social reforms have been of a "prophylactic" rather than a progressive nature, they argue; they have preempted rather than provoked any truly "fundamental" changes. But although such criticisms of past social reforms clearly rest on some implicit alternative, the exact nature of that alternative, that is, what *would* constitute "fundamental" change, remains remarkably elusive, as speculation about such matters would be tantamount to designing "utopian blueprints." At the same time, however, both the major European Communist parties and the bulk of the Marxist theorists of the state have recently come to advocate various "democratic" roads to socialism which are, for all intents and purposes, indistinguishable from "bourgeois" reformism. Thus, the current consensus—from which only the consistently revolutionary Trotskyists dissent—seems to be that whereas *past* reforms could only be "prophylactic" in nature, *future* reforms may well be more "fundamental."

The recent Marxist literature, which I begin to discuss in Chapter 3, is, however, almost exclusively concerned with proving that past social reform was virtually *bound* to be of a system-maintaining rather than a system-transforming nature. According to the oldest of the theories purportedly showing this, the now discredited "instrumentalist" approach, past social reforms could not be of the "fundamental" kind because, despite the trappings of formal democracy, the state is in fact the covert instrument of the capitalist class. Hence, only reforms approved by the bourgeoisie are ever implemented by governments in capitalist societies.

I review two versions of the theory. The simpler version, developed by Ralph Miliband, claims that the capitalist class is virtually united on matters that touch its common "fundamental" interests and that, as a result, given its superior resources and access to government officials, it always gets its way on such issues. Such a theory can be tested empirically, I have argued, by selecting cases in which the preferences of the united bourgeoisie clearly clashed with those of the majority of the electorate on a "fundamental" issue and taking any defeat of the bourgeoisie in such a case as a successful refutation of the theory, provided, of course, that we first define what the "fundamental" issues are—which Miliband, true to his "anti-utopian" heritage, fails to do. Moreover, Miliband further complicates things by claiming that the bourgeoisie may well be able to prevent any opposition to its "fundamental" interests from arising in the first place, by means of the massive "process of legitimation" carried out continuously by upper-class-controlled media, educational institutions, churches, and the like. This makes it even *more* imperative that the "fundamental" interests of the bourgeoisie be clearly defined, as well as the implicit alternative (the "fundamental" interests of the public which the "process of legitimation" prevents it from recognizing). But these are not, of course, questions that tax the "anti-utopian" Marxist mind very greatly. Like most Marxists after Lenin, Miliband simply equates *any* reform short of the complete transition to "socialism"—in itself rather an elusive criterion—with "system maintenance" and hence with the "fundamental" interests of the capitalist class.

G. William Domhoff offers a more subtle version of "instrumentalism" known as the "corporate liberalism" thesis. Essentially the argument is that, although the major corporate business interests in the United States are ideologically split between an archconservative antireform and a liberal proreform wing, it is the more powerful, better organized liberal wing that generally gets its way. Apparent defeats of "business" by "labor" in the passage of social-reform legislation are, in reality, merely cases of the liberal wing of business defeating the archconservatives. But, since the liberal wing is in fact merely the more farsighted of the two—accepting limited reform by coopting moderate representatives of labor and other potential opposition groups into carefully worked out compromises that damage the basic interests of big business as little as possible—it is business as a whole that eventually benefits from such limited, stabilizing reform.

I criticize Domhoff's approach on both empirical and theoretical grounds. Domhoff fails to document the superior strength and resources of his liberal "power elite." His own evidence in the crucial case of the Wagner Act fails to support his case. All he appears to be doing is to show that virtually all reforms enjoyed the backing of *some* wealthy or well-connected person(s). He does not confront the crucial question of the *degree* to which the "power elite" controls the organizations and associations he designates as part of the liberal policy-making network. But, most important for present purposes, Domhoff does not provide any convincing grounds for considering what *appear* to be compromises between those representatives of business *and* labor (or other nonbusiness interests) as unmitigated victories for business. This is clearly based on some implicit assumption of the feasibility or desirability of some more radical alternative resolution than the one arrived at by "moderate" business and labor representatives, but, although not himself a doctrinaire Marxist in any way, Domhoff is as silent on this implicit criterion of judgment as are the other theorists discussed here. Meanwhile, the policy-making process he describes does not differ materially from that depicted by the more sophisticated liberal pluralists who acknowledge great differences in power but none that are such as to let the most powerful interests get by without making at least *some* significant concessions and compromises.

Interestingly, the objections raised by more orthodox Marxists against "instrumentalism" are somewhat similar to mine. As discussed in the third section of Chapter 3 ("Marxist Criticisms of 'Instrumentalism' "), these objections are essentially twofold: "instrumentalism" is empirically untenable, and it is theoretically still too close to the reformism it supposedly seeks to refute. On the empirical side, these authors concede to "bourgeois" pluralism that the capitalist class is in fact rarely united on any issue, let alone the "fundamental" ones. Far too preoccupied with their own short-term, parochial interests, the capitalists are too systematically fragmented to be able to grasp their own, common, long-term "fundamental" interest in the maintenance of the overall system, let alone formulate the complex and subtle reform policies that are necessary to realize it. Thus, the state can often be observed to *impose* such policies on a reluctant capitalist class, yet these reforms *do* end up serving the bourgeoisie's long-term interest in the preservation of the system. On the theoretical side, the critics charge that "instrumentalism" does not conclusively refute reformism since if the capitalists can use the state as an apparently neutral instrument that will do their bidding, why should not the workers or their political parties be able to do the same thing after a decisive electoral victory? The trouble with the "instrumentalist" approach is, these critics agree, that it is altogether too "voluntaristic" and too "subjectivistic" to account for the clearly more "structural" manner in which the capitalist state manages to safeguard the interests of the capitalist class.

I am not going to repeat my criticisms of these invariably abstruse arguments here. Two things about them are worth noting in the present context, however. First, like all other Marxist antireformist arguments, they are based on the implicit, unexplained presupposition that *anything* short of the complete destruction of capitalism and its replacement with "socialism" is tantamount to the "maintenance" of the capitalist system and, *ipso facto* in the exclusive interest of the capitalist class. Again, an entirely unelucidated alternative state of affairs is tacitly taken to be the *only possible* alternative. Second, it is little short of astonishing that arguments as obscure and uncompelling as these were able to persuade virtually the entire body of Marxists concerned with the state to drop the venerable "instrumentalist" model almost without hesitation as now obviously utterly out of date and untenably "vulgar."

In Chapter 4 I discuss the most famous of the "structural" theories arising out of the critique of "instrumentalism": Poulantzas's theory based on Althusser's "structuralist" Marxism. Although Althusser's structuralism has since fallen into disrepute for its sheer theoretical vacuousness, Poulantzas's theory is still widely perceived as the "Copernican revolution" in Marxist thinking about the state. His major achievement, it is claimed, is that he has superseded the pluralist-instrumentalist debate by showing that the empirical evidence that appears to support the pluralist argument can in fact be reconciled with the Marxist doctrine that the state serves the interests of the capitalist class. However, on closer inspection of his arguments it turns out that although Poulantzas does indeed grant a great deal to pluralism in terms of empirical evidence—beyond most pluralists' wildest dreams, in fact—and although he also does indeed constantly reiterate Marxist doctrine concerning the state, he fails completely to produce even the slightest *hint* of an argument to reconcile the two. On the one hand he concedes that the members of the capitalist class are habitually divided and fragmented and that, as a result, democratically elected governments can often be observed to pursue policies that are *opposed* by some or even most of the members of the capitalist class. On the other hand, Poulantzas firmly maintains that the capitalist state is nevertheless "structurally" compelled to remain *"relatively* autonomous" from the capitalist class only, meaning that it can *only* impose such policies on the bourgeoisie as are in the latter's real, long-term interests, however unknown to its members. This raises two crucial questions which Poulantzas must adequately answer if his approach is to be a credible alternative to pluralism and "instrumentalism": what *are* the "fundamental" interests of the bourgeoisie and how can they be determined if not by the bourgeoisie's own preferences; and what is the structural mechanism that compels the state, in spite of all appearances to the contrary, to observe them?

I have reviewed the answers Poulantzas gives to these questions, or rather fails to give, in considerable detail. They consist essentially of an endless barrage of (re)definitions, conceptualizations, taxonomies, tautologies, circular arguments, and non sequiturs, all of which have the effect of bringing *any* possible empirical evidence within the purview of received Marxist doctrine on the state, that is, of turning the latter into a completely unfalsifiable and hence totally meaningless, formalized dogma. The process of immunizing the doctrine that the capitalist state will not and cannot act against the "fundamental" interests of the capitalist class against the possibility of empirical refutation, a process that began with the refusal on the part of the "instrumentalist" theorists to specify the nature of these "fundamental" interests, is carried to its extreme by Poulantzas's steadfast refusal *either* to define those interests *or* to explain why the state will not violate them.

On the other hand, Poulantzas's arguments display some of the same significant features we have encountered in the earlier theories. There is the same claim to a special ability to determine the "objective" interests of social classes, including the bourgeoisie this time, based on undisclosed "scientific" credentials. Second, presumably on the basis of this Higher Insight, Poulantzas concurs with other Marxists in equating *anything* short of the definitive realization of "socialism"—which remains as undefined as ever—with the maintenance of the "cohesion" and "unity" of the "social formation" and *hence* in the exclusive interest of the capitalist class. Once again, the tacit assumption is that, first, capitalism has been and is permanently teetering on the brink of its demise and, second, that its *only* conceivable successor is the "socialist" millennium.

Much the same can be said of the second version of a Marxist structural-functionalist theory of the state, discussed in Chapter 5. Interestingly, although the main advocate of this approach, Claus Offe, comes out of the Frankfurt School tradition of Hegelianized Marxism, that is, in a sense from the very opposite end of the Marxist spectrum as "scientific" Althusserian "structuralism," the similarity with Poulantzas's theory of the state is quite striking.[4] Offe, too, argues that the state *needs* to be "rel-

4   I am merely referring to what are *conventionally* presented as the polar opposites within Marxism: on the one hand, the Hegelian, "critical," "humanistic" variant stressing the role of consciousness, and the "superstructure" generally; on the other hand, the "scientific," economistic tradition which

atively autonomous" of the bourgeoisie *in order to* be able to impose policies on it that serve its long-term class interests but that
its members are too shortsighted and divided to recognize as
such. The state does this by using the legitimacy deriving from
formal democracy to overcome bourgeois opposition. However,
this imposes another function on the state, namely, that of concealing the fact that it mainly serves the interests of capital accumulation. This is the so-called legitimation function by which
the state tries to maintain its appearance of class neutrality by
making strategic concessions to noncapitalist groups whenever
necessary. Unlike Poulantzas, Offe explicitly asserts that ultimately the contradiction between the two is irresolvable and
that, hence, conflicts and struggles about the class character of
state policy and eventually the capitalist system as such constantly threaten to erupt and destroy the state's appearance of
neutrality.

As I argue in the second section of Chapter 5 ("State 'Functions' as Marxist Dogma"), Offe's argument suffers from the
exact same weaknesses as Poulantzas's. He simply fails to provide a plausible argument to show *why* the state is confined to
policies that "stabilize" and "legitimate" the existing system
rather than policies that "fundamentally" transform it. Second,
like Poulantzas and others, Offe also does not bother to explain
what the difference between "legitimation" and "fundamental"
change is, other than treating anything short of a complete abolition of capitalism as, *ipso facto*, its "legitimation," thus once
again displaying that tacit assumption of capitalism's inherent
fragility. In practice, however, as in the case of Poulantzas's theory, this boils down to turning Marxist doctrine into a hollow
phraseology that is compatible with *any* evidence (except the realization of an undefined "socialism") and thus totally unfalsifiable.

But of more interest, I argue in the third section ("The Unex-

maintains a strictly determinist model of the relation between the economic
base and the superstructure (see, e.g., Gouldner 1980; Jacoby 1981). As
should be clear from my arguments here and elsewhere (see van den Berg
1984), I obviously do not subscribe to this dichotomous view of Marxism.
This view, I believe, grossly overstates the differences and ignores the far
more important—that is, fateful—similarities.

amined Presuppositions of Marxism and the Appeal of Structural Functionalism"), Offe's approach reveals even more clearly the tacit "domain assumption" that seems to underlie the turn toward structural-functional theorizing and much of Marxist theory in general. Although the claim that the state would have to conceal its "accumulation function" flies in the face of all empirical evidence and common sense, it may be a bit more plausible if you start with the basic assumption that capitalism is, however modified by social reforms, *in and of itself* repugnant to "the masses"; that it is *inherently*, that is, quite irrespective of the known alternatives, fragile because always under the threat of mass disaffection and rebellion. This is the very same "immanent" assumption that Marx had originally made. But if the assumption was not particularly compelling in Marx's own day, it is infinitely less so now. The turn toward functionalism, however, appears to be designed to avoid having to question this original "domain assumption." In a theoretical development that runs remarkably parallel to Parsons's famous resolution of the Hobbesian "problem of order," these Marxists have developed extremely elaborate theoretical structures to explain what has kept their implicit model of rationality (the rise of a revolutionary proletariat) from being realized, rather than questioning whether the model ever *was* very rational to begin with.

The result of all this is a very curious theoretical hybrid. On the one hand, as the basic domain assumption has not changed since Marx, neither can the final conclusion: since the massive majority is sooner or later *bound* to find the continuation of capitalism intolerable, capitalism and democracy are ultimately incompatible. The failure of this prediction to materialize in the years since Marx first issued it represents merely an unfortunate but temporary historical detour. On the other hand, since all of the theoretical effort has gone into decrying the former gravedigger designate's reluctance to live up to its billing, and no obvious new "historical subject" seems in sight, the theory has become a somewhat faint replica of its rather more muscular predecessor. It is not exactly clear how the clash of "organizational principles" or the rise of "decommodified sectors" is going to be able to carry the theoretical weight of the erstwhile "class struggle."

This last somewhat disturbing conclusion also seems to underlie the attempts to develop a more dynamic "class struggle" theory of the state, the latest theoretical development in Marxist theorizing about the state, discussed in Chapter 6. The "class struggle" theorists, who include Poulantzas in his later work, consider the structural-functional approaches too static and the "instrumentalist" approach too voluntaristic. Seeking a middle road, they propose to view state policy as the product of a class struggle whose outcome is not necessarily always in the bourgeoisie's best interest. But it is really hard to see how this differs from standard liberal-pluralist accounts of democratic politics, except for the radical rhetoric and the somewhat narrow focus on *class* struggle. Whereas Poulantzas and Offe are indistinguishable from pluralism in the empirical implications of their theories, the "class struggle" approach does not even seem to differ from pluralism in the hallowed realm of theory itself.

This rather embarrassing state of affairs seems to have escaped notice only because, steeped as they are in the recent arcane debates on the theory of the state, Marxists have long ceased to take the pluralist alternative seriously, as can be seen from the cursory treatments of pluralism by those who consider it at all.[5] But whenever they *are* confronted with the uncomfortably "bourgeois" implications of their own approach, the "class struggle" theorists, too, invariably retreat to more comfortable instrumentalist or structuralist sanctuaries to show that not even their "class struggle" can "really" affect the "fundamental" interests of the capitalist class, as is plain, of course, from the very fact of capitalism's survival. Thus, even the advocates of this crypto-pluralist theory of the state share that basic domain assumption of their fellow Marxists, namely that the workers would surely have overthrown the capitalist system and replaced it with "socialism"—and that they, or some other

---

5   In addition to the cases mentioned in Chapter 6, see van den Berg (1981)
     for more examples of pluralist defenders and radical critics of "bourgeois"
     democracy largely talking past each other.

group or "contradiction," are still poised to do so—if it were not for . . .

Marxism: Creeping Embourgeoisement?

What, then, are the more general conclusions that can be drawn from all this? Much has been made of the great theoretical strides made in the past decades of intense theorizing and debate about the capitalist state. It has been claimed that "there is at present more room for wide-ranging and meaningful debate *within* Marxism as a theoretical *cum* political practice than within any of the contending liberal/conservative frameworks" (Panitch, ed. 1977, ix). By now, one is entitled to expect, all this "wide-ranging and meaningful debate" should be bearing some tangible fruit. In particular, one might expect such debate to have produced a credible alternative to the traditional archrival, liberal-reformist pluralism. Whether or not it has is the question dealt with in this section.

Recently, a few authors have noted how the history of Marxism, especially the "Western" variety, is in part the history of the gradual, incremental adoption of elements of "bourgeois" traditions in order to resolve growing "paradigm anomalies" (see, e.g., Alexander 1982b, ch. 10; Anderson 1976; Gouldner 1980; Parkin 1979). This observation is confirmed in the theories reviewed here. In fact, the trend that is manifested in the successive attempts at formulating a better theory of the state—from "instrumentalism" to "structural" theories to the "class struggle" theory—is one of *a slow but incremental capitulation to the liberal pluralist description and understanding of "democratic politics."* At the same time this convergence with "bourgeois" theory is accompanied by a seemingly increasingly militant-sounding reassertion of Marxist orthodoxy. The result is a theory that is not distinguishable from its "bourgeois" rivals on empirical grounds but only by its purely rhetorical, almost ritual declarations of fidelity to an orthodox doctrine that is emptied of all substantive content in the process.

Ironically, with respect to the "orthodox" doctrine in question, the rejection of all reformism, Marx himself was rather more heterodox than his followers. In fact, in spite of his distinctive general theory of the state predicated on his anticipation of an eventual society without class conflict, his understanding of the workings of bourgeois democratic politics was not very different from that of the latter-day liberal pluralists. Marx viewed the state in general as nothing but an agency for the forcible suppression of class conflict to the advantage of whichever class can successfully gain control of this agency, which seemed to imply that once class conflict were abolished, so would the state be. This general view is, of course, a far cry from the "bourgeois" perception of the state as an agency of conflict resolution, which can be abolished as little as conflict can. In fact, Marx's general position is close to the anarchist view of the state. But this did not, for Marx, imply that existing states were necessarily immune to "capture" by the working class, and he took the possibility quite seriously that, under favorable conditions, this might occur legally and peacefully in some democratic countries. In this respect, then, Marx's position did not differ materially from that of the modern-day "bourgeois" reformists.

Only with Lenin does categorical rejection of *any* kind of reformism become a necessary condition of orthodoxy, and even the slightest wavering on this point a telltale indication of a secret or unwitting support for the cause of the bourgeoisie. As Lenin suspected that, contrary to the original expectations, capitalism and bourgeois democracy might well be capable of an indefinite period of peaceful coexistence, he simply proclaimed *all* existing states, especially the bourgeois democracies, to be *inherently* capitalist. Lenin thus managed to condemn all democratic states to be "smashed" rather than captured, and all reformists to doctrinal excommunication.

The development of what has become known as the "instrumentalist" theory of the state by such authors as Miliband and Domhoff was an attempt to provide a more coherent and convincing account of how formally democratic political institutions could be systematically perverted into serving the interests of the capitalist minority, thereby thwarting any reformist attempts to use those institutions to transform the capitalist system "fundamentally". The "instrumentalist" theory has one obvious and considerable merit: it clearly predicts empirical outcomes that differ from those predicted by liberal pluralists. Whereas pluralists assert that majority opinion can and, when it is well organized and vociferous, occasionally does defeat capitalist-class opposition even when the capitalists are united, "instrumentalism" claims that, because of the overwhelming advantages enjoyed by the capitalist class this never happens. But, as we have seen, "instrumentalist" theorists have introduced certain additional qualifications—restriction of the argument to undefined "fundamental" issues only; the possibility of "mass indoctrination" by the capitalist class so that no clear conflict of preferences can arise in the first place; the introduction of factions of the capitalist class the more successful of which are, for reasons that are not fully explained, deemed the "true" representatives of the class as a whole—that tend to make the theory either unfalsifiable because of failure to define crucial variables ("fundamental" issues) or indistinguishable from pluralism except for the relabeling of "consensus" and "compromise" as "indoctrination" and "cooptation" by the liberal faction of the capitalist class, on grounds that remain undiscussed. But still, even these more elusive versions of "instrumentalism" could at least in principle be refuted by any evidence of majority opinion prevailing over a *united* bourgeois opposition.

Not so for the "structural" theories of the state, which claim to have overcome the weaknesses of "instrumentalism": these weaknesses, the proponents of the "structural" approaches claim, are the result of the "instrumentalists'" inability to shake certain aspects of "bourgeois" thought, its "voluntarism" and "subjectivism." Rather ironically, however, these critics then proceed to replace such "bourgeois" impurities by a "structuralism" or structural functionalism that is hardly any less bourgeois in origin. Moreover, their approach does little more than carry the relabeling of "bourgeois" concepts and notions to extremes. In the process, they in effect adopt the pluralist depiction of empirical reality *en bloc*. Governments do force the members of the capitalist class, whether united or divided, to accept policies they perceive to be against their interests, and they do this in response to pressures exerted by public opinion, the unions, and so on through the institutions of formal democracy. But, according to these "structural" theorists, this does not at all refute the Marxist theory of the state. On the contrary, it only *confirms* the theory, when correctly specified.

Clearly there is no way of deciding between this "structural" Marxist theory of the state and "bourgeois" pluralism on purely empirical grounds since in this respect they are virtually identical. Therefore, if this approach is to prove itself superior to "bourgeois" theory in a rational manner, that is, on some basis other than sheer faith or ritual incantation, it must show that it is theoretically more coherent, consistent, or comprehensive. As we have seen, however, both versions of the "structural" theory are anything *but* these things. Their strategy is to turn empirical evidence that to pluralists, "instrumentalists," and most other mortals for that matter, would plainly signify the defeat of capitalist-class interests, into evidence *supporting* Marxist theory, by simply relabeling it with terms ostensibly derived from a Marxist theoretical scheme. What might look to others like a sound defeat of the bourgeoisie now turns out to be merely a case in which it is "forced to make the sacrifices necessary for maintaining the cohesion and unity of the social formation" or, for short, an exercise in "legitimation." Yet, what the purpose, significance, or theoretical origin of these new labels is we are simply not told. Nor do these theorists even *try* to specify the "structural" mechanism that presumably compels the state to do what it does, however one wishes to label it. Thus, all we are left with is a description of reality that is indistinguishable from that given by pluralists and a "theory" that consists of nothing more than a set of thoroughly vacuous but vaguely militant-sounding labels to replace those used by the pluralists, combined with the dogmatic assertion that the state always serves the interests of the capitalist class. Besides this, the "structural" approach offers little more than such banalities as that governments, especially democratic ones, usually seek to maintain some minimal degree of social order (Poulantzas's "cohesion"), and that social conflicts of some sort will probably continue to erupt from time to time (Offe), which hardly serves to distinguish it from pluralism. As Domhoff has been one of the few to notice, "Marxists . . . start out with definitions that sound very different from those of pluralists, but they end up saying that the State apparatus does what pluralists say it does" (1983, 214).

The "class struggle" approach, which seeks to avoid the flaws of *both* the "instrumentalist" and the "structuralist" theories, does so only by reinventing liberal pluralism *in toto*. Not even the terminology is all that different anymore, and not even the dogmatic, though plainly meaningless, insistence that the state necessarily serves only the interests of the bourgeoisie is retained. This approach is truly a perfect replica of the pluralist theories long espoused by such arch "bourgeois" theorists as Dahl or Lipset, a fact that could have only escaped the attention of the advocates of the "class struggle" approach because they did not find it necessary to consider seriously such remnants of a bygone era after two decades of "wide-ranging and meaningful debate *within* Marxism." Meanwhile, as I have tried to show in Chapter 6, whenever these "class struggle" theorists are faced with the plainly reformist implications of their general statements, they quickly retreat to quasi-structural or quasi-instrumentalist arguments after all. This, of course, *does* serve to differentiate them from the likes of Dahl and Lipset, but hardly on grounds of superior consistency or coherence.[6]

In addition to this gradual embourgeoisement of the Marxist theory of the state, the attitude toward reformism among the theorists has, like that of the "Eurocommunist" parties of Italy, France, and Spain, become rather ambivalent, even incoherent, despite the incessant antireformist posturing. Although social-democratic reformism remains anathema, several of these theorists have come to advocate a "democratic road" to socialism, whose differences from the reformism of the social-democratic parties remain far from clear. There is a lot of talk of "radical breaks" and "sweeping changes" but little about what exactly these will consist of or how to get a majority of the electorate to support them where social democrats have failed to find majorities for many of the rather modest reforms *they* have sought to introduce. In fact, these recent converts to the "democratic road" offer little more than the assertion that, although in the past reformism could not possibly succeed, in the future it can—without even beginning to suggest what might account for

6   Interestingly, Marxist debates concerning "bourgeois" law have followed a trajectory remarkably similar to those on the capitalist state in recent years (see Cotterrell 1981).

this rather radical difference between the past and the anticipated future. Again, except for the somewhat curious persistence of some of the shibboleths and phrases of past orthodoxy there is nothing that clearly differentiates this from "bourgeois" reformism.

Thus, if the years of intense theorizing about the state are to be judged by whether or not they have produced a theory that could conceivably pose a credible *alternative* to conventional liberal pluralism, or even just the faint promise of one, they must be judged nothing short of a resounding failure. Far from producing a viable *alternative* to pluralism, the various debates add up to little more than a rather roundabout way of *reinventing* it. After two decades of debate and literally hundreds, perhaps even thousands, of learned articles and books, Marxist theorists of the state have produced exactly this: (1) a complete capitulation to the pluralist depiction of reality and, largely, its interpretation; (2) a purely dogmatic insistence on the claim that the state serves the interests of the capitalist class nonetheless; and (3) a complete failure to produce even the shadow of a rational argument to link the two together, so that the orthodox doctrine has become something like a ritual incantation whose soothing effects are completely unrelated to its rational content, as it has long ceased to possess any.

Marx and the Marxist Theory of the State: Some Continuities

The conclusion of the last section also implies that the Marxist theory of the state can not be judged to have made much of an advance over Marx's own comments on the state either, however fragmentary those comments may have been. In fact, even on the purely rhetorical—that is, nominally still Marxist—side, the elaborate "theorizations" of the recent past boil down to little more than rather laborious and obscure restatements of Marx's simple assertion that the "executive of the modern State is but a committee for managing the common affairs of the whole bourgeoisie" (Marx 1977, 223; cf. Balbus 1982, 87), the differences between them having primarily to do with the question of whether the bourgeoisie *knows* this to be the case or not.

But even this bit of apparent doctrinal fidelity rests on a basic misunderstanding of Marx's argument. It rests on a confusion between Marx's theory of the state in general, according to which class division is a necessary and sufficient condition for the existence of the state, and the more specific question of whether or not certain existing democratic states can become the instrument of the working class to abolish the capitalist system and establish socialism, *after which*, in accordance with the general theory, the state would necessarily "wither away." The above famous phrase was only a corollary of that other famous phrase, according to which "political power, properly so called, is merely the organizing power of one class for oppressing the other" (Marx 1977, 238), a corollary of the *general* theory, that is. For Marx it did not at all imply, as I have tried to show in Chapter 1, that the proletariat could not *also* use this organizing power to oppress the bourgeoisie and that it might not gain control of this organizing power by legal means in certain countries with strong traditions of parliamentary democracy. But *this is* how later Marxist theorists, beginning with Lenin, have in fact interpreted the phrase. Yet, in a tradition that habitually seeks the answer to every question by consulting the writings of its founders, the confusion is perhaps understandable since there were no other instructions anywhere in those writings on how to deal with the unanticipated eventuality of a proletariat that is reluctant even to *try* to use the "organizing power" of the state to execute its historical mission.[7]

But even this is being too kind. For in one crucial respect the more recent theories amount to a plain retrogression from Marx. They exhibit a process of theoretical degeneration that is noticeable in other areas of Marxist theorizing as well (see, e.g., Van Parijs 1980): *rather than seeking to maintain the "scientificity" of received doctrine by revising it in the light of unanticipated empirical evidence, Marxists have opted for immunizing it against any possible*

7   Perhaps it is also because of this confusion between the theory of states (and politics) in general and the theory of specific bourgeois-democratic states that recent theorists insist on speaking of "the state" when they are obviously referring to the government or at best the polity (i.e., executive plus legislature). After all, these theorists are, in fact, rightly or wrongly, applying Marx's general theory of the state to the behavior of particular governments in democratic capitalist countries.

refutation whatsoever. This can be seen quite clearly in the successive "theorizations" of the capitalist state since the late 1960s. The initial flurry of theoretical debates was primarily a reaction against the "instrumentalist" theory, which had formulated received doctrine in a moderately refutable form. This model was criticized for not providing sufficient "theoretical guarantees" that the state necessarily serves the capitalist class under all circumstances, that is, for being too easily refutable. The subsequent theoretical advances essentially boil down to successive efforts to reduce the risk of refutation to the minimum feasible. The introduction and immediate popularity of the notion of the "relative autonomy" of the capitalist state, and the associated functionalist obscurantisms, clearly devised to safeguard Marxist dogma from any threat of falsification once and for all (Pemberton 1983, 303), constitute something of a high point—or low point for those still committed to the old-fashioned notion that a theory ought to be designed to convince those not yet convinced by appealing to their sense of logic and empirical reality—in this process. This hardly amounts to a great theoretical advance over Marx's fragmentary but at least in principle empirically refutable remarks.

As a result of these efforts "the" Marxist theory of the state now consists of a convenient grab bag of theories from which one can pick and choose as the occasion requires. Whenever business gets its way this proves that the state is the "instrument" of the bourgeoisie; when labor gets its way this shows how the state fulfills its function of "legitimating" and maintaining the "cohesion" of the system; whenever policies appear to be the result of compromise after some overt conflict this shows either that the farsighted fraction of the bourgeoisie has come to recognize its true, long-term interests, or that the state is an "arena of class struggle." Thus, one can conveniently switch from the more to the less refutable "theories" whenever the defense of received doctrine requires, thus rendering the Marxist theory of the state *doubly* irrefutable (for some examples of this "synthetic" approach, see Frankel 1979, 205; Mandel 1975, 474–99; 1978, 150–87; Miliband 1977, 90–106; Szymanski, 1978). Ollman even provides an explicit rationale for this sort of procedure: "These apparently contradictory views of the state are equally true ... representing as they do different tendencies inside the state relation. Dialectical truth does not fit together like the pieces of a puzzle, but allows for the kind of multiple one-sidedness and apparent contradictions that results from studying any subject from perspectives associated with its different aspects" (1982, 43).

To those not privy to the intricacies of "dialectical truth," however, this sounds an awful lot either like the banality that all things are possible or like downright intellectual dishonesty. At any rate, in neither case is it much of an improvement over Marx's own rather less "dialectical," more falsifiable arguments.[8]

But not all the shortcomings of the recent Marxist theories of the state are due to ill-conceived departures from the Marxian originals. Some, in fact, are the result of *certain continuities between Marx and his present-day followers*. One obvious case in point is the *virtually exclusive preoccupation with classes*. As we have seen, Marx's own "general" theory of the state attributes the very existence of politics and the state to the existence of class division *alone*: political power is "*merely* the organizing power of one class for oppressing the other" (emphasis added). By implication, when classes, and therefore social conflict, will have disappeared, so will political power and its institutional embodiment, the state. Lenin simply repeated the basic formula, only adding that even in a bourgeois democracy it is necessarily the bourgeoisie that controls "the organizing power for oppressing the other" classes. Later, in the "instrumentalist" theories of Miliband and Domhoff, there is no doubt about the fact that it is the capitalist *class* that controls the actions of governments from both the inside and the outside, and that it controls it to the detriment of all other *classes*. Poulantzas *defines* power completely arbitrarily, though in this respect remaining relatively faithful to Marx and Lenin, as belonging to classes only, and

8   Ollman, like others among the faithful, finds it necessary to attribute his own theoretical stew, which is obviously a "synthesis" of the recent debates, to Marx himself, who, he claims, conceived the capitalist state "as a complex social relation of many different aspects, the main ones being political processes and institutions, the ruling class, an objective structure of political/economic functions, and an arena of struggle" (1982, 41).

couches his theory of the capitalist state exclusively in terms of dominant and dominated classes and fractions of classes, other "social categories" such as civil servants appearing only as "hindrances" and "resistances." There is also no question in Offe's theory who the main beneficiary of the state's accumulation and legitimation functions is: the bourgeoisie. Yet, sharing the Frankfurt School's total disillusionment with the proletariat, Offe replaces it with the "organizational principle" of "use value production" represented by an assortment of "progressive" forces. The "class struggle" approach may be a virtual replica of liberal pluralism, but it does differ from the latter in that it, too, seems to be wholly concerned with the struggle between *classes* only.

There is nothing new about this excessive class reductionism in the Marxist literature, and it has been rightly and adequately criticized many times from various perspectives (see, e.g., Balbus 1982; Jessop 1982; Johnston 1986; Mouzelis 1980; Parkin 1979; Przeworski 1977). What I wish to point out here, however, is that this exclusive preoccupation with social classes and their conflicts is in part to blame for what Miliband quite rightly describes as "an extraordinarily complacent view of the ease with which political problems (other than mastering bourgeois resistance) would be resolved in post-revolutionary societies" (1977, 11). Since, after the abolition of classes the cause of "major" social conflict would be eliminated, there would only remain a need for the relatively simple "administration of things" whose exact organization it was hardly worth worrying about (cf. Chase-Dunn 1980, 511; Parkin 1979, 178–79). As I have tried to show, throughout his life Marx truly believed that after the abolition of classes (or, in the earliest writings, the attainment of true "universality") there would be no need for a conflict-resolving agency at all, not even a democratic one (cf. Balbus 1982, 109–15). The transitional phase might have to be quite despotic, he thought, but this would only be a relatively insignificant interlude as it could only lead to the abolition of classes and hence political power itself. Similarly, Lenin need not have felt any great inconsistency between arguing for direct democracy, immediate recall, and the like as the features of the "higher democracy" of the transitional "dictatorship of the pro-

letariat" at one time and demanding the ruthless suppression of
any democracy only a few months later. All that mattered was
which *class* was in power, and as long as his Bolsheviks, armed
with the infallible truths of "scientific Marxism," were in power
it was by definition the proletariat that ruled. How exactly that
rule was organized was a matter of minor detail.

What is far more astonishing, however, is that this incredibly
cavalier attitude toward postrevolutionary political organization
persists even now, decades after it has become clear how much
damage and suffering it has caused (cf. Bobbio 1978a, b). Both
the stubbornly revolutionary Trotskyists and the various recent
converts to the "democratic road" to socialism routinely invoke
the "higher form of democracy" that will result from the "unfurling of self-management" in all spheres of life, without bothering to give even the slightest indication of how this "higher
form" will deal with large-scale issues and societywide (let alone
worldwide) conflicts and problems. But although this remarkable carelessness is clearly partly rooted in a narrow focus on
class conflicts, this is not, as I argue below, its only source.

The other intriguing continuity between the work of Marx
and the writings of recent Marxists that I have tried to bring
out and which is, I believe, of equal significance, although it has
received much less critical attention, is *the habit of judging and
criticizing the present by the yardstick of an incomparably better future.*
Throughout his life Marx more or less consciously sought to
analyze and criticize the status quo from the standpoint of what
he took to be its future alternative. As Luxemburg once noted,
"it is only because Marx looked at capitalism from the socialist's
viewpoint, that is from the historical viewpoint, that he was enabled to decipher the hieroglyphics of capitalist economy"
(quoted by Holloway and Picciotto 1978, 27). Clearly, this is no
less true for Marx's theory of the state which is, I have tried to
show, entirely predicated on the belief that in the future realm
of "true universality," aka "socialism," there will be no further
need for an agency to resolve or suppress social conflict. There
was little doubt in Marx's mind that "socialism" was the only
possible historical alternative to the capitalism of his day, and
that its arrival was sufficiently near to base his condemnation of

that capitalism on it without having to resort to moralistic trans-historical appeals (cf. Popper 1966b, 137–43).[9]

Later Marxist theorists of politics and the state have adopted this feature, too, from Marx's "general" theory and applied it to the particular case of bourgeois democracy. In fact, the tendency to judge government policies by the yardstick of a better, "socialist" alternative is so persistent and pervasive that it often appears to be the very essence of those theories. Lenin's fateful claim that there can only be two kinds of ideology, either "bourgeois" or "socialist," since "mankind has not created a 'third' ideology," as well as his denunciation of the "democratic republic" as merely a front for class rule when compared to the infinitely "greater and more perfect democracy" that would exist after the socialist revolution are obvious cases in point. But the tendency is just as obvious in the later theories of the state. Miliband's main point is that the capitalist class will allow the state to implement only such reforms and make only such concessions to labor as are not "fundamental," that is, do not transform the system in the direction of "socialism." Similarly, Domhoff's claim that the compromise solutions pursued by "corporate liberals" and moderate representatives of labor constitute unqualified victories for business as a whole is clearly predicated on a more radical alternative that would be a "real" defeat of the interests of the big corporations. Poulantzas equates *any* policy that does not entirely "transform" the "social formation" with, *ipso facto*, the maintenance of its "unity" and

---

9   According to Popper, however, this was only a tacit assumption of Marx's, a bit of "wishful thinking" (1966b, 139) in an otherwise commendable attempt to develop a social science in the Kantian sense. As I have argued before and continue to argue in the next section, the assumption was anything *but* a minor inconsistency. It did and still does constitute part of the very theoretical core of Marxist thinking. There is one place, in the *Communist Manifesto*, where Marx and Engels express some doubt as to whether class struggles always produce progressive change. There they claim that the class struggles of which "all hitherto history" has consisted have ended either in "a revolutionary reconstitution of society at large" *or* "in the common ruin of the contending classes" (Marx 1977, 222). There is, however, no indication that either they or any of their followers ever took the latter possibility seriously with respect to the predicted struggles between proletariat and bourgeoisie in the capitalist mode of production (but see pp. 161–62).

"cohesion," which is, obviously, to the exclusive benefit of the "dominant class." Offe, also, simply takes the sheer maintenance of the "conditions of accumulation" to be in the exclusive interest of the capitalist class and describes anything short of a *total* transformation as, *ipso facto*, "legitimation" of the *existing* system. The "class struggle" theorists, finally, also assume that there is only one basic dichotomy, namely that between government policies that are "reproductive" of the capitalist system and those that are "nonreproductive," that is, those that lead naturally to "socialism."

These are just the more prominent examples of the tendency to judge the present by taking a "fundamentally" better future state as the relevant "contrast model" (see also van den Berg 1981, 92–102). Many more could be mentioned.[10] Here I only want to point out the remarkable consistency of this basic theme from the early, Hegelian Marx to the most recent Marxist theories of the capitalist state. Whatever else they may have in common, *for a century and a half Marxists have taken it for granted that it is reasonable and worthwhile to criticize the existing world and its shortcomings by implicitly or explicitly holding it up against the "socialist" ideal on the apparent assumption that the latter constitutes the only historical alternative to the status quo.* For Marx, of course, this assumption was based, in turn, on the firm belief that the working class would soon become the overwhelming majority and would be irresistibly drawn toward the cause of socialism as the only possible salvation from its suffering under capitalism. Some sort of similar assumption also clearly underlies the arguments of recent theorists of the state that past reforms have helped to

10   The persistent habit of blurring the distinctions between fascist and bourgeois democratic regimes, as manifested, for instance, in Poulantzas's treatment of "totalitarianism" as typical of the capitalist state and merely an extension of its inherent tendencies, is, according to Miliband, the result of "an attitude of mind to which Marxists have been prone. This is the belief that because A and B are not *totally* different, they are not *really* different at all" (1977, 83). The same could be said for the curious arguments that seek to redefine Soviet-type socialism as ("state") capitalism because it does not fully meet the expectations of a "genuine" socialist society (cf. Nove 1983). In both cases the basic "attitude of mind" is that there are only two possible conditions, the "socialist" ideal and "capitalism." Anything short of "socialism" is, therefore, capitalist and to be condemned as such (see also Maravall 1979, 279-83).

"maintain" or "reproduce" the capitalist system. As Wright correctly points out, the notion of "reproduction," which is so central to "Western" Marxism, clearly implies that the phenomenon so described helped prevent some change that would have occurred in its absence (E. O. Wright 1978, 18–19). And the social change in question is, of course, none other than "fundamental" change, the total "transformation" of the system, the realization of "socialism."

Thus, the common tendency among Marxists to evaluate the present in terms of a "socialist" future appears to rest on another common assumption that informs their arguments throughout, namely *the assumption that the working class is naturally drawn toward "socialism" and that, hence, it poses a constant threat to the survival of the capitalist system.* Marx and Engels themselves simply took it for granted that the workers' every experience, whether it be dire misery or temporary prosperity, political victory or defeat, would inevitably make them more and more conscious of their world-historical mission and more and more desirous of executing it. Significantly, the theme of the impending *prise de conscience* of the proletariat is much less prominent in Lenin's writings, but Lenin *did* obviously and firmly believe that capitalism was constantly teetering on the brink of its demise, and there was no doubt in his mind that once the workers had been shaken from their habitual "trade-unionist" slumber by the imminent revolutionary crisis they would enthusiastically and overwhelmingly support the socialist revolution. It was probably in part because of this firm belief that Lenin did not in the least foresee the postrevolutionary disagreements, conflicts, and lack of majority support that were to force him to choose between the suppression of democracy, even for the workers, or the surrender of power.

Similarly, the later theories of the state, which are all primarily concerned to show that past reforms have served to "maintain," not to "fundamentally transform" the capitalist system, all clearly presuppose that the system is, or at least was, constantly on the verge of being overthrown by a socialist working class. Thus, Miliband claims that social reforms have been "an essential prophylactic against . . . [the] advance towards socialism" (1977, 155), no more than the "relatively low . . . price which the dominant classes knew they would have to pay . . . for the maintenance of the existing social order" (1969, 100). Clearly, he assumes that the advance toward socialism *would* have taken place if it had not been for these reforms and a generous dose of "mass indoctrination" to keep the workers from rallying to the socialist cause. Similarly, when Domhoff asserts that the "liberal" wing of the corporate world is the more farsighted one, recognizing what compromises and concessions are *necessary* for the long-term preservation of corporate power and privilege, he obviously assumes that *without* such minimum compromise labor and its allies would have *insisted on and obtained* much more radical reforms.

Poulantzas starts with precisely the same assumption when he claims that the state forces the dominant class to make the "compromises and sacrifices . . . necessary for the realization of [its] political class interests" (1973b, 285). His whole argument hinges on his assumption that the state's "isolation effect" is far more effective in dividing and fragmenting the capitalist class than it is in preventing the working class's "organized political struggle" (284). Therefore, he argues, the state must constantly *dis*organize the working class, that is, prevent it from following its "natural" inclination toward "socialism" by well-timed concessions and compromises. The tacit assumption that the working class is perpetually on the verge of becoming an irresistible force for "socialism," runs throughout Poulantzas's endless definitions, taxonomies, and conceptualizations, from his definition of "power" to his designation of the state as the "factor of cohesion" of the "social formation." They all rest on the taken-for-granted assumption that however great the concessions made to the workers, they are always the very least the "dominant class" could have gotten away with, given the workers' easily provoked dissatisfaction, which would naturally have cost the dominant class far more dearly (see also Balbus 1982, 97–100).

Similarly, Offe, O'Connor, and Wolfe take it to be self-evident that the state has to "conceal" from the masses its complicity in the maintenance of the "conditions of capitalist accumulation" by means of cleverly designed "legitimation" policies. Otherwise, they claim, those masses would surely start asking why the state should "help one class accumulate capital at the expense of other classes" (O'Connor 1973, 6). The theory is predicated on the assumption that the capitalist mode of production is naturally repugnant to the workers and in the long run intolerable. This is why Offe predicts the eventual "repoliticization" of class conflict. Whereas, true to his Frankfurt School heritage, he considers the members of the working class, at least those in the most highly commodified sectors,[11] a spent force as far as the "fundamental" class struggle is concerned, he definitely *does* believe that capitalism almost automatically produces strong revulsion and opposition against its own "organizational principle" among large sections of the population. This is quite clear from his argument that sheer exposure to any "organizational principle" other than exchange must obviously lead to a critical questioning of that principle and thus a dangerous politicization of the very foundations of the capitalist system. From his answers to critics who have suggested that mere acquiescence may be sufficient for the survival of capitalism or that many "legitimating" symbols are in practice available to the defenders of the status quo (see Edelman 1975; Mann 1975; Mayntz 1975), it is obvious that Offe simply cannot imagine that anything short of complete encapsulation in the "commodity form" could possibly *fail* to produce profound and widespread opposition to the capitalist system *as such* (see Offe 1975a).

Even the "class struggle" theorists, however indistinguishable they may otherwise be from plain bourgeois pluralism, still assume as a matter of course that the working class "naturally moves towards political struggle for socialism" (Esping-Ander-

11 As I have already pointed out, Offe's argument appears rather un-Marxist here and in some respects closer to the nineteenth-century "utopian" socialists who still lacked a "historical subject" to realize their visions of the good society. He claims that people in the *least* commodified sectors are most likely to rebel against a society dominated by the "organizational principle" of exchange, whereas the workers in the *most* commodified sectors, especially the monopoly sector, are least likely to do so. This is somewhat odd on two counts. First, labor in the monopoly sector would appear to be *less*, not more "commodified" than in the more competitive sector, and, second, the whole point of Marxism has always been precisely that subjection to the "commodity form" does ultimately cause workers to unite to overthrow the capitalist system.

sen, Friedland, and Wright 1976, 206). Yet few things would be harder to document than this presupposed "historically appointed affinity between the working class and socialism," as Goldthorpe aptly calls it (quoted by G. Marshall 1983, 285). There have been a few celebrated upheavals, such as that of 1848, the Paris Commune, the Russian Revolution and, the "near revolutions" in Germany, Italy, and Hungary between 1918 and 1920, all of which have contributed a great deal to the persistence of *the great myth of the radical worker* which continues to underlie Marxist theory. But on closer examination, none of these famous episodes was really an instance of, or the result of, working-class socialist radicalism at all, so that they—let alone the intervening periods of relative calm—could hardly serve to confirm this basic Marxist belief. (See also R. F. Hamilton 1972, 190; B. Moore 1978; Przeworski 1977, 383; Stephens 1979, 68, 86.)[12] If anything, the historical record seems to suggest that "enthusiasm for revolution has been much more widespread among intellectuals and other groups generally cut off from the main body of workers than it has been among the working class" (Calhoun 1983, 902).

This should only surprise the Marxists themselves, however. As I have argued in Chapter 1, Marx himself never supplied a coherent, much less a very convincing, argument to explain why or how the working class in capitalism should eventually come to support, and be prepared to go to the barricades for, that uncertain ideal called "socialism." He knew full well that "there is no guarantee that exploitation, or just plain human misery, will somehow secrete its own antidote" (B. Moore 1978, 475). He rejected all arguments based on some fixed notion of human nature or justice since they would inevitably founder on their inability to explain why "socialism" had not found any widespread support in previous epochs. Instead, however, Marx's own belief in the eventual adoption of the socialist cause

12   For the definitive refutation of the socialist mythology surrounding the events of 1848 in France, see Traugott (1985). Marshall suggests that the Marxist reluctance to undertake studies of working-class consciousness from a historical perspective stems largely from their unwillingness to question this great myth, toward whose preservation all their efforts appear to be aimed (G. Marshall 1983, 284-85). My analysis of Marxist theories of the state certainly provides no grounds for questioning this verdict.

by the working class seems to have been ultimately based on a faith in the rationality of history itself, which is hardly more compelling.[13] Since then the reasoning has hardly become any *more* compelling. In fact, once the argument comes to revolve around "organizational principles" that are for some reason incapable of "systemically" coexisting, the reasoning becomes very nebulous indeed.

In sum, there appear to be three interrelated continuities between Marx's own writings and more recent Marxist theorizing about the capitalist state. First, the more recent theories are as narrowly focused on *classes* as any of Marx's writings, which helps to account for the persistence of an incredibly nonchalant lack of concern for the question of how political decision making and conflict resolution will be organized in the presumably classless postrevolutionary society. Second, there is the intriguing finding that, like Marx before them, the more recent Marxist theorists of the state criticize contemporary, "bourgeois" democracy on the basis of an implicit comparison with the infinitely better "socialist" alternative of the future. Whereas the comparison is rarely made explicit, it does form the crucial underpinning of much of their theories—an underpinning without which they would not, in fact, be plausible at all. Third, what underlies this willingness to hold up the imperfect present against a supposedly far better future is the equally implicit basic assumption that the proletariat constitutes at all times a profound threat to the continued existence of capitalism as such. This, too, is an assumption that clearly derives from Marx himself, although the historical record since his day has hardly increased its plausibility.

This leads to a rather paradoxical conclusion: Marxist theory appears to be almost entirely based on, and in a sense increasingly inspired by, one crucial assumption—the proletariat's "natural" affinity with "socialism"—for which it has never been able to supply even a vaguely plausible rationale and for which the historical evidence is overwhelmingly negative. This curious

13   For some recent criticisms of the inadequacies of Marx's theory of the proletariat's conversion to socialism that, from three remarkably differing perspectives, nicely complement mine, see Alexander (1982a, 192-98), Balbus (1982, 48-54), and Calhoun (1983, 889-92).

condition is at least in part due, I believe, to another, perhaps even more profoundly characteristic attribute of Marxism, its adherence to Hegelian "immanentism" with the associated prohibition of "utopian blueprints."

Marxism: The "Immanentist" Core

The commitment to "immanent" critique runs through Marx's writings from the very first to the last. It is derived from the Hegelian argument that any ideal that claims to be more than the merely arbitrary, utopian fancy of an isolated individual must show that it is a necessary and essential "moment" immanent in presently emerging objective reality, in other words, that its time has really come. As opposed to a "utopian" critique of existing reality based on allegedly timeless standards of "justice" and detailed blueprints of a future society organized in accordance with those standards, "scientific" criticism of the present society must be based on the standards that can be demonstrated to be already immanent in it and about to become predominant. Marx fully absorbed this Hegelian position at a very early age, and only perfected it, once he had discovered the "material weapon" of his philosophy in the nascent proletariat, by stipulating that the objective conditions from which the ideal was to be realized would have to be material, economic conditions. To Marx and Engels, their "scientific socialism" was distinct from, and superior to the "utopian socialisms" of Owen, Fourier, and their ilk, precisely in that it did not depend on the supposedly timeless moral appeal of utopian blueprints of a perfect society designed by a single visionary, but on the "scientific" demonstration that present material conditions would inevitably produce a class struggle which, in turn, would inevitably produce a socialist society. This is perhaps the single most significant distinguishing feature of Marxism since *it* is the reason for its preoccupation with classes and class struggle.

Thus, the basic assumption of Marxism discussed in the preceding section is not so much that workers are "naturally" attracted by the appeal of a projected future socialism but that they are propelled or driven *toward* socialism by the objective material conditions the capitalist system imposes on them. The specific form that the future socialist society will take is entirely irrelevant, and to try and predetermine it is to engage in futile utopian speculation, as it belongs to the "realm of freedom" which cannot be scientifically predicted. What can be so predicted is how the present "realm of necessity" forces the proletariat to engage in a struggle that will eventually issue in that "realm of freedom" (cf. Giddens 1976, 102; Popper 1966b, 104–5). Thus, the "objective" class interests of the proletariat are not something it may or may not choose to adopt; they are "objective" precisely in the sense that sooner or later it will be *forced* to adopt them by its objective conditions of existence (cf. Ollman 1971, 122–24). The taboo on "utopian blueprints" within Marxism, as well as its claim to be "scientific," are, then, traceable to its ultimately Hegelian "historicism" (cf. Popper 1966b, 193–98, 318–19).[14]

Few of Marx's doctrines have remained as unquestioned and unchallenged as this curiously "anti-utopian" insistence on immanent critique.[15] After Marxism's "utopian" rivals had practically disappeared from the labor movements, Marxists came to take it for granted as entirely uncontroversial, hardly in need of an explicit justification anymore. Even some of Marxism's harshest critics accepted its "anti-utopianism" as no more than an indication that it sought to be hard-nosed, realistic, and

14   Even Alexander, who otherwise strongly emphasizes the difference between the "mature" Marx and Hegelianism, agrees: "If Marx is still a Hegelian, he is so only in one sense. He will use a historical standard of rationality to evaluate the putative excellence of contemporary life . . . Marx's proletarian, indeed his capitalist too, is irrational only in the special Hegelian sense of not knowing his world-historical interest, an ignorance caused by his lack of insight into the inner layer of capitalist production" (1982b, 186-87).
    The idea that ultimate recognition of that "world-historical interest" is in no way based on the putative excellence of *future* life but must, instead, be entirely the result of inescapable forces operating in the present—an idea Alexander identifies as Marx's "instrumental" and determinist conception of social action and order—is, however, just as Hegelian in origin.

15   Although, as may be suspected from the nature of the "revisionism" debates and the persistent temptation of "reformism" discussed in Chapter 2, while labor-movement leaders and spokesmen abandoned various brands of "utopian" socialism for "scientific" Marxism, the rank-and-file workers probably became, or remained, exclusively concerned with pragmatic efforts to obtain some partial improvements from governments and employers, that is, not terribly taken by either bucolic blueprints or "scientific," "anti-utopian" revolutionary theory.

firmly grounded in empirical reality.[16] If Marxists boast of their "anti-utopianism" at all, it is usually merely in a passing remark expressing the author's contempt for "detailed blueprints," clearly assuming that the futility of such things is self-evident (see, e.g., Freeman 1979, 24; E. O. Wright 1974, 90; 1978, 204; cf. Kolakowski 1978b, 282, 359; for a more elaborate statement see Cerroni 1978, 241–42, 252).

The underlying "immanentism" has remained as active and significant an ingredient of Marxist theory as ever. The orthodox and left-wing attacks on Bernstein were clearly attempts to preserve it. Lenin's lack of preparation for the postrevolutionary era was partly its result.[17] And all the theories of the state I have reviewed turn out to be based on the assumption that the working class would have (or should have) rallied to the socialist cause entirely for "immanent" reasons, that is, without requiring any clear previous information concerning "socialism's" an-

16   The most remarkable example of this is Popper, the great critic of "historicism" (1957, 1966a, b) who wrote: "Marx fought against what he called 'Utopianism', and rightly so" as its "attempts at rational planning" were "admittedly immature" (1966b, 333, n. 4). And elsewhere he argues: "Marx was to a certain extent justified in his refusal to embark upon social engineering. To organize the workers was undoubtedly the most important practical task of his day. If such a suspect excuse as 'the time was not ripe for it' can ever be justly applied, it must be applied to Marx's refusal to dabble in the problems of rational institutional engineering. (This point is illustrated by the childish character of the Utopian proposals down to and including, say, Bellamy)" (337, n. 21). Popper also attributes Marx's refusal to base himself on moral commitment to a desire to avoid the hypocritical moralizing he observed all around him (199-211). However, he also notes how "strikingly" the famous "anti-utopian" passage from *The Civil War in France*, in which Marx proclaims that the Paris Communards had "no ideals to realize, but to set free the elements of the new society with which the old collapsing bourgeois society itself is pregnant," exhibits "the historicist lack of plan" (337, n. 21). Moreover, Popper repeatedly criticizes Marxism and other "historicist" philosophies for restricting themselves to long-term, remote, and hence unfalsifiable prophecies, while ignoring the organizational details of the society-to-be (e.g., 1957, 36-39; 1966a, 9, 160-61, ch. 9; 1966b, 82-86). However, for Popper this is only a minor aspect of his critique of the "holistic" tendency in "historicism."

17   Significantly, even as he himself was advocating the most naive of utopian "blueprints," Lenin found it necessary to insist that "there is no trace of Utopianism in Marx, in the sense of inventing or imagining a 'new' society. No, he studies, as a process of natural history, the *birth* of the new society *from* the old, the forms of transition from the latter to the former"(1932, 42).

ticipated features, if it had not been for the successful preemptive maneuvers by the state or the capitalist class. In fact, the assumption appears to be so deeply ingrained that none of the authors discussed even *bother* to justify their failure to describe the "socialism" or "fundamental" change against which they measure the performance of the "capitalist state" (cf. Maravall 1979, 278–79, 285–87).

But the suggestion that it might not be unreasonable for real workers—as opposed to the mythical variety inspiring Marxist theorizing—to require a little more detailed information concerning the nature and feasibility of the goal before they will join the no doubt arduous and dangerous struggle for its realization, is not, after all, *that* far-fetched. In fact, non-Marxist students of social movements have long argued that for that kind of mass mobilization one needs not only a sense of shared interests, a sense of conflict with the interests of other classes, and a sense of solidarity with those sharing one's interests, but also, last but not least, some idea of a feasible alternative, of a way, that is, to actually *realize* those interests.[18] Not even the revelation of the proletariat's glorious historical mission is likely to persuade many workers to join a cause they consider hopeless or unclear (see, e.g., Bottomore 1979, 47; Giddens 1973, 111–14; Mann 1973, 13). Thus, the obvious reluctance of most workers in advanced capitalism to embrace revolutionary, or even merely radical "socialism" may well result simply from the fact that they have yet to be convinced of its feasibility (cf. Abercrombie, Hill, and Turner 1980, 140–55).[19]

While Marxist theorists have been busy denouncing modest social reform as a mere "prophylactic," the overwhelming majority of workers in most capitalist countries always seems to

18   For some evidence suggesting the importance of practical "utopian blueprints" as a way of gaining mass support for the German and Austrian Social Democratic parties before World War I—in spite of the "scientific" party theoreticians' contempt for such blueprints—see Calkin (1982).

19   Although, as Pinard and Hamilton (1984, 15-16) point out, "the lack of any expectancy of success, more than any other mobilization problems, is no doubt immediately responsible for the failure to act of innumerable groups throughout history," this obvious point is rarely explicitly considered even in the non-Marxist literature on social movements. Notable exceptions are Korpi (1974) and Oberschall (1980).

have supported cautious incrementalism as the most promising strategy for achieving some tangible improvement of their lot, even during the purportedly most "revolutionary" periods (see, e.g., Bottomore 1965, 67; Gay 1952, 109; B. Moore 1978, 185–226).[20] In fact, "revolutionary" ideologies and organizations appear to enjoy some worker support only when the workers are effectively excluded from the political process altogether. Once formal access to the polity has been won, the working-class rank and file appears to have been generally more eager than the "revolutionary" cadres and leaders to use this access to gain incremental improvements, with the leaders and their official ideologies usually following suit only reluctantly and after some delay (see, e.g., Feher and Heller 1983, 216–17, 226–27; Gay 1952; B. Moore 1978, 247–56, 474–79; Roberts et al. 1977, 173–75; Stephens 1979, 133). The reason for this would seem to be fairly obvious: wherever there was a choice between the invariably abstract, vague, and remote goal of "socialism" advocated by Marxist intellectuals and the concrete, tangible, immediate, and possibly incremental gains that appeared to be feasible and obtainable through political and industrial organization, most workers were understandably inclined toward the latter (cf. Abercrombie, Hill, and Turner 1980, 140–55; Benson 1978, 163–64, 170–71; Elster 1985, 530; Hamilton and Wright 1986, 402–10; Korpi 1983, 232). As Moore concludes, "If the workers refused some of the suggestions, and by and large displayed a reluctance to become revolutionary cannon fodder for the sake of ideals they had not created out of their own experience, who can blame them for that?" (B. Moore 1978, 479).[21]

20   The slightly absurd implication (for a Marxist) of Poulantzas's argument that the working class pressuring the state into imposing "necessary sacrifices" on the "dominant class" has become capitalism's best friend and the capitalist class its worst enemy, appears to be a tacit admission of this (see also Rich 1976, 658-61).

21   I am not suggesting in any way here that cautious incrementalism necessarily *is* the most fruitful policy for the working class in democratic capitalist countries. I am only saying that the choice in favor of incrementalism seems logical to me *in the absence of any well-defined alternative*. Thus, although there is much in Popper's critique of "historicism" that I can agree with, I do not share his dogmatic commitment to "piecemeal" as opposed to "utopian engineering" (see esp. Popper 1957, pt. 3; 1966a, 157-68). He rejects the lat-

As has become clear on several occasions in my discussions of Marxist criticisms of "reformism," what the Marxists object to most in the cautiously incrementalist strategy is not so much that it accepts the institutions of "bourgeois" democracy for the purpose of obtaining limited improvements for the working class, but that it is not part of a broader overall plan for an

---

ter on the following grounds: "What I criticize under the name of Utopian engineering recommends the reconstruction of society as a whole, i.e. the very sweeping changes whose practical consequences are hard to calculate owing to our limited experiences. It claims to plan rationally for the whole of society, although we do not possess anything like the factual knowledge which would be necessary to make good such an ambitious claim" (1966a, 161-62). Now, it is no doubt almost by definition easier to guess the likely feasibility, costs, and benefits of piecemeal, incremental change than of more sweeping transformations, and this is precisely why I have argued that, *without* a good case for the latter, workers, or anyone other than Marxist intellectuals for that matter, will naturally opt for the former. However, moderation and reformism obviously also have their problems and (opportunity) costs (see Martin 1975 for an intelligent, nondogmatic discussion of some of the problems of social-democratic reformism), and, although not easy, it is neither impossible nor fruitless to try and gauge the likely feasibility, (opportunity) costs, and benefits of more sweeping alternatives, and weigh the two options off against one another. In fact, this is precisely what any policy maker or would-be strategist is constantly doing, whether consciously or not. Even Popper's own dogmatic incrementalism is in fact an expression of his tacit belief that what he calls "holistic" change is *always* more costly and *less* beneficial and feasible than "piecemeal" change (for a brilliant critique of Popper along these lines, see Rule 1978, 82-107), although, as Eidlin (1984) appears to argue, this may not be a necessary inference from Popper's own critique of "utopian engineering" which only criticizes attempts at radical change without the requisite knowledge to avoid unacceptable risk. But at any rate, unlike Popper, I do not criticize Marxism's "dangerous dogmatic attachment to a blueprint for which countless sacrifices have been made" (Popper 1966a, 163; cf. Eidlin 1984, 513), but for demanding such sacrifices without even *bothering* to design a reasonably convincing blueprint. It is of interest that Przeworski, one of the few to be aware of the problem, ends up committing the same error. He argues that from the standpoint of purely economic interests it is not rational for workers to opt for socialism instead of incremental economic improvements under capitalism because the transition to socialism would initially be extremely costly in terms of living standards. Therefore, he reasons, the case for socialism will have to be based on the more radical need for complete freedom (Przeworski 1980; Przeworski and Wallerstein 1982). Yet here, too, the "rationality" of opting for "socialism" does not depend only on the cost involved in getting there, but equally on the total amount of benefits that can be expected from it, i.e., on the nature and feasibility of this "socialism," whether the desired or expected benefits be purely of a material or a more "radical," intangible kind.

eventual complete transition to "socialism." But, of course, such criticism only suggests *more* strongly the need for a well-designed, plausible alternative to incrementalism. Occasionally, some Marxists appear to sense the problem. Block, for instance, after distinguishing several levels of "working class consciousness," admits that the highest level, "a revolutionary consciousness that recognizes the necessity of socialist revolution" which "involves a strategic sense of precisely what needs to be done to produce a society that satisfies the needs of the working class" is, in fact, "only rarely achieved" (1978a, 213). But it is a rarity indeed to find a Marxist wondering whether this might have something to do with Marxism's *own* refusal to reveal "precisely what needs to be done to produce a society that satisfies the needs of the working class."

Unaware of how agonizingly acute it would soon become, Engels once formulated the major question confronting future generations of Marxists quite clearly: "If, in all the longer revolutionary periods it was so easy to win the great masses of the people by merely plausible false representations of the forward-thrusting minorities, why should they be less susceptible to ideas which were the truest reflection of their economic condition, which were nothing but the clear, rational expression of their needs?" (quoted by Zeitlin 1981, 231). In trying to answer it, Marxists did not, of course, doubt for a moment that the ideas in question *were* in fact the "truest reflection" of the "economic condition" of the "great masses of the people" and "nothing but the clear, rational expression of their needs." Instead, the firm conviction that they already *knew* what was rational and possible for the masses to do, combined with the masses' reluctance to do it, "paved the way for a succession of Marxist theorists, from Lukács and Gramsci to the Althusserian and Frankfurt schools, offering a diagnosis implying in the most oblique and scholarly manner that the proletariat was suffering from a kind of collective brain damage" (Parkin 1979, 81).

Marxists have claimed all along that they had an infallible, "scientific" method for establishing the real, "objective" interests of a class, and, therefore, what is possible and rational for it, especially for the working class, whether the actual members of that class agreed or not (cf. Gouldner 1985, 137–40). As Oll-man rightly notes, "for Marx, 'interest' refers to what it makes sense for people to want and do, given their overall situation, the most important element of which is their relation to the mode of production" (1971, 122–23). Similarly, for Lukács "class consciousness consists in fact of the appropriate and rational reactions 'imputed' [*zugerechnet*] to a particular typical position in the process of production" (1971, 51). This is not a position limited to Leninist-Lukácsian authoritarian Marxism. The American Marxist sociologist Erik Olin Wright maintains that "class interests in capitalist society are those potential objectives which become actual objectives of struggle in the absence of the mystifications and distortions of capitalist relations. Class interests, therefore, are in a sense hypotheses: they are hypotheses about the objectives of struggles which would occur if the actors in the struggle had a scientifically correct understanding of their situations" (1978, 89). Moreover, the "fundamental interests" of the working class consist of "socialism," of course, so that any limitation of the ongoing struggles to lesser causes "reflects an incomplete understanding of capitalist society as a whole, for it fails to grasp the possibility of transcending the entire system of capitalist exploitation through socialism" (91; see also E. O. Wright 1980, 339). As we have seen, time and again, all the various theories of the state, however much they may differ in other respects, share this basic assumption that the only "true," "objective" interest of the working class, its only rational goal, consists of the realization of "socialism."

If, then, the only rational thing for the proletariat to pursue is "socialism," its persistent refusal to recognize this must be a form of irrationality, the result of "mystifications and distortions" and of the absence of "a scientifically correct understanding" by the proletarians of their own situations. This is what is meant when Marxists, beginning with Marx and Engels themselves, speak of the "dominant ideology," "commodity fetishism," "false consciousness," "reified consciousness" (Lukács), "bourgeois hegemony" (Gramsci), and so on (see also, e.g., Corrigan, Ramsey, and Sayer 1978, 19–23; Genovese 1967, 300–303; Israel 1971, 90). The theories of the state that I have reviewed, too, are without exception attempts to explain how government policies have kept the workers from doing the rational thing. They all argue in one way or another that the timely reform policies implemented by governments in the advanced capitalist countries, together with the "massive indoctrination" undertaken by the "Ideological State Apparatuses," have succeeded again and again in convincing the workers of the basic "legitimacy" of the political and economic system. In other words, they have succeeded in keeping the workers in a state of irrational acceptance of the status quo (cf. Friedrichs 1980, 548).[22]

Somewhat ironically, this tends to turn Marxism into an angry version of Parsonsianism. The same formal reasoning leads to the same essentially normative conception of social order. Like Parsons, Marxists start out with the basic domain assumption that if social actors acted rationally in their best interests they would end up destroying (the present) social order. The problem then becomes how to explain the actors' *failure* to do so. Since both rule out sheer coercion as a sufficient force to keep the actors from pursuing their rational interests, both Parsons and these Marxists resort to powerful forces of normative "internalization" which are capable of making the social actors ignorant of their rational interests or unwilling to pursue them. That is to say, in both cases the otherwise inexplicable persistence of social order is explained as the result of a nonrational, normative force that keeps the actors' very goals and wishes in harmony with the social order. Both see social order as based on some form of normative integration, the only difference between them being that what Parsons considers a highly desirable form of nonrationality the Marxists view as an imposed form of *ir*rationality.

But many of the objections that have been raised against the Parsonsian conception of the social order as resting on the "internalization" of norms supporting that order are equally valid with respect to the angry, Marxist version. There is, in fact, no

---

22   Interestingly, "class consciousness" is also treated differently by class, in accordance with the tacit assumption of capitalism's ever-imminent demise discussed earlier. Whenever the capitalist class compromises, this is proof of its remarkably farsighted class consciousness, whereas when labor compromises this is equally strong proof of its "false consciousness"!

evidence for any widespread value consensus strong or specific enough to sustain a social order that would not have existed without it. The norms apparently subscribed to by the "masses" are neither particularly supportive of the status quo, nor particularly coherent or articulate. It would seem that only intellectuals are terribly and consistently preoccupied with articulating coherent systems of norms for themselves (see, e.g., Abercrombie, Hill, and Turner 1980; R. F. Hamilton 1972, 102–10; Mann 1970, 1975; Parkin 1971; Roberts et al. 1977, ch. 5; J. D. Wright 1976; Wrong 1961). Moreover, the evidence that the media of mass communication and other agencies of indoctrination have anywhere near the profound effect on people's values, particularly those of "the masses," as is claimed, is simply nonexistent (see, e.g., R. F. Hamilton 1972, 79–80; 1975, 183–217; B. Moore 1978, 100–102; Neuman 1981, 1266). All this, of course, raises the rather fundamental question, Does social "order" really require anything like a normative consensus? Do people really have to believe in the essential justice or "legitimacy" of the social system they live in to refrain from destroying it? Is it not possible, and even far more likely, that although many people feel they and others are subject to a great deal of injustice and inequity, few people have any very clear ideas of what could be done to remedy the situation, and even fewer have the resources to do it? Is it not far more likely, in other words, that whatever social order exists generally rests on its pragmatic acceptance by most people, on the acquiescence of those who do not like it but do not know how to change it either, rather than on the "internalization" of norms supporting that order (cf., e.g., Abercrombie, Hill, and Turner 1980, 158–69; Giddens 1981, 65–67; Goldthorpe 1972, 359–62; B. Moore 1978, 438; Plamenatz 1963, 360–63; Polan 1984, 187)?

But to confront such issues would for Marxists be tantamount to questioning their own most cherished domain assumptions, namely that "socialism" is both realizable and in the "objective" interest of the working class, and that this "objective" interest derives solely from the present, empirical condition of that class and in no way from any premature notions concerning the actual social arrangements that "socialism" might consist of. Rather than questioning such basic assumptions, Marxists have chosen the safer route of charging the proletariat with some form of irrationality and even stupidity (cf. Abercrombie, Hill, and Turner 1980, 158).[23] That the price of preserving doctrinal certitude in this way may well be an elitist arrogance toward the very "masses" Marxism wishes to see "emancipated" and the danger of authoritarianism is amply borne out by Lenin's political practice and Lukács's philosophical justification for it. Yet, as I have pointed out earlier, it is not obvious how else they could have preserved Marxist doctrine once the close marriage between its "immanent" critique and the anticipated struggles of the proletariat, taken for granted

23   I disagree, therefore, with Alexander's neo-Parsonsian explanation for the increasing recourse to normative and superstructural factors among Marxists to make sense of a world that refuses to act according to their specifications. According to Alexander (1982b, chs. 2, 3, 6, 10, but esp. 192-98, 343-70), after his break with Hegelianism, Marx became committed to a "presuppositional logic" which views social action as exclusively instrumental-adaptive. Consequently, Alexander argues, Marx was never able to provide a convincing theory to explain how the workers would evolve from a purely instrumental, self-interested attitude to a humanistic commitment to socialism and communism. To resolve this anomaly, and to account for the failed forecasts, Alexander continues, Marxists were forced to import more and more normative elements into the theory, but they have done so while trying to remain faithful to the original instrumental-materialist logic by invoking the dominance of the economic factor "in the last instance," in the manner of Engels and Althusser. Contrary to this, I have argued that Marx's determinism and his preoccupation with "objective" economic conditions and trends were a result of his commitment to establish the eventual arrival of "socialism" on more certain grounds than mere unpredictable human whim and fancy. Thus, it was because of his commitment to the Hegelian "immanentism" that Marx first discovered in the proletariat the "material weapon" of philosophy and subsequently became preoccupied with "the economic conditions of production, which can be determined with the precision of natural science" (Marx 1974, 426). And it was also because of *this* commitment that Marx simply *failed* to examine the human-motivational process by which the workers would come to translate their suffering from these "conditions of production" into a commitment to "socialism." My interpretation is further strengthened, as compared to Alexander's, by the fact that, as I have shown, both Marx's prematerialist Hegelian writings and his "mature" (in Alexander's terms "instrumentalist") thought are characterized by this "anti-utopianism." Moreover, as Habermas's recent attempts to "reconstruct" historical materialism on the basis of an evolutionary theory of normative development show, this commitment to "anti-utopianism"—i.e., this desire to safeguard one's moral and ideological commitments from the contingencies of voluntarism—can be served just as well by a normative determinism (cf. van den Berg 1980).

by Marx and Engels, had definitely become unraveled. Unwilling to give up their certainty about the coming of "socialism," which was originally based on the "scientific" prediction that the proletariat would be compelled, by its own suffering, to become its champion, yet unable to convince the same proletariat of its historic destiny, precisely *because* of this "anti-utopian" refusal to allow the coming of "socialism" to depend on such notoriously unreliable factors as moral convictions and "utopian" blueprints, Marxists had no choice but to assert the "true" interests of the proletariat *against* the proletariat if necessary.

Significantly, as I have argued before (see also van den Berg 1984), this elitist, potentially authoritarian claim to a higher insight is no less characteristic of the Hegelian, "critical" versions of Marxism, which are often depicted as more "humanist," "emancipatory," and democratic (see, e.g., Bottomore 1981, 2–5; Feenberg 1981; Gouldner 1980, 1985; Howard and Klare 1972; Jacoby 1981; Piccone 1983), than it is of their more "scientific" and presumably less democratic counterparts. Few, after all, have claimed to possess this privileged insight more explicitly and bluntly than the father of "Hegelianized" Marxism, Georg Lukács.[24] Those "critical theorists" who have tried to maintain *both* the notion of "objective" interests *and* a commitment to democracy, moreover, end up caught in the "dilemma of democratic radicalism": they simply waver between dogmatic elitism and democratic acceptance of the verdict of the "masses" without resolving the tension between these two positions (see van den Berg 1980).[25]

24 By contrast, among the most consistent opponents of the increasing authoritarianism of Soviet rule beginning under Lenin—an opposition that was to cost him dearly under Stalin—was none other than Nikolai Bukharin, the "mechanistic" economic determinist who served as a foil for Gramsci's theoretical ruminations. In fact, my arguments in Chapters 1 and 2 suggest that economic-determinist Marxists such as Bukharin and Kautsky are, because of their firm conviction that the overwhelming majority of the working class will *inevitably* come to its senses sooner or later, *less* likely to revert to authoritarian-elitist thinking and practices than those Marxists who have come to embrace a more "voluntaristic" version of Marxism in order to make sense of the persistent "false consciousness," "fetishism," etc., of the working class. Moreover, there is no necessary link between Hegelianism and voluntarism-humanism at all, as Gouldner seems to have thought (1980, 1985; cf. Berki 1983, 71).

25 Habermas has long recognized the connection between Lukácsian-Leninist vanguardism and its "consequences unveiled in Stalinist terror" (1984, 364),

But although such claims to intellectual superiority may allow Marxist theorizers to retain their belief in the "objective" validity of their critique of capitalism, they do little to convince the workers of the feasibility of the "socialist" alternative. Instead, such workers will be more inclined to look at Eastern European "really existing socialism" for clues concerning the likely costs and benefits of "socialism." This is, after all, not so illogical as these countries have by now accumulated up to seven decades of experience with Marxist-inspired social systems. But the results are hardly overwhelmingly favorable. Whatever the great achievements of "really existing socialism," it remains a far cry from the heralded "society free of inequalities, privileges and prejudices" (Przeworski 1981, 48) or "the realm of freedom, the final triumph of man over necessity and alienation" (Anderson 1966, 225). In many respects its performance may well appear to many workers to be decidedly inferior to that of advanced capitalism (cf. Heilbroner 1970, 79–114). If this is so, then the sheer existence of "really existing socialism" constitutes yet another powerful reason for the Western working classes to be wary of Marxist promises of redemption. As Bottomore cautiously puts it, "It seems probable, indeed, that the example of authoritarian socialist states has been a major factor in promoting the transformation of socialism in Western Europe into the defence of sectional interests, or at most a moderate reformist doctrine of trade unions" (Bottomore 1982, 270; cf. Aronson 1985; Bottomore 1984a, 48; 1984b, 157; Parkin 1979, 198–200).

The case of "really existing socialism" is in more than one respect a remarkable illustration of the significance of Marxism's ban on "utopianism." First, whatever other reasons and mitigating circumstances there may have been (see, e.g., Anderson 1966, 225–30), its authoritarian features are, at least in part, also the product of Marxism's prohibition of "utopian blueprints" which left Lenin with incredibly few and vague ideas about what to do *after* he had successfully attained power and with little more than a vanguard party and explicitly elitist

---

but he nevertheless persists in his search for a way to identify the real interests of those to be emancipated as distinct from their merely subjectively felt interests (see also van den Berg 1987).

claims to privileged insight to work with (cf. Bell 1961, 374–75; Popper 1966a, 143–45).[26] But no less indicative of their persistent "anti-utopian" lack of concern with the precise features of "socialism" is the astonishingly cavalier manner with which Marxists have ever since treated the problematic existence of "real socialism" which is so obviously crucial to their critique of capitalism. As I have noted before, some Marxists have simply decided to relabel it as a form of ("state") capitalism, which, of course, preserves the purity of the socialist ideal but hardly helps to convince anyone of its feasibility (cf. Balbus 1982, 103–4, 165, 208). Others simply ignore it (cf. Miliband 1977, 14–15, 29). In neither case, however, is the crucial significance of the lessons of "really existing socialism" for the critique and eventual transformation of capitalism acknowledged.[27]

Western Marxists appear to take it for granted that the experiences of Eastern Europe do not really affect the possibility of a "true" socialism in the advanced capitalist countries. Yet, as Parkin sarcastically points out, "in the case of the real socialism . . . the snag is that those assigned the burdensome task of making it come about are much more likely to be impressed by what is *empirically probable* than by what is merely *theoretically possible*" (1979, 199). Thus, in order to convince these people of the validity of their critique of capitalism, Marxists *first* have to estab-

---

26   But Popper appears to believe that things might well have turned out much better "but for the somewhat accidental fact that Marx discouraged research in social technology" (1966b, 198). As I have tried to show, this was anything *but* "accidental."

27   A partial exception here are the Trotskyist critics of the "bureaucratic degeneration" of socialism under Stalin and his successors. But they are more notable for the stubbornness with which they cling to Marxism's pre-Leninist "innocence" than for their persuasiveness in seriously trying to draw lessons about how "socialism" should be organized to provide a plausible and feasible goal for Western workers to struggle for. According to the Trotskyists things only started to go wrong when Stalin lost faith in the natural and unlimited revolutionary energies of the "toiling masses" of the world and launched his retrenchment policy to save "socialism in one country." But while advocating a vaguely articulated system of direct "council democracy" based on the "toiling masses'" undying revolutionary fervor, Trotskyists do not question the need for a "vanguard" firmly leading those same "masses" in the least (see, e.g., Mandel 1978; 1979). Clearly this unstable theoretical compound is not very likely to sway those workers who are *not yet* overcome with revolutionary fervor.

lish the empirical probability of realizing the alternative they have in mind. This need not involve silly bucolic utopias at all. On the contrary, what it requires is thorough examination of the various alternative social arrangements on the basis of the best empirical evidence and the soundest arguments available, in which the lessons of Eastern Europe would, of course, take a prominent place indeed. How can we combine workers' control and planning, freedom and equality, central control and individual liberty, regulation and efficiency? Moreover, what are the likely distributions of costs and benefits of different combinations? What are the likely balances of costs and benefits of different strategies to realize them? These questions cannot be answered easily or definitively, but they can certainly be addressed with rational arguments and large amounts of empirical evidence (cf. Anderson 1976, 103–21; Dahl 1985; Giddens 1981, 248; Heilbroner 1970, 127–46; 1980, 147–74; Rule 1978, 73–81, 163–71). Most people no doubt require at least *some* reasonably plausible and empirically grounded argument concerning their chances of success before they enthusiastically join the struggle for "socialism." Yet Marxists have always had a ready-made excuse for *not* addressing these questions: that would be mere utopian speculation.[28] But ironically, in the *absence* of such speculation it is the Marxist critique of advanced capitalism that is bound to seem far *more* hopelessly utopian in the eyes of its purported beneficiaries.[29]

Instead of dealing with these nuts-and-bolts questions of socialist organization, Marxist theorizers have indulged in scholastic debates about "epistemological breaks," the dominance of

28   Even when the explicit intent is to draw a realistic picture of the society Marxism strives to achieve, it is apparently impossible to go beyond listing a few farfetched *desiderata* such as the abolition of any division of labor and all coercion, the elimination of all social constraints, the transformation of work into "self-activity," and so on, which, *in the absence of any attempt to show how they might be practically realized*, sound utopian in the extreme (see, e.g., Hunt 1984, 212-65; Ollman 1977; Przeworski 1980, 147-53).

29   Moreover, by virtually ignoring those "bourgeois" writings that *do* address these questions, from welfare economics (e.g., Sharp 1973) and normative democratic theory (e.g., Dahl 1970) to arguments for a reinvigoration of the free market economy, Marxists have left the field entirely to liberal reformers and (neo)conservatives (e.g., Berger 1986), thereby further reinforcing the impression of the impossibility of more radical social change.

the economy "in the last instance," the true definition of "forces" and "relations" of production, the exact size of the pro- letariat, the measurement of the "rate of exploitation," and, generally, the "authentic" meaning of Marx's every written word. It has often been remarked that Marxism seems to be more an expression of the aspirations and "objective" condi- ᵛ| tions of intellectuals than of the working class (see, e.g., Becker 1983, 273; Feher and Heller 1983, 223; Goldthorpe 1979; Gouldner 1985; Kolakowski 1978b, 94–95; see also Mattick 1983). I believe this is essentially a correct assessment, and it, too, has a lot to do with Marxism's longstanding commitment to "immanentism." The attempt to demonstrate "scientifically" the necessary advent of "socialism" by arguing that the proletariat would be compelled by the force of its own miserable working and living conditions to realize it, seems to have been, from the outset, better suited to convince secularized intellectuals of the "objective" validity and inevitability of their hopes and ideals than to convince workers to do what History has commissioned them to do. In fact, this doctrine in effect treats the workers as of importance only to the extent that they serve as the "weapon of philosophy," as the "material force" that raises Marxism above its utopian competitors. The wishes and needs of the workers are of no significance in their own right except insofar as they drive the workers irresistibly toward the "socialist" cause. The workers are not to be convinced to join the cause by open and rational argument and debate about the various alter- native plans and strategies in the course of which they might reject their mission or seek to modify it, but to be driven by blind compulsion. Under these assumptions, as Popper rightly notes, *"reason can have no part in bringing about a reasonable world"* (1966b, 202).

But it is not reason in general that is being ruled out here, just the notoriously fallible reason of the ordinary mortals on whom the glorious mission of fulfilling the Plan of History has been bestowed. Reason, or the "scientific" knowledge of all this, is something that remains as yet reserved for those intellectuals who have been initiated into "scientific socialism." This does in- deed seem to be a faith tailor-made to appeal to the secularized, chronically somewhat disaffected (see Mann 1975) intellectuals of capitalist society. Like other religions, it offers a promise of salvation that is beyond verification because its consummation lies in the indefinite future. Yet, unlike conventional religions it does not resort to divine revelation or a higher morality which have become somewhat discredited in the eyes of the secular intelligentsia. Instead it is based on what appear to be purely rationalistic grounds, exclusively concerned with the here and now, and in no way dependent on the precise form the ultimate salvation will take. Thus, Marxism appears to offer the best of both worlds: the satisfaction of being "the confidants of history" (Gouldner 1985, 22), privy to a Higher Knowledge without fear of refutation, *yet* this Knowledge still appears to be firmly based on the sort of "scientific" rationalism that the modern intelligentsia claims as *its* special field of competence. If ever there was an "opium for the intellectuals" this must surely be it, as Raymond Aron (1957) pointed out long ago.

Only this can, I think, explain Marxism's remarkable insensitivity to the hard and uncertain choices continuously confronting the "masses" whose benefactor it claims to be. Only this can explain how Marxists can routinely dismiss tangible improvements that have required long and hard struggles as insignificant compared to the unspecified "fundamental" transformations they had in mind.[30] Only this, finally, can explain their incredible inability to understand that the "masses" might want to know, however incompletely, *what* they are fighting for before they risk being blown off the barricades erected in the name of "socialism."[31]

Marxism is not alone in holding present reality up against a tacit or explicit alternative. As I have argued elsewhere, any evaluation is necessarily based on what is considered to be the most likely or most worthy "contrast model," or "utopia" (see van den Berg 1981). Nor do I criticize Marxism for employing a utopia that is too sweeping or otherwise inherently unattain-

30   As Wolfe notes, *"the welfare state is more easily denounced by intellectuals than by workers"* (A. Wolfe 1974, 143; see also Stephens 1979, 174-75).

31   In addition, many of the strategic errors and failures committed by Marxist-inspired organizations can be traced to the rigid theoretical dogmatism of the intellectuals who invariably lead such organizations. For a wealth of particularly disturbing examples, given their outcome, see R. F. Hamilton (1982, ch.11).

able to be a reasonable basis for a critical analysis of an imperfect reality, as Popper and others have done. Rather, I criticize it for refusing even to *discuss* the implicit utopia on which its every argument is nevertheless crucially based. Marxism is not distinguished by its dependence on a tacit utopia but by its success in withdrawing this utopia from any form of rational debate or critical inspection. It thereby becomes, as Lukes notes, an "irrational endeavour" (1985, 145).[32]

Moreover, the ban on discussing "utopian blueprints" and the *de facto* disregard for the "really existing socialist" experience have not exactly increased our practical understanding of how to create a better society. As Irving Howe comments in regard to Marxism's past record, "An intellectual scandal has been its paucity of thought regarding the structural workings of socialist society: most Marxists, in fact, have not thought it worth the trouble" (1981, 493). I have tried to show here that this "intellectual scandal" is very much rooted in one of Marxism's core doctrines, perhaps *the* distinguishing doctrine: its peculiar "immanentism" and the resulting taboo on "utopian blueprints." This raises a somewhat subversive question: if this is truly the *differentia specifica* of Marxism, has Marxism itself perhaps been one of the major obstacles in the search for a genuine socialist alternative?

32 Lukes is worth quoting at length on the subject: "Because it inhibits the specification of its ultimate aim, while presuming to foresee the future, in which its eventual realization is somehow guaranteed, it foreswears both the clarification of the long-term consequences by which alternative courses of action are to be judged and, as Dewey put it, the 'open and unprejudiced' examination of those alternatives" (1985, 145-46).

Bibliography

[handwritten annotations in top margin: "Aronowitz", "Cohen", "3rd World? Chile?", "Grunge?", "Policy domains—ed", "L'pr??"]

Abercrombie, Nicholas; Hill, Stephen; and Turner, Bryan S.
 1980 *The Dominant Ideology Thesis*. London: Allen & Unwin.
Abercrombie, Nicholas, and Urry, John
 1983 *Capital, Labour and the Middle Classes*. London: Allen & Unwin.
Alexander, Jeffrey C.
 1982a *Theoretical Logic in Sociology*. Vol. 1, *Positivism, Presuppositions, and Current Controversies*. Berkeley: University of California Press.
 1982b *Theoretical Logic in Sociology*. Vol. 2, *The Antinomies of Classical Thought: Marx and Durkheim*. Berkeley: University of California Press.
Alford, Robert R.
 1975 "Paradigms of Relations between State and Society." In Lindberg et al. 1975: 145–60.
Alford, Robert R., and Friedland, Roger
 1975 "Political Participation and Public Policy." *Annual Review of Sociology* 1: 429–79.
 1985 *Powers of Theory: Capitalism, the State, and Democracy*. London: Cambridge University Press.
Althusser, Louis
 1969 *For Marx*. London: New Left Books.
 1971 *Lenin and Philosophy and Other Essays*. New York: Monthly Review Press.
 1976 *Essays in Self-Criticism*. London: New Left Books.
Althusser, Louis, and Balibar, Etienne
 1970 *Reading Capital*. London: New Left Books.
Altman, Andrew
 1981 "Is Marxism Utopian?" *Philosophy and Social Criticism* 8, no. 4 (Winter): 389–403.

Anderson, Perry
  1966 "Problems of Socialist Strategy." In Anderson and Blackburn 1966: 212–90.
  1976 *Considerations on Western Marxism.* London: New Left Books.
  1977 "The Antinomies of Antonio Gramsci." *New Left Review,* no. 100 (November 1976-January 1977): 5–78.
  1980 *Arguments within English Marxism.* London: New Left Books.
  1983 "Trotsky's Interpretation of Stalinism." *New Left Review,* no. 139 (May-June): 49–58.
Anderson Perry, and Blackburn, Robin, eds.
  1966 *Towards Socialism.* Ithaca, N.Y.: Cornell University Press.
Appelbaum, Richard P.
  1979 "Born-Again Functionalism? A Reconsideration of Althusser's Structuralism." *Insurgent Sociologist* 9, no. 1 (Summer): 18–33.
Armitage, Andrew
  1975 *Social Welfare in Canada: Ideals and Realities.* Toronto: McClelland & Stewart.
Armour, Philip K., and Coughlin, Richard M.
  1985 "Social Control and Social Security: Theory and Research on Capitalist and Communist Nations." *Social Science Quarterly* 66, no. 4 (December): 770–88.
Armstrong, Hugh
  1977 "The Labour Force and State Workers in Canada." In Panitch, ed. 1977: 289–310.
Aron, Raymond
  1957 *The Opium of the Intellectuals.* London: Secker and Warburg.
Aronson, Ronald
  1985 "Historical Materialism, Answer to Marxism's Critics." *New Left Review,* no. 152 (July-August): 74–94.
Avineri, Shlomo
  1968 *The Social and Political Thought of Karl Marx.* London: Cambridge University Press.
Bachrach, Peter
  1967 *The Theory of Democratic Elitism.* Boston: Little, Brown.

Bachrach, Peter, and Baratz, Morton S.
1962 "Two Faces of Power." *American Political Science Review* 56, no. 4 (December): 947–52.

Badie, Bertrand, and Birnbaum, Pierre
1983 *The Sociology of the State*. Chicago: University of Chicago Press.

Balbus, Isaac D.
1982 *Marxism and Domination: A Neo-Hegelian, Feminist, Psychoanalytic Theory of Sexual, Political and Technological Liberation*. Princeton, N.J.: Princeton University Press.

Baran, Paul A.
1957 *The Political Economy of Growth*. New York: Monthly Review Press.

Barry, Brian
1978 *Sociologists, Economists and Democracy*. Chicago: University of Chicago Press.

Bauman, Zygmunt
1983 *Memories of Class: The Pre-History and After Life of Class*. Boston: Routledge & Kegan Paul.

Becker, Werner
1983 "Die rückwärtsgewandte Utopie: Eine kritische Bilanz der Gegenwartsbedeutung von Karl Marx." *Politische Studien* 34 (May-June): 269–78.

Beedle, Paul, and Taylor-Gooby, Peter
1983 "Ambivalence and Altruism: Public Opinion about Taxation and Welfare." *Policy and Politics* 11, no. 1: 15–39.

Bell, Daniel
1961 *The End of Ideology: On the Exhaustion of Political Ideas in the Fifties*. Rev. ed. New York: Free Press.
1976 *The Cultural Contradictions of Capitalism*. New York: Basic Books.

Benhabib, Seyla.
1981 "Modernity and the Aporias of Critical Theory." *Telos*, no. 49 (Autumn): 39–59.

Benson, Leslie
1978 *Proletarians and Parties*. London: Tavistock.

Benton, Ted
1984 *The Rise and Fall of Structural Marxism: Althusser and His Influence*. New York: St. Martin's Press.

Berger, Peter
  1986 *The Capitalist Revolution: Fifty Propositions about Prosperity,
  Equality, and Liberty*. New York: Basic Books.
Berki, R. N.
  1983 *Insight and Vision: The Problem of Communism in Marx's
  Thought*. London: J. M. Dent.
Berlin, Isaiah
  1969 *Four Essays on Liberty*. Oxford: Oxford University Press.
Berman, Edward H.
  1983 *The Influence of the Carnegie, Ford, and Rockefeller Foundations on American Foreign Policy: The Ideology of Philanthropy*.
  Albany: State University of New York Press.
Bernstein, Eduard
  1909 *Evolutionary Socialism*. New York: Huebsch.
  1922 *Der Sozialismus einst und jetzt*. Stuttgart: J.H.W. Dietz
  Nachfolger.
Best, Michael H., and Connolly, William E.
  1979 "Politics and Subjects: The Limits of Structural Marxism." *Socialist Review*, no. 48 (vol. 9, no. 6, November-December): 75–99.
Birnbaum, Pierre
  1985 "Universal Suffrage, the Vanguard Party and Mobilization in Marxism." *Government and Opposition* 20, no. 1 (Winter): 53–69.
Blackburn, R., ed.
  1972 *Ideology in Social Science*. London: Fontana.
Blanke, Bernhard; Jürgens, Ulrich; and Kastendiek, Hans
  1978 "On the Current Marxist Discussion on the Analysis of
  Form and Function of the Bourgeois State: Reflections on
  the Relationship of Politics to Economics." In Holloway and
  Picciotto, eds. 1978: 108–47.
Block, Fred
  1977a "Beyond Corporate Liberalism." *Social Problems* 24, no.
  3 (February): 352–61.
  1977b "The Ruling Class Does Not Rule: Notes on the Marxist Theory of the State." *Socialist Revolution*, no. 33 (vol. 7, no.
  3, May-June): 6–28.
  1978a "Class Consciousness and Capitalist Rationalization: A

Reply to Critics." *Socialist Review*, nos. 40–41 (vol. 8, nos. 4–5, July-October): 212–20.

1978b "Reply to 'Before Radical Rejection.' " *Social Problems* 25, no. 3 (February): 350–51.

1980 "Beyond Relative Autonomy: State Managers as Historical Subjects." *Socialist Register, 1980*: 227–42.

1981 "The Fiscal Crisis of the Capitalist State." *Annual Review of Sociology* 7: 1–27.

Bobbio, Norberto

1978a "Are There Alternatives to Representative Democracy?" *Telos*, no. 35 (Spring): 17–30.

1978b "Is There a Marxist Theory of the State?" *Telos*, no. 35 (Spring): 5–16.

Boggs, Carl

1976 *Gramsci's Marxism*. London: Pluto Press.

1984 *The Two Revolutions: Antonio Gramsci and the Dilemmas of Western Marxism*. Boston: South End Press.

Boggs, Carl, and Plotke, David, eds.

1980 *The Politics of Eurocommunism: Socialism in Transition*. Montreal: Black Rose Books.

Bottomore, T. B.

1965 *Classes in Modern Society*. London: Allen & Unwin.

Bottomore, Tom

1975 *Marxist Sociology*. London: Macmillan.

1979 *Political Sociology*. New York: Harper & Row.

1981 "Introduction." In Bottomore, ed. 1981: 1–22.

1982 "The Political Role of the Working Class in Western Europe." In Giddens and Mackenzie 1982: 265–75.

1984a *The Frankfurt School*. London: Tavistock.

1984b *Sociology and Socialism*. London: Wheatsheaf Books.

Bottomore, Tom, ed.

1981 *Modern Interpretations of Marx*. Oxford: Basil Blackwell.

Bottomore, Tom, and Nisbet, Robert, eds.

1978 *A History of Sociological Analysis*. New York: Basic Books.

Bowles, Samuel, and Gintis, Herbert

1976 *Schooling in Capitalist America*. New York: Basic Books.

Braverman, Harry

1974 *Labor and Monopoly Capital*. New York: Monthly Review Press.

Breines, Paul
1981 "The Two Marxisms: Vintage Gouldner." *Theory and Society* 10, no. 2 (March): 249–64.

Bridges, Amy Beth
1974 "Nicos Poulantzas and the Marxist Theory of the State." *Politics and Society* 4, no. 2: 161–90.

Buchanan, Allen E.
1982 *Marx and Justice*. Totowa, N.J.: Rowman and Littlefield.

Buci-Glucksmann, Christine
1975 *Gramsci et l'état: pour une théorie matérialiste de la philosophie*. Paris: Fayard.

Burawoy, Michael
1978 "Contemporary Currents in Marxist Theory." *American Sociologist* 13 (February): 50–64.

Burris, Val
1979 "The Structuralist Influence in Marxist Theory and Research." *Insurgent Sociologist* 9, no. 1 (Summer): 4–17.

Burstein, Paul
1981 "The Sociology of Democratic Politics and Government." *Annual Review of Sociology* 7: 291–319.

Calhoun, Craig
1982 *The Question of Class Struggle: Social Foundations of Popular Radicalism during the Industrial Revolution*. Chicago: University of Chicago Press.
1983 "The Radicalism of Tradition: Community Strength or Vulnerable Disguise and Borrowed Language?" *American Journal of Sociology* 88, no. 5 (March): 886–914.

Calkin, Craig
1982 "The Uses of Utopianism: The Millenarian Dream in Central European Social Democracy before 1914." *Central European History* 15: 124–48.

Callinicos, Alex
1976 *Althusser's Marxism*. London: Pluto Press.

Caplan, Jane
1977 "Theories of Fascism: Nicos Poulantzas as Historian." *History Workshop*, no. 3 (Spring): 85–100.

Carrillo, Santiago
1978 *Eurocommunism and the State*. Westport, Conn.: Lawrence Hill.

Carnoy, Martin
1984 *The State and Political Theory*. Princeton, N.J.: Princeton University Press.

Carter, Robert
1985 *Capitalism, Class Conflict and the New Middle Class*. London: Routledge & Kegan Paul.

Carver, Terrell
1980 "Marx, Engels and Dialectics." *Political Studies* 28, no. 3: 353–63.
1984a *Marx and Engels: The Intellectual Relationship*. Bloomington; Indiana University Press.
1984b "Marx, Engels and Scholarship." *Political Studies* 32, no. 2: 249–56.

Castells, Manuel
1980 *The Economic Crisis and American Society*. Princeton, N.J.: Princeton University Press.

Cerroni, Umberto
1978 "Democracy and Socialism." *Economy and Society* 7, no. 3 (August): 241–83.

Chang, Sherman H. M.
1931 *The Marxian Theory of the State*. Philadelphia: published by the author.

Chase-Dunn, Christopher K.
1980 "Socialist States in the Capitalist World-Economy." *Social Problems* 27, no. 5 (June): 505–25.

Chorney, Harold, and Hansen, Phillip
1980 "The Falling Rate of Legitimation: The Problem of the Contemporary Capitalist State in Canada." *Studies in Political Economy*, no. 4 (Autumn): 65–98.

Clarke, Simon
1977 "Marxism, Sociology and Poulantzas' Theory of the State." *Capital and Class*, no. 2 (Summer): 1–31.

Clarke, Simon; Lovell, Terry; McDonnell, Kevin; Robins, Kevin; and Seidler, Victor Jeleniewski
1980 *One-Dimensional Marxism: Althusser and the Politics of Culture*. London: Allison & Busby.

Clement, Wallace
1977 "The Corporate Elite, the Capitalist Class, and the Canadian State." In Panitch, ed. 1977: 225–48.

Cohen, G. A.
   1978 *Marx's Theory of History, A Defence.* Oxford: Oxford University Press.
Cohen, Marshall; Nagel, Thomas; and Scanlon, Thomas, eds.
   1980 *Marx, Justice, and History.* Princeton, N.J.: Princeton University Press.
Colletti, Lucio
   1975 "Introduction." In Marx 1975: 7–56.
Collins, Randall
   1975 *Conflict Sociology: Toward an Explanatory Science.* New York: Academic Press.
   1985 *Three Sociological Traditions.* New York: Oxford University Press.
Connell, R. W.
   1982 "A Critique of the Althusserian Approach to Class." In Giddens and Held 1982: 130–47.
Connor, James E.
   1968 "Introduction." In Lenin 1968: xi–xxvii.
Corrigan, Philip; Ramsay, Harvie; and Sayer, Derek
   1978 *Socialist Construction and Marxist Theory: Bolshevism and Its Critique.* London: Macmillan.
Cotterrell, Roger
   1981 "Conceptualizing Law: Problems and Prospects of Contempoary Legal Theory." *Economy and Society* 10, no. 3 (August): 348–66.
Cottrell, Allin
   1984 *Social Classes in Marxist Theory.* London: Routledge & Kegan Paul.
Craib, Ian
   1984 *Modern Social Theory: From Parsons to Habermas.* Brighton: Wheatsheaf Books.
Craven, Paul
   1980 *"An Impartial Umpire": Industrial Relations and the Canadian State 1900–1911.* Toronto: University of Toronto Press.
   1983 "Reply to van den Berg and Smith." *Canadian Journal of Sociology* 8, no. 3 (Summer): 329–32.
Crossman, R., ed.
   1950 *The God That Failed: Six Studies in Communism.* London: Hamish Hamilton.

Crozier, Michel
1964 *The Bureaucratic Phenomenon*. Chicago: University of Chicago Press.
Cuneo, Carl J.
1978 "Class Exploitation in Canada." *Canadian Review of Sociology and Anthropology* 15, no. 3: 284–300.
1979 "State, Class, and Reserve Labour: The Case of the 1941 Canadian Unemployment Insurance Act." *Canadian Review of Sociology and Anthropology* 16, no. 2: 147–70.
1980 "State Mediation of Class Contradictions in Canadian Unemployment Insurance, 1930–1935." *Studies in Political Economy*, no. 3 (Spring): 37–65.
1982 "Class Struggle and Measurement of the Rate of Surplus Value." *Canadian Review of Sociology and Anthropology* 19, no. 3: 377–425.
1984 "Reconfirming Karl Marx's Rate of Surplus Value." *Canadian Review of Sociology and Anthropology* 21, no. 1: 98–104.
Curtis, James E., and Scott, William G.
1979 *Social Stratification: Canada*. 2d ed. Scarborough, Ont.: Prentice Hall of Canada.
Dahl, Robert A.
1956 *A Preface to Democratic Theory*. Chicago: University of Chicago Press.
1958 "A Critique of the Ruling Elite Model." *American Political Science Review* 52, no. 2 (June): 463–69.
1961 *Who Governs?* New Haven: Yale University Press.
1970 *After the Revolution? Authority in a Good Society*. New Haven: Yale University Press.
1971a *Democracy in the United States: Promise and Performance*. 2d ed. Chicago: Rand McNally.
1971b *Polyarchy, Participation and Opposition*. New Haven: Yale University Press.
1982 *Dilemmas of Pluralist Democracy: Autonomy vs. Control*. New Haven: Yale University Press.
1985 *A Preface to Economic Democracy*. Berkeley: University of California Press.
Dahl, Robert A., and Lindblom, Charles E.
1953 *Politics, Economics and Welfare*. New York: Harper & Row.

Dahrendorf, Ralf
1959 *Class and Class Conflict in Industrial Society.* Stanford: Stanford University Press.
Dawe, Alan
1978 "Theories of Social Action." In Bottomore and Nisbet 1978: 362–417.
Deaton, Rick
1973 "The Fiscal Crisis of the State." In Roussopoulos 1973: 18–58.
Devine, Joel A.
1985 "State and State Expenditure: Determinants of Social Investment and Social Consumption Spending in the Postwar United States." *American Sociological Review* 50, no. 2 (April): 150–65.
DiTomaso, Nancy
1982 " 'Sociological Reductionism' from Parsons to Althusser: Linking Action and Structure in Social Theory." *American Sociological Review* 47, no. 1 (February): 14–28.
Dobb, Maurice
1964 *Studies in the Development of Capitalism.* New York: International Publishers.
Domhoff, G. William
1967 *Who Rules America?* Englewood Cliffs, N.J.: Prentice-Hall.
1970 *The Higher Circles.* New York: Random House.
1972 "Some Friendly Answers to Radical Critics." *Insurgent Sociologist* 2, no. 2 (Spring): 27–39.
1974 *The Bohemian Grove and Other Retreats: A Study in Ruling-Class Cohesiveness.* New York: Harper & Row.
1976 "I Am Not an 'Instrumentalist.' " *Kapitalistate*, no. 4–5: 221–24.
1977a "More on the Democratic Party: A Rejoinder to Plotke." *Socialist Revolution*, no. 31 (vol. 7, no. 1, January-February): 51–58.
1977b "Why Socialists Should Be Democrats: A Tactic for the Class Struggle in Corporate America." *Socialist Revolution*, no. 31 (vol. 7, no. 1, January-February): 25–36.
1978 *Who Really Rules? New Haven and Community Power Re-Examined.* New Brunswick, N.J.: Transaction Books.

1979 *The Powers That Be: Processes of Ruling Class Domination in America.* New York: Random House.

1980 Reply to O'Connor letter. *Insurgent Sociologist* 10, no. 1 (Summer): 81–83.

1983 *Who Rules America Now? A View for the '80s.* Englewood Cliffs, N.J.: Prentice-Hall.

1986 Review of *The Influence of the Carnegie, Ford, and Rockefeller Foundations on American Foreign Policy: The Ideology of Philanthropy*, by Edward H. Berman. *Contemporary Sociology* 15, no. 1: 131–32.

Draper, Hal

1962 "Marx and the Dictatorship of the Proletariat." *New Politics* 1, no. 4: 91–104.

1974 "Marx on Democratic Forms of Government." *Socialist Register, 1974*: 101–24.

1977 *Karl Marx's Theory of Revolution.* Vol. 1, *State and Bureaucracy.* New York: Monthly Review Press.

1978 *Karl Marx's Theory of Revolution.* Vol. 2, *The Politics of Social Classes.* New York: Monthly Review Press.

Dubiel, Helmut.

1985 *Theory and Politics: Studies in the Development of Critical Theory.* Trans. Benjamin Gregg. Cambridge, Mass.: MIT Press.

Edelman, Murray

1975 "The Shaping of Beliefs through Politics" In Lindberg et al. 1975: 309–20.

Edwards, Richard

1979 *Contested Terrain: The Transformation of the Workplace in the Twentieth Century.* New York: Basic Books.

Ehrenburg, John R.

1980 "Dialectics of Dictatorship: Marx and the Proletarian State." *Social Praxis* 7, nos. 1–2: 21–39.

Eidlin, Fred

1984 "L'aspect radical et révolutionnarie de la théorie sociale et politique de Popper." *Canadian Journal of Political Science* 17, no. 3 (September): 503–20.

Elster, Jon

1979 *Ulysses and the Syrens: Studies in Rationality and Irrationality.* New York: Wiley.

1982 "Marxism, Functionalism, and Game Theory: The Case for Methodological Individualism." *Theory and Society* 11, no. 4 (July): 453–82.

1983 "Reply to Comments." *Theory and Society* 12, no. 1 (January): 111–20.

1985 *Making Sense of Marx*. London: Cambridge University Press.

Engels, Friedrich

1939 *Anti-Dühring*. New York: International Publishers.

1972 *The Origin of the Family, Private Property, and the State*. New York: Pathfinder Press.

Esping-Andersen, Gosta

1985 *Politics against Markets: The Social Democratic Road to Power*. Princeton, N.J.: Princeton University Press.

Esping-Andersen, Gosta; Friedland, Roger; and Wright, Erik Olin

1976 "Modes of Class Struggle and the Capitalist State." *Kapitalistate*, nos. 4–5: 186–220.

Fairley, John

1980 "French Developments in the Theory of State Monopoloy Capitalism." *Science and Society* 44, no. 3 (Fall): 305–25.

Feenberg, Andrew

1981 *Lukács, Marx, and the Sources of Critical Theory*. Totowa, N.J.: Rowman and Littlefield.

Feher, Ferenc, and Heller, Agnes

1983 "Class, Democracy, Modernity." *Theory and Society* 12, no. 2 (March): 211–44.

Fernbach, David

1974 "Introduction." In Marx 1974: 9–72.

Festinger, L.; Riecker, M.; and Schachter, S.

1956 *When Prophecy Fails*. Minneapolis: University of Minnesota Press.

Fetscher, Irving

1961 "Marx, Engels, and the Future Society." *Survey*, no. 38 (October): 100–110.

Filo Della Torre, Paolo; Mortimer, Edward; and Story, Jonathan, eds.

1979 *Eurocommunism: Myth or Reality?* Harmondsworth: Penguin Books.

Fine, Ben, and Harris, Lawrence
1976 "Controversial Issues in Marxist Economic Theory." *Socialist Register, 1976*: 141–78.

Finegold, Kenneth, and Skocpol, Theda
1980 "Capitalists, Farmers and Workers in the New Deal—The Ironies of Government Intervention." Paper presented at the American Political Science Association annual meeting, Washington D.C., August 1980.

Finkel, Alvin
1977 "Origins of the Welfare State in Canada." In Panitch, ed. 1977: 344–70.

Fisher, Donald
1983 "The Role of Philanthropic Foundations in the Reproduction and Production of Hegemony: Rockefeller Foundations and the Social Sciences." *Sociology* 17, no. 2 (May): 206–33.

Flacks, Richard, and Turkel, Gerald
1978 "Radical Sociology: The Emergence of neo-Marxian Perspectives in U.S. Sociology." *Annual Review of Sociology* 4: 193–238.

Flew, Antony
1978 *Thinking about Social Thinking*. Oxford: Basil Blackwell.

Form, William
1983 "Sociological Research and the American Working Class." *Sociological Quarterly* 24, no. 2 (Spring): 163–84.

Frankel, Boris
1979 "On the State of the State: Marxist Theories of the State after Leninism." *Theory and Society* 7, nos. 1–2 (March): 199–242.

Freeman, Harold
1979 "Toward Socialism in America." *Monthly Review* 31, no. 4 (September): 21–29.

Friedrichs, David O.
1980 "The Legitimacy Crisis in the United States: A Conceptual Analysis." *Social Problems* 27, no. 5 (June): 540–55.

Fromm, Erich
1961 *Marx's Concept of Man*. New York: Frederick Ungar.

Gabbert, Mark A.
1985 "Stalinism, Soviet Society and the 'Workers' State': Trotsky's Theory Re-examined." *Contemporary Crises* 9: 169–82.

Gagliani, Giorgio
1981 "How Many Working Classes?" *American Journal of Sociology* 87, no. 2 (September): 259–85.
Garner, Larry, and Garner, Roberta
1981 "Problems of the Hegemonic Party: The PCI and the Structural Limits of Reform." *Science and Society* 45, no. 3 (Fall): 257–73.
Gay, Peter
1952 *The Dilemma of Democratic Socialism: Eduard Bernstein's Challenge to Marx.* New York: Columbia University Press.
Genovese, Eugene D.
1967 "On Antonio Gramsci." In Weinstein and Eakins 1967: 284–316.
Geras, Norman
1977 "Althusser's Marxism: An Assessment." In Stedman Jones et al. 1977: 232–72.
1985 "The Controversy about Marx and Justice." *New Left Review*, no. 150 (March-April): 47–85.
Gerstenberger, Heide
1976 "Theory of the State, Special Features of the Discussion in the FRG." In von Beyme et al. 1976: 69–92.
1978 "Class Conflict, Competition and State Functions." In Holloway and Picciotto, eds. 1978: 148–59.
Geyer, Felix R., and Schweitzer, David R., eds.
1976 *Theories of Alienation: Critical Perspectives in Philosophy and the Social Sciences.* Leiden: Nijhoff.
Gibbon, Peter
1983 "Gramsci, Eurocommunism and the Cominterm." *Economy and Society* 12, no. 3 (August): 328–66.
Giddens, Anthony
1971 *Capitalism and Modern Social Theory: An Analysis of the Writings of Marx, Durkheim and Max Weber.* London: Cambridge University Press.
1973 *The Class Structure of the Advanced Societies.* London: Hutchinson.
1976 *New Rules of Sociological Method.* London: Hutchinson.
1977 *Studies in Social and Political Theory.* New York: Basic Books.

1979 *Central Problems in Social Theory: Action, Structure and Contradiction in Social Analysis.* Berkeley: University of California Press.

1980 "Classes, Capitalism, and the State." *Theory and Society* 9, no. 6 (November): 877–90.

1981 *A Contemporary Critique of Historical Materialism.* Vol. 1, *Power, Property and the State.* Berkeley: University of California Press.

Giddens, Anthony, and Held, David, eds.

1982 *Classes, Power, and Conflict; Classical and Contemporary Debates.* Berkeley: University of California Press.

Giddens, Anthony, and Mackenzie, Gavin, eds.

1982 *Social Class and the Division of Labour: Essays in Honour of Ilya Neustadt.* London: Cambridge University Press.

Girardin, Jean-Claude

1974 "On the Marxist Theory of the State." *Politics and Society* 4, no. 2: 193–223.

Glenn, Evelyn Nakano, and Feldberg, Roslyn L.

1977 "Degraded and Deskilled: The Proletarianization of Clerical Work." *Social Problems* 28, no. 1 (October): 56–64.

Glucksmann, André

1977 "A Ventriloquist Structuralism." In Stedman Jones et al. 1977: 282–314.

Glyn, Andrew, and Sutcliffe, Bob

1972 *British Capitalism, Workers and the Profits Squeeze.* Harmondsworth: Penguin Books.

Gold, David A.; Lo, Clarence Y. H.; and Wright, Erik O.

1975a "Recent Developments in Marxist Theories of the Capitalist State." *Monthly Review* 27, no. 5 (October): 29–43.

1975b "Recent Developments in Marxist Theories of the Capitalist State, Part 2." *Monthly Review* 27, no. 6 (November): 36–51.

Goldthorpe, John H.

1972 "Class, Status and Party in Modern Britain: Some Recent Interpretations, Marxist and Marxisant." *European Journal of Sociology* 13: 342–72.

1979 *Intellectuals and the Working Class in Modern Britain.* Colchester: University of Essex, Fuller Bequest Lecture.

Gorz, André
  1968 "Reform and Revolution." *Socialist Register, 1968*: 111–43.
Gough, Ian
  1975 "State Expenditure in Advanced Capitalism." *New Left Review*, no. 92 (July-August): 53–92.
  1979 *The Political Economy of the Welfare State*. London: Macmillan.
Gouldner, Alvin W.
  1971 *The Coming Crisis of Western Sociology*. London: Heinemann.
  1980 *The Two Marxisms: Contradictions and Anomalies in the Development of Theory*. New York: Seabury Press.
  1985 *Against Fragmentation*. Oxford: Oxford University Press.
Gramsci, Antonio
  1971 *Selections from the Prison Notebooks of Antonio Gramsci*. Ed. Quintin Hoare and Geoffrey Nowell Smith. New York: International Publishers.
Griffin, Lancy J.; Devine, Joel A.; and Wallace, Michael
  1981 "Accumulation, Legitimation, and Politics: The Growth of Welfare Expenditures in the United States since the Second World War." Paper presented at the American Sociological Association annual meeting, Toronto, August 1981.
Guest, Dennis
  1980 *The Emergence of Social Security in Canada*. Vancouver: University of British Columbia Press.
Haas, Gordon
  1979 "Claus Offe and the Capitalist State: A Critique." *Alternate Routes* 3: 25–48.
Habermas, Jürgen
  1968 *Technik und Wissenschaft als Ideologie*. Frankfurt a.M.: Suhrkamp.
  1971 *Theorie und Praxis*. 4th enl. ed. Frankfurt a.M.: Suhrkamp.
  1973a *Kultur und Kritik*. Frankfurt a.M.: Suhrkamp.
  1973b *Legitimationsprobleme im Spätkapitalismus*. Frankfurt a.M.: Suhrkamp.
  1976 *Zur Rekonstruktion des Historischen Materialismus*. Frankfurt a.M.: Suhrkamp.

1984 *The Theory of Communicative Action*. Vol. 1, *Reason and Rationalization of Society*. Boston: Beacon Press.

Halfpenny, Peter

1983 "A Refutation of Historical Materialism?" *Social Science Information* 22, no. 1 (February): 61–87.

Hall, Stuart, and Hunt, Alan

1979 "Political Parties and the Crisis of Marxism: Interview with Nicos Poulantzas." *Socialist Review*, no. 48 (vol. 9, no. 6, November-December): 57–74.

Hamilton, Peter

1983 *Talcott Parsons*. Winchester, Sussex: Ellis Horwood.

Hamilton, Richard F.

1972 *Class and Politics in the United States*. New York: Wiley.

1975 *Restraining Myths: Critical Studies of U.S. Social Structure and Politics*. New York: Sage.

1982 *Who Voted for Hitler?* Princeton, N.J.: Princeton University Press.

Hamilton, Richard F., and Wright, James D.

1986 *The State of the Masses*. New York: Aldine.

Hammond, John L.

1978 "The Consciousness of the Ruling Class: Comment on Block." *Socialist Review*, nos. 40–41 (vol. 8, nos. 4–5, July-October): 208–11.

Harding, Neil

1977 *Lenin's Political Thought*. Vol. 1, *Theory and Practice in the Democratic Revolution*. London: Macmillan.

1978 *Lenin's Political Thought*. Vol. 2, *Theory and Practice in the Socialist Revolution*: London: Macmillan.

Hayek, Friedrich, A.

1944 *The Road to Serfdom*. Chicago: University of Chicago Press.

Heilbroner, Robert L.

1970 *Between Capitalism and Socialism: Essays in Political Economics*. New York: Random House.

1980 *Marxism: For and Against*. New York: W.W. Norton.

Heller, Agnes

1981 "Labour and Human Needs in a Society of Associated Producers." In Bottomore, ed. 1981: 188–201.

Hewitt, Christopher
1974 "Policy-Making in Post-War Britain: A Nation-Level Test of Elitist and Pluralist Hypotheses." *British Journal of Political Science* 4, pt. 2 (April): 187–216.

Hirsch, Joachim
1978 "The State Apparatus and Social Reproduction: Elements of a Theory of the Bourgeois State." In Holloway and Picciotto, eds. 1978: 57–107.

Hoare, Quintin, and Nowell Smith, Geoffrey
1971 "General Introduction." In Gramsci 1971: xvii–xcvi.

Hobsbawm, Eric J.
1977 *The Age of Capital, 1848–1875*. London: Abacus Books.

Hodgson, Geoff
1974 "The Theory of the Falling Rate of Profit." *New Left Review*, no. 84 (March-April): 55–82.

Holloway, John, and Picciotto, Sol
1977 "Capital, Crisis and the State." *Capital and Class*, no. 2 (Summer): 76–101.
1978 "Introduction: Towards a Materialist Theory of the State." In Holloway and Picciotto, eds. 1978: 1–31.

Holloway, John, and Picciotto, Sol, eds.
1978 *State and Capital: A Marxist Debate*. London: Edward Arnold.

Holloway, Steven
1983 "Relations among Core Capitalist States: The Kautsky-Lenin Debate Reconsidered." *Canadian Journal of Political Science* 14, no. 2 (June): 321–33.

Horowitz, Irving Louis, and Hayes, Bernadette
1980 "For Marx against Engels: Dialectics Revisited." *Social Praxis* 7, nos. 1–2: 59–75.

Howard, Dick, and Klare, Karl E., eds.
1972 *The Unknown Dimension: European Marxism since Lenin*. New York: Basic Books.

Howe, Irving
1981 "On the Moral Basis of Socialism." *Dissent* 28, no. 4 (Fall): 491–94.

Howe, Irving, ed.
1976 *Essential Works of Socialism*. New Haven: Yale University Press.

Hunt, Richard N.
1974 *The Political Ideas of Marx and Engels*. Vol. 1, *Marxism and Totalitarian Democracy, 1818–1850*. Pittsburgh: University of Pittsburgh Press.
1984 *The Political Ideas of Marx and Engels*. Vol. 2, *Classical Marxism, 1850–1895*. Pittsburgh: University of Pittsburgh Press.

Huntington, Samuel P.
1968 *Political Order in Changing Societies*. New Haven: Yale University Press.

Isaac, Larry, and Kelly, William R.
1981 "Racial Insurgency, the State, and Welfare Expansion: Local and National Level Evidence from the Postwar United States." *American Journal of Sociology* 86, no. 6 (May): 1348–86.

Israel, Joachim
1971 *Alienation from Marx to Modern Sociology: A Macrosociological Analysis*. Boston: Allyn and Bacon.
1976 "Alienation and Reification." In Geyer and Schweitzer 1976: 41–57.

Jacoby, Russell
1979 "The Inception of Western Marxism: Karl Korsch and the Politics of Philosophy." *Canadian Journal of Political and Social Theory* 3, no. 3 (Fall): 5–33.
1981 *Dialectic of Defeat: Contours of Western Marxism*. London: Cambridge University Press.

Jain, Ajit, and Matejko, Alexander, eds.
1984 *Marx and Marxism*. New York: Praeger.

Jessop, Bob
1977 "Recent Theories of the Capitalist State." *Cambridge Journal of Economics* 1, no. 4 (December): 353–73.
1980a "The Capitalist State and Political Practice." *Economy and Society* 9, no. 1 (February): 108–27.
1980b "The Gramsci Debate." *Marxism Today*, Vol. 24, no. 2 (Feb.): 23–25.
1982 *The Capitalist State: Marxist Theories and Methods*. Oxford: Martin Robertson.
1985 *Nicos Poulantzas: Marxist Theory and Political Strategy*. New York: St. Martin's Press.

Johnson, Leo A.
  1979 "Income Disparity and the Structure of Earnings in
  Canada, 1946–74." In Curtis and Scott 1979: 141–57.
Johnston, Les
  1986 *Marxism, Class Analysis and Socialist Pluralism: A Theoretical and Political Critique of Marxist Conceptions of Politics.* London: Allen & Unwin.
Kalecki, M.
  1971 *Selected Essays on the Dynamics of the Capitalist Economy,
  1933–1970.* London: Cambridge University Press.
Kautsky, Karl
  1964 *The Dictatorship of the Proletariat.* Ann Arbor: University
  of Michigan Press.
Kaye, Harvey J.
  1981 "Antonio Gramsci: An Annotated Bibliography of
  Studies in English." *Politics and Society* 10, no. 3: 335–53.
  1983 "History and Social Theory: Notes on the Contribution
  of British Marxist Historiography to our Understanding of
  Class." *Canadian Review of Sociology and Anthropology* 20, no. 2:
  167–92.
Keane, John
  1978 "The Legacy of Political Economy: Thinking with and
  against Claus Offe." *Canadian Journal of Political and Social
  Theory* 2, no. 3 (Fall): 49–92.
  1984 "Introduction." in Offe 1984a: 11–34.
Keat, Russell
  1981 *The Politics of Social Theory: Habermas, Freud and the Critique of Positivism.* Chicago: University of Chicago Press.
Kesselman, Mark
  1983 "From State Theory to Class Struggle and Compromise:
  Contemporary Marxist Political Studies." *Social Science Quarterly* 64, no. 4 (December): 826–45.
Kline, George L.
  1984 "The Myth of Marx's Materialism." *Annals of Scholarship*
  3, no. 2: 1–38.
Knei-Paz, Baruch
  1978 *The Social and Political Thought of Leon Trotsky.* Oxford:
  Clarendon Press.

Koch, Koen
   1980 "The New Marxist Theory of the State or the Rediscovery of the Limitations of a Structural-Functionalist Paradigm." *Netherlands' Journal of Sociology* 16: 1–19.
Kolakowski, Leszek
   1971 "Althusser's Marx." *Socialist Register, 1971*: 111–28.
   1978a *Main Currents of Marxism.* Vol. 1, *The Founders.* New York: Oxford University Press.
   1978b *Main Currents of Marxism.* Vol. 2, *The Golden Age.* New York: Oxford University Press.
   1978c *Main Currents of Marxism.* Vol. 3, *The Breakdown.* New York: Oxford Unversity Press.
Kolko, Gabriel
   1963 *The Triumph of Conservatism.* Chicago: Quadrangle Books.
Korpi, Walter
   1974 "Conflict, Power and Relative Deprivation." *American Political Science Review* 68, no. 4 (December): 1569–78.
   1978 *The Working Class in Welfare Capitalism: Work, Unions and Politics in Sweden.* London: Routledge & Kegan Paul.
   1983 *The Democratic Class Struggle.* London: Routledge & Kegan Paul.
Krieger, Joel, and Held, David
   1978 "A Theory of the State? A Comment on Block's 'The Ruling Class Does Not Rule.'" *Socialist Review,* nos. 40–41 (vol. 8, nos. 4–5, July-October): 189–207.
Kriesberg, L., ed.
   1980 *Research in Social Movements, Conflicts and Change.* Vol. 3. Greenwich, Conn.: JAI Press.
Laclau, Ernesto
   1975 "The Specificity of the Political: the Poulantzas-Miliband Debate." *Economy and Society* 5, no. 1 (February): 87–110.
Lane, David
   1976 *The Socialist Industrial State: Towards a Political Sociology of State Socialism.* London: Allen & Unwin.
   1982 *The End of Inequality? Class, Status and Power under State Socialism.* London: Allen & Unwin.

Lenin, V. I.
1932 *State and Revolution*. New York: International Publishers.
1968 *Lenin on Politics and Revolution: Selected Writings*. Ed. James E. Connor. New York: Pegasus.
Lenski, Gerhard
1966 *Power and Privilege: A Theory of Stratification*. New York: McGraw-Hill.
Levi, Margaret
1981 "The Predatory Theory of Rule." *Politics and Society* 10, no. 4: 431–65.
Levine, Norman
1975 *The Tragic Deception: Marx contra Engels*. Oxford: Clio Press.
1983 "The Engelsian Inversion." *Studies in Soviet Thought* 25: 307–21.
1985 "Lenin's Utopianism." *Studies in Soviet Thought* 30: 95–107.
Levine, Rhonda F.
1981 "State Policy, Class Struggle, and the Restructuring of Capitalist Development in the 1930s." Paper presented at the American Sociological Association annual meeting, Toronto, August 1981.
Levitt, Cyril
1978 "Karl Marx on Law, State and Collectivity." *Catalyst* 12: 12–21.
Lewis, Alan
1981 "Nicos Poulantzas and the Autonomy of Politics." *Catalyst* 14: 23–44.
Lichtheim, George
1965 *Marxism, An Historical and Critical Study*. 2d rev. ed. New York: Praeger.
Lindberg, Leon N.; Alford, Robert R.; Crouch, Colin; and Offe, Claus, eds.
1975 *Stress and Contradiction in Modern Capitalism*. Lexington, Mass.: Lexington Books.
Lindblom, Charles E.
1977 *Politics and Markets: The World's Political-Economic Systems*. New York: Basic Books.

Lindsey, J. K.
1980 "The Conceptualization of Social Class." *Studies in Political Economy*, no. 3 (Spring): 17–36.

Lipset, Seymour Martin
1960 *Political Man*. Garden City, N. Y.: Doubleday.

Little, Daniel
1981 "Rationality, Ideology, and Morality in Marx's Social Theory." *Social Praxis* 8, nos. 3–4: 73–88.

Lockwood, David
1981 "The Weakest Link in the Chain: Some Comments on the Marxist Theory of Class Action." In Simpson and Simpson 1981: 435–81.

Long, Tom
1980 "Marx and Western Marxism in the 1970's." *Berkeley Journal of Sociology* 24–25: 13–66.

Lowenthal, Richard
1976 "Social Transformation and Democratic Legitimacy." *Social Research* 43, no. 2 (Summer): 246–75.

Löwith, Karl
1982 *Max Weber and Karl Marx*. Ed. Tom Bottomore and William Outhwaite. London: Allen & Unwin.

Lukács, Georg
1971 *History and Class Consciousness: Studies in Marxist Dialectics*. Trans. Rodney Livingstone. London: Merlin Press.

Lukes, Steven
1974 *Power: A Radical View*. London: Macmillan.
1985 *Marxism and Morality*. Oxford: Oxford University Press.

McCarthy, George
1985 "Marx's Social Ethics and Critique of Traditional Morality." *Studies in Soviet Thought* 29: 177–99.

McInnes, Neil
1979 "From Comintern to Polycentrism: The First Fifty Years of West European Communism." In Filo Della Torre, Mortimer, and Story 1979: 35–68.

MacIntyre, A.
1967 "Herbert Marcuse." *Survey* no. 62 (January): 38–44.

McLellan, David
1969 "Marx's View of the Unalienated Society." *Review of Politics* 31, no. 4 (October): 459–65.

1980 *The Thought of Karl Marx.* 2d ed. London: Macmillan.
McNall, Scott G.
   1983 "Variations on a Theme: Social Theory." *The Sociological Quarterly* 24, no. 4 (Autumn): 471–87.
McNall, Scott G., ed.
   1985 *Current Perspectives in Social Theory.* Vol. 6. Greenwich, Conn.: JAI Press.
McNall, Scott G., and Howe, Gary N., eds.
   1982 *Current Perspectives in Social Theory.* Vol. 3. Greenwich, Conn.: JAI Press.
Macpherson, C. B.
   1977a "Do We Need a Theory of the State?" *Archives européennes de sociologie* 18: 223–44.
   1977b *The Life and Times of Liberal Democracy.* New York: Oxford University Press.
McQuarie, Donald, and Amburgey, Terry
   1978 "Marx and Modern Systems Theory." *Social Science Quarterly* 59, no. 1 (June): 3–19.
Magnussen, Warren
   1981 "Metropolitan Reform in the Capitalist City." *Canadian Journal of Political Science.* 14, no. 3 (September): 557–85.
Maguire, John M.
   1978 *Marx's Theory of Politics.* London: Cambridge University Press.
Mandel, Ernest
   1968 *Marxist Economic Theory.* London: Merlin Press.
   1975 *Late Capitalism.* London: New Left Books.
   1978 *From Stalinism to Eurocommunism: The Bitter Fruits of "Socialism in One Country."* London: New Left Books.
   1979 *Revolutionary Marxism Today.* London: New Left Books.
Mankoff, Milton
   1970 "Power in Advanced Capitalist Society: A Review Essay on Recent Elitist and Marxist Criticism of Pluralist Theory." *Social Problems* 17, no. 3 (Winter): 418–30.
Mann, Michael
   1970 "The Social Cohesion of Liberal Democracy." *American Sociological Review* 35, no. 3 (June): 423–39.
   1973 *Consciousness and Action among the Western Working Class.* London: Macmillan.

1975 "The Ideology of Intellectuals and Other People in the Development of Capitalism." In Lindberg et al., 1975: 275–307.

Maravall, José M.

1979 "The Limits of Reformism: Parliamentary Socialism and the Marxist Theory of the State." *British Journal of Sociology* 30, no. 3 (September): 267–90.

Marglin, Stephen

1974 "What Do Bosses Do? The Origins and Functions of Hierarchy in Capitalist Production." *Review of Radical Political Economics* 6, no. 2 (Summer): 33–60.

Marshall, Gordon

1983 "Some Remarks on the Study of Working-Class Consciousness." *Politics and Society* 12, no. 3: 263–301.

Marshall, T. H.

1964 *Class, Citizenship and Social Development*. Garden City, N.Y.: Doubleday.

Martin, Andrew

1975 "Is Democratic Control of Capitalist Economies Possible?." In Lindberg et al. 1975: 13–56.

Marx, Karl

1961 *Selected Writings in Sociology and Social Philosophy*. Ed. T. B. Bottomore and Maximilien Rubel. Harmondsworth: Penguin Books.

1963a *The Eighteenth Brumaire of Louis Bonaparte*. New York: International Publishers.

1963b *The Poverty of Philosophy*. New York: International Publishers.

1964 *Early Writings*. Ed. T. B. Bottomore. New York: McGraw-Hill.

1967a *Capital*. Vol. 1. New York: International Publishers.

1967b *Capital*. Vol. 3. New York: International Publishers.

1973 *Grundrisse: Introduction to the Critique of Political Economy*. Trans. Martin Nicolaus. New York: Random House.

1974 *The First International and After*. Ed. David Fernbach. New York: Random House.

1975 *Early Writings*. Ed. Quintin Hoare. New York: Random House.

1977 *Selected Writings*. Ed. David McLellan. Oxford: Oxford University Press.

Marx, Karl, and Engels, Friedrich
1947 *The German Ideology*. New York: International Publishers.
1959 *Basic Writings on Politics and Philosophy*. Ed. Lewis S. Feuer. Garden City, N.Y.: Doubleday.

Marx, Karl; Engels, Friedrich; and Lenin, V. I.
1967 *On Scientific Communism*. Moscow: Progress Publishers.

Mattick, Paul
1983 *Marxism: Last Refuge of the Bourgeoisie?* Armonk, N.Y.: M.E. Sharpe.

Mayntz, Renate
1975 "Legitimacy and the Directive Capacity of the Political System." In Lindberg et al. 1975: 261–74.

Meiksins Wood, Ellen
1981 "The Separation of the Economic and the Political in Capitalism." *New Left Review*, no. 127 (May-June): 66–95.

Merrington, John
1977 "Theory and Practice in Gramsci's Marxism." In Stedman Jones et al. 1977: 140–75.

Merton, Robert K.
1957 *Social Theory and Social Structure*. Rev. and enl. ed. Glencoe, Ill.: Free Press.

Mewes, Robert
1976 "On the Concept of Politics in the Early Work of Karl Marx." *Social Research* 43, no. 2 (Summer): 276–94.

Miliband, Ralph
1965 "Marx and the State." *Socialist Register, 1965*: 278–96.
1969 *The State in Capitalist Society*. London: Weidenfeld & Nicolson.
1970 "The State and Revolution." *Monthly Review* 21, no. 11 (April): 77–90.
1972 "Reply to Nicos Poulantzas." In Blackburn 1972: 253–62.
1973 "Poulantzas and the Capitalist State." *New Left Review*, no. 82 (November-December): 83–92.
1975 "Political Forms and Historical Materialism." *Socialist Register, 1975*: 308–18.

1977 *Marxism and Politics*. London: Oxford University Press.

1982 *Capitalist Democracy in Britain*. Oxford: Oxford University Press.

1983 "State Power and Class Interests." *New Left Review*, no. 138 (March-April): 57–68.

Miller, Richard W.

1984 *Analyzing Marx: Morality, Power and History*. Princeton, N.J.: Princeton University Press.

Mills, C. Wright

1956 *The Power Elite*. New York: Oxford University Press.

Milner, Henry

1977 "The Decline and Fall of the Quebec Liberal Regime: Contradictions in the Modern Quebec State." In Panitch, ed. 1977: 101–32.

Mizruchi, Mark S.

1983 "At Last, A Solution to the Pluralist-Elitist Debate." *Contemporary Sociology* 12, no. 6 (November): 645–47.

Mizuta, Hiroshi

1984 "Marx's Place in the History of Thought." In Jain and Matejko 1984: 11–20.

Mollenkopf, John

1975 "Theories of the State and Power Research." *Insurgent Sociologist* 5, no. 3 (Spring): 245–64.

Moore, Jr., Barrington

1978 *Injustice: The Social Bases of Obedience and Revolt*. White Plains, N. Y.: M.E. Sharpe.

Moore, Stanley W.

1957 *The Critique of Capitalist Democracy: An Introduction to the Theory of the State in Marx, Engels and Lenin*. New York: Paine-Whitman.

1980 *Marx on the Choice between Socialism and Communism*. Cambridge, Mass.: Harvard University Press.

Mosley, Hugh

1978 "Is There a Fiscal Crisis of the State?" *Monthly Review* 30, no. 4 (May): 34–45.

Mouzelis, Nicos

1980 "Types of Reductionism in Marxist Theory." *Telos*, no. 45 (Fall): 173–85.

Müller, Wolfgang, and Neusüss, Christel
  1978 "The 'Welfare-state Illusion' and the Contradiction between Wage Labour and Capital." In Holloway and Picciotto, eds. 1978: 32–39.
Münch, Richard
  1981 "Talcott Parsons and the Theory of Action. I. The Structure of the Kantian Core." *American Journal of Sociology* 86, no. 4 (January): 709–39.
  1983 "From Pure Methodological Individualism to Poor Sociological Utilitarianism: A Critique of an Avoidable Alliance." *Canadian Journal of Sociology* 8, no. 1 (Winter): 45–77.
Navarro, Vincente
  1980 "The Nature of Democracy in the Core Capitalist Countries: Meanings and Implications for Class Struggle." *Insurgent Sociologist* 10, no. 1 (Summer): 3–15.
Neuman, W. Russel
  1981 "Differentiation and Integration: Two Dimensions of Political Thinking." *American Journal of Sociology* 86, no. 6 (May): 1236–68.
Nielsen, Kai
  1985 "If Historical Materialism Is True Does Morality Totter?." *Philosophy of the Social Sciences* 15, no.4 (December): 389–407.
Nielsen, Kai, and Patten, Steven C., eds.
  1981 *Marx and Morality*. Supp. vol. 7 of the *Canadian Journal of Philosophy*. Guelph: Canadian Association for Publishing in Philosophy.
Nisbet, Robert A.
  1967 *The Sociological Tradition*. London: Heinemann.
  1978 "Conservatism." In Bottomore and Nisbet 1978: 80–117.
Noble, Charles
  1985 "Class, State, and Social Reform in America: The Case of the Occupational Safety and Health Act of 1970." In Zarembka and Ferguson 1985: 145–62.
Nordahl, Richard
  1985 "Marx on Moral Commentary: Ideology and Science." *Philosophy of the Social Sciences* 15, no. 3 (September): 237–54.

Nove, Alec
1983 "The Class Nature of the Soviet Union Revisited." *Soviet Studies* 35, no. 3 (July): 298–312.
Oberschall, Anthony
1980 "Loosely Structured Collective Conflicts: A Theory and an Application." In Kriesberg 1980: 45–68.
O'Connor, James
1973 *The Fiscal Crisis of the State.* New York: St. Martin's Press.
1978 "More on the Fiscal Crisis of the State." *Monthly Review* 30, no. 6 (November): 54–57.
1980 Letter to the Editor. *Insurgent Sociologist* 10, no. 1 (Summer): 81.
Offe, Claus
1972a "Advanced Capitalism and the Welfare State." *Politics and Society* 2, no. 4: 479–88.
1972b "Political Authority and Class Structures—An Analysis of Late Capitalist Societies." *International Journal of Sociology* 2, no. 1 (Spring): 73–108.
1972c *Strukturprobleme des kapitalistischen Staates.* Frankfurt a.M.: Suhrkamp.
1973a "The Abolition of Market Control and the Problem of Legitimacy I." *Kapitalistate*, no. 1: 109–16.
1973b "The Abolition of Market Control and the Problem of Legitimacy II." *Kapitalistate*, no. 2: 73–75.
1974 "Structural Problems of the Capitalist State, Class Rule and the Political System: On the Selectiveness of Political Institutions." In von Beyme 1974: 31–57.
1975a "Introduction to Part III." In Lindberg et al. 1975: 245–59.
1975b "The Theory of the Capitalist State and the Problems of Policy Formation." In Lindberg et al. 1975: 125–44.
1976a "Crises of Crisis Management: Elements of a Political Crisis Theory." *International Journal of Politics* 6, no. 3: 29–67.
1976b *Industry and Inequality.* London: Edward Arnold.
1980 "The Separation of Form and Content in Liberal Democratic Politics." *Studies in Political Economy*, no. 3 (Spring): 5–16.
1983 "Political Legitimation Through Majority Rule?" *Social Research* 50, no. 4 (Winter): 709–56.

1984a *Contradictions of the Welfare State*. London: Hutchinson.
1984b "Korporatismus als System nichtstaatlicher Makrosteu-
erung? Notizen über seine Voraussetzungen und demokra-
tischen Gehalte." *Geschichte und Gesellschaft* 10: 234–56.
1985 *Disorganized Capitalism: Contemporary Transformations of
Work and Politics*. Ed. John Keane. Cambridge: Polity Press.

Offe, Claus, and Ronge, Volker
1975 "Theses on the Theory of the State." *New German Critique*, no. 6 (Fall): 137–47.

Ollman, Bertell
1971 *Alienation: Marx's Conception of Man in Capitalist Society*.
Cambridge: Cambridge University Press.
1977 "Marx's Vision of Communism: A Reconstruction." *Critique*, no.8 (Summer): 4–41.
1982 "Theses on the Capitalist State." *Monthly Review* 34, no.
7 (December): 41–46.

Olson, Mancur
1965 *The Logic of Collective Action*. Cambridge, Mass.: Harvard
University Press.
1982 *The Rise and Decline of Nations: Economic Growth, Stagfla-
tion, and Social Rigidities*. New Haven: Yale University Press.

Ornstein, Michael D., and Stevenson, H. Michael
1981 "Elite and Public Opinion before the Quebec Referen-
dum: A Commentary on the State in Canada." *Canadian Journal of Political Science* 14, no. 4 (December): 745–74.

Pachter, Henry
1981 "The Ambiguous Legacy of Eduard Bernstein." *Dissent*
28, no. 2 (Spring): 203–16.

Pal, Leslie A.
1986 "Relative Autonomy Revisited: The Origins of Canadian Unemployment Insurance." *Canadian Journal of Political
Science* 19, no. 1 (March): 71–92.

Palmer, Ian
1985 "State Theory and Statutory Authorities: Points of Convergence." *Sociology* 19, no. 4 (November): 523–40.

Panitch, Leo
1977 "The Role and Nature of the Canadian State." In Panitch, ed. 1977: 3–27.
1979 "Trade Unions and the Capitalist State: Corporatism

and Its Contradictions." Toronto: Structural Analysis Programme, Department of Sociology, University of Toronto, Working Paper Series no. 6.

Panitch, Leo, ed.

1977 *The Canadian State: Political Economy and Political Power.* Toronto: University of Toronto Press.

Parkin, Frank

1971 *Class Inequality and Political Order.* London: MacGibbon & Kee.

1979 *Marxism and Class Theory: A Bourgeois Critique.* New York: Columbia University Press.

1980 "Reply to Giddens." *Theory and Society* 9, no. 6 (November): 891–94.

Parsons, Talcott

1937 *The Structure of Social Action.* New York: McGraw-Hill.

Pedraza-Bailey, Silvia

1982 "Talcott Parsons and Structural Marxism: Functionalist Theories of Society." In McNall and Howe 1982: 207–24

Pellicani, Luciano

1981 *Gramsci: An Alternative to Communism.* Stanford: Hoover Institution Press.

Pemberton, Alec

1983 "Marxism and Social Policy: A Critique of the 'Contradictions of Welfare.' " *Journal of Social Policy* 12, pt. 3 (July): 289–307.

Perez-Diaz, Victor M.

1978 *State, Bureaucracy and Civil Society.* Atlantic Highlands, N.J.: Humanities Press.

Piccone, Paul

1983 *Italian Marxism.* Berkeley: University of California Press.

Pierson, Christopher

1984 "New Theories of State and Civil Society: Recent Developments in Post-Marxist Analysis of the State." *Sociology* 18, no. 4 (November): 563–71.

Pinard, Maurice, and Hamilton, Richard F.

1984 "The Motivational Dimensions in a Nationalist Movement: The Quebec Case." Paper presented at the American

Sociological Association annual meeting, San Antonio, Texas, August 1984.

Piven, Frances Fox, and Cloward, Richard A.
1971 *Regulating the Poor: The Functions of Public Welfare.* New York: Pantheon.

Plamenatz, John
1963 *Man and Society: A Critical Examination of Some Important Social and Political Theories from Machiavelli to Marx. Vol. 2.* London: Longmans.

Plotke, David
1977 "Marxist Political Theory and the Problem of Revisionism." *Socialist Revolution,* no. 36 (vol. 7, no. 6, November-December): 79–93.

Polan, A. J.
1984 *Lenin and the End of Politics.* Berkeley: University of California Press.

Polanyi, Karl
1957 *The Great Transformation.* Boston: Beacon Press.

Pontusson, Jonas
1980 "Gramsci and Eurocommunism: A Comparative Analysis of Conceptions of Class Rule and Socialist Transition." *Berkeley Journal of Sociology* 24–25: 185–248.

Popper, Karl R.
1957 *The Poverty of Historicism.* London: Routledge & Kegan Paul.
1966a *The Open Society and Its Enemies.* Vol. 1, *The Spell of Plato.* 5th rev. ed. Princeton, N.J.: Princeton University Press.
1966b *The Open Society and Its Enemies.* Vol. 2, *The High Tide of Prophecy: Hegel, Marx, and the Aftermath.* 5th rev. ed. Princeton, N.J.: Princeton University Press.

Porpora, Douglas V.
1985 "The Role of Agency in History: The Althusser-Thompson-Anderson Debate." In McNall 1985: 219–41.

Potter, Mike
1981 "The State as Welfare." *Economy and Society* 10, no. 1 (February): 102–14.

Poulantzas, Nicos
1967 "Marxist Political Theory in Great Britain." *New Left Review,* no. 43 (May-June): 57–74.

1972 "The Problem of the Capitalist State." In Blackburn 1972: 238–53.

1973a "On Social Classes." *New Left Review,* no. 78 (March-April): 27–54.

1973b *Political Power and Social Classes.* London: New Left Books.

1974 *Fascism and Dictatorship.* London: New Left Books.

1975 *Classes in Contemporary Capitalism.* London: New Left Books.

1976 "The Capitalist State: A Reply to Miliband and Laclau." *New Left Review,* no. 95 (January-February): 63–83.

1978 *State, Power, Socialism.* London: New Left Books.

Przeworski, Adam

1977 "Proletarian into a Class: The Process of Class Formation from Karl Kautsky's *The Class Struggle* to Recent Controversies." *Politics and Society* 7, no. 4: 343–401.

1980 "Material Interests, Class Compromise, and the Transition to Socialism." *Politics and Society* 10, no. 1: 125–53.

1981 "Democratic Socialism in Poland?" *Studies in Political Economy,* no. 5 (Spring): 29–53.

Przeworski, Adam, and Wallerstein, Michael

1982 "The Structure of Class Conflict in Democratic Capitalist Societies." *American Political Science Review* 76, no. 2 (June): 215–38.

Quadagno, Jill

1984 "Welfare Capitalism and the Social Security Act of 1935." *American Sociological Review* 49, no.5 (October): 632–47.

1985 "Two Models of Welfare State Development: Reply to Skocpol and Amenta." *American Sociological Review* 50, no.4 (August): 575–78.

Rader, Melvin

1979 *Marx's Interpretation of History.* New York: Oxford University Press.

Radosh, Ronald

1972 "The Myth of the New Deal." In Radosh and Rothbard 1972: 146–87.

Radosh, Ronald, and Rothbard, Murray N., eds.

1972 *A New History of Leviathan: Essays on the Rise of the Corporate State.* New York: Dutton.

Rich, Harvey
1976 "Marxism as Dogma, Ideology, and Theory in Contemporary Political Sociology." *Canadian Journal of Political Science* 9, no. 4 (December): 654–67.

Roberts, K.; Cook, F. G.; Clark, S. C.; and Semeonoff, Elizabeth
1977 *The Fragmentary Class Structure*. London: Heinemann.

Robinson, Joan
1966 *An Essay on Marxian Economics*. 2d ed. London: Macmillan.

Ross, George'
1978 "Marxism and the New Middle Classes." *Theory and Society* 5, no. 2 (March): 163–90.

Roussopoulos, Dimitrios I., ed.
1973 *The Political Economy of the State*. Montreal: Black Rose Books.

Rowthorn, B.
1980 *Capitalism, Conflict and Inflation*. London: Lawrence and Wishart.

Rule, James B.
1978 *Insight and Social Betterment: A Preface to Applied Social Science*. New York: Oxford University Press.

Runciman, W. G.
1966 *Relative Deprivation and Social Justice*. London: Routledge & Kegan Paul.

Salvadori, Massimo
1979 *Karl Kautsky and the Socialist Revolution: 1880–1930*. Trans. Jon Rothschild. London: New Left Books.

Sardei-Biermann, Sabine; Christiansen, Jens; and Dohse, Knuth
1973. "Class Domination and the Political System: A Critical Interpretation of Recent Contributions by Claus Offe." *Kapitalistate*, no. 2: 60–69.

Schacht, Richard
1970 *Alienation*. Garden City, N.Y.: Doubleday.

Schecter, Stephen
1977 "Capitalism, Class, and Educational Reform in Canada." In Panitch, ed. 1977: 373–416.

Schmidt, Manfred G.
1983 "The Welfare State and the Economy in Periods of Eco-

nomic Crisis: A Comparative Study of Twenty-Three OECD Nations." *European Journal of Political Research* 11, no. 1: 1–26.

Schorsch, Louis
1983 Review of *Genealogies of Capitalism*, by Keith Tribe. *Science and Society* 47, no. 1 (Spring): 104–6.

Schott, Kerry
1984 *Policy, Power, and Order: The Persistence of Economic Problems in Capitalist States*. New Haven: Yale University Press.

Schroyer, Trent
1975 "The Re-politicization of the Relations of Production: An Interpretation of Jürgen Habermas' Analytic Theory of Late Capitalist Development." *New German Critique*, no. 5 (Spring): 107–28.

Schumpeter, Joseph A.
1950 *Capitalism, Socialism and Democracy*. 3d. ed. New York: Harper & Row.

Shapiro, H. Svi
1981 "Functionalism, the State, and Education: Towards a New Analysis." *Social Praxis* 8, nos. 3–4: 5–24.

Sharp, Margaret
1973 *The State, the Enterprise and the Individual: An Introduction to Applied Microeconomics*. London: Weidenfeld & Nicolson.

Shaw, Martin
1974 "The Theory of the State and Politics: A Central Paradox of Marxism." *Economy and Society* 3, no. 4 (November): 429–50.

Sica, Alan
1983 "Parsons, Jr." *American Journal of Sociology* 89, no. 1 (July): 200–219.

Silva, Edward T.
1978 "Before Radical Rejection: A Comment on Block's 'Beyond Corporate Liberalism.'" *Social Problems* 25, no. 3 (February): 345–49.

Simpson, Richard L., and Harper, Ida, eds.
1981 *Research in the Sociology of Work*. Greenwich, Conn.: JAI Press.

Sirianni, Carmen
1983 "Councils and Parliaments: The Problems of Dual

Power and Democracy in Comparative Perspective." *Politics and Society* 12, no. 1: 83–123.

Skocpol, Theda
1979 *States and Social Revolutions: A Comparative Analysis of France, Russia, and China.* London: Cambridge University Press.
1980 "Political Response to Capitalist Crisis: Neo-Marxist Theories of the State and the Case of the New Deal." *Politics and Society* 10, no. 2: 155–201.

Skocpol, Theda, and Amenta, Edwin
1985 "Did Capitalists Shape Social Security?" *American Sociological Review* 50, no. 4 (August): 572–75.

Smith, Steven B.
1984 *Reading Althusser: An Essay on Structural Marxism.* Ithaca, N.Y.: Cornell University Press.

Sowell, Thomas
1985 *Marxism: Philosophy and Economics.* New York: William Morrow.

Spencer, Martin E.
1979 "Marx on the State: The Events in France between 1848–1850." *Theory and Society* 7, nos. 1–2 (March): 167–98.

Springborg, Patricia
1984 "Karl Marx on Democracy, Participation, Voting, and Equality." *Political Theory* 12, no. 4 (November): 537–56.

Stanley, John L., and Zimmerman, Ernest
1984 "On the Alleged Differences between Marx and Engels." *Political Studies* 32, no. 2: 226–48.

Stearns, Peter
1975 *Lives of Labour.* London: Croom Helm.

Stedman Jones, Gareth; Löwy, Michael; Therborn, Göran; Merrington, John; Gorz, André; Aronson, Ronald; Geras, Norman; Glucksmann, André; and Colletti, Lucio
1977 *Western Marxism, A Critical Reader.* London: New Left Books.

Steedman, Ian
1975 "Value, Price and Profit." *New Left Review*, no. 90 (March-April): 71–80.

Stephens, John D.
1979 *The Transition to Socialism.* London: Macmillan.

Stevenson, Garth
1977 "Federalism and the Political Economy of the Canadian State." In Panitch, ed. 1977: 71–100.
Stewart, A.; Prandy, K.; and Blackburn, R. M.
1980 *Social Stratification and Occupations*. London: Macmillan.
Stinchcombe, Arthur L.
1968 *Constructing Social Theories*. New York: Harcourt.
Stojanovic, Svetozar
1981 "The Ethical Potential of Marx's Thought." In Bottomore, ed. 1981: 170–89.
Stone, Katherine
1974 "The Origins of Job Structures in the Steel Industry." *Review of Radical Political Economics* 6, no. 2 (Summer): 61–97.
Swank, Duane
1981 "Between Revolution and Incrementalism: The Growth of the Welfare State in Advanced Capitalist Democracies." Paper presented at the American Sociological Association annual meeting, Toronto, August 1981.
Swartz, Donald
1977 "The Politics of Reform: Conflict and Accommodation in Canadian Health Policy." In Panitch, ed. 1977: 311–43.
Sweezy, Paul M.
1942 *The Theory of Capitalist Development: Principles of Marxian Political Economy*. New York: Monthly Review Press.
Szymanski, Albert
1978 *The Capitalist State and the Politics of Class*. Cambridge, Mass.: Winthrop Publishers.
Taylor-Gooby, Peter
1982 "Two Cheers for the Welfare State: Public Opinion and Private Welfare." *Journal of Public Policy* 2, pt. 4 (October): 319–46.
Taylor-Gooby, Peter
1983 "Legitimation Deficit, Public Opinion and the Welfare State." *Sociology* 17, no. 2 (May): 165–84.
Teeple, Gary
1972 " 'Liberals in a Hurry': Socialism and the CCF-NDP." In Teeple, ed. 1972: 229–50.

1984 *Marx's Critique of Politics, 1842–1847*. Toronto: University of Toronto Press.

Teeple, Gary, ed.
1972 *Capitalism and the National Question in Canada*. Toronto: University of Toronto Press.

Therborn, Göran
1976 "What Does the Ruling Class Do When It Rules? Some Reflections on Different Approaches to the Study of Power in Society." *Insurgent Sociologist* 6, no. 3 (Spring): 3–16.
1977 "The Rule of Capital and the Rise of Democracy." *New Left Review*, no. 103 (May-June): 3–41.
1978 *What Does the Ruling Class Do When It Rules? State Apparatuses and State Power under Feudalism, Capitalism and Socialism*. London: New Left Books.

Thompson, E. P.
1978 *The Poverty of Theory and Other Essays*. New York: Monthly Review Press.

Tilly, Charles
1978 *From Mobilization to Revolution*. Reading, Mass.: Addison-Wesley.

Titmuss, Richard
1976 *Commitment to Welfare*. 2d ed. London: Allen & Unwin.

Tocqueville, Alexis de
1955 *Democracy in America*. New York: Vintage Books.

Todd, Jennifer
1982 "The Politics of the Public Service: Some Implications of Recent Theories of the State for the Analysis of Administrative Systems." *European Journal of Political Research* 10, no. 4: 353–66.

Traugott, Mark
1985 *Armies of the Poor*. Princeton, N.J.: Princeton University Press.

Turner, Bryan
1986 *Citizenship and Capitalism: The Debate over Reformism*. London: Allen & Unwin

Vaillancourt, Pauline Marie.
1986 *When Marxists Do Research*. New York: Greenwood Press.

van den Berg, Axel
1980 "Critical Theory: Is There Still Hope?" *American Journal of Sociology* 86, no. 3 (November): 449–78.

1981 *Equality versus Liberty? Radical and Reformist Theories of Capitalist Democracy.* Sociologisch Instituut, University of Amsterdam.

1983 "Social Theory, Metatheory, and Lofty Ideals: A Reply to Wexler and Parker and to Ashley." *American Journal of Sociology* Vol. 88, no. 6 (May): 1259–70.

1984 "Marx and Marxism: The Hegelian Core." In Jain and Matejko, eds. 1984: 279–99.

1987 "Habermas and Modernity: A Critique of the Theory of Communicative Action." McGill University. Photocopy.

van den Berg, Axel, and Smith, Michael R.

1981 "Review Essay: The Marxist Theory of the State in Practice." *Canadian Journal of Sociology* 6, no. 4 (Fall): 505–19.

1982 "On 'Class Exploitation' in Canada." *Canadian Review of Sociology and Anthropology* 19, no. 2: 263–78.

1983 "On Saying What You Mean and Meaning What You Say: A Response to Craven." *Canadian Journal of Sociology* 8, no. 3 (Summer): 333–37.

1984 "Correcting Cuneo's Corrections." *Canadian Review of Sociology and Anthropology* 21, no. 1: 92–97.

Van Den Berghe, Pierre.

1963 "Dialectic and Functionalism: Toward Reconciliation." *American Sociological Review* 28, no. 5 (October): 695–705.

van der Linden, Harry

1984 "Marx and Morality: An Impossible Synthesis?" *Theory and Society* 13, no.1 (January): 119–34.

Van Parijs, Philippe

1980 "The Falling-Rate-of-Profit Theory of Crisis: A Rational Reconstruction by Way of Obituary." *Review of Radical Political Economics* 12, no. 1 (Spring): 1–16.

Verba, Sidney; Nie, Norman H.; and Kim, Jae-on

1978 *Participation and Political Equality; A Seven-Nation Comparison.* London: Cambridge University Press.

von Beyme, Klaus

1985 "Karl Marx and Party Theory." *Government and Opposition* 20, no. 1 (Winter): 70–87.

von Beyme, Klaus, ed.

1974 *German Political Studies.* Vol. 1. London: Sage.

von Beyme, Klaus; Kaase, Max; Krippendorf, Ekkehart; Rittberger, Volker; and Shell, Kurt L., eds.

1976 *German Political Systems: Theory and Practice in the Two Germanies. German Political Studies 2.* London: Sage.

Walker, Pat, ed.
1978 *Between Labor and Capital.* Montreal: Black Rose Books.

Wallerstein, Immanuel
1974a *The Modern World-System: Capitalist Agriculture and the Origins of the European World-Economy in the Sixteenth Century.* New York: Academic Press.
1974b "The Rise and Future Demise of the World Capitalist System: Concepts for Comparative Analysis." *Comparative Studies in Society and History*, no. 16: 387–415.

Walters, Vivienne
1982 "State, Capital, and Labour: The Introduction of Federal-Provincial Insurance for Physician Care in Canada." *Canadian Review of Sociology and Anthropology* 19, no. 2: 157–72.

Warshay, Leon H.
1981 "General Theory." *International Review of Modern Sociology* 11 (January-December): 25–79.

Weber, Henri
1978 "The State and the Transition to Socialism: Nicos Poulantzas Interviewed." *Socialist Review* no. 38 (vol. 8, no. 2, March-April): 9–36.

Weber, Max
1947 *The Theory of Social and Economic Organization.* Trans. and ed. A. M. Henderson and Talcott Parsons. New York: Oxford University Press.
1958 *The Protestant Ethic and the Spirit of Capitalism.* New York: Charles Scribner's Sons.

Wedderburn, Dorothy
1965 "Facts and Theories of the Welfare State." *Socialist Register, 1965*: 127–46.

Weiner, Richard
1980 *The State in Capitalist Society.* Livermore, Calif.: Red Feather Institute for Advanced Studies in Sociology.

Weinstein, James
1968 *The Corporate Ideal and the Liberal State, 1900–1918.* Boston: Beacon Press.

Weinstein, James, and Eakins, David W.
1967 *For a New America: Essays in History and Politics from "Studies on the Left." 1959–1967.* New York: Vintage Books.

Westergaard, John
1978 "Social Policy and Class Inequality: Some Notes on Welfare State Limits." *Socialist Register, 1978*: 71–99.
Whitaker, Reg
1977 "Images of the State in Canada." In Panitch, ed. 1977: 28–68.
Whitt, J. Allen
1979a "Can Capitalists Organize Themselves?" *Insurgent Sociologist* 9, nos. 2–3 (Fall-Winter): 51–59.
1979b "Toward a Class-Dialectical Model of Power: An Empirical Assessment of Three Competing Models of Political Power." *American Sociological Review* 44, no. 1 (February): 81–99.
1982 *Urban Elites and Mass Transportation: The Dialectics of Power.* Princeton, N.J.: Princeton University Press.
Wilensky, Harold L., and Lebeaux, Charles M.
1965 *Industrial Society and Social Welfare.* Enl. ed. New York: Free Press.
Wirth, Margaret
1977 "Towards a Critique of the Theory of State Monopoly Capitalism." *Economy and Society* 6, no. 3 (August): 284–313.
Wolfe, Alan
1974 "New Directions in the Marxist Theory of Politics." *Politics and Society* 4, no. 2: 131–59.
1977 *The Limits of Legitimacy: Political Contradictions of Contemporary Capitalism.* New York: Free Press.
Wolfe, Bertram D.
1965 *Marxism: One Hundred Years in the Life of a Doctrine.* New York: Dial Press.
Wolfe, David A.
1981 "Mercantilism, Liberalism and Keynesianism: Changing Forms of State Intervention in Capitalist Economies." *Canadian Journal of Political and Social Theory* 5, nos. 1–2 (Winter-Spring): 69–96.
Wood, Allen W.
1972 "The Marxian Critique of Justice." *Philosophy and Public Affairs* 1, no. 3 (Spring): 244–82.
Woodiwiss, Tony
1978 "Critical Theory and the Capitalist State (review of Jür-

gen Habermas, *Legitimation Crisis*)." *Economy and Society* 7, no. 2 (May): 175–92.

Wright, Erik Olin
1974 "To Control or to Smash Bureaucracy: Weber and Lenin on Politics, the State, and Bureaucracy." *Berkeley Journal of Sociology* 19 (1974–1975): 69–108.
1975 "Alternative Perspectives in Marxist Theory of Accumulation and Crisis." *Insurgent Sociologist* 6, no. 1 (Fall): 5–39.
1976 "Class Boundaries in Advanced Capitalist Societies." *New Left Review*, no. 98 (July-August): 3–41.
1978 *Class, Crisis and the State*. London: New Left Books.
1980 "Varieties of Marxist Conceptions of Class Structure." *Politics and Society* 9, no. 3: 323–70.
1983 "Capitalism's Futures." *Socialist Review*, no. 68 (vol. 13, no. 2, March-April): 77–126.
1985 *Classes*, London and New York: Verso and Schocken Books.

Wright, James D.
1976 *The Dissent of the Governed: Alienation and Democracy in America*. New York: Academic Press.

Wrong, Dennis H.
1961 "The Oversocialized Conception of Man." *American Sociological Review* 26, no. 2 (April): 183–93.
1979 *Power, Its Forms, Bases and Uses*. New York: Harper & Row.

Yaffe, David S.
1973 "The Marxian Theory of Crisis, Capital and the State." *Economy and Society* 2, no. 2 (May): 186–232.

Zarembka, P., and Ferguson, T., eds.
1985 *Research in Political Economy*. Vol. 8. Greenwich, Conn.: JAI Press.

Zeitlin, Irving
1981 *Ideology and the Development of Sociological Theory*. 2d ed. Englewood Cliffs, N.J.: Prentice-Hall.

Name Index

Szymanski, Albert, 6, 154, 491

Taylor-Gooby, Peter, 399
Teeple, Gary, 16–19, 46, 159, 168
Therborn, Göran, 4, 77, 83, 89, 153,
    159–61, 165, 166, 169–71, 182, 183,
    223, 224, 234–39, 261n, 280, 309
Thompson, E. P., 246, 253n, 281,
    297n, 301n, 339
Tilly, Charles, 349
Titmuss, Richard, 161, 404
Tocqueville, Alexis de, 154
Todd, Jennifer, 378, 410
Traugott, Mark, 35n, 500n
Turkel, Gerald, 4, 224, 367n, 382
Turner, Bryan, 148, 149, 156, 337,
    404, 422, 449n, 505, 506, 511, 512

Urry, John, 7

Vaillancourt, Pauline Marie, 7
van den Berg, Axel, 70n, 76, 94, 108,
    152–54, 161, 186, 221, 238, 297n,
    309n, 367, 371, 373, 389n, 394,
    397n, 400, 402, 414, 416n, 419n,
    428, 450n, 458, 481n, 483n, 496,
    512n, 513, 514n, 518
Van Den Berghe, Pierre, 242
van der Linden, Harry, 51n, 76
Van Parijs, Philippe, 13, 165, 286n,
    296n, 490
Verba, Sidney, 154
von Beyme, Klaus, 46n, 90

Wagner, Senator Robert, 199, 200,
    202, 203
Walker, Pat, 7
Wallace, Michael, 446
Wallerstein, Michael, 507n
Walters, Vivienne, 398
Warshay, Leon H., 7

Weber, Henri, 288, 289
Weber, Max, 13, 122n, 306, 310, 350,
    419
Wedderburn, Dorothy, 167, 420
Weinstein, James, 196
Weitling, Wilhelm, 44
Westergaard, John, 167
Whitaker, Reg, 159, 161, 401
Whitt, J. Allen, 241, 430, 442–45, 447,
    448, 451n, 459, 460, 463
Wiener, Richard, 5n, 28, 168, 228, 241,
    280, 297, 364n, 368
Wilensky, Harold L., 161, 404, 420
Wilson, Woodrow, 214
Winant, John G., 199, 201
Wirth, Margaret, 115, 117n
Wolfe, Alan, 205, 228, 253n, 280n,
    281, 284, 385, 386, 388n, 402, 407n,
    410–12, 418, 419n, 428, 498, 518
Wolfe, Bertram D., 14, 36, 38, 46, 52,
    66, 68, 72, 75, 76, 81, 82, 84, 92, 94,
    115, 136
Wolfe, David A., 368n
Wood, Allen W., 5n, 51n
Woodiwiss, Tony, 382n
Wright, Erik Olin, 4, 7, 122n, 154, 159,
    161–68, 171–73, 222–24, 228, 255n,
    261n, 264, 279, 281, 286n, 301n,
    367n, 368, 381, 382, 384, 394, 403,
    407n, 409, 411, 430–32, 433n, 434–
    36, 437n, 447–50, 451n, 452, 453,
    462, 497, 500, 504, 509
Wright, James D., 179, 210, 399, 506,
    511
Wrong, Dennis H., 155, 156, 309n,
    421n, 511

Yaffe, David S., 296n

Zeitlin, Irving, 508
Zimmerman, Ernest, 3n

Subject Index